THE AGE OF SOCIAL DEMOCRACY

THE AGE OF
SOCIAL DEMOCRACY

Norway and Sweden in the Twentieth Century

Francis Sejersted

Translated by Richard Daly with editing by Madeleine B. Adams

PRINCETON UNIVERSITY PRESS

PRINCETON AND OXFORD

Published by Princeton University Press, 41 William Street, Princeton, New Jersey 08540
In the United Kingdom: Princeton University Press, 6 Oxford Street,
Woodstock, Oxfordshire OX20 1TW
press.princeton.edu

Library of Congress Cataloging-in-Publication Data

Sejersted, Francis, 1936–
 [Sosialdemokratiets tidsalder. English]
The age of social democracy : Norway and Sweden in the twentieth century /
Francis Sejersted ; translated by Richard Daly ; with editing by Madeleine B. Adams.
    p.cm.
Translation of v. 2 of revised version of: Norge og Sverige gjennom 200 år /
Bo Stråth. Oslo : Pax, 2005.
Includes bibliographical references and index.
ISBN 978-0-691-14774-1 (hardcover : alk. paper)
1. Sweden—Politics and government—1905–1950. 2. Sweden—Politics and government—1950–1973.
3. Norway—Politics and government—1905–. 4. Socialism—Sweden—
History—20th century. 5. Socialism—Norway—History—20th century. 6. Sweden—
Social policy. 7. Norway—Social policy. 8. Democracy—Sweden—History—20th century.
9. Democracy—Norway—History—20th century. I. Adams, Madeleine B. II. Title.
 DL861.S45 2011
 948.104—dc22   2010031673

British Library Cataloging-in-Publication Data is available

This work received support from the Norwegian Ministry of Cultural Affairs

This book has been composed in Adobe Garamond

Printed on acid-free paper. ∞

Printed in the United States of America

10 9 8 7 6 5 4 3 2 1

CONTENTS

Acknowledgments   ix

Introduction   1
  The Many Faces of Modernization • The Scandinavian Solution • Three Phases •
  National Characteristics • Overview of the Book

PART I
1905–1940: Growth and Social Integration

CHAPTER 1
Dreaming the Land of the Future   15
  Norsk Hydro • Science and Modernization • Industrialization, a Natural Process
  for Sweden • Norway Follows Hesitantly • Emigration and Industrialization •
  The Norrland Debate • The Norwegian Concession Laws • Electricity, the Basis
  for Technological Modernization • War and Structural Problems • Thrust for
  Socialization • Consolidation of Two Different Structures • Rationalization •
  Technocracy • Dreaming the Land of the Future

CHAPTER 2
National Integration and Democracy   50
  The Question of Political Democracy in the Period around 1905 • Mobilizing the
  Public • Training for Democracy • Toward an Integrated School System in Norway •
  Contrasting the Two Countries • Karl Staaff and the Question of Suffrage in Sweden •
  Arvid Lindman and the Question of Universal Suffrage • The Difficult Road to
  Parliamentarianism • Gunnar Knudsen and State Capitalism • Currents of
  Antiparliamentarianism • The Farmers and Modernization • Farmers on the Offensive:
  Norway • Farmers on the Offensive: Sweden • Crisis Settlement in Both Countries •
  Women and Civil and Political Rights • The Integration of Minorities: The Sami •
  The Integration of Minorities: Refugees from Germany • National Integration
  and Democracy

CHAPTER 3
Assistance for Self-Help   99
  The Conceptual Basis for Social Policy • A Great Preventive Project • Health Insurance •
  National Pension Plans • Unemployment Insurance • Population Crisis? • The Politics
  of Sterilization • Assistance for Self-Help

CHAPTER 4
Revolution or Reform 122
The Last Great Popular Movement • Working-Class Culture • Marxist Rhetoric and
Reformist Practice • An Indistinct Policy • From One's Own Home to the People's
Home: The Labor Movement and the Land Question • Hjalmar Branting • The Big
Strike of 1909 • The Party Is Split • Martin Tranmæl • Worker Scandinavianism •
How Radical? • "A Peculiar Legalization Activity" • The Level of Conflict Escalates •
The Solidarity Game Is Established • Per Albin Hansson and the "People's Home" •
Johan Nygaardsvold and the People's Party • The Expansionism of the Crisis Policy
as Ideology • Revolution or Reform

CHAPTER 5
Distance and Proximity 173
Distance • Proximity • World War I • An Expanded Home Market? • A Nordic
Defense Alliance?

PART II
1940–1970: The Golden Age of Social Democracy

CHAPTER 6
Cooperation in a Menacing World 185
Not the Same War • The Cold War—Still Not the Same War? • The Internal Danger
and Surveillance • A New Drive for a Nordic Customs Union • SAS: A Success Story •
Despite Everything, a Flourishing Collaboration • Cooperation in a Menacing World

CHAPTER 7
"The Most Dynamic Force for Social Development" 205
Class Society in Transformation I • Class Society in Transformation II • "The Most
Dynamic Force for Social Development" • The Vision of the Atomic Age • Sweden:
A Winner Nation • The Wallenberg System • Swedish Labor Market Policy • The
Norwegian State and the Labor Market • Focusing on Natural Conditions • To "Play
Wallenberg" in Norway • An Attempt to Create a Norwegian Knowledge Industry •
Successful Industrial Policy? • The Social Democratic Urban Landscape • The
Suburban Towns • Who Can Save the City? • The Triumph of Reason

CHAPTER 8
The Crowning Glory 241
Technocracy and the Welfare State • Children and the Family • The Radicalism of the
Myrdals • The Era of the Nuclear Family • The Housewife Contract under Pressure •
The Struggle over the Compulsory General Supplementary Pension (ATP) •

Agreement on Social Security • Why Standard Security? • The "Evangian" Health Policy • Swedish Health Policy • Good Family Housing • Social Democracy's Happy Moment

CHAPTER 9
What Kind of People Do We Need?   267
Sweden and Norway, One School-Nation • A Break with the Past? • What Kind of Equality? • Integration and Normality • Several Dilemmas under the Surface • An Unsuccessful Integration Drive • Marginalized Universities • Swedish University Reform • Norwegian University Reform • The Social Democratic People's Church • Church and Morals • Which Is More Important—Health or Salvation? • What Kind of Human Being?

CHAPTER 10
Capitalism, Socialism, and Democracy   289
Tage Erlander and Einar Gerhardsen • The Struggle over the Planned Economy in Sweden • The Struggle over the Planned Economy in Norway • A Social Democratic Constitution • Corporatism and Economic Democracy • The New Administrative Corporatism • How Democratic? • The Double Strategy of Business and Industry • An Ideological Counterthrust • Social Democracy as a Consumer Society • Taxation Socialism • Capitalism without Capitalists? • Credit Socialism or Indicative Planning? • An Order in Its Own Right

PART III
1970–2000: A Richer Reality

CHAPTER 11
A Difficult Modernity   333
A Decade of Conflict • The Social Democrats Reply • The Risk Society • Sweden and Nuclear Power • Norway and Natural Gas Energy • The Nordic Energy Market • Norway Becomes an Oil Nation • Heavy-Handed Discrimination • Sweden Loses Its Leading Position • New Policy: A Turnabout? • Successful Policy? • A Difficult Modernity

CHAPTER 12
What Happened to Economic Democracy?   361
Corporatism under Pressure • Nevertheless, a Change of Model? • Industrial Democracy • Self-determination • Wage Earner Funds—a Radical Move • Weakened Administrative Corporatism • Labor Power for a Better Competitive Edge • Social Democracy in a Globalized Economy • A Weak Milieu of Private Ownership • State Ownership • An Ambiguous Development

CHAPTER 13
From Equality to Freedom   388

The Welfare State under Pressure • The Changing Character of Social Policy • The
Hunt for the Lost Sense of Community • The Jewel Is Removed from the Crown •
Does Norway Follow Suit? • From an Emigration Society to an Immigration Society
• The Establishment of an Immigration Policy • A Political Minefield • The Policy Is
Revised • Toward the Two-Income Family • The Great Dispute over the Cash Benefit
Plan • Gender Equality Lite • A School for the Weakest • Gudmund Hernes—a
Parenthesis • Toward the Dissolution of the Comprehensive School • The Universities
and Market Logic • From Equality to Freedom

CHAPTER 14
The Return of Politics   431

Two Perspectives • Is Democratic Power Disintegrating? • A Weakened Party
System • New Forms of Participation • Social Democracy's Media System • The Great
Release • Threats to Independence • The Media-Biased Society • The Decay of the
General Public? • The Youth Rebellion • Feminism • Marxism-Leninism • Constitu-
tionalism Rediscovered • The Return of the Values Debate • Jesus—a Social Democrat? •
The Common Good • A Showdown with the Past • The Return of Politics

CHAPTER 15
The Last "Soviet States"?   468

A Large-Scale Cooperative Effort • The Volvo Agreement: Another Unsuccessful
Campaign • Toward a Nordic Economic Region? • Europe • Why Did Sweden Reverse
Its Policy on Europe? • The Last "Soviet States"?

AFTER SOCIAL DEMOCRACY:
Toward New Social Structures?   484

A Success—but Not Exclusively So • Social Democracy's Liberal Inheritance •
The Institutional Structures under Pressure • The Freedom and Rights Revolution •
What Kind of Freedom? • High Score • Toward New Structures? • Politics Matter

Bibliography   503

Index   533

ACKNOWLEDGMENTS

This book is a thoroughly revised version of a book with the same title published in Norwegian and Swedish in 2005 as the second volume in a two-volume work written to commemorate the dissolution of the Swedish-Norwegian union in 1905. The first volume, written by Bo Stråth, covered the history of the two countries during the time of the union from 1814 to 1905, and the second volume the period after the dissolution. It was a natural choice to concentrate the history of the twentieth century on the parallel development of Social Democracy in the two countries.

The present volume has profited enormously from numerous discussions with friends and colleagues and from presentations of aspects of the book in lectures and seminars in Norway and Sweden through many years. I can but mention some of the many to whom I am indebted. A close contact with my friend and colleague Rune Slagstad has been a continuous inspiration. My interest in and knowledge of Swedish history has been developed by the close friendship with my Swedish colleague Göran B. Nilsson. The manuscript of the early version was read and commented on by Torbjörn Nilsson, Thorsten Nybom, and Bo Stråth. Single chapters have been read and commented on by Erling Annaniassen, Ole Berg, Grete Brochmann, Jon Erik Dølvik, Anne Lise Ellingsæter, and Klas Åmark. I have benefited from reviews of the early version, in particular reviews by Jan Heiret and Knut Kjeldstadli. Three expert readers chosen by Princeton University Press have written invaluable comments, not least the only non-anonymous of the three, Bo Rothstein. I also want to thank all those who helped prepare the book for publication, in particular Ian Malcolm of Princeton University Press, who took interest in the book, and Madeleine Adams for her thorough editing of the English text.

Throughout the many years I have worked on the book, the Institute for Social Research in Oslo has provided me office space in an extremely stimulating milieu. The directors of the institute, Fredrik Engelstad and Ann-Helen Bay, the librarians Sven Lindblad and Jon Hustad, and all their staff have given me the impression that what they most wanted was to help me in every possible way. Last but most important a sincere thanks to my wife Hilde for support and stimulation, a sine qua non for whatever I have achieved throughout our nearly half-century-long companionship.

Francis Sejersted
Oslo, March 2010

THE AGE OF SOCIAL DEMOCRACY

INTRODUCTION

The Many Faces of Modernization • The Scandinavian Solution • Three Phases • National Characteristics • Overview of the Book

In the 1930s the Social Democratic parties of Sweden and Norway came to power and formed governments in their respective countries. This marked the beginning of a stable period of Social Democratic hegemony. These parties had taken root at the beginning of the twentieth century as revolutionary Marxist parties. They gradually shook off their Marxism, and by the beginning of their period of hegemony they had managed to wrest the great modernization project from the non-Socialist parties and put their own stamp on it. The result is what we might call the Social Democratic order—also called the Scandinavian model, or simply the Swedish or Nordic model. The Social Democratic order reached its zenith in the 1960s; thereafter it declined. This book presents an account of the development of this order in Sweden and Norway.

THE MANY FACES OF MODERNIZATION

Sweden was one of the European great powers during the seventeenth century. By the beginning of the twentieth century this status was only a distant memory, but a more modern ambition was taking shape, "a new, forward-looking and benign great power dream: the vision of Sweden as a cutting-edge industrial and economic world power."[1] In contrast, to find a period when one could possibly call Norway a great power, one would have to go back to the Middle Ages. In the early twentieth century Norway had no great-power dream; its ambitions were more limited. Nevertheless, there is a parallel between the two countries' national projects, or "the new working day," as it was called in Norway. At the beginning of the twentieth century we find a new nationalism in both countries—an industrial and commercial nationalism linked to industrialization and economic development. This reflected a general tendency in Europe. The German historian Hans-Ulrich Wehler writes of "business nationalism as development ideology."[2] Something that is

---

[1] Mithander 2000, 205. See also Elzinga et al. 1998.
[2] Wehler 1974. His concept is "Wirthschaftsnationalismus als Entwicklungsideologie."

more unique to Scandinavia—and particularly to Norway—is the very central place that democratization occupies in the conception of modernization. Modernization is a vague concept that tends to dissolve when one focuses on the concrete historical process, but its comprehensiveness makes it a useful starting point.

Four key aspects of the modernization project should be noted. First, modernization revolves around a *liberation project*, a liberation from oppressive structures both of the people by democratic institutions and of the individual by the idea of human rights. Liberation is closely linked to scientific rationality, or the demythologizing of the world. This rationality has nourished instrumentalist modes of thought and new ambitions for society building. In other words, in the wake of the Enlightenment the Western world developed an ambitious project to build a free "modern" society. Consequently, freedom has "not come to be associated with *dismantling* or *liquidating* but with the *building* and *expanding* of society."[3]

There is a paradox, however, in the idea of modernization, a dilemma that springs out of these great ambitions. The struggle to build the ideal society can pose a threat to freedom. All modern societies are faced with the need to find a balance between policies that are democratic, tolerant, and inclusive and those that seek to mold individuals to fit the new society. The contrasts among modern societies are partly due to the different ways in which they have balanced these aims. Hitler's Germany and Stalin's Soviet Union are extreme examples of how the modernization project and its ambition of liberation can be perverted to totalitarianism.

Second, modernization stands for *economic development through technological progress*. This is part of the liberation project: technological development should release people from poverty and from the oppressiveness of work. Here we encounter another dilemma analogous to the first: how to build institutions to serve as the foundation for this technological and economic progress. The many approaches to balancing the objectives of freedom and targeted development have varied from capitalist market solutions to East European command economies.

Third, modernization implies a *differentiation process*, that is, a move from a homogeneous society with a common worldview to a society divided into many functionally distinct entities with their own systems of values and customary forms of communication. This process has to do with areas such as politics, science, economics, aesthetics, and the judicial system but also with subcultures independent of society's formal institutions. This means that individuals are bound to different institutions or cultural contexts, and

[3] Christoffersen 1999, 234.

within these they seek meaning in their lives. At the same time, economic development implies increasing interdependence among specialized entities. Once again we find a paradox within the modern: fragmentation has its antithesis in the programmatic construction and expansion of an interdependent society.

Finally, modernization implies a *consolidation of the nation-state*. Modernization projects seek to build up the nation-state as a functional framework within which to construct the new society, often with a focus on improving national infrastructure and broadening citizens' rights. Nationalism goes hand in hand with modernization. Thus the differentiation of sections of society is counterbalanced by national affiliation. Social integration within the framework of the nation-state, carried out through democratization and the development of a general public, is a central aspect of the modernization project. A good example of the interaction between the differentiation process and national consolidation is the growth of the working class as a nation within the nation—an entity with its own class identity—and its subsequent integration into the greater national community.

The driving force behind the great modernization project grew out of a shared understanding that, though not always clearly articulated, found its way into policy. In order to understand the historical process and post–World War II social stability, we must recognize the importance of this modernization project so characteristic of the Western world. Furthermore, there is every reason to subscribe to what Sheri Berman calls "the primacy of politics."[4] The realization of the Social Democratic order was the result of conscious policy based on a shared idea of what a modern society should look like. A false picture would be painted by any historical account that described the modern period as a random result of the struggle among various interests in a process driven by either technological or economic necessity.

Today many believe that development has taken another turn and is now moving toward a postmodern society. The critique of the modernization project, or of the form it took, has been clearly articulated. Industrialization has led to pollution and is breaking down the boundaries of nation-states. The individual is tugged by competing loyalties. Social integration on the national level is threatened from within, and we see signs of disintegration. Social integration has also been challenged by new demands for a more equitable distribution of wealth on the international level. National boundaries are also challenged by globalization. These and other related tendencies can be interpreted as the completion of modernization or as a turn away from it. These interpretations are not necessarily in conflict. It is common to change course

---

[4] Berman 2006. The title of the book.

at the moment of a project's completion. The final part of this book uses these general tendencies as background in an account of development and change in Sweden and Norway.

Our account begins at the threshold of the twentieth century—in other words, at a point when the modernization process in Western countries had reached the halfway point and had encountered a social crisis. The way forward was problematic. It would not be long before World War I cast its shadow over Europe. The period that followed saw huge new crises and wars. Totalitarian ideologies took root in popular thought. In retrospect the twentieth century, in most ways the century of modernity, reveals a Janus face. On the one hand, it was the century of extremes and great crises and confrontations. This is the thrust of the historian Eric Hobsbawm's bleak description.[5] On the other hand, the twentieth century was also the century of economic growth, the development of democracy, and increasing welfare in more and more countries.[6]

THE SCANDINAVIAN SOLUTION

A central question is what happened to the modernization project when it was adopted and implemented by the Scandinavian countries. Here it was possible relatively peacefully to develop a mixed economy, democracy, and human welfare in what has been called the Scandinavian model. In the interwar years the Scandinavian countries succeeded in averting both the Communist and the Fascist threats by modifying capitalism to eliminate its less attractive aspects. In brief, the Scandinavian model posed a "better" solution to the problems of modernity than either of the two totalitarian movements or purer capitalism did. This success was partly, but far from exclusively, attributable to the influence of the Social Democratic parties.

Sheri Berman has made a comparative analysis of the Social Democratic movements in five European countries (Germany, Austria, France, Italy, and Sweden) up to World War II. According to her, "social democracy emerged out of a revision of orthodox Marxism." The fact that this is the case in these five countries is one of her reasons for choosing them.[7] Among these countries Sweden is the exception, as it was only in Sweden that Socialists "were

---

[5] Hobsbawm 1995.

[6] Torbjørn L. Knutsen 2001. Knutsen's view is that historians tell the somber story while social scientists tell the light one.

[7] Berman 2006, 18. Using this criterion she could have added Norway and Denmark to the list. Reformist Social Democracy had of course other roots than Marxism, such as nonrevolutionary socialism and radical liberals, not least the Fabians and the English labor movement in general.

able to outmaneuver the radical right and cement a stable majority coalition, escaping the collapse of the left and democracy that occurred elsewhere in Europe." Berman continues, "The key to understanding the Swedish SAP's [the Swedish Social Democratic Labor Party's] remarkable success in the interwar years lies in the triumph of democratic revisionism several decades earlier." Berman identifies Sweden with Scandinavia.[8] If she had considered Norway, she would have had to modify her conclusions, as we shall see. Norwegian Social Democrats clung to their Marxism for a long time but were nevertheless almost as successful as the Swedes.

Berman is certainly right in maintaining that Sweden became a model for Western Europe after World War II, as the Western European countries were developing the democratic mixed-economy welfare state as we know it. Criticizing the common view that the mixed economies that emerged after World War II were a modified version of liberalism, Berman writes that "what spread like wildfire after the war was really something quite different: social democracy."[9] She argues convincingly that Social Democracy must be regarded as a separate order in its own right. But whether this view applies to all of Western Europe is another question. Tony Judt has a different take: the post–World War II history of Europe includes more than one "thematic shape," and it was not until "the crab-like institutional extension of the European Community" that we can discern something like a "European model"— a model born "of an eclectic mix of Social Democratic and Christian Democratic legislation."[10]

There were differences among countries, of course. One reason for choosing to concentrate on Sweden and Norway is that although the Social Democratic *model* became important for many countries in Western Europe, it was only in Sweden and Norway that the Social Democratic *parties* won an undisputed hegemonic position and thus configured the model in a way characteristic of those two countries. During the 1930s to 1960s Sweden and Norway became what has been called Social Democratic "one-party states." This book explores what became of the political visions of the Social Democrats in a situation of hegemonic power. It also uses comparative analysis to deepen understanding of the dynamics involved in the development of the Social Democratic order in Scandinavia. The best way to compare is to search for differences between the two most similar entities; thus we will compare developments in Sweden and Norway in detail, and only occasionally glance at developments outside the Scandinavian Peninsula.

---

[8] Berman 2006, 152.

[9] Berman 2006, 6.

[10] Judt 2007, 7.

Because the Social Democratic parties of Sweden and Norway regarded themselves as revolutionary Marxist parties to begin with, it was not obvious that they should avoid the pitfalls of totalitarianism and choose democratic reformism. The beginning of the twentieth century was a time of crisis in the Scandinavian countries as well as in the rest of Europe, and in such times deep conflicts can easily lead countries along undesirable paths.

Two conflicts were predominant: those between traditionalists and modernists and between capital and labor. Among the traditionalists we find both representatives of the old agrarian society and critics of civilization who viewed all "progress" with skepticism. The latter were present but of marginal importance at the beginning of the twentieth century. The former were more prominent, as both countries had large peasant populations. The other conflict, between labor and capital, divided society just as deeply and threatened social stability in the early twentieth century. But "solutions" were eventually found.

In the 1930s two social pacts were established that were to form the basis of hegemonic Social Democracy—the pacts between labor and farming and between labor and capital, the first in the form of an agreement between the labor and farmer parties on how to handle the crisis, and the latter in the form of an agreement between the two working-life parties on how to settle conflicts peacefully. As Tony Judt points out, "The social services and other public provisions that came to characterize the Scandinavian 'model' reflected these origins."[11]

But what actually is the Scandinavian model, and how does it differ from the social orders developed in the other Western European countries that attempted to copy this model? The Scandinavian model is marked—to cite just a few of its characteristic traits—by comprehensiveness of social security systems, institutionalized universal social rights, a high level of public support, and a high level of equality, which grew out of a combination of public commitment to the principle of universalism and equality of income distribution, which, in turn, is partly attributable to the strength of trade unions.[12] But what kind of social formation are we talking about?

In Norway three leading historians of the generation that wrote during Social Democracy's zenith in the 1960s characterized the same Social Democratic regime in three startlingly different ways. For Sverre Steen it was *the great reconciliation*, that is, the successful realization of the great social integration project. This characteristic corresponds to the Swedish concept of *folkhemmet* (lit. the "people's home"). For Jens Arup Seip, in contrast, the Social Democratic order represented *the Leninist one-party state*. He empha-

[11] Judt 2007, 365–366.
[12] Kautto et al. 1999, 10–14.

sized the dark underside of the integration project, the dominance of one party, state management, and paternalistic tendencies toward molding individuals into the type of human beings that "we need in this modern society."[13] And finally Edvard Bull Jr. characterized the Social Democratic regime as *ultimate capitalism*.[14] This view implies that social integration had not been successful and that class society persisted. Earlier I asserted that the Social Democratic order is an order in it own right, but here we are faced with a lack of concepts suitable to capturing and describing this social order.

We can list some historical starting points that are useful for delineating Social Democracy. Recent research has concentrated on historical lines of descent, especially in relation to the particularities of countries with a Lutheran background where Social Democracy has taken root and represents modernity. "Social democracy works best on ground fertilized by simultaneous emphases on the principles of human equality, individual responsibility, industriousness, and solid respect for state power."[15] Church and state were conjoined after the Reformation, which implies not only that spiritual and temporal authority reached a higher degree of unity but also that the state took over the social welfare function. From this conjunction springs a historical line of descent leading to the modern Scandinavian universalist welfare state.

With the Reformation, religion became a private, personal matter. This individualization would be retained as a constituent feature while society gradually became secularized. Seen in this light, it is noteworthy that cultural radicalism appeared in Scandinavia at the end of the nineteenth century.[16] Cultural radicalism took a critical stand toward the established social authorities, but on an individualistic and antitotalitarian basis. Relations between cultural radicalism and Socialism are complex, but it is reasonable to assume that cultural radicalism helped vaccinate the special Scandinavian variant of Socialism—Social Democracy—against totalitarian tendencies despite its Marxist roots.

This liberation of the individual was linked to the strong demand for social integration by the powerful ideal of equality. The emphases on equality and social integration, combined with the state's dominant presence, help to explain why Socialism in these societies "is not an oppositional but an orthodox way of looking at things."[17] Thus we have gathered some elements of an explanation of how Socialism could be peacefully incorporated into Scan-

[13] Alva and Gunnar Myrdal 1934, 261.
[14] Francis Sejersted 2003a, cf. chapter titled "Historiefagets fortellinger."
[15] Christoffersen 1999, 237. He further cites Tim Knudsen 2000, 47. See also Slagstad 1998, 112.
[16] Nolin 1993. In particular, see Skoglund 1993. The concept has somewhat different meanings in different Scandinavian countries.
[17] Witoszek 1998, 58–60.

dinavian society and become hegemonic by assuming a Social Democratic form. Moreover, in this form the state's sovereign power was constrained by its liberal, rights-based protection of the individual.

THREE PHASES

The twentieth-century history of the Scandinavian model, or the rise and decline of Social Democracy, can be divided into three phases. The first phase ran to the end of the 1930s. This period started with the crisis at the beginning of the century and moved toward a gradual integration and mutual understanding that could serve as the foundation for the Social Democratic order. After extremist tendencies had been overcome, the working class was integrated into the nation with the labor parties of the two countries becoming the governing parties. As Walter Korpi writes, "At the end of the 1930s, they [the major opposing forces in society] came to what might be called a historic compromise between capital and labor."[18] As we have seen, this occurred at the same time as the compromise (or pact) between farming and labor.

We may ask, however, whether these pacts were merely compromises. Didn't they also have elements of consensus, that is, Sverre Steen's "great reconciliation"? One foreign observer, Marquis W. Childs, wrote, "It seems to me that capitalism in the Nordic countries has been modified and in a way, controlled. In many areas the profit motive has been drastically limited or eliminated—repressed is perhaps a better word. Thus the economy is organized to a considerable degree so as to bring the greatest good to greatest number."[19] Remarkably, this was written in 1936, at the moment when Social Democracy was about to assume governmental power. The foundation of a society we associate with Social Democracy had already been laid. Obviously, many forces were working together to establish this special form of Nordic capitalism.

The second phase stretched from the end of the 1930s to the 1970s. Korpi writes, "That the formula for the historic compromise stood for well over thirty years shows that 'the Swedish model' dealt in many ways successfully with the opposing interests of capital and labor."[20] During this phase the Social Democratic order was built on the foundation of this historic compromise. Again it is a question of how much one emphasizes underlying opposing interests versus consensus. The various characterizations of the Social Democratic order by the historians Steen, Seip, and Bull indicate that different interpretations are possible. One feature that stands out is how similar the

---

[18] Korpi 1981, 25.
[19] Childs 1936, xii.
[20] Korpi 1981, 27.

Nordic welfare societies were during this phase. This is due not only to their development from a common historical starting point but also, to a large degree, to their influence on one another, particularly the mutual influence of Sweden and Norway. This is one reason why we in some respects can consider Scandinavia, or at least Sweden and Norway, as a single entity.

The final phase, the postmodern or the "second modernity," stretched from the 1970s to the end of the twentieth century. This period was marked by disintegration. Common understanding and unity were fractured, and development seemed to go in many different directions. What is perhaps most remarkable is that the omnipresent state—in which people had such faith, which had been entrusted with the task of nation building, and which had continually expanded from far back in the 1800s on—began to draw back. What could fill the resulting vacuum? The market, naturally, but not only that. State and society had become identical concepts, but now that the state was weakening we could begin to see the hazy contours of civil society.

It is one of the ironies of history that precisely under the conditions when the Social Democratic order became a reality, apparently fully developed— precisely at Social Democracy's zenith or "happy moment"—the edifice began to crack. It seems that a new individualism began to blossom and this threatened the old solidarity. The liberation of the individual had been an underlying theme throughout the modernization process. We can view this last phase as the completion of modernization, and Social Democracy as only a step along the way, not toward Socialism but toward the "modern" society, whatever that might be.

Moreover, these features of development during Social Democracy's last phase were not limited to Scandinavia. They reflect a general development. With these later developments, Scandinavian Social Democracy lost some of what made it distinctive, what had characterized the Scandinavian model. This seems to be part of a process in which we can, as Judt says, "discern something like a 'European model.'"

The distinctive Scandinavian Social Democratic features were not completely obliterated, however. Today there are tendencies in Norway and Sweden toward a rehabilitation of certain Social Democratic traits. There also seems to be a renewed interest in the Scandinavian model internationally. It is praised, for example, by the influential American economist Jeffrey Sachs: "It is possible to combine a high level of income, growth, and innovation with a high degree of social protection. The Nordic societies of Northern Europe have done it. And their experience sheds considerable light on the choices for others." He adds, "The social-welfare states tend to outperform the other countries on most economic and governance indicators."[21]

---

[21] Sachs 2008, 258, 265. See also Dølvik et al. 2007, 32.

NATIONAL CHARACTERISTICS

I mentioned earlier the importance of Sweden and Norway's common historical heritage from the Reformation. But when we look more closely at history,
we find clear differences between the two countries. For four hundred years,
up to 1814, Norway had been a province of the Danish-Norwegian composite state, and from 1660 on it had been under the absolute rule of the king in
Copenhagen. In 1814, in the wake of the Napoleonic Wars, Norway became
an independent state in a union with Sweden. The absolute monarchy was
replaced with a constitutional monarchy, with a constitution that was one of
the most democratic in Europe at that time. In the Middle Ages, Norway had
been a strong independent state. The Danish period was viewed as a break
in continuity in the development of the Norwegian nation—a wound to be
healed. This view of national history was important for the nation building of
the nineteenth century, a period that came to an end in 1905 with the peaceful dissolution of the union with Sweden.

The dissolution of the union meant national consolidation for both countries, that is, consolidation of the boundaries within which modernization
would take place. The union had left different impressions on the two countries' conceptions of modernization. During its nineteenth-century struggle
for full national independence, Norway's nationalism had been linked to progressive democratic forces. Its project of nation building and modernization
at the beginning of the twentieth century was therefore strongly colored by
democratic norms.

Sweden did not suffer such a break in its historical continuity; that is, the
country had achieved a constitution in 1809 that did away with the absolute
monarchy. But the absolute monarchy was replaced with a form of "aristocratic constitutionalism." Thus Sweden's problem was the opposite of Norway's. Sweden dragged a large part of its old social order along with it, right
up to the beginning of the twentieth century. Therefore it was important for
the modern progressive forces to break with the old and begin on a fresh page.
Sweden's break in continuity began at the beginning of the twentieth century
and was different from Norway's. Sweden had no wound to heal but rather an
inheritance to shake off. The Swedish nationalism that sought nourishment
in national history was not linked as in Norway with the progressive forces. It
was primarily conservative forces that mobilized history for their own goals.
In Sweden's progressive nation-building project, national identity was not
linked to historical continuity as much as to modernity itself, and to being
modern and belonging to the avant-garde.[22]

[22] Alf W. Johansson 2001, 8.

By starting the account of Sweden and Norway at the beginning of the twentieth century, we break into the modernization process halfway through the race. The considerable differences in historical background provide the context for specifying what is involved in this half-run race. In other words, we can ask about which typical modern institutions were in place at the time of the dissolution of the union in 1905. We find characteristic differences that reflect the two countries' different historical experiences. What modern institutions did Sweden have that Norway lacked? Sweden already had a national heavy-industry sector that asserted itself internationally. The country had a banking system capable of serving such industry. Moreover, it had had technical universities for a long time. It also had a Companies Act that regulated the modern forms of capital association with limited liability. None of this was to be found in Norway.

What did Norway have that Sweden lacked? Norway had universal male suffrage beginning in 1898 and a more parliamentary form of governance. Neither of these features were found in Sweden. In essence, Sweden already had fairly typical industrial capitalist institutions in place but not democratic ones; Norway was the opposite. At the risk of oversimplifying, one could say that Norway was democratized before it was industrialized, while the opposite was the case in Sweden.[23] This difference has distinguished the two countries' development trajectories up to the present day, not least in the conspicuous strength of democratic norms in Norway. In other words, in Norway it has been difficult to legitimate social power other than through democratic procedures. For example, Norwegian business has had to subordinate itself to political leadership to a much greater degree than Swedish business has. The strong industrial bourgeoisie in Sweden has a legitimacy—based partly on tradition and partly on performance—that has allowed it to exercise social power. In other words, Swedish business has gained legitimacy as the effective modernizing force in the high-tech economy. In contrast, the Norwegian Sonderweg (special way) is characterized by the weakness of big business and the corresponding strength of the democratic petite bourgeoisie.[24]

As we can see in relation to historical inheritance and continuity, the differences between the two countries have clear implications for their modernization projects. Sweden began with a more routine conception of modernization, centered on economic modernization—that is, industrialization. It has been argued that Norway had a better-rounded conception of moderniza-

[23] Naturally enough, a complete picture is not so simple. Sweden had taken steps in the direction of parliamentarianism in 1905, and Norway had developed a vigorous light industry sector. It might be argued that it was precisely this vigorous light industry that shut Norway away from the development of heavy industry. See Francis Sejersted 2002a, chapters 2 and 11.

[24] Francis Sejersted 2002a; see chapter titled "Den norske 'Sonderweg.'"

tion. In any case, democratization was more prominent in Norway than in Sweden. The characteristic differences in the two countries' conceptions of modernization have been reflected in many areas right up to the present day.

OVERVIEW OF THE BOOK

Social Democracy's growth and development through most of the twentieth century is the story of how a grand-theory political project gradually was formulated and finally realized in Social Democracy's happy moment. The last phase, since the 1970s, is the story of how this Social Democratic order was overtaken by history and its development shifted direction. The account is divided into the three phases described earlier. This prepares for an ongoing comparison of development in the two countries, Sweden and Norway. The comparison is intended to cast light on the dynamics of development toward a social order that, despite the differences en route, has been quite similar in the two countries.[25]

I emphasize two themes. The first is how the two countries accomplished industrialization, based on their shared desire for economic modernization. The second central theme is how democratization gained strength from a project of social integration of all groups into one nation. The development of the welfare state reflects the same social integration project through its generous disbursements and universalist character. So does school policy: in the standardized school system one finds a particularly clear expression of the ideal of equality.

Behind these and other policies we see the image of humanity characteristic of Social Democracy. In other words, we dimly perceive an answer to the question that the influential Social Democratic politician Alva Myrdal posed at the beginning of Social Democracy's happy moment: "Precisely what kind of human being do we need in modern society?"[26] The ambition was to change both society and the people. The "freedom revolution" that followed the happy moment was a reaction to the paternalistic tendencies lurking behind such questions—and behind the passionately pursued ideal of equality. Equality and freedom are not always easy to combine.

---

[25] Comparison as a method requires attention to the question of dependence/independence between the two entities being compared. Thus the comparison itself must be linked to an investigation of relations between the two entities compared. See Kaelble 1999, 21 and Francis Sejersted 2003c, chapter titled "Sammenligning er ikke bare sammenligning."

[26] A. and G. Myrdal 1934, 261.

PART I

1905–1940: Growth and Social Integration

CHAPTER 1

Dreaming the Land of the Future

Norsk Hydro • Science and Modernization • Industrialization, a Natural Process for Sweden • Norway Follows Hesitantly • Emigration and Industrialization • The Norrland Debate • The Norwegian Concession Laws • Electricity, the Basis for Technological Modernization • War and Structural Problems • Thrust for Socialization • Consolidation of Two Different Structures • Rationalization • Technocracy • Dreaming the Land of the Future

NORSK HYDRO

An extremely large and audacious industrial gamble led to the founding of the major company Norsk Hydro in 1905, the same year that the union between Sweden and Norway was dissolved. Norsk Hydro was to some degree both the fruit of that union and a symbol of the dawning of the "new working day" in Norway. Moreover, the initial establishment phase provided glimpses of expectations about the industrial development of the two countries and the political problems associated with industrialization. Hydro was based on the latest breakthroughs in the fields of electrical technology and chemistry. Through the use of Norway's large hydroelectric power resources and a new cutting-edge, science-based invention, nitrogen would now be extracted from the air in a way that allowed it to be chemically bound. In the belief that fertilizer produced by this means would revolutionize world food production, many researchers had been exploring methods of extracting and binding nitrogen from the air. Professor Kristian Birkeland at the University of Oslo developed the world's first commercially useful method of doing this, which provided the basis for the formation of Hydro. Birkeland's method had been undergoing industrial testing in the period before 1905, when construction began on Hydro's large-scale plants.

In 1911, in a remote valley in Telemark, Norsk Hydro's Vemork power station was finished. For several years it was the world's largest hydroelectric power station. The large hydroelectric power station at Trollhättan in Sweden had been finished the year before.[1] The mammoth dimensions of these

---

[1] For the Swedish state involvement in hydro power construction, see Jakobsson 1996; Fridlund 1999; and Vedung and Brandel 2001.

projects appealed to the popular imagination. Moreover, both power stations were graced with spectacular architecture that contributed to their becoming physical symbols of a golden future. But there was a significant difference between them: the Trollhätte power station was built by the Swedish state, while Vemork was built by private foreign—including Swedish—interests. Under the terms of the union between Sweden and Norway, each country had the right to establish businesses in either country.[2] A precondition for the building of a large-scale hydroelectric power station in a side valley in Norway was the fact that the Swedish banker Marcus Wallenberg had become engaged in the project and had been able to mobilize his international financial networks.[3] There was no comparable banking system in Norway. During the union with Sweden, Norwegians had been able to rely on the Swedish system. Thus, to a certain degree, the Scandinavian Peninsula was industrialized by means of economic and institutional unity—unity that broke down with the dissolution of the union. Norway never managed to develop a banking system equal to Sweden's.

SCIENCE AND MODERNIZATION

At the beginning of the twentieth century, "society was permeated by science and the scientific outlook."[4] The natural sciences were then contributing in an entirely new way to the formation of our view of the world and our way of relating to it. The new scientific rationality pervaded all aspects of human life at the expense of the old humanistic disciplines. Not least, political life became identified with the process of demythologizing the world, and the critical attitude of science became the norm. The ideal was factual and unbiased argumentation.

In this period Darwinism went far beyond biology. It became a way of thinking about both people and nations. It stimulated thinking about how a nation ought to throw itself into the struggle for existence. Scientific brilliance became a source of national pride. In this way the new sciences became linked to the aggressive nationalism of the day.[5] The new scientific rationality also provided fertile ground for ideas on how to harness science for practical

---

[2] The specific clause is part of the law concerning Norwegian citizenship rights, ratified 21 April 1888, which reads (§ 9) as follows: "Without permission granted by the King, or whoever he thereby authorizes, henceforth and in the future, permanent ownership here within the realm cannot with full legal effect be transferred to other than Norwegian or Swedish citizens or corporations." Regulations of this type presupposed mutual agreement. From the Swedish side, one finds this in a decree of 4 June 1868.

[3] See Gasslander 1959, 2:172–226, on Wallenberg's involvement in the formation of Norsk Hydro.

[4] Gunnar Eriksson 1978, 203: "samhället genomträngs av vetenskapen och den vetenskapeliga andan."

[5] Gunnar Eriksson 1978, 199.

purposes. In the early twentieth century this was most clearly observable in mapping the different nations' natural resources. The Norwegian W. C. Brøgger expressed this spirit when he argued that a scientific approach to resource management consisted of knowledge about the nation—not just its history, its people, and its culture, but also its natural conditions. And in this knowledge one also found national identity.[6] Brøgger was a geologist. He had been a professor at the Royal Technical College in Stockholm. When he returned home to a professorship in Kristiania (Oslo) in 1890, he was one of the most prominent mappers among natural scientists.

Scientific mapping was applied not simply to the different nations' own natural resources. We find as well expanded mapping and inventorying "in new, and from various different points of view, potentially exploitable fields."[7] Sweden and Norway's parallel development was shown in their expeditions to the Arctic, the Antarctic, and elsewhere. All of these were scientific and thereby united in the heroic struggle *against* nature by conducting scientific investigation *of* nature. It became a kind of sport in both Norway and Sweden to map the most inaccessible parts of the globe. In this field the most prominent Swede was Adolf Nordenskiöld, who, among his many other expeditions, was the first to sail through the Northeast Passage, north of Siberia, in 1878–1880. In the period 1894–1902 the Swedish explorer Sven Hedin undertook legendary expeditions through central Asia.[8] The Northwest Passage, north of Canada, was first traversed by ship in the period 1903–1906 by the Norwegian Roald Amundsen. In 1911 he was the first to reach the South Pole, a feat that made an important contribution to strengthening his young nation's sense of identity. Beyond this, the greatest Norwegian figure of the time was Fridtjof Nansen, preeminent national hero, man of science, master of the forces of nature, politician, and humanist.

Sweden had a more solid tradition in the natural sciences than Norway did. Nevertheless, it is striking that the situations in Norway and Sweden were similar. This no doubt had something to do with relatively conspicuous cross-border cooperation. Among other things, beginning in 1836 there were regular meetings of Scandinavian natural science researchers. The fact that the Swedish newspaper *Social-Demokraten* refers with great enthusiasm to such a meeting in 1898 is symptomatic of the hegemony of scientific thought in society. According to that newspaper, the spirit of science, and all that was presented at the meeting, ought to be directed out into society at large, which was still unfamiliar with both the essence and the existence of science. In this

[6] Hestmark 1999, 14.
[7] Gunnar Eriksson 1978, 105.
[8] Gunnar Eriksson 1978, 140.

Figure 1. Roald Amundsen and his men at the South Pole on December 14, 1911. Amundsen was the first human to reach the South Pole—an achievement that created excitement and strengthened the self-image of the newly independent Norwegian nation otherwise tormented by social conflicts. (Photo: Olav Bjaaland, The National Library of Australia.)

we see modern science and the modern labor movement standing shoulder to shoulder.[9]

As in Sweden, the modernization process had begun in Norway far back in the nineteenth century. In both countries there was a wave of reform around midcentury in which one found a combination of liberal positions—such as support for free enterprise and free trade, strong defense of the rights of ownership, and so forth—and demands for a strong and active state. The state played the role of executive strategist for modernization.[10] It was also characteristic that traditionalists and modernists were united in their concern for the primary industries (agriculture, fisheries, and forestry). In both countries there was close cooperation between, on the one hand, the natural sciences and the focus of their research and, on the other hand, the development of the primary industries. Applied agricultural and oceanographic research was prominent in both countries. In neither country did the state hesitate to support these industries by means of research grants. But here the parallels between the two countries end.

[9] Nils Eriksson 1991, 326. The meeting in 1898 was, moreover, the last for a long time.
[10] Göran B. Nilsson 2003; Torbjörn Nilsson 1994, 138.

Compared with Norway, Sweden had a completely different tradition of interest in, and attention being paid to, technological development and the modern manufacturing industries. A clear expression of this is the fact that, beginning in the 1820s, Sweden had an institute of polytechnical education with the clear goal of stimulating industrial development. And it actually achieved this goal. Around the middle of the nineteenth century the polytechnical institute developed into a technical university. The first two decades of the twentieth century were called "the age of engineering science," referring to a shared development in the Western countries.[11] Sweden followed the typical pattern in this development.

This interest in technological development did not imply the existence of direct links between the natural sciences and technology. In relation to the academic sciences and the applied sciences involved in the primary industries, "the conditions for technical science directed toward modern manufacturing industries were . . . modest."[12] Naturally, this link did exist wherever modern industry was largely based on scientific breakthroughs in chemistry or physics (electricity, for example). In Norway as well there were examples of links between science and industry, such as Kristian Birkeland's discovery of the process for nitrogen extraction that was the basis for Norsk Hydro. Nevertheless, it is important to point out that, institutionally, science and technology were relatively isolated from each other. Hence the difference between Sweden and Norway lay not so much in differences in the development of the natural sciences as it did in the development of technology and the technological environment. In this area Sweden was much more advanced, while Norway lagged far behind the level of general development found in the developed countries.

INDUSTRIALIZATION, A NATURAL PROCESS FOR SWEDEN

Toward the end of the nineteenth century the West entered what is often called the second industrial revolution, marked by science-based technology and large industrial corporations. That was the period in which the United States and Germany overtook England to become the leading industrial nations in the world. Sweden followed the new "organized" industrial capitalism and surged ahead of Norway.

Sweden industrialized quite rapidly after 1870, and per capita income rose by 131 percent in the period 1870–1910. Norway lagged behind, with a cor-

---

[11] Sundin 1981.
[12] Sundin 1981, 43.

responding increase in per capita income of 61 percent.[13] Sweden developed a number of technology-based firms that were able to assert themselves in the international arena, such as the Nobel Industries, Atlas Copco, L. M. Ericsson, ASEA, Alfa-Laval, and SKF. Norway followed along to some degree in wood processing, but here too Sweden was more advanced. Sweden was on the verge of converting its old dream of being a political and military great power into a dream of becoming an industrial and economic great power.

This political plan was reflected in Sweden's protectionist breakthrough in 1888. This breakthrough represented a new and aggressive economic nationalism, a defense of Swedish labor and employment. Originally it had been agrarian interests that had agitated for the grain tax, but the battle gradually acquired broader dimensions. Behind the breakthrough stood an alliance of agrarian and industrial interests, and the tax was introduced on both food products and industrial goods. The termination of the Swedish-Norwegian trade agreement in 1895 can be seen as a consequence of this new line. The termination became a nail in the coffin of the union between the two countries. What was the use of a union if it did not even include a common market?

The successful industrialization at the end of the nineteenth century had brought to the fore the idea that it was "*natural* that Sweden was now in a position to achieve a highly advanced level of industrial development."[14] It was also natural—and traditional, to boot—that the state stepped in to lend support. Sweden had long had a National Board of Trade (Kommerskollegium), which had been successively modernized until it became a modern industry-supporting public institution. After 1905 there followed "a face-lift wherein responsibility for trade and industry became more pronounced and better organized."[15] A rather typical result of this industrial policy was, for example, the fact that the private company ASEA was awarded by the Swedish state the contract for hydroelectric-power construction. This and related agreements expressed conscious and systematic positive discrimination by the state in its efforts to create world-class industrial enterprises.

This strong wave of industrialization in Sweden at the end of the nineteenth century was also premised on the system of authority—the power structure—in Swedish society. Not only were the engineers in place, but also this new industrial Sweden was able to continue in the old tradition of the great ironworks. "It might be said that the owners' power is the result of an ancient tradition."[16] The nineteenth-century revolution of the bourgeoisie

---

[13] Jörberg 1973, 386.
[14] Angell 2002, 280.
[15] T. Nilsson 1994, 219.
[16] Glete 1991, 239.

did not eliminate the traditional authority structures in Sweden in the same sweeping manner it did in Norway. As has been noted with regard to Germany, Sweden's new capitalists and industrialists were able to build on the structures of traditional authority.

In addition to the authority that could be built on existing tradition, industry was also able to draw on the legitimacy that emerged from *performance*. Quite simply, the industrialists had been very skillful in carrying out their "assignment," namely, the creation of modern industry. They managed to establish their own sphere of power, and came to represent a consolidated social power that had a degree of legitimacy within Swedish society that Norwegian industrialists had never possessed. While the leaders of Norwegian trade and industry were obliged to adapt themselves to the prevailing democratic political organs, their counterparts in Sweden were able to negotiate with the same organs on an equal footing. This reflected the stronger democratic tradition in Norway. Norway had what has been called "democratic capitalism."[17]

As mentioned in the introduction, Norway started the democratization process early and was late with its industrialization. Sweden was the opposite. With regard to the structures of authority, there is much evidence that Sweden's late democratization was one of the factors that contributed to its strong and successful industrialization in the late 1800s. The relationship between democratic development and industrialization was not unambiguous, even if from a larger perspective these are two aspects of the same project of modernization.[18]

NORWAY FOLLOWS HESITANTLY

In the course of the nineteenth century Norway had developed a viable light industry typical of the first phase of industrialization. As a result, by 1870 it was more urbanized and somewhat richer per capita than Sweden. In the following period, however, Sweden overtook Norway, which did not manage to take the next step into "organized capitalism." With the dissolution of the union between the two countries in 1905, Norway lacked important institutional foundations for the development of modern industry. The "new working day" relatively quickly allowed Norway to put a number of these institutions into place, however.

Norway established a technical college in 1910. The first proposal to establish such an institution had been presented in Parliament as early as 1833,

---

[17] Francis Sejersted 2002a. The title of the book.
[18] Edling 1996, 31.

but it inspired vehement opposition for a long time—a *very* long time. This lack of technological higher education, unique to Norway, is one of the reasons why the country did not develop a strong technological environment in which to build systematic cooperation between science and its industrial application. The reason was said to be "a lack of political power behind . . . this type of education." The farmer and the worker were educated by public schooling, and the civil servant and middle-class nontechnical professional received education at the university. But the economic middle class did not possess the political power necessary to establish its own educational institutions.[19] Behind this, of course, lay various constellations of interest politics.

One way to explain the interest politics is to examine the lack of a technical college in light of the nature of the Norwegian "discourse on modernization." In other words, it was not simply a question of the political influence of the various groups but, above all, a question of shared ideas. The Norwegian modernization discourse maintained that political and cultural modernizations were just as important as economic modernization. As far as the economy was concerned, the country was attached to the more traditional structures, that is, to the modernization of the primary industries and light industry as it had developed during the course of the nineteenth century. And in following this course there was no strong demand for a technical college. It was "these intersecting motivations in the Norwegian modernization process that neutralized the demand for higher technical education."[20] But in 1910 Norway too got its technical college, a half century after Sweden, and it did so as a natural component of the "new working day" proclaimed in 1905.[21]

What is usually stressed in regard to this period of organized capitalism is the strategic role played by the largest banks. Not only in Sweden but also in Denmark and Finland there were large banks serving the whole country by the beginning of the twentieth century. In Norway, by contrast, there were only small local savings and mercantile banks. In Sweden in particular, but also in Denmark, we see how the large banks entered into business networks that, precisely on the basis of this structure, were able to become strategists for establishing and developing the large modern industrial firms. The establishment of such network structures was characteristic of organized capitalism. The most prominent example in Scandinavia is the Wallenberg family of Sweden. Its central role in the founding of Norsk Hydro was not fortuitous.

In Norway people certainly desired banks and industry, but they viewed *big* banks and *big* industry with skepticism. Carl Kierulf's comment is typical of this attitude: "It is not a healthy policy to allow the larger banks easy

[19] Jens Arup Seip 1971, 118–119. Hanisch and Lange 1985, 33–34, have the same explanation.

[20] Angell 2002, 251; see as well p. 265.

[21] Sweden had higher technical education about 1860 at the Teknologiska Institutet, which in 1876 was formally constituted as a technical college. See also Hult et al. 1989, 223, 260.

access to the setting up of branches, whereby they have the opportunity to stretch their tentacles over the whole country and by this means draw in deposits, removing them from those regions of the country that otherwise would actually make good use of them."[22] We suspect that this is one of the reasons why Norway did not manage to develop organized capitalism but, rather, remained lodged within a structure that was developed under classic nineteenth-century industrial capitalism.[23]

The country lacked not only modern institutions for capital accumulation but also appropriate regulations concerning limited liability. Sweden had already enacted its Companies Act in 1848, which was updated in 1895. By that time a need for limited-liability regulation was felt in Norway, too, and a discussion about creating it was under way, yet this did not result in anything tangible before the Companies Act of 1910. Norway did possess many limited-liability share companies. The stock exchange was founded in 1881 for trading stocks and bonds, and during the 1890s there was an upswing in the number of industrial shares on the market.[24] Lack of regulation, however, permitted considerable abuse, particularly among small firms that could easily be milked by their owners and in reality operated with the risk falling on creditors.[25] Warnings against Norwegian companies were issued abroad.[26]

These anarchistic conditions in Norway constitute another example of how far away the country was from organized capitalism. Certainly Norway did get its technical college and its statutes regarding share trading in 1910, but there were no large banks, and the difference in economic structure between Sweden and Norway persisted through most of the twentieth century.

EMIGRATION AND INDUSTRIALIZATION

During this period the political arena in Sweden was distinguished by a debate about emigration. An underlying theme of this debate was the conflict between traditionalists and modernists. But here we also see a conflict between different modernization strategies, or different ideas about what society should be.

---

[22] This quotation has been taken from bank director Carl Kierulf's comments in *Report from a Committee Appointed by the Ministry of Finance* 1921, 90 (annex 3). The report is incorporated as an addendum to St. forh. (Parl. Proceedings) 1923, Ot. Prp. 13. From its context, this appears to have been a rather common point of view. I am indebted to Sverre Knutsen for this reference.

[23] Francis Sejersted 2002a. See especially the chapter titled "Den norske 'Sonderweg.'"

[24] Kili 1996, 4. See also the subheading titled "Aksjeloven av 1910 og dens konsekvenser," Kili 1996, 94–99.

[25] *Udkast til Lov om Aktieselskaber* (Proposal for an Act Concerning Companies), Kristiania 1894, 13, 28. The proposal is incorporated as an addendum to St. forh. (Parl. Proceedings) 1900–1901, Ot. Prp. 28.

[26] St. forh. (Parl. Proceedings) 1910, Ot. Prp. 5, p. 3.

The Swedish emigration to America followed roughly the same pattern as the Norwegian: in three large waves, the first in the 1860s, the next during the 1880s, and a somewhat smaller one after the turn of the century. Like Norway, Sweden had a rather ambivalent attitude toward emigration. This alternated between a negative attitude toward the loss of human resources and a positive attitude toward the possibilities that emigration offered for regulating population growth. Around the beginning of the twentieth century in Sweden the negative view of emigration dominated. The National Association against Emigration was founded in 1907 and became an influential organization that at its highest point had sixteen thousand members. In connection with the own-your-own-home movement and thus with the state's Own Home Fund, the National Association against Emigration was an early example of what would become typical of twentieth-century corporatism, in which interest organizations were drawn into the management of society by means of state subsidies.[27]

In relation to the political agenda, the antiemigration movement found expression in the major public report on emigration. The dominant person involved in this report was the statistician Gustav Sundbärg. He published a 900-page final report in 1913. Before this, twenty associated documents (totaling 3,800 pages) were published. All this comprehensive work contributed to establishing a pattern with regard to the use of social science in public reports.[28] According to the report, emigration showed that something was wrong with Swedish society. Active state intervention was demanded.

From the beginning, the antiemigration movement was associated with the traditionalists and their agrarian romance and critique of civilization: "Emigration stood out, alongside industrialization, urban growth, and the expansion of the labor movement, as another expression of hatred directed against the old society."[29] The remedy should be found in new cultivation within the homeland, or the development of a class of small farmers who owned their own enterprises. Both Sweden and Norway had enough uncultivated arable land to make this feasible.[30]

But there were also voices that maintained from the beginning that industrialization was a better solution to emigration than renewed cultivation of land. The latter position was Sundbärg's own, and it was presented forcefully in the conclusion of the report: the building up of industry would make it as attractive to remain in Sweden as to travel to America. As it was put before the Riksdagen, the Swedish Parliament, Sweden would become "the land of

---

[27] Patrik Hall 2000, 238.
[28] P. Hall 2000, 241.
[29] Cited in P. Hall, 2000, 230.
[30] Randen 2002, 41.

the future"—but only by moving America to Sweden could one prevent the citizens of Sweden from moving to America.[31] The report met halfway not only the progressive industrialists but also the Social Democrats. In the report's conclusion there was no longer talk of defending the old Sweden but rather of building the new.

In relative terms, Norwegian emigration was greater than Swedish emigration. One found the same anxiety in Norway, and a report on emigration comparable to the Swedish report was prepared, but the debate never developed the way it did in Sweden. In Norway emigration did not become grist for an argument for speeding up industrial development.

The emigration debates reflected the project of nation building insofar as they constituted a good example of "how race constituted the obvious object of policy."[32] One might certainly expect that an effort would be made to balance emigration with increased immigration. But, contrary to such an expectation, an initiative was taken to limit immigration as well as emigration. As the Swedish conservative intellectual Rudolf Kjellén put it, "We must find a way to lock both doors, stop the clear flow going out and the muddy one coming in."[33] The Norwegian report included corresponding arguments that, among other reasons for apprehension, "the Slavic and half-Asian elements" reproduced much faster than "the Norwegian race." At a time when class identities based on differences of material circumstance were so prominent in society, this shows that beneath the political surface it is indeed possible to find identifications that stemmed from other dimensions. The relationship between the modernization project and nationalism is clear. We also see how the nation-building project presupposed a division between "us" and "them." Minorities became "dangerous" because they blurred this national identity.[34] This was the underbelly of the integration project. "Everybody" should be integrated, but this certainly did not mean just *anybody*.

THE NORRLAND DEBATE

This period was also distinguished by two other modernization debates. Their theme was management and control of the use of natural resources. In Sweden this had to do with what was called the Norrland debate, and in Norway it was the debate about the concession laws.[35] The Norrland debate broke

---

[31] Sundbärg 1913, 9.
[32] Soltvedt 2000, 34.
[33] P. Hall 2000, 229.
[34] Sirnes 1999, 34–35, 59.
[35] Gasslander 1959, 2:267; page 409 also draws parallels between the two issues.

out when it became known that the dominant forest-products industry had acquired ownership of vast tracts of forest in Norrland and Dalarna, two of Sweden's northern regions. This gave birth to a new and broad political protest movement comprising representatives from the affected areas, urban radicals and liberals, and moderates such as various conservative agrarian interests and Socialists from Socialdemokratiske Ungdomsförbundet, the Association of Social Democratic Youth. The response shows that the issue acquired symbolic value, and it demonstrates the relative autonomy of policy decisions in relation to established interests.[36] What was effective was the argument that the very existence of the individual landowning population was at stake and the existing social order was under threat.

The issue was also linked to the emigration question. Acquisition of land by industry had forced northern Swedes to break ground along the Mississippi instead of in the territory of Norrland. At the same time, the issue was especially important for the own-your-own-home movement, and thus for advancing the concept of the "people's home". The Social Democratic leader Hjalmar Branting saw in the demand for state intervention a healthy "defense against the corporate might of the favored class," despite his general skepticism toward the movement's anticapitalist tendencies.[37] As a radical Social Democrat he was closely bound up with the logic of industrial capitalism.

Another issue that affected national control of natural resources had to do with the rich deposits of iron ore in the north of the country. Around 1905 a public mood for nationalizing the large mining companies developed. This involved the companies Luossavaara-Kiirunavaara AB (LKAB) and Grängesberg. In 1907 the moderate conservative government under Arvid Lindman presented to Parliament a proposition that included severe regulation of Grängesberg's operations, as well as, over the course of several years, the gradual takeover of LKAB by the state. As Emil Uddhammar writes, the latter involved "transferring private ownership to the public at a level of compensation lower than the estimated future market value, and thus constituted a partial confiscation."[38] Nevertheless, there was broad political agreement about this policy.

The Norrland debate and the regulations that followed in its wake modified the predominant "thesis of the new export-oriented large-scale enterprises' ability to make their interests prevail in state and society."[39] Anti-industrial

---

[36] Edling 1994, 291.

[37] Edling 1994, 280.

[38] Uddhammar 1993, 394.

[39] Edling 1994, 267–295, 268. Since that time, Edling has modified this point of view in the sense that this could mean that there was a *certain degree* of limitation to the large participants' ability to pursue their own interests, and that this did not reflect a common industrywide skepticism (personal communication).

forces were at play and, above all, there were limits to how far one could go in the direction of giving large industry and foreigners a free hand; indeed, anything else would have been exceedingly odd. Natural resources had to be protected by the state.

The major impression, however, is that there was strong agreement about the building of heavy industry as a strategy, since the agrarian skeptics of industry had been marginalized. Those on the industrial right, as well as liberals and the business world, had in the process acquired the labor movement as an ally in the struggle to build heavy industry—an alliance that was more important than the agrarians' resistance. The policy concerning the iron ore fields showed that there was agreement covering the whole political spectrum that it was possible to go quite some distance in the direction of limiting and regulating the market with regard to those natural resources required for national industry. In Norway, too, there was considerable agreement in this direction.

THE NORWEGIAN CONCESSION LAWS

The situation in Norway was different from that of Sweden in that the agrarian interests were not organized at an early point; on the contrary, they were part of a liberal movement that aspired to social integration.[40] The Liberals made it a virtue not to be a party of special interests. And various matters, not least the union with Sweden, allowed the Liberal Party to unite ostensibly disparate interests. As a result, the modernization policy became more of a compromise than in Sweden. This meant that agricultural interests in Norway were dragged into modernization in a different way than in Sweden, where they had been marginalized early on (even though they had won a number of protective regulations in the wake of the Norrland debate). Owing to the necessity of compromise, Norwegian modernization had a different profile. Cultural and, above all, social and political modernization—advocated by small farmers, urban radicals, and workers—were balanced with economic and industrial modernization so that one got "a well-rounded conception of modernization."[41] Perhaps some would say that Norway developed a weaker and less distinct concept of modernization. This lack of clarity is demonstrated in the debate about the concession laws.

While emigration was worrying the Swedes, something entirely different was causing anxiety in Norway. This had little to do with Norwegians forsaking their country but rather with the invasion of foreigners—that is, foreign

---

[40] Angell 2002, 321.
[41] Slagstad 1998, 142; see also Nordby 1983, 393.

capitalists seeking the use of Norwegian natural resources. The great buying up of waterfalls and all the publicity around Norsk Hydro provided the background for what became known as the "panic laws" of 1906. These laws were launched by the Liberal-Conservative government under the leadership of Christian Michelsen, who a year earlier had been the hero of the dissolution of the union with Sweden. The issue got on the agenda following the publication of an article in the newspaper *Verdens Gang* about an alleged conspiracy "by foreign capital to buy up all the available Norwegian waterpower sources for the purpose of speculation."[42] The panic laws placed strict requirements for concessions on the purchase of natural resources by foreigners.

A new law came into effect in 1909, and another in 1917. During this whole period the concessions issue was a major political question. Like the emigration debate in Sweden, the concessions debate in Norway can be seen as the central debate about the content of the modernization project. The debate exposed the complete spectrum of positions from the ardent anti-industrialists, on one side, all the way to the adherents of free access to foreign capital for the purposes of building large-scale industry, on the other. The majority, however, were in favor of industrialization and a certain degree of public control of its development. The disagreement was over the basic form of control, and behind this we glimpse various degrees of skepticism toward industrialization, heavy industry, and the tempo of development and expansion.

The politician who expressed a point of view closest to that of the Swedish industrial right was the Conservative Party leader Francis Hagerup: "A country cannot be an industrial land without also opening itself up to large-scale industry. . . . Big industry is the bearer of contemporary culture much as the Viking raids were in the earlier Middle Ages."[43] And even if the Norwegians had wanted to industrialize using their own available resources, this was impossible. Foreign capital had to be invited to participate alongside Norwegian capital.

The Michelsen government's proposal to enact the panic laws was more restrictive. The proposal was formulated from a national capitalist standpoint; that is to say, the government was of the opinion that the laws should slow down *foreigners'* buying up of Norwegian natural resources and thereby favor capitalists of Norwegian nationality. In principle there was a great degree of agreement on this issue, so much so that the Conservatives came to adopt this point of view.

But the 1909 laws enacted by Gunnar Knudsen's Liberal Party (Venstre, literally "Left") government did not favor the Norwegians. The general tone

---

[42] *Verdens Gang*, 21 March 1903. Cited by Thue 1996, 41.
[43] St. forh. (Parl. Proceedings) 1905–1906, O. Tid. p. 903.

of the Venstre government's laws was more radical since the strict requirements for concessions applied not just to foreign capitalists but to capitalists
in general. The laws of 1917 followed up and reinforced this line. This was
called a "braking law" since part of its explicit intention was to prevent too
rapid development. Accordingly, the proposition stated:

> In every society, as in the life of the individual, every headlong development is dangerous.
> The society must have time to accept the new gradually. The many new factory centers must
> have time to settle down peacefully and learn to lead and develop their private conduct and
> the conduct of the local communities.[44]

What in principle was new and radical in these laws was, first, their anticapitalistic tendency and, second, their inclusion of "social institutional demands." They paved the way for creating the conditions for the concessions,
such as the obligation to use Norwegian workers and Norwegian materials, as
well as the obligation to provide cheap electricity to local communities. The
law of 1917 was worked out by the Liberal (and social radical) cabinet minister Johan Castberg. In general he tried with his policy to counter the social
disintegration that followed industrialization by introducing "socially reinte-
grating institutions."[45] This radical opening to provide far-reaching provisions
for concessions should be viewed in this light. Castberg won approval in Parliament for this skepticism toward capitalism by building a coalition of social
radicals, Socialist industrialists, and farmers who were skeptical of industry.

One radical element of the 1917 law consisted of what was called "the right
of reversion." This maintained that the state should take over waterfalls and
electrical generating plants after a certain number of years (sixty to eighty)
without paying compensation to the concession holders. The principle had
been put forward by the opposition but then applied only to foreigners. In
the 1917 law it applied to all. It was the prime minister, the engineer Gunnar Knudsen himself, who fathered the right of reversion: when waterpower
becomes commonly owned by the people through the reversion law, "the
Norwegian people [will] have the conditions necessary for a material success
enjoyed almost nowhere else in the world."[46]

The matter was tested before the Supreme Court in a landmark decision
in 1917. The premises of this decision, formulated by a conservative judge,
were as follows: "It is clear that the legislative power has and must have comprehensive justification for limiting the rights of ownership, such that the
owner's possession in law be exercised with respect to various considerations,

---

[44] St. forh. (Parl. Proceedings) 1915, Ot. Prp. 15, p. 3.
[45] Slagstad 1998, 138.
[46] Fuglum 1989, 120.

that social conditions and the development of society necessarily be taken into consideration at every point in time." As Rune Slagstad has commented, in this way "the sharp struggle over the new interventionist state and its relationship to acquired rights, set off by the formulation of the concession laws, . . . was supplemented by the Supreme Court in the formulation of modern ownership rights."[47]

There are valid reasons for claiming that the Norrland laws in Sweden represented a similar tendency in the direction of "modernizing" rights of ownership. Thus Karl Staff, Liberal prime minister and minister of justice, said with regard to these laws that the state had the right to make changes to the rights of joint stock companies "that the state, from other and higher points of view, may find necessary."[48] The gradual takeover of LKAB by the Swedish state is parallel to the final takeover of the waterfalls by the Norwegian state. It must be added, first, that regulations of a similar kind were to be found in many European countries and, second, that both states exercised these "modern ownership rights" in a liberal manner so as not to hamper the main goal—industrialization.

ELECTRICITY, THE BASIS FOR TECHNOLOGICAL MODERNIZATION

Waterpower, electricity, and energy production were central to this technological and economic modernization process. Whereas in the nineteenth century the steamship and the railway symbolized modernity and the future, in the twentieth, it was electricity more than anything else that symbolized technological modernity. As we have seen, this gained concrete expression in the construction of the two great power stations at Vemork and Trollhättan. Sweden and especially Norway stood in favorable positions with regard to their waterpower resources.

The starting points for regulating rivers were different in the two countries. In Norway there was virtually no regulation. Water was under private ownership, and there were few obstacles to using it for whatever one desired. In Sweden, as across Europe for that matter, rivers had affected agricultural and transportation interests differently than in Norway, a fact reflected in Sweden's regulations. These presented grave obstacles to the development of hydroelectric power. First, there was the principle that for transportation

---

[47] Rettstidende [Court Proceedings] 1918, 405; Slagstad 1989, 349.
[48] Edling 1994, 288.

Figure 2. The large hydroelectric power stations Trollhätte in Sweden, *top*, and Vemork in Norway, *bottom*, were put into operation in 1910 and 1911. The monumental style of architecture reflected national pride and faith in electricity as the foundation for future material well-being. For eight years Vemork was the world's largest hydroelectric plant. (Photo of Trollhätte: Vattenfall. Photo of Vemork: Norsk Industriarbeidermuseum.)

needs the state "owned" one-third of the water in the larger rivers, which made it extremely complicated to build dams across the whole river. Second, there was the principle of preserving "the natural flood," which meant that one could not regulate the flow of water according to the needs of the power plant. It is perhaps not so strange that Swedish and other foreign private interests coveted Norway's cascades and waterfalls.

The construction of the Trollhätte power station at Trollhättan marked a turning point. The Göta River, between the large lake Vänern and the city of Gothenburg, is Sweden's largest river with regard to water flow, and the waterfall at Trollhättan, right at the outflow from Vänern, was most suitable for the construction of a hydroelectric facility.[49] It was decided in 1906 that the dam and spillway should be built, and in 1908 the Royal Hydro Power Authority (Kungl. Vattenfallsstyrelsen) was established for the construction and operation, not only of Trollhättan, but also for all subsequent state hydroelectric power projects. In this way the state created "a powerful actor, an entrepreneur capable of taking care of and actively promoting the state's interest in hydroelectric power construction."[50] The Trollhätte power station was completed in 1910. The same year also saw the beginning of the Great Kopparberg (Stora Kopparberg) project at Bullerforsen. This power station, finished in 1913, was larger than Trollhätte. Moreover, in 1910 the Swedish Parliament decided to build a series of power plants along the Great Lule River under the management of the Royal Hydro Power Authority. The proposal was submitted by the conservative Lindman government and received full support in Parliament. The Social Democrat leader, Hjalmar Branting, wrote in relation to this issue: "When faced with such a question, as always when actual national future prosperity is at stake, the political conflicts give way on our side. Such a gigantic undertaking to make use of the riches of nature will be an inspiration for generations."[51]

Evert Vedung's commentary is that we are here facing "a deep mutual understanding," "an unadulterated, hegemonic extended alliance" that "strikes wonder in the social researcher." Was it not the case that the period between 1910 and 1917 was marked by the most powerful of political oppositions? Yet we note that when it came to the question of Sweden's "actual national future prosperity," there was agreement among everyone from "the industrial right" to the Socialists that the country had to be electrified with waterpower and the state had to take responsibility to see that this happened.

As we have seen, it was easier to build in Norway than in Sweden, where the old regulations stood in the way. Old regulations do not allow themselves to be unceremoniously swept away. The time was ripe, however, and with Sweden's Water Enactment in the year 1918 a modern regulation came into being and prepared the ground for hydroelectric construction.[52] It so hap-

---

[49] Jakobsson 1996, 93–94. It was a unique case. The judicial decision was based on considerations of "regal rights" which means that old pre-liberal rules of law were used to put limits on a liberal private right of ownership, and give reason for "modern ownership rights."

[50] Vedung and Brandel 2001, 30.

[51] Vedung and Brandel 2001, 35.

[52] Vedung and Brandel 2001, 43ff.

pened that at roughly the same time Norway had managed to get its own system in place with the concession laws. The processes had followed different trajectories in the two countries. In Norway uneasiness about such major construction had driven the issue, and the result was a "braking law." Conversely, in Sweden the desire to do away with hindrances that lay in the way of such a construction project served to move the issue forward, and the result was a law that opened up new possibilities. The two countries came out of their respective and different corners and moved toward regulations that were similar in their consequences.

In both countries the hydroelectric systems had a mixed economic character. "System-builders could move between the private and the public sphere, and in this way implement their technological visions."[53] The construction was extensive in both countries, despite the limitations imposed by the crises of the interwar period. But here the similarities end.

According to the Swedish historian Eva Jakobsson, "The Norwegian model distinguishes itself to a remarkable degree from the Swedish system." From the beginning the Norwegian system had a clear binary structure based on the division between supplying power to the general public and supplying electricity to large-scale electrochemical and electrometallurgical industries. The legal framework tended to favor the supplying of public power. It is important to be aware that this public supply also included electricity for light industry and that this was an important precondition for this part of the system being favored. As it was expressed in a government proposition of 1910: "It is such, that access to cheap electrical power will become very significant not simply for the advancement of industry in general, but also in particular for advancing what, on a social basis, is the most desirable form of industry, small industry."[54]

In line with traditional Norwegian localism, municipalities were exempted from the restrictions imposed by concessions from the state and had the right to expropriate waterways. The municipalities became the large builders. In 1923 they generated 83 percent of the public electricity supply. When it came to supplying new power-consuming industries, however, 90–95 percent of the power installations were private. Many of them were in foreign hands. They were subject to the conditions of the concession laws and the right of reversion. The concession laws were enforced cautiously, so that foreign capital was not excluded. Nor had such exclusion been the intention.[55] The strong-man behind the laws was Prime Minister Gunnar Knudsen, who was one

---

[53] Jakobsson 1996, 102.
[54] St. forh. (Parl. Proceedings) 1910, Ot. Prp. 44. Cited here from Thue 1996, 45.
[55] Annaniassen 1983, 229ff.

of the great strategists of modernization. The state also bought several river locations capable of generating power. This involvement gradually expanded, and in 1921 Norway acquired its counterpart to Sweden's Vattenfallsstyrelsen (Royal Hydro Power Authority), namely, Vassdrags- og Elektrisitetsvesen (Waterways and Electricity Authority). Even the relatively modest state-run constructions were above all directed toward providing electricity for general consumption.[56] In Norway the really extensive building by the state did not happen until the hegemonic period for Social Democracy after World War II.

In Sweden there was no comparable bipartite system such as we find in Norway. Consequently, there was no political will to give the municipalities any advantages, for example, in the form of rights of expropriation. There was no right of reversion, and concessions were not laden with social demands.[57] On the other hand, the state was involved as a very active builder right from the beginning. Even though the municipalities played a more passive role than in Norway, they were borne along with the private interests as holders of share capital and as potential consumers of electric power. In this way nonstate power producers were established. This construction has been described as "a new form of enterprise." In contrast to the many small Norwegian municipal power companies, some of the Swedish ones were gathered together in larger enterprises. This applied above all to Sydkraft (Southern Power) and Gullsprångs Kraft (Gullsprång Power). The Swedish system was thus dominated by the state's Hydro Power Authority, on the one hand, and the semimunicipal companies, on the other.

It is important to point out that the foundation for this system was rooted in an integrated ideology, namely, in an industrial-friendly, large-scale model—a belief in large rational systems. Despite this strong public engagement, the Swedish system was less politically directed than the Norwegian, which through the concession laws was characterized by strong political influence. In Sweden, in spite of strong state engagement, there was a conscious political choice to abstain from the influence of current political power.[58] Thus the two systems were different, but the result, in the form of a publicly initiated and managed electrification, was the same in both countries.

In order to understand the significance of electrification for the dynamics of economic and technological development, it is important to be aware that the starting point for the projects undertaken was not an articulated demand for electricity. When the initiative was taken to begin the venture that became Norsk Hydro, it was not decided what the power would be used for, simply that it would be used to build up modern industry. The starting point was an

---

[56] Thue 1994, 230.
[57] Jakobsson 1992, 253, 257.
[58] Jakobsson 1992, 66, 103–104, 108.

awareness of the superiority of waterpower. This attitude penetrated far into the Social Democratic state. When Norway's Social Democratic prime minister Einar Gerhardsen gave his May First speech in 1946, at the inception of Social Democracy's great period, when the Social Democrats were preparing for the state to deliver a strong stimulus to hydroelectric power construction, he said the same thing: "We should not ask what we are going to use the electricity for. We have to build it up so that industry will follow along behind."

It is important to bear in mind that the systems of hydroelectric construction and distribution were in place when the interwar crises hit. Construction continued during this time, although at a slower pace. The point, however, is that in both countries there was a resource that now demanded application. This became an impetus for development and an important preparatory step on the road out of the crises.[59]

WAR AND STRUCTURAL PROBLEMS

World War I made itself felt in more or less the same way in the two countries. They were both neutral and experienced a strong and, to some extent, speculative economic boom. The currency became inflated, and the gold standard was suspended. Violent inflation together with difficulties in the importing of foodstuffs due to the restrictions placed on trade and transport led to hunger and social unrest. From a purely economic point of view, what was most remarkable was the fact that the two countries managed to repay the large outstanding foreign debt that had accumulated during the previous great period of construction. In 1910 Sweden was "possibly the world's most indebted nation."[60] The foreign debt may well have been settled but, on the other hand, the state debt increased significantly in both countries, and this weakened the state's ability to step in during the crises that followed World War I.

The speculative element of the economic boom period during the war led to irresponsibility and bad investments, and both Sweden and Norway endured serious bank crises after the war. All the same, it is in all probability correct to say that the bad investments of the boom period were limited, not least by the continuing investment in hydroelectric power construction.[61] Furthermore, the crisis that began in 1920 cleaned up the bad investments by getting rid of old companies tied to traditional methods and structures. In Sweden there was an extensive *bruksdöd* (death of the old ironworks).

---

[59] Schön 2000, 355. Childs (1936) also devotes great attention to the importance of "a national power system."

[60] Schön 2000, 270.

[61] Schön 2000, 277–278.

Wartime inflation was "sorted out" by means of a back-to-par policy. This parity was reached in Sweden in 1924 and in Norway in 1928. In 1931, however, both countries followed Great Britain in giving up the gold standard they had fought so hard to reinstitute. Many regard the fall of the gold standard as a decisive dividing line in the European politico-economic development of the period.[62] By giving up the reestablished "normal conditions" from before World War I, one opened the way for an ongoing "process policy" or political intervention in the economy by means of monetary policy.

World War I led to the creation of a cooperative relationship between the state and industry in both countries. In Sweden this meant following a traditional line; in Norway it represented, to a greater degree, a new orientation. Closely linked to this construction work was the breakthrough in thinking about the special responsibility of the state for applied research geared to industrial goals. It was incumbent on those holding power to find substitutes for raw materials and goods that earlier it had been possible to import—above all, coal.[63] In 1918 the Swedish *Affärsvärlden* (Business World) wrote that "necessity created by the war" had yielded good results "through the combination of scientific research and practical work."[64] One also could observe how the countries that had gone to war—especially Germany—had organized research at the national level. Great Britain and the United States followed suit and built up public institutions for industrial research. Other institutions followed, and public resources were channeled into research for industry. In some areas research institutions were gradually established for individual branches of industry. All these initiatives were based on cooperation between the public and private sectors.

This policy received a setback during the interwar crises. Government paralysis caused by crises—especially the crisis in state finance—led to abandonment of plans and even to liquidation of some institutions. Nonetheless, the principles of public-private cooperation lived on. In many ways World War I signified a lasting breakthrough for the idea of closer cooperation between the state and the business world, the idea of science being applied to the needs of industry, and the state's responsibility in fostering both connections. The real breakthrough in practice came during the boom period following World War II with, among other things, the founding of the research councils.

In addition to the many similarities in the two countries' post–World War I development, there were also differences. Sweden was the first country in

---

[62] See, for example, Polanyi 1944. He maintained that giving up the gold standard necessarily led to the formation of a new form of economy with the markings of fascism.

[63] Francis Sejersted 2002a, chapter titled "Moderniseringsstrategier i Norge 1900–1940."

[64] Sundin 1981, 195.

Europe able to reestablish the gold standard at its old rate following the war. The country quickly recovered from the deflation crisis and was able to make use of the boom years in the latter part of the 1920s. Norway had a longer way to go and was the last country to reestablish the gold standard parity. Therefore the deflation crisis had far more serious consequences for Norway. This is the background to the different turns that the structural changes took in the two countries.

Tendencies toward concentration and monopolization in the form of large enterprises, amalgamations and takeovers, price-fixing agreements (cartels), and the use of holding companies or other means of circumventing the market were all features of "organized capitalism," and these tendencies were further exaggerated during World War I and the crises that followed. In Sweden this tendency was clear and strong, while in Norway it was less visible. The United States was far in advance, and there one also found a reaction in the form of strong antitrust laws, not that they were particularly helpful. In Europe, by contrast, there was a tendency to look at the amalgamations as a desired rationalization and as a way of defending against the destructive power of competition. Thus Sweden experienced a long period of widespread contentment with the strong tendencies toward concentration of capital because they were regarded as a precondition for successful industrialization. People were more skeptical in Norway. There, small-scale light industry was preferred.

In spite of the general tendency toward concentration, the high prices and speculation during the war had created a certain skepticism toward concentration. This skepticism led to the creation of Sweden's Trust Foundation Committee and Norway's Trust Commission "for dealing with questions concerning opposition to trust formations and other concentrations of capital accused of abolishing freedom of competition and artificially raising prices, among other things." Both commissions came out with their findings in 1921.[65] The findings reflect the skepticism toward the regulation of competition. In the Norwegian commission, however, the young radical man of the left, Wilhelm Thagaard, maintained that the concentrations were positive and saw them as preconditions for a future transition to "social management" wherein the state would play an active role.[66]

While on the one hand the war had given rise to skepticism, on the other the interwar crises contributed to an expanding awareness of the positive character of these concentrations. They were increasingly seen as an initiative

---

[65] Hermansson 1965, 16–20; Magnusson 1997, 362–363. Trustkommisjonens instilling (The Trust Commission's report) was appended to St. forh. (Parl. Proceedings) 1924, O. Prp. 46.

[66] St. forh (Parl. Proceedings) 1924, O. Prp. 46. Appendix, 48.

against destructive competition. Thus it was in character that when the trust laws were finally enacted in 1925 in Sweden and in 1926 in Norway, the original commission recommendations were considerably watered down. At no point was there ever a "trust commission" established in Sweden, and in Norway the law was so open that Thagaard, as chairman of the Trust Control Commission, was able to conduct a policy based on a positive view of the regulations on competition.[67] Similarly, we find examples of the state in both countries going into the compulsory formation of cartels as a way of dealing with crises. There was thus a clear tendency in the direction of economic planning and state intervention in the sphere of production, something that pointed toward the future Social Democratic state.

THRUST FOR SOCIALIZATION

Socialization commissions were established at the same time the trust commissions were. These had the support and participation of parties representing the business world in both countries. This participation by the non-Socialists has to be seen against the background of fear of revolution that haunted this whole period, when the demands of the radicals led to a certain degree of accommodation by the non-Socialists. But there were also elements of reform optimism among many of the non-Socialists.

A precondition for being able to make use of the positive potential inherent in the concentration of capital was one or another form of public control. For some, and under some circumstances, this meant public or national takeover of companies. Nationalization or, as Thagaard put it, "socialized management" was thus joined with the process of concentration. Given this development, the radicals were able to see the contours of a new social formation. The Liberals and liberal Conservatives could see the necessity of taking initiatives with regard to certain firms so that capitalism would function better. In this area there were significant differences between Sweden and Norway.

The issue of public ownership began in Norway when the workers at Norsk Hydro approached Parliament in 1919 with a demand that the company be nationalized as quickly as possible. Within the labor movement at this time, public ownership, or "socialization," was not identified with "nationalization," or state takeover of companies. The state was still bourgeois, so socialization took the form of a kind of self-management in which the majority of the board of directors would be chosen by the employees, the

---

[67] SOU 1940, 35, *Organiserad samverkan inom näringsliv* (Organized Cooperation in Business Life), pp. 312f.; Kili 1996, 108–109.

consumers would also have a representative, and Parliament would appoint an administrative director.[68] Parliament responded by setting up the Socialization Commission, which had the task of looking into the desirability of making public certain types of companies. At this point it was still clearly not difficult for the radical non-Socialists to be part of the socialization effort. However, after a number of replacements, the committee found itself with a majority representing the labor movement and, among them, some of the foremost theorists of socialization.[69]

The Norwegian Socialization Commission report came out in 1924. The majority of the committee, representatives of the labor movement, had "an ambivalent relationship toward capitalism."[70] Mature capitalism, they thought, should give birth to socialism, but the problem was that Norwegian capitalism was immature; that is, it lacked the objective conditions essential to capitalistic accumulation—the concentration of capital. "Therefore the first step was not socialization, but rather to hasten the maturing process" by means of a socially controlled creation of trusts. The labor movement had to postpone socialism for the time being in order to contribute to the development of a mature capitalism that functioned better.[71]

The non-Socialist members of the committee shared the same worries as did representatives of the labor movement. Both sides were worried that Norway was falling behind in developing a modern structure of production, and they were both willing to go a long way in the direction of social management. The positions within the committee reflected the positions of the industry magnate Walter Rathenau and the Marxist Karl Kautsky. They were both engaged in the question of socialization of ownership in Germany, and from their respective sides they both advocated extensive concentration and strict rationalization. Rathenau's organic production collectives under scientific leadership could have been exchanged for technocratic socialist models.[72] Rathenau's and Kautsky's thinking was well known in the Norwegian committee and was used in arguments by both sides.

Naturally enough there was not full agreement. The premises on which the common worries were based differed. Those representing the non-Socialists and the business class certainly did not see concentration as a step toward Socialism; moreover, they put forward their own minority positions. Nevertheless, this relative agreement is striking. We might say that the reason why such agreement was reached was because the committee, including

---

[68] Myrvang 1996, 55.
[69] Myrvang 1996, 70.
[70] Myrvang 1996, 75.
[71] Myrvang 1996, 80, 93.
[72] Myrvang 1996, 130.

the representatives of the labor movement, confined itself to a discourse of industrialism, leaving aside the traditional Socialist discourse of capitalism. When one first engages in a collaboration, one has to communicate on the basis of a common discourse, and in this case the goal for both sides was the development of well-functioning modern industry. Or to put it another way, the committee was preparatory not to a *project of socialization* but rather to a *project of modernization.*

Sweden had a socialization commission that worked parallel to that in Norway, but the results were different. The background to Sweden's setting up of the commission was that the Social Democrats had launched a socialization drive in conjunction with the establishment of the first Social Democratic government in 1920. The Swedish commission's 1924 recommendation was to concentrate on the organization of the country's largest undertaking, Statens Järnvägar (the National Railway). One difficulty for the Social Democrats was that the state initiatives taken during the war had been deemed ineffective, whereas private business, despite the unfortunate speculations during the war, could still float along on the legitimacy that effective performance was able to provide. Thus we see "that economic liberalism came to dominate economic thinking not only on the right but also in the labor movement."[73] Or, as the historian Klas Åmark writes, it was "striking how quickly those in the LO (Landsorganisationen—the trade union central) developed a way of thinking that runs in the direction of cooperation and compromise with the employers, since this implied that the trade union movement not only lived in peaceful coexistence with capitalism but also strove for as effective development of capitalism as possible."[74]

The different fates of the two socialization committees reflected the fact that the formation of trusts had become much more extensive in Sweden and consequently that Swedish capitalism was considered so much more mature. Seen through Swedish Social Democratic eyes, this was positive. Thus in 1908 the Social Democrat—and later leader of the Swedish Socialization Commission—Rikard Sandler was able to say that "in socialism's Sweden the creator of trusts . . . almost merits a statue."[75]

The same year that Sandler made his statement, the Labor Party of Norway, from the opposite side, warned against amalgamations of capital that could place power in the hands of major capitalists. This warning came in the context of one of the concession issues.[76] In contrast to their Swedish counterparts, the Norwegian Socialists allied themselves with traditional anticapital-

[73] Myrvang 1996, 173–175; Lundh 1987, 111.
[74] Åmark 1998, 363.
[75] Myrvang 1996, 178; Tingsten 1967, 1:207.
[76] Myrvang 1996, 32.

ist movements, the roots of which were in the old agrarian society. It seems that Norwegian Socialists were more anticapitalistic than Swedish Socialists, but whether they were more Socialistic is another question. That Swedish capitalism was so much more mature should perhaps indicate that Sweden was in a position to take the next step—the socialization of production. The degree of maturity was precisely the argument of Sweden's Communists when they advocated socializing industry in 1945.[77] But for the Social Democrats this was too radical, in the 1920s as well as in 1945. Socialization as a policy was rejected in both countries. Paradoxically, the public industrial sector in Social Democratic Sweden remained among the smallest in Europe.[78]

We should nevertheless be reticent about concluding from this review that the Social Democrats gave up socialization as a strategy once and for all. *Socialization* is a term that can include many different forms of curtailment or takeover of the power of capitalists. It remains as an ideological element, a part of the identity of the labor movement, that can be pushed away in certain situations for pragmatic reasons but can always be brought forward in various disguises and can actually determine action. The ongoing debate on economic or industrial democracy that continued throughout the twentieth century reflected this element, and in the 1970s, with the proposal about the "wage-earner funds," the idea of socialization appeared again in a comparatively pure form (see chapter 12).

CONSOLIDATION OF TWO DIFFERENT STRUCTURES

The interwar crises contributed to consolidating the different economic structures in the two countries. In Sweden there was a strengthening of the special networks that had developed within business life. Three banks stood at the center of these networks: Skandinavbanken, Handelsbanken, and the Stockholm Enskilda Bank of the Wallenbergs. Even though these large banks had their problems in relation to the crisis of the 1920s, in the end they gained wider influence over industry. They played a vital role in the changes of concentration and the restructuring of Swedish large industry during that period. Perhaps the best example of this is the formation of Svenska Cellulosa AB (Swedish Cellulose Inc.) in 1929, when the Swedish industrialist Ivar Kreuger purchased a series of wood-processing plants that, following the crisis of the 1920s, had fallen into the hands of Handelsbanken. Under the management of the bank a comprehensive restructuring had taken place, including ratio-

---

[77] Lewin 1992, 233.
[78] Judt 2007, 555.

nalization and modernization, partly by establishing new factories.[79] Something similar occurred in the iron and steel industry. An important part of the technological renewal was the replacement of coal by electricity for heating.

The areas of industrial growth in the interwar period were above all those associated with the production of the new durable consumer goods of the period such as telephones, automobiles, vacuum cleaners, kitchen ranges, refrigerators, radios, and so on. Swedish industry made good use of these interwar possibilities (for example, the companies L. M. Ericsson, Volvo, and Electrolux). The world economic crisis also hit Sweden in 1931, of course, but like the crises of the 1920s it was overcome with surprising speed. In brief, Sweden became a "winning nation," as Lennart Schön writes.[80] The reason for this has been much discussed. Most now believe that it did not lie in the expansive Social Democratic finance policy, as previously maintained. Schön continues, "Accordingly, behind this fortunate economic policy there lay a longer-term set of structural conditions that allowed mobility of response to the new possibilities and to the fact that relatively favorable conditions could be sustained for a longer period."[81] In other words, during the crises the country's economic structure proved to be well suited for structural rationalization and the creation of new enterprises.

This history is very different from Norway's in the same period. Even Norway's flagship, Norsk Hydro, had difficulties because during World War I the Germans had developed a much more efficient method of extracting nitrogen from the air.

There were certainly some positive cases in Norway. Elektrokemisk AS (Electrochemical Inc.) can be viewed as another example of what in Sweden was called *snilleindustri* (literally, an enterprise of genius). Elektrokemisk was established in 1904 with the idea of industrial development based on hydroelectric power. During the war years the company developed the so-called Söderberg electrode, which was critically important for the ability to use electricity in the heating and refining processes of the metal industry.[82] The company represents the starting point for what later was to become the very extensive Norwegian aluminum industry. Activities of this type were too few or of insufficient weight to affect the general trajectory of development, however.

[79] Schön 2000, 295, 308, 344–345. Kreuger also had interests in other parts of Swedish industry. The great Kreuger crash in 1932 contributed to the consolidation of the old constellation of ownership in the industrial sector.

[80] Schön 2000, 295. See particularly the chapter titled "Varför klarade Sverige trettiotalskrisen så bra?" pp. 348ff.

[81] Schön 2000, p. 351.

[82] Nerheim 1980; Francis Sejersted 2002a, the chapter titled "Moderniseringsstrategier i Norge 1900–1940," pp. 298–299.

But, in the interwar years, Norwegian maritime shipping developed because of a successful transfer from steam power to internal combustion en-
gines, among other reasons. The Norwegian shipbuilding industry did not
manage to follow this up, however. This expansion and restructuring of *Norwegian* maritime shipping was, by contrast, an important precondition for
the extensive renewal and refitting of the *Swedish* shipbuilding industry in
the interwar period, and consequently demonstrates the amazing ability of
Swedish industry to regenerate, in comparison to its Norwegian counterpart.

Even though the effects of the crisis were great in Norway and unemployment was very high at times, the country did not come out so badly in the
broader perspective. Thus, between 1933 and 1939, industrial employment
increased at the rate of 6.7 percent per annum. This was due to the development of a powerful movement in the small-firm sector of industry. The rate of
establishing new industrial firms at this time was high. This had a great deal to
do with the fact that firms developed in close contact with the local markets
and showed that they could accommodate themselves to the new patterns
of consumption in a flexible manner. One might say that the structure of
Norwegian industry, with its small entities linked to local markets, showed its
strength during this late phase. The strength lay in what was later called "flexible specialization"—that is, small companies, with their restructuring ability
and their flexibility in adapting to changes in the market, may have had an
advantage over the large, mass-producing firms. This certainly was the case
during the 1930s, when a new consumer pattern was emerging. In addition,
as we noted earlier, light industry was able to make good use of the cheap and
abundant electric power.

The Norwegian industrial entrepreneur Joakim Lehmkuhl is illustrative of
the prevailing conditions. He established a company to manufacture electric
refrigerators. He also was a very articulate adherent of Taylorism or scientific
management (discussed in the following section). He gave up the attempt to
implement these principles in his own company, however, because he came
to realize that they were ill suited to Norwegian business conditions. Referring to the strong, democratically minded Norwegian petite bourgeoisie, he
rejected "the principle of dictatorship," as he put it, and worked instead to
advance light industry with the assistance of the state. In 1940 he went to the
United States, where he took over a watch and clock firm later named Timex.
After World War II he rationalized the firm's production according to modern
principles of production of durable consumer goods.[83] Whether he would
have been able to do the same thing with equal success in Sweden we do not
know, though it is not unlikely. But in Norway it turned out to be impossible.

---

[83] Jakobsen 1994, 79 f.

RATIONALIZATION

The tendencies toward monopolization were closely linked with the rationalization efforts of the time, called "scientific management." This movement was linked to Fredrick W. Taylor and the management approach he invented, Taylorism. Taylor was an American engineer with experience in industry. He believed that resources were poorly utilized in American industry, partly because of ineffective organization and partly because of the conflict between capital and labor. By means of scientific experimental methods (time and motion studies), he argued, one should be able to find a functional division of labor and the most effective labor processes. By managing individual performance and performance incentives, a firm's leadership ought to be able to create solidarity within the company.

Taylor was an opponent of trade unions, and his methods immediately met with opposition from workers. Nevertheless, the idea of rationalization, in various forms, spread widely. This idea was gradually combined with psychological studies that paid greater attention to the human factor. The principles of rationalization were markedly instrumental. Human labor was to be shaped to suit the needs of production. Despite this, the labor movements in many countries gradually came to view scientific management in a positive light because some rationalized American firms paid higher wages, and scientific management principles were being applied in the Soviet Union.[84]

The efficiency programs of the United States entered the Swedish debate in 1907 without reference to Taylor. His book, *Principles of Scientific Management*, was not published until 1911, but it awakened immediate notice in Sweden. The book came out in Swedish in 1913.[85] Scientific management also was quickly given an institutional basis by the consulting firm Industribyrån (the Industry Bureau) in 1912 and subsequently became a central concern of the Academy of the Engineering Sciences, which was founded with public support in the wake of World War I. During the 1930s efforts in this field were considerable.[86]

The Swedish variant of scientific management was adapted to Swedish conditions. "On those points that were uniquely and specifically Tayloristic—the functional supervision, the wage system, the reluctance to accept the workers' organizations—it never thoroughly took root in Sweden."[87] A conscious rationalization movement developed, however, based on systematic time studies and professionalization of the leadership functions at all levels.

[84] Geer 1978, 52.
[85] Geer 1978, 69, 81–82.
[86] Geer 1978, 117–118.
[87] Geer 1978, 237.

The efficiency of Swedish industry increased significantly in the interwar period. Erik Dahmén maintains, "It is very likely that the '20s were unparalleled on fundamental progress in the area of production methods." He mentions Taylor's influence in this connection.[88]

It is striking to see how much the Social Democrats were preoccupied with production problems at the expense, to a certain degree, of the traditional preoccupation of the Socialists with problems of redistribution. Not least, they showed concern for industrial efficiency. A precondition for this was the fact that this rationalization—like monopolization and concentration, which can be viewed as part of rationalization—was linked to the idea of public responsibility for employment as well as for the structure of industry in general. The implication is that rationalization pointed to the development of *the planned economy* in general and to the special Swedish organization of the labor market (see part 2).

It is also fruitful to analyze Social Democratic *political* practice from the end of the 1930s on the basis of management theories. The government fastened onto a form of management that in its essential features was well known in the business and non-Socialist world: it viewed itself as a professional corporate leadership for the nation.[89] This professionalization of the function of leadership made a significant contribution to lessening the conflict between capital and labor at all levels.

The scientific management wave also reached Norway. In 1920 the industrial entrepreneur Joakim Lehmkuhl, whom we met earlier, published the book *Rationel arbeidsledelse* (Rational Labor Management), which was the real introduction to the theme in Norway. Nonetheless, Tayloristic ideas did not gain an institutional foothold in Norway in the interwar period the way they did in Sweden. They made a certain breakthrough, however, in the 1950s, when it was possible to observe engineers going around with stop-watches in many Norwegian factories.[90] Yet ideas of this type did play an ideological role as part of the general rationalization project, and thereby part of the modernization project.[91] There was worry and concern whenever they did not achieve a breakthrough in practice.

We have already seen that Lehmkuhl gave up his attempt to establish a rationalized mass-production factory for durable consumer goods in Norway. He also modified his Tayloristic ideas in a book that he published in 1933, *Norway's Road: An Attack on Norwegian Nonsocialist Policy—and a Proposal for a National Labor Plan* (Norges vei—Et angrep på norsk borgerlig politikk—

---

[88] Dahmén 1950, 128, 362.
[89] Geer 1978, 339.
[90] Heiret et al. 2003, 137.
[91] Halvorsen 1982; Jakobsen 1994, 6.

og et forslag til nasjonal arbeidsplan). Here he advocates a state-supported light-industry sector as part of a program of economic expansionism. At this time Lehmkuhl was a central figure in the Fatherland Association (Fedrelands-laget), a bourgeois nonparliamentary organization established out of frustration with the non-Socialist parties' lack of initiative during the crises. The book presents the point of view of the Fatherland Association—a Norwegian variant of a modernization project that later, to some degree, was taken over and implemented by the labor movement.[92]

There are two things to note about Lehmkuhl's books from 1920 and 1933. First, in the 1920 book, where he introduced Taylor, Lehmkuhl expressed certain doubts. Rational labor management "reduces individuals to mechanisms," as he put it.[93] This humanistic reaction to the instrumentality of modernism entered here as an afterthought or a reflection. Second, his modification of the program to fit light industry in his 1933 book can perhaps be viewed as a concession to this reflection. But above all it is an ideologizing of the factual development of light industry. There was no talk, however, either by Lehmkuhl or by others, of the general breakthrough of such ideologizing, which became apparent after World War II, when Lehmkuhl realized his mass-production ideal in America and the Labor Party's economic plans tried to live up to the ideals of the time by preparing for heavy industry in Norway.

TECHNOCRACY

The fact that applied industrial research developed so late obviously had something to do with the dispute about how closely technology should be linked to the natural sciences. Here we can detect the existence of a dilemma that seems to have been resolved around the time of World War I:

> By emphasizing the technical sciences as independent and distinctive sciences that, among other things, take into consideration economic factors, it became possible to do away with the contradiction between theory and practice.
>
> The scientific aura around the work of the engineer was preserved, while at the same time the economic and practical interests were satisfied, so to speak, in theory.[94]

Thus from a position somewhere between the devil and the deep blue sea, the engineer's enterprise developed into its own type of enterprise, a new practice. During this period the engineer became in a special sense the representative

---

[92] Jakobsen 1994, 50.
[93] Lehmkuhl 1920, 19.
[94] Sundin 1981, 84.

of modern society. From an unclear social position on the sidelines, he moved to a central place in modern society's social hierarchy. This is symptomatic of the fact that to an increasing degree engineers were becoming directors of modern companies, and to this extent they served to reduce the influence of capitalists or owners. This was what came to be called managerial capitalism. It could just as well have been called engineer capitalism. This is the basis for the designation "the epoch of engineering science," and it is here that one finds the starting point for technocracy.

Technocracy, or "the art of social engineering," implies that the character-istic ideals of the engineer become generalized.[95] The ideas of rationalization and the instrumentalism of engineering ideology were promoted on the so-cietal level, but this does not mean that the engineer assumed a central posi-tion. On the societal level the engineer had to compete with other experts who, by acquiring the ideals of the engineer, had developed aspirations to become the generalists of the planned economy—experts such as economists, doctors, and architects. The man who expressed this new social political ide-ology most clearly was the Swedish economist Gunnar Myrdal. He presented his vision of technocracy in an article in 1932. This new ideology was "intel-lectual and coolly rationalistic," in contrast to the old sociopolitical ideology, which, he says, was sentimental. The romance of the new ideology was "that of the engineer."[96]

Myrdal discusses the architect as an example. This was perhaps not com-pletely coincidental, as 1930 had been Stockholm's exposition year and this had left traces on Myrdal's thinking. The exposition represented the break-through of functionalism and the new Nordic simplicity and matter-of-factness. It was here that Sweden's "project of the future was born."[97] This was a new society marked by good sense, rationality, and planning. The physical environment was to be formed according to the functional aesthetic, which was expressed briefly and powerfully by Otto Carlsund, the cubist painter re-sponsible for the art exhibition titled L'art concret: "Nature is dead; long live geometric concrete art." The history of Sweden was brought to life by Lud-vig Nordström, who declared that the great industrial corporations signified "what once in the venerable past the old King Gustav Wasa, or King Gustav II Adolf stood for"—in other words, industry had given the Swedish people "the highest degree of spiritual freedom that any nation could aspire to."[98]

[95] Jakobsen 1994, 138. Jakobsen refers to F. A. Hayek 1964, 94, where he draws out three features on the engineer's horizon: the importance of planning, a tendency (conditioned by education) to forget social conditions, together with efficiency analyzed in terms of energy.

[96] Gunnar Myrdal 1932, "Socialpolitikens dilemma," in Spektrum. Cited here from G. Nilsson 1990.

[97] Zander 2001, 240.

[98] Norman 2001, 215.

The project was born in a spirit of considerable social feeling. The new aesthetic, the new technology, and objective common sense were all intended to come together to serve both the masses and the project of social integration. If one were to believe these statements, society had already come a long way toward realizing the emigration report's project: building the land of the future. Sweden was the avant-garde; it stood in the forefront, especially in the physical formation of the environment.

Gunnar Myrdal enthusiastically supported functionalism's program. He was one of the trendsetting Social Democrats, and the program gained great influence within Social Democracy. Myrdal has, however, been criticized for his instrumentalism.[99] We must also be careful not to identify functionalism too closely with the labor movement.[100] The ideal of the modern functional apartment block with a kitchen that was ergonomically constructed to improve the efficiency of housework had constantly to compete with the romantic image of the "little red cottage," which represented another ideal way of living. The art of social engineering had to compete with the anti-instrumentalism of the humanist tradition, even within the labor movement.

The new modernist objectivity also took root in Norway. Characteristically, however, this breakthrough occurred later and was less pronounced than in Sweden. Functionalism in Norway had to wrestle with nationalist values to a much greater extent than in Sweden.[101] Sweden was a country at the cutting edge, the avant-garde that enthusiasts of functionalism in Norway could only regard with envy. In a general sense there also developed a type of social engineering in Norway represented particularly by the Social Democrats. But, as indicated, special conditions made the concept of modernization in Norway more moderate than it was in Sweden.

DREAMING THE LAND OF THE FUTURE

By the beginning of the twentieth century both countries found themselves in what some have called "the situation of an incomplete society."[102] It was a period marked by industrial and economic growth but also by the social crisis created by the new industrial society. The new scientific developments and the promises of industrialization and electrification all contributed to shaping

[99] G. Nilsson 1990.
[100] Zander 2001, 247.
[101] Slagstad 1998, 182.
[102] Slagstad 1998, 168.

the dream of a future society. This dream was particularly strong in Sweden, which was ahead in the process of industrialization. There it nurtured a great-power dream of becoming Europe's vanguard.

Ambitions were more modest in Norway, and the modernization concept itself was less clear. There were also differences between the two countries' starting points and ideals for material structure. Sweden was deeply into organized capitalism, with several large heavy-industrial ventures. In Norway light industry predominated both in reality and in the country's vision of the ideal. At the same time, there developed in both countries an agreement between industrialists and Socialists that industrialization was necessary and that it should be based on hydroelectric power, something to which both countries had abundant access. Concrete initiatives were taken with a high degree of agreement about major issues. In relation to these initiatives, we have also observed that the Socialists veered away from the Marxian discourse of capitalism and toward the discourse of industrialism, a shift that opened the way for class cooperation.

The "romance of the engineer" was the new ideology. Techno-economic modernization and the scientific mode of thinking came to characterize what has been called "the art of social engineering." Although technocracy became a central element in what was later the Social Democratic order, it would never be completely dominant. It came to stand for a tense relationship with democratic ideals, on the one hand, and with humanistic ideals, on the other. From the standpoint of the new professional expertise, insight and scientific methods were capable of banishing politics, with its meaningless squabbles. Experts had a tendency to believe that experts could lead more effectively than either politicians or the people in general. And even though most of them would not admit to being antidemocratic, the tension persisted. Humanists reacted warily to instrumentalism, or to the tendency to shove aside the old ideal about the morally formed human being in favor of the physically healthy and happy person as the acculturated ideal standing for the good future society. The question became one of the relative strength of the democratic or humanistic critiques, or to what degree these critiques came to modify technocracy. Here we discern a difference between the countries, since the democratic norms were stronger in Norway than in Sweden.

CHAPTER 2

National Integration and Democracy

The Question of Political Democracy in the Period around 1905 • Mobilizing the Public • Training for Democracy • Toward an Integrated School System in Norway • Contrasting the Two Countries • Karl Staaff and the Question of Suffrage in Sweden • Arvid Lindman and the Question of Universal Suffrage • The Difficult Road to Parliamentarianism • Gunnar Knudsen and State Capitalism • Currents of Antiparliamentarianism • The Farmers and Modernization • Farmers on the Offensive: Norway • Farmers on the Offensive: Sweden • Crisis Settlement in Both Countries • Women and Civil and Political Rights • The Integration of Minorities: The Sami • The Integration of Minorities: Refugees from Germany • National Integration and Democracy

THE QUESTION OF POLITICAL DEMOCRACY IN THE PERIOD AROUND 1905

The struggle for political democracy came partly from below, by means of popular movements, and partly from above, from modernist reformers. Political democratization was part of nation building. Political democratization began in the early 1800s with the fall of absolute monarchy in Sweden in 1809 and in Norway in 1814. But it was not until the end of the nineteenth and the beginning of the twentieth centuries that the countries approached what we recognize today as political democracy with parliamentary systems and universal suffrage. Nor was the battle then won once and for all. The parliamentary system came under threat from totalitarian movements during the interwar period. Besides, although the parliamentary system and universal suffrage constituted the major step on the road to real political democracy, there were still obstacles to overcome.

According to the theory of nation building put forward by Stein Rokkan, the next step after the right to vote is parliamentary representation.[1] The farmers were the first to be integrated into the first two steps, and then the workers. The integration of the farmers followed the national revolution and

---

[1] Rokkan 1970, 79. Rokkan actually operates with four "institutional thresholds": the first is the legitimacy of opposition, the second is participation in voting, the third is representation, and the fourth is participation in the exercise of power.

that of the workers followed the industrial revolution.[2] We will also turn our attention to other groups, which took longer to integrate.

The process of democratization at this phase referred to the *political* sphere. Democratization of the *economic* sphere influenced the capitalist social order in a different manner. In most European countries the struggle over economic democratization would continue throughout the twentieth century. The outcome of this struggle has been ambiguous, something to which we will return (see part 3).

The introduction stated that Norway was democratized before it was industrialized and that the reverse was the case in Sweden. The explanation of this difference lies in the two countries' social structures and political institutions. "In Sweden one found a powerful upper class, which consisted of higher-level civil servants, landowners, mill owners and industrialists. These people occupied a strong position in [Parliament's] upper house and constituted a restraining power for a long time."[3]

Norway did not possess the social foundation needed to establish an upper house with "restraining power." This was one of the reasons why the Norwegian Constitution of 1814 was one of the most democratic in Europe. The fact that the king who reigned over the union between the two countries was Swedish also contributed to the democratization insofar as it was popular representatives and not the king who stood for the values of the nation. In 1884 Parliament voted for impeachment, which forced the government in Norway to resign—a huge step toward parliamentarianism, that is, toward the government's power deriving from the support of popularly elected representatives. After 1884 it was only a matter of time until universal suffrage was granted to male Norwegians in 1898.

In Sweden the old Parliament based on the estates of the realm was replaced by a two-house parliamentary system in 1866. The agrarians had a strong position in the new Parliament. Moreover, the rules of eligibility to vote led to a situation in which the Swedish upper house of Parliament became "more highly aristocratic and plutocratic than 'Riddarhuset' (the organization of the nobility)."[4] For a long time this upper house remained a barrier to democratization. Universal suffrage for men did not come into effect until 1909 and parliamentarianism until 1917.[5] Universal suffrage for women was granted in Norway in 1913. In Sweden the women's vote came as part of the great reforms in 1918.

---

[2] Rokkan 1970, 101.

[3] Hadenius 2000, 44.

[4] Lewin 1992, 77.

[5] Stjernquist 1996, 83, 254. The departure of the Swartz government and the appointment of the Edén government that year is considered the definitive breakthrough for parliamentarianism.

MOBILIZING THE PUBLIC

Democracy, as it was developing at the beginning of the twentieth century, acquired many of its characteristics from the "society of voluntary organizations" or the great popular movements that sprang up after the middle of the nineteenth century in both countries. To quote the historian Sverre Steen,

> [These voluntary organizations were] involved in creating or developing the democratic environment, shaping and working up the democratic way of thinking, generalizing the democratic technique. They played a special role in preparing for parliamentarianism, by carrying through universal suffrage for men and women and by introducing a whole series of social reforms. The organizations also functioned to even out social differences. Within the same association "everybody was equal." . . . These voluntary organizations were particularly important for democratic developments as the circle of active politicians more and more frequently were recruited from the trained cadres of organizations.[6]

Steen was writing about Norway, but he could equally have been referring to Sweden. In Scandinavia the idea of *folket* (the people) as a community became "a characteristically democratic force." This stood in contrast to Germany, for example, where the same idea was mobilized for the glorification of dictatorship.[7]

The most important popular movements were the revival movements, the temperance movement, and the labor movement. In Norway there was also the language movement, the struggle to replace the Danish-influenced written language with one that was closer to the Norwegian dialects. All these movements had features of protest—they were opposed to traditional authority—and they had great influence in the sphere of politics.[8] It was a sort of democratization before democratization. This process unfolded differently in the two countries.

In Norway the support and influence of these movements were quickly channeled into the Liberal movement. The reason why the Liberal Party (Venstre) managed to embrace so many different tendencies was that it represented the nationalist movement in the struggle over the union with Sweden.[9] The Liberal Party would dominate the political arena for a long time. The most paradoxical alliance within the party, perhaps, was that between the pietists of the counties on Norway's west coast and the radical freethinkers in the urban sector. At that time revivalist Christianity represented an indi-

---

[6] Steen 1958, 195–196.
[7] Slagstad 1998, 93.
[8] Lundkvist 1977, 55, *in passim*.
[9] Angell 2002, 67.

vidualizing and democratizing opposition within the state church, and the struggle against the dominant clergy of state officials was seen as part of the general struggle against the old civil service regime.

In Sweden the two houses of Parliament acted as a barrier to a similar development such that the movements operated more freely in relation to the political parties but nonetheless exerted significant influence on policy. Kjell Östberg writes that in the years around the turn of the century the temperance committees "played almost the role of a political party for ordinary people. . . . There were few Liberals or Social Democrats chosen for Parliament or for municipal posts without the authorization of the temperance committees."[10] When the political parties in Sweden developed into modern national parties around 1910, they could in many ways copy the structure of the popular movements and take over their political functions. This applied to the revivalist movements and particularly the temperance movement.[11]

TRAINING FOR DEMOCRACY

Almost without exception, the great popular movements at the end of the nineteenth century had as an integral part of their programs the development of popular refinement.[12] Different education societies, study circles, and "folk" colleges based on these movements were found both in Sweden and in Norway. Popular refinement had "two motives—the romantic-expressive: a contemporary identity-creation anchored in the past; and the rationalist-instrumental: a useful instruction" that was bound to a democratic motive, namely, the training of a "mature human being" for participation in "the country's public affairs."[13] Although the different motives carried different weights in the various movements, they still had noticeable common features. One thing that they held in common was opposition to the old traditional ideas of the educational process with roots in the pedagogy of class. These ideas called for everyone to be formed and educated to be integrated into his or her own social stratum. The scholarly class represented the highest formative degree and was associated with the classical ideals symbolized by Latin.

The modern concept of popular training and education broke with such class-oriented pedagogy: class divisions were to be broken down, the core of refinement should be unified, and everyone should be able to take part in a

---

[10] Östberg 1996, 12.

[11] Lundkvist 1977, 222.

[12] This is a translation of the Norwegian concept *folkedannelse* or the Swedish *folkbildning* (Cf. German *Volksbildung*). In the following we will alternate between "refinement," "education," and "enlightenment."

[13] Slagstad 1998, 95.

common culture. The history, culture, and language of the homeland were central elements; Latin was to be replaced by modern languages; and the natural sciences should be taught. During the crisis at the turn of the century, when "the labor question" became a pressing social problem, the issue of social integration also left its mark on popular education.

Consequently, a conflict developed between the "crystal core" of the old society—the university and the academic gymnasia—where the classical ideals had their strongest defenders, and the new culture of popular education. Like the "folk" movements in general, popular enlightenment was also a democratic opposition movement. It took a critical position toward the universities and the old culture of the civil service. This "became an important feature of the program of cultural radicalism."[14] Popular enlightenment represented a movement from a classical to a democratic regime of social refinement.

There has been debate on whether the roots of present-day democratic ideas lie in the ethnic-national realm or in the more liberal general European one with its emphasis on "citizen enlightenment that gives priority to the link between the people, democracy and the state."[15] Both aspects were present and, over time, they developed into an *educational compromise*—between the popular and the intellectual or learned culture, between romanticism and enlightenment. The compromise came earlier in Norway than in Sweden, and the mixture was not the same in the two countries.

The popular or folk colleges were the most striking expression of the project for the social and educational refinement of the people. This was a uniquely Nordic schooling effort, which, on the basis of pedagogical freedom, was to give mature youths a general education beyond that of the obligatory school system. In Norway we see how the folk colleges became institutions that emphasized acculturation and refinement more than education. They had as their starting point a liberal public-mindedness together with the romantic vision of the Dane N.F.S. Grundtvig about "the formation of the heart." Folk colleges with a different orientation—especially pietistic Christianity—gradually developed as well. The Norwegian folk colleges, however, maintained much of their original foothold in the alternative culture of popular education and kept their unique identity in contrast to the system of general schooling and to university education.[16]

In Sweden this development took a different direction. The person who more than anyone else put his mark on the Swedish popular refinement tradition was Hans Larsson in Lund. Unlike Grundtvig, whose emphasis on Norse

[14] Frängsmyr 2000, 149.
[15] Dale 2003, 172.
[16] Högnäs 2001, 34.

mythology, language, and culture permeated the Norwegian folk colleges, Larsson was no romantic but rather an enlightened philosopher with great faith in progress, science, and common sense. Folk refinement, as defined by Larsson, came to acquire great importance for the Swedish labor movement. The Social Democrat Tage Erlander, who later became prime minister, was a student at the University of Lund during Larsson's time there. We find a little sigh in his diary when, much later in life, he read a book about Larsson, with whose world of ideas he clearly was able to identify: "What could I have been thinking not to have joined the circle around Hans Larsson? Too awkward and lazy and nobody gave me a nudge."[17] Like the practical and vigorous Johan Castberg in Norway, Hans Larsson was one of those who thought social-democratically before Social Democracy had matured.

A unique example of a Swedish folk college is Brunnsvik College, established by the Swedish labor movement in 1906, which came to play an important role for the movement. The driving force behind its establishment was Rickard Sandler. Sandler's ideal of social refinement had its roots in the critical position of the folk movement toward the specialization of knowledge. His thinking moved away from the original view of the folk college as "a school for the illumination of life" and toward "a school for planned refinement for citizenship." He came to place decisive weight on "the objective pole in the concept of refinement." Indeed, the broader and deeper the refinement of a society's general population, the more democratic that society could become, according to Sandler. And it was precisely the democratizing process that made popular education such a topical issue. But for Sandler it was also important to emphasize the socialistic character of this education. Democracy required a special type of social competence.[18] Brunnsvik Folk College maintained high standards and was a characteristic expression of the important role of academics in the mainstream of the Swedish labor movement.[19] In contrast to Norway, it was said about Sweden that "in the Swedish labor movement the meeting between workers and popular enlightenment of various kinds saw the early acceptance of the intellectual in social democracy."[20]

In Norway, however, a different type of schooling initiative was to build a bridge between cultures—the rural gymnasia. The old university-preparatory gymnasia or grammar schools had been in the cities. For young people from the countryside this was a significant barrier against attending a grammar school in order to go on to university education. One such class transformation is described by Arne Garborg in his important coming-of-age novel

17 Erlander 2001, journal entry 26/03/1950.
18 Gustavsson 1991, 98, 103, 115–116.
19 Hagtvet 1970.
20 Forser 1993, 151.

The Peasant University Students. The main character, Daniel Braut, meets the formal requirements of the urban grammar school, but he fails in the refinement process. In his meeting with the hegemonic urban bourgeois culture he undergoes an identity crisis. The struggle for rural gymnasia was inspired by Garborg, and its aim was to create a road to higher education for rural youths that would make it possible to maintain respect for one's own roots and cultural antecedents.

Following a period of political struggle, a law regarding rural gymnasia was enacted in 1914. They were established outside the cities and had an attendance requirement one year shorter than in the normal grammar schools. Arguments that these would come to stand for a professionally inferior alternative proved wrong. The rural gymnasia came to constitute an elite school system for gifted rural youths. Striking numbers of such youths became civil engineers or, to put it another way, became the vanguard agents of modernization for the society that was to be built up. The conflict between the rural grammar school and the folk college was obvious.[21] The former was a school for cramming and the latter a pure institution of betterment and refinement. The demands of the everyday prevailed in the former, and of the Sunday world in the latter. Both sprang from the alternative movement for popular education, however.

In the previous chapter we saw that, in relation to industrialization, the Socialists had to argue on their opponents' premises. They experienced this discursive pressure just as all counterhegemonic projects do. The case was the same here. Just as the Socialists' project did not become a socialization project but rather a modernization project, so too the rural grammar schools did not become a countercultural project but rather an integration project. Nevertheless, it is clear from a long-term perspective that early Socialism as well as the counterculture came to function as a kind of sourdough within established society and contributed to changing it in the direction of Social Democracy.

TOWARD AN INTEGRATED
SCHOOL SYSTEM IN NORWAY

The most important instrument in the great integration project was, naturally, the general school system from early childhood on. With time, both countries developed a unitary or integrated public school system.[22] The inte-

---

[21] Høidal 2003.

[22] The term in Norwegian is *enhetsskole*—literally "unitary school." We will most often use the term "integrated school," sometimes also "comprehensive school system," in particular when not only primary but also secondary school is included.

grated school was the school arising from the democratically oriented regime of education and was intended to break radically with class-based pedagogy. The thinking behind the integrated school was to create a school system that was the same all over the country and that students from all social classes would attend together. The aim was also to link lower and higher education. Differentiation was to be undertaken as late as possible, and everyone should have equal opportunity for higher education.

The notion of standardization arose partly from social integration and partly from arguments for equality—for equal opportunity. Children from the lower classes should be given a chance at the education that was best for both the child and society. The latter "recruitment" perspective was important. The thinking was that the longer children were kept together, the greater the chance that many of them would pursue higher education. Naturally enough, behind all this lay the thinking of the Enlightenment—a strong belief in the advantage of education. The integrated school was thus the core element of the democratic regime of popular refinement, taking over from the old school system built on class-based pedagogy. The transition was a long process, running through much of the nineteenth and into the twentieth century.

The professional content and the pedagogical principles of the integrated school were not clearly defined. There were tensions, and there would be struggle over principles. We mentioned the two motives: the creation of a contemporary identity anchored in the past, and the fostering of mature human beings equipped to participate in public life. These two motives were anchored, respectively, in romanticism and rationalism. In parallel with this dichotomy there was also a tendency toward antagonism concerning what would develop the individual personality and what was the more collectivist goal—to foster fellow citizens.[23] There was also what has been called "the pedagogical paradox," namely, that a free and mature person should be fostered by placing him or her under the tutelage that the school (necessarily) represented.[24] It was this paradox that the reform pedagogy tried to resolve by building on the student's own experience and activity, in contrast to the principle of the "knowledge school" based on the idea that there existed a body of knowledge that should be communicated to the students. This paradox also affected the role of the teacher and the nature of the teaching. Finally, there were conflicts about the content of social equality, so closely linked to the democratic motive. What kind of equality should the school system strive for? Should the school sort out those who were clever, and would this be democratic? All these tensions followed school policy through-

---

[23] Gustavsson 1996, 193.
[24] Slagstad, Korsgaard, and Løvlie 2003, 23.

out the twentieth century. One has been obliged to choose, and the choices have varied according to the opportunities of the period. We will follow the major contours of this development through three phases that unfolded during the twentieth century.

The same groups agitated for the integrated school system in both countries: the middle-class radicals ultimately in alliance with the labor movement. This alliance happened very late, however. And yet the road taken toward a unitary school system turned out to be very different in the two countries. In Norway the integrated school was established early on; in Sweden it was established late. At the end of the nineteenth and beginning of the twentieth century—that is, during the Liberal Party's period in power in Norway—the characteristics of Norwegian school policy were "an almost extreme radicalism, a departure that quickly became associated with the view that Norway as a school nation said no to Europe," writes Alfred Oftedal Telhaug.[25] And a no to Europe was also a no to Sweden.

The old parallel school system with its roots in the ranked society was phased out with surprising speed in Norway. What was of decisive significance was the parliamentary resolution of 1896 that introduced a five-year integrated school system to Norway and at the same time repealed the Latin requirement for university entrance. Norway was the first country in Europe to introduce this reform. It was, as a classical philologist was later to express it, "a reform that is presumably without parallel in the history of schooling in Europe, at least if we exclude the revolution in Russia in 1917."[26] The integrated school was expanded further in 1920 when all Norwegian children between the ages of seven and fourteen were brought within a common seven-year primary school system. As one commentator said about the reform, "This, together with the fact that prior to 1920 one after the other the private schools were bought up by the municipalities, meant that the separate class-based upbringing of the bourgeoisie's children through schooling was almost suppressed."[27] Thus, long before the Social Democrats assumed governmental power in Norway, the liberal state had liquidated the class-based upbringing of children and instituted unitary schooling.

The integrated school of the liberal state retained many of the characteristics of the knowledge school. The ideal teacher was charismatic and could fire up the students. In many places the teacher was accorded the same role of culture-bearer for the local community that the priest had played in the old, rather rigid class society. This role would later be eschewed by the professional

---

[25] Telhaug 2003, 1.
[26] Eilif Skard, as cited by Slagstad 2000, 98.
[27] Fredriksen 1979, 28.

pedagogues.[28] And, finally, it was a school that clearly emphasized equality of opportunity, not equality of results.

Like all the other parts of the great social integration project, the integrated school system had its dark side. Inclusion required certain qualifications; in other words, some had to be excluded. The integrated school as it developed in the late 1800s was not a very generous place. Those children who at the time were considered to be "retarded," "abnormal," "neglected," or "morally corrupted" were to be kept away. In a word, it was seen as necessary to clear the common school of "problem children."[29]

The integrated school should no longer sort children by social standing or class, but what occurred was the sorting of children by new criteria, into normal or abnormal. The background of this phenomenon lay partly in the necessity of making the school attractive to those who had the alternative of private schooling, and partly in the teaching profession's strong new professional policy. But there was also a deeper motive to the normative uniformity of popular education—a motive that points toward the paternalism of the Social Democratic state.

CONTRASTING THE TWO COUNTRIES

The constellations were the same in both countries—parallel schooling versus integrated schooling. In Sweden the type of integrated school such as that in Norway was articulately defended by Fridtjuv Berg in his 1883 book *Folk School as Basic School.* The overriding idea was social integration. The intensity of support for the old system was much stronger in Sweden than in Norway, however, and it would take a long time before thinking such as Berg's made a breakthrough. Class-based pedagogy lived on, concealed partly through other ideological discourse.[30] Classical upbringing had to be limited to the few; a learned proletariat would only disturb the peace and harmony of society. Even the minister of education in the Social Democratic government of 1932, the radical Arthur Engberg, himself classically educated, was no supporter of integrated schooling. In Sweden, it would take a whole new generation of Social Democrats to establish standard integrated schooling after 1945.

The explanation for the differences between the two countries lies, on the one hand, in the relatively strong leftist movement in Norway and, on the

---

[28] Ahonen and Rantala 2001, 15.

[29] Froestad 1998; Tove Stang Dahl 1974, 135.

[30] Runeby 1995, 64.

other, the relative strength of traditional educational ideals in Sweden. The liberal forces were much stronger in Norway, especially institutionally. It was possible for the cultural radical to ally him- or herself with the counterculture coalition that included the language nationalists, the temperance supporters, and the low-church revivalists. On this basis the liberal forces captured the teacher seminars, which thus became an institutional intellectual foundation that provided an alternative to the university in line with the folk colleges, and which could be used to reform schooling from within.

At the same time, the oppositional elements could be brought into the political arena through the strong Liberal Party much more quickly than was possible in Sweden. Another feature was that teachers constituted a considerable presence among the politicians. It might be argued that the Liberal Party state in Norway could also have been called the "school state" or the "teacher state." This democratic populism left its mark on the general public in both countries, but in Norway it was more easily institutionalized because the traditional forces were so much weaker.[31] The early development of the standard integrated school in Norway and the early development of political democracy are two sides of the same coin.

In the movement for popular education there was a tendency toward loosening the close relationship between profession and education that had been so characteristic of class-based pedagogy. In the new democratic school system an opposition developed between refinement and social integration, on the one hand, and education or vocational training, on the other. "According to those late bourgeois ideas from around the turn of the century, being cultivated meant creating a Sunday world for oneself, away from the grind and the duties of everyday life."[32] Where the main weight should lie in schooling—on the everyday demands or on the Sunday world—was not solved once and for all.

What was left of the central role that the university had played in the formative process? The old university had been the "crystal core" of a state dominated by the official class. The university had been at the center of a great refinement project. The normative disciplines, or the "moral sciences" of theology, law, and the humanities, had predominated. The new popular education project, however, set this "crystal core" aside as an institution of cultural formation. This meant that the universities had to renegotiate the social contract with the new democracy. The basis for the new contract was a combination of "the instrumentalization and the autonomy of science."[33]

---

[31] This contrast is analyzed in Telhaug 2003.
[32] Theodor Geiger cited in Runeby 1995, 77.
[33] Slagstad 2000, 53.

To put it another way, science achieved its autonomy by pulling away from politics. What the sciences, and thus the university, should deliver was positive knowledge that society could use. This "contract" between university and society that was negotiated around the beginning of the twentieth century was to prevail for a long time; that is, the universities managed to exist in a manner that was both independent and relatively marginalized. But there were two sides to this coin. The interwar period was a period of stagnation for the universities.

KARL STAAFF AND THE QUESTION OF SUFFRAGE IN SWEDEN

The great political struggle of the 1880s in Sweden was over customs, whereas in the 1890s it was over the right to vote. At first the issue was brought forward by a popular movement. Sweden's Universal Suffrage Society was founded in 1890. This society organized two "folk parliaments" in 1893 and 1896, based on universal voting rights for women and for men. We see here how the folk movements operated on the leading edge of the formal democratization of the political system. A number of prominent politicians took part in the folk parliaments.[34]

It did not take long before the question of universal suffrage broke into the political system and contributed to changing the constellation of parties. In the election of 1905 the Liberals under the leadership of Karl Staaff stood as a modern party with a parliamentary group and a national organization. They gained many seats, and Staaff was able to form a government. The way now seemed open for universal suffrage and generally for a democratic modernization of the political system. This turned out, however, to be no easy task.

In addition to the right to vote, two other questions demanded attention, namely, the question of defense and what in a vague sense may be called "the worker question." Staaff was confronted with these questions almost immediately. The worker question lay behind what was being advanced at the time in the field of social reform. But it was also associated with the simultaneous threats to the social order itself. In 1906 the government adopted laws (known as the Staaff laws) that increased the punishment for incitement to riot and instituted strong controls on antimilitaristic agitation. These laws were strongly criticized in radical circles, but Staaff got them ratified with support from the political right, which weakened his radical Liberal Party.

[34] Stjernquist 1996, 60.

It was characteristic of the liberal left parties in Sweden as in Norway that even though they could be radical when it came to suffrage and social policy, they were noticeably legalistic and willing to go to great lengths to defend the social order. It has been said that a particular character trait of Staaff was to veer "from a rigid standpoint of legality to a warmth of humanity."[35] This may be correct, but it must be stressed that this attitude was consistent with the general behavior of the radical bourgeoisie. In distinction to the Social Democrats, the radical non-Socialists viewed the (bourgeois) state as rising above political interests. Staaff's point of indictment against the labor movement was that it was anarchistic, that it tended toward becoming a state within the state. This would also come to the fore during his handling of the great strike of 1909. He was against both strikes and lockouts and was of the opinion that the strike represented a breach of contract by the labor organizations.[36] That such legalism along with the previously mentioned view on the state constituted a natural point of view for the progressive bourgeoisie will be confirmed when we turn our attention to Norway.

The most important issue after 1905 was the right to vote, and in this matter Staaff and the Liberals came to collaborate with Hjalmar Branting and the Social Democrats. Here it is worth noting the contrast with Norway, where universal suffrage for males had been carried out by the Liberal Party before the Social Democrats attained representation in Parliament (Stortinget). Therefore the issue of the right to vote did not have the same unifying effect on the relationship between the Liberals and the Social Democrats that we see in Sweden, where the Social Democratic Party stood for universal suffrage. Thus the paradox emerges that precisely the strong democratic tradition in Norway was part of the reason why it took such a long time for the Socialists (Social Democrats) to accept liberal democracy.

In 1906 the Staaff government presented a proposition for universal suffrage and majority elections to the Second Chamber (the lower house of Parliament), which passed it. By this time the First Chamber (upper house), which had not been included in the proposition, also was prepared to give concessions on the suffrage question but wished to link the right to vote to *proportional elections* rather than *majority elections*. Consequently, the First Chamber voted against the proposition.

Proportional elections mean representation according to relative strength in the overall election tallies. The alternative, majority election, would normally in "winner takes all" constituencies give disproportionate representation to the strongest party (such a system is found, among other places, in Great Britain). The proportional electoral system was set up as a guarantee against

---

[35] Palme 1964, 220.
[36] Palme 1964, 158.

"the tyranny of the majority." In Norway the Conservative Party (Høyre) took the same position as the right did in Sweden: from 1888 on, it linked a condition of proportional election to the expansion of the right to vote "in order to procure a truer expression of the various opinions and interests in state and municipality."[37] The old Norwegian electoral system, which in all essentials was the system dating to the establishment of the Constitution in 1814, was in principle a majority system. The Liberals consistently rejected proportional representation in Norway, despite the fact that it was, according to the Conservatives, a "howling injustice" to grant only "representation to the majority."

After their great election victory in 1898, the Norwegian Liberals were able to force through universal suffrage for men and majority representation. The Liberals' insistence on majority representation contributed to the fact that the Conservatives held back on the issue of the right to vote.[38] In Sweden the political right had, through its control of the First Chamber, an institutional means of stopping the corresponding initiative for universal suffrage with majority elections. After the First Chamber rejected the proposal in 1906, the Staaff government resigned. Staaff's successor was Arvid Lindman, who formed a liberal-conservative government.[39]

ARVID LINDMAN AND THE QUESTION OF UNIVERSAL SUFFRAGE

Based on liberal-conservative premises, Lindman's project was one of modernizing society.[40] His party, Allmänna Valmansförbundet (Association of the General Electorate or Conservative Party), had sprung out of the ranks of the traditional right, but under the strong influence of Lindman it became a progress-oriented liberal-conservative party. He is thus reckoned to be the founder of the modern conservative party—his "most impressive creation," as has been said.[41]

[37] Kaartvedt 1984, 158.

[38] Kaartvedt 1984, 159. With a reform in 1905, the Conservative Party fell in line with the principle of majority elections. The reason for this changed stance by the Conservatives was among other things the desire to limit the representation of the social democrats. See Danielsen 1964, 16–18.

[39] Sten Carlsson 1980, 461. See also Anderson 1956, 102. This was not a party government but rather, according to Pettersson in Påboda, a coalition of "persons of a substantially moderate and popular disposition."

[40] Torbjörn Nilsson 2002, 82. Nilsson underlines Lindman's significance for the influence of liberalism in the Conservative Party.

[41] Palme 1964, 260. The party changed its name, in 1930, from Allmänna Valmansförbundet to Högerpartiet (the Party of the Right) and changed it again, from 1969 onward, to Moderata Samlingspartiet (the Coalition Party of Moderates). In the following we will normally refer to it, and to its twin party in Norway, Høyre (the Party of the Right), as the Conservative Party.

Lindman has been described as having an extrovert nature with a winning disposition "exceedingly well suited to unite entrepreneurs, civil servants, and farmers around a practical conservative program."[42] Besides this, he had a rare ability that is of great service in politics. His close friend and colleague Hugo Hamilton describes this in his diary: "It is characteristic of L. that the greater the difficulties that pile up in his way, the more brilliant become his spirits."[43] He had been a naval officer, and before he became prime minister he had been a parliamentarian and cabinet minister. He also had a background in the business world and was able to give himself the title of director general. On the Norrland question he had originally represented the timber companies against the farmers. But as a leader of the right, he came to pay more attention to agriculture's point of view. Lindman's ties to Swedish industry were strengthened, however, especially after 1912 when he became chairman of several large companies. Gradually an informal network formed around Lindman, which came to be identified by the term *the industrial right*, suggesting close contact between the liberal-conservative party and core sectors of the business community.

Lindman's government continued where the Staaff government left off, but with a somewhat changed presentation. Lindman's liberal-conservative government in 1907 put forward the proposition that would lead to universal suffrage for men in elections to the Second Chamber. The conservatives were split over the question. There were strong forces represented by weighty orators in the First Chamber who were opposed to democratization. Nevertheless, with great political ingenuity Lindman managed to pilot the government's proposition through both chambers.

Several conditions contributed to why universal suffrage for men was a liberal-conservative initiative. It was one element in a strategic accommodation with the radical demands during an unstable social situation. But there were also positive grounds. As we have seen, political democracy was a natural part of nation building. Furthermore, there was nothing unnatural about this in the eyes of the progressive industrialists to whom Lindman was linked. Many of them saw the transition to political democracy as a necessity.[44] There were also clear voices among the liberal conservatives that argued that universal suffrage followed naturally from the general compulsory military service that had been instituted in 1901.[45]

On the other hand, there was an old fear that giving the right to vote to the unpropertied would lead to societal upheaval and undermining of the

---

[42] S. Carlsson 1980, 461.
[43] Hamilton 1955, 9, 25/2–11.
[44] Söderpalm 1969, 201; Hadenius 2000, 48.
[45] Elvander 1961, 140–141.

rights of ownership, as Socialist agitators demanded. Therefore it was necessary to have guarantees that this would not be allowed to happen. The Lindman government's system also had more conservative guarantees than one finds in the Norwegian system instituted by the Liberal Party in 1898. In contrast to the Norwegian system, the Swedish had proportional representation, which was seen as a conservative guarantee. Moreover, there was still a First Chamber, however modified democratically, and full parliamentarism was still not possible while the two-chamber system was open to royal intervention. The experiences of other countries—especially Norway—were also used to argue that universal suffrage had not led to such corrosive tendencies as many had feared.[46]

Lindman's government also took several social policy initiatives. Among other things, it released a white paper on a national pension plan. When Staaff and the liberals regained governmental power, they followed up with a series of social policy initiatives. On the question of a national pension plan, they put forward a proposition based on the Lindman government's white paper. The matter went through, gaining approval from all parties in Parliament. "In this way the foundation was laid for modern Swedish social legislation."[47] And this had occurred on the basis of agreement across political lines.

Liberal ideas about political equality or democracy are historically linked to ideas about political unity, that is, a sense of national fellowship. Equality and unity—democracy and fellowship—belong together. The liberal ideal envisioned a society of equal individuals. The point is that given the liberal— and thus also liberal-conservative—ideas of the day, it was difficult to think of a modern society in which the political arena had not been democratized. The process of integration in national fellowship occurred through democratization. The question was when and how it should happen. How impatient should one be, and what could damage the process along the way? What legal guarantees could and must one have?

The contribution of the Scandinavian liberal-conservative parties to the Scandinavian form of society was precisely their insistence that modern democracy must be based on legal limits to the power of the majority. Democracy had to guarantee the rights of minorities and individuals. This liberal antitotalitarian argument was used against the left's most radical proponents of democracy, and against the socialist danger liberals thought they perceived in the background.

---

[46] Stjernquist 1996, 80. Branting's view was that one should reassure the right that universal suffrage would not lead to "any great upheaval in our society" (Lewin 1992, 89–90).

[47] Elvander 1961, 469.

THE DIFFICULT ROAD TO PARLIAMENTARIANISM

Following the election of 1911, the Liberal Staaff was returned as prime minister. The dominant political theme during the tense international situation leading up to World War I was defense. In this the traditionalists found an issue around which they could unite and which found its strongest expression in the farmers' march of 1914.[48] Thirty thousand farmers from all over the country traveled to Stockholm, where they marched to the palace courtyard where the king gave a vigorous defense-friendly speech that was a direct polemic against Staaff and the majority in the Second Chamber. "Once again the peasants stand in the vanguard of the monarch when king and country are in danger."[49] The royal power and the old society had raised their heads. Two days later fifty thousand people participated in a counterdemonstration. The main speaker at it was the leader of the Social Democrats, the antimilitarist and modernist Hjalmar Branting. He supported Staaff.

In this special situation it appears that the moderate forces were pushed to the sidelines. The underlying conflict between traditionalists and modernists came to the fore. We see a confrontation between what once was and what was coming into being, or between agrarian society and industrial society. The farmers' march led to a political crisis with Staaff resigning in protest at the king's behavior. The king appointed a generally defense-friendly government under the apolitical Hjalmar Hammarskjöld. The Hammarskjöld government had a conservative tinge but was hardly reactionary. Quite the reverse: it contained a noticeable element from modern business life. The farmers' march represented a traditional undercurrent, with some support in Parliament, but on the political level this was an isolated episode. Modernization, in the form of both industrialization and democratization, continued along its path in accord with the moderate national spirit of mutual understanding, and with Lindman's Conservative Party as an active partner.

It is striking that at a certain period around 1907 Lindman managed to wrest from the non-Socialist radicals the initiative for democratic political modernization. By means of the final great suffrage reform of 1918, however, the left managed to retake the initiative. The reform gave universal suffrage to women and democratized the First Chamber so that in reality it came to have the same social basis as the Second Chamber. In this way, what had been called "chamber dualism" almost disappeared, opening the road to parliamentarianism. Sweden kept this weakened version of the two-chamber parliamentary

[48] Hadenius 2000, 35.
[49] T. Nilsson 2002, 89.

system through the Social Democratic period and right up to 1970. Ironically, in its final phase it was the Social Democrats who demonstrated how to use the possibilities afforded by what remained of the two-chamber system. With an absolute majority in the First Chamber, they managed to stay in power right up to the end of the "golden age of Social Democracy," despite their loss of absolute majority in the Second Chamber in 1949.[50]

The suffrage proposition was put forward during the autumn of 1918 and was dealt with by a special committee of Parliament. Branting played a central role in the rapid handling of the issue. He was the chairman of the committee and wrote the report himself. Characteristically, it opened with a reference to "the exceptional events out in the world" and proclaimed that the world stood at "a turning point in the history not only of Europe but of all humanity." The right demanded conservative "guarantees," and there was a bit of a tug-of-war over these. There was also opposition from the leftist Socialists to parts of the reform. Branting acted with great ingenuity in the role of negotiator and managed to get a united Social Democratic parliamentary group behind the reform.

It has been said that the suffrage reform was a great compromise between the left and the right. Nils Stjernquist is of a different opinion. Certainly the right received a number of "guarantees," but they were relatively insignificant. One of the most important guarantees, proportional representation, had already been provided by Lindman. In Norway we saw that the Liberal Party had trumped on the issue of majority representation. It is worth noting that this unstable situation of 1918 was accompanied by an endorsement of proportional representation in Norway as well. Elections with proportional representation—or the rights of minorities to representation, as it was called— have been an important part of Scandinavian parliamentarianism ever since.

Parliamentary democracy in Sweden was the result of an internal process by which reform gradually gained great support. The point at which it was carried through should also be seen as a response to the wave of democratization that rolled across Europe following World War I.[51] In Sweden, as in other countries, there was a feeling of facing a revolutionary threat. The situation was unstable, and the governing coalition of liberals and Social Democrats made use of "the psychological moment," as Prime Minister Nils Edén called it. There was also a radicalizing of the Swedish Parliament. With the 1919 election to the First Chamber, the Social Democrats became the largest party in this chamber as well as in the Second Chamber. In this situation Branting was able to form the first Social Democratic government in 1920.

[50] Hadenius 2000, 270–271. Steinmo 1993, 130–131.
[51] This paragraph builds on Stjernquist 1996, 82–99.

We have followed how the Swedish liberals drifted over and became more or less integrated with the moderate Social Democrats, while Lindman's conservatives took over the inheritance of the liberals. Lindman himself said that the Swedish liberals had "all the more approached Socialism with their demand for the state's intervention and regulation in all areas," while the Conservative Party had "taken over the old liberal idea built on genuine liberal-mindedness and maintaining the freedom of the individual."[52] In Sweden it was the Conservatives along with the Social Democrats who politically directed the technological and economic modernization. This was not the case in Norway. There, the Social Democrats were still not "integrated" into politics as they were in Sweden. The Norwegian Liberal Party (Venstre) was the largest party and would hold on to the political initiative up to 1920. This Liberal government was followed by a Conservative government, not, as in Sweden, by a Social Democratic one.

GUNNAR KNUDSEN AND STATE CAPITALISM

After the peaceful breakup of the union between the two countries in 1905, Prime Minister Christian Michelsen became a national hero in Norway. His background was in the Liberal Party, but his government was a coalition of bourgeois interests with a mandate to lead Norway out of the union. After this task had been fulfilled, he continued as prime minister. Michelsen explained that it was his duty to continue to rule since there was no clear parliamentary majority that could take over. There is an explanation that goes deeper, however: the government remained in power in order to further develop non-Socialist unification politics.[53] This "dream of bourgeois unification" had the aim of establishing a cross-political coalition against the Socialists and socially radical leftist forces in society. These were to be isolated. The dream also represented a desire for economic modernization.[54] The union question had shoved these aims to one side, but now one had to concentrate on modernization. Michelsen's plan was to utilize his great prestige from 1905 to carry through this policy. He had the Conservative Party with him. The party was willing to give up its identity in return for a broad bourgeois coalition under Michelsen. Michelsen did not have his own party on board, however. The great Liberal Party, which had championed democratization and union issues and had united so many conflicting tendencies under its

---

[52] Elvander 1961, 467.
[53] Kaartvedt 1984, 227.
[54] Kaartvedt 1984, 183.

wing, split into several factions after 1905. Only a small group followed Michelsen in the formation of a new liberal party (Samlingspartiet, or the Coalition Party), which, together with the Conservative Party, came to represent the right in Norwegian politics.

There was another dream of unification. This dream was to unite all the social radical forces from the Social Democrats and far left into the liberal ranks, and to isolate the reactionary right-wing forces. In the forefront of trying to realize this dream was Johan Castberg. In 1900 he had been elected to Parliament, where he was the leader of a small group of radical left representatives, later organized as the Labor Democrats.[55] Castberg came to play an important role in Norwegian politics, even though his great dream of a large social radical (Social Democratic) unification party was not realized—or, to be more precise, was not realized during his lifetime or on the basis of his Labor Democrats.

Common to both Michelsen's dream of a moderate coalition and Castberg's dream of a social radical coalition was that they both considered the main part of the Liberal Party to be ripe for their respective reformations.[56] But they were both wrong in this. To the contrary, the Liberal Party was consolidated in 1908 under the leadership of Gunnar Knudsen. Knudsen was successful in gathering a majority of the Liberal Party parliamentary group into a new leftist association under bylaws that declared, "Political or parliamentary cooperation with the Right [the Coalition Party] or with the Socialist Party [the Labor Party] . . . is something our association cannot participate in."[57] He thus established clear fronts against both the Social Democrats and the Conservatives in coalition with Michelsen's group. The election of 1912 was a victory for Knudsen's consolidated left. Because this was a majority election, they, together with a small group of Labor Democrats, won an absolute majority in Parliament. Knudsen's government was in power until 1920. "Knudsen's system was for a long time attractively strong, stable, and cleverly led."[58] But what did this regime really stand for?

Gunnar Knudsen was a capitalist and big businessman. He inherited a shipping company that he managed to turn into one of the leading firms in the country. He had been educated as an engineer in Sweden and then had practiced in England. Throughout his life he maintained a great interest in technology and was involved in a series of industrial ventures. Among other things, he was active in establishing Norway's first electrical plant in 1885. Electrification and the possibilities it provided for industrial development ab-

---

[55] Aasland 1961. A general history of the Labor Democrats.
[56] Nordby 1983, 11.
[57] Fuglum 1989, 21.
[58] Knut Kjeldstadli 1994, 37.

Figure 3. In Norway the foundation for a Social Democratic society was laid down under the Liberal (Left) Party government, particularly under the great industrialist Gunnar Knudsen's efficient and strong regime up to 1920. It stood for a strong state, industrialization, extensive social reforms, and struggle against class struggle. The photo shows, from the left, Prime Minister Knudsen and his closest associate, cabinet minister Johan Castberg.

sorbed him throughout his life. In his youth he attached himself to the radical part of the Liberal Party, and he was a member of the Labor Commission of 1885 that prepared a report on supervisory and security schemes for the new industries. He was a member of Michelsen's coalition government in 1905 but, as a republican, he resigned from the government. As prime minister beginning in 1912, he built up great personal prestige. With the consolidation of the Liberal Party, he decided to reject the moderate Michelsen and take the radical Castberg into the government. The government carried forward its democratization line by instituting universal suffrage for women. It formulated the concession laws and other business statutes. This government also stood for some sweeping initiatives within the field of social legislation. Here the driving force was Castberg.

If one presupposes a fundamental conflict between capital and labor, it is difficult to understand a man like Gunnar Knudsen, a large-scale capitalist who placed himself in the social radical wing of politics. It is still more difficult than it is with Lindman to explain Knudsen's position as strategic accommodation arising from opportunistic motives. Like Lindman, he was a strategist with a positive program of modernization. In his eyes democratization and industrialization with social guarantees constituted a natural unity. One is not able to enter the world of Knudsen's thinking by regarding him as a capitalist or from the dichotomous perspective of capital/labor. What he was, was an *engineer*. His mind-set was that of an engineer, and precisely for this reason he had a resonance with the times in which he lived. It is perhaps not coincidental that right at this time we find an engineer sitting in the prime minister's seat—the only engineer who has ever sat there.

In his book *The National Strategists*, Rune Slagstad portrays Johan Castberg as the great strategist. There is no doubt that Castberg was a driving force in the Knudsen government for both the concession laws and social legislation. He did not get his most radical proposals enacted, however. Slagstad's main reason for emphasizing Castberg is that he sees in Castberg's view of society something fundamentally new in relation to the established liberal line. What was fundamentally new was "the radicalization of the state sector—the state sector that had a tendentious identity with the social, this stately sociality. From here a direct line runs to the Social Democratic regime of modernization, in which the state and society were interchangeable quantities."[59] With his "state socialism" Castberg represented what with time would be a fundamental characteristic of the victorious Social Democracy—before the Social Democrats themselves had formed this vision. His dream of this great social radical party of unification would be realized in the form of the post–World War II Social Democracy. It was Knudsen who gave Castberg the elbow room he needed, however, and it was Knudsen who held back when he felt that was necessary. At that time it was Knudsen's approach that won.

During the debate on the concession laws Knudsen was accused by Michelsen, among others, of being a "state socialist."[60] Even though he did not want to go as far as Castberg, Knudsen saw the state as an institution that could be fully used for the modernization strategy. He had the engineer's mistrust of the market and the action-oriented strategist's mistrust of being tied down by legal restrictions. These two positions together made it necessary to set boundaries against the Conservatives. At the same time he regarded with disapproval the Social Democrats' unclear stance regarding property rights and their unclear position on the state, which they still looked on as a bourgeois state. In Knudsen's eyes the state, and thereby he himself, stood above

---

[59] Slagstad 1998, 146. See also Angell 2002, 211. Parallel points of view are found among radical liberals in Sweden such as Axel Schotte.

[60] Nissen 1957, 176.

society's antagonisms between interests. On this basis he was able to declare a "struggle against class struggle."[61] The Liberal Party's insistence on solving labor conflicts by means of compulsory arbitration also demonstrates this technocratic, state-friendly point of view. His response to Michelsen's charges that he was a "state socialist" is characteristic: "If one finds that one should undertake a government measure that in and for itself is in agreement with the interests of the State and the common good, then one does so, when it is reasonable and accords with healthy good sense, and does not let oneself be scared off by the concept of socialism or state socialism."[62]

Much of the discord over the concession laws arose from the notion of their being "enabling acts," acts by which Parliament delegates much of its authority to the government, giving it a great deal of room to maneuver.[63] Seen from this perspective, this was a Social Democratic feature established by the Liberal government before the Social Democrats themselves took it up. The real struggle over these principles was the big conflict over the enabling acts after 1945 (see chapter 12). But it was Knudsen who provided the prelude to this.

The government used its enabling laws in a way that modified tendencies toward state capitalism. Knudsen himself implied that a shift in policy had taken place from the original initiative for the concession laws to the relatively liberal way the concession laws were later applied, for which he came to stand—especially the liberality with regard to foreign capital.[64] The primary point of Knudsen's strategy was to achieve controlled but strong industrialization. Even though the domain of state intervention had been expanded in relation to things such as social policy, redistribution, and organization for production, and even though the state was seen as a good and powerful instrument, the state nonetheless hesitated to enter the production sphere. Barriers were broken, however, and these would not be allowed to rise again. The Liberal Party's active, interventionist state had time on its side.

Sweden never did get a "Left-Liberal state" like Norway's. The bourgeois radicals did not have the political opportunity that this would have required. In Norway the Liberals had a grip on political modernization and to a large degree on economic modernization as well. An important precondition for the strong Left-Liberal state in Norway, and the absence of the same in Sweden, was that in Norway the Social Democrats did not allow themselves to become integrated into the system as they did in Sweden. Precisely during this period the Norwegian Labor Party presented itself as a revolutionary

[61] K. Kjeldstadli 1994, 33.
[62] Nissen 1957, 176.
[63] Nordby 1983, 404ff.
[64] Nordby 1983, 414.

party outside established society (see chapter 4). In other words, there was more room for radical bourgeois elements in Branting's Labor Party than there was in the Norwegian Labor Party.

The real tug-of-war, especially on the issue of the concession laws, was over the role of the state in the capitalist order. In Norway the radical bourgeois elements had their own party—the Left or Liberal Party—that would come to define this role. The state socialist Gunnar Knudsen regarded himself as a national strategist, not as a representative of business and industry. The primary strategic responsibility for economic modernization would lie with the state.

Views of the state were not exactly the same in the two countries. One legacy of the Left-Liberal state in Norway was the belief that the state was the best instrument for solving nearly all problems. In Sweden much more political power resided in the private economic sphere. Sweden was, if one likes, a more capitalist country. In contrast to Norway, Sweden took the step to "organized capitalism."

CURRENTS OF ANTIPARLIAMENTARIANISM

A period of political instability began in 1920. In Norway Gunnar Knudsen had to resign, and in Sweden Nils Edén's coalition government of liberals and Social Democrats disintegrated. Compared with Knudsen's stable leadership in Norway, there had been more turbulence in Sweden. The collaboration between the liberals and Social Democrats for the great universal suffrage reform had stamped Swedish politics with unity, direction, and progress. When the reform was implemented, however, the Social Democrats broke off their collaboration with the liberals. During the 1920s the major split in the political arena was between the Socialists and non-Socialists—as it was in Norway. The political constellations made a stable coalition government impossible. From 1920 until the Social Democrat Per Albin Hansson became prime minister in 1932, there was a total of twelve prime ministerial changes in Sweden. There was precisely the same number of prime ministerial changes in Norway from 1920 until the Social Democrat Johan Nygaardsvold became prime minister in 1935. A new stability arrived with Hansson and Nygaardsvold.

This politically chaotic period had its dismal background in economic and social crises. During the 1920s none of the parliamentary parties had any solutions to the crises, and mistrust of the parliamentary system spread. The most serious threat came from the left. When the crisis began in 1920, however, the fear inspired by the Russian Revolution had weakened. Nonetheless, the labor movement and the ever-stronger Social Democratic parties retained much of their revolutionary rhetoric, especially in Norway. They represented, however, a gradually weakening threat to the system. The threat from the right had a weaker footing insofar as the Fascistic or Nazi-oriented parties had no representation in the Parliament of either country. But naturally there was a danger that they would come to have influence in the established right-wing parliamentary parties. The situation itself, that the conservative parties' attention was fixed on the totalitarian threats from the left, must have made them vulnerable to totalitarian influences from the right. But they would stand in opposition to this.

The crises and poorly functioning minority parliamentarianism made the system vulnerable. In this difficult situation it was very easy for criticism to slide over into criticism of the system, that is, into antiparliamentarianism or in the direction of totalitarianism. Thus in both countries there were those who wanted a strongman who could govern more independently of the parties and the Parliament. It was thought that a strong leader would speak out directly for the popular will. Parliament was seen as blocking this. In Norway the yearning for a strongman was attached to a particular person, Fridtjof Nansen, "the only star of the first order."[65] Nansen himself was passive but not unsympathetic, but upon his death in 1930 the idea of a strongman became marginalized.

The non-Socialist antiparliamentarianism, with its roots in trade and commerce circles and its links to the financing of the bourgeois parties, was of greater significance. Niklas Stenlås has introduced the concept of "the inner circle" in relation to Scandinavia. This has to do with a circle of the prominent and politically active from the economic elite who have connections to the organizations of the business world or to large economic enterprises. Moreover, they act not on behalf of these formal organizations but rather through a more informal network.[66] These networks acquired a certain degree of formal expression in both countries during the 1920s, however, through the organizations Vort Land (Our Country, organized in 1923) in Norway and Unitas (organized in 1928) in Sweden.[67] These were organizations that channeled money to the non-Socialist parties. That the business community itself coordinated the raising of funds for the non-Socialist parties implied that it had its own political agenda, and this organizing provoked anxiety in the parties. The aim was to mobilize a common non-Socialist or bourgeois front against Socialism, if necessary by having "parliamentarianism and Parliament relieved of its duties for a period, party politics repealed, and government power taken over by a bourgeois coalition government entrusted with

---

[65] Torstendahl 1969, 121, Danielsen 1984, 184.
[66] Stenlås 1998, 30.
[67] Stenlås 1998, 124; see also Danielsen 1984, 173ff.

the highest authority," as Vort Land's spokesman put it in an editorial.[68] Yet this declaration represented no more than a tendency. What was characteristic of the situation was widespread dissatisfaction combined with a fundamental lack of clarity on alternatives to the parliamentary system.

One Norwegian organization that had no counterpart in Sweden was Fedrelandslaget (the Fatherland Association), founded in 1925 by Joakim Lehmkuhl. In chapter 1, he appeared as a central man of industry and as the person who brought Taylorism to Norway. Fedrelandslaget reflected the widespread dissatisfaction about partisan political wrangling. It was intended to be "a constituent organization across party lines whose aim was to force the parties to cooperate," and by "the parties" one was to read "the bourgeois parties." Lehmkuhl's dream was to build Federlandslaget into a modern mass organization, and to some extent he succeeded. Around 1930 the membership was said to have been about one hundred thousand. Distaste for this organization was very strong within the Conservative Party. In the 1930 election the Conservatives made marked gains, which helps to explain Fedrelandslaget's simultaneous loss of support and influence. Some of the central figures from Fedrelandslaget found refuge in the Conservative Party, and others in Vidkun Quisling's Nazi-inspired party, Nasjonal Samling (NS, National Unification Party), which was founded in 1933.

In Sweden the formal expression of extraparliamentary tendencies on the bourgeois side was weaker than in Norway. This does not necessarily mean that dissatisfaction with the parliamentary system was any weaker. Here we find the same worries as in Norway. One of the clearest attacks on the system came from Sweden's Nationella Ungdomsförbund (SNU, National Youth League of Sweden). The association was organizationally independent, but in practice it operated as the youth organization of the Conservative Party. It grew to be a strong organization by the end of the 1920s, with a membership of thirty thousand. It then began to develop conflicts with its mother party. SNU demanded a tougher, more activist form of politics. The Conservative Party broke off contact with SNU in 1934 and established its own youth organization. SNU transformed itself into Sweden's Nationella Förbund (Swedish National League), which presented itself as a Nazi-style party. The break was directed by the leader of the Conservative Party, Arvid Lindman. The Norwegian Conservative Party never had such a clear threat within the organization itself, even though its general secretary expressed anxiety that the Young Conservatives would follow the Swedish example and form a national youth league.[69] On the other hand, the Swedish nazis never had the same ho-

---

[68] Stenlås 1998, 178. The citation was taken from the journal *Vor Verden* 1923/24, p. 329.
[69] Danielsen 1984, 234.

mogeneous organization as in Norway under Vidkun Quisling. In addition
to SNU, smaller groups formed around, for example, Birger Furugård and
Sven Olof Lindholm.[70]

The historian Rolf Danielsen has argued against a fairly common view in
Norway that the threat from right-wing activism was strongest in the 1930s,
above all from the founding of Quisling's party, the NS, in 1933. Rather,
Danielsen argues, the formation of the NS was "closer to an expression of
the defeat and isolation of activism, rather than evidence of its growth."
Conversely, activism in the 1920s "had a greater breadth and represented a
more serious threat to the political system."[71] A vague and rather widespread
antiparliamentarian activism with a number of Fascistic features was thus
replaced in the 1930s by a clearer drawing of lines by the formation of the
Nazi-style party NS. After this there followed isolation and marginalization;
the Nazi-style parties never achieved anything close to a breakthrough. To the
contrary, parliamentary democracy became consolidated and strengthened.

The same analysis can be applied to conditions in Sweden. This has further implications for the analysis of how the parliamentary system had such
power of resistance to the totalitarian currents. One common explanation
has been that it was due to Social Democracy. The Social Democrats modified themselves in order to be part of a common front against Fascism.[72] This
is certainly part of the explanation, but if Danielsen's analysis is correct, the
transition of the labor parties to reformism must also be seen in relation to the
fact that Fascism was rejected in the bourgeois quarters.[73]

Why did Fascism not take hold in Scandinavia? Ulf Lindström in Sweden
thinks that it is surprising that it did not take deeper root when one takes
into consideration the level of unemployment, the crisis in agriculture, and
the difficulty of establishing stable coalition governments. He goes on to list
nine reasons why Fascism did not gain ground. What was especially important was that there were no deep socioeconomic tensions in the Scandinavian
countries. In agreement with the Norwegian Bernt Hagtvet, Lindström also
stresses that the countries had not been defeated in any wars. Nor were there
any religious conflicts. The social institutions were intact. When the threat
arose, the political field was not polarized.[74]

The question can be sharpened: Why did the Scandinavian conservative
parties not fall under the influence of Fascism? The prominent leaders of the

[70] Hansson 2001.

[71] Danielsen 1984, 203.

[72] Jakobsen 1994, 157. He cites Bjørgum 1993, 158, and Maurseth 1987, 564. In the Swedish connection, see Alf W. Johansson 2000, 148ff.

[73] Jakobsen 1994, 158.

[74] Ulf Lindström 1983; Hagtvet 1980. The debate is summed up by Hansson (2001, 84).

conservative parties in the interwar period, Arvid Lindman in Sweden and C. J. Hambro in Norway, were both confirmed anti-Fascists and anti-Nazis.[75] They had at the same time turned against both Communist and Fascist dictatorships. It has been formulated as a criticism of Lindman that his arguments "against dictatorial thinking never included a defense of the principles of democracy but were always based on the problem of the freedom of the individual."[76] This could also be said of Hambro. "In truth," he wrote, "it is equally impossible for the Nordic way of thinking to assimilate the ideas of dictatorship as it is to stand for law and order as a flexible tool in the hand of the powerholder, and not as a framework for absolute principles."[77] Hambro and Lindman were both democrats and parliamentarians, but for both of them the most powerful and crucial argument against fascism lay in the tradition of liberal constitutional government, with its emphasis on the limiting of power and the defense of minorities, of the individual, and of individual rights from both majorities and state power. The conservative parties of Sweden and Norway were liberal-conservative; that is, *antitotalitarianism* was part of their soul. On this point they overlapped with the cultural radicals (see the introduction).

This also applied to the liberal-leftist parties. The leader of the Norwegian Liberal Party and three-time prime minister Johan Ludvig Mowinckel was just as clearly a parliamentarian and anti-Fascist as Hambro. When the Swedish liberals founded Folkpartiet (we will refer to it hereafter as the Liberal Party) in 1934 on the basis of a renewed alliance of the radical liberal factions, there was a certain degree of antiparliamentarianism in the draft of their platform. In its final form, however, the platform maintained that "every tendency toward the aspirations of dictatorship must be rejected."[78] On the other hand, the agrarian parties had to a greater degree been exponents of antiparliamentarianism. In the (Swedish) Farmers Association platform of 1933 one finds certain racist tendencies. The Farmers' Party in Norway also existed in a gray zone but, as we shall see, it finally chose to collaborate with the Social Democrats.

Above all others, it was the bourgeois parties that defended the democratic parliamentarianism that they themselves had created. At the same time, the most consistently anti-Fascist bourgeois politicians were those who demonstrated the least ability when it came to political and economic reform. The appeal of Fascism during the interwar period lay in the fact that the economic and economic-institutional fields were in need of genuine reform. In rejecting

---

[75] T. Nilsson 2002, 93.
[76] Torstendahl 1969, 97.
[77] Hambro 1937, 37.
[78] Vallinder 1984, 66, 68.

Fascism, however, the bourgeois politicians created room for another force pushing for reform to maneuver, namely, the Social Democrats.[79]

When the parliamentary system survived and emerged from the crisis period strengthened, this was partly ascribed to a deep-rooted liberal legacy. Besides, the non-Socialist parties showed themselves to be relatively open and flexible and never gave provocative responses to provocative initiatives. To the contrary, they functioned in an absorbing and decent manner, and thereby dampened the conflicts in society. The Socialists got to prove themselves in government positions and, as we have seen, were granted concessions in the socialization campaigns.

Nor did the system function as miserably as the many changes of government might suggest. Along the way the parliaments undertook leadership and delegated the executive power to parliamentary committees. In Sweden they referred to "parliamentarianism by committee," and it was said about Norway that "Parliament assumed power and governed with the help of parliamentary committees, of which the most important was the cabinet collegium."[80]

The politics that emerged from this situation greatly softened the results of the social crises. Despite the fragile financial foundation, an attempt was made to build up the social state. Moreover it has to be stressed that despite the crises, the period was within a time of economic upturn. Technological and economic modernization continued through the crises. Life became better for many. This was also the period when farmers and workers were brought into the system of political leadership.

THE FARMERS AND MODERNIZATION

The new political stability that came with the takeover of power by the Social Democrats in both countries during the 1930s had two causes. First, the Social Democratic parties had developed away from class-based parties and toward popular parties. The implications of this are that they took over to a considerable degree, and carried further, the policies of the radical bourgeoisie. Second, the new stability was built on a compromise with pertinent parliamentary support from the other class parties, namely, the agrarian parties. One might perhaps have expected a compromise with the liberal parties from which the Social Democrats had stolen so much of their policy; however, this was not the way things went. A new alliance was set up between farmers and

---

[79] Jakobsen 1994, 158.
[80] Jens Arup Seip 1994, 204. He provides the caveat that this was an extreme formulation.

workers, which would shove aside the old—radical and conservative—bourgeois parties. And this could happen by prescribed parliamentary means that had been laid down precisely by these old bourgeois parties.

The beginning of the twentieth century fell within what has been called "the great political period of farmers," which in Sweden stretched from 1867 to 1914.[81] This also applied to Norway. The liberal-leftist movements that led to political modernization in both countries were largely built on the votes of the farmers. Great concessions had also been given to the farmers. In matters such as the Norrland issue and the land question (see chapter 3), agricultural policy received a form of precedence. Even so, the description of this as a "great period" for farmers is true only if modified. The farmers never took leadership in politics. The liberal-leftist movements were very complex in their makeup, but when it came to setting the agenda and formulating the program of modernization, the leadership and defining power lay with the radical bourgeoisie, and even though the farmers' demands were met, there was an internal tension in the leftist movements that sooner or later would lead to disruption.

There was a difference here between Norway and Sweden. The period of political unrest leading up to 1914 in Sweden and the large farmers' march that year showed clearly that "the great political time of the farmers" was over. The farmers' march was a class-based manifestation and an expression of how, with respect to this "grievance," there was no longer a real agricultural party in the Parliament.[82] For various reasons the great leftist alliance held together better in Norway, a fact that gave the farmers somewhat greater influence than in Sweden. But after World War I this blew up as well. Farmer representation became less in both countries, but there was an even greater "weakening of *farmer interests*."[83]

Despite their relatively strong position in politics, farmers in both countries had long felt on the defensive—their world was in danger. The threats came from all sides: from the growing industrial sector, which competed for labor and made it more costly; from international competition, which drove down the price of agricultural goods; and above all from the mentality of the modernist society. Agriculture was no longer considered "the mother industry," and the social norms and structures of agrarian society were considered obsolete. A conflict arose between traditionalists and modernists. In this conflict the modernist bourgeoisie stood on the same side as the new industrial working class.

[81] S. Carlsson 1956, 389.
[82] S. Carlsson 1956, 491.
[83] S. Carlsson 1956, 468.

The new turbulence over the Socialists' attack on property rights and the many strikes shook the old agrarian society just as much as the modernization drive of the progressive bourgeoisie did, and the tension between farmers and workers would for a certain period be an important factor in politics. In brief, the farmers felt that they were struggling with their backs against the wall, that they were in the process of becoming marginalized. Along with the integration of the new class—the industrial workers—this marginalization of the old peasant farmer class represented a great challenge to the national project of social integration that had sprung forth from the ideas of a modern nation-state.

FARMERS ON THE OFFENSIVE: NORWAY

Sharp conflicts of interest within agriculture made political mobilization difficult. There was no clear class identity. But this was to change. In 1920, the year that Knudsen's stable Left-Liberal regime fell, the initiative was taken to establish a political party—the Farmers' Party.[84] Above all, the motivating reason was the farmers' dissatisfaction with the thoroughgoing policy of price and production regulations undertaken by the authorities during the war. This dissatisfaction worked as a unifying factor and was kindled as well by a general feeling that the farmers were now losing the ear of the bourgeois parties. It was said that the bourgeois parties had become more interested in showing goodwill toward the workers, who would "undermine society," than toward the farmers, who wanted to defend it.[85] The Farmers' Party took an appreciable number of votes away from the Liberals, and over the course of the 1920s the Farmers' Party's share of the vote increased from 13 percent to 16 percent, which made it an important player in the chaotic parliamentary political arena.

The Farmers' Party's preeminent figure during the 1920s was the prosperous farmer Johan E. Mellbye. Mellbye's rhetoric was colored by the traditionalists' view that agrarian society was the basis of the whole society. It was said that he preached the "leaf-mold gospel." Among his less romantic parliamentary colleagues he was referred to as "lord of the fog." His main enemy was the labor movement. Despite the party's increasing proportion of votes and despite Mellbye's having created a visible party profile, there was no way to hide the fact that he led a movement that looked back in nostalgia and was on the defensive.

---

[84] Aasland 1974. This study follows the process up to the formation of the party.
[85] May-Brith Ohman Nielsen 2001, 9.

Mellbye stepped down as chairman of the party about 1930, and great changes happened. The background was very somber. Agriculture was suffering a deep international crisis brought about by overproduction and sinking prices. This had been aggravated in Norway by the parity policy of the 1920s, which was an important reason for the credit crisis that drove many farmers off their land. The crisis gave birth to two initiatives that became important to the integration of the farmers into modern society. These were the establishment of central marketing boards for farm animal products and of the organization Rural People's Crisis Relief.

The initiative for central marketing boards was taken by the Farmers' Union, the farmers' interest organization, and this campaign rapidly united the "great farming masses." The movement raised a demand concerning public authorization of, and state contributions to, interest organizations in general and, in this particular case, to the Farmers' Union. This was realized with the Joint Marketing Law of 1930.[86] The principle was that the state should channel tax money to the private interest organizations to distribute to the farmers. The law was passed with votes from the Liberal and Labor parties and most of the Conservative Party. Some members of the Conservative Party wanted no law since they were opposed to the compulsory organizing that it entailed. The Farmers' Party wanted to go further but finally conceded and voted for the majority proposition.

The Conservatives and Liberals had both feared compulsory organizing and therefore hesitated, and the Labor Party had hesitated, on behalf of consumers, over this form of producers' cooperative, but owing to the force of circumstances they conceded. The issue simply revolved around saving the agricultural sector and the farmers as a social group. It was typical that the spokesperson for the Liberal Party commented that "one is forced into proposing strange things and going along with them in these times."[87] The Labor Party cautiously maintained that the law had resulted in a positive reference to cooperative thinking in general.[88] The central marketing institutions and the initiatives linked to them helped to check the falling prices of farm animal products.[89] This effort represented an effective regulation of prices, and to a certain degree production, with redistributive consequences that favored the farmers.

The marketing law was a sensational development. First, it involved a significant shift of power to the organizations, and therefore it constituted a milestone in the development of corporatism; second, it would become

[86] Furre 1968, 3.
[87] St. forh. (Parl. Proceedings) 1930, O. Tid. p. 1009.
[88] Furre 1968, 278, 396.
[89] Furre 1968, 333.

permanent and typical of the Social Democratic order; and third, it was brought into being by bourgeois forces with the reluctant endorsement of the Labor Party.

The Rural People's Crisis Relief was an extraparliamentary activist organization for the victims of debt. It was established in 1931 and represented a protest against the established parties. Being confronted with such an organization was a particularly cold shower for the Farmers' Union and the Farmers' Party.[90] Mellbye and the Farmers' Party had been against the writing off of debts, but in 1932 the party reversed its position and supported debt relief. The debt relief movement would eventually put pressure on both the farmers' movement and the labor movement. Already, in the election of 1927, the Labor Party had become the largest party among the rural population, and with the election of 1933 debt relief was a major point in the party's platform, together with employment. The election allowed for a big step forward. The crisis had brought the debtor parties together, and "bourgeois politics faced a fateful time."[91]

The Rural People's Crisis Relief had by this time slid toward Quisling's NS party, and after the election it quickly dissolved, but it had made its mark on politics. In 1934 there was a breakthrough in debt policy when Parliament ratified a state loan fund for agriculture. A struggle against compulsory auctions of farms in foreclosure had been successful. By means of public intervention and public funds, the problems were solved through writing off loans and debt conversion. The crisis had put the whole nation-building project in danger since an entire sector of the population was in acute need. Given such a situation, the common interest prevailed over special interests.

FARMERS ON THE OFFENSIVE: SWEDEN

Developments in Sweden in many respects paralleled those in Norway. In 1921 the first modern interest party was formed, the Farmers' Union (Bondeförbundet). But, as in Norway under the pressure of the crisis around 1930, the farmers went on the offensive politically, beginning with the different farmers' organizations and gradually gathering a high degree of political unity.

As in Norway, there were demands for help with the credit crisis. This problem did not reach the same severity in Sweden as in Norway, however, and did not affect the debate in the same way.[92] The most important demands

---

[90] Nerbøvik 1991, 81.

[91] Nerbøvik 1991, 28, 71, 253, and 256.

[92] Thullberg 1977, 197, 255.

had to do with import, price, and production regulations and, as in Norway, they were premised on public funds and a close cooperation between the farmers' organizations and authorities, which in one form or another meant public authorization of the organizations.

Bo Rothstein has argued against the common view that it was the Social Democrats who in the 1930s introduced the collectivist ideal of democracy with a strong corporatist element. This has been said to have happened with the crisis settlement of 1933 (see below) with opposition from the non-Socialists.[93] The decisive event in the development of the crisis policy and a democratic corporatism had, however, happened *before* the crisis settlement, according to Rothstein. The precise time was June 10, 1932, when the non-Socialist parties decided "in principle on a mandatory collectivization of the Swedish farmer class." The Social Democrats stood on the sidelines as amazed bystanders. The issue had to do with a proposal from the major farmers' organization that the state powers sanction the organization's "decisive influence on price and production conditions" in the area of milk marketing. In other words, the organization would be given the right to collect fees even from producers who had chosen to remain outside the organization. State coercion was necessary. The crisis had put a knife to the country's throat. As a conservative politician said, "The existing economic class faced a threat to its existence," and thus one would rather "modify one's principal misgivings a little."

This is parallel to what happened in Norway, except in Sweden the Social Democrats voted against the proposal. What is interesting, however, is the implication immediately enunciated by the Social Democrats: the non-Socialist parties wanted to solve the crisis in agriculture by building up and *lending support to* the agrarian organizations, whereas the non-Socialists' solution to unemployment involved *weakening* the trade unions. Furthermore, support for the agrarian organizations was support for the attempt to keep prices high, whereas weakening the trade unions was intended to help hold prices—or, rather, wages—low. Thus the Social Democrats accused the non-Socialist parties of pursuing an inconsistent policy by claiming that the mechanism of the market could not solve the agricultural crisis but it could solve the unemployment crisis. Similarly, the conservative Arvid Lindman, unconsciously prophetic according to Rothstein, came to argue strongly for the theory of purchasing power, in relation to the proposition that farmers' purchasing power had to be maintained in order to maintain their demand for industrial goods.[94] Naturally, this was in principle the same argument that

[93] The following is built on Rothstein 1992, 110–135.

[94] Rothstein 1992, 125. Torstendahl (1969, 44f.) has also noted Lindman's inconsistency (pp. 61–62) and pointed to theoretical purchasing-power reasoning in the Farmers' Union.

the Social Democrats used for their labor market program, in which one of the main points was to maintain workers' purchasing power by keeping wages high. The inconsistency in the bourgeois argument reveals the transitional nature of the situation.

Along with Rothstein, and based on the actual use of the reasoning inherent in the theory of purchasing power, one has grounds for criticizing the common view that the breakthrough of this reasoning reflected new economic insight. The context was more important than many have thought. One does not find this type of reasoning in relation to the debate in Norway over the central marketing law of 1930, not even among the Social Democrats. It could be that this point of view had matured and had wider currency among the Swedish Social Democrats. In all probability this reasoning enabled them quickly to see the implications of the proposed legislation and to use them in the debate. But this should not obscure the fact that this reasoning had its first political impact in the course of the bourgeois parties' resolution of June 10, 1932. The resolution was predicated on a clear argument based on the principle of purchasing power—an argument that was developed independent of the theorists and the Social Democrats, and that was created out of the need to shape and legitimize a crisis policy.

CRISIS SETTLEMENT IN BOTH COUNTRIES

In 1932 Per Albin Hansson formed a Social Democratic government in Sweden. The Hansson government introduced a new stable period. The basis for this stability was the 1933 "cow trade" between the Social Democrats and the political party of the farmers, the Farmers' Union. (*Cow trade* refers to a crisis settlement by means of "horse-trading.") The Social Democrats got support for their new active labor market policy, while the Farmers' Union was assured of continuing support for the extension of state assistance to agriculture. For example, farmers ended up with guaranteed fixed prices for grain and butter!

It is noteworthy that the farmers entered into a coalition with their old enemy, the Social Democrats. Indeed, the previous year the Farmers' Union had carried out the compulsory formation of cartels with the help of the bourgeois parties—an important contribution to alleviating the agricultural crisis. Could they not have gained just as much by remaining within the traditional bourgeois front against the Socialists?

The key person in the Farmers' Union's break from the bourgeois front was Axel Pehrsson of Bramstorp.[95] He entered the decisive crisis year 1932

---

[95] Thullberg 1977, 272f., in reference to this paragraph.

Figure 4. Swedish Farmers' Union leader Axel Pehrsson of Bramstorp, *left*, and Social Democratic leader Per Albin Hansson warmly shake hands on the occasion of forming a coalition government with Pehrsson as prime minister in 1936. Hansson had led a purely Social Democratic government with the support of the Farmers' Union since 1932 and was soon to take over as prime minister for the coalition.

in a relatively modest position and came to occupy a central position, becoming the main player in the development of the "cow trade." He became party leader in 1934, and in a brief three-month period in 1936 when Hansson's and the Social Democratic Party's leadership was interrupted he became prime minister, and after that he was minister of agriculture in Hansson's coalition government until 1945. Pehrsson was a man of compromise and a pragmatist who came to enjoy great confidence among wide circles. According to the Social Democratic minister of finance Ernst Wigforss, with whom he worked closely, he viewed "the state's intervention in economic life as a purely practical problem, without any ideological coloring," which, naturally, greatly pleased Wigforss's ideological "coloring."

On the other hand, the Social Democrats had been skeptical of the farmers' demands because they felt acceding to them would oppose consumers' interests. Because it was necessary to do something about the agricultural crisis, because the Social Democrats had received many votes in rural areas, because they were willing to pay a price to get their labor market program enacted, and finally because of a mutual sympathy and desire to take action, especially on Pehrsson's side, the "cow trade" could be carried out. Per Thullberg stresses that Pehrsson "consistently set the question of the economy above any form of ideology," and he refers to Pehrsson's "purely professional aims."[96]

A corresponding "crisis settlement" occurred in Norway in 1935. As we have seen, the organizational development of agriculture was analogous in the two countries. The Farmers' Party in Norway was a typical interest party that sprang from, and had a close relationship to, the Farmers' Union interest organization. Following the Norwegian pattern, there was a drive to establish an "implementation of Norway's Farmers' Union idea in Sweden." Thereupon in Sweden the National Association of Rural People (Riksförbundet Landsbygdens Folk) adopted many of its new bylaws from those of the Norwegian Farmers' Union.[97] But the settlement of the crisis occurred first in Sweden. In this way Norwegians learned that farmers and workers could share common interests and transcend the old ideological barriers. One of the reasons this happened later than in Sweden was that it was not until after the election of 1933 that the Labor Party and the Farmers' Party jointly held a majority in the Norwegian Parliament.

In both countries the farmers had the most to gain in their compromise with the Social Democrats. The subsidies to agriculture increased considerably. The two interest parties had fewer inhibitions about increasing the budget than the old bourgeois parties did. Indeed, this was in keeping with the new tendencies of the time. But these two interest parties also broke with the bourgeois parties on questions related to the social order. The Norwegian Farmers' Party believed that the state should actively intervene to ensure the viability of agriculture. Here the farmers were in line with the Social Democrats, whereas the Liberals, after the party had participated in the "mandatory cartelization" in the early 1930s, now maintained that public intervention in free production could weaken the vitality of agriculture.[98] The farmers seem to have gotten the idea that the threat to their well-being came not from workers and Socialists but rather from capital and liberalism.[99] And in the struggle against these latter threats, the bourgeois parties were not to be

[96] Thullberg 1977, 306.
[97] Thullberg 1977, 272ff.
[98] Bjørgum 1970, 9.
[99] M.B.O. Nielsen 2001, 143.

trusted. Moreover, there was a common interest between the farmers' parties and the workers' parties "in view of the state's relationship to the interest organizations that lay closest to the parties from which they drew, or came to draw, their chief support."[100] Here we glimpse a political paradigm shift.

Corporatism was not new, but the corporatist schemes that the farmers drew up and that had (in part) been implemented during the crisis stood for a significant step in the direction of the corporative pluralism that came to be so characteristic of the Social Democratic order. It is not by accident that this important step in the corporatist direction came in tandem with the two interest parties finding themselves together able to take over government power through the process of crisis settlement. The old bourgeois parties, the Conservatives and Liberals, had made a virtue of not defining themselves as interest parties. Politics, they believed, should deal with forming a society that benefited all, and the state was not to be a tool of various interests but rather should stand above such things. The fact that one can glimpse interest positions behind this ideology does not mean that it was insincere. For the interest parties, however, politics was more a question of the state acting as a facilitator of compromises between different interests, especially by means of corporatist projects.

This breakthrough of the interest parties, the disregarding of the old bourgeois parties, located and strengthened the corporatization process, which had begun around the middle of the 1930s. The Main Agreement and the Saltsjöbad Agreement, which together represented an important step in the direction of strengthening the interest organizations in relation to traditional political institutions, followed naturally in the wake of the interest parties' assumption of political power (see chapter 4). The key to understanding this whole movement toward the idea of politics as compromise among differing interests lies just as much in developments on the bourgeois side as in developments among the Social Democrats.

Thus it is worth noting that the farmers moved from a defensive position, in which they were fighting to avoid marginalization in modern society, to an offensive one precisely in the depths of the crisis. They actively helped to give a more concrete shape to the Social Democratic variant of modern society—a shape that would have room for farmers as well, at least for a while. In this context it is significant that this paradigm shift reflected the integration of the farmers and workers into modern society through a more direct participation in the exercise of political power. This involved an important step toward further democratization. This (final) step they had had to manage themselves. But not all groups became so effectively integrated.

---

[100] Rothstein 1992, 130.

WOMEN AND CIVIL AND POLITICAL RIGHTS

The dissolution of the union between the two countries was significant for the development of democracy, especially with regard to the mobilization of women. When Parliament in Norway had decided that the dissolution of the union would be confirmed by plebiscite, it was recommended to the government that women should get the right to vote. This was rejected. Women then sprang into action with a petition campaign. In this way a total of 280,000 women, or half of those with the potential right to vote, gave their approval to the dissolution of the union. According to Kari Melby, the action was "an example of the fact that women were able to act politically even before they achieved full political rights. Women found their place in the public arena and demonstrated their membership in the national community. They took the right to express themselves despite their sex."[101] By using what they considered to be their democratic right in this manner, women contributed to paving the way for universal suffrage for women. A direct path led from the action in 1905 to the introduction of limited women's suffrage in 1907 and to full voting rights in 1913. In Sweden women's suffrage did not come until the great constitutional reform in 1918.

The issue had been on the agenda for a long time. A series of women's associations were formed toward the end of the nineteenth century, partly to perform social work and partly to struggle for women's rights and women's suffrage. Arguments for women's liberation have been integral to the general liberal rights argument that sees the individual as the primary unit of society. The concept of rights revealed itself to be an important and explosive force in the long run: the individual, whether woman or man, has the right to participate in the life of the nation. In this manner women's liberation could be linked to nation building. It was equally important that women, through their associations and through their topical actions such as that of 1905, were able to win for themselves a place in the public space. The opposition, however, was strong.

The concept of individual rights was never universal, even among liberals. When one examines the way that thinking about society developed through the whole modernization process, one finds various combinations of individualist and collectivist ideas. The most important for our purposes was that this thinking about individual rights had to compete with ideas of *the family* as the basic unit of society.[102] Loyalty to this little collective was one of the

---

[101] Melby 2001, 40.
[102] Esping-Andersen 1999.

most common arguments against women coming out into the public sphere and getting the right to vote.

The family sphere was characterized by more than the fact that women were shut out of the public sphere. The family was also patriarchal insofar as the man continued to be its head. For civil and political rights, emancipation efforts followed two lines. On the one hand, these efforts attempted to break down patriarchy in the intimate sphere by placing women on an equal footing with men on questions of financial circumstances, parental authority, and marriage and divorce. On the other hand, these efforts also attempted to secure for women a place in the public sphere.

In 1909 the Swedish government took the initiative to get a common Scandinavian statute in the field of family law. Women were consulted, and in 1915 they formally attained representation in a Scandinavian committee appointed by the three governments to propose such a statute. For women from Denmark and Sweden, this happened even before they attained the right to vote. The initiative led to new marriage laws regulating the entering into and leaving of marriage, and laws about financial circumstances that put both parties on a par with one another.[103] "Patriarchy fell" in the face of these laws, at least in a formal sense. This "Nordic model" was "sensational in the international context."[104] But this model implies no breakthrough on the other front, of women in the public sphere; almost the reverse was true.

Thus man and woman were formally on an equal footing inside the family, but according to the established customary "housewife contract" they had different roles and responsibilities. The man had responsibility for financially supporting the family; the woman had responsibility for housework and children. The housewife contract was predominant in both Sweden and Norway from 1920 until about 1960. It is somewhat unclear whether one could speak of a similar contract prior to 1920, because it was not until the beginning of the twentieth century that the bourgeois idea of the family was generalized. In the 1960s the housewife contract gradually faded from its dominant position in the demarcation of family relationships in favor of an "equality contract" that, among other things, assumed that a two-income family was the norm and that society had a far-reaching responsibility for children.

Thus the housewife contract was dominant throughout the golden age of Social Democracy. Unemployment in the interwar years contributed to consolidating these social expectations through the demand that one family should not have two incomes. On the other hand, there was an effort to professionalize and upgrade "the housewife profession," as it came to be

---

[103] Danielsen and Lödrup 1988, 566.
[104] Melby 2001, 45; Danielsen and Lödrup 1988, 567: the law was "in many ways ahead of its time."

called. A typical representative of this housewife ideology and the gender-based division of labor was Olivia Nordgren, a leading Social Democratic politician in Sweden. She explicitly opposed "complete equality between man and woman" and spoke warmly in favor of not regarding "women's work in the home as inferior to other work."[105] Even though patriarchy had fallen and there was gender equality, so far as it went, this by no means implied the end of the traditional role distinctions between the sexes. We see this clearly at the political level.

The first election in Sweden following the introduction of universal women's suffrage took place in 1921. According to the historian Yvonne Hirdman, this election transformed "a century-long threat into a mere bagatelle, insofar as only a mere handful of women entered Parliament and the numbers did not increase throughout the interwar period." The conflict over suffrage had been solved, but it was followed by "the rapid, disappointed realization that [women] were still as much outsiders as ever."[106] These observations were even more applicable to Norway than to Sweden. What happened, for example, to the women who had mobilized in 1905 in Norway? They had asserted themselves in the public arena and obtained the right to vote, but they did not use this to further distinguish themselves in public life.

In Sweden as well, women mobilized before the introduction of universal women's suffrage, especially during the years of scarcity, 1917–1918. According to Kjell Östberg, "The events of the spring of 1917 probably without comparison constitute the most extensive example of women's collective political actions seen in the country up to that point, and perhaps even up to the present." That was about the physical survival of the family, and it demonstrates that the actions initiated by women had a tendency to develop into acts of violence. But "when need disappeared, this type of independent action by women also ceased."[107] The Swedish mobilization of women was linked to what was women's particular area of responsibility, the family. That this mobilization did not leave deeper traces, and that women in general did not capture more positions in civil society, not only was due to opposition from men, but also was related to the fact that many women accepted the established pattern of gender roles.

The development of women's networks continued from the end of the nineteenth century through the first half of the twentieth as well. Special women's organizations developed within the parties, for example. The fact that women got their own organizations has been viewed as a weakness, a

---

[105] Hagemann and Åmark 1999, 191.
[106] Hirdman 1998, 124.
[107] Östberg 1997, 24, 26, 27, 20.

kind of substitute for the possibility of doing something through those associations and groupings central to the life of society that traditionally were dominated by men. Recent research in Sweden has called attention to the complexities of the phenomenon, however. Not only do we see development in women's organizing but also that a network had developed across the divisions in society, precisely through these special women's associations. This latter point is interesting from the perspective of integration. Since gender segregation crossed the lines of social segregation, it has served to some extent to soften the problems of social integration between women in different positions in society. A special women's public sphere was formed.[108] And this women's network had a significant influence on politics.[109] Here there are marked differences between Norway and Sweden.

During the interwar unemployment crises a demand was made that married women stay out of the workforce. No one family should have two incomes. This met with strong opposition in Sweden, especially within the Swedish labor movement, where, among other bodies, the Women's Labor Committee, which counted Alva Myrdal as one of its leading figures, came to play an important role. Especially because of their input, in 1939 Sweden got what was at the time unique legislation outlawing measures that would prohibit women from working.[110]

It was a different situation in Norway. Norway had given women suffrage early on, and the right to assistance in childbirth was introduced as early as 1909, long before it was introduced in Sweden. Norway was also involved from an early date in the dismantling of patriarchy in the family sphere. Despite such initiatives, however, there persisted a stronger family ideology in Norway than in Sweden. This was accompanied by strong distinctions between social gender roles.[111] This family ideology dominated both the labor movement and the bourgeois women's movement. It is thus characteristic of Norway that, in contrast to Sweden, there was no momentum behind the campaign against keeping married women out of the workforce during the crisis of the 1930s.

Nor did Norway ever form a special women's public sphere as the Swedish did with their active collaboration across social boundaries. There was an attempt to establish a women's united front following the Swedish pattern, but it was of no importance.[112] The absence of cooperation between working-class and bourgeois women like that in Sweden has been ascribed, for example,

---

[108] Östberg 1997, 200; Hagemann 2002, 155.

[109] Östberg 1997, 101f. He refers particularly to Frangeur 1995.

[110] Hagemann 2002, 156–157; Frangeur 1995, 215; Peter Johansson 2002.

[111] Sainsbury 2001, 118. Sainsbury has a penetrating analysis in which she strongly underlines the great difference between Sweden and Norway.

[112] Following the initiative of Ella Anker (Soltvedt 2000, 112).

to the fact that there had not been cooperation on the question of women's suffrage. In contrast to the process in Sweden, voting rights for Norwegian women were introduced in two steps. The first step in 1907 left out working-class women and led to a split in the women's movements.[113]

Part of the explanation for the hegemonic housewife contract not having been contested the same way in Norway as it was in Sweden lies on the level of the historical actor. Norway had no Alva Myrdal.[114] The most important explanation, however, lies with the fact that the mixture of individualism and collectivism is different in the two countries. The lukewarm attitude in Norway toward the emancipation of women demonstrates how the Norwegian labor movement has stood in opposition to the liberal movements. Put simply, it has been more Socialist or collectivist in its orientation than the Swedish labor movement, which in many ways should be viewed as a radical-liberal bourgeois movement. And this applies as much to relations within the family as to class. This also helps to explain why working-class women in Norway did not cooperate with their bourgeois counterparts despite the fact that they were in agreement about family politics.

THE INTEGRATION OF MINORITIES: THE SAMI

We must also glance at the small groups in society, the cultural or ethnic minorities. Were they integrated into the nation? Sweden and Norway were ethnically and culturally homogeneous societies in the sense that each had a completely dominant national culture. This cultural dominance can make it difficult to catch sight of the minorities who are there, and their invisibility must leave its mark on policy directed toward these groups. How strong was the demand to conform to the norms of the wider society? How did the greater society set boundaries between inclusion and segregation? We will examine in particular the policy toward the Sami.

The tension between the nomadic Sami and the sedentary Nordic agriculturalists was of long standing. It acquired a new feature toward the end of the nineteenth century, however. By then social Darwinism and the idea that the nomadic culture was doomed to extinction had penetrated the two countries. It is characteristic of this change that whereas formerly civil servants had a tendency to consider the Sami skilled and enterprising, now, under the influence of social Darwinism, the Sami came to be considered immoral, indolent, dirty, and alcoholic. This was the background for both countries going in

---

[113] Sainsbury 2001, 123.
[114] See Hagemann and Åmark (1999) for a discussion on the reasons for the difference.

for a heavy-handed "civilization process." In the latter half of the nineteenth century the Sami language disappeared as a language used in the schools; the Sami were to be integrated into the national culture. This policy had the greatest consequences in Norway. One question that has been discussed is the degree of "success" these intentions have had. It has even been suggested that in reality school policy strengthened Sami culture, thus achieving an effect opposite to that intended.[115]

Even though the ideological basis was the same in the two countries, Sweden's Sami policy changed direction in the 1900s, which gave it a completely different character from Norway's Sami policy. The decline and fall of the nomadic culture was a given, according to social Darwinism; but, as was maintained in Sweden, one need not hasten this decline; it could be allowed to happen by means of "a free historical process."[116] In this way it was possible to give social Darwinism a more positive character. Leaving the Sami to themselves was seen as being in their own best interest. As Lennart Lundmark writes:

> This new line implied that one could minimize the Sami's contact with "civilization," something that could very well tempt them to abandon the mountains and reindeer herding for good. The policy came to be described in the slogan "the Lapps will be Lapps" and clearly had racist motives. According to the politicians, the Sami had certain qualities that made them entirely suited to nomadic reindeer herding because "the reindeer were created for the Lapps and the Lapps for the reindeer." If the Sami turned to anything else, they ended up in destitution and wretchedness.[117]

The Swedish policy involved setting aside certain mountain areas where the Sami could live, preserving their nomadic culture. With regard to the comprehensive land clearing that gradually took place in Norrland, the areas set aside for the Sami were much smaller than the areas over which they had originally extended their herding. In addition, after 1905 Norway restricted the admission of Swedish Sami to summer pasture on the Norwegian side of the border.

The clearest expression of the "Lapps will be Lapps" policy in Sweden is found in the school sector.[118] Sami children were sent to mobile nomadic schools set up especially for them. The policy was to make this schooling inferior to that of the normal primary schools so that the Sami children would not be able to get a taste of the conveniences that other children had a right to. The scheme was linked to the family's pattern of life: children of sedentary

---

[115] Lorenz 1991, 81.
[116] Lorenz 1991, 79.
[117] Lundmark 2002, 63. "Lapps" is an old word for "Sami."
[118] Lundmark 2002, 76ff.

Sami were considered not to be "real Lapps," and therefore went to ordinary primary schools. The difference between Sweden and Norway was tangible. In Norway the village schools were closed down, and centralized residential schools were constructed for Sami children. The goal was to "civilize" them— that is, to wipe out the Sami culture through integration.

Another feature of the "Lapps will be Lapps" policy was the opposition to allowing Sami to till the land and build houses. There were of course many sedentary Sami. This created problems for the Sami policy because in many situations it could be difficult to define who was Sami and who was not. The problem was thus that in both Sweden and Norway all sorts of hindrances were put in the way of Sami who wanted to cultivate the land, whether they were young people who came from reindeer herding or from the sedentary community. At this time arrangements were made for land clearance in both countries. But this did not benefit the Sami. Quite the reverse: in Norway there was a conscious policy to Norwegianize the county of Finnmark, that is, to prepare for the settlement there of the country's ethnic majority population.[119] The result of this policy was that those Sami who did not herd reindeer were almost without any rights. Meanwhile the Sami population declined. Poverty, a high mortality rate, and sinking self-esteem were characteristic of the Sami in the interwar period.

Given the great nation-building and integration project, how should a country act in relation to an ethnic minority like the Sami? It is noteworthy that Swedish and Norwegian policies were so different. To put it bluntly, we could say that Norway chose *integration*, while Sweden chose *segregation*. The ideological starting point in social Darwinism could lead equally well to either one. The difference could be accidental, to some extent. Yet certain conditions can help to explain the difference. First, in Sweden the territories were large, and the pressure on resources was less than in Norway. Thus Sweden had room for segregation. Second, in Norway there was a strong wave of nationalism that pushed for a policy of national consolidation. Norwegianization was a natural extension of this. Third, in Norway considerations of political security came to play a much greater role than in Sweden. There was great fear of danger from the east, from the Russians and the Finns. In this connection an ethnically unstable Finnmark, Norway's northernmost county, represented poor defense. Hence it was not only the policy toward the old aboriginal population, the Sami, that was different in the two countries but also policy toward the immigrant Finns (called, in the Norwegian context, Kvener). In Norway there was a tendency to regard the Sami and immigrant Finns as together constituting a risk in relation to national defense

---

[119] Lundmark 2002, 122; Eriksen and Niemi 1981, 336.

policy. In addition to being a factor behind the Norwegianization policy, this fear led to surveillance and inspections, especially of the immigrant Finns. In Sweden, by contrast, the policy toward immigrant Finns was colored by the feeling that the Finns were an old kindred folk.[120]

In fact, it would turn out that the greatest threat came not from Russia, the Soviet Union, or Finland but rather from Germany, with the German occupation of Norway during World War II. One might perhaps have expected that the minorities would benefit from the situation and cooperate with the occupying forces against their old oppressors, but the opposite happened. The Sami in Norway in particular took a courageous stand against the occupiers, which was one of the reasons for the change in Sami policy after 1945.[121]

In the main, the policies sketched here were followed until the outbreak of World War II. It must be added, however, that these policies were softened somewhat in the 1930s, for several reasons. First, it became "necessary" to do something about the depletion of the Sami population, which by then had fallen drastically. Second, the Sami mobilized themselves by forming Sami associations, partly across national borders. A weakness of the Sami's own mobilization, however, was their internal disagreement over the greater society's integration project.

In 1906 the Sami Isak Saba was elected as member of Parliament for Finnmark from the Labor Party's list of candidates. An important issue for Saba and the local party organization was the struggle against Norwegianization. Yet this was controversial among the Sami themselves, and the central powers of the Labor Party did not support the issue. To the contrary, the ideas of social Darwinism hung over the Labor Party, so that the Labor Party government from 1935 on followed the previous government's policy on minorities. It was not until after the war that social Darwinism began to loosen it grip on the public mind, which allowed a new minority policy to be adopted. This was the same in both countries.

THE INTEGRATION OF MINORITIES: REFUGEES FROM GERMANY

Nation building involved the marking of national boundaries. We have seen that in Sweden both emigration and immigration were viewed with skepticism. The same thing applied to Norway as well. Immigration in particular

---

[120] Eriksen and Niemi 1981, 335, 346–349.
[121] Otnes 1970, 156–157.

could be disturbing to integration and nation building. As a preview of the great wave of immigration that began around 1970, we can examine a special group of immigrants in the interwar years, namely, refugees from Germany. How were they received and how did people relate to them? In the view of Frank Meyer, there were significant differences between the Scandinavian countries on this issue—differences, he argues, that reflect differences in national character, that is, in "the individual's disposition to react, to feel, be, and think that are colored by the national society."[122] On this basis he has looked for fundamental differences between Sweden and Norway.

From about 1933 until around 1940, 7,200 German refugees went to Sweden, while 2,680 went to Norway. Of these, relatively more Jews went to Sweden than to Norway.[123] At the outset, conditions regarding passports and visas were roughly the same. Both Norway and Sweden had passed new immigration legislation in 1927. Gradually, as the number of refugees increased, more stringent requirements were introduced. The stream of refugees was considered a problem to be solved by limiting immigration. In both countries the Jews were considered economic, not political, refugees; they were not particularly welcome. Sweden entered into an agreement with Germany that notice be given in the passport that the holder was Jewish.[124] In the documentary sources pertaining to Norway and Sweden there were no signs of empathetic defense of the right to seek asylum, as, by contrast, there were in Denmark.

Norway was always the most defensive, the most careful in regard to taking in refugees. When the stream of refugees did appear, what might be considered a panic reaction broke out. As quickly as possible, "the Norwegian authorities pulled in the gangplank and signed out of the game."[125] Nevertheless, when the refugees first came to the country, the alarm was switched off. This was in clear contrast to what happened in Sweden, where the borders were (relatively) more open and supervision was more strict. The Swedes developed a bureaucratic system with both coarse and refined instruments for limiting the stream of refugees and, above all, supervising the refugees as they entered. According to Meyer, in the years up to 1940 the Swedes developed a kind of paranoia. The authorities tended to see enemies and dangers everywhere. There was a sort of dialectical reversal from rationality to irrationality.[126]

With the German occupation of Denmark and Norway, Sweden became a neutral state and, as well, a recipient of refugees from both of these countries.

[122] Frank Meyer 2001, 271. Meyer built on Norbert Elias's concept of "habitus."
[123] F. Meyer 2001, 40, 68.
[124] F. Meyer 2001, 63; Isaksson 2000, 368.
[125] F. Meyer 2001, 73.
[126] F. Meyer 2001, 83.

The inclination to take in Jewish refugees was not very strong, but this would change. The many reports of the persecution of Jews, and in particular the deportation of more than five hundred Jews from Norway to Germany in the late autumn of 1942, led to a new policy in Sweden. In the autumn of 1943 the border was opened to about eight thousand Danish Jews, who fled across Öresund. "With this move Sweden became in fact the first state to offer the Jews of a German-occupied country free entry."[127] The stream of refugees from Denmark was made possible by the organized efforts of patriotic Danes, but perhaps also because the occupying power did not go all out to stop it. In Norway this did not happen. Norway had a very small Jewish population—in 1940 barely eighteen hundred, of whom six hundred were refugees who had arrived within the preceding decade. There was no organized underground mobilization to save the Jews, as there was in Denmark. Conversely, "good" Norwegians allowed themselves to be used in the deportation of the Jews, which led to completely different figures, in relative terms, from those for Denmark. Only slightly more than half of the Jewish population of Norway was saved.[128]

There were thus clear differences between the Swedes' and the Norwegians' ways of dealing with the problem of refugees. Meyer believes it is possible to find an explanation for this in differences of national character. The egalitarian Norwegian social structure with great social mobility created a strong sense of fellowship combined with free and open internal relations but assiduously guarded external boundaries. Conversely, the Swedish social structure was characterized by a fusion of aristocratic and bourgeois behavior. The first was marked by liberality and the second by rationality and control.[129]

As soon as the immigrant groups began to be viewed as a risk to security policy, the Norwegian authorities could also take refuge in surveillance and internal control, as they did with regard to the immigrant Finns in the county of Finnmark. It was precisely a case of exaggerated fear. Here we can speak of a Norwegian paranoia that parallels Sweden's paranoia as perceived by Meyer. The national characters of the two countries were not so very different when it comes right down to it. Actually, it would later be revealed that what really did pose a threat—namely, the German fifth column—was not feared at all. In Norway there was a blissful ignorance of this danger. Precisely on this point the Swedes seem to have been better informed and more rational.

---

[127] Isaksson 2000, 374.
[128] *Om Sveriges förhållande till nazismen . . .* (On Sweden's Relationship to Nazism) 2001, 137.
[129] F. Meyer 2001, 282ff.

NATIONAL INTEGRATION AND DEMOCRACY

Democratization is partly a question of the right to vote, but it is also much more than that. It has to do with social integration and national fellowship. There was general agreement about this primary goal, and the roots of this nation-building project stretch far back in time. The problem of integration became pressing at the beginning of the twentieth century, a time of great social tensions. The strategies of the liberal society for nation building were demonstrably inadequate. The new working class was beating on the door leading to national fellowship. In retrospect we can see that eventually the problem was solved and the door was opened. But the process was convoluted and difficult.

A key to understanding these developments lies in the great popular movements at the end of the nineteenth century. They were essentially oppositional and represented a mobilization of a broad stratum of the population—a form of democratizing before democratization. The popular education or refinement project brought along by these movements was of particular importance. Education and democratization are indissolubly linked. The more broadly and radically the population is educated or refined, the more deeply the society can be democratized, as the Socialist Richard Sandler said. Naturally enough, there was disagreement about the content of this project. In Norway there was an early, clean break with the educational ideas of the old class-based pedagogy, a fact that reflects the earlier democratizing process in Norway. In Sweden this break came later.

A special problem from the perspective of integration was the peasant farmers, the dominant class of the old society. They had become integrated politically during the national revolution in Norway, but they were pushed to the sidelines by the industrial revolution. The interwar crisis forced through radical moves, however, which contributed partly to the integration of this class into modern society. A next step in integration came directly from the alliance of old antagonists, the farmers and the workers, who were able to take over government power in both countries during the 1930s. A precondition for this to happen was the fact that right-wing extremism had been rejected by the bourgeois side and leftist extremism by the Social Democratic side. When the two characteristic interest parties of the farmers and the workers took over government power, the political scene turned in the direction of corporatism and compromise politics.

CHAPTER 3

Assistance for Self-Help

The Conceptual Basis for Social Policy • A Great Preventive Project •
Health Insurance • National Pension Plans • Unemployment Insurance •
Population Crisis? • The Politics of Sterilization • Assistance for Self-Help

THE CONCEPTUAL BASIS FOR SOCIAL POLICY

Social policy became one of the most important arenas of the nation-building project with its emphasis on social integration, which over time would lead to what came to be known as the welfare state. As development takes its course we catch glimpses of the new principles of self-help and universality behind the various social welfare plans.

The old poor relief (mostly local government assistance to the poor) was an institutionalization of alms, the old "piety relations" between the financially comfortable and the needy. With social integration, the foundation for poor relief changed. The state's mandate was to integrate all individuals into the nation. The state had to take care of its citizens, educate them, make sure they had an acceptable standard of material well-being, defend them against danger, organize them into well-functioning collectives, and so forth. Once they were defined as citizens, everyone was to be equal. These benefits were not to be given as charity but rather as something to which every citizen had a right. We could call this a new social citizenship. This view came into being at the end of the nineteenth century and was the basis for developing social policy in the twentieth. It did not reach ascendancy until the second half of the century, however.

The principle of *assistance for self-help* (that is, public assistance to enable individuals to better their own situations), which had been the principle of the bourgeois radicals, became the dominant principle of the new social policy from the end of the nineteenth century to the 1930s. This "social assistance state" was a transitional form between the "self-responsibility" of the nineteenth century and the later welfare state.[1] The old social principle of

[1] Anne-Lise Seip 1984, 12.

responsibility for one's self was gradually replaced with the idea that the state should step in and assist, yet the state's responsibility was limited, since the prevailing principle was that things should be arranged to facilitate self-help. In other words, it was preferable to rely on security plans to which the individual client was expected to contribute. Self-help was inexpensive for the state, of course, and it was argued that with these plans one avoided the stigmatization that came with poor relief. In practice, the public sector had to contribute as well, so usually these social safety nets were mixed plans. As long as social security plans were based on assistance for self-help, there was no notion that these would be socially redistributive. To a certain degree, however, this is what they became in their transitional form.[2]

The principle of *universality* was attached to the new concept of rights. It would also come to distinguish the Scandinavian welfare states. The principle holds that everyone has an equal right to social benefits. Here the new thinking separated itself radically from the old form of poor relief, which had been based on means tests and thus functioned as a form of social segregation; in other words, those who accepted assistance could not at the same time be considered full and adequate citizens. Conversely, from the new point of view, assistance would have an integrative function, elevating the recipient to full citizenship. The principle of universality was crucial to destigmatizing the acceptance of assistance.

Indeed, it took a long time to establish the principle of universality. This was due in part to the high cost involved and the necessity of postponing implementation while facing the crises of the interwar period. In addition, it takes time for new, radical principles to become accepted. During the whole interwar period we see, first, that poor relief operated alongside the new social security plans and, second, that means testing crept into many of the new initiatives. What has been said of the Swedish Unemployment Commission (AK), which was active in the interwar period, characterizes other programs of the time as well: it lay "right in the middle between the old poor relief policy and the new welfare policy."[3]

At the beginning of the twentieth century the greatest problem confronting society was frequently defined as "the worker problem." Some of the new initiatives were directed only toward the emerging group of industrial work-

---

[2] It is also possible to view the welfare state system as having an element of assistance for self-help since in principle everyone was expected to contribute through the tax system. It has also been argued that the developed welfare state from the 1960s on was not redistributive. Rothstein (2002, 179ff.) argues persuasively however that a policy based on the principle of universality was more redistributive than a policy based on means testing.

[3] Isaksson 1996, 222. Cf. Rothstein (1986, 160f.) on the commission's "unfortunate" practice.

ers. The labor movement maintained that this was a form of class discrimination and soon began to argue for the principle of universality. By demanding that the state should take a greater responsibility through tax-based financing and by supporting the principle of universality, the labor movement launched plans that would come to characterize the later welfare state. In practice, however, the labor movement was willing to give way on the principles, setting the principle of universality aside and approving means testing as a transitional arrangement when economic pragmatism demanded it. The most important point, after all, was to obtain a reasonable degree of material security for those most in need, preferably through plans that implied transfers from those who were better off.[4]

This new social policy led to a paternalistic paradox. The individual citizen should, on the one hand, be *helped* and *elevated* and yet, on the other, *formed* and *educated*. The social security plans were to some degree marked by a normative apparatus. The construction of "the conscientious worker" was one of the goals of the social policy.[5] This implied that public subsidies could be linked to moral quid pro quos, as in the Swedish National Pensions Plan of 1913, in which supplementary pensions could not be awarded to those who "clearly do not have the capacity to try honestly to contribute to their welfare or who have surrendered themselves to inebriation."[6] In this way the state could "at one and the same time take social responsibility and hold fast to the liberal ethic of responsibility for oneself."[7] This paradox becomes an especially strong feature of the social assistance state. When one comes to the fully developed welfare state, these normative aspects are bleached out. It is not surprising that they reappeared after 1970, following a period during which the welfare state was under pressure.[8]

The new social policy at the end of the nineteenth century was, first, a natural part of the nineteenth century's nation-building project and, second, a response to a perceived social crisis that people considered in part a result of industrialization. Bismarck's Prussia provided the model for this new social policy. It was partly a policy for social pacification. In other words, it was thought that social policy should be an answer to threats to the social order. This was undoubtedly one consideration, and it was explicitly stated by the conservatives. But this negative motivation for policy was only the obverse of

---

[4] Petersen and Åmark 2002, 28.
[5] Ambjörnsson 1988.
[6] Berge 1995, 34.
[7] Berge 1995, 66.
[8] In some circumstances it seems as though means testing is the road back for an overburdened system. On the other hand it seems that living on social assistance is less stigmatizing that it was previously.

the prevailing ideas about positive social development—the nation-building project's idea of social integration. It was here that the actual inspiration for the new social policy lay.[9]

The paradox of the new social policy springs, on the one hand, from a principle of autonomy: the individual ought to be able to form his or her own life project and to sell his or her own labor on the market. On the other hand, it also springs from a communitarian principle: when the state steps in and guarantees the citizen's social status, it also takes a stand on what constitutes a desirable life project. By engaging in the construction of the "conscientious worker," the state contributes not only to increasing his or her quality of life but also to maintaining or enhancing his or her exchange value in the market and thereby ensuring that the production system functions satisfactorily. The economy depends on the fact that the labor force is being taken care of. This new social policy was based on the general mistrust of the market's ability to develop the "conscientious worker." And when neither the market nor the family could shape individuals into "conscientious workers," the state had to step in.

This mistrust of the labor market's ability to function satisfactorily found its clearest expression in the market-regulating initiatives that constituted the second part of early social policy. This had to do precisely with looking after the status and value of the individual worker. These initiatives were carried out through laws governing working conditions, child welfare, minimum wages, limits on the number of working hours, and similar issues.[10] These were laws that paralleled the new social welfare policies in both Sweden and Norway. Sweden was first out of the gate: it had regulated the use of children in working life as early as 1846, whereas Norway's first regulations did not come into effect until 1892. Worker protection legislation was enacted in Sweden in 1889 and in Norway in 1892. Both countries also acquired industrial accident insurance. In addition, the legislation for the eight-hour workday was enacted in both countries in 1918.

A highly influential text about social policy in the interwar period was the book *Kris i befolkningsfrågan* (The Population Crisis) by the Swedish husband-and-wife team of Gunnar and Alva Myrdal. The Myrdals argued for a shift away from social policy that addressed symptoms and toward a *preventive* social policy that could solve the underlying problems. This had to include "a real qualitative increase in the living and development possibilities of the rising generation" and, "at the same time, a shifting of the costs and responsi-

---

[9] Rothstein 2002, 193, supports the same view: "the question is not 'how shall we solve the problem they pose' but rather closer to 'how shall we solve our common problem (care of the sick, construction, pensions, etc.)."

[10] Rothstein 2002, 15, 38ff.

bilities from the individual family providers to the whole nation."[11] Here the concept of "social policy" came closest to embracing the reconstruction of the social order as a whole. We are able dimly to perceive the Social Democratic vision of the nation as an extended home—the "people's home" (*folkhemmet*).

A GREAT PREVENTIVE PROJECT

A special project occupied a central position at the outset of the twentieth century, a project that demonstrates the preventive and assistance for self-help principles and gives us a glimpse of the dynamics of developing social policy in a broad sense. This project involved the forerunner of the people's home— namely, what was called "one's own home."[12]

The project's starting point was the question of whether the rural proletariat (from whose ranks came the largest sector of society's poor) should be assisted to obtain their own land and thus become small peasant farmers. But gradually this developed into a more comprehensive question concerning workers'—including industrial workers'—housing and self-help possibilities in general. Making it easier to get one's own home with greater or lesser amounts of arable land was, for a time, the most important positive (preventive) strategy for bringing about the fundamental integration project.

The land question touched the relationship between traditionalists and modernists. The great response to small-farmer thinking demonstrates the primarily agrarian nature of the culture. But gradually it also became a question about how industrial society should be organized. The land question affected ownership rights and access to the means of production, and it affected the relationship between the agrarian and the industrial proletariats—the city and the countryside.

It was the radical liberals who put the own-home policy on the agenda during the 1890s; they also were the driving force in carrying the policy forward until it received acceptance from most political circles. The own-home policy was the first great social policy project of the liberal Folk Party in the Second Chamber of the Swedish Parliament.[13] In Norway the question of land was the starting point for a group of radical leftists who later established their own party—the Labor Democrats. "The Labor Democrats perceived the land question as the core of their social reform program."[14] The party leader Johan Castberg, whom we have met in other connections, was the driving force.

---

[11] Alva and Gunnar Myrdal 1934, 203–204.
[12] Edling 1996, 384 (about the relationship between "people's home" and "own home").
[13] Edling 1996, 150.
[14] Aasland 1961, 44. See also Rovde 2000, 58–59.

Furthermore, on this question we also see how he drew the Liberal Party along with him. This policy had its breakthrough with the public credit plan established in 1903–1904. In Norway the Workers' Smallholding and Housing Bank was founded by law in 1903 as a state-guaranteed bank. In Sweden Parliament decided in 1904 to establish a similar public lending plan that could be administrated by the local agricultural societies. Both countries built on earlier plans that had, in part, accommodated the same needs.

Built into the lending plans of both Norway and Sweden was a dilemma: what should actually be given priority, workers' housing or self-supporting small farms? Should modern society's workers be integrated through this plan, or should agriculture be given support in order to slow the rate of industrialization and hence the rate of modernization? The solution was a compromise. In other words, practice varied between different parts of each country as well as between the two countries. Small "combination farms," where the father of the family had work off the farm, in the forest, as a fisherman, or in some other venture, were quite usual. The route to paid labor was not long. In Sweden the center of gravity was family smallholdings for workers in modern industries, whereas in Norway it was self-supporting small farms, or "combination farms" within the primary industries (agriculture, fisheries, and forestry).[15]

The policy was inspired by the American economist Henry George's ideas, which were being widely discussed at this time.[16] A central element was a land value tax that involved state capture of the increase in the value of land that was not the result of improvements (work on the land). The argument was that full rights to private ownership and disposition of land would lead to speculation and increasing injustice in land distribution. George's ideas did not achieve full acceptance in politics.[17] As they bore on proprietary rights to land, however, the land question and Georgism caught the interest of the Social Democrats. Generally speaking, the land question became "a difficult nut for the Social Democrats to crack."[18] We will return to this issue later.

There is something paradoxical about the concentration focused on the land question. Small-scale agriculture was certainly not the solution for the future. As Edling writes, "From our perspective, with access to the benefits of twentieth-century social mobility, the own-home plans are somewhat vague

[15] Explained by Erling Annaniassen.

[16] Edling 1996, 282.

[17] Among the central parliamentarians in Norway there was only one, Tore Myrvang from the Labor Democrats, who was a Georgist. See Aasland 1961, 47. In other respects it is worth noting that the very old Norwegian rights of allodial possession ("odel") must have had some of the same effect as Henry George's land tax in that they limit the owner's right of selling land.

[18] Morell 2001, 133.

and incomprehensible."[19] In hindsight the attempt to solve this social problem by establishing new small-scale agriculture appears to lead into a blind alley. Thus, for a time, the state was forced into a program that had little future. On the other hand, the own-home plans served as an important tool during the social crises at the end of the nineteenth century and into the interwar period. From 1910 onward the establishment of small-scale farms through land clearance was viewed in both countries as a weapon against emigration, and in the jubilee celebrations of the Norwegian Constitution in Oslo in 1914 the model of small-scale agriculture was proudly shown off. During the 1930s the policy of promoting small-scale agriculture was practically phased out in Sweden.[20] The process was more protracted in Norway, where there was still major land clearing during the 1930s.[21] The social aspects of land ownership were still current, only now the social fabric was threatened not by emigration but rather by unemployment.

One element of the land question that should not be underestimated was the depiction of small-scale agriculture as an ideal way of life. This view has been very tenacious, and to a certain degree it has survived up to the present day in dreams about "the little red cottage." This begs the question of whether small-scale agriculture really is a good way of life. Was the County of Norrland an ideal society of happy peasant farmers? Olav Randen has discussed the question as it pertained to the rural population in Norway. Sympathetic to farming as a way of life, he concludes that "farming on new land in the interwar period was a rational and future-oriented policy." To the extent that it, among other things, was practiced with an overly heavy emphasis on self-reliant production, however, "the pressure on the small farmers was . . . too hard and the idealization of exhausting work was too strong."[22] In a richer society small-scale agriculture was not a realistic tool for building a preventive social policy.

From a sociopolitical point of view, small-scale agricultural thinking was an answer to both an employment problem and a housing problem. In the post–World War II period, although other solutions were pursued in relation to both problems, the idea that the good family dwelling was the basis of a good society persisted. The housing problem was old; it seemed to have dogged the footsteps of industrial society from the beginning. Housing as a field of social policy was correspondingly venerable, and remained as current as ever. In a more modern form it became an important policy area within the Social Democratic state in both Sweden and Norway.

[19] Edling 1996, 12; A.-L. Seip 1984, 128.
[20] Morell 2001, 140.
[21] Randen 2002, 82.
[22] Randen 2002, 320.

HEALTH INSURANCE

A key concern of social policy is compensation for loss of income because of illness, age, or other reasons. The welfare state that developed in Sweden and Norway would eventually give almost full compensation for loss of income. The appointment of the labor commissions in Sweden in 1884 and in Norway in 1885 is generally viewed as the genesis of this type of insurance. But, for a long time, the level of compensation was far too low to adequately support vulnerable groups. This meant that "the liberal democrats in reality were incapable of solving the welfare problem of capitalist wage labor."[23] This problem was not solved until the development of the welfare state plans from the 1930s on. The social assistance state was an important phase of this development, however. Beyond these parallels, the similarities between Sweden and Norway cease. In fact, institutional conditions were so different that the two countries devised quite different solutions. We shall examine two very central areas, health insurance and national pension plans.

Health insurance was introduced by law in Norway in 1909. The labor commission of 1885 had viewed health insurance as "the basis of a new social security system."[24] A bill was proposed in 1890, but so many problems had to be solved before the insurance plan could be instituted that the law did not take effect until 1909. First, there was the issue of whether the insurance system would be voluntary or mandatory. In the end it was made mandatory. Second, there was the question of who should be covered. Ultimately the program was limited to wage earners in enterprises related to factory production. The insurance plan was organized as a unitary cash transaction system with a regional fund in each municipality. The financing was based on assistance for self-help, with the recipients themselves paying 60 percent of the costs, and the employer and the municipality together paying the remainder. One important feature of the law was its basis in the "family insurance principle." This principle was emphasized in the revised law of 1914, which extended coverage to maternity benefits, including maternity cash assistance and free midwifery. In addition to payments for loss of income, costs of nursing and medical care were also covered for both the insured and their dependents.[25] In Sweden payments of this type were not instituted until 1931.

The labor movement had opposed several aspects of the law. To limit coverage to wage earners was to make it class-based. To make it mandatory was to place workers under public guardianship, and assistance for self-help meant

---

[23] Åmark 1999, 12–13.

[24] A.-L. Seip 1994, 96.

[25] Sainsbury 2001, 116: "By the end of the 1910s the social rights of Norwegian women stood out in an international perspective." A.-L. Seip 1984, 105, 197.

placing "a new burden on the backs of the workers." But the Socialists gradually became defenders of the law as they came to view it as the first step in a
process toward a more distant goal. And so it was. In the larger perspective
this development followed "a well-known pattern," with the law gradually
evolving from a class-based law to a law for all.[26] In 1956 this mandatory
health insurance became applicable to all.

Sweden followed a different pattern. Beginning in 1891, that country had
a law concerning public grants to private voluntary health insurance funds.
Despite extension of this system in 1910 with larger grants from the public
sector and expanded public management, the law was very limited. It seems
that Sweden was behind Norway on this point. The explanation, however, is
closer to the reverse. In Sweden there was traditionally a much more developed system of private health insurance funds than in Norway. In 1909 this
system had 630,000 members in Sweden,[27] compared with 60,000 members
in Norway. But with the introduction of the mandatory class-based insurance law, Norway had an estimated 220,000 who were covered by health
insurance.[28] Considering that Sweden's population was approximately double
Norway's, Sweden's voluntary plan was actually more inclusive.

Nevertheless, the Swedish plan was also limited. Even with increasing subsidies from the public sector after 1910, only 21 percent of the adult population had insurance by 1930, compared with 65 percent in the corresponding
voluntary plan in Denmark.[29] Moreover, the Swedish plan in reality had a
class character as well: whereas the Norwegian paternalistic plan was for the
working class, the Swedish plan was largely for the middle class. Experience
shows that it is difficult for voluntary plans to get participation by those who
need them most. Indeed, the Swedish system remained voluntary until 1955,
although there was no dearth of pressure or attempts to make it mandatory.
The fact that these attempts did not succeed is blamed partly on institutional
inertia and partly on a fear that a mandatory system like Norway's would
reduce the Swedish middle class's opportunity for state-subsidized voluntary
coverage. In addition, the economic crisis of the 1920s strengthened misgivings about the state's financial ability to provide mandatory coverage for all.[30]

Health insurance in Norway and Sweden was thus very different. In Sweden this could be attributed to the existence of a relatively well-organized
private system at the outset—a system that the state had little alternative but
to support. In Norway the system had to be built from the ground up. It is

[26] Bjørnson and Haavet 1994, 72.
[27] Edebalk 1996, 20. Some were double-registered. The total with health coverage came to only 14
percent of the adult population (those over the age of 15).
[28] A.-L. Seip 1984, 97.
[29] Edebalk 1996, 50.
[30] Peter Johansson 1999.

noteworthy, however, that with the changing of the laws in 1955 (Sweden) and 1956 (Norway) the countries moved from these very different systems to plans that were almost the same. This meant, in effect, that the class-based, mandatory Norwegian plan was made general while the general, voluntary Swedish plan was made mandatory.

NATIONAL PENSION PLANS

In 1913 Sweden enacted the world's first national pension plan—preceding even parliamentarism and universal suffrage for women. "Normally," perhaps, universal suffrage should have come first. As we have seen, social insurance plans are rooted in the old paternalistic society. Experience everywhere shows, however, that there is a connection between democratization and the further development of modern social insurance. These are two sides of the same coin insofar as both democratization and social insurance policies have socially integrative functions. Moreover, the social policy reforms have to be seen as a result of competition for votes, especially the votes of the new industrial workforce.

In Sweden the issue of a national pension plan had been under debate for some time. With the 1905 election, the issue was taken up by the party manifestos of both the Liberals and the Social Democrats, and in 1908 it was also taken up by the Conservative Party. By then Lindman's liberal-conservative government had already appointed an "old-age pension committee."[31] In addition to the general issues that have already been mentioned, the pension committee debated the goal of diminishing emigration. It was thought that a clever social policy might contribute to such a diminution. In addition, the committee considered the issue of lessening the burden on the system of poor relief, which was financed through municipal taxes. A social security system would be financed through fees or through state taxation. Hjalmar Branting, the leader of the Social Democrats, was on the committee and, together with the chairman, was its driving force. The committee's report came out in 1912 and was dealt with rather quickly in Parliament since there was broad political agreement on the issue.

The resulting plan had elements taken from various models. It was "a gifted compromise."[32] First, it was built on the invalid principle: everyone who was

[31] The paragraphs concerning this general pension scheme are based to a large extent on Edebalk 1996, 69–82.

[32] Edebalk 1996, 76. In the previous chapter we saw the significance of Branting in unifying around the question of voting reform in 1917. His importance on the personal level in getting the gifted compromise through seems to have been considerable. On the other hand, Petersen and Åmark (2002, 27) stress

permanently unable to work and everyone over the age of sixty-seven should be entitled to a pension. The plan was further divided into two parts: a small basic pension directly related to fees paid into the fund, and a tax-financed, means-tested supplementary pension, which would be reduced for those with higher incomes. The system was not entirely universal. Groups with other pension plans could remain outside the system. The right to such special plans was removed, however, in 1935. The great support for what was called "the death of separatism" has been seen as a victory for an incipient new norm of solidarity.[33] In 1935 and 1937 the individual premium was eliminated as the plans became tax financed. The supplementary pension was the most important part of the plan. It must be stressed, however, that pensions were low, scarcely enough to survive on. The dual system existed until 1948.

There was sufficient agreement in the political arena so that the solution could be arrived at quickly and easily. Certain conflicts came to the forefront, however, in a vehement public debate that had weak links to the political system. Opposition came from "the people behind poverty relief," who had their social base in the leading economic stratum of the Stockholm area.[34] They felt that the social problem, which they acknowledged had become serious, should be solved by reforming the poor relief system rather than by instituting a modern pension plan. Their thinking was paternalistic and based on moral considerations. They regarded it as unfortunate that, under the new plan, children's duty to financially support their aged parents would be abolished and the "undeserving" would be eligible to receive pensions.[35] They felt that this undermined the general moral order. They also criticized what they viewed as discrimination against women. The poverty relief supporters were not intrinsically opposed to assistance for self-help. Their main principle, however, was support according to individual means testing. Part of their critique was that the proposed system would not meet actual needs to the same extent that continuing the poor relief system would. In their view, developing poor relief into a system based on individual means testing would not only take account of the old pietistic relations but also be more effective than the proposed system.

This critique is useful for putting the new national pension plan in context. As we have seen, the new plan was an amalgamated system. Even this new system demanded a certain moral consideration and presupposed a continu-

---

in this connection that the Swedes' "ability for reform" through compromise was characteristic of Swedish political culture.

[33] Berge 1998, 36.

[34] Edebalk 1996, 77ff.

[35] We have seen that the final system gave certain concessions to these objections couched in terms of moral concession.

ation of the poor relief system. The Swedish national pension plan of 1913, however, with its element of universalism, represented a small but important step away from the old paternalism and toward what would become the modern welfare state.

It would be a long time before Norway enacted a national pension plan.[36] The idea that creating a national pension system was part of general modernization had been advanced long before old-age pension committees were set up in both countries in 1907. Both committees reported their main findings in 1912. But whereas in Sweden the issue was swiftly addressed with adoption of a law the following year, in Norway no such proposition was put forward until 1918. One of the reasons for the difference was undoubtedly that while the Swedish committee had united around a solution, the Norwegian committee had been so divided that both the majority and the minority submitted separate reports, each of five hundred closely written pages.[37] Here there was no Hjalmar Branting to pave the way for "a gifted compromise." Both factions proposed mixed forms with a certain redistributive effect, yet the majority's proposal emphasized the insurance principle while the minority proposal gave more weight to the tax principle. The proposition advanced by the government followed the majority's proposal.

As in Sweden, the proposition was heatedly debated. The main attack, however, came, not from the supporters of poor relief, as in Sweden, but from the Socialists. In the 1918 election campaign they proposed a means-tested, tax-financed pension for everyone over the age of sixty-five. The battle was fought on different fronts in the two countries not because of differences between the proposals but because of differences in timing: in Sweden the discussion and reform happened before World War I, whereas in Norway they happened after the war. The Norwegian Social Democrats had gained strength in 1918 and were in their most radical phase; they felt less committed to the social system and thus were less predisposed to compromise than at any other period. What was radical in their proposal was tax-based financing, which meant moving away from the assistance for self-help principle and toward welfare state solutions. It turned out that the Social Democrats' proposition was not so forbiddingly revolutionary after all; in fact, it also had appeal among the representatives of the bourgeois parties—among others, the Conservatives' social policy spokesman, Odd Klingenberg.

Parliament did not deal with the proposal in 1918, but the government set up a new committee to investigate and report on a tax-based pension plan. The committee presented its findings in 1920, and in 1923 Klingenberg, who

---

[36] This paragraph is built largely on A.-L. Seip 1994, 257–280.
[37] St. forh. (Parl. Proceedings) 1918, Appendix to Ot. Prp. 11 (1918).

was now a cabinet minister, put forward a proposition based on tax financing. The Liberal Party stood firmly for the previously discussed social security principle—fostering self-respect through assistance for self-help. Nonetheless, Klingenberg's legislative proposal was ratified by the Social Democrats, the Conservatives, Christian Michelsen's Coalition Party of freethinking liberals, and some votes from Johan Castberg's Labor Democrats. By this time economic crisis had overtaken the country, and therefore implementation of this bill was postponed, which meant, in effect, that the issue was dead. In 1936 old-age social security was instituted, based on means testing and essentially tax-financed.[38] But there was still a way to go to a universal pension system.

The Conservatives came out in favor of a tax-financed arrangement for a universal pension plan partly owing to the social unrest of the time. The situation led to concessions from the bourgeois parties in many areas. But this must also be seen as an early concession to the principle of the welfare state's extensive responsibilities. In this light, we can ask whether Norway could have established a general old-age pension in 1913 if this large coalition had united around a proposal. This is a possibility, albeit rather meager. After all, Sweden had greater economic carrying capacity, and Norway did not completely lack social security plans.

In the period up to 1940 the health insurance plan was implemented in Norway but not in Sweden, while the social pension plan was implemented in Sweden but not in Norway. In both countries, however, these laws were considered components of a greater body of legislation that together would encompass all instances of loss of income. The assumption was that Norway would eventually institute an old-age pension plan and Sweden would institute health insurance. We saw that Sweden did have a health insurance plan that was just as inclusive as Norway's, but its starting point was private and voluntary. This was not accidental. Sweden traditionally had a better-developed civil society than Norway did. We have seen the great significance of popular movements, especially in Sweden. This process of democratizing before democratization had its counterpart in social assistance before the advent of the welfare state, that is, in private collective plans that took care of the population's most vulnerable groups. That these duties were not politicized as they were in Norway was due to the late development of formal democracy in Sweden. This applies especially at the municipal level, which is clearly seen in comparison with Norway.

Self-governance at the municipal level was more extensive in Norway than in Sweden. Voting regulations were also more democratic. It has been said that Norway was composed of seven hundred self-governing republics. This

---

[38] Bjørnson and Haavet 1994, 154.

implies that some of the municipalities achieved relatively unconstrained radical power at an early date, particularly in the cities and larger towns where social problems were pressing. A series of demands were placed on municipalities—including the organization of relief work, job creation, construction of housing for workers, provision of free school materials and free medical assistance, and building of extended-care institutions, orphanages, municipal tramlines, and so on. Some of these tasks were actually accomplished. The result has been called "municipal socialism."

The trend toward municipal socialism caused considerable concern in Norway, and in 1911 a law was enacted limiting the right of municipalities to increase taxation. During the relatively prosperous years between 1916 and 1920 this limitation did not prevent an avalanche of municipal pension plans—primarily old-age pension plans but also pensions for the disabled and, in some cases, widows and maternity cash assistance. In 1922, 40 percent of the Norwegian population lived in municipalities with publicly financed welfare plans.[39] In Sweden the "wasteful" Norwegian municipalities were used as object lessons to scare and alarm the public, even by the Social Democrats.[40] The 1936 law instituting old-age social security was enacted partly to relieve the burden on those municipalities that had fallen into economic difficulties.

UNEMPLOYMENT INSURANCE

Unemployment insurance was generally among the last of the central security plans to come into being in the European countries. Again the difference between Norway and Sweden is great. Norway was early and Sweden late. In 1906 Norway instituted an insurance plan that included state and municipal contributions to a publicly approved voluntary unemployment fund (the so-called Gent System). In Sweden there was no public support before 1934, when a corresponding system came into being, almost a generation after the creation of the system in Norway. Four years later Norway abandoned its voluntary system and introduced mandatory insurance, while Sweden kept the Gent System.

Of all the early welfare plans, the Norwegian unemployment insurance system of 1906 was the only one in which the labor movement's mobilization had a decisive effect on the outcome. The plan was unique in that the trade unions would be responsible for the administration of the law. It was argued

---

[39] Grønlie 1991, 46.
[40] Östberg 1996, 115, 121.

that only unions were capable of proper management, since they had an intimate knowledge of their members' situations. The strict rules for approving payments meant that several unions did not make use of the law. Gradually, as public subsidies increased, the majority of unions began to make use of it. In 1914 it was estimated that approximately 50 percent of union-organized workers were covered by unemployment insurance. There were arguments against the voluntary component because it left out the low-wage earner. During the massive unemployment of the 1920s the system more or less broke down.

During the interwar period it was the Liberal Party that pushed for a mandatory plan. The Labor Party was originally opposed, but it shifted position in the 1930s. In other words, the mandatory plan that was introduced in 1938 enjoyed broad support. This drastically expanded the number of workers covered by the insurance plan, while it was taken out of the hands of the trade unions and placed within the state health insurance apparatus. There are grounds for asking why the Norwegian labor movement gave in so readily to its loss of control over the unemployment insurance funds. First, it had to do with the need to draw employers into the financing. Second, there were many in the labor movement, including the trendsetting Martin Tranmæl, who were skeptical of a system that created divisions within the ranks of workers between those with coverage and those without.[41]

It is perhaps more difficult to clarify why it took so long to bring about a public mandatory plan in Sweden. In the next chapter we shall see that in Sweden there was a norm that the public sector should not involve itself in relations between capital and labor. During the 1920s, however, the issue was overshadowed by conflict over the public Unemployment Commission (AK). The strict practices of the commission, and the fact that it had become a permanent institution, came under the relentless attack of the LO (trade union central). The difficulty of achieving agreement on whether the plan should be voluntary or mandatory also dragged out the issue. Naturally, underlying the whole issue was the question of how large the public contribution should be.[42]

When the Social Democrats were enjoying their first breakthrough following the 1932 election, it became possible to ratify a plan in 1934; in addition, Gustav Möller, the central personality regarding social policy, had negotiated a compromise that allowed for a common position within the labor movement in support of a voluntary plan that conformed to the Gent System.

[41] Bjørnson and Haavet 1994, 100. This paragraph relies rather heavily on Bjørnson's presentation in which he also makes comparisons with Sweden (81–100).

[42] Isaksson 2000, 194f.

The administration of the funds was given to the trade unions. There was also a provision giving unorganized workers an opportunity to participate. Unlike in the mandatory state-organized Norwegian system instituted four years later, employers in Sweden did not contribute to financing the plan. Payments were low, and there were restrictive rules governing eligibility. Initially several large trade union federations did not participate in the plan, but once payments and state contributions were significantly increased after 1941, they closed ranks around the system. According to Möller's strategy, this was precisely the way things ought to evolve.

By allowing the trade unions to administer these important public funds, the state gave them what in reality was a tax-enacting right parallel to that we saw given to the agrarian organizations in relation to the crisis relief plans. These voluntary plans came close to being compulsory. Viewed in a different light, the unemployment insurance system gave the trade unions significant power and was an important step in the direction of corporatism. It is apparent that the level of organization was noticeably greater in countries (such as Sweden) that had voluntary funding with state support than in countries (such as Norway) that had mandatory plans administered by the state.[43]

As we saw earlier, social policy grew from below. In Norway the welfare municipality preceded the welfare state. Something similar happened in Sweden, but the initiative there came more from nonpolitical civil society, and it could build on a stronger tradition of private collective plans. This difference is also evident in the two countries' unemployment insurance plans.

POPULATION CRISIS?

The large wave of childbirths throughout Europe at the beginning of the twentieth century caused concern, which led to an intense struggle over birth control. Birth control was also an important issue related to women's liberation because women had to bear the burden of giving birth to many children. Equally important, however, was the positive argument that separating sexuality from conception was part of modernization's overall project of liberation. According to the Norwegian medical doctor Karl Evang, it was by living out one's sexual life without feelings of guilt that the individual could reveal his or her real nature.[44] The use of birth control methods was entirely in keeping with the technological optimism of the times, the faith in humans' ability

---

[43] Rothstein 1992, 310f.
[44] Soltvedt 2000, 163.

to gain "technical mastery over the sources of life." The conservative counter-forces were strong, but birth control within marriage gradually became accept

What had been the starting point of the debate in the interwar period radically changed. Fear of overpopulation was replaced by the opposite fear. The relatively dramatic decline in birthrates during the 1930s was a general European phenomenon. It came up first, and in a most pronounced way, in France but soon spread to other countries. This decline in birthrates occasioned the book *Kris i befolkningsfrågan* (The Population Crisis) by Social Democrats Gunnar and Alva Myrdal. As they wrote, "The radical neo-Malthusians have certainly had their prayers granted beyond their wildest dreams."[45] There had to be something fundamentally wrong with society—and the institution of the family—when birthrates sank below replacement levels.

The context in which the Myrdals set the population question is important to grasp. It says something about intention. Their book can be read as an effort to influence public opinion in favor of a radical politics of social reform:

> From a social point of view, the mere rate of fertility in and of itself is not important without taking into account the deeper thoroughgoing changes in society's economic, psychological, and moral structures. The decline of the fertility rate is merely among the more obvious signs of the mighty sociologically dynamic processes that will leave what are perhaps deeper traces on the overall development of our civilization than anybody can anticipate.[46]

It is possible to read this as a gloomy view of the future. But behind the statement lies an optimistic belief that it is possible, with the help of science and technology, to counteract these unfortunate tendencies and send development in a positive direction. The whole book presents a program for carrying out the project of building the good society. Its motives go far beyond counteracting the decline in the birthrate. Rather, this new problem merely strengthened the old motives of creating a socially integrated nation. In other words, the population question gave new life and reality to modernization's society-building project and, to some degree, gave it a new Social Democratic direction.

The Norwegian Karl Evang was skeptical that there was any population crisis at all. Rather, he used it for tactical advantage by emphasizing the population question in a lecture given to the national women's conference of the Labor Party in the spring of 1936, claiming that what was "new and exceedingly gratifying about the situation is that the labor movement has,

---

[45] A. and G. Myrdal 1934, 10.
[46] A. and G. Myrdal 1934, 79.

so to speak, captured the argument about the sinking birthrate and put it to use for the benefit of solving societal questions." The solution lay in "the labor movement's general political and economic program."[47] His reasoning paralleled that of the Myrdals. They were less concerned about the population question itself than about the greater Social Democratic society-building project.

THE POLITICS OF STERILIZATION

Attention soon shifted from the need to increase the number of births to an increased awareness of the *quality of the population*, and thus the quality of the children born into it. There was talk of forming individuals for the society of the future through social and biological approaches, focusing on both the schooling and the upbringing of children and on improving the quality of the gene pool by weeding out poor hereditary material. There was then a tendency to biologize these social questions. This led to initiatives that we are now inclined to view as social and political blunders.

Both Norway and Sweden enacted sterilization laws in 1934 with broad political support. These were abolished in Sweden in 1975 and in Norway in 1977.[48] During these years there were more than forty-four thousand sterilizations performed in Norway and sixty-three thousand in Sweden. In 1997 the newspaper *Dagens Nyheter* "laid bare" the fact that the "model state" of Sweden had, during the period that the sterilization law was in effect, carried out compulsory sterilizations of thousands of people for the purpose of creating a purer race. This "news" spread around the world. By implementing a policy to rid the population of inferior genes, the world's most advanced welfare state had crossed a moral line, a transgression that would not be tolerated in a later epoch of history. As is so often the case with such "exposures," the reality was less dramatic than the exposure. Moreover, this was not news, since the main facts of this development had long been known and were available to those who were interested.

The practical application of the sterilization laws in the two countries seems to have been roughly parallel. About half of the sterilizations had been undertaken voluntarily. In other words, sterilization was being used as a means

---

[47] Soltvedt 2000, 227.

[48] New laws were enacted. In Sweden consent is now required for sterilization. In Norway there is still a limited approach to sterilization without consent (Haave 2000, 114). During the occupation between 1940 and 1945, the Nazis established racially hygienic "laws" in Norway, and this prepared the way for forced sterilization of the population known as Itinerants. However, the Nazis did not manage to accomplish the sterilization before the war ended (Haave 2000, 322).

of birth control. For the most part, the remaining cases were conducted on the basis of indirect coercion, that is, with the use of different forms of pressure or persuasion. A certain number were carried out by means of direct (but not necessarily physical) coercion. "Eugenic" arguments played a central role—the goal of these interventions was to prevent transmission of undesirable genetic traits to future generations. The other major coercive argument was social—parental lack of opportunity to give children a good upbringing. Sometimes these arguments were indistinguishable. It has been pointed out that practical social considerations carried more weight at the level on which individual concrete decisions about sterilization were made.[49] This means that concern for a child's chances of having a good upbringing had more influence on practical decisions to undergo sterilization, even though eugenic arguments weighed heavily at the political level.

Since the concept of "racial hygiene" has taken hold, we should stress that the eugenic indications of poor genetic inheritance (mental illness, feeble-mindedness) are independent of what we understand by the word *race*.[50] In a very real sense, racism was quite widespread in Europe between the two world wars, but it scarcely provided orientation to population policy in Scandinavia.

Yet there seems to be one possible exception: Itinerants.[51] Their ethnic background is mixed. In Norway a total of 155 applications were put forward regarding the sterilization of Itinerants, of which 128 were carried out. In Sweden there were between 600 and 700 applications, of which 450 to 500 were carried out.[52] The numbers are low; the percentage of Itinerants sterilized (voluntarily or by coercion) in Norway under the sterilization law was only about double the percentage of the general population sterilized. The figures are highly disputable, as there also were other sterilizations carried out without prior application, possibly 200 to 250 Itinerants.[53] The possibility of sterilization was definitely much higher for the Itinerants than for the population at large. Nevertheless, neither in Norway nor in Sweden was there anything like ethnic cleansing. The Itinerants were, however, also subject to other encroachments, such as having children taken from their families and sent to orphanages. The special attention to which the Itinerants were subjected certainly had something to do with their way of life, which was at odds

---

[49] Haave 2000, 233.

[50] "Eugenic" and "racial hygiene" are often used as synonyms. See the Norwegian dictionary *Norsk Riksmålsordbok* under "rasehygiene." This can amount to an unfortunate usage. See the dictionary *Kunnskapsforlagets Leksikon* under "evgenikk."

[51] In Norwegian *omstreifere* or *tatere*; in Swedish *tattare*. They are not identical with Gypsies, of which there are very few in Norway and Sweden before World War II.

[52] Tydén 2002, 62.

[53] Communicated by Per Haave.

with the surrounding society. This made it easy to use social justifications, even though an underlying racist motive may have existed.

The Myrdals' book includes a chapter titled "Social Policy and Population Quality," with a section called "The Question of Sterilization." The book, which endorsed the sterilization law, was published in 1934, the year the law was enacted. Despite the authors' technological tone, a reader detects in the book a note of warning against going too far. The law ought to have "as strict [a] legal application as possible," and "the area for sterilization intervention [must] itself be very restricted," for two reasons. Regarding eugenic factors, there was a lack of essential knowledge about the role of genetic inheritance in illnesses and moral characteristics. The Myrdals were therefore inclined to emphasize environmental factors in the development of illnesses and moral characteristics. Regarding social factors, they also urged prudence, maintaining that it was usually better for society to take care of the children than to sterilize the parents.[54] This attitude reveals their real agenda. As we have seen, their entire book powerfully advocated for a comprehensive, preventive social policy incorporating deep and thoroughgoing reforms, of which promoting population purity was a very small part. The state needed to build up the school system, the health care system, and the entire social support sector in all its aspects. This would create a healthy, happy, productive, and (especially) reproductive population. Sterilization was acceptable in certain cases, but it was of marginal utility in relation to the greater project.

The same year that the Myrdals' book appeared in Sweden, Karl Evang's book *Rasepolitikk og reaksjon* (Race Policy and Reaction) was published in Norway. Above all else, it was a sharp attack on racial politics in Germany. He wrote that the aim of a conservative racial policy was to support existing power relations since this view presupposed that the upper class possessed the most desirable qualities. Racial politics was subordinate to class politics. Here we find a clear line of demarcation against the more extreme proponents of racial hygiene. Evang was not, in principle, opposed to sterilization for eugenic purposes, however. Limiting the reproduction of bearers of poor genetic material was "a completely rational thought that Socialism has always supported."[55] But such a policy could be effectively carried out only in a Socialist society, where, with equal conditions of upbringing for all, it would be possible to distinguish those with desirable or undesirable genetic makeups.[56] Here the revolutionary is speaking.

---

[54] A. and G. Myrdal 1934, 217–226.

[55] Evang 1934, 130.

[56] Soltvedt 2000, 166. Here we are following Soltvedt's analysis of Evang.

Evidently, however, when Evang became Social Democracy's powerful director of health, he easily accommodated himself to reformist practice. Although eugenics was a marginal tool for men like Evang, it was an integral part of his social policy. As late as 1955 he would say that Norway perhaps had been too cautious in evaluating the potential of the sterilization law as a tool for eugenics.[57] Moreover, it is important to be aware that the aim and practice of sterilization changed over time. The system developed from predominantly coercive to predominantly voluntary, and from primarily serving the interests of society to serving the interests of the individual.[58]

Eugenics (to the extent that it was carried out) was a particularly noticeable outcome of a technocratic or social engineering way of thinking, in which citizens were divided into subjects and objects. Some—the majority—became objects of technocrats' social interventions in the same way that nature became the object of natural scientists' or engineers' experiments (see chapter 1). This reduction of people to objects had an element of *invasiveness*. Today it has become relatively common to criticize the great Social Democratic project for its technocratic tendencies. Regarding invasion of personal integrity—which sterilization is when carried out for eugenic purposes—the Social Democrats were not the driving force, and it can scarcely be viewed as part of their project even though they made certain concessions to such practices. This technocratic thinking was "more widespread in the right-wing radical contributions to the debate about the population" than among Social Democrats.[59]

The Swedish historian Mattias Tydén, too, argues against the view that sterilization was integral to the welfare policy projects.[60] As the argument went among many Social Democrats, the issue could actually be turned around: sterilizations represented a welfare state's *preliminary state*. In a rich, mature welfare state such as that described by the Myrdals and at least partly realized some decades later in both Sweden and Norway, sterilization was not technically (in terms of birth control) or socially "necessary." Moreover, Tydén asks whether today's abortion of fetuses with Down syndrome "in principle is something different from doing away with 'the mentally deficient,' which among other things was the aim of sterilization."[61]

There were misgivings about sterilization within the labor movement. Nevertheless, when "blunt supporters like Per Albin [the prime minister] were

---

[57] Soltvedt 2000, 170–171.
[58] Soltvedt 2000, 522; Haave and Giæver 2000, 65.
[59] Soltvedt 2000, 319.
[60] Tydén 2002, 553.
[61] Tydén 2002, 14.

carried along by the current," it was due to their project for thoroughgoing social change. This project was linked to a pragmatic political procedural stance that regarded population as a practical issue lent legitimacy by majority resolutions in the Swedish Parliament.[62] We find the clearest institutionally anchored opposition to this type of social engineering in countries with deeply ingrained individual rights. Maciej Zaremba notes that Sweden, unlike the United States, kept the issue of sterilization out of the sphere of jurisprudence and the court system: "The few parliamentarians who in the 1920s and 1930s raised their voices against racial hygiene were most often jurists, and the principle they referred to—that the individual possessed certain rights that the state under no circumstances could legitimately violate—was viewed by Social Democracy as a hindrance to progressive reforms."[63] This parallels the opposition to Nazism that had its roots in liberal rights thinking within liberal and conservative circles.

ASSISTANCE FOR SELF-HELP

We have discussed some of the central focuses of the great social policy initiatives beginning in the early twentieth century and continuing into the interwar period. These initiatives must be viewed in connection with the great modernization project. Social integration, or lifting all social groups up to the level of full national citizenship, was one part of this bifurcated project. The other part was the technological and economic modernization that was to form the basis for the integration project. The democratizing process was the clearest expression of the concept of a society in which members were equal. From this perspective, democratization and social policy were two sides of the same coin; they followed one another naturally. The goal of social policy was to help those in need. It represented the self-organizing of the social collective, an expression of the collective will to remedy unfortunate consequences arising from the free interplay of forces; social policy was a way of building society collectively. There was a sort of fundamental agreement about this that predated the conflicts and contradictory interests that also came to mark the development of social policy. It was important to find a way out of the social crises that these societies had experienced at the close of the nineteenth century.

Social policy contains two paradoxes. One arises from what we might call the positive part of the project: helping and raising up groups and individuals within the societal fellowship must be balanced with certain demands placed

---

[62] Isaksson 2000, 103.
[63] Zaremba 1999, 218.

on those who are to be included; one has to be morally mature, healthy, productive, and reproductive. We have illustrated how these demands and this formative will arose in various contexts, especially in relation to the population question. Integration presupposed a certain degree of segregation.

This points us to a second paradox: accepting help, even when it is given for the most honorable reasons, almost necessarily carries an element of degradation. Accepting help would thus be counterproductive to the greater purpose (achieving social equality). Assistance for self-help and the emphases on universality and rights in relation to the assistance one receives were all ways of trying to escape this paradox. When assistance for self-help became a dominant feature of the incipient welfare state, the social assistance state, it was still, above all, for economic reasons. Universality was too costly; it had to wait.

Sweden emerged more quickly than Norway did from the interwar crises. It rapidly became richer than Norway and could therefore, even before World War II, implement a wave of social reforms that pointed the way toward the welfare state. The period between 1937 and 1939 became "a harvest season for a series of social reforms that previously for the most part were dreams for the future." As Prime Minister Per Albin Hansson wrote, "1937 loosened things up. That is when a pension amendment indexed to the cost of living was enacted, child support, mothers' assistance, maternity assistance, far-reaching improvements in preventative mother and child care, the housing loan fund. The regulation of farm labor was improved. 1938 gave us compulsory holidays, the national dental plan, and the Institute for Health Insurance. 1939 saw the regulation of working hours . . . [and] housing for pensioners was created for the aged."[64] In this period Sweden was ahead of Norway and, indeed, most European countries.

The largest and most important of the popular movements, the labor movement, appeared last. Against the background of the decisive role that this movement would come to play in the later phase of Social Democracy, it is important to remember that around the beginning of the twentieth century it played a relatively marginal role, particularly in Norway. As we have seen, while the Social Democratic parties were preoccupied with shaking off their Marxism and class-based identity, other forces, to a large extent, were developing the foundations of what came to be the Social Democratic order. This move from Marxism to reformism, and eventually to governmental power, will be examined in the next chapter.

[64] Isaksson 2000, 355–356.

CHAPTER 4

Revolution or Reform

The Last Great Popular Movement • Working-Class Culture • Marxist Rhetoric and Reformist Practice • An Indistinct Policy • From One's Own Home to the People's Home: The Labor Movement and the Land Question • Hjalmar Branting • The Big Strike of 1909 • The Party Is Split • Martin Tranmæl • Worker Scandinavianism • How Radical? • "A Peculiar Legalization Activity" • The Level of Conflict Escalates • The Solidarity Game Is Established • Per Albin Hansson and the "People's Home" • Johan Nygaardsvold and the People's Party • The Expansionism of the Crisis Policy as Ideology • Revolution or Reform

THE LAST GREAT POPULAR MOVEMENT

The labor movement was the last of the great popular movements in Scandinavia at the beginning of the twentieth century. In this chapter we will see how the labor movement originated outside the established society, gradually became integrated into society, and, in the end, came to shoulder the great modernization project, taking it out of the hands of the middle classes and putting the movement's own mark on it. Social Democracy, as it developed and adapted in order to bring about "the Social Democratic order" in the 1960s, was formed in confrontation and cooperation with other forces in society. In its final form it had roots in both the liberal and the socialist and reformist traditions. It grew into a hegemonic "order." In other words, by the 1960s in Sweden and Norway there was a high degree of agreement about how society ought to look. But this was certainly not the case at the beginning of the century.

In the late 1800s industrialization carried much promise, but with the great crisis in the 1880s the shady side of industrial society threatened to predominate. A new industrial proletariat arose; an underprivileged class formed, a class that, not without reason, felt left out of the national fellowship. At the same time, agrarian society was being threatened by the new industrial society. The situation was pregnant with social problems, and pessimism and unrest were in the air. It was out of this situation that the labor movement grew.

The mainstream Social Democratic parties of Norway and Sweden were established in 1887 and 1889 respectively. (In Norway: Det Norske Arbeiderparti, mostly referred to in the short version, Arbeiderpartiet—the Labor Party. In Sweden: Sveriges Socialdemoratiska Arbetarparti, mostly referred to as Socialdemokraterna—the Social Democrats. In the following we will use the short version.) The parties were based on preexisting local political organizations and trade union activity. The idea as it was proposed in Norway in 1887 was that all real labor associations—including the trade unions—should be organized under a coordinated leadership. At that time there was no distinction between the political party and the trade unions. Their beginning was not very spectacular, but the organizations grew, and we shall see how they developed a political strategy. In 1897 the decisive step to separate the trade unions from the political organization was taken at a Scandinavian Labor Congress in Stockholm. There it was decided that a trade union central should be established in each of the three Scandinavian countries, with a separate secretariat for each country. These came into being in 1898 in Sweden and 1899 in Norway, and in due course they would be called LO (*Landsorganisasjonen* in Norwegian and *Landsorganisationen* in Swedish) in both countries. Discussions took place about how close the relationship should be between the party and the LO and whether they should operate by means of collective party membership.

England had the longest tradition of trade union organization in Europe. Toward the end of the nineteenth century the trade unions took initiatives in English party politics, for example, by having their own candidates in parliamentary elections. Out of this the Labor Party developed little by little after the turn of the century. In France, on the contrary, many of the trade unions were under the influence of the revolutionary syndicalists and therefore "antiparliamentarian" for a long time. Scandinavia adopted the German model, which was something in between. Until World War II almost all Swedish and Norwegian trade unions were members of the LO and thus closely linked to the labor parties in the two countries. But that does not mean that they always moved in tandem.

Collective party membership (union membership including party membership) was introduced in both countries but became better established as a form of organization in Sweden. Sweden was more industrialized and had developed a stronger central trade union than Norway. With a population half the size of Sweden's, Norway had national trade union membership totaling 15,000 by 1905, compared with 104,000 in Sweden.[1] The relative strength

---

[1] Elvander 1980, 40f.

of trade union organizing in Sweden was important in turning the policy of the Social Democrats in the direction of reform. The Norwegian case was somewhat different.

WORKING-CLASS CULTURE

In the period leading up to World War II a working-class culture developed counter to the dominant bourgeois culture. This evolving way of life was closely associated with a number of specific working-class institutions established by the labor movement, the most important being the labor parties and trade unions. But there were others in addition, such as the labor press; children's, women's, and sports organizations; and choirs. All these were collectives existing somewhat outside the larger society. Arising alongside these were educational institutions, a body of working-class literature, publishing houses, and special meeting places known as *Folkets hus* (houses of the people).

So along with the labor movement the underprivileged and marginalized got their own culture. And through its labor organizations and cultural institutions the working class eventually developed self-esteem and self-awareness as a class. As Øyvind Bjørnson writes: "From a raw and uncivilized mass the labor movement had created a well-disciplined and sound army of orderly, well-bred workers who systematically worked toward their long-term goals."[2]

A special feature in Sweden was the rich and important proletarian literature, with writers such as Ivar Lo-Johansson, Moa Martinsson, and Wilhelm Moberg. This literature "gives a different picture of the world than bourgeois literature does and it tells about experiences that have not been given due place in the official histories."[3] In addition, many of the books were of a very high literary quality. This could not be said of Norway, although there were a few examples of high-quality proletarian literature.[4]

As we have seen, all the popular movements developed institutions for public education. Education and enlightenment were the most important cultural activities of the labor movement. So-called workers' academies organized as courses of study were common far back in the nineteenth century. Later there were evening schools. We have also seen that a folk college that later came to play an important role was established by the Swedish labor movement in 1906. Inspired by the Swedes and the Danes, a similar initiative

---

[2] Bjørnson 1990, 246.

[3] *Magnus Nilsson i Nationalencyplopedin* 2008, "Arbetarpressen." Furuland and Svedjedal 2006. The proletarian literature should not be confused with the radical intellectual literature.

[4] Larsen and Sandvik 1980, 22. Here Hans Heiberg mentions the best books by Johan Falkberget and Kristofer Uppdal and the poet Rudolf Nilsen.

was taken in Norway in 1918, but it did not come to much. A folk college was eventually established in 1939.[5] A Workers Educational Association to coordinate the many initiatives was established on a national level in Sweden in 1912. In Norway a Central Committee for Socialist Education was established in 1920, and a Workers Educational Association using the Swedish model was created in 1931. The educational programs of the labor movements were great successes, continuing to expand after World War II.

According to Arne Kokkvoll, the educational programs of the labor movement held two ideals. On the one hand, the workers should acquire the traditional culture of the larger society. It was important to heighten the general cultural level of the working class in order for it to be integrated into the national fellowship. On the other hand, the workers were supposed to be the bearers of a different culture with new values that could replace the old bourgeois culture. The two ideals existed side by side, but after World War II the countercultural dimension almost vanished,[6] partly because the labor movement had come to feel that it had the opportunity to leave its own stamp on the national culture.

The sports movement, the last and smallest of the popular movements, provides an example of these changing attitudes. Around 1940 the large comprehensive sports organizations had about 390,000 members in Sweden and 300,000 in Norway.[7] These rather high figures are characteristic for Scandinavia. In Norway, however, the sports movement gained greater political significance than it did in Sweden. The development of the Norwegian movement is part of the history of the development of the labor movement from a class struggle ideology into a popular movement reflecting the idea of national integration. Thus we have an illustration of the typical difference between the labor movements in the two countries.

At the turn of the twentieth century the interest in sports and athletics was growing, and many sports organizations were established. There were different views as to the purpose of these activities.[8] Typically the English Olympic sports ideal with its emphasis on competition was confronted with the traditional ideal of physical training, the latter being closely linked to military needs. Many of the leaders in the early sports movements were military men, particularly in Norway. Out of this complex situation with many different or-

---

[5] Kokkvoll 1981, 117f., 226.

[6] Kokkvoll 1981, 36–37.

[7] Lindroth and Norberg 2002, 36. Olstad 1987, 257. For Norway, both associations (see below) are included. Lindroth and Norberg give higher numbers for the Norwegian National Association than does Olstad.

[8] For the general development see Lindroth and Norberg 2002, in particular chapter 2 by Norberg: "The Extensiveness, Affiliation and Composition of the Sports Movement" pp. 25–57, and Olstad 1987.

ganizations grew comprehensive national associations. The Swedish National Sports Association was founded in 1903, and in Norway a national association was founded in 1910. These organizations were especially a consequence of a growing political interest leading to increasing public grants. An example of the new political interest is evidenced in Sweden's participation in the London Olympic Games of 1908. According to the minister in charge, the state had to grant money so that "we will not be defeated by the Norwegians." Obviously the loss of prestige in connection with the dissolution of the union in 1905 was still felt.

The breakthrough of the sports movement in popular culture occurred in the interwar years. Then the class struggle also impressed itself on the development of the sports movement. Separate sports organizations within the labor movement had already been formed in Germany and Austria before the turn of the century. But in no other Western European country did workers' sports associations became as strong as in Norway. In 1924 the Workers Sports Association in Norway was founded. In 1928 one of the association's leading sports ideologues said that "the worker-athletes form the army of the working class—the Red Army—which will know how to outfight the army of the bourgeoisie."[9] The idea of physical training in order to build military strength was taken from the bourgeoisie. In 1933 the revolutionary perspective had vanished, but the antagonism remained: "Sports for the champions, top-level performance, sensation-seeking in nationalistic clothing are the contributions of the bourgeoisie to the health of the people."[10] The workers' participation in the new sports activities made it a true popular movement, but unlike Swedish worker-athletes, Norwegian workers participated through their own separate sports organization. In 1940 the Workers Sports Association was about half the size of the National Sports Association.

The physical conditioning of the masses was also part of the bourgeois ideology, so the two sports movements could converge on this basis. Up to 1940 the antagonism between the two faded as the general idea of national integration gained ground within the workers' sports associations. According to Finn Olstad, the threat of war was a contributing factor in the reconciliation between the two movements. The German occupation made a further contribution, and in 1946 a joint comprehensive sports association was founded in Norway without opposition.[11]

A separate Workers Sports Association was also established in Sweden. But contrary to Norway's experience, the response was negligible. Most of the

[9] Olstad 1987, 244.
[10] Olstad 1987, 245.
[11] Olstad 1987, 322, 324.

workers who took part in organized sports activities chose the comprehensive national association. Historians who have written about the history of sports "emphasize the reformist policy of the Swedish Social Democratic Party and the acceptance of the bourgeois ideology of the sports movement."[12] This is a particularly clear expression of the difference that we have pointed out in other connections between the Swedish and the Norwegian mainstream development of the labor movements. Class struggle ideology and antagonism toward the bourgeois institutions were more deeply rooted in the Norwegian than in the Swedish movement. In Sweden the labor movement was more "bourgeois."

After 1945, during the hegemonic period of Social Democracy, the sports movements were united in both countries. Now, as Rune Slagstad writes, the Social Democrats could realize their vision "to develop democratic popular sports activities as an independent part of the socialist educational project."[13] In the Swedish context it has been pointed out how the human body became a focal point in the Social Democratic state: "The people must be cleansed, sanitized, modernized, and physically trained in order to be set loose from the old collectives and be fit for integration in the new society."[14] Thus the Social Democratic state "became a sports state" by building a sports network "with the intention of furthering national integration."[15]

MARXIST RHETORIC AND REFORMIST PRACTICE

The societal model and the politics taken up by the Scandinavian Social Democratic movement had been borrowed from the German Social Democratic Party (SPD). The Marxist Karl Kautsky, the leading ideologue of the SPD, was behind what was known as the Erfurt Program of 1891, which set the tone for several European Social Democratic parties. The program was revolutionary in the sense that it was based on historical materialism and the necessity of class struggle. There was, however, a second aspect drafted primarily by Eduard Bernstein, the man who would be the main ideologue of reformist Socialism. This second part listed several practical reforms. Thus the program was fundamentally unclear, for example, as to whether economic or political forces were the driving forces in history.

There has been discussion about how radical or revolutionary the labor movement truly was in this founding phase. In his book about the ideo-

---

[12] Lindroth and Norberg 2002, 39.
[13] Slagstad 1998, 342.
[14] Ehn, Frykman, and Löfgren 1993, 167.
[15] Slagstad 1998, 338.

logical basis of Swedish Social Democracy, Herbert Tingsten maintains that
the movement was marked by the developmental fatalism of historical materialism, which meant that it was unable to work out any reform strategy
until well into the 1900s.[16] This point of view was later modified by several
researchers. Sheri Berman, emphasizing the contrast between the passivity
of materialism and the primacy of politics, argues that compared with the
development of the Social Democratic parties on the Continent, the Swedish
party chose democratic revisionism or "the primacy of politics" at an early
stage, which again explains the success of the party in the interwar years.[17]
Ingrid Millbourn has argued from a looser concept of the ideological. She
distinguishes between manifest and latent ideology and has described the
development more as a continual process of adaptation and conflict. From
this point of view, reform and the significance of practical experience can be
traced back to the beginning, together with drawing forward more or less
manifest ideological antagonisms within the movement.[18]

Up to 1905 the Norwegian labor movement developed in tandem with
that of Sweden; thereafter it took a more radical direction than the Swedish
movement. Recent research in Norway has been oriented toward accentuat-
ing the movement's actual reformist character in this early phase, however.[19]
Owing to a traditional feeling of fellowship in the homogeneous Scandinavian societies, it appears as though there have not been any real revolutionary
spirits within Scandinavian Socialism.

We do not need to answer the question of what the movement "really" was,
of course. It is not necessary to reduce it to its "deepest foundation," either
reformist or revolutionary. The movement from the beginning carried within
itself a duality, and such was the case for a long time. Thus the eventual victory of reform can be viewed as the outcome of a historical process. In other
words, one should "try to understand how reform in its struggle with other
tendencies successively took form and came to dominate the movement."[20]

Nonetheless, in this early phase the Social Democratic parties presented
themselves as revolutionary. On the other hand, the movement also operated
within the established political system. This positioning between the inside
and the outside, or the (apparent) opposition between what the parties said

---

[16] Tingsten 1967, 1:127ff. Lewin 1992, 171f., follows up on the work of Tingsten.

[17] Berman 2006, 152f.

[18] Millbourn 1990, 30ff. Here she goes through, after Tingsten, the debate that broke out in Sweden.
Much of the discussion is about whether the Marxism that Tingsten writes about or that the leading ideologues such as Hjalmar Branting and Axel Danielsson stood for was a correct interpretation of Marx or
not. In our context this debate is not relevant. They themselves refer to their ideology as Marxist.

[19] With regard to the big discussion of the 1980s on the radicalism of the early labor movement, see
below.

[20] Ekdahl and Hjelm 1981. See also Östberg 1990, 17f.

and what they did, has been observed by several writers and described in various ways. Most common has been simply to maintain that the movement had a Marxist ideology and a reformist practice.[21] And Per Albin Hansson, who was to be the Swedish party's leading figure in the interwar period, was "an avowed Marxist but a practicing reformist" during his youth.[22] Notwithstanding how this positioning has been understood, it must of course have been a problematic starting point for formulating the political line of these parties. And with this we have perhaps reached the core of the problem.

AN INDISTINCT POLICY

From the outset there were two possible political strategies. One could work toward an overthrow of the existing form of society through extraparliamentary actions and mass mobilization, or work to improve the conditions of the workers and solve the problems of industrial society through parliamentary democracy via reforms. Thus it was that the movement faced a classical dilemma: should it reform, thereby contributing to the defense of capitalism by making it more palatable, or should it seek a more system-critical revolutionary line? In brief, was it correct to stand inside or outside established society? For some time the parties refused to make the choice—in the case of Norway, for a very long time. Thus practical politics became somewhat hesitant. Marxism "constrained the possibilities of the party to fully play its cards in its parliamentary work."[23] But this was not so much because the parties were Marxist. The point is that they could not make up their minds whether they were Marxist or not.

Many of those within the ranks of established society feared that universal suffrage would bring those without property to power, resulting in a revolutionary social upheaval. But in 1900, with the first election based on universal suffrage for men in Norway, only 3 percent of the votes cast went to the Labor Party, and it achieved no parliamentary representation. At the next election in 1903 there was a small breakthrough in the North that resulted in four representatives in Parliament.

In Sweden Social Democratic Party leader Hjalmar Branting had come into the Second Chamber on a liberal list in 1896. For a long time he was the lone Social Democrat in the Swedish Parliament, but in 1903 the Swedish Social Democrats also had a group of four in Parliament—prior to universal

---

[21] Elvander 1980, 47.
[22] Isaksson 1985, 201.
[23] Isaksson 1985, 199.

suffrage. Thus on the parliamentary level these two Social Democratic sister parties in Norway and Sweden were both very small at the beginning of
the century.

Voter response increased significantly in the years following 1905. Sweden
instituted universal suffrage for men and adopted proportional representation
in 1909, a factor that contributed to a marked increase for the labor movement. By 1915 the Social Democrats were the largest group in the Second
Chamber with eighty-seven representatives, or 38 percent of the total number.[24] With the election in Norway in the same year the Labor Party had nine-
teen members of Parliament. From the number of votes cast, the party would
have had at least double that number, or 33 percent of the representatives,
with proportional representation. But the majority system of electing representatives kept the number down. Thus from 1915 the Social Democratic
parties became a force to be reckoned with, especially in Sweden.

In 1911 Liberal prime minister Karl Staaff invited his old friend Branting to take part in a coalition government. Branting refused, but in 1917 he
went into the government of the Liberal Nils Edén, and in 1920 he was able
to form the first purely Social Democratic government. About a year earlier
the German Social Democrats had formed a government, but it constituted
something more like an episode. Branting's short experience in forming a
government in 1920 was, in contrast, an important step in the direction of
integrating the labor movement into Swedish society. It would end with the
Social Democrats assuming governmental power in the 1930s, roughly at the
same time that Hitler seized power in Germany.

On some issues the Social Democrats' policy was unambiguous. First, it was
modernist, in the sense that they thought and argued from scientific norms
of rationality and argumentation. "Socialism is a science, built through studies of the society and on principles based on experience," wrote the founder
of the Norwegian Labor Party in 1891.[25] Wherever it dealt with the conflict
between traditionalists and modernists, the movement stood on the side of
modernity; the labor movement wanted industrialization. Furthermore, the
standpoint of the labor movement was for universal suffrage, at least in Sweden. Here it stood together with, and to some extent pushed further than, the
radical liberals. In Norway we shall see that the party was more ambiguous
on this point.

In general it is characteristic that the policy of the Social Democrats was
ambiguous on several issues in this period. Up until the dissolution of the

[24] Greve 1964, 4. Stjernquist 1996, 122–123.
[25] Cited by Terjesen 1991, 44.

union between Sweden and Norway in 1905 the issue of this union dominated politics, particularly in Norway. On this issue the Norwegian labor
movement took a nationalist stand. It has been said that it took what almost
amounted to the line of the Conservative Party.[26] Because the union was not
so important for the movement, it was able to contribute to achieving a peaceful solution. At the Swedish Social Democratic Congress in Stockholm in
February 1905 the parliamentary leader of the Norwegian Labor Party, Alfred
Eriksen, was allowed to make a speech about the union question as seen from
the Norwegian side. The congress then adopted a statement that called for
"an unqualified recognition of the Norwegian people's right to freedom, and
without interference, to decide their own affairs."[27] It was also important that
Branting became personally engaged in calming the nationalistic passions of
Sweden. When the agreement to dissolve the union came before Parliament
in the autumn of 1905, the Norwegian minister of foreign affairs was able
to say, "What he [Branting] and the Swedish social democrats have to their
credit for having dampened the fires of war in Sweden is immeasurable."[28]

On the other hand, there were also certain Labor Party representatives in
the Norwegian Parliament, led by Alfred Eriksen, who whipped things up
in the direction of ultranationalism. They voted against the settlement that
set out the conditions for the peaceful dissolution of the union. The hot-
test point of contention was Norway's duty to pull down its border defenses
against Sweden. The Social Democrats were not to emerge from this episode
with impunity.

Out of the great complexity of issues that blossomed forth in Norwegian
politics after 1905, one might well have expected a solid engagement on the
part of the Social Democrats with regard to the concession laws. Indeed, these
laws dealt with placing limits on the capitalist mode of production. Nevertheless the Social Democrats played a role of little distinction. There too they sat
on the sidelines of an issue that most people were absorbed by. In 1907 the
parliamentary leader of the Social Democrats was able to declare that "the
fundamental thinking" that was the basis for the Liberal Party's attack on
the government "actually springs from Socialist ideas." And when the Liberal
Party's radical proposal on the concession laws was put forward in 1909, the
historian of the Labor Party, Halvard Lange, could only note that the party's
parliamentarians did not make "any effort to step into the vanguard."[29] Even

---

[26] Halvard Lange 1937, 1:259. Bjørgum 1985.

[27] Scheflo 1964, 252.

[28] Lange 1937, vol. I: 277. Later Branting got the Nobel Peace Prize from the (Norwegian) Nobel Peace
Prize committee.

[29] H. Lange 1937, 2:30, 35.

on this issue there was a certain passivity. Where the Social Democrats managed to define the Liberal Party's policy as "Socialistic," this meant in reality that they linked this concept to a reformist parliamentary practice. There was, however, still no general transition to reform.

FROM ONE'S OWN HOME TO THE PEOPLE'S HOME: THE LABOR MOVEMENT AND THE LAND QUESTION

The land question was discussed in chapter 3. This issue is particularly suitable for illustrating the strategic-political dilemma that we have outlined since here the labor movement was forced to take account of the real conditions of Scandinavia and break with some of the most central Marxist dogmas.[30]

The Marxism embraced by the Social Democratic parties of the two countries before the turn of the century implied their acceptance of the *theory of concentration*, which maintained that development was moving in the direction of large production entities and that this was progressive because only by means of such large entities could production be efficient. Second, it implied their acceptance of the *theory of depletion*, which saw development toward a society that in all essentials was increasingly composed of capitalists and proletarians since the middle strata would be either squeezed out or proletarianized.

In Scandinavian society, whose population was actually largely composed of lower-middle-class tradespeople and small farmers, there were still very few who felt comfortable with a description of society based on the two Marxist categories—capitalist and proletarian. Nor did this capture the imagination of landless agrarian proletarians. Instead of the overthrow of the existing system of ownership in favor of collective ownership, they dreamed of having their own smallholdings. The imported concepts collided with homegrown experience. The confrontation with Scandinavian reality almost necessarily led to revisions of the ideological profile. Such revisions are not carried out overnight, however. The Social Democrats hesitated.

In 1886 Branting had written that the future belonged to large-scale agriculture, and at the Third Scandinavian Labor Congress in 1890 a resolution was adopted that denounced "all efforts to preserve the class of small farm-

---

[30] Tingsten (1967, vol. 1), Björlin (1974), and Odhner (1989) have treated the Social Democrats' attitude toward the land question. In contrast to the situation in Sweden, the question has received little attention by researchers of the history of the labor movement in Norway, although Fure (1983) has a short account of the programs concerning the land question (pp. 90ff). Rovde, who had dealt with the question in a comprehensive article, mentions that Halvard Lange's treatment (1937) remains the fundamental account (Rovde 2000, 77, note).

ers—through loans on favorable terms or the parceling out of land or leasing of state lands—[which] are, from a Socialist point of view, to be condemned since these efforts, even if they are not completely without success, merely contribute to prolonging the existence of the middle class, which tenaciously and with utmost prejudice holds fast to private ownership and therefore has become the bearer of reaction against the revolutionary labor movement."[31]

The own home movement was viewed as pronouncedly bourgeois. Those who owned their own homes would never become those who stormed the ramparts of society. This position was not completely without ambiguity, however. In the course of the 1890s certain concessions were given in relation to small farmers' rights of ownership.[32] The Federation of Social Democratic Youth developed a line of thought about small-scale, earth-bound socialism, so the dilemma was recognized.[33] As the well-known Swedish radical economist Knut Wicksell said, "Social Democracy hesitates about how to treat the small farmer, as exploiter or as exploited, and whether he should be treated as the capitalist or consoled as the proletarian."[34]

In 1904 the Social Democrats took their first initiative toward a solution that took the form of "one's own home." They avoided criticizing the loan plan that had been ratified in Parliament the same year. On the other hand, they considered it sufficient to have a state rent-and-lease system; the state should own the land, but the user should be guaranteed rights of usufruct. The proposal was Henry George–inspired. In 1907 Branting undertook a final retreat on the land question. Developments had shown, as he said, that his position from the 1880s, that large-scale production was the solution of the future, had been wrong. Marx's generalization had not been borne out. The form of production that had captured the future was intensive small-scale agriculture.[35] Thus it was that the Social Democrats clung hesitantly to the policy of the liberals and the farmers. They also did so in Norway, at least for a brief period.

Within the Norwegian labor movement the discussion took place between the farmer Christopher Hornsrud and one of the founders of the Labor Party, the craftsman Carl Jeppesen, who was a Marxist. According to Jeppesen, primitive reality stood against the development tendencies of Socialism.[36]

---

[31] Tingsten 1967, 1:174; H. Lange 1937, 1:112.

[32] Tingsten 1967, 1:175.

[33] Edling 1996, 131.

[34] Isaksson 1985, I1:170.

[35] Edling 1996, 370. See also Björnlin 1974, 72: "The altered point of view on small-scale farming was the result of a long process of development under which the labor movement came to accept the political rules of the game held by the established society."

[36] H. Lange 1937, 1:239.

In 1895, however, Hornsrud managed to have "Socialist common landhold-ing" replaced with "modern agriculture" in the program.[37] In 1901 Hornsrud managed to set up a committee with himself as the chair to deal with the ag-ricultural question. The committee's proposal was adopted in 1902. The debt problem and the question of interest were pushed into the foreground, as they were shortly thereafter in Sweden as well, and the Social Democrats were able to come around to supporting the loan plan that was then launched. Whether it would be common landholding or individual holding was described as a pragmatic question. In reality it allowed for individual ownership.[38]

What was most remarkable about the program of 1902 was the fact that it was open to *cooperation* in agriculture as a Socialist initiative. One of the arguments against small-scale agriculture from the industrialists and Social-ists was that it could not be economically efficient. Small-scale agriculture condemned the farmer to poverty and exhaustion. It represented a primitive reality. The new idea, in Sweden as well as in Norway, was that this problem of efficiency could be solved by replacing the policy of collectivization with cooperation between smallholders. As Tingsten writes, "To a certain degree the advantages of unified large-scale enterprises could be achieved through cooperation."[39] From developments in Denmark one could find confirmation that this thought was correct.

Earlier on the labor movement had rejected thoughts about such coopera-tive production. According to Karl Kautsky, cooperative production was a threat to unity and Social Democracy. It was anarchism's form of produc-tion.[40] But the land question thrust forward a revision of this point of view. The experience of Sweden and Norway was somewhat similar and was con-firmed in the Scandinavian Labor Congress in Copenhagen in 1901. The party historian wrote: "With the revision of the program in 1901 and the framing of the land program in 1902, the Norwegian Labor Party had shown its willingness to move from being a pronounced agitational party to a practi-cal political party of reform."[41] Christopher Hornsrud was considered to be the man who had solved the dilemma for the party, and he became party chair in 1903.

In 1906, however, there was a shift of line in Norway—back to Kautsky's version of Marxism. The policy of small-scale agriculture was rejected, and Hornsrud was shoved back to the periphery. He came forward again, how-ever. In 1928, after the party had shaken itself free of Marxism, he became the

---

[37] Ole Peder Kjeldstadli 1973, 103.
[38] H. Lange 1937, 1:240.
[39] Tingsten 1967, 1:192.
[40] Millbourn 1990, 271, 160.
[41] H. Lange 1937, 1:241–242, 208, 239, 240, 242. See also Edling 1996, 237.

first Social Democratic prime minister of Norway. That same year the Labor Party became one of the active driving forces for the Agricultural Act, which was to give the municipalities broad and comprehensive powers to expropriate land for those who wanted to establish themselves as small-scale farmers. The "modernization" of the concept of ownership, which the concession laws represented, was thus followed up by the Agricultural Act. Sweden had managed to get a radical expropriation act following a proposal by Swartz's Conservative government of 1917. The Social Democrats had then wanted to go further in the direction of what would become the Norwegian Agricultural Act a decade later,[42] but Sweden did not go that far.

"The Agricultural Act was a milestone that marks the Norwegian Labor Party change from a revolutionary party, or perhaps a party of revolutionary phrases, to a party of reform eager to hold power," writes the historian Olav Randen.[43] This commentary is almost identical to that of the party historian concerning the events of twenty-six years earlier, in 1902. The Marxist interlude was over, and once again the party had abandoned the revolutionary line. The land question was a central feature on both occasions.

Now, as a signal of the approaching good way of life under Social Democracy, small-scale agriculture would fade away. As far as it went, Branting was correct in his position of the 1880s (when he wrote that the future belonged to large-scale agriculture), not in his position of 1907 (when he held that the form of production that had captured the future was intensive small-scale agriculture). From the beginning the Social Democrats had looked to the practice of capitalism for their model and, as we know, that was where the future would lie. One might argue, however, that the policy regarding small-scale agriculture was a necessity, in the conditions at the beginning of the twentieth century and on into the late 1930s, as a solution to the social problems of the time. In addition, it was by building the unity of workers and farmers that the Labor Party managed to become so powerful—indeed, that the Social Democratic order came to power in the two countries. This stands in contrast to Germany, where the Social Democrats did not build a corresponding alliance. When the Social Democrats of Sweden and Norway were forced to accept the possibility of producer cooperation and property rights to land, and thereby land rights in general, this was in accordance with common attitudes in Scandinavia and in agreement with what would become the future.

The problem of the inefficiency of smallholdings had producer cooperation as its theoretical "solution." But there are also grounds for stressing small-scale agriculture as a way of life. Millbourn has drawn out a contradiction within

---

[42] Uddhammar 1993, 348.
[43] Randen 2002, 91.

Social Democracy between the ideal of the disciplined worker in an effective large firm and the ideal of decentralization and working for oneself as a strategy for liberation.[44] She does not take up small-scale agriculture policy in this connection, but it seems clearly relevant. The idea of the free, self-directed enterprise is expressed nowhere more clearly than precisely here. It might have been necessary to argue for the efficiency of small-scale agriculture, but much of the strength of the small-scale agricultural policy lay exactly in the idealization of smallholdings as a way of life.

We find the notion of the self-run enterprise or self-direction within industry as well, just as Millbourn has pointed out. Among other places, we see that this idea gained ground as a democratization strategy for the trade union movement during the heyday of the Social Democratic order in the 1960s. Throughout the latter half of the century this has provided direction for several attempts at reorganization within the field of modern industry, above all in the form of self-governing groups but also more generally in relation to the control and management of the labor process. Thus, self-governance on the micro level has some of is roots in the land question and the "own home" policy. At the macro level the "people's home" had its roots here as well.

HJALMAR BRANTING

The troublesome dilemma of the land question had its parallel in the troublesome dilemma concerning whether the party should follow a parliamentary or an extraparliamentary strategy. Branting was the predominant leadership figure in the Swedish Social Democratic Party, from its foundation until his death in 1925. If any one person can be said to have solved the dilemmas and establish Social Democracy as the leading parliamentary reform party, it was Branting. On the whole, if anyone could be designated as having dominated the national strategy of Sweden in the twentieth century, Branting would be a strong candidate.

Branting came from the upper echelons of the bourgeoisie. He had an impressive presence and a brilliant intellect. During his student days at Uppsala he took part in all the student activities—professional, intellectual, political, and social—but never managed to complete his studies, since politics and journalism completely consumed him. Branting's inheritance was not inconsiderable, yet it disappeared relatively quickly. He was generous toward his friends (the writer August Strindberg received a Branting "loan"), but his generosity was first and foremost toward the Social Democratic movement.

[44] Millbourn 1990, 244, 281.

Figure 5. Hjalmar Branting was the undisputed leader of the Swedish Social Democrats. He had a solid bourgeois background, entered Parliament in 1897, and led the labor movement with a firm hand in its transition from a revolutionary to a reformist path. The picture shows the old revolutionary as minister of finance in a coalition government with the Liberal Party formed in 1917, when the revolutionary spirit swept over Europe. (Photo: Erik Holmén.)

Initially he characterized himself as a liberal, and during his student days he developed a close friendship with Karl Staaff, who later became the Liberal Party prime minister. Nonetheless, Branting became a Socialist relatively early on and had a burning zeal for his points of view, although he was not aggressive by nature. The poet and writer Gustav Fröding has given us a brief portrait written after a visit by Branting:

There are few people in this country whom I value as highly as this "Socialist hooligan." Of course he takes pains to make himself look as underclass as possible—goes around in rough clothing and has a shagginess to his moustache—presumably so as not to irritate his party friends excessively. But his fine nose, his intelligent and tactful glance, and his characteristic forehead are things he cannot democratize—just as he cannot amputate and cast aside his great knowledge and his considerable gifts. He was mild-tempered in his discernment of people—even the worst of his opponents—and by no means one-sidedly biased politically.[45]

This description accords with many others. "Branting was surely an agreeable but indecisive and somewhat disorganized man," wrote Anders Isaksson.[46] How could this indecisive and disorganized upper-class person be the sovereign leader of the Social Democrats in a period when they were few and marginalized, all the while standing in a situation of struggle and making use of a revolutionary rhetoric? Are we facing the irony of history, or is the question wrongly put? Was it not necessary to have precisely such a person to fill the role?

In 1886 Branting gave his famous Gävle speech, "Why the Labor Movement Must Be Socialist," a speech said to have "constituted the Swedish labor movement's declaration of independence and the first program document of Swedish Socialism," to cite Branting's antagonist and later biographer Zeta Höglund.[47] Branting's speech was full of the Marxist rhetoric of the time. Both the theory of concentration and the theory of depletion were there, along with the notion that socialism was to be realized through revolution (that is, by introducing a new social order). But if by revolution one meant "something that has to do with street riots, murder, and plunder, then Socialism is so far from being revolutionary that, to the contrary, it has to be reckoned as, in the real sense, conservative."[48]

This speech has been interpreted in different ways. Herbert Tingsten considered it Marxist. Per Nyström maintained that it was German academic Socialism (*Kathedersozialismus*), meaning that it was reformist. Sten O. Karlsson sums up as follows: "Branting borrows lustily from different sources. He cooks up a brew with the major communitarian ingredients consisting of a solid pinch of [Ferdinand] Lassalle, a tablespoon of general evolutionism, and a handful of unspecified German academic Socialism. The dish is flavored with certain spicy Marxist phrases. Above all, as a statement of independence the Gävle speech puts forward its autonomy from Marx."[49] Branting also mentions universal suffrage as the prerequisite for the bourgeoisie to purchase a peaceful passage into the future. This was formulated as an ultimatum: only by means of universal suffrage could the Social Democrats work for their visions of the future within the bourgeois democratic system.

[45] Franzén 1985, 139.
[46] Isaksson 1985, 199.
[47] Tingsten 1967, 1:137.
[48] Tingsten 1967, 1:137f. and 2:15.
[49] Karlsson 2001, 252–259.

THE BIG STRIKE OF 1909

The strike has always been an extraparliamentary tool of the labor movement, and it can take many forms. The general strike, which was much discussed at the beginning of the twentieth century, represented direct action through which the social revolution was to be realized. At the Second Congress of the Internationale in 1904, however, the majority, including Branting, rejected the general strike because it was considered to be a revolutionary means, opting for the "big strike" as their tool for the defense or capture of special rights.[50]

In Norway and Sweden in the 1890s there were many strikes and very little in the way of institutionalized procedures. In other words, strikes were seen from both sides as a threat to the existing social order. Naturally enough, Branting came down on the side of the workers, while at the same time warning them against rash actions that they were doomed to lose. He also frequently acted as a mediator and arbitrator. As we have already seen, universal suffrage was long in coming to Sweden. In conformity with what Branting had said in 1886, this had led to the routine practice of extraparliamentary forms of action. In 1902 and again in 1907 a major strike for the purpose of bringing to a head the issue of universal suffrage was discussed but rejected.[51] In 1909, however, a big strike occurred.

The big strike of 1909 did not have to do with the right to vote. The background was complicated and had to it a certain element of struggle over the social order. In other words, the strike had certain features of the general strike; indeed, the distinction between the big strike and the general strike was not always easily made. The immediate cause was the major lockout by the Employers Association. But of course this too had a previous history. A number of years of economic downturn, with falling wage rates and increasing unrest, had led to a series of local strikes and lockouts. In this situation the Employers Association took matters into its own hands, declaring that if peace could not be brought about on the labor front in specifically determined ways, there would be a lockout.

The central issue was what was then called the freedom to work, which implied the employers' full right to hire and fire as they saw fit and their right to organize the work. Among other things, this opened the way for strikebreaking, something that the trade unions naturally refused to go along with. The LO (trade union central) replied by deciding to call a large-scale strike.

[50] Schiller 1967, 209–210.

[51] Simonson 1985, 77–166, gives an account of the lengthy discussions within the party on the use of major strikes as a means in the struggle for universal suffrage. According to Hentilä (1979), the rejection of this strategy marks the victory of reformism in the party.

This was carried through with a broad response, and its actions took peaceful forms. After some weeks had passed, however, the strikers went back to work without having achieved anything. The conservative Lindman government had been passive during the strike, and the Liberal Party leader Staaff, in accord with his positive view of compulsory arbitration, came out against the strike.[52]

By choosing what they considered a suitable time for their lockout, the Swedish employers hoped that they could push for an agreement that was more on their own terms. Such an agreement did not transpire. There is no doubt, however, that it was the employer side that demonstrated its strength in the big strike of 1909. The initiative had been in their hands and was based precisely on the recognition of their strength.[53] The result served to weaken the trade union movement. The LO lost half of its members, and it would be a decade before it reached the level of support it had enjoyed before the strike.

The leadership of the trade union movement had been against the big strike. The chairman of the LO, Herman Lindquist, stood close to Branting and shared his skepticism toward the big strike as a weapon; a year earlier he had declared that the big strike was comparable to suicide.[54] Both men knew that they were weak and that they would likely lose. The trade unions were weakly centralized, there was currently an economic downturn, and the strike fund was limited. Nonetheless, when the LO did declare the big strike, it was largely because the trade union organization had to respond in some way to what it considered a provocation from the employers' side. This was also the general view within the movement. The strike was urged on by workers on the grassroots level in the decentralized trade unions.[55]

Even though the labor movement was the loser and the contradictions in society became sharper, this is not to say that from a long-term perspective things moved in the direction of sharper conflicts. First of all, the employers did not get the agreement they wanted, so they too were somewhat on the losing side. Additionally, a rather general feeling existed that there was no desire for this type of confrontation politics, which in the final analysis caused losses to everyone. Conflicts continued, but with a characteristic reserve based on an underlying agreement not to destroy the foundations and development of a well-functioning industrial society. In this light, Nils Elvander concludes that "the big strike in Sweden strengthened reform in the labor movement. Thanks to it having come up at such an early stage, it was able to constitute an exemplary warning when the LO and the party were exposed to the pressure

[52] Palme 1964, "Karl Staaff and the Big Strike of 1909."
[53] Schiller 1967, 206.
[54] Franzén 1985, 239.
[55] Schiller 1967, 235.

of the revolutionary atmosphere of 1917–1918." And he is able to write with an eye to Norway—"the corresponding big strike defeat was first encountered in 1921."[56] Ironically enough, the big strike was a step on the road toward the hegemony of the Social Democratic order. We will later revisit the Norwegian experience "under the pressure of the revolutionary atmosphere."

THE PARTY IS SPLIT

Branting had taken over as leader of the Social Democratic Party in Sweden in 1908. At that time the tensions within the movement were noticeable. Before the big strike the following year one of the trendsetting young men wrote to Branting about his worries that those leading the party tended toward "steering us into a *much too* revisionist, opportunistic, and unprincipled fold. Despite your revisionist temperament, I still always regard you as the strongest force that could counteract this dangerous tendency. . . . Developments among the masses are shifting to the left, the working youth are all becoming radicalized."[57] Here respect is mixed with veiled threats. It was a warning about what was on the horizon.

The contradictions within the movement came to a head during World War I, particularly after Zeta Höglund from the Federation of Social Democratic Youth was elected to the Second Chamber of Parliament. In 1915 Höglund managed to split the party over the question of rearmament. That same year he traveled to the Zimmerwald Conference, a meeting of oppositional Socialists from several European countries. Lenin was one of the delegates. Following the Russian Revolution, the Zimmerwald movement laid the basis for the Communist International (the Comintern) under the leadership of Moscow. Right from the beginning Branting distanced himself from the movement.

The great confrontation came at the Social Democratic Party Congress in February 1917. The meeting was directed by Branting and ultimately led to the splitting of the party. On a vote of no confidence the party leadership received 136 votes of confidence against the opposition's 42. Out of the eighty-seven members of the parliamentary group of Social Democrats, the opposition had only fifteen members.[58] The minority then formed Sweden's Social Democratic Left Party under Zeta Höglund. This faction welcomed the October Revolution in Russia and eventually joined the Comintern. The

[56] Elvander 1980, 45.
[57] This was Fredrik Ström. Franzén 1985, 265.
[58] Franzén 1985, 304.

Figure 6. Hjalmar Branting as a lightning rod against Bolshevism. King Gustav of Sweden is shouting to the kings of Denmark and Norway: "Why didn't you get your lightning rods organized in time?" (Drawing: Ragnvald Blix.)

road taken by Branting and the majority of the Social Democrats was different. In the autumn of 1917 he entered a coalition government with the Liberals and clearly and immediately distanced himself from the Bolshevik seizure of power in Russia.

The year 1917 was marked by the winds of revolution. During the spring the food supply was precarious, and hunger demonstrations broke out over much of Sweden. At the same time, labor councils and soldier councils were established following Soviet models.[59] It is doubtful that there was a real revolutionary threat in 1917; it has also been debated whether there was a revolutionary threat in December 1918 as a response to the revolutionary situation

[59] Andræ 1998, 297.

in Germany and in relation to the voting rights reform.[60] But by this time both the October Revolution in Russia and the Finnish civil war in February and March had provided forbidding examples of what Communism could lead to.[61] The voting rights reform was brought safely to conclusion thanks, especially, to Branting, who among other things made use of the fear of revolution. The trade union organization characteristically kept itself out of political disputes, ensuring that the situation was kept under control. The old party leadership under Branting was thus able to seize the day in spite of the force of both the emergency situation and the revolutionary pressure.

With voting rights in place, Branting broke away from the liberal coalition and formed the first Social Democratic government in 1920 with the idea of pursuing a more Socialist policy, and socialization was put on the agenda. The election that same year led to a setback for the party, however, and the government resigned. As we have seen, very little came out of the socialization drive. If anything, it revealed that having capitalism function well was a major consideration of the Social Democrats. When the party launched socialization again in 1928, it experienced a new setback.[62] Socialization became at most a parenthesis on Sweden's steady course toward reform, so these attempts at radicalization cannot overshadow the fact that, in the turbulent years after World War I, the revolutionaries were left on the sidelines. Branting's leadership was not insignificant to this steady course toward reform. This becomes clearer when one compares the Swedish situation with developments in Norway.

MARTIN TRANMÆL

The nationalistic zeal of those who represented Social Democracy in Parliament in 1905 received rough treatment at the annual national conference of the Norwegian Labor Party in 1906. This revealed itself, however, to be a mere cover for another plan—the radical wing of the party's use of the situation to capture positions.[63] The focus of criticism was parliamentary collaboration with the non-Socialist bourgeois parties in connection with the dissolution of the union with Sweden and the obscuring of the class struggle aspect that this involved. Party chairman Christopher Hornsrud had been unclear in the way he conducted these questions and was now pressured to resign. Taking a swift kick at farmer Hornsrud and his land policy, the party's

---

[60] Isaksson 1990, 269f.
[61] Isaksson 1990, 257.
[62] Simonson 1985, 219–220.
[63] Bjørgum 1998, 44.

leading ideologue, Edvard Bull Sr., wrote disapprovingly that the party had been in the process "of losing its character as a pure labor party—in any case, losing its character as the party of the industrial workers—and thus being changed into a large populist party."[64]

The "dogmatic veterans" used the occasion to "recapture the party."[65] They received support from young delegates to the national conference, of whom one of the most active was Martin Tranmæl, who had just returned from America. His conduct led to his election to the national board of the party in the same meeting. "The events of 1905 [gave] a man such as Martin Tranmæl greater opportunities to build up his opposition, his antireformist project, than had corresponding oppositional trends in other socialist parties."[66] This also gave rise to a course that extended from the dissolution of the union in 1905 to the capture of the party by Tranmæl's radical opposition in 1918.

Tranmæl was a painter's apprentice. He was charming and enthusiastic; besides being a charismatic speaker well versed in revolutionary rhetoric, he was also an ingenious politician. He was revolutionary insofar as he was all for a transformation of society through mass actions, yet he was not as completely revolutionary as myth would have it. He maintained that parliamentary work was important, and throughout his long political life he managed to keep within the established party and the established trade union movement.[67]

Tranmæl built up his position partly on the basis of the trade unions of his home region of Trøndelag and partly on the basis of the Youth Union. As in Sweden, the Norwegian Youth Union was a hotbed of the most radical elements. Tranmæl distanced himself from the Swedes, however, claiming that "this young Socialism that has been translated from the Swedish as antiparliamentarianism, the rejection of military conscription, sabotage, 'action propaganda' and so on" had to be combated. This political direction was "reactionary, stupid and harmful to the workers' struggle for liberation."[68] This statement has to be interpreted in light of the fact that his strategy was to remain within the mother party. Nevertheless his critique against the party leadership was equally clear. When it came right down to it, the "dogmatic veterans" were insufficiently radical. With great dexterity he managed to defend the Youth Union within the mother party—as a radical opposition.

In 1911 the party undertook a program calling for successive reforms to the parliamentary form of government that, over time, would lead to a quali-

---

[64] Bjørgum 1998, 532.

[65] Bjørgum 1998, 509.

[66] Bjørgum 1998, 44.

[67] Bjørgum 1998, 496–497. Bjørgum feels it is possible to reject the common position that Tranmæl was a syndicalist.

[68] Bjørgum 1998, 56. This statement was made in 1909.

tatively new society. This was a reformist program, and not sufficiently radical for the impatient. Among other things, Tranmæl, inspired by the great wave of strikes that had gripped England the same year, formulated a resolution that became the starting point for the nationwide organization of a "Trade Union Opposition" group within the national trade union organization in 1913. The resolution stated that organizational work had to be put on a "more revolutionary basis than before." Taking a swipe at the agreement of 1907 (see below), the resolution stated that "written binding agreements are to be rejected." The means of struggle were to be the strike, the sympathy strike, boycotts, obstruction, sabotage, and cooperation. Mass action was not mentioned, but it was a clear possibility. Another characteristic of his plan was that trade councils at the district level were to be given considerable influence.[69] Tranmæl's strategy was unique in that he wanted to give the leading political role to the trade unions rather than to the party.

The radical wing gained considerable influence in the wake of World War I and the Russian Revolution, events that sharply affected radicalization all over Europe. Many felt that the world was facing the great crisis of capitalism. In contrast to Branting, Tranmæl welcomed the Bolsheviks' seizure of power in Russia, and at the Labor Party's annual general meeting of 1918 he and his supporters achieved victory. At the annual general meeting the following year Tranmæl maintained that "revolution and dictatorship are an unavoidable necessity."[70] The party subsequently joined the Comintern, and was one of the few mainstream Social Democratic parties in Western Europe to do so. (As it happened, this occurred at the same time that Branting and the Swedish Social Democrats were collaborating with the liberals over the great reform of voting rights.) In 1921 a minority of reformist Social Democrats broke away, subsequently forging the Norwegian Social Democratic Party.

The next act was played out amid great drama in 1923. The Comintern had sent one of the leaders of the Soviet Communist Party, Nicholai Bukarin, as its representative at the Labor Party's yearly general meeting. Tranmæl clashed with Bukarin over what had been labeled "the Moscow theses," which maintained that the Communist parties were to be elite groups of professional revolutionaries subordinate to a central leadership in Moscow.[71] The Moscow theses split the labor movement throughout Europe. According to Eric Hobsbawm, this strategy chosen by the Russian Bolsheviks was their fatal misstep.[72]

---

[69] Bjørgum 1998, 83.

[70] Haakon Lie 1988, 296.

[71] The split of 1923 has been much discussed. See, for example, Egge (2003). H. Lie (1988) gives an exhaustive portrayal of the split (354f.).

[72] Hobsbawm 1995, 69.

Figure 7. Martin Tranmæl, *right*, a journeyman painter, became the great strategist of the Norwegian Labor Party from around 1910 into the post–World War II period. His revolutionary line was victorious within the party in 1918. Later he led the party out of the Comintern and onto a reformist path. The man with the pipe is his foremost protégé, Einar Gerhardsen, who became prime minister in 1945 and personified like no one else the golden age of Social Democracy. (Photo: Arbeiderbevegelsens arkiv.)

The conflict over the Moscow theses resulted in Tranmæl, who had led the Labor Party into the Comintern five years earlier, now receiving majority support from the party to leave that organization. With a view to the ill-defined conditions for party cooperation with the farmers, and in light of the fact that it was through the support of the farmers' parties that the Social Democrats in both Sweden and Norway were able to seize power in the 1930s, it is worth noting that in 1923 Tranmæl rejected the Comintern's call for a worker-peasant government. On this issue Tranmæl stood together with Zeta Höglund, leader of the breakaway Communist Party in Sweden. Eventually Höglund also broke with the Comintern.

Thus there were three Socialist parties in Norway after 1923, a result of the breakaway of the reformist wing in 1921 followed by the breakaway of the Communist wing in 1923. In the parliamentary election of 1924 the three parties competed against one another. The mainstream Labor Party received more support than the two breakaway parties combined, and Tranmæl found himself a representative in Parliament, where he sat for one term. Gradually a period of calm ensued, and in 1927 the Labor Party merged with the small reformist Social Democratic Party. At last the mainstream Social Democrats were caught up with the strong democratic tradition in Norway. This was a precondition for the success that followed.

WORKER SCANDINAVIANISM

There was a particularly close cooperation between the labor movements of Scandinavia at the beginning of the twentieth century, especially between Norway and Sweden. This had its roots back in the nineteenth century and had been formalized at the First Scandinavian Labor Congress, held in Gothenburg in 1886. "Worker Scandinavianism" soon became a popular concept.[73] It is reasonable to view this fellowship in its early phase as expedited by the relative marginalization of the Socialists in the national context, on the one hand, and their common link to the German Social Democrats and the Kautskyian Marxists, on the other. Herbert Tingsten has pointed out that the international links gradually had to yield as the labor movements became more integrated within their national contexts. This was not applicable to the links between the Swedish-Norwegian movements, however. There were certain oscillations in the relationship between the two labor movements due to national considerations or diverging strategies, but in the larger perspective the relationship remained close, even during periods in which the mainstream Social Democratic parties each chose their own road.

[73] Fostervoll 1935, 8.

The close cooperation between the two labor movements was partly destroyed when nationalistic considerations became too strong during the dissolution of the union between the two countries in 1905. The Scandinavian labor congresses continued after 1905, however. In 1907 one such congress was held in Kristiania (which twenty years later would change its name to Oslo) even if there were still "certain wounded feelings among the Swedes toward their Norwegian party comrades."[74]

There was a new congress held in Stockholm in 1912, but now divergent views that moved beyond national were being articulated. At this meeting Tranmæl put forward the program of the Norwegian Trade Union Opposition, but he suffered a crushing defeat on a resolution based on the proposal he had advanced. The leader of the Norwegian LO, Ole O. Lian, gave a two-hour speech that in all essentials was a refutation of Tranmæl's position. The discussion of the Norwegian opposition's point of view came to dominate this particular Scandinavian congress. Although Tranmæl's defeat was a crushing blow, he had a much friendlier reception at the Socialist youth congress that had been arranged in conjunction with the main labor congress. Later the same year he toured Sweden for three weeks spreading his message.[75]

Tranmæl's behavior in 1912 is symptomatic of the joint public arena for the labor movement that existed in Scandinavia, and especially for the Swedish and Norwegian labor movements. This meant that the confrontations between the wings of the Norwegian movement were able to take place partly on Swedish ground. Scandinavia and the Scandinavian congresses became a common central battlefield for both the reformists and the revolutionaries.[76]

Despite this struggle between the revolutionaries and the reformists, the Scandinavian dimension was unifying. In the 1912 congress a statement was adopted that called on the Social Democratic parties of Scandinavia to take the lead in the further development of cooperation between the Nordic nations.[77] Moreover, cooperation between the labor movements was institutionalized with the establishment of the Committee for Scandinavian Cooperation.

On the other hand, clear boundaries were drawn against having an amalgamation that was too close. As Branting put it, "to a certain degree the different preconditions involved different responses."[78] The showdown between the Norwegians at the congress had served to chill their blood. Tranmæl's revolutionary line in the Norwegian party would also make cooperation more

---

[74] Grass 1988, 80.
[75] Bjørgum 1998, 102–106.
[76] Fostervoll 1935, 9.
[77] Henning Nielsen 1938, 3:30.
[78] Grass 1988, 80.

difficult in the years following 1917. The Committee for Cooperation lay comatose for some time. Cooperation between the trade union organizations, both centrally and in terms of the local unions, continued, however, and in 1932 the Committee for Cooperation was revitalized. Initially the Norwegians participated only as observers.[79] But cooperation became particularly close after 1945.

Cooperation within the labor movement gave birth to a similar collaboration between Scandinavian employer organizations. The first meeting was held in 1907, and meetings were held rather frequently thereafter. We have seen that the times were conflict laden, and cooperation was not attributed to "blue-eyed Scandinavianism, but to hard realities."[80] Both of the sides were involved in working life and thus sought to strengthen their fellowship across the borders.

Despite the differences we saw in the previous chapter, there is scarcely any area in which mutual influence has been of greater significance than in relations in working life. The road to the parallel crisis settlements (1933 in Sweden and 1935 in Norway), the Main Agreement (1935 in Norway), and the Saltsjöbad Agreement (1938 in Sweden; see below), and further to political cooperation once a hegemonic position had been secured in each country, is difficult to understand without being aware of the close relations between the labor movements in Sweden and Norway, partly on the personal level, that extended through the whole history of the movements. "Worker Scandinavianism" was realized to a high degree—perhaps not so much by coordinated activities as by mutual influence within what we might call a Scandinavian worker-public.

HOW RADICAL?

Discussion has taken place partly concerning *why* the Labor Party and the workers in Norway stood firmly with revolutionary Marxism for so long, in contrast to the mainstream of the Swedish labor movement, and partly about *whether* the Norwegian industrial workers really were as radical as their rhetoric would indicate. How should the events be interpreted? First, it is important to note that, compared with the Social Democratic parties on the Continent, Sweden was an exception.[81] Norway was closer to the general development in Europe even though most of the Social Democrats on the

[79] Blidberg 1984, 10–11, 39f.
[80] H. Nielsen 1938, 3:29.
[81] This is one of the main points with Berman (2006).

Continent stayed outside the Comintern. It has nevertheless been considered most problematic to explain the radicalism of the Norwegians.

One common theory stems from Edvard Bull Sr.—a historian and a follower of Tranmæl through the various phases from Marxism to reformism—who maintains that the Norwegian working class resulted from a late and rapid industrialization and this made it more rootless than, for example, the Swedish, and therefore more predisposed toward "revolutionary thinking." Bull also points out that the early democratization of Norway made cooperation with the radical liberals of no current interest. In addition he stresses the decentralized structure of the Norwegian movement (in contrast to the more centralized movement in Sweden) and the fact that, unlike Sweden, the opposition had its roots not merely in the youth movement but also in the trade union movement.[82]

Beyond this, Bull mentions the role played by Tranmæl himself, a feature that has been mentioned by several writers.[83] Sweden had no Tranmæl. But this argument can be turned on its head: Norway had no Branting. In their eagerness to explain, historians often have a tendency to present the course of events as predetermined, as something that had to happen. Historical coincidence is seldom accorded a place. In reality, history is full of coincidence. The chance actor will, under given conditions, be able to affect the course of history. Branting and Tranmæl both were such actors or "action ideologues," a term coined by Rune Slagstad. They were bearers of effective ideology and entered positions and situations in which they could convert their ideas into political actions that had great consequences.[84]

The revolutionaries built their project on the basis of imported social analysis; that is, they had no analysis of the conditions in Norway. As a result, it is not clear how revolutionary the Norwegian working class actually was. It does not seem "necessary to assume that the working class in Norway was more radical than in other countries."[85] Conversely, it is possible to view the situation in Sweden as opposite of Bull's perception, namely that the working class was more radical or action-oriented in Sweden than in Norway. Under the pressure of the prevailing revolutionary spirit, violence was immanent and close at hand. It "was found in rich measure in Finland and it was found in the form of disturbances and plundering, in fact more in reformist countries such as Denmark and Sweden than in leftist Norway."[86] The Norwegian

[82] Bull Sr., 1922.

[83] See, for example, Bjørgum 1998, 511.

[84] Slagstad 1998, 447. This is parallel to what Berman calls "programmatic beliefs"—"ideational framework within which *programs* of action are formulated." Berman 1998, 21.

[85] Olstad 1998, 87.

[86] Andræ 1998, 321.

Labor Party scarcely had the support of the working class. No one, either in Sweden or Norway, had any strategy or made any practical preparations with a view to taking revolutionary mass actions.[87] One cannot ignore the fact that the conditions themselves might have set actions in motion but, to put it mildly, there is very little likelihood that such actions could have led to the replacement of parliamentary democracy with a Soviet-style republic based on workers' and soldiers' councils. Moreover, even though the Socialists' parliamentary work during this radical phase has been considered of lesser importance, breaking this work off was out of the question.

The strategy of the bourgeois society was to follow two lines in relation to the labor movement. First there was organized surveillance and a military buildup in anticipation of a revolutionary situation.[88] The second, and more important, line from the larger perspective was to increase flexibility and compliance with regard to the demands of the workers. In other words, the non-Socialist bourgeois society continued a policy, rooted far back in the nineteenth century, that aimed to integrate the workers, or the new society's proletariat, into the national society. This was carried out by means of democratizing the political field through regulating working life, instituting corporatist procedures, being compliant toward economic demands, and establishing increasing numbers of welfare plans. For a long time the Labor Party had stood on the sidelines in relation to this reform work, while at the same time becoming increasingly aware that perhaps there was most to gain by working within this parliamentary democracy.

"A PECULIAR LEGALIZATION ACTIVITY"

The central trade union organization in Sweden split, with leftist factions peeling off. The most important of these leftist groups was the syndicalist Workers Central Organization of Sweden, which had been founded following the big strike of 1909, and in 1920 it had more than thirty thousand members.[89] The importance of the split should not be exaggerated; the Swedish trade union movement was in general homogeneous.[90] This was also the case in Norway, where there was no splitting along political lines.[91] Tranmæl's radical Trade Union Opposition remained within the mother organization; however, it never managed to gain control over the organization in the same

---

[87] Fure 1983, 58, passim.
[88] Fure 1983, 527f., 543f.
[89] Nycander 2002, 36f.
[90] Åmark 1998, 365.
[91] Maurseth 1987, 349.

way it did over the party. At its height in 1918 the membership of the Trade Union Opposition was one-fifth of the total membership of the entire LO.[92] "[L]oss of the trade union movement was more important than victory in the party."[93] To be sure, at the LO congress of 1920 several of the points of the Trade Union Opposition's platform had their breakthrough.[94] But the significance of this was no more than a marginal political radicalization. The economic crisis that began that same year did not nourish the revolutionary tendencies; the reality was closer to the reverse.

A key question for the trade union movement was how far one could go in terms of corporatist collaboration. A breakthrough of sorts for such cooperation to be known as the "September Compromise" took place in Denmark in 1899 after a major labor dispute. The compromise was a general agreement between employers and employees requiring the mutual acceptance of the respective organizations and an allocation of rights and duties. It was a compromise between two formally equal partners—a collective agreement intended to contribute to peace in the workplace.

The first step in a similar direction was taken in Sweden with the "December Compromise" of 1906. For the first time the Employers Association engaged in direct negotiations with the LO. The compromise affirmed management rights of work control while at the same time acknowledging the workers' right to organize.[95] Nevertheless, the agreement was not clear when it came to the rights of governing and control, particularly the employers' rights to hire and fire. Thus the LO found it necessary to stress that the unions would not consider it a breaking of the agreement if workers refused to work alongside strikebreakers. Within the ranks of both parties to the agreement, the "December Compromise" led to strife and unpleasantness. Some felt that the compromises had gone too far. Nor was the compromise a deterrent to the big strike three years later. Despite this, it has been considered an important step in the direction of establishing a legal system for the labor market.

The following year, in 1907, a nationwide wage agreement was entered into for the first time in Norway. This occurred in the metal trades. The "Iron Agreement" held a status in Norway similar to that of the December Compromise in Sweden. With this agreement the right to organize was specifically ratified. Managerial rights of employers and the minimum wage principle were adopted.[96] As had been the case in Sweden, a considerable amount of internal discord broke out among the Norwegian signatories in the wake of

[92] Maurseth 1987, 280.
[93] Olstad 1998, 89.
[94] Maurseth 1987, 121ff.
[95] Nycander 2002, 24f.
[96] Bjørnhaug et al. 2000, 19f.: "An epoch-making agreement."

the agreement. Opposition to allowing the employers full management rights was particularly strong and persistent in Norway.[97] Overall, the employers were in a weaker position than their counterparts in Sweden. After the big strike of 1909 the Swedish employers' rights to dictate working conditions were strengthened, while the organized workers in Norway collectively made use of the opportunity for individual negotiations under the agreement. The problems this created for employers led them to a greater tendency to seek support from the state and the ordinary legislative process.[98]

In the wake of the 1906 and 1907 agreements attempts were made to replace local struggles with central negotiations and settlements. As has been said, these agreements were a "starting point for a historical compromise between capital and labor."[99] They point toward the system that would acquire its final structure with the Main Agreement in Norway in 1935 and the Saltsjöbad Agreement in Sweden in 1938, and thereby toward the strong corporatist elements of the Social Democratic order.

The state played a subordinate role in developing these agreements: "The collective labor legislation in Sweden was created by the civil society."[100] In Norway Paal Berg, the Liberal minister who soon would become a driving force for the new labor legislation, referred to the process as "a remarkable and peculiar legalization activity that has redeemed itself in the wage agreements."[101] There were, however, some significant differences between the two countries.

Like the radical liberals of Sweden, the Norwegian Liberal Party saw the state as holding superior interests and wanted to use it for all it was worth. Since the Liberals were much stronger in Norway, the state corporatist feature became more noticeable there than in Sweden. As Norwegian Liberal prime minister Gunnar Knudsen said in 1915: "The banner of the future must be the struggle against class struggle. One step in this struggle is *compulsory arbitration* of industrial disputes—to obtain a judgment instead of resorting to strikes and lockouts."[102] In Knudsen's view, the strike was a foreign element intruding into parliamentary democracy. Thus it was that the Liberals made compulsory arbitration integral to their program, just as the Liberal leader Karl Staaff did in Sweden as well. The difference was simply that Knudsen would achieve a breakthrough for his policy, unlike Staaff and the Swedish Liberals. The question of compulsory arbitration of industrial disputes never

---

[97] Heiret et al. 2003, 6.
[98] Heiret et al. 2003, 48, 62.
[99] Olstad 1991, 66.
[100] Nycander 2002, 25.
[101] Paul Knutsen 1994, 61.
[102] As cited by P. Knutsen 1994, 56.

really arose in Sweden. Norway passed the first legislation regarding compulsory arbitration in 1916. Paal Berg would later warn Knudsen against coming on too strongly in favor of compulsory arbitration such that it would provoke the major organizations on both sides. Nevertheless, it has been used ad hoc in many conflicts right up to the present.

Paal Berg was the man behind the Industrial Disputes Act in Norway in 1915. With this law, both *compulsory mediation* and the Labor Court were established.[103] Sweden had to wait until 1928 to get corresponding legislation. This was put forward by Liberal prime minister C. G. Ekman (the first prime minister from a working-class background) and provoked strong opposition from the Swedish LO. It came to function to the satisfaction of everyone, however. In his book about the development of the labor market, Svante Nycander could state that "[t]he campaign against the legislative procedure for collective agreement came to be viewed as one of the labor movement's greatest political mistakes."[104] Thus in both Sweden and Norway we find an activity that set up legal frameworks through collective agreements that, in turn, would gradually prepare the ground for a well-functioning mediated corporatism.

THE LEVEL OF CONFLICT ESCALATES

Of course the road to corporatization and regulation of the labor market was not straight and smooth. Many felt that too much had been given up in the agreements, and that there had been an acceptance of class collaboration within capitalist society. The big strike in Sweden followed not many years behind the "December Compromise." The alleged breaking of the agreement became a central theme, as well as the main reason that the radical liberal Karl Staaff went out against the strikers.[105] And we saw that the Trade Union Opposition in Norway demanded that written binding agreements should not be entered into. In addition, even though the threat of revolution was more remote during the crises after 1920, the unrest in the labor market was not; the reverse was closer to the truth. The crises led to the employers' demand for a drop in wages, which gave rise to many labor conflicts. This was the case in both countries but particularly in Norway, where the crisis was more prolonged.

Norway found itself under the weight of great conflict in the spring of 1920. Negotiations had not moved forward, and the government opted for compulsory arbitration. To a large extent the judges concurred with the de-

---

[103] P. Knutsen 1994, 63.

[104] Nycander 2002, 33. Isaksson 1996, 323. (P. A. Hansson had originally been in favor of the legislation [ibid., 321].)

[105] Palme 1964, 157ff.; Nycander 2002, 35.

mands of the workers, providing confirmation of the established society's accommodating attitude toward the workers' demands. It also strengthened the confidence of the workers in the state as superior to particular sectional interests. No sooner had the judges made their decision than crisis occurred, however, bringing both new wage-related demands and new conflicts. As a result, 1921 became a year of lockouts and strikes, with the loss of 3.5 million working days. The big strike that broke out that year brought to mind the big strike in Sweden in 1909. It "came as close as possible to being the mass action that Martin Tranmæl had spoken about with such glee."[106] As with the big strike in Sweden, this one was on the whole a victory for employers.

In Norway the dramatic iron strike of 1923 represented "the most significant attempt to carry through a labor action according to classic Bolshevik guidelines."[107] The strike broke out in the iron industry following warning of a wage cut of 5 percent that had been authorized according to the relevant wage agreement. The strike was thus illegal. At the outset it was limited, but it grew rapidly and triggered a lockout that, in turn, triggered a sympathy strike. This episode provided "a forbidding example of what could happen when the class struggle went out of organizational control."[108] As one might expect, there was conflict over strategy among both workers and employers. Central figures in the leadership on both sides wanted rapprochement and moderation.

The decisive action in resolving the strike was the intervention of the Conservative government. The settlement called for a show of accommodation by the employers because the period of the wage agreement had run out, making the strike legal; moreover, changing economic developments made the wage cut less crucial. Thus "the rapprochement between the moderate, legally legitimate, and society-building forces in the LO and the Conservative government [involved] a constellation of interests that set the decisive stamp on the conclusion of the great conflict." In all essentials the conclusion was a victory for the workers while at the same time marginalizing the more aggressive elements on both sides, and once again it was demonstrated that there was scarcely any basis for "instrumental interpretations of the state as a tool of the ruling class."[109]

The role of the state in labor conflicts was not clarified by these events. In fact, a step was taken in the opposite direction in Norway in 1927 with the ratification of what has been called "labor-hostile" legislation. This referred to a new law on compulsory arbitration (also called "the jailhouse law"), a sharp-

---

[106] H. Lie 1988, 333–334.
[107] P. Knutsen 1994, 96.
[108] P. Knutsen 1994, 156.
[109] P. Knutsen 1994, 163.

ening of the penal code to strengthen the protection of rights of strikebreakers and a change in the Labor Disputes Act that sharpened the demands on the trade unions with respect to the question of their liability in connection with the breakdown of tariff negotiations. For the most part, however, the LO referred the struggle against labor-hostile laws to the parliamentary arena, which meant that serious conflict was avoided.

In 1928 there was a large conflict in response to an arbitration decision representing a 4 percent wage reduction in the Norwegian building trades. This led to an unlawful strike, and compulsory arbitration became discredited for a lengthy period of time. There was a large-scale lockout in 1931 that ended in a "draw" and a strong resolve from both sides to avoid such conflicts in the future. In the course of this otherwise rather peaceful conflict, what was called the Menstad confrontation (named after the Norsk Hydro port at Skien, where the conflict took place) between striking workers and army troops occurred in response to contending views about strikebreaking.

There were also great conflicts in Sweden during the crisis at the beginning of the 1920s, breaking out in 1923 and 1925. Things became calmer after this period but, once again, there was a powerful upsurge in the level of conflict at the beginning of the 1930s, this time in relation to the new Depression.[110] Throughout the 1920s and beginning of the 1930s attempts were continually made to regulate the labor market through legislation, but there were great chasms between all of the proposed laws and what was actually put into effect.[111] The collective agreement of 1928 was one exception but, as we have seen, it came too late and was met with skepticism. Characteristically for Sweden, the trade unions together with the employers' organizations took on the role of regulating the labor market while the state generally stood on the sidelines. As Nils Elvander writes, "the opposition of the Swedish trade union movement to legislated interference in conflict resolution was even more solid and consistent than that of Norway's Labor Organization."[112]

One of the most dramatic events in the history of labor conflict in Scandinavia took place in 1931 when an unarmed column of Swedish demonstrators in Ådalen was fired upon by army troops. Five demonstrators were killed and an equal number wounded. The shots in Ådalen and a confrontation in Menstad, Norway, the same year had great symbolic value in their respective countries. Concrete and dramatic events of this type will always be used in the struggle over the interpretation of history. These two events can thus be

---

[110] Nycander 2002, 71; Westerståhl 1945, 153f.

[111] Westerståhl 1945, 417f.

[112] Elvander 1980, 72.

fashioned to strengthen class-based identities. Naturally enough, this is more applicable to Ådalen than to Menstad, where no lives were lost. The shots fired at Ådalen led to a spontaneous series of demonstrations. This was followed by a prohibition on demonstrations in Stockholm and the imposition of long prison sentences for several of the workers who had been involved in the events. The leader of the Communist Party and several of the party's editors received sentences. The events at Ådalen did not lead to further confrontations, however.

It is not impossible to consider that an event such as the Ådalen confrontation could have had different consequences if it had taken place in the revolutionary atmosphere of 1917–1918. But in 1931 the general attitude was in favor of peace in the workplace. This meant that the Social Democratic leadership under Per Albin Hansson did not want to use the confrontation to sharpen the class struggle. Hansson maintained that the event was the result of unfortunate circumstances and that much of the responsibility lay with the Communists. For him, isolating the Communists was a primary concern. He felt that the conflict should prompt broad political cooperation across party boundaries; that is, among the Social Democrats and the non-Socialist parties. It seems that he garnered relatively strong support for this interpretation and that the issue of Ådalen contributed to the election breakthrough of the Social Democrats in 1932.

Hansson's interpretation became the hegemonic view throughout the Social Democratic regime's "happy moment," right up to approximately 1970. Then Ådalen was again brought out as "something of an icon." In the struggle between the Social Democrats and the Liberal opposition over the interpretation of Swedish history, it has been important to exploit this icon.[113] From our point of view, however, the most important thing to note is the fact that the dramatic events of Ådalen did not obstruct progress toward the Saltsjöbad Agreement and relative peace in the workplace.

THE SOLIDARITY GAME IS ESTABLISHED

The confusing mix of revolutionary and reformist positions that one finds far into the interwar period can perhaps be explained if we take as our starting point the notion that modernization was a common project. The labor movement was not only willing to peacefully coexist with capitalism; it wanted a form of capitalism that was as effective as possible, as we saw in chapter 1. We

---

[113] Roger Johansson 2001, 447f.; Nycander 2002, 59.

have seen how relatively easily progressive bourgeois forces were able to collaborate with leading forces within the labor movement, preferably remaining in the wings in a "partnership of top people."[114]

Furthermore, a comparison between Sweden and Norway invites us to analyze the conflicts as a kind of "solidarity game"; that is, we can find a connection between the fact that Swedish capitalism functioned better than the Norwegian form, while at the same time the Norwegian labor movement was more radical than the Swedish. In order to have a well-functioning capitalism—something that both parties were interested in—it is assumed that the two parties, capitalist and labor, must play their respective roles in the game. If one of the parties, for instance the capitalists, does not do so, then the system does not function, and the opposing party's opposition has to take the form of a critique of the system; in other words, it has to become more revolutionary.

The story of the Aker Mechanical Works by the Norwegian writer Dag Solstad is illustrative.[115] He takes up the rise of what he calls "the compromise" in 1919 between the declared revolutionary workers and the owner of the Aker plant, the shipping magnate Fred Olsen. The compromise was expressed externally when Olsen handed over the stock dividends for 1918–1919 to the workers, and again when the workers gathered money for a wreath of silver following the death of Olsen's wife shortly thereafter. In addition to spurring this demonstration of self-consciousness, the compromise formed the prelude to a mutual undercurrent of sympathy between the two parties. One condition for this compromise was clearly that Fred Olsen was extremely clever in steering the plant through the difficult interwar period. By being a skilful capitalist, Olsen was thus able to behead the revolutionary hydra.

This solidarity game began with the December Compromise in Sweden in 1906 and the Iron Agreement in Norway in 1907, and it found its final ratifications in Norway's Main Agreement of 1935 and the Saltsjöbad Agreement of 1938 in Sweden. This latter pair of agreements represented a comprehensive symmetrical framework anchored in both non-Socialist and Social Democratic opinion.[116] The agreements framed how negotiations between parties in both working life and labor conflicts were to be handled. The agreements of 1935 and 1938 constituted the second of the two "social pacts" we referred to in the introduction as the basis of the hegemonic rule of Social Democracy, that between labor and agriculture and that between labor and capital. We have seen (chapter 2) how the first of these pacts was reached earlier in the 1930s in the wake the crises settlements.

---

[114] This expression is from Edvard Bull Jr. P. Knudsen (1994) has shown that this phenomenon goes further back in time than Bull had thought.

[115] Solstad 1990.

[116] Nycander 2002, 83.

Two conditions thrust their way into negotiating the last phase of the agreements in 1935 and 1938 and contributed to their final ratification. First, political initiatives had been taken in both countries to ensure more comprehensive legal regulation of the labor market, but both parties were against this. They wanted to keep the initiative and demonstrate that they themselves were able to keep peace in the workplace by means of agreements between the organizations. In other words, we see an element of defensive strategy in relation to state power. Second, the Social Democrats had recently taken over the governments in both countries. Consequently, the labor organizations had to adapt their policies to the society-building project of Social Democracy.[117]

We have seen that the Swedes steered clear of state intervention to a greater degree than did the Norwegians. Another characteristic difference was that centralized trade union leadership was utilized in Sweden to secure peace in the workplace.[118] In Norway trade union opposition within the labor movement was stronger, and correspondingly the central coordinating leadership was weaker.[119] Despite the differences, it is the similarities in the two countries' agreements that leave the strongest impression. Additionally, it can be shown that the agreements largely functioned as intended. Both countries entered a period of relative peace in the workplace. Thus these agreements are viewed as national treasures, cornerstones upon which the Social Democratic order was built.

PER ALBIN HANSSON AND THE "PEOPLE'S HOME"

In 1932 Per Albin Hansson formed a purely Social Democratic government in Sweden. Coupled with the crisis compromise with the farmers the following year, this signaled the beginning of Social Democracy's period of hegemony. In the words of the biographer Anders Isaksson: "Through his own actions Per Albin was Social Democracy's foremost pioneer, both a shrewd tactician and a careful strategist who little by little and with great persistence changed the self-image of the Social Democrats from a class party to a broad people's party; indeed, a symbol of modernity, rationality, Swedishness, patriotism and national pride."[120] Hansson was to become the "father of the country," leading the way into the long period of Social Democratic hegemony in Sweden. It might almost sound as though transforming the workers' party from class party to people's party was the work of one man, which of course it was not.

[117] Heiret et al. 2003, 96, 99.
[118] Elvander 1980, 73.
[119] Heiret et al. 2003, 47.
[120] Isaksson 2001, 232.

First, the soil for a national people's party was prepared by young thinkers of the labor movement such as Ernst Wigforss, Rickard Sandler, and Nils Karleby, among others. Especially influential was Karleby's book *Socialism in Confrontation with Reality*, which was published in 1926 (the same year that Karleby died at age thirty-four). He points to the common ground of Socialism and liberalism, but above all he emphasizes the demand for full integration of the working class into all aspects of national life.[121] It should also be noted that the same transformation of the Labor Party took place in Norway, although there one did not find a completely comparable gestalt to Hansson. But the manner in which the transformation unfolded in Sweden can perhaps be ascribed to the person: Hansson demonstrated how "to seize Time by her flowing locks and lead her down the right path."[122]

Hansson came from modest circumstances and became interested in the labor movement early in life. He was a pronounced organization man, intelligent and articulate, but no theoretician; he was radical. Isaksson's second volume bears the title *The Revolutionary*, covering the World War I years through 1918. Hansson followed "to be sure, a revolutionary line," Isaksson writes, but it was "a revolution that was tactical and determined by the times." Hansson was critical of the Bolshevik Revolution, and there was no doubt that he would follow Branting and the main current when Höglund and those consorting with him broke away to the left. On the other hand, he was "uncontrollably revolutionary" during the hunger demonstrations of 1917 and during the suffrage negotiations in 1918. He did not hesitate to advocate extraparliamentary means. All democratic drives had occurred "under the pressure of mass movement from outside the Parliament," he declared.[123] In relation to Branting he was the young radical critic, but nevertheless followed in Branting's footsteps.

Hansson entered Parliament in 1918 and held the post of defense minister in all three Branting governments. Following Branting's death in 1925 Hansson became acting chairman of the party, winning the position by election in 1928. He became prime minister in 1932 and gradually was hailed as "father of the country." At first he was viewed to some extent with patronizing skepticism by the party's group of strong intellectuals (Arthur Engberg, Rickard Sandler, and Ernst Wigforss, among others), who registered the course of his career with amazement. Hansson's strength lay in his energy, steadfastness, desire for power, and good contacts at the grassroots level of the party. It is

---

[121] Bergström 1989, 54. English edition 1992, 169.
[122] This turn of phrase belongs to Esaias Tegnér and here is cited from Göran Nilsson 1990, 171.
[123] Isaksson 1990, 93, 209–210, 19.

perhaps not particularly fruitful to ask whether he was actually a revolution-ary or a democrat. When the suffrage reform had been carried through and he was seated in Parliament, he became captivated by the system and soon became an extremely skilful parliamentarian. It was apparently easy for him to set aside his Marxist rhetoric.

In 1928, the same year he was elected party chairman, Hansson gave the famed speech in which he made use of the notion of the "people's home" (*Folkhemmet*), which would eventually become the great unifying metaphor of Swedish Social Democracy. The concept was not new;[124] it had been used around 1900, for example, by Rudolf Kjellén, the leader of the Young Con-servatives. Hansson thus had links to a conservative tradition—or rather, perhaps, to a general way of thinking about society in Sweden. In addition, the term has been shown to have roots in the own-home politics in evidence around the beginning of the twentieth century.[125] Hansson was able to pick up the rhetoric from these traditions and lift it to the national level.

Still, the 1928 speech did not represent a radical break in Hansson's rheto-ric. Initially the "people's home" concept was used only provisionally, and at times interchangeably with the notion of "compatriot home," and we find related rhetoric further back in time. According to Isaksson, the "Per Albin line" was born from an improvised election speech in 1921 in which Hansson ended with the words: "For a Sweden that is a just and happy place for the people—long live the fatherland!" "The fatherland," like "the people's home," belonged to the rhetoric of the conservatives; it verged on breaking with eti-quette for a Social Democrat to use it in this manner in 1921.[126]

By shoving aside the class-struggle rhetoric in favor of a rhetoric of national fellowship, Hansson contributed to removing the social integration proj-ect from the hands of the bourgeoisie. It was Social Democracy that would lead to and define the foundation for integration in the final phase of nation building. The whole conception of the workers standing on the periphery of established society was replaced by the idea that they represented a natural part of it, and that they should reform it from within. This was the crux of a turning point in the mentality of the movement.

Hansson's rhetoric reflected his manner of thinking about politics. It was natural for him to talk about the "people's home" and the "fatherland." That he managed to get his startled fellow party members to go along with this change is something that Isaksson attributes to Hansson's legitimacy as a rev-

---

[124] For example, in general, see Isaksson 1996, 172ff., and Zander 2001, 221ff.
[125] Edling 1996, 384.
[126] Isaksson 1996, 185f.

olutionary proletarian. No one could suspect him of being the errand boy of the bourgeois class. Therefore he was precisely the one to lead the movement on this quite dramatic about-face in redefining the party, turning it from a class struggle party into the people's party. Credibility gives maneuvering room to those who are audacious. A parallel event occurred when Arvid Lindman managed to take the conservatives with him on the issue of universal suffrage for men in 1907.[127]

"Democracy" was the central word in Hansson's rhetoric; however, he never systematically expanded what he meant by the term. The issue is discussed by Anders Isaksson in the volume of his biography titled *Father of the Country*. In several places Isaksson comes back to Hansson's characteristic paternalism. He had a tendency to consider the freedoms of democracy as a gift given to the people by the state in return for their loyalty: "In his role as the prime interpreter of the people's will, he put himself at the center of the political universe and later came to equate points of view critical to his own public stewardship as malicious attempts to undermine democracy itself." According to Isaksson, these patriarchal traits were rooted in the old authoritarian methods of governance.[128] They certainly also had a basis in Hansson's personality and emerged gradually as he took pleasure in his role as "father of the country." But it is also possible that this behavior was relatively easy to accept in Sweden, with its long, unbroken tradition of authoritarian forms of rule.

JOHAN NYGAARDSVOLD AND THE PEOPLE'S PARTY

It is quite natural to compare Per Albin Hansson and Norwegian Johan Nygaardsvold. They were born about the same time, in 1885 and 1879 respectively. They both came from modest backgrounds, and throughout their lives they were linked to the mainstream of the Social Democratic movement, which meant that they had both experienced revolutionary periods. They entered their houses of parliament (the Swedish Riksdag and the Norwegian Storting) in 1918 and 1916 respectively, each becoming comfortably and effectively ensnared within the parliamentary process. They were both political practitioners who looked skeptically at long-winded theorizing. Each introduced the hegemonic Social Democratic regime in his own country when he became prime minister (Hansson held the office from 1932 to 1946 and

[127] Isaksson 1990, 18.
[128] Isaksson 1990, 352, 313, 127.

Nygaardsvold from 1935 to 1945). Like Hansson, Nygaardsvold was central in turning the Labor Party from a class struggle party to a popular people's party. Nygaardsvold felt himself to be deeply rooted in things Norwegian, and the fatherland rhetoric rested lightly on his tongue.[129]

Yet there were several notable differences. Nygaardsvold did not seek power; to the contrary, he was almost shoved into the positions he came to occupy. And he was shoved into them—and out of them—by Tranmæl, who was the great strategist in the party through the interwar period and into the postwar period. Nygaardsvold had his base in the local party organization and in the parliamentary group, where he became the natural leader. Unlike Per Albin Hansson, he was never party chairman, nor did he aspire to be. According to the party's bylaws, the parliamentary group was subject to party control, which in reality meant "the triumvirate of Youngstorget."[130] Youngstorget, in Oslo, was the Labor Party headquarters, and the triumvirate consisted of Tranmæl and his two protégés, party chairman Oscar Torp and party secretary Einar Gerhardsen. But gradually the role of Nygaardsvold and the parliamentary group matured into something more independent in relation to the triumvirate. This was particularly the case following the election of 1927, when the Labor Party became the largest party in the Storting.

Government crisis occurred in 1928, and the Liberal government had to resign. The Labor Party, as the largest party, was asked by King Haakon to form a government. The party accepted, and Nygaardsvold was asked to take the job of prime minister. He refused, and the task fell to Christopher Hornsrud. The new government's platform was demonstrably radical. When it was insinuated that capital was fleeing from the country, the non-Socialist majority took up the affair and threw out the new government after it had been in power for only eighteen days. This episode was construed by the radical Social Democrats within the party as evidence that the parliamentary route was not the way forward, thereby strengthening the extraparliamentary forces within the party.[131]

This renewed emphasis on class struggle led to a setback in the following election, requiring the development of a new direction for the party. By the election of 1933 it had abandoned the antiparliamentary line and begun to concentrate on an active crisis policy. The party made a strong advance in that election, and Tranmæl immediately launched Nygaardsvold as the party's prime ministerial candidate.[132] Nygaardsvold emerged at this point

---

[129] Berntsen 1991, 299.
[130] Berntsen 1991, 264.
[131] Berntsen 1991, 264–272.
[132] Berntsen 1991, 344.

as an independent and powerful politician and compelled general respect as a parliamentarian. Great strategist that he was, Tranmæl understood to the fullest extent how valuable Nygaardsvold was for the party in the current situation. With the crisis compromise of 1935, Nygaardsvold was able to form a pure Labor Party government with the support of the Farmers' Party, just as Per Albin Hansson had done in Sweden three years earlier.

The year 1935 became the "remarkable year" according to the historian Sverre Steen. The bitter conflicts had been settled: "With Nygaardsvold's government in the lead and with the support of the young Farmers' Party, the Norwegian people turned back to their old society." But while Isaksson sets Hansson in the tradition of the old patriarchal form of rule, Steen sets Nygaardsvold in the tradition stemming from "the fathers of Eidsvoll."[133] (The phrase "fathers of Eidsvoll" refers to those who gathered at Eidsvoll to draw up the Constitution of Norway in 1814.) Here the contrasts are, in all probability, characteristic of both personality types and governing traditions. This difference should still not overshadow the central point that in many ways Nygaardsvold played the same role in Norway as Hansson did in Sweden when it came to taking the great national social integration project out of the hands of the bourgeoisie. His fate was, however, different from that of Hansson.

Tranmæl continued the line of keeping the party leadership at arm's length from responsibility for the necessary compromises in Parliament. On the other hand, it is clear that the Nygaardsvold and his government now became the real center of power.[134] Nygaardsvold sat as prime minister for ten years, the last five as leader of the coalition government-in-exile in London. When Nygaardsvold came home in 1945, Tranmæl and his men at Youngstorget found that the time was ripe for the party to take over the leadership, and Nygaardsvold was outmaneuvered in favor of someone from the party's, and Youngtorget's, inner circle: Einar Gerhardsen.

In both countries we see how the Social Democrats were captured by the ordinary democratic political process after entering into parliamentary work and receiving an increasingly great response from the voters. The Swedish Social Democrats took the lead in this regard. They had already become the largest group in the Second Chamber by 1915, and in the First Chamber in 1921. The Norwegian Social Democrats became the largest parliamentary group for the first time in 1927. Within the parliaments it was possible to observe that the bourgeois state they struggled against was not hostile toward labor. There were areas in which it was possible to collaborate, and much could be achieved by means of the parliamentary route.

[133] Steen 1977, 86.
[134] Berntsen 1991, 362.

Figure 8. The Norwegian government-in-exile coming home from London in 1945. The man in front is the Social Democratic (Labor Party) prime minister Johan Nygaardsvold, who was soon to be pushed aside by younger party members. Behind him is the minister of foreign affairs, Trygve Lie, who became the first general secretary of the United Nations in 1946. (Photo: Scanpix.)

But there were also some characteristic differences in both countries in this process of developing from class struggle parties to people's parties. In Sweden Hansson was able to seize the baton directly from Branting and become party chair, while the more radical Norwegian party established an extraparliamentary center with the goal of defending its virtue as a party of class struggle. In one of the ironies of history, this eased the transition to a people's party. When Nygaardsvold's government showed that it was stable and strong, the party center at Youngstorget became somewhat marginalized—until it seized the reins again in 1945. And here we see how different processes in the two countries led to the same results when the basic conditions were the same.

In Norway Per Albin Hansson's metaphor of the "people's home" never took hold. Isaksson feels that since Hansson, with his eye on the tasks of state, stood "closer to the old-fashioned patriarchal conservatism than to liberalism," the collective "home" metaphor fit quite naturally.[135] Nygaardsvold could hardly be characterized as an old-fashioned patriarch. Thus the Swedes held a different view of national fellowship. In addition, the Norwegians

[135] Isaksson 2000, 127.

carried more of their history with them. They had a whole arsenal of accumulated metaphors, pictures, and ideas that expressed national fellowship. In short, they had the whole rhetoric about "the fathers of Eidsvoll" and the Constitution of 1814, which was the most democratic constitution at that time and which today is the oldest constitution in Europe, and they had the legacy from the struggle for full national independence right up to 1905. This historical legacy the Labor Party too, although certainly late, but effectively, associated itself with and made use of. In Sweden there were no national symbols tied to history that were comparably applicable. Sweden was the land of the future, destined to create new symbols of fellowship from the currency of the times.

THE EXPANSIONISM OF THE
CRISIS POLICY AS IDEOLOGY

One condition that enabled the labor movement to take the social integration project out of the hands of the bourgeoisie was that the movement developed what it considered to be a solution to the critical problems of the 1930s. We have indicated that the traditional bourgeois parties did not have any real answer to the problems, but there were two currents that believed they did have solutions: on the one hand, a bourgeois current that was Fascistically tinged, and on the other, the labor movement. The former became marginalized, clearing the way for the solutions of the latter. But what did the labor movement actually have to contribute? According to revolutionary Marxism, crisis was unavoidable in a capitalist society. But Marxism had been abandoned by the labor parties in these two countries, thereby creating an ideological vacuum. We see that in the 1920s the Social Democrats had no alternative to bourgeois economic orthodoxy, which is to say they did not have an answer to the crisis. The new crisis at the beginning of the 1930s was another situation, however.

There has been a great debate in Sweden based on the crisis policy that the Social Democratic government launched upon its inception in 1932.[136] The Social Democrats themselves felt that they were introducing a new policy—they had something to contribute, and they were certainly right up to a point.[137] This concerned an expansionist policy directed toward combating unemployment. Minister of Finance Ernst Wigforss received much

[136] The literature on this theme is considerable. One concise overview is given in Beckman et al. (1974). A fresh overview of a more subjective character has been given by Karlsson (2001).
[137] Karlsson 2001, 610.

of the credit for introducing the modern crisis policy. In 1932 he authored an election pamphlet titled *Can We Afford to Work?*—"a thin little print job of twenty-four pages that, with its simple words, punchy similes, and effective polemic against the predominant doctrine of economizing with the taxpayers' money and balancing the state budget, became his masterpiece of agitation."[138]

With regard to the development of Social Democratic ideology in these years, Wigforss was certainly among the most influential, along with thinkers such as Sandler and Karleby. But he combined this role with that of political practitioner to a greater extent than did the others, and a relatively comprehensive Wigforss literature has blossomed forth.[139] Wigforss was an associate professor who had presented a dissertation in linguistics. He entered the Social Democratic movement early on. Although not a Marxist, he derived inspiration from various forms of democratic Socialism, such as those espoused by Eduard Bernstein and the academic Socialists of Germany, the English Fabians, and the American pragmatists' undogmatic action ideology.[140] One could hardly say that he developed a unified system of thinking. Wigforss was an "action ideologue" who combined political positions with a reflective ideological engagement.

There has been discussion as to whether Wigforss's new crisis policy was based on a new economic theory. Wigforss was hardly a groundbreaking economist, but he benefited from the help of a series of progressive young economists who constituted what has been called the Stockholm School, names such as Gunnar Myrdal, Erik Lindahl, and Bertil Ohlin. These men made an indubitable contribution to the development of an expansionist countercyclical theory paralleling that of John Maynard Keynes, whose internationally known name has been linked to this development.

Questions arise as to what this theoretical innovation consisted of, where it originated, and to what degree it preconditioned the new policy. It may be said that the most important contribution by economists during his early phase was the liberation of economics from the old orthodoxy rather than the advancement of an already-developed countercyclical theory. What was important to this "liberation process" was the devaluation of 1931, which followed the lead of Great Britain in both Norway and Sweden. In both countries, but especially in Norway, there had been great sacrifices made during the 1920s to carry through a parity policy for reinstating the

[138] Isaksson 2000, 199.

[139] Karlsson (2001, 27–32) gives a short review of this literature.

[140] Karlsson (2001) is the one who stressed the role of the pragmatists. In an interview conducted by Bernt Hagtvet, Wigforss emphasized the inspiration he derived from the English historian R. H. Tawney and his book *Equality*. Communicated by Hagtvet.

old gold standard. The devaluation now meant that these sacrifices had been for naught, and it also kicked the legs out from under the basis for the parity policy. It was a liberation from the old normative ideas and the old standards. The fact that one now felt free to act enabled one to follow a pragmatic policy directed toward immediate problems.

Everyone knew that it was possible to fight the crisis with an expansionist policy. The problem was how to finance it. The orthodox answer was what came to be called the *theory of leveling economic cycles*—one should save when the cycle was in an upswing in order to spend expansively in the downturn. An already indebted state had little with which to pull itself up. In general form, this mode of thinking had been developed, among other places, in Britain by the Fabian-inspired Minority Report of 1909, which had strongly influenced Scandinavia.[141] The Keynesian conception diverged from this theory by turning the problem the other way: rather than saving to invest, one should invest in order to save—the investments were to pay for themselves. One needed only to print the currency and invest it in order to get the system working again.

No one went to the Keynesian extreme. As late as 1934 we see that Gunnar Myrdal took account of the theory of leveling economic cycles—state finances had to be balanced within a ten-year period.[142] The cabinet minister Gustav Möller had aired the same point of view during the budget debates of 1933—too much borrowing by the state would only create more unemployment in the future.[143] But the point was that governments became more willing to engage in deficit financing.

In addition to the theory of deficit financing, the *theory of purchasing power* was another important foundation of the crisis policy. One could not stimulate production without maintaining demand by, among other methods, paying the farmers and workers decent wages. We have already noted that the theory of purchasing power was taken up by the Social Democrats and that, among other places, it appeared when Arvid Lindman argued in favor of good prices for farm products. The theory of purchasing power also underlay the Social Democrats' crisis solution when they advocated fighting unemployment by setting up large-scale emergency work programs at standard open-market wages. Nor was the theory of purchasing power new. Elements of it underlay the old underconsumption theory, but it could still be brought up again, systematized, and used to legitimate an emergency policy.

---

[141] In Sweden Wigforss was well known for this position, and in Norway, Wilhelm Thagaard.

[142] Karlsson 2001, 612.

[143] Beckman et al. 1974, 64.

Most important about this liberation, and visibly most revolutionary, was the breakthrough of short-term perspectives in policy that the new theory was based on, and that have managed to survive to the present time: One should not do what the old orthodoxy prescribed (namely, think much about the distant future). One had to solve present problems today and tomorrow's problems tomorrow. Keynes's famous dictum, "In the long run we are all dead," is part of an argument against the long-term perspective of the old orthodoxy. Thus we can observe a process through which one gradually learned to think in new ways about the economy.

Developments in Norway were rather analogous. Two books, *A Norwegian Three-Year Plan* and *Saving and the Regulation of Circulation*, were published in 1933; the former was written by a geographer and a mathematician and the latter by the well-known economist Ragnar Frisch. These books formed the basis for the Labor Party's crisis program in 1934, which was brought to life in part following the formation of the government in 1935. The Norwegian crisis policy was similar to but somewhat more modest than the Swedish policy. As with the Swedish policy, one is impressed by its practical orientation. Thus it is completely in character that Frisch did not talk about a new theory but rather about a new "active basic view."[144]

As we have seen, there was much of this new manner of thinking floating around, to be borrowed from when needed. But, even though it was at hand, it is interesting to ask where it had originated. One might perhaps believe that the Social Democrats in Norway, who lagged somewhat behind their Swedish colleagues in this field, had received inspiration for the Norwegian crisis policy from Sweden. This seems not to have been the case, however. It has been pointed out that one of the authors of the first of the two aforementioned books, Ole Colbjørnsen, had as his model the German crisis plan, worked out early in 1932 by Gregor Strasser, second in the Nazi hierarchy: "State-based expansion of credit by means that were not indemnified was conducted and promoted as a German specialty!"[145] Colbjørnsen did not actually announce where he had found his model. In his eyes, it was a question of fighting the Nazis by removing the crisis policy from their hands.

As we have seen, the new expansionist policies in Norway and Sweden must be explained by, above all, practical necessity. The contribution of the economists was more one of legitimizing rather than generating policy. Also of some significance was the fact that the Social Democrats were rather more

---

[144] Francis Sejersted 2002a. Cf. chapter titled "Keynes in Norway." Frisch was the first to be awarded the Nobel Memorial Prize in Economics in 1969.

[145] Ketil Gjølme Andersen 2003, especially 125f., 128, 133.

unfettered by the old orthodoxy. Moreover, the policy was apparently successful. Over the course of the 1930s unemployment declined. Sweden came forward first. In addition to the active labor market policy, the Swedes were able to set in motion a series of social reforms. Norway followed along slowly. The main reason for the economic upswings in both countries was not the new policy, however. This myth-enshrouded crisis policy became only "a short parenthesis" because the state budgets were rapidly balanced.[146] The decisive factor was the improving economic cycle and the ability of the economic system itself to work its way out of the crises.[147] Nonetheless, the Social Democrats, especially in Sweden, were able to benefit from the notion that they had turned things around. But this is the truth only with great modifications.

There was another effect of Keynesianism that should not be undervalued, namely, the ideological function of the new theory. The Social Democrats were pleased to take delivery of this new theory, not only because they were more unfettered with regard to economic orthodoxy, but also because they had a powerful need to fill the ideological vacuum that appeared when Marxism was no longer of current interest. The reformist Social Democrats, like the bourgeoisie, had lacked a policy with which to meet the crisis. Keynesianism was able to give legitimacy to an expansive policy regarding the labor market and the social sector. "The Keynesian 'new economic policy' was a godsend to a party that was ideologically approaching a dead end."[148] Keynes's theories were thus "just the theoretical superstructure that the party required in order to fit capitalism into its own doctrine."[149]

Another telling example of how the expansionist theory filled an ideological vacuum has to do with the Norwegian economist Johan Vogt. In contrast to Sweden, in Norway there were few openings for intellectuals within the Labor Party.[150] For some years we find an intellectual Marxist power center in the organization Mot Dag (Toward the Day) that played a role for the party in the 1920s but was later excluded. Like Evang, Vogt had been a part of this group. As one might expect, the members of the group remained faithful to their Marxism for a long time. For instance, in 1933 Vogt published a book titled *The New Technical Revolution and Its Social Consequences*, a Marxist analysis of the deepening effect of new technology on a crisis that was already insoluble within capitalist society. By 1937 the tone was different: Mot Dag

---

[146] Isaksson 2000, 263; Schön 2000, 349; Furre 1992, 157.
[147] Cf. J. A. Schumpter's "creative destruction." Francis Sejersted 1982b. Schön 2000, 352f.
[148] Ulf Olsson 1994, 47.
[149] Isaksson 2000, 203. See as well Lewin 1992, 182.
[150] Forser 1993, 150–151. He builds on Bernt Hagtvet 1973.

had been disbanded, and Vogt wrote a new book, *The Breakdown of Dogma in the Science of Social Economy*, in which he embraced "the upheaval within bourgeois social economy" that made the acquisition of a social scientific objectivity possible, such that both bourgeois and Marxist could "meet one another on one and the same platform."[151]

This platform was the expansionist theory that had been integrated with Social Democracy. With a view toward how the Social Democratic order would develop, it is perhaps appropriate to note one element in the expansionist theory that Myrdal stressed as early as 1934: "maximal production is based on maximal consumption, and vice versa."[152] Expansionism points toward *the consumer society*.

REVOLUTION OR REFORM

The last of the great popular movements, the labor movement, organized itself at the end of the nineteenth century. At that time the industrial revolution had led to a social crisis. It had created a working class that stood outside the boundaries of established society, a propertyless class marked by poverty and lacking the right to vote. In little more than a human lifetime, characterized by great turbulence, the mainstream labor parties in Sweden and Norway had shifted from small, revolutionary, class struggle parties to big, national, unifying parties ready to take over a hegemonic role in the respective countries. The strength of the labor parties rested not least on a close cooperation with particularly strong trade unions. These developments in the two countries followed different paths, however.

Contrasting the paths followed by the Social Democrats in Sweden (SAP) and in Germany (SDP), Sheri Berman has emphasized the early choices made by the SAP to be a reformist people's party, setting aside Marxian fatalism and working actively to democratize the undemocratic Sweden in collaboration with the progressive non-Socialists. Later the SAP managed to offer a creative response to the economic chaos in the interwar years. In Germany the SDP did neither, setting the stage for the Nazi Party.[153]

The Norwegian path was somewhere in the middle. Even more than the SPD in Germany, the Social Democrats in Norway held on to the Marxist legacy after World War I. On the other hand, in Norway, as distinct from Sweden, there was a very strong liberal democratic tradition. We have seen

---

[151] Vogt 1937, 129.
[152] Alva and Gunnar Myrdal 1934, 177.
[153] Berman 1998, 215 f.

how the Norwegian Labor Party was transformed to a people's party in the course of the interwar years, identifying itself with this democratic tradition and, like the Social Democrats in Sweden, offering a response to the economic problems of the 1930s. In Norway the final success of the Labor Party cannot, however, be explained by any particularly early breakthrough of democratic revisionism.

The explanation of how the Social Democrats in Sweden and Norway turned to reformism and won their strong position is complicated. The development can be understood only by following the historical process in some detail for each of the two countries. When that has been said, it is important to note that the labor movements of the two countries did not develop completely independent of each other. There was a certain mutual influence that is part of the explanation of how they reached the same position in spite of the many differences in the paths chosen. There is for instance a striking parallel in the way in which the two Labor parties in Norway and Sweden joined with the farmers' parties in the 1930s in organizing a crisis settlement and in the way in which the trade unions subsequently reached a comprehensive general agreement with the employers' associations, securing a relative peace in the workplace in the following epoch of Social Democratic hegemony.

Last but not least, there seems to be an underlying precondition for the Social Democratic successes in a tradition of fellowship that existed in these small homogeneous societies and was manifested in a common project, namely the creation of a modern, socially integrated industrial state. As the then "revolutionary" Branting was able to say in 1911: "when actual national future prosperity is at stake, the political conflicts give way on our side" (see chapter 1). There is thus much truth in the saying of Nina Witoszek that Socialism in these countries "is not an oppositional but an orthodox way of looking at things" (see the introduction).

CHAPTER 5

Distance and Proximity

Distance • Proximity • World War I • An Expanded Home Market? •
A Nordic Defense Alliance?

The nation-state was the framework for modernization—for technical modernization, for the great social integration project, for democratization, and for the welfare plans. For both Sweden and Norway, the dissolution of their union in 1905 was the culmination of their development into autonomous nation-states. Consequently, the dissolution of the union provided an impulse for a further modernization process, in both the technical-industrial and the political-democratic fields, in the two countries. The notion that each country was autonomous was subject to modifications, of course. Both countries had to act within the context of the world around them, especially the context of their neighboring countries. Even though we have focused on the differences between Sweden and Norway, there were also striking similarities. This makes it natural to ask how independent of each other the two countries actually were. Which similarities resulted from parallel but independent development and which from mutual influence? Was there not something that bound the two countries together? Could they not perhaps be considered a single entity in certain areas?

After 1905 the relationship between Sweden and Norway developed largely within a Scandinavian context, sometimes with Denmark playing the role of mediator between these two former union partners. A collaboration among three parties in which no one party is able to dominate can, under certain circumstances, be easier to accomplish than a collaboration between two. Yet the relationship between Sweden and Norway also had its own separate dynamic—for better or worse—following the dissolution of the union.

DISTANCE

The dissolution of the union in 1905 immediately precipitated a cool climate between Sweden and Norway, with a series of ruptures that affected many civil networks. It was less the dissolution of the union, in itself, than the manner in which it was carried out that created bad feelings on the Swedish side. Scandinavianism had originally blossomed from 1840 until the Danish-Prussian War of 1864 as a student movement based on romantic ideas of Nordic fellowship. Sweden and Norway's lack of support for Denmark in the Danish-Prussian War in 1864 severely wounded the movement, but it did not die. Another type of Scandinavianism arose in its place, nonpolitical and more practically oriented. It proved much more effective in terms of building up networks precisely because it was so practically oriented.[1] This Scandinavianism flowered in the years following 1864, especially up to 1905, when Nordic cooperation was enjoying an "Indian summer."[2] Scandinavian societies and Scandinavian journals were established. Professions such as economics, law, and the natural sciences held regular regional meetings. To a certain degree these meetings developed in the direction of a common cultural public arena. Naturally enough, this was decisively based on proximity and a common linguistic foundation. Swedes, Danes, and Norwegians could use their own languages in their contacts with one another and be understood.

The atmosphere markedly changed with the dissolution of the union. "In 1905 and 1906, one after another planned and arranged meetings were called off."[3] It has been said that Nordic cooperation suddenly went from "Indian summer" to "Nordic winter."[4] Nor was the tone any better at the political level. In 1905 Sweden and Norway prepared for war with one another, and there has been much discussion of how close they actually came to war. The union was ultimately dissolved peacefully, but a deep-seated antagonism remained. Norway clung to its old image of Sweden as a potential military threat and in 1912 carried out its most extensive military exercises since 1814, "based on a war scenario with Sweden as the aggressor."[5]

Sweden's image of its enemy was different. Its greatest threat came from Russia. To protect its rear flank, Sweden needed a guarantee from Norway about its response in the event of a conflict with Russia. This had been a weighty military strategic consideration when the union was initiated in 1814. An event in 1913 increased the tension. It came to light that Norwegian and Russian officers had been cooperating on military intelligence directed against Sweden. The Norwegian foreign minister expounded the Norwegian point of view: Norway desired good relations with Russia and could not rule out the possibility "that Norway, instead of fighting alongside

---

[1] Hemstad 2005.
[2] Erik Rudeng in the foreword to Eliæson and Björk 2000, 11.
[3] Hemstad 2005.
[4] Hemstad 2005.
[5] Hobson and Kristiansen 2001, 75.

Sweden, was at war with it."[6] There was still a great amount of suspicion between the two countries, and not without cause. We now know that the policy of neutrality worked for the Scandinavian countries during World War I, but if we look ahead a couple of decades we see a certain irony. From the mid-1930s to the mid-1940s it was Germany, not Russia, that threatened, and it was Norway, not Sweden, that was threatened. What about the defense of the rear flank then?

The idea of economic cooperation was also weakened in the years that followed 1905. Traditionally, the two countries had followed a policy of trade cooperation. A Scandinavian monetary union had been established in 1876. Plans for a Nordic common market—never realized—went back to 1866. A common market had been established within the Swedish-Norwegian union, however, but it was liquidated in 1897 following an initiative by the Swedes. In 1905 Norway enacted new protectionist customs legislation. One issue that embittered relations between the two countries after 1905 was conflict over the traditional right of the Swedish Sami to use summer pasturing in Norway for their reindeer herds. Thus one could feel the cold of this Nordic winter in the field of economics. Perhaps this was a natural consequence of the intensification, which we have been tracing, in both Sweden and Norway of the national consolidation process around the modernization program.

PROXIMITY

The picture should not be painted in tones that are too dark, especially concerning networks of civil society, which, despite everything, proved remarkably stable during this new "winter." Relations between Sweden and Norway improved noticeably beginning in 1912. New networks developed, and political relations improved after the Swedish election of 1911, which brought the Liberals to power. The threatening international situation also made the Scandinavian countries stand together. With the Balkan wars as background, Sweden, Norway, and Denmark adopted common neutrality statutes in 1912, and Norway and Sweden started negotiating reindeer pasturing. In 1919 the two countries signed a convention that for a long time would eliminate this source of conflict. (Whether this convention was in the interests of the Sami people is another question.) With this new convention, "Norway's goal-driven work over many generations to drive the Sami culture out of those areas in the north that were suitable for agriculture took a big step forward."[7]

---

[6] Hobson and Kristiansen 2001, 187.
[7] Roald Berg 1995, 138.

The joint work to create legislation continued as well in fields such as family law and the economy.[8] Joint legislation is especially interesting because it reflects Nordic civil society, which springs from a common view of society and makes social intercourse between the nations easier. Mutual influences here were direct and important. At the same time, we have to remember that differences existed, for example in the regulation of the labor market, in which, we have seen, state legislation played a larger role in Norway whereas civil society took the lead in Sweden. Nonetheless, the results in the two countries were rather similar.

WORLD WAR I

Initially, World War I increased the tension between Sweden and Norway, owing to their fundamentally different geopolitical orientations. The Swedes' sympathy lay with the Germans: "During the war, England emerged as Sweden's number one enemy."[9] In contrast, Norway became Britain's "neutral ally."[10] Furthermore, both countries found through experience that it was not easy to be neutral during a war between the great powers of Europe. They were exposed to considerable pressure in developing, or breaking off, trade relations with the belligerent powers and placing resources at their disposal. The considerable danger that the two countries could be drawn into opposite sides in the war led to military preparedness and planning, particularly by Sweden. Old plans from 1905 and earlier for an attack on Norway were updated. Politicians in Norway clung to old scenarios in which Sweden was the most likely aggressor.[11]

The situation was paradoxical insofar as neither country wanted to be drawn into the war, especially against the other.[12] The very idea was frightening, and the two countries' foreign ministers consequently made contact to reassure each other that they respected each other's right to make arrangements "so that they would not come to shoot at each other." This mutual reassurance was followed by governmental statements from both sides applauding the fact that the mistrust from 1905 was gone.[13] The meeting between the Swedish, Danish, and Norwegian monarchs at Malmø, Sweden, in 1914 was a further manifestation of Nordic cooperation on the policy of neutrality.

---

[8] Fredrik Sejersted 1998, 218; Henning Nielsen 1938, 3:17–19.

[9] Gihl 1951, 94.

[10] Riste 1965. The title of Riste's book is *The Neutral Ally.*

[11] Ericson 2000, 86f.

[12] Holtsmark and Kristiansen (1991, 7) say that they both had the same foreign policy but different policies on security.

[13] R. Berg 1995, 186.

A series of events occurred in 1917 that changed the situation in a way that would bring the Scandinavian countries together. In January, Germany launched its unlimited submarine war, hitting neutral countries as well as the Allies. This was a major reason behind the United States' entry into the war on the side of the Western powers in March. In the same month, the Russian Revolution opened the way for Finland's independence. Seeking an ally in their bid for independence from Russia, the Finns contacted the Germans, who thus came to have a strong influence in the Baltic region. The Åland Islands between Sweden and Finland became a hot potato. The Finns wanted the Germans to occupy Åland, while the people of Åland wanted to be under Swedish rule.

In November 1917 the Bolshevik revolution broke out in Russia, followed by Russia's cease-fire with Germany and Finland's declaration of independence. The revolution also put an end to what the Swedes, and particularly the Swedish radicals, saw as the Western powers' compromising collaboration with czarist Russia. The changes in Sweden's government were also important because they led to a coalition government of Liberals and Social Democrats coming to power, "whereupon it was no longer possible to place an equal sign between Swedish opinion and German-friendly opinion."[14] Sweden was thus slowly turning away from its friendship with Germany and toward the Western powers. In many circles in Sweden, however, German-friendly opinion and links to Germany remained strong. It was not easy for the new Liberal government to turn public sympathy toward the Western powers, although, as it gradually became clear who would eventually win the war, it became easier. The danger that Sweden and Norway would be drawn into opposite sides in the war disappeared, and cooperation between the two countries could be expanded.

One important area of cooperation was working for peace. Inter-Scandinavian groups were appointed to work out proposals furthering the work of the peace congresses in The Hague in 1899 and 1907, including development of international arbitration, organization of new peace congresses, and strengthening of international law institutions. The idea was to get the neutral states to support cooperative peace efforts. According to this thinking, the prestige that the Scandinavian countries had gained as neutral and peaceful nations should be put to use. The work of the inter-Scandinavian groups would later be expanded through initiatives taken by the war's victors, ultimately leading to establishment of the League of Nations. In the Scandinavian countries working for international peace became enshrined as a policy for the future, as these countries assumed the role of peace negotiators in the international arena.

[14] Gihl 1951, 108.

AN EXPANDED HOME MARKET?

A whole series of new cooperative initiatives were put forward in 1918–
1919. Once more we see how robust Scandinavia's tight-knit civil networks
were, symbolized by the establishment of the Norden organizations in
Denmark, Sweden, and Norway in 1919. The Norden organizations would
work for mutual enlightenment and cultural cooperation among the Scandinavian countries. On the political level, however, cooperation invited considerable problems. In the interwar period the political agenda was dominated
by two contentious issues: creation of a Scandinavian customs union and
common defense. Despite significant efforts on both projects, they failed to
come to fruition.

The war, by hindering trade with non-Scandinavian countries, led to an
increase in trade among the Nordic countries. As soon as the war was over,
however, trade reverted to its customary routes. None of the Nordic countries had a Nordic neighbor as its most important trading partner. The question of Nordic economic cooperation arose, particularly creation of a Nordic
customs union, engendered by the idea that significant advantages might
accrue to an expanded home market. Creating a single domestic market
out of the Nordic bloc, or Scandinavia, was a natural and tempting idea,
as witnessed by the innumerable (unsuccessful) attempts to establish such a
regional collaboration.

Everyone might agree on the advantage that an enlarged home market
would provide, especially as the basis of expanded international trade beyond Scandinavia. But again and again it proved difficult to implement this
natural and tempting idea because it would mean curtailing national control
over trade policy, and this was hard to accept, especially once the crisis of
the 1920s began and especially for the Norwegians. The Norwegians feared
competition, particularly from their nearest neighbors, that is, competition
from Danish agriculture and Swedish industry. It also appears that Norwegians still suffered from a union complex. After their successful struggle for
full national independence culminating in the dissolution of the Swedish-
Norwegian union in 1905, they hesitated to redevelop closer political cooperation with the bigger and stronger Sweden. Johan Castberg was among
the central Norwegian politicians who warned against trusting the Swedes,
recalling their unilateral annulment of the Swedish-Norwegian common
market in 1897.[15]

---

[15] *Tidens Tegn*, 15 April 1922. *Dagbladet*, 12 April 1922.

A NORDIC DEFENSE ALLIANCE?

The increasing international tensions in the 1930s led to closer relations among the Nordic countries. Like the idea of a customs union, the idea of a Nordic defense alliance cropped up repeatedly. It never came even close to realization, however, primarily because the countries' geopolitical orientations were so different. Finland and Denmark both saw themselves as threatened by great powers, but by different great powers. Sweden and Norway did not feel particularly threatened, Sweden because of its strength and location (which proved realistic) and Norway because it felt itself to be under the protection of Great Britain (which proved unrealistic). The main explanation for the failure to organize a defense alliance, consequently, is the "lack of one common threat. Why should one risk war against somebody one did not consider oneself threatened by?"[16] Particularly in Norway there was broad political consensus against entering into any Nordic defense alliance, due to fear that such an alliance would act as a guarantor of Swedish interests. On the other hand, there were forces arguing for a defense collaboration as a means of defending neutrality, no matter where the threats might come from.[17] This was not unrealistic, as Norway's experience during World War I proved. It is possible that Norway might have been able to remain neutral in World War II if such a collaboration had been established.[18]

The problem is illustrated by the Soviet Union's attack on Finland in November 1939, which immediately set off a government crisis in Sweden. Sweden's foreign minister, Rickard Sandler, thought that Sweden ought to send troops to Åland. Sweden's prime minister, Per Albin Hansson, hard-pressed by finance minister Ernst Wigforss, put his foot down: Sweden would above all defend its neutrality, and sending troops to Åland would mean being drawn into the war.[19] Sandler was forced to step down, and the whole government was reshuffled to form a coalition government that remained in office until 1945.

Nevertheless, activism on behalf of Finland was strong in Sweden and much help was sent, such as credits, humanitarian aid, and even war materials. In addition, many Swedish soldiers signed up voluntarily to defend

---

[16] Alf W. Johansson 1984, 141. Hobson and Kristiansen (2001, 234–235) brush aside the possibility rather quickly.

[17] Holtsmark and Kristiansen 1991, 38–39.

[18] Holtsmark and Kristiansen 1991, 319–324. There is a discussion here about the possibilities that the April 9, 1940, invasion of Norway by Nazi Germany could have been avoided. The alternative of a Nordic defense alliance, however, is not mentioned.

[19] Salmon 1997, 205.

Finland. The Swedish government authorized up to twelve thousand men to fight for Finland. The war ended in March 1940, with the Finns having to accept a humiliating peace with the Soviet Union. The same month—a little more than a week before the Germans' assault on Denmark and Norway on April 9—a Nordic defense alliance was again discussed in Stockholm. The idea was still alive, but it was far from being realized. "There was bitterness from the Finns, lack of concern from the Norwegians, resignation from the Danes, and from the Swedes—sober-mindedness."[20] This sober-mindedness was demonstrated again on April 9. The Swedes' main consideration at that moment was to keep out of the war. Unlike Sweden's "Finland activism" of the previous year, there was scarcely any "Norway activism." Coming to the rescue of the old union partner was not politic in the current situation, and official Sweden was completely dismissive of the idea. Some Swedes (presumably a few hundred) voluntarily fought in defense of Denmark and Norway.[21] If the union had not been dissolved, the situation would have been different. One fact that helps to explain why Swedish activism on behalf of Finland was strong but activism on behalf of Norway was minor is that the former was directed against Sweden's traditional main enemy—Russia/Soviet Union—whereas the latter was directed against Germany, with which Sweden had always been closely aligned.

Rickard Sandler belonged to a small group of prominent intellectuals who were at the center of the Swedish Social Democratic Party. Upon Hjalmar Branting's death in 1925, Sandler had taken over as prime minister and then served as foreign minister from 1932 to 1939 (apart from a short break in 1936). Sandler was an ardent advocate of the Nordic cause. His idea was to "attempt to set the whole of Swedish foreign policy on a Nordic path, but this disappeared like a whisper when the gravity of the situation [the Soviet attack on Finland] broke through and the content of the [pan-Nordic] rhetoric was ready for testing."[22] It is not certain, however, that things had to go the way they did. Sandler's Nordic policy was based on the tradition of "worker Scandinavianism" and on the fact that Social Democratic governments had come to power in all the three Scandinavian countries.[23] He believed that solidarity among the Social Democratic governments ought to be strengthened. The governments had also gone a long way toward a common foreign policy based on a clear rejection of Nazism. As Sandler said in a speech on May 1, 1939, "Those who find it shabby that Swedish battalions are not out in the battle-

---

[20] A. W. Johansson 1984, 140.

[21] Sjöstedt 1999, 29.

[22] A. W. Johansson 1984, 87. Regarding Sandler's policies in general, see Salmon 1997, 202.

[23] Holtsmark and Kristiansen 1991, 54. Conservative politicians talked about a "Marxist Scandinavianism."

fields when the fate of freedom and democracy in Europe is being decided have to be reminded that our contribution should be reserved, and must be reserved, for the defense of freedom and democracy in the Nordic countries. By utilizing all resources, what is necessary can be achieved."[24] Swedish battalions were also missing from the battlefield in the Nordic countries, however. Sandler was forced to resign long before Germany's attack on Norway and Denmark on April 9, 1940, and Per Albin Hansson held firmly to neutrality. The Norwegian government would have done the same if it had been given the chance.

National identity was very strong in the different Scandinavian countries. But everyone has multiple identities. It was clear that a Scandinavian identity did exist. There was a feeling of fellowship between Sweden and Norway that had its roots in their shared Scandinavian identity. The most important basis for this sense of regional identity lies in proximity and the language community. At a fundamental level between the two countries there were also extensive networks in the labor movement and the academic world, among the professions, within management and administration, among local entities, and so forth. Even with regard to defense, on which the Scandinavian countries never managed to come close to a binding agreement at the political level, technical cooperation developed with the exchange of intelligence and coordinated aerial surveillance.[25] The sense of community also found expression in the rhetoric of fellowship. It was unusual in Norway to speak of Sweden as a "foreign country," and vice versa. In the economic arena Norwegians and Swedes spoke only of "an expanded home market." Rhetoric reveals mental conceptions. On the other hand, we see how Scandinavian identity collided with national identity. In both the economic and the defense policy arenas, the individual countries' national interests were in conflict.

Political distance remained between the two former union partners. In cultural matters and civil networks, however, proximity predominated. In spite of their different historical experiences and a certain political distance that resulted from these differences, Sweden and Norway shared a strong inclination to copy each other. The two countries developed in tandem.[26] The close relationship between them would become particularly marked after 1945, during the heyday of Social Democracy in both countries.

---

[24] Wahlbäck 1990, 31.

[25] Holtsmark and Kristiansen 1991, 71.

[26] Kaelble 1999, and see Francis Sejersted, "Sammenligning er ikke bare sammenligning" (Comparisons Are Not Merely Comparisons) in Francis Sejersted 2003c. It is argued here that comparative description must be supplemented with a description of the relationship between the entities that are compared.

PART II

1940–1970: The Golden Age of Social Democracy

CHAPTER 6

Cooperation in a Menacing World

Not the Same War • The Cold War—Still Not the Same War? • The Internal Danger and
Surveillance • A New Drive for a Nordic Customs Union • SAS: A Success Story •
Despite Everything, a Flourishing Collaboration • Cooperation in a Menacing World

NOT THE SAME WAR

Norway was invaded by Germany on April 9, 1940. The official Swedish reaction to the invasion was expressed in Prime Minister Hansson's radio broadcast three days later. He stressed that Sweden was "firmly resolved to continue to follow the strict line of neutrality." This meant that Sweden not only refused to come to the rescue of its former union partner but also, for fear of German reprisal, went a long way toward fulfilling Germany's demands. The Swedish government also rejected the request by Haakon, the Norwegian king, for asylum in Sweden without being interned, and when he spent some hours on the Swedish side of the border during his flight from the Germans, this was viewed ungraciously.

Sweden by and large followed the demands of neutrality during the struggle in Norway during the summer months, but once the fighting was over Sweden allowed the movement of German soldiers and war matériel across its territory. During the three years that this occurred, approximately two million German soldiers were transported via the Swedish railway system. Even the Swedes recognized that this exceeded the rules of neutrality. Prime Minister Hansson's journal notation for June 18, 1940, the date when his government yielded to the transit demands of the Germans, provides an example: "And thus it was that our cherished and strict course of neutrality was broken due to the understanding that it was impossible to maintain in this situation without risking war."[1] Other issues contributing to the souring of relations between Sweden and Norway included the rights of disposition of Norwegian vessels in Swedish ports and diplomatic representation to the Norwegian government-in-exile in London.

---

[1] Åselius 2001, 47.

During World War I the possibility had existed that Sweden would be drawn into the war on the German side. This was scarcely a possibility during World War II. To fight side by side with the Nazis, as the Finns were doing, was no alternative, at least not for the Social Democrats. Nonetheless, Sweden had close—and problematic—relations with Germany and Finland. The ambivalence of Sweden's relationship with Germany was summed up in the title of Gunnar Richardson's book on that relationship between 1940 and 1942, *Admiration and Fear*.[2] In this book Richardson emphasizes the considerable civil and military contact between the two countries during this period. There were strong forces in Swedish society that wanted to maintain close ties with Germany, if not with the Nazis. Moreover, Sweden's relationship with Norway reportedly was distinguished by persistent attitudes dating back to the dissolution of their union in 1905: "The 1905 complex was a reality in both countries."[3] According to the Swedes, the Norwegians were finding out how stupid they had been to break out of the union. And on this they scored a point.

The frictions between Norway and Sweden also reflected differing views on what sort of war was actually being fought. For Norwegians, it was a war between democracy and dictatorship. They saw themselves as fighters in a heroic struggle—even though they had not decided to enter the war and clearly would have preferred to be in the same situation as the Swedes. For Sweden, the situation was more complicated. There too we find the war viewed as a struggle between democracy and dictatorship, at least according to Rickard Sandler in 1939. The picture became more complicated after the Soviet Union entered the war on the side of the Allies, however. This lent weight to the view that the war was an "ordinary war" between the great powers, in which one should not get involved.[4] There was also a feeling among the Swedes that they had "a strong responsibility to keep the fire of the modern project burning while other countries sent their youth to the front."[5]

Moreover, Sweden's close relationship with Finland made the situation increasingly difficult. Sweden clung to its traditional fears of the great neighbor to the east—Russia/the Soviet Union. Swedish public opinion was divided on whether Germany or the Soviet Union represented the greater threat.[6] These differences of opinion and the many conflicting considerations made a pragmatic, nonheroic attitude a natural stand to take in the existing situa-

---

[2] Richardson 1996; see also Åselius 2001, 25, where an oscillation is described between "enthusiastic love and anxious self-justification."

[3] Sverdrup 1996, 181; Riste 1990.

[4] Åselius 2001, 31.

[5] Ehn, B. et al. 1993, 145.

[6] Sverdrup 1996, 163.

tion. Consequently, there were differences between the Norwegian and Swedish ways of interpreting the situation, differences that made communication more difficult. The two countries were not talking about the same war.

Some Swedes, such as the well-known editor Torgny Segerstedt, viewed the war as a just war against totalitarian Germany, and they took Norway's side. The Swedish central trade union (LO) also came out early in support of Norway,[7] and in 1943 Sweden's official policy changed. By then Germany was on the defensive, and it was clear that the Allies would eventually win the war. Yet Sweden's major consideration was to keep out of the war. But whereas the policy of neutrality was originally broken to the advantage of the Germans, in the later phase of the war it was broken to the advantage of Norway and the Allies.

The amount of Swedish help received by Norway was considerable, overshadowing the previous controversies. For Norway, it was a great advantage to have a neutral Sweden on the other side of their long mutual border, as almost sixty thousand Norwegians were able to flee to Sweden during the war. In Sweden it was possible to organize a refugee society under Norwegian control. It also was possible to use Sweden as a base for the resistance struggle inside Norway. And toward the end of the war the Swedes allowed the establishment of Norwegian infantry units of more than ten thousand men on Swedish soil. In addition, Sweden sent foodstuffs to Norway through Swedish Norwegian Aid, which had been organized in 1942. Many close personal relations between Swedes and Norwegians developed during this period.

Right after the war both countries began investigating and documenting the development of their wartime policies, with a view to illuminating those policies and to answering the questions that were being raised about them in Norway, naturally, but also in Sweden. In both countries this process led to the same conclusion: that both countries' wartime policies had been the right ones. Both countries perceived a need to find agreement, avoid conflict, and look to the future. Therefore they were cautious about dredging up difficult and traumatic relations from the war years—despite the commissions of investigation.

Now Norway had to deal with the events of 1940. The government had displayed its weakness when Germany invaded, and the military defense had not been particularly glorious. On these and many other points the government was sharply criticized. Norway also had to go through a rather extensive national political tribunal. In all, 92,805 charges were brought (of which 37,150 were dismissed). Passive membership in Vidkun Quisling's National Unity Party was sufficient grounds for being taken before the court. The ju-

---

[7] Alf W. Johansson 1984, 285.

dicial determinations were based on regulated procedures, however. In all essentials Norway avoided the forms of local vigilante justice that were witnessed in other countries, and the sentences, with the exception of a few death sentences, for the most part were light. This reflected the national desire to leave these traumatic events quickly behind and establish a consensus about the heroic struggle. But this was accomplished at a cost: many of the less heroic events were swept under the carpet rather than resolved, and one was left with a sharp division between those who had been members of the National Unity Party or had collaborated with the enemy in some other way and everyone else.

In Sweden, which had not been at war, such a settling of accounts was not deemed "necessary." Naturally enough, criticism arose in the wake of the war. The decision to allow transit of German troops and matériel across Sweden was criticized, along with what was generally agreed to have been excessive press censorship. For the most part, however, it was possible in Sweden to put the traumatic events to rest and establish a national consensus based on the fact that the government's pragmatic policy of compliance with Germany had been reasonable and necessary. It was seen as being to the credit of the coalition government that Sweden had managed to avoid being drawn into the war. Unlike in Norwegian society, no lines of demarcation between innocent and guilty were drawn.

The result was that each people could live with its respective past, conscious that it had done the right thing. The premises each maintained for this were different: the Norwegians had lived up to the moral demands of the situation, whereas the Swedes had acted pragmatically. Thus the war came to contribute to the two countries' national self-portraits in different ways.

One might perhaps have thought that the difference in national consciousness that flowed from different war experiences would have had greater influence on the relationship between the two countries, but this does not seem to have been the case. Both countries desired to put their war experiences behind them in order to further develop Social Democratic society. In both Sweden and Norway the Social Democrats consolidated their position in 1945. The consolidated Social Democrats were thus able to concentrate on building on the foundations they had laid during the 1930s. From this perspective, the war stood as a parenthesis in the process of development, and the two countries could seek support and inspiration from each other. Still, this cooperation and mutual support was limited by the fact that the war had given neutral Sweden a great economic advantage. In other areas, especially with regard to the international order, the two countries would go separate ways.

THE COLD WAR—STILL NOT THE SAME WAR?

On May 3, 1948, the Swedish minister of foreign affairs Östen Undén visited Oslo to propose reconsidering the old idea from the interwar period of establishing a common Scandinavian defense alliance. Negotiations were initiated, but once again no such alliance materialized. About a year later Norway joined NATO while Sweden decided not to do so.

The background for Östen Undén's approach reflected Sweden's political security situation following World War II. The Communist coup in Czechoslovakia in February 1948 had sharpened the conflict between East and West and contributed to placing the Scandinavian countries in a more vulnerable position. "In a single blow the political situation has changed," Sweden's Social Democratic prime minister Tage Erlander noted in his diary. Two days later he referred to the many rumors that "speak about how the nearby Russians are driving toward Scandinavia. The whole thing sounds completely absurd, but the Communist Party's behavior both here and in Finland is ominous."[8]

Originally, both Sweden and Norway had relied on a neutral bridge-building policy within the United Nations system of collective security. They felt that they were in a position to contribute positively toward peace by dampening conflicts between the great powers. Underlying the bridge-building policy was the ideology of small states: small states had none of the interests of the large states; they were, by definition, moral and peaceable. Another consideration that played a material role in both countries' neutrality was the fact that many in the labor movement had difficulty choosing sides at the beginning of the Cold War. Even though the Social Democratic mainstream in both countries was anti-Communist, there was a certain degree of sympathy for the great social experiment in the Soviet Union, and at the same time there was a degree of skepticism toward the capitalist United States. A document prepared within the Labor Party of Norway by, among others, the future foreign minister Halvard Lange warns against "the supercapitalist Atlantic powers" and against entering into an adversarial relationship with the Soviet Union.[9]

At the beginning, therefore, both Norway and Sweden decided not to choose sides. Even during the powerful confrontations between the United States and the Soviet Union at the United Nations in the autumn of 1947, both Sweden and Norway stood together in not supporting either side, even on important issues. Moreover, during negotiations over what would become assistance from the Marshall Plan (officially, the European Recovery Pro-

---

[8] Erlander 2001, 8 and 10 March 1948.
[9] Sverdrup 1996, 197.

gram), they stood together in their efforts to dampen the conflict between the United States and the Soviet Union.[10] A policy of active bridge building was dependent on a relatively relaxed atmosphere in the international arena, however. Eventually circumstances brought the conflicts between the superpowers to a head, and both Sweden and Norway had to revise their policies of bridge building.

For Sweden, it seems that the choice, once it had to be made, was simple: to fall back on its traditional policy of neutrality. This had worked well during two world wars. In addition, by this time Sweden had also built up a strong defense force. The country had its own military-industrial complex of a type that otherwise only the superpowers possessed. Among other things, Sweden relied on its own home-produced fighter jets for national defense.[11] In comparison to Sweden's defense forces, Norway's were miserably underequipped.

That the traditional policy of neutrality, even in the new situation confronting Sweden in 1945, could have its "moral" costs was demonstrated when the Soviets demanded that the Baltic soldiers who had fought on the German side and had moved to Sweden during the final phase of World War II be handed over to them. The decision regarding the extradition gave rise to an extremely hot debate. In particular, Undén was exposed to sharp criticism for his compliance with the Soviet demands. It later came to light that he had tried to reverse the decision to extradite but had been overruled within the government.

Sweden not only chose neutrality but also made a clear and strong case that Norway and Denmark should do the same. Sweden regarded itself as the leading representative of the Nordic bloc.[12] This was the background behind Undén's visit to Oslo, which represented "a bold attempt to expand the Swedish policy of neutrality to include both Norway and Denmark."[13] From a military point of view, Sweden had little to gain by including the two neighboring countries in a neutrality alliance. On the political front, however, the Swedes believed that a Scandinavian alliance could strengthen neutrality and thus the likelihood of keeping the three countries out of a war between the superpowers.

The policy of neutrality had deep roots in Norway as well. It became difficult for Norway to choose between a Scandinavian neutrality policy and a Western alliance policy. The Norwegians did not immediately embrace the

---

[10] Sverdrup 1996, 284.

[11] Magnus Petersson 1999, 145. Petersson refers to the speech by the central Swedish diplomat Erik Bohemen in which he said that Sweden had one thousand fighter jets as against Norway's ninety.

[12] Riste 1990, 126.

[13] Sverdrup 1996, 304f.

idea of participating in a Western defense bloc. There were many Norwegian Social Democrats who thought as the Swedes did and would have preferred a Nordic defense alliance as the basis for a policy of neutrality. Norway wanted it both ways: Scandinavian cooperation with a Western guarantee. A Western guarantee, however, violated the idea of neutrality, a violation the Swedes could not countenance. Again, war experiences colored national strategic considerations. "Neutrality" was an honored word in Sweden, whereas in Norway the concept had become somewhat discredited.[14] The old contradiction between Swedish pragmatism and Norwegian moralism reared its head once again. The Swedish prime minister Erlander could become irritated by the Norwegian foreign minister Lange's "pronouncement about the different morals in Sweden, which looked only to its own interests, and Norway, which looked to the world's—which shows that he [Lange] had now burst onto the stage with every thought clogged with phrases and histrionic effects."[15]

The differing war experiences of the two countries conditioned their different evaluations of the political security situation. Norwegians thought that Scandinavia lay in a strategically vulnerable position and it would be difficult, if not impossible, to keep Scandinavia out of a potential superpower conflict. As Erlander notes with a touch of bitterness, "The Norwegians obviously consider it completely unreasonable that the Nordic countries could stay neutral in the event of a war."[16] The Norwegians concluded that one had to take sides. The Swedes' assessment was the opposite. For them it was important "to save the Nordic countries from the grip of the superpowers."[17] The Norwegians believed that a guarantee from, or an endorsement of, a Western alliance would have a deterrent effect, preventing the Soviet Union from attempting a limited annexation in the Scandinavian region. Conversely, the Swedes maintained that entering a Western alliance in itself would constitute a provocation of the Soviet Union and thus contribute to increased tension.

To explain why each country chose its own road, many have invoked the legacy of the 1905 dissolution of the union. It has been said that Norway was afflicted with a "union syndrome" and Sweden with a "disloyalty syndrome."[18] The Norwegians were unable to go along with anything that resembled a union, and the Swedes could not bring themselves to treat Norway as an equal. The historian Olav Riste maintains that the earliest point

---

[14] Sverdrup 1996, 326.
[15] Erlander 2001, 23 December 1948.
[16] Erlander 2001, 19 May 1948.
[17] Erlander 2001, 7 January 1949.
[18] Noreen 1994, 16f.

when Sweden really acknowledged Norway's independence was 1949.[19] In any case, the impossibility of reaching any compromise became apparent. Norway together with Denmark joined NATO in the spring of 1949. Sweden remained outside.

The history of the different security policies was not, however, concluded with Norway and Denmark joining NATO in 1949. The Swedes had to evaluate the possibility of being drawn into a great war, and there was no doubt about which side they inevitably would find themselves on. It also became evident that, despite their differing positions, the Swedes and the Norwegians could cooperate unofficially but constructively and unproblematically on security policy when the pattern of formal alliances was established. First, the Norwegians naturally viewed the strong Swedish defense as a shield against the Soviet threat. Second, there was established a comprehensive, albeit unacknowledged, Swedish-Norwegian military cooperation to make the defense of the Scandinavian Peninsula as effective as possible. This was particularly true in the northern regions, where close cooperation took place "without [political] fuss," as a Norwegian defense leader later expressed it. Third, in the late 1940s and early 1950s the Norwegians worked systematically among their allies toward an understanding of the Swedish position in order to prevent Sweden from being isolated politically and militarily.

At that time Norway was Sweden's channel of military communications with Great Britain and the United States, although Sweden gradually increased its direct contact with the United States and NATO. Magnus Petersson, who has investigated the collaboration between Sweden and Norway, concludes, "This Swedish-Norwegian intelligence cooperation during the 1950s and 1960s stands out, like their collaboration in other fields (for example, in aviation), as conspicuously extensive and well constructed if one recalls that Sweden was outside any alliance and Norway was a member of NATO."[20]

There has been debate over the existence of a hidden Swedish NATO membership. The conclusion so far is that "no convincing documentation or consistent argument for a silent alliance policy has yet been furnished."[21] What is clear, however, is that Sweden was in close contact with Norway and was prepared to receive assistance from NATO and eventually to coordinate with it on defense. On this basis Magnus Petersson concludes: "Never before, not even during the hardening of the world situation in the 1930s, had Carl Johan's conception of the Scandinavian Peninsula as a well-bounded strategic

[19] M. Petersson 2003a, 68.
[20] M. Petersson 2003b, 291.
[21] M. Petersson 2003b, 226.

entity had such an effect on Swedish and Norwegian security thinking and action, and this during a period when Norway's and Sweden's security policies were, officially, more divergent from each other than they had been at any point since 1814."[22]

Sweden's and Norway's different decisions on joining NATO in 1949 did not mean that the discord concerning security policy was over. Parallel to Sweden's allegedly seeking clandestine alliances, Norway's politics was split by the struggle over joining NATO. In both countries the raging internal disagreements reached their climax in the mid-1950s, on the question of re-arming with nuclear weapons.

In Norway the conflict had to do with NATO's plan to place tactical atomic weaponry on Norwegian soil during peacetime, which evoked considerable opposition within the Labor Party. In 1957 the Soviets demanded assurance from Norway that no such thing would happen. This developed into a struggle between Minister of Foreign Affairs Halvard Lange and Prime Minister Einar Gerhardsen. Gerhardsen's policy emerged victorious: there would be no nuclear weapons on Norwegian soil during peacetime. Throughout the 1960s this policy was respected by NATO.

But before this issue was resolved, NATO policy had lasting consequences for the Norwegian Labor Party because it spurred the splitting off of a new radical party, the Socialist People's (SF) Party, in 1961. The SF Party's platform was to reject atomic weapons and military alliances and to embrace Socialism. In the 1961 election two SF Party representatives were elected to Parliament, creating a small sensation.

Swedish and Norwegian security policies were interwoven in some cases. On the one hand, the Swedes had opposed the placement of NATO bases on Norwegian soil and atomic weapons in Denmark and Norway. On the other hand, Sweden's neutrality policy was based on strong defense; indeed, the country deliberated developing its own atomic weaponry. In all probability a majority in the government, led by Prime Minister Erlander, supported this and Foreign Minister Undén opposed it. Thus in Sweden as well as in Norway the prime ministers and the foreign ministers clashed over the question of atomic weapons, but with opposite polarities in the two countries. It is clear that Swedish foreign minister Undén had close contact with Norwegian prime minister Gerhardsen about this question, based on their shared recognition that the introduction of atomic weapons in either country would be a powerful argument for introducing them in the other country.[23] Undén's

---

[22] M. Petersson 2003b, 298. (Carl Johan was Napoleon's Marshall Bernadotte, who became king of Sweden and Norway in 1818.)

[23] Eriksen and Pharo 1997, 276.

position on the question was victorious in Sweden, just as Gerhardsen's was in Norway. Neither country obtained atomic weapons, a result produced by some degree of political coordination between the two countries.

The opposition to atomic weapons within the labor movement gained strength both from traditional antimilitarism and from traditional distaste for allying too closely with the West. And the history of the nuclear weaponry debate was "worth considering," according to the historian Karl Molin, because it "was in fact the undisciplined opposition that turned out to have been right from the start"[24] We note, however, that this undisciplined opposition got the support of a few in the party leadership in both Sweden and Norway. But Sweden, unlike Norway, avoided a party split.

THE INTERNAL DANGER AND SURVEILLANCE

The Communist coup in Czechoslovakia in February 1948 immediately fed fear of a coup in Scandinavia as well. Recall that in Sweden Prime Minister Erlander characterized the Communist Party's conduct in the wake of the coup as "ominous." In Norway Prime Minister Gerhardsen's view was that "the most important task in the struggle for Norway's independence, democracy, and legal protection is to reduce the Communist Party and the influence of the Communists as much as possible."[25] The Communist parties in both countries had made certain advances immediately following World War II. After the coup in Czechoslovakia, however, they quickly became marginalized, and fear of an internal coup disappeared.

In contrast, fear of a Soviet attack remained, along with fear of fifth-column activity. Intense vigilance against this potential internal danger during the Cold War was primarily characterized by rather comprehensive surveillance, which was a particular feature of Social Democracy in its heyday. This surveillance was conducted in service of national interests, but not exclusively so. The boundary between government policy and party policy became fluid in the Social Democratic state.

Following the coup in Czechoslovakia, the Social Democratic leaders in the two countries came together to discuss the struggle against Communism. In Norway there was a certain fear of Communist sabotage.[26] Swedish prime minister Erlander was skeptical, however: "I cannot seriously believe that they are planning a coup, but I can well imagine that the Communists are building

---

[24] Molin 1989, 336. English edition 1992, 401.
[25] Cited from Eriksen and Pharo 1997, 57.
[26] Bergh and Eriksen 1998, 2:149.

up an organization in response to the Norwegian turn toward the Western bloc."[27] Erlander was again riding his hobbyhorse—claiming that Norway's orientation toward the West made Scandinavia more vulnerable to threats from the East. Nevertheless, Norway's and Sweden's military security services and civilian surveillance agencies cooperated very closely on surveillance of Communists. In this case, Sweden was more important to Norway than were its NATO partners.[28]

When the Cold War ended, commissions were set up in both Sweden and Norway to critically examine how this action against internal dangers had been conducted. Despite disagreement about how deep such criticism should be, these investigations took on the character of coming to terms with the past. They concluded that although a threat had undoubtedly existed, the seriousness of the threat did not fully explain the extent of the surveillance. "The fixation on the threat prevents us from coming to an understanding of what happened; it does not help us at all," wrote the historian Klas Åmark. The surveillance "would never have been possible if it had not been for the responsible politicians—this applied above all but not exclusively to the Social Democrats—not respecting the fundamental rights of citizens."[29]

In 1994 the Norwegian Parliament set up a commission to investigate whether after 1945 the secret services had engaged in *illegal* political surveillance and registration of Norwegian citizens suspected of Communist Party membership or Communist sympathies.[30] The commission found that up to the end of the 1960s there had been an almost total mapping of the activities of the Communist Party. The building of dossiers on persons went far beyond the party, however. "Possible Communists" were also registered and investigated. When it came to the SF Party, which was viewed as an heir to the Communist Party, all the party's election candidates were under surveillance and indexed right up to 1964. In 1973 the number of dossiered Norwegian citizens in the civil intelligence service's files alone was thirty-nine thousand.[31]

More sensitive than indexing was surveillance. Undercover police activity was not illegal and was employed to some degree. Interior listening devices were used systematically in central meeting rooms despite the fact that they were illegal throughout this period. Their use continued until approximately 1958, when quite likely the top political leadership was informed about this

[27] Erlander 2001, 7 May 1948.

[28] Bergh and Eriksen 1998, 2:516f.

[29] Åmark 2003a.

[30] St. forh. (Parl. Proceedings) 1995–1996, document 15. In 1993 the Norwegian Department of Justice had taken the initiative to launch an investigation of the surveillance (Bergh and Eriksen 1998) and the Department of Defense an investigation of military intelligence (Riste and Moland 1997).

[31] St. forh. (Parl. Proceedings) 1995–1996, document 15, 45.

activity. Telephone wiretapping was illegal up to 1960, but thereafter it could be undertaken with a court order, which was summarily issued. In this way telephone wiretapping, although "in conflict with constitutional law, [has] been seen as a possibility for following the activities of the organization."[32]

In addition to surveillance, another sensitive issue was how the intelligence information had been used. The most serious criticism was of the exchange of information between the surveillance service and military intelligence, on the one hand, and the labor movement, on the other. The commission condemned this as "a gross incidence of indictable public activity."[33] It was plain that the surveillance services had been involved in the internal struggles of the Labor Party, which led to the exclusion of left-leaning party members and contributed to the establishment of the SF Party. "Surplus information" about the first party leader of the SF, Knut Løfsnes, fell into the hands of "the right people in the DNA [Norwegian Labor Party]," that is, those who were interested in having "Løfsnes yanked out by the hair."[34] This "surplus information" was used for political purposes that had nothing to do with the security of the realm. Intelligence gathered about individuals could also come into the hands of shop stewards in specific firms, implying illegal involvement by the security service in the conflicts between the left and right wings of trade unions. Moreover, the security service gave intelligence gathered about individuals to their employers.

The Swedish commission's mandate differed from that of the Norwegian commission. Whereas the Norwegian commission was charged with investigating *illegal* political surveillance, the Swedish commission was charged with giving "an integrated, exhaustive, and definitive clarification of the internal activities of the security service."[35] The documentation of dissidents was extensive. According to the historian Klas Åmark, the commission's numbers were too low; he estimates that the total number of persons investigated and documented in the period between 1950 and 1970 was about two hundred thousand.[36] Secret internal listening devices were applied in a variety of circumstances. This had been prohibited during the entire period, although the prohibition was not set out in its own paragraph in the criminal code until 1975. Telephone wiretapping had been used in the same way as in Norway, and the Swedish commission found that the courts "in many instances [had] not to a sufficient extent lived up to their obligation to protect the legal rights of the individual."[37]

---

[32] St. forh. (Parl. Proceedings) 1995–1996, document 15, 19.
[33] St. forh. (Parl. Proceedings) 1995–1996, document 15, 36.
[34] St. forh. (Parl. Proceedings) 1995–1996, document 15, 37.
[35] SOU 2002, 87, p. 45.
[36] Åmark 2003a.
[37] SOU 2002:87, p. 386.

Regarding the close relationship between the secret services and the Social Democrats and the irregular use of "surplus information" for political ends, there was a particularly close link, partly of a personal nature, with the military intelligence service. Information concerning conditions at workplaces flowed in both directions, and the identities of those who had access to the intelligence information were kept hidden from those who gave the information. One example of the political use of such "surplus surveillance information" relates to the attempt to found a Socialist People's Party in Sweden. Such a party had been founded in Denmark in 1958 and in Norway in 1961. There was a great fear that something similar would happen in Sweden, since many considered "the formation of Socialist People's parties in the Nordic countries as a form of advanced Soviet infiltration." On the basis of information received from secret surveillance, it had been possible to prevent the leader of the Socialist People's Party of Denmark from being invited to visit the Social Democratic Youth Movement in Stockholm.[38] In 1973 the secret surveillance organization was exposed, leading to a housecleaning and reorganization— and to the imprisonment of those who did the exposing!

In the wake of these commissions' findings, there has been a discussion in both Norway and Sweden about whether extensive political surveillance was reasonable, given the perceived threat at the time. The Swedish commission has been criticized by some for "being an apologist of history." The opposite has also been maintained, that the commission lost sight of the level of threat during the period when this surveillance took place and was therefore *too* critical.[39]

The question remains whether the politicians and the secret services would have had public support for the practices that were developed if these practices had been publicly known. In Norway there was great publicity about an issue that indicated how far, in that threatening situation, public opinion was willing to go in granting to the authorities full powers involving curtailment of citizens' legal protections. A proposal for a defense law was put forward in 1950 following the outbreak of the Korean War.[40] The bill proposed use of a court of treason, the death penalty, internment without trial, and press censorship in the event of war, under the threat of war, or when "the independence or security of the kingdom is in danger as a result of aggressive or threatening hostilities between foreign states or on other grounds."

Opposition to this proposed act quickly appeared. One of the leading critics was the old cultural radical and writer Sigurd Hoel. The government, he

---

[38] SOU 2002:87, p. 595.
[39] Åmark 2003a.
[40] Cf. Sejersted 2001, 323–326, "Striden om beredskapslovene" (The Struggle over the Defense Laws).

wrote, had turned its "back on the Norwegian Constitution and everything that could be called a free democratic state governed by constitutional law, and has begun to march down the wide main road of dictatorship." In particular, the final phrase of the proposed legislation, *or on other grounds*, waved the red flag of provocation. The proposal was withdrawn, and a new, less specific act was adopted.

The reaction to the defense laws indicates that these comprehensive and semi-illegal acts of surveillance could not be completely excused by virtue of the perceived threat. Even in the most menacing situations there were limits to how much infringement of their civil rights the majority of people would tolerate.

The similarity between Sweden and Norway on the handling of surveillance, partly rooted in their close cooperation, is striking. Even though the parliamentary commissions put an end to some of the worst rumors of abuse of security powers, their extensive inquiries ascertained that illegal clandestine surveillance had taken place in both countries and that "surplus surveillance information" had been unlawfully used for political purposes. These revelations of comprehensive surveillance have fed the conception that arrogance of power was characteristic of the Social Democratic state.

A NEW DRIVE FOR A NORDIC CUSTOMS UNION

Toward the end of World War II it was clear to most that international economic cooperation was necessary to avoid a repetition of the unfortunate state of affairs that had occurred in the wake of World War I. Thus the Bretton Woods Agreement, which regulated monetary policy and lay the foundation for the World Bank and the International Monetary Fund, came into force in 1944. In 1947 the American secretary of state George Marshall launched the European Recovery Program (commonly called the Marshall Plan), which offered American aid to Europe under the condition that the European countries coordinate their efforts at postwar reconstruction. The foundation of the organ of European economic cooperation, the Organization for European Economic Cooperation (OEEC, later renamed the Organization for Economic Cooperation and Development, OECD) was laid by the European Recovery Program. In all, a total of twelve billion dollars in gifts and loans was disbursed in the program.

Both Sweden and Norway hesitated to participate in the program. During this time of bridge building, both desired to remain independent of the two great political blocs. During this period there was also in both countries considerable skepticism toward a comprehensive economic integration of Europe. Therefore Sweden and Norway stood together in rejecting the American drive for a European customs union in 1947. The Social Democrats wanted to control the development of their own social economy, and closer international cooperation could easily frustrate that goal. Ultimately, however, both countries joined the European Recovery Program.[41] Norway received $460 million in subsidies and loans, while Sweden received approximately $120 million in loans. Participation in the Marshall Plan and the OEEC left its mark on the relatively moderate form of planned economy that the Social Democrats eventually implemented.[42]

The idea of a Nordic customs union turned up again in discussions about the European Recovery Program. The Danes were inclined to regard a Nordic customs union as a step on the road toward European economic cooperation. In contrast, Sweden and Norway were inclined to regard this Nordic solution as an alternative to the European one. The three countries also disagreed about the form economic cooperation would take. Sweden (and Denmark) wanted to have a customs union, while Norway feared free trade. Put more concretely, Norway feared competition from Danish agriculture and especially from Swedish industry.

Norway wanted a planned economy–oriented collaboration that could dampen competition through a division of labor and at the same time secure a supply of capital and technology for further industrialization. Or, to put it differently, a Scandinavian Social Democratic bloc, as the bourgeois and private business communities feared, was exactly what the Norwegian Social Democrats desired, while the Danes and Swedes both supported a form of free trade. The Swedish and Norwegian positions reflected the differences in the two countries' economic structures.

In the 1950s various reports about Scandinavian economic cooperation were presented and distributed, none of which yielded any results. Through it all Norway was the most skeptical. What eventually "derailed the Nordic train" was the European Free Trade Association (EFTA) formation process, which began in earnest during the summer of 1959.[43] In 1957 the Treaty of Rome among the Inner Six (Belgium, France, Italy, Luxembourg, the Netherlands, and West Germany) was signed, and the European Economic Community (EEC, which later developed into the European Union) was established. In 1958 French president Charles de Gaulle rejected the possibility that Great Britain and the Nordic countries should be allowed to enter into the EEC— and his opposition strengthened the discussions about a free trade region for

[41] Eriksen and Pharo 1997, 125f.
[42] Eriksen and Pharo 1997, 126–127.
[43] Eriksen and Pharo 1997, 304.

the "outer seven" (Austria, Denmark, Norway, Portugal, Sweden, Switzerland, and the United Kingdom). These negotiations intensified in 1959 and led in 1960 to the establishment of EFTA (the European Free Trade Association). For most, EFTA was considered a step on the road to membership in the EEC, and in the summer of 1967 Norway and Denmark (but not Sweden) sought membership in the EEC. In the autumn of 1967, however, de Gaulle again vetoed the expansion of the EEC. This led to a new round of negotiations on Nordic economic cooperation (NORDØK).[44] But when de Gaulle retired in 1969, it was again possible to seek membership in the EEC. Denmark and Great Britain joined and Norway made the attempt, but a Norwegian plebiscite conducted in 1972 rejected the proposal. Sweden remained aloof.

The idea of a Nordic customs union had very deep roots, but the continuous efforts to establish such a union, or at least a common market, did not succeed for a variety of reasons. The EEC was a more attractive option. Trade with Europe was more significant than inter-Nordic trade. As we have seen, it was impossible to achieve agreement about what Nordic economic cooperation would consist of. Should structural rationalization be brought about with the help of market exposure, or on the basis of planned economic management? That the Norwegians were always the most skeptical could be attributed not only to fear of competition from neighboring countries but also to the old union complex.

It soon became apparent that a Scandinavian common market for industrial goods was emerging within EFTA as the Nordic countries cut their customs tariffs among themselves more rapidly than set out in the EFTA agreement. Inter-Nordic trade increased more strongly than trade with Europe. It also became apparent that Norwegian industry had less to fear than it had thought at the start, and the idea of a Scandinavian home market was clearly articulated in 1968. Within the Norwegian business community, it was said that the Swedish market was a "training zone": "Sweden is one of the most demanding markets in the world—and if one is able to compete there, it is a good sign."[45] Even in Norway, self-confidence about trade and commerce slowly grew.

SAS: A SUCCESS STORY

A successful example of a concrete initiative taken by the three Scandinavian Social Democratic governments was the establishment of the Scandinavian Airlines System (SAS) in 1951. Bearing in mind that both the Nordic defense alliance and the Nordic customs union had gone on the rocks in 1949, there

[44] Tamnes 1997, 167f. See also Wendt 1979.
[45] Svein Olav Hansen 1994, 158.

were grounds for pessimism. Were attitudes changing? Erlander noted in his diary that he had received reports about "the whole Norwegian government seriously working for mutual understanding and cooperation with Sweden" and that "the Norwegian people had begun to overcome their doubts about us." He added, "S.A.S. is the first test."[46]

In addition to a number of smaller private airline companies in the three Scandinavian countries, there were three national companies in which the state was a significant partial owner, to the extent of 20 percent in Denmark and Norway, and 50 percent in Sweden. The three airlines had attracted state support for their operations in different ways, and they had collaborated (under the designation SAS) on certain international routes since 1946. The 1951 proposal had to do with transforming these national airlines into holding companies for a new common SAS in which the Swedes would own three-sevenths and the other two would each own two-sevenths. Even though this arrangement involved companies with large amounts of private capital, there was a precondition that the new SAS would get significant public support through concessions, guarantees, and subsidies.[47] The argument for state involvement was partly that this was an investment in the future and partly that it was an infrastructural initiative.

The initiative was Social Democratic; the three national governments were thinking along parallel lines. At the same time, it was based on close cooperation with private investors. Business leaders had been involved in the negotiations—on the Swedish side, Marcus Wallenberg among others. When the collaboration was first considered in 1946, there had been a certain amount of opposition in Sweden, but in December 1950 it slipped through Parliament without debate.[48]

It was a different story in Norway, where the strongest opposition came from the Conservative Party. The anti-Scandinavianism of the Conservative Party was based on skepticism toward both the Social Democrats and the Swedes (and partly the Danes). The old union complex was still there. When the Conservatives were accused of exaggerated mistrust, their parliamentary leader replied that they had every reason to be suspicious: "We have still not managed to share the inheritance of our common historical past with Denmark and Sweden in such a way that we have the basis for putting aside all mistrust."[49] Many years later Wallenberg commented on the negotiations in connection with Per Gyllenhammar's initiative in the Volvo negotiations: "He should have known what a [big] job we had with SAS. To work across the border with the Norwegians—I don't think he knows what he is letting him-

---

[46] Erlander 2001, 2 November 1950.
[47] St. forh. (Parl. Proceedings) 1950, S. Prp. 138, appendix 1.
[48] Buraas 1972, 60, 105.
[49] St. forh. (Parl. Proceedings) 1951, S. Tid., p. 81.

self in for."[50] But SAS was one political initiative that yielded results. Maybe Erlander was correct when he commented in his diary that "the Norwegian people had begun to overcome their doubts about us," despite the setbacks with the customs union.[51]

DESPITE EVERYTHING, A FLOURISHING COLLABORATION

It was during the period between 1945 and 1972 that this new Nordic cooperation expanded most rapidly.[52] In fact, one might consider that the many unsuccessful attempts to build defense and customs unions or a common market gave rise to other forms of cooperation through a type of compensatory mechanism. The defeat of the customs union and the defense alliance in 1948–1949 led to the foundation of the Nordic Council in 1952 and the freedom of Nordic citizens to travel without passports in all the Nordic countries. When the Nordic countries split over the question of seeking EEC membership in 1961, as compensation they got the Helsinki Agreement, a vague but rather comprehensive agreement that primarily prepared the region for economic cooperation. In 1971, in the wake of the breakdown of negotiations on the NORDØK economic cooperation initiative, other collaborations emerged, including a strengthened Nordic Council, the founding of the Nordic Ministerial Council, and the signing of a cultural agreement and a transportation treaty. And more examples of this compensatory mechanism could be mentioned.

The most important institutional innovation in this period was the founding in 1952 of the Nordic Council, a permanent parliamentary assembly. As is often the case, the Danes were the prime movers while the Norwegians were the most skeptical. The Norwegians, afraid of every form of extranationality, insisted that the council be involved only in cooperative efforts and that there be no intimation of signing away sovereignty. This is exactly what the council became—an organ of practical cooperation. The Nordic Council has been criticized for being a "chattering organ," but one should probably not undervalue the significance of being able to talk together. It has also come to light that the majority of the council's recommendations have been acted on by the national assemblies.[53]

---

[50] Ulf Olsson 2000, 412.
[51] Erlander 2001, 2 November 1950.
[52] S. O. Hansen 1994, 136.
[53] S. O. Hansen 1994, 149–152.

Figure 9a. Election poster for the Swedish Social Democratic (Labor) Party in 1940. The party's former antimilitarism was abandoned. The text says: "Safety for the home, freedom for the country. Vote for the Labor Party."

COOPERATION IN A MENACING WORLD

Arguably, the realization of the great Social Democratic project began in the 1930s, when, with conditions favoring them, the Social Democratic parties came to power in Sweden and Norway, but World War II broke out before these Social Democratic regimes had even consolidated their positions. Neither government was prepared for war, mentally or militarily. They had inherited an antimilitaristic bent, from which they had to free themselves for good.

But the conditions of war also introduced political dilemmas of a moral character. The Swedish and Norwegian governments had to find solutions based on the opportunities offered by the times—different solutions, as they

Figure 9b. Election poster for the Norwegian Labor Party in 1945. Reconstruction and industrialization were on the agenda. The text says: "We are building the Norway of the future.
Join in! The Norwegian Labor Party." The functional aesthetic of the day is evident in both
this poster and the poster on the previous page. (Photo: Arbeiderbevegelsens arkiv.)

were confronted by the war in different ways. The war also tested the relationship between the two countries. By and large they passed the test and could
put the war behind them, each country convinced that it had done the right
thing in its own way. Thus, in the decades following the war, they could re-
sume the task of realizing the Social Democratic society in both countries,
partly by means of cooperation across the border. In this era of reconciliation
the Scandinavian countries achieved prosperity and developed welfare states
and a political order admired throughout the world. Scandinavia gradually
became an idyllic place of comfort, peace, and contentment but retained a residual flavor of what we have called the Social Democratic arrogance of power.

CHAPTER 7

"The Most Dynamic Force for Social Development"

Class Society in Transformation I • Class Society in Transformation II • "The Most Dynamic Force for Social Development" • The Vision of the Atomic Age • Sweden: A Winner Nation • The Wallenberg System • Swedish Labor Market Policy • The Norwegian State and the Labor Market • Focusing on Natural Conditions • To "Play Wallenberg" in Norway • An Attempt to Create a Norwegian Knowledge Industry • Successful Industrial Policy? • The Social Democratic Urban Landscape • The Suburban Towns • Who Can Save the City? • The Triumph of Reason

CLASS SOCIETY IN TRANSFORMATION I

One day in August 1945 in the small town of Halden, Håkon Nyland left the large brick apartment block where he lived, mounted his old black-painted bicycle, and cycled off to his first day of work in newly liberated Norway. Nyland was thirty years of age and worked in a footwear factory, which he had done since he turned fifteen. His wife and two small boys remained at home in the apartment consisting of two small rooms and a kitchen. The weather was beautiful and—"Nothing is going to be as it was before." This is the opening scene in Dag Solstad's novel titled *September 25th Square*. This young worker was a Socialist and dreamed of a golden future that was to begin now that the workers were in the process of taking power. Halden lies on the Norwegian side of the Swedish-Norwegian border, so Nyland could see the material prosperity of the future that already existed on the other side. "People who had been in Gothenburg or Uddevalla [in Sweden] told stories of a land of abundance, a land of milk and honey, a wonderland."

In the course of the 1950s Håkon Nyland built a duplex home, occupying one half and renting out the other, and he bought a car. He and his family took part in the journey of the working class from poverty to the consumer society, which took place surprisingly quickly. Within a couple of decades Norway had almost caught up with the fairy-tale land of Sweden. Nyland also remained faithful to the Labor Party, and his three sons became workers. The eldest, like his father, remained with the Labor Party, but the two younger sons joined the youth revolt around 1970.

With this novel, Solstad, who was himself one of the "rebels," turned the searchlight of social criticism on the well-established Labor Party. Despite great material progress, developments had not been quite as people had dreamed. But the novel does not end in gloom. On September 25, 1972, almost a whole generation after Håkon Nyland had cycled to his first day of work in poor-but-liberated Norway, the well-established Labor Party suffered defeat when the population voted against joining the European Economic Community. This was a rebellion against the Social Democratic order. According to Solstad—and the two younger sons of Nyland—the 1970s heralded a new phase in the social development.

In 1945 Ronny Ambjörnsson was nine years old, a little older than Nyland's eldest son. Ambjörnsson, unlike Nyland, was not a character in a novel but a real figure. He grew up in a working-class home with one room and a kitchen in Gothenburg in western Sweden, which at the time perhaps was not such a wonderland place as it seemed from the vantage point of Norway. In his autobiographical sketch titled *My First Name is Ronny*, he describes how his parents got a larger apartment and a car: "Consumerism lifted my parents as though through the back door into a world that hitherto they had seen only from the outside."[1] The main theme of the sketch, however, is his own class journey. He would become a professor, teaching the history of ideas and knowledge. We recall Garborg's fictional figure Daniel Braut, who took the class journey from peasant to priest half a century earlier. On the surface it was a success, but on a psychological level it was highly disturbing to Braut's personal identity. The identity problematic, this admittance to two worlds that created "a distance from both," is the theme that runs through Ambjörnsson's reflections as well. The book ends with the family photograph taken at his investiture as professor:

> here we stand confronted by eternity: three generations, mama delighted with the situation … papa … as usual a little withdrawn, no doubt his thoughts far away … my children … happily liberated from the vicissitudes and self-imposed restrictions of the class journey; and then me, myself there, the traveler and the careerist, dangling between the obvious generations and classes, gripped by a problematic that hopefully is no more than a historical parenthesis.[2]

Both in Ambjörnsson's memoir and in Solstad's novel we notice the great material lift during what we have called the hegemonic period of Social Democracy, a lift that brought the workers into a world that had excluded them. But at the same time we are reminded that class was not only an economic reality but also a cultural construction. Class consciousness does not disappear,

---

[1] Ambjörnsson 1996, 74.
[2] Ambjörnsson 1996, 109.

at least not for those among the upwardly mobile who have roots reaching into the depths of the poor working class, whether the journey is a journey of the class out of poverty or an individual rise to the upper classes. But what about the longer-term perspective; what about Ambjörnsson's children, the happily liberated? What happens to the cultural construction when the material conditions have changed? Sweden and Norway were both to be characterized by a high degree of equality and openness.[3] The workers soon assumed the material standards of the lower middle class. Moreover, in Ambjörnsson's university institute the majority of the staff had made the class journey as he had done. Daniel Braut had been the exception, whereas in Ambjörnsson's society the exceptions were strikingly numerous and in some places became the rule. In such a society it is not unreasonable to think that the class journey problematic could be a parenthesis. But this would not reveal itself until the next phase of development. When the great leap was taken in the Social Democratic period, class as a cultural construction was still a reality. It marked the manner of thinking in that period.

CLASS SOCIETY IN TRANSFORMATION II

During the wartime elections in Sweden the Social Democrats had won an absolute majority in the Parliament, and with the election of 1945 this occurred in Norway as well. The dissolution of the wartime coalition governments enabled Social Democrats in both countries to form pure governments and carry forward the policies they had begun in the 1930s.[4] They were able to maintain this dominant position until around 1970. This was the happy moment of Social Democracy, or the period of the "one-party state," as some have called it. Much of the strength of the parties in both countries was based on their close relationship with the LO—the strong trade union central of the labor unions. The dominant position of the parties was, however, also dependent on their ability to attract non-working-class votes. Although both parties were labor parties in their hearts, they defined themselves, as we have seen, as "people's parties." Because the Swedish Social Democratic (Labor) Party was more successful in attracting middle-class voters than its Norwegian counterpart, the Norwegian Labor Party, its domination was somewhat stronger and lasted somewhat longer.[5]

---

[3] Erikson and Goldthorpe 1992, 177–178 and passim.

[4] In Denmark the Social Democrats never won an absolute majority in the Parliament.

[5] The dominating position of the SAP was somewhat strengthened by its taking advantage of what was left of the two-chamber Parliament after World War II. The two-chamber system was done away with in 1970.

Before World War II industrial workers constituted 45 percent of the working population in Sweden, whereas farmers constituted around 30 percent and salaried employees around 20 percent. After the war the percentage of industrial workers remained about the same, whereas the other two groups changed positions. This means simply that before the war the Social Democrats had to seek support among farmers (or peasant farmers) but after the war they turned to salaried workers. To cite Torsten Svensson, "the political dominance can be explained by a carefully designed Social Democratic multiclass strategy."[6]

We have seen how the strategy was designed in the 1930s, when the Swedish Social Democrats not only recruited voters from among the farmworkers but also cooperated with the Farmers' Party, with whom they competed for votes. After the war the Social Democrats had to compete more intensely with the other non-Socialist parties, the liberal Folkpartiet and the conservative Högerpartiet, for the votes of the salaried employees. The Swedish Social Democrats did not cooperate with these two parties, however. They were opposition parties, just as they had been before the war. In fact, when the Swedish Social Democratic leader and prime minister from 1946 Tage Erlander formed a coalition government in 1951, it was once again with the Farmers' Party, as was the case with the Social Democratic prime minister Per Albin Hansson in 1936. The cooperation with the salaried employees took place in another arena.

In 1944 salaried employees had formed a trade union central (TCO, Tjänstemännens Centralorganisation), which soon became an important political actor. The strategy designed by the Social Democratic LO, which turned out to be successful, was not to compete with the TCO for the membership of the salaried employees but to cooperate with the nonpolitical TCO. The crucial event toward political cooperation was the struggle over the supplementary pension plan (ATP) in the 1950s, which ended with the TCO giving its approval to the Social Democrats' standard security reform. The model was taken from the normal pension systems for salaried workers and implied that pensions should vary according to a worker's income before retirement. (A detailed analysis of the political process toward ATP is given in chapter 8.) To cite Svensson again: "The old understanding of equality was replaced by new visions, emphasizing social security. This is the beginning of the 'middle-class welfare state.'. . . The following election in 1960 showed an electoral breakthrough [for the Social Democrats] among the salaried employees."[7]

---

[6] Torsten Svensson 1994, 308.
[7] T. Svensson 1994, 310.

The multiclass strategy was not without risks and costs. In the first place there was the risk that the Communists could appear as the only real labor party. And after the war there was the risk that the support of the peasant farmers would be lost. When the Social Democrats succeeded in keeping most of its core voters while at the same time attracting new votes from among the salaried employees, it was partly due to the established strong position of the party. For many of the core voters there was hardly any alternative. But it was also due to the fact that the salaried employees had become as positive toward social reforms as were the workers. Thus it was that the labor movement, by a skillfully designed strategy, could move the coalition of white-collar and blue-collar workers beyond class-based distinctions and on to a wage earners' movement. The concept "workers" was replaced by "wage earners."

The Norwegian labor movement had greater organizational difficulties. Like the Swedish LO, the Norwegian LO had a spectacular increase in members after 1945, although less than that of the Swedish LO, which also had a higher proportion of trade union members in general (relative to the total population). As for the Norwegian Labor Party, it was on a par with the Swedish sister party around 1950, but thereafter the Norwegian party lost members while the Swedes more or less held position until around 1975. By that time they had three times as many members as the Norwegian party (relative to the total population).

The reason for these organizational difficulties was partly that the Norwegian LO never had gained the same strength as the Swedish LO, which, as we have seen, was more intimately integrated into the corporatist structures. The Swedish trade unions were, for instance, given the task of administering the unemployment insurance, and they had greater responsibility in the labor market since the opposing parties in industrial disputes could not be overruled by the state through compulsory arbitration, as was the case in Norway.

The challenges presented to the Social Democrats by the growing number of salaried employees were the same in the two countries. As in Sweden, the salaried employees in Norway established a trade union central, called FSO (Funksjonærenes Sentralorganisasjon), outside the LO, in 1951. This was modeled after the Swedish TCO. But in contrast to the Swedish experience, the Norwegian LO, rather than cooperating with the FSO, started a fierce competition with the group to capture salaried workers as members. The LO was indeed successful up to a point, but only to a point. Many salaried employees chose to be organized in unions outside the LO. This was in accordance with the Norwegian labor movement's hold on its identity as a *labor* movement to a greater degree than the Swedes. For instance, the Labor Party in Norway never joined in a coalition government with other parties as Branting did with the Liberals and Hansson and Erlander with the farmers in Sweden.[8] It also seems as though the undercurrent of antagonism toward salaried workers was stronger among Norwegian industrial workers.[9]

Reactions to the supplementary pension plan differed in the two countries as well. It did not bring about a real struggle in Norway as it did in Sweden; nor was it initiated by the Social Democrats. It was introduced by a non-Socialist government that had taken the Swedish system as its model. Klas Åmark concludes that the "consensus policy in Norway seems to have contributed to relative political stability, while at the same time denying the Norwegian Labor Party any traction for mobilization."[10] Whereas the pension issue smoothed the way toward positioning the Labor Party as a multiclass party in Sweden, it did not do so in Norway. Even though consensus on the issue was more marked in Norway than in Sweden, the process still did not have any impact on the party system. The strategy of the Norwegian Labor Party turned out to be less successful in capturing voters than the strategy chosen in Sweden, where the Social Democrats got more salaried workers' votes without trying to organize them!

With the growth in numbers of salaried employees and decrease in numbers of industrial workers, the somewhat more traditional Labor Party in Norway lost more ground than did its counterpart in Sweden. This difference should not be overemphasized, however. Up until around 1970 the Social Democrats dominated in both countries, and even if the Social Democrats in Norway were not quite as dominant as in Sweden, it does not mean that Norway was less Social Democratic.

The long period of dominance meant that the Social Democrats of both countries had a unique opportunity to realize their visions, and the more so since the period was characterized by a long and stable international economic upturn. The generation that took the reins in 1945 was also marked by youth, vitality, and the desire to lead, and they had few hesitations about using the power that their absolute majority in Parliament had afforded them. Their freedom, however, was limited by several contextual factors. We have seen how the Cold War forced them to give up the traditional Socialist antimilitarism and seek allies in the international arena, and how they had to take into account their multiclass bases, or their new identity as "people's parties." They also (wisely?) hesitated to undermine an economic system that functioned well. Nevertheless there are good reasons to emphasize the uniqueness of the situation, and we shall follow closely what became of their Socialist political legacy in the various arenas within this new situation of domination.

---

[8] The exception was the Norwegian exile government in London during the war.

[9] Messel 2000, 249, 251.

[10] Åmark 2005, 202.

"THE MOST DYNAMIC FORCE FOR
SOCIAL DEVELOPMENT"

After 1945 citizens in Sweden spoke of *harvest time*. Now was the time to harvest what had been sown earlier. Such a concept could not have taken root in Norway. Having been through the war, Norwegians referred to the period after 1945 as the *period of reconstruction*, the time to start anew. But there can be advantages to starting with a blank page.

At the beginning of the twentieth century we find that the Western societies were "permeated by science and the scientific outlook." And during the interwar period there came the growth of an even more consistent scientific ideology, along with the beginnings of a technocracy. These tendencies found expression in the 1939 book by the radical physicist John D. Bernal titled *The Social Function of Science*. He proclaimed the potential of science: "It is now evident that enough is known, both of natural science and of techniques making use of it, to solve all the major problems of the world economy."[11] This ideological direction certainly marked the postwar period. Inspired by Bernal among others, the Swedish minister of education said in 1959 that science was "the most dynamic force for social development."[12] A weak variation of "Bernalism" became one of the overriding ideologies of the Social Democrats.[13] This was particularly true of Sweden. Research and study was taken up systematically as the basis for reforms in almost all areas of society. "The welfare state ought to be built with the help of science."[14]

So we observe a shift in ideological trends, away from the old sentimental sociopolitical ideology to one that was cooler and more rational. In this "scientification" of society and politics there was a tendency to repeal policies and redefine political issues as questions that ought to be solved by experts. There is value in this depoliticizing insofar as experts and the sciences have had genuinely new insights to contribute. Those who know how to make use of these insights for the shaping of policy can become winners in relation to both realism and legitimacy. In Sweden and Norway this is what the Social Democrats did, allying themselves with science and expertise. This alliance undoubtedly contributed to the Social Democratic hegemony as well as the high degree of agreement that marked this epoch.

On the other hand, reliance on science and experts can be problematic. In politics, as elsewhere, it can be difficult to differentiate between means and ends, or between political and factual content. Experts could easily go

---

[11] Bernal 1969, 901.
[12] Edenman's speech in SOU 1959, 45, 39.
[13] Nybom 1997, 35.
[14] Frängsmyr 2000, 300.

beyond the limits of their expertise and into the realm of defining goals or establishing guidelines for resolving political conflicts. Moreover, different professions—economists, doctors, architects, engineers, pedagogues—positioned themselves as best able to respond to the complexities of a changed society. The doctors "knew" how to create a happy and healthy population; the architects emphasized the designing of the physical surroundings; the engineers had a vision of a technological future; the pedagogues "knew" how human material should be formed. In the various professions there existed aspirations to be something more than an expert in one's own field. The fact that competing holistic perspectives could break onto the scene, or such tugs-of-war between "generalist experts" could occur, demonstrates precisely how expert discourse could move into the actual field of politics.

Now there is scarcely any doubt that it was the social sciences, particularly the economists of the Keynesian tradition, who became the generalists and reform technocrats par excellence in the new Social Democratic society. The Social Democratic regime consequently completed the slow transformation from cultural humanism to economics as the society's dominant perspective. Economic, political, and welfare policies became more important than cultural policies; economic growth, industrialization, and equalization more important than symbolic production and identity politics. It is also characteristic that this new regime acquired clearly paternalistic features—the experts knew best. Reformist technocracy had to come into a tense relationship with the democratic motive.

In the industrialization drive in the postwar period the Social Democrats got a new ideological injection. Leif Lewin writes:

> Once more ... Swedish Social Democracy has been guided in its practical policy by a theoretician who works within radical international liberalism. In the 1930s with the high unemployment it was John Maynard Keynes. In the affluent society of the 1960s it is John Kenneth Galbraith.[15]

Galbraith's most articulate exposition of the modern society is in his two books *The Affluent Society* and *The New Industrial State*. The influence has, however, been reciprocal. Beginning in the late 1930s Galbraith became a close friend of Gunnar Myrdal and, as he himself has written, "With the possible exception of Great Britain, Sweden is the country with which I have had the closest contact."[16] We have seen that rather early on the Social Democrats cleansed themselves of Marxism. This meant that they abandoned the critical discourse on capitalism and, therein, the idea of a necessary contradiction

---

[15] Lewin 1967, 430.
[16] Galbraith 1996, in the foreword to the Swedish edition of his *My Economic History*.

between capital and labor. The "capitalism discourse" was replaced by the "industrialism discourse," in which the contradiction between capital and labor faded away.

Galbraith is the foremost example of one who worked within the industrialism discourse and thereby was able to launch the vision of a melding of the Soviet command economy with American capitalism in a new synthesis—the new industrial state: "nothing in our time is more interesting than that the erstwhile capitalist corporation and the erstwhile Communist firm should, under the imperative of organization, come together as oligarchies of their own members."[17] A social formation based on planning and neither Communist nor capitalist is precisely what the Social Democrats intended to stand for. Galbraith put words to their vision, and he was widely read, especially in Sweden. Although his work was known in Norway as well, the direct influence was less since Norway lacked an influential group of institutional economists such as the one we find in Sweden (Gunnar Myrdal, Erik Lundberg, and others).

It is a short road from Bernal's ideology of science to Galbraith's view of technology as "the most dynamic force for social development." According to Galbraith, "The imperatives of technology and organization, not the images of ideology, are what determine the shape of economic society."[18] At the same time, he stressed that the industrial system was profoundly dependent on the state. A strong state was especially necessary to ensure that the industrial state, propelled forward at the imperative of organization and technology, would serve a good society. We also see that by underlining technology as the real motive force, Galbraith went a long way toward the abolition of politics. The irony lies in the fact that when Galbraith published *The New Industrial State* in 1967, the Social Democratic state was facing new challenges that would change the direction of development and lead to a policy regeneration. But that is another story.

Circles of rationalists and scientifically inspired technocrats constituted the most important part of the prepolitical area between the private and public spheres during the Social Democratic period. On the one hand, these rationalists and technocrats had great influence on most people's view of the world: it became normal to believe in the imperative of science and technology. On the other hand, they had great influence on political solutions devised in order to accommodate these imperatives. We shall meet them again in their various arenas—the planning of the physical environment, the welfare state, schooling, economic policy, and industry.

[17] Galbraith 1967, 397.
[18] Galbraith 1967, 19.

THE VISION OF THE ATOMIC AGE

The research engineers constituted a central group of reform technocrats in both countries.[19] They operated in a vast gray zone between the public system and the private business community such as we saw earlier in relation to hydroelectric construction. Their basis was in a new form of organization—the research councils. At the top of their agenda was the inexhaustible source of future energy—nuclear power. Immediately after World War II considerable resources were channeled into atomic research in both Norway and Sweden. The seriousness of this effort is attested to by the fact that in 1951 Norway was the first small nation-state in the world to put an atomic reactor into operation. And in Sweden in 1965 ASEA (Allmänna Svenska Elektriska Aktiebolaget) was the only European enterprise able to deliver an atomic energy plant without U.S. licenses.[20]

Perhaps one might not think that atomic energy would be so high on the agenda in Sweden and Norway since both countries were so rich in waterpower. Sweden already had a supply situation that spurred interest in seeking out a new source of energy, however. Of equal importance, Sweden had reached a point where the future society had to be planned. The political regime shift gave extra impetus in this direction. It was natural for the Social Democrats to take the lead in a common effort to develop the technology of the future. And the voices of the experts were heeded. In a huge meeting at the concert hall in Stockholm in 1955, in a presentation titled "Atomic Power—Annihilation or Well-being?" the former Social Democratic prime minister and foreign minister Rickard Sandler maintained that atomic power was a moral force; it represented "a victory for reason, which transforms the demon of annihilation that lives in the nucleus of the atom into a powerful, obedient servant of mankind."[21]

Nuclear power did not become a political issue at this early stage. It was taken as given in Sweden and in Norway that the future lay in atomic power. There is scarcely any other area where technological determinism or "industrial fatalism" found clearer expression. Science and technology were seen as creative constructive subjects, the motivating, but also liberating, forces in history: "No, it is not possible to find any turning back from the atomic age; it is irrevocably writing a new page in history."[22]

[19] Slagstad 1998, 295.
[20] Schön 2000, 387.
[21] Sandler, in his speech "The Dawn of the Atomic Age," *Morgontidningen*, 16 February 1955. Cited by Anshelm 2000, 39.
[22] Anshelm 2000, 61.

In 1945 the Swedish government appointed an Atomic Committee that was to "find suitable methods to harness atomic energy." The committee was dominated by natural scientists, including no fewer than four former and future Nobel Prize winners. The idea to expand nuclear energy received extensive private as well as public support. The epoch-making decision that Sweden should pursue nuclear power was taken by Parliament in 1956. A state-owned company, Atomenergi (Atomic Energy) was to have the main responsibility for development and production of reactors and fuel, while the private ASEA was to take responsibility for running the power plants. The state was now prepared to increase its involvement significantly. The importance of the 1956 decision is underlined by Stefan Lindström:

> "Atoms," along with "automation," were prominent symbols in the politics of the future— for tomorrow's society—that made an important contribution to the Social Democratic initiatives before 1956's election to the Second Chamber. With some justice the decisions of 1956 can be described as among the most important and most interesting political decisions made during the 1950s.[23]

At this time the idea that Sweden should develop its own nuclear defense was still prevalent. The development of civilian use rapidly came to be a driving force, however. There was a close relationship between the civil and military programs, even though there was gradually less and less said about the military application. The need for coordination between the civil and military programs seems to have been the reason that the state took full control over further development of the nuclear program with the parliamentary decision of 1956. With this decision the "Swedish line" for development of nuclear energy was determined right up to 1970. We will come back to what has happened since that time.

Swedish research was ahead of Norwegian research in general—and the field of nuclear research was no exception. All the same, Norway had two elements to build on. For one, they had strong connections that were of benefit to them. Certain Norwegian researchers had developed a network among their allies while refugees during the war. And they had close contacts with their own government through the legendary Jens Christian Hauge. Hauge had been the very young leader of the home front military organization. He became minister of defense in 1945 and was to become one of Social Democracy's great strategists. Norway's second advantage was Norsk Hydro's heavy-water plant. Alongside uranium, heavy water was a strategic material necessary to the development of nuclear power, and both were difficult to obtain on the international market.

[23] Stefan Lindström 1991, 17.

In Norway the Defense Research Institute took up the nuclear issue. After a certain amount of jurisdictional dispute with members of the university research community among others, atomic research was handed over to the newly formed civil Atomic Energy Institute. The defined goal was to build an experimental reactor and conduct research into the practical civilian use of atomic energy in Norway. Close contact was developed with partly state-owned Norsk Hydro, which invested in the development of the first reactor by supplying the necessary heavy water. The Norwegians produced their own heavy water but lacked uranium. Conversely, the Dutch sat on uranium and lacked heavy water. A barter system came into effect between the two countries, forming the basis for a relatively quick commissioning of the Norwegian atomic reactor in 1951.

Both Sweden and Norway devoted considerable resources to the atomic project, but the future did not turn out as expected. To a great extent the effort was a dead end. Indeed, Sweden got its atomic energy plant, whereas Norway never got that far—owing largely to Norway's great hydroelectric resources. In addition, a powerful public reaction developed against nuclear energy, meaning that the research engineers had to cede part of the sub-political arena, with which they had so freely had their way, to the environmental movement.

In 1956 Åke Rusck, the general director of the Swedish Vattenfall, revealed plans to build the first atomic energy plant, to be called Adam, and then take "a rib" from this and create an atomic energy plant called Eve. "The atomic age was likened to the dawn of civilization, and the new society to Eden's garden of pleasures, 'a paradise of atoms,'" went Jonas Anshelm's commentary, ironically concluding: "Hardly any of those who took part in the discourse would have been ignorant of what happened to Adam and Eve in the Garden of Eden, that they were punished for having eaten from the Tree of Knowledge, cast out of Paradise by God and forced to live a difficult and painful life. . . . Åke Rusck and Vattenfall, it must be said, had been virtually and unintentionally clairvoyant when they launched the metaphor."[24]

SWEDEN: A WINNER NATION

Sweden had come relatively quickly out of the crises that beset the interwar period, largely because of the networks that had been built up within Swedish business life. In this connection the large commercial banks played a decisive role. On the basis of these networks it had been possible to meet the crises

---

[24] Anshelm 2000, 39, 66–67.

with modernization and restructuring, allowing Sweden to become "a winner nation." As a result, they had positive experiences to build on. The wartime experiences also added elements to this picture. There "happened a shifting of power toward the state and politics, which had . . . far-reaching consequences." The coordination of efforts during the war had paid off: the production of electrical power had doubled, and a military-industrial complex was expanded on the basis of the advanced engineering industry.[25] Swedish industry demonstrated its flexibility and strength through its collaboration with the political leadership. This was to be the basis for development after 1945.

In both Sweden and Norway the business communities were now challenged by a consolidated Social Democracy. There were disputes over regulatory policies. In both countries the business communities wanted to show that they themselves could deal with the emerging challenges. The only difference was that the Swedes managed to do so, in contrast to the Norwegians. To cite Leif Lewin: "Through energetic reconstruction work after the war, the entrepreneurs would show how unfair and unmotivated it was not to accept the ability of the private sector to keep up production and employment. The Social Democrats' distrust also turned out to be unfounded. Trade and commerce were showing a boom period such as had never been seen before. 'Productive labor' was triumphing over 'bureaucracy.'"[26]

The period between 1950 and 1975 represents the golden age of industrialism in Sweden.[27] Growth was rapid and stable. Although this was occurring throughout the industrialized world, Sweden was among the leaders. This development has been attributed to a concurrence of fortunate factors. The international economic cycles constituted one of the conditions, but of equal importance were the internal structural relations. The new consumer society, complete with electrification and the culture of the automobile, gave motive force to new markets.

As before, the state took direct initiative in hydroelectric power construction. While atomic power was projected for a distant future, hydroelectric power was for use more immediately. That it could still be further developed was "in the eyes of the experts something so self-evidently positive that no special arguments were needed. They merely noted that hydropower for many years into the future truly would be central to 'an exaggerated level of development, and thus would be of highest priority from the general point of view.'"[28] This was reiterated in a 1947 memorandum; in this case the experts were not research engineers but rather social economists and politicians with

[25] Schön 2000, 359–360.
[26] Lewin 1992, 245.
[27] Schön 2000, 375.
[28] Vedung and Brandel 2001, 54.

broad support in terms of public opinion. Hydroelectric power was increased almost fivefold from 1946 to 1975, with the public sector being the developer and driving force.

One characteristic of Sweden was its unusually high number of international industrial corporations. The traditional heavy steel industry was modernized; organized in larger units of production, it flourished. Engineering was the leading sector of industry up to 1970. As we have seen, in the interwar period Sweden had already developed a significant shipbuilding industry. Shipbuilding reached its high point in the 1960s, accounting for about 10 percent of the world's production of ships.[29] One of the important preexisting conditions for this activity was the strong link between Swedish shipbuilders and Norwegian shipowners. Old enterprises like ASEA and L. M. Ericsson also launched mighty expansions.

Close ties between the state and the public sector, with its strong involvement in infrastructure, were an important condition for this expansion. Thus it was that ASEA cooperated closely with the public company Vattenfall, and L. M. Ericsson with the public telecommunication company Televerket. SAAB was developed by public commission as part of the armaments industry. On this foundation the firm was able to expand as a successful producer of automobiles. The largest automobile producer was Volvo, which, together with ASEA, became Sweden's largest industrial producer during this period. Scania-Vabis, which produced trucks and buses, also expanded significantly. Vehicles were Sweden's most important export article.

In general Sweden developed a very strong position with regard to the production of various consumer durables for a rapidly growing international market. In addition to the automobile, this applied to refrigerators, kitchen ranges, vacuum cleaners (Electrolux), office machinery (Facit), radio, and, later, television equipment (Luxor). Older firms such as SKF (ball bearings), Alfa-Laval (agricultural machinery), and Atlas Copco (motors and jackhammers) also experienced strong growth. On the whole, the continuity was just as striking as the renovation and renewal; the reconstruction was carried out to a great degree on the basis of the old structures. In short, Social Democratic Sweden became an industrial model country—until about 1970–1975.

THE WALLENBERG SYSTEM

The network structures we described earlier, which had their roots back in the industrialization period at the end of the nineteenth century and expanded

---

[29] Schön 2000, 421.

in the interwar period, continued and also were consolidated after the war. Characteristic for Sweden, the ownership structure of the large industrial firms was concentrated in a few groups, sometimes referred to as the "fifteen families." Typically these ownership groups held close relationships to the largest Swedish banks. The Wallenbergs were the dominant group, having a controlling interest in several of the above-mentioned firms (Alfa-Laval, ASEA, Atlas Copco, Electrolux, SAAB, Scania-Vabis, L. M. Ericsson, and SKF). An important feature in the structure was their bank, the Stockholms Enskilda [Private] Bank. The group members typically held ownership positions in their bank, which was simultaneously their most important source of loans. Ulf Olsson characterizes the group as an "entrepreneurial group"; that is to say, they were actively engaged in the individual companies, and the activities of the bank were subordinate to their industrial goals. "In a somewhat schematic form one can explain the state of affairs thus: the Wallenberg group acted at a middle level—a "meso level"—between private enterprise at the micro level and the national macro level." Thanks primarily to their bank, the Wallenberg group had great opportunities "to act at this meso level. Coordination between enterprises, in both the horizontal and vertical senses, and transfers of capital or production between firms were relatively easy to accomplish. The initiative to perform mergers or make other structural changes could be arranged. Activity at this level, above the individual firm, had features of both organized management and free entrepreneurship such that it involved both influence and an exchange of ideas—upward toward the macro level and downward toward the micro level. The expansion of the Wallenberg group indicates that their composition and methods have been well adapted to their purposes."[30]

Not only structural factors stood behind the success of the Wallenbergs; they also were extremely capable. This is particularly true of Marcus Wallenberg Jr., who acquired a unique position in the history of Swedish industry after 1945, at the peak of Social Democratic hegemony. His was the third generation of the family's extensive business activity. In addition to participating in trade and commerce, he had been Sweden's tennis champion before the war, and during the war he had been involved with the government in its trade negotiations with Great Britain.

It is rather remarkable that this clever supercapitalist achieved such a position in Social Democratic Sweden: "In his industrial activities MW obviously worked right into the 1960s in unison with both the country's political and professional leadership." For example, when Prime Minister Erlander and Wallenberg both attended a conference in 1957 to discuss the country's eco-

[30] Ulf Olsson 1986, 263.

Figure 10. Tage Erlander, *right*, became prime minister in Sweden in 1946 and personified like no one else the golden age of Social Democracy in Sweden, as Gerhardsen did in Norway. Here he is conversing with the legendary business leader Marcus Wallenberg Jr. It was said that they were the two most powerful men in Sweden, representing the public and the private sectors respectively. Sending the photo to Wallenberg, Erlander hinted that it could perhaps arouse suspicion of a too close relationship between capital and labor. (Photo: The Foundation for Economic History and Research within Banking and Enterprise, Stockholm.)

nomic future, this was portrayed in the media as a collegial meeting between "Sweden's two leading persons, each with responsibility for his respective part of the country, the public and the private."[31]

The interplay between Social Democracy and the business world—the public and the private—functioned well. Sweden was able to further develop its research-based industry, and it flourished as an industrial nation. The country stood as an example of the land of the future that Galbraith would later describe; it had become the avant-garde nation that the country had been preparing for at the beginning of the century. As many have remarked, in this

[31] U. Olsson 1986, 339.

period Sweden was able to demonstrate that Social Democracy could function more in accordance with the logic of industrialism than could liberal capitalism, simply by acting more rationally than the latter.[32]

SWEDISH LABOR MARKET POLICY

What particularly characterized Sweden was the way its public sector rapidly established mechanisms for development of an effective labor market policy that played a decisive role in industrialization and the general modernization of Swedish society. The policy, which came to be known as the Rehn-Meidner Model (after LO economists Gösta Rehn and Rudolf Meidner), was adopted by the Trade Union (LO) Congress of 1951. The aim of this model was to establish a system allowing for full employment, a stable level of prices and wages, freedom for the participants in working life to undertake agreements on their own premises, and, last but not least, consideration of the need for structural rationalization in trade and commerce and, thereby, economic growth. The means to this end involved a tight financial policy, a labor mediation authority with extensive powers, and a solidarity wage policy.

Naturally enough, sociopolitical motives lay behind this labor market policy. This applies above all to the solidarity wage policy and unemployment insurance provisions. Significantly, behind the policy lay also a strong macroeconomic motive. The desired goal was planned economic management of the input factor "labor." This was clearly announced in 1954 by the social minister, who later became the strong minister of finance Gunnar Sträng: "The motive of the social policy has shifted. . . . Now, when conditions for new social reforms are to be discussed, it is the problem of production and effectiveness, the question of making the common cake larger, that comes to the fore."[33]

From the macroeconomic perspective the most remarkable thing has been the active and effective labor mediation that the labor market regime Arbetsmarknadsstyrelsen (AMS) came to stand for. This had roots back in the communally organized labor relations from the beginning of the twentieth century. It was further expanded during the war when a great need for a redistribution of the workforce arose and when, because of the extraordinary situation, extensive public-sector management was legitimate. The main feature of this redistribution was that it was neutral in relation to organized class interests. It was accepted by both sides involved in working life, and it effectively

---

[32] Stephens 1979, chap. 4; Erikson and Goldthorpe 1992, 18.
[33] As cited Åmark1999, 44.

eliminated disputes, despite the fact that many difficult conflicts arose in other areas of working life.[34] With the development of this labor mediation, which was consolidated in the AMS in 1948, it is said that "modern state interventionism was introduced into Swedish public administration."[35] The AMS became an effective instrument of economic policy insofar as it actively contributed to the movement of the workforce, and thereby the restructuring and rationalization of Swedish industry. The system has been emphasized as a symbol of the Swedish model, and it has been regarded with admiration in other countries, yet no one has managed to copy it.

What made such an institution so effective? Labor mediation was systematically developed as an alternative to the traditional state bureaucracy. To a large degree the personnel were recruited from the trade unions, that is, from people familiar with the labor market from the ground up, or "street bureaucrats" as opposed to ordinary bureaucrats. They operated selectively, considering the local conditions in each case, and had a large arsenal of different means of achieving satisfactory ends. Bo Rothstein emphasizes in particular the use of ideological means. In this connection he cites the chief economist of the Swedish Employers Association, K. O. Faxén, in his commentary on the possibility of relocating the unemployed when circumstances warranted:

> In Sweden we consider such movement to be a self-evident issue. Especially since Chairman Mr. Bertil Olsson's energetic public relations activity on the subject, the fact that one is supposed to move has gone right into public consciousness. It is considered to be something almost criminal not to be flexible, so to speak. It has become so self-evident that we do not even reflect about how odd it actually is. If one were to look at other countries I do not believe by any means that one would find the same general attitude. There, on the whole, one finds a considerable amount of romantic talk about the district and the tradition and about how important it is to plow the same fields as one's forefathers, that one ought to uphold the local culture of a certain district and not ruthlessly say—as we do here in Sweden, and which we consider to be the moral thing to do—that when an area no longer has great economic potential we then arrange a mobility-promoting labor market policy that makes it easier for people to move away.[36]

To direct labor power "ruthlessly" is therefore something unique to Swedish Social Democracy among Western democracies. It was made possible because it was laid down as a norm of society, thus giving rise to relative agreement. The politician Bertil Olsson, above all others, was the implementer of this policy. He was a Social Democrat and had risen up through the ranks since

---

[34] Rothstein 1986, 109.
[35] Rothstein 1986, 119–120.
[36] As cited by Rothstein 1986, 151.

he was first employed by AMS in 1940, eventually becoming director general of the organization. It was especially under his leadership in the 1960s that the areas constituting the Swedish periphery were downgraded and to a large degree depopulated.

Sweden's ability to move the workforce was an important foundation for the strengthening and restructuring of Swedish industry during the Social Democratic epoch. In this area the contrast between brutal Sweden and kind Norway is striking. It would be very strange indeed if Faxén did not have Norway in mind when he contrasted the Swedish system with that of "other countries" where there was much talk about the district and tradition. The goal above all others in Norway was to defend "the pattern of residence," as it was called. The idea was not to move people.

The other main element in the Rehn-Meidner Model in addition to labor mediation was the solidarity wage policy.[37] The problem for the LO was determining the trade unions' role in a context of full employment and of labor's movement into governmental power. There was an urgent danger that strong inflation would undermine the economy. "We do not have any theoretical and technical apparatus for meeting the problem of full employment. . . . We have had this full employment; we have been taken unawares by it. But there is no theory to be found," as Meidner wrote.[38] To utilize the boom periods of the economic cycle by following the traditional policy of pushing workers' wages up as high as possible would have been irresponsible. Nor was it an alternative, according to Meidner, simply to turn the policy around and hold down wage demands, as William Beveridge in Great Britain had recommended. That would be to assume the role that rightfully belonged to the employers and the political authorities. In addition, the organization would lose credibility among its members. In short, what should the trade union's role be in the Social Democratic society with full employment?

The solution was a radical curtailment of purchasing power through financial and taxation policies, which was the task of the political authorities, and the establishment of a solidarity wage policy, which was the task of the trade union organization. The solidarity wage policy meant equal pay for equal work regardless of the carrying capacity of the individual firms. In this way high wages could be held back while agitating for wage increases for the low paid. The problem with such a policy was that it would knock out the weaker firms and threaten the jobs that they had provided. But this problem was turned into something positive—it was an advantage to the economy that the weaker firms were eliminated. A solidarity wage policy simply meant

---

[37] The following is largely built on Johansson and Magnusson 1998, 43f.
[38] Ekdahl 2001, 248.

that one used "the wage policy as an instrument for increasing production and improved effectiveness." The precondition, however, was that the workers who lost their jobs were to be rapidly placed in profitable work at good wages in other firms at other locations. This is where the necessity of having an effective labor market policy came in.

One of the reasons that the strategy succeeded as well as it did was the mutual understanding between the two sides that were involved in working life regarding how the game was to be played. Control was gained by substituting negotiations on the branch level with centralized negotiations. Furthermore, the Employers Association no longer had reason to fear "that the trade union movement would go to the government and Parliament to seek support in wage negotiations."[39] On the other hand, the Employers Association contributed to the function of the model by developing a solidarity cost policy, the employers being careful not to compete for labor. Likewise, on the LO side the solidarity policy presupposed a high degree of centralized power within the organization. In this way unique to Sweden "the internal solidarity within the two opposing collective bodies worked in the same direction and toward improved wage structuring."[40] Thus Sweden developed a pure and well-functioning negotiated corporatism while remaining at arm's length from the state. In Norway it was inconceivable that the state should relinquish such a central political domain to the working-life organizations in this way.[41]

THE NORWEGIAN STATE AND THE LABOR MARKET

Following World War II the development of the economic management structure in both Sweden and Norway was marked by two experiences—the crisis of the interwar period following the failure of the market economy, and the effectiveness of the wartime command economies of belligerent countries. This formed the background for the "economic planning debate" that was to become very intense in both countries. It is important to be aware that this dual experience had shifted the basis for the debate. Everyone now felt that it was necessary to have more planning than had been the case in the interwar years. There remained the question, however, of who should be the planners.

In Norway this combination of agreement on the need for planning and disagreement regarding who should do the planning is illustrated by an ini-

---

[39] Ekdahl 2001, 325–326.
[40] Nycander 2002, 142.
[41] Heiret et al. 2003, 126–127.

tiative taken by a certain circle of business leaders during the war. In 1943, during the German occupation, one of the most prominent of these leaders, Gunnar Schjelderup, wrote a "private memo regarding a confidential study society for the elucidation of new industrial projects, planning to form a nationally accented holding company whose mandate would be to bring these projects to life at the moment peace returned." The experiences of the 1930s were frightening for, as Schjelderup wrote, if the business community did not show more initiative than it had shown it would have only itself to blame "for a little-desired development." And this little-desired development would consist of "many state companies, which will and must exist if the men of trade and commerce do not themselves show adequate initiative."[42]

This "Study Society for Norwegian Industry" received broad support but did not manage in any way to live up to its original intentions. It was more a demonstration of the powerlessness of the Norwegian industrial bourgeoisie when it came to taking organized national initiatives for building up the organization of production. Precisely as Schjelderup had predicted, and characterized as "a little-desired development," the state moved in, compensating for the weakness of the commerce bourgeoisie. This was close to the opposite of what happened in Sweden, where the business world "triumphed over bureaucracy."

Like Sweden, Norway also benefited from the international trade prosperity of the times and had a similar rate of growth from the late 1940s until 1970, but the similarities ended here. Norway's starting point was lower; in 1945 Norway had employment for 160,000 industrial workers, compared with 1,000,000 in Sweden.[43] We have already seen, as well, that the interwar crises hit Norway harder. In addition, the war had given Sweden a head start. During the war Sweden had a growth rate of 2.5 percent, while national wealth in Norway was reduced by an estimated 18.5 percent. In other words, Norway faced a significant reconstruction. In contrast to Sweden, the Norwegian state had to compensate for the lack of a strong private bourgeoisie. The Social Democrats had few hesitations about taking up the role. But just as the business community had groped around, so too did the state.

It was a long time before a labor market policy was developed in Norway. And even then it was tied first and foremost to social rather than economic policy.[44] Sweden had built up an effective employment service during the war. The need to move the workforce also arose in Norway, and certain initiatives were set in motion as early as 1940 by the Administration Council (a non-

---

[42] The memo is included in Sevje 1977.
[43] Lindboe 1990, 170.
[44] Helgesen 1997, 311.

Nazi civilian transition administration of 1940). The labor exchange under the Administration Council was quickly Nazified, however, and when it became clear that to a great degree it was being used to benefit the building and construction projects of the Germans, the resistance movement called for a boycott and ordered sabotage actions. This provided a poor starting point for building up the management of labor mediation following 1945.

Norway's regional policy also had a completely different profile from Sweden's. Most prominently, whereas in Sweden, for economic reasons, workers were moved from the districts to central areas, the opposite was the case in Norway. There, to a much greater degree, an effort was made to move investments out to the workforce in the districts. In Norway social importance was attached to preservation of the residential demographic pattern. The North Norway Plan from 1952 provides a typical example—"an industrially subdued modernization plan" that received broad support.[45] It led to significant investment in the most northerly regions of the country through public credit institutions. This occurred approximately simultaneously with Sweden's planned near depopulation of its northerly regions. The general trend in Norway was, of course, the same as in Sweden—a depopulation of the rural and northern regions and a general migration to the cities. The difference between the two countries was that while the Swedes adapted their policy to the general trend and even strengthened it, the Norwegians tried to strive against it.

Norway also had its solidarity wage policy on the agenda. As in Sweden, branch-level negotiations were substituted for centralized negotiations. The wage policy was not coordinated with a planned restructuring of industry, however. Moreover, in contrast to Sweden, a state-guaranteed system emerged in Norway. Until the end of the 1950s its wage-moderating regime was, nevertheless, more successful than the Swedish one. This "corporative social contract" implied that the state dictated wages to a great degree through compulsory arbitration. The precondition for the success of this policy, and for abstention from high wage demands, was the voluntarism of the reconstruction period: moderation today would yield well-being tomorrow.

In the long run, however, the active role of the Norwegian state in wage policy became problematic. With the state acting as third party, wage policy was a chip in the political game. From having been in the lead in wage equalization around 1950, Norway gradually fell behind Sweden.[46] Additionally, Norway developed what would later be called "the front professions model" as the basis for a common wage policy, utilizing wages in the

45 Slagstad 1998, 269.
46 Alf O. Johansson 2000, 209.

competition-exposed export industries as the norm for defining responsible wage levels.

Consequently, Sweden and Norway had quite different systems. Sweden had a bipartite collaboration—"a trust-based social contract"—with the state in an arm's-length relationship. In Norway there was a tripartite collaboration, with the state as the third party, controlling and subsidizing—"a corporative social contract."[47] Among other things, the difference lay in the fact that the employer party was weaker in Norway and therefore "needed" the state. But part of the reason also lay on the employee side. Indeed, the stronger and more nationally coordinated the trade union organizations are, the greater the chance that they "will adopt some awareness of and consideration for the consequences their demands and strategies entail for the employment prospects of workers in general, as well as for the rate of inflation and their industry's competitiveness."[48] This was the case to a greater degree in Sweden than in Norway. The Norwegian trade union movement had a relatively strong shop steward institution, a stronger local right to negotiate, and a stronger influence from the membership than did the Swedish.[49] In other words, the Norwegian trade unions were not organized to take care of superordinate national interests in the same way the unions were in the centralized Swedish movement. Therefore the state had to become involved. Both the Swedish and the Norwegian systems of working-life relations functioned reasonably well in terms of wage moderation and peaceful working conditions, however.

FOCUSING ON NATURAL CONDITIONS

But where should the focus of further industrialization be placed? The obvious choice in both Norway and Sweden was on increasing the generation of electricity, a task that was assumed by the public sector itself. By 1945 the two countries had built up approximately the same amount of hydropower, which meant that Norway produced twice as much power per capita as did Sweden. By 1975 we find that Sweden had increased its hydroelectric production fivefold while Norway had a sevenfold increase. Some of this energy was directed toward domestic consumption, but more was used for industrial purposes. Unlike Sweden, however, Norway at the outset did not have an active and dynamic industry that could utilize the power. With the exception

[47] Frøland 1992; Alf O. Johansson 2000; Heiret et al. 2003, 118.
[48] Offe 2006, 10.
[49] Heiret et al. 2003, 141.

of Norsk Hydro and a couple of other companies, Norway had to create new
industrial enterprises. This is the background for the Labor Party's "energy
Socialism." Between 1945 and 1947 the party adopted a series of parliamentary initiatives that clearly indicated it was heavy industry that should best
utilize abundant and cheap state-produced hydropower.[50] In the years that
followed there developed an extensive, power-intensive metallurgical industry. The first initiative was a large state-controlled steelworks at Mo i Rana in
northern Norway. Norway had lacked a steel industry, which was considered
to be an important part of the infrastructure of a modern industrial state. In
addition, Norway needed to save its dollar currency holdings and wanted to
develop industry in the rural districts. A/S Norsk Jernverk (the Norwegian
Ironworks Corporation) was thus set up on the basis of political agreement.
But it gobbled up significant amounts of capital and never came to pay its
own way, eventually closing down in 1989.

The heaviest concentration of Norwegian effort, however, was invested in
a series of primary aluminum plants spread around the rural regions. In 1970
Norway had become the largest exporter of aluminum in Europe. Plant construction took place partly under shared state and private management. In
1959 the former UN general secretary Trygve Lie was appointed Norway's
"dollar ambassador"; in other words, he was to entice foreign investors to
Norway using cheap power as the incentive. The work of Trygve Lie and his
committee was a model of Social Democratic economic planning, characterized by taking strategic control of the structure of the aluminum industry.[51]
These initiatives must be viewed as successful.

Norway developed a characteristic dual industrial structure. On the one
hand, we find further development of traditional Norwegian light industry that essentially produced for a protected home market—and that feared
Swedish competition. On the other hand, there was an enclave of heavy industries that were energy intensive, were publicly initiated and directed, and
that sold semiprocessed goods on the export market. But, as was increasingly
evident in comparison to Sweden, Norway lacked a research-based industry
and an industry for durable consumer goods that might be competitive on
the international market.

The Norwegian merchant marine represented one of the greatest items of
investment in the Norwegian economy after the war. In 1948 the gross tonnage carried by marine vessels had risen to its prewar level—4.4 million tons.
But the scarcity of hard currency led the Social Democratic government at

[50] Thue 1996, 61.
[51] Sogner 2003, 161–164.

first to demand that the shipowners finance their building contracts with 100 percent self-earned hard currency and thereafter to put a stop to contracting in 1948–1949. It has been argued that, as a result, Norwegian shipping lost momentum and fell behind its competitors. Nevertheless, by 1970 the gross tonnage was 20.1 million. As far as it went, the shipping industry managed to make use of the good times despite restrictions and heavy taxation.

TO "PLAY WALLENBERG" IN NORWAY

In comparison with Sweden, Norway lacked institutionalization of the strategic middle level between the firms and the state. It had no powerful co-ordinating entity such as the Wallenbergs provided in Sweden. Schjelderup had seen this weakness and attempted to repair it, without success, as did Johan Melander. Under Melander's direction Den norske Creditbank became Norway's largest bank, although it was still small compared with the large Swedish banks. Nevertheless, Melander shouldered the burden of "playing Wallenberg," as he himself put it.

Melander was a lawyer with a background in public service. Early in the 1950s, before he took over as bank director, he had been given the important commission to lead the negotiations for the first General Agreement on Tariffs and Trade (GATT). Although Melander and Wallenberg differed in background, both men held international reputations and considered themselves to be national strategists. Melander's attempt to "play Wallenberg" began with the large aluminum works on the western coast, at Husnes, in 1962. Melander had visions: "For the first time we want to have an example that a Norwegian bank, too, can solve problems that the great European 'Banques d'Affaires' have solved in Europe."[52] The initiative was successful, but this was more a result of Trygve Lie's initiatives, and Melander can be viewed to some extent as a chip played in Lie's game.

A number of Melander's lesser moves were quite successful, but two spectacular initiatives did not succeed. The first involved an attempt to bring about a structural rationalization of wood-processing plants on two of the largest waterways in southern Norway. (Sweden had carried out such a structural rationalization a generation earlier.) The attempt was necessary, but eventually it failed. The other failed initiative was a large-scale reorganization of the urban district of Vaterland in Oslo. Melander did not lack invitations to take up this strategic role—from the private business sector itself but es-

---

[52] Sejersted 2002a, 397f.

pecially from prominent Social Democrats such as Erik Brofoss (the head of Norges Bank, former finance minister, and architect behind the postwar economic policy of the Labor Party) and Oslo's Social Democratic mayor, Brynjulf Bull. But opinion reversed itself as soon as Melander's bank began to operate. Its activity became defined as large capital that was simply following its own interests, and both of these initiatives had to be abandoned. When it came to making the play, Melander lacked sufficient legitimacy not only in the realm of public opinion but also among the political authorities and the businesses that were to be restructured. In Norway economic strategies on a national level were the responsibility of the public sector, even such tasks as industrial strategy at the middle level.

The state's industrialization initiatives were, above all, compensatory. In other words, the motive driving these initiatives was not socialization but rather industrialization, which meant that the state stepped in where the private sector did not manage, or was not expected, to solve the problems. Within some segments of the labor movement there had initially been a certain will toward socialization. Thus we do find some examples of this, such as the aluminum works at Årdal that the state took over from the Germans after the war. For a certain period the ambition was to make a public company into a kind of demonstration model for the industrial firm of the future. This ambition was quickly laid aside, however, when the apolitical industrialist Jens Bache-Wiig became the chairman: he "saw it as his job to make sure that Årdal did not become an experiment in Socialism."[53]

Bache-Wiig had been a professor at Norway's Technical College (NIT). He had broad international industrial experience and had been vice president of the American corporation ITT, with responsibility for activities in the Nordic countries. Early in the war he had been a member of the Administration Council. Later he took part in Schjelderup's clandestine initiative and took over as chairman and functioning general director of Norsk Hydro during the final year of the war. He steered Hydro clear of German influence, just as later he would steer the Årdal and Sunndal plants clear of Socialist experimentation. He was engaged in getting the German ownership portion of Norsk Hydro transferred to the Norwegian state as a war reparation in 1945, and continued as chairman of Hydro and of the state-owned Årdal works for several years. He enjoyed strong support in the government, which used him as a policy expert on industry. The way Bache-Wiig was utilized demonstrates precisely that the project of the Social Democrats was not socialization but rather industrial modernization.

---

[53] Slagstad 1998, 292. Slagstad presents him as one of the national strategists.

AN ATTEMPT TO CREATE A
NORWEGIAN KNOWLEDGE INDUSTRY

A powerful initiative was taken in the 1970s to build up a Norwegian knowledge industry in the field of electronics. This initiative came from the research engineers' milieu, in collaboration with key Labor Party people, especially Jens Christian Hauge. Three companies that had been reasonably successful in their own areas within the field of electronics were selected for expansion and development into what were called "cornerstone firms," thereby providing the core of a new structure. These were the privately owned radio factory Tandberg, the state-owned Kongsberg Våpenfabrikk (Kongsberg Weapons Factory), and the telecommunications firm Elektrisk Bureau (Electric Bureau). It was thought that these three companies had the technological and administrative competence needed to further develop a modern knowledge-based industry.

As a precondition to cornerstone designation these companies were to clean up the structure of three smaller crisis-ridden companies. Following the challenge posed by the state, Tandberg took over the radio company Radionette, Elektrisk Bureau took over Nera, and Kongsberg Våpenfabrikk took over Noratom-Norcontrol. The three "cornerstone firms" were promised considerable state support if they followed the strategy issued by the authorities. But "compelling" them to take over these crisis-ridden companies was scarcely a good solution.

The instrument of the authorities was that of the Industry Foundation, established in 1973 through the amalgamation of several more or less goal-oriented, state-run industrial foundations. In addition, this initiative was closely associated with a planned state-owned holding company for industry that would consolidate the state's proprietary interests. The company was modeled after an American corporate paradigm, which meant that in a certain sense it broke with traditional state planning. It was, consequently, to work at arm's length from the government department.[54]

This initiative to build a more powerful Norwegian knowledge-based industry turned into a fiasco. First of all, the proposal for a state-owned holding company met with political opposition and had to be abandoned, and the Industry Foundation had neither the financial means nor the political strength to carry the initiative further. Second, the initiative was overtaken by difficult times, and Tandberg went bankrupt in 1978. The failure of the initiative had political consequences and discredited the idea of public industry. The construction of the initiative itself created unclear relations of responsibility.

---

[54] Sogner 2002, 51. See also Tveite 1995.

How far should the state's responsibility extend regarding the chosen "cornerstone firms"?

Returning to the difference between the two countries with regard to the linkage between technical–natural science research and industry, Sweden already had a knowledge-based industry that was able to make use of the state commitment to research for industry. In Norway there was no such starting point, nor was it ever possible to coordinate the important efforts in the field of industrial research by means of an active public-sector industry policy. The difference between the two countries finds expression in that Sweden stood well above average among the Organization for Economic Development (OECD) countries when it came to research efforts, while Norway stood well below average. And this was attributed not so much to differences in public commitment as to differences in the industries' own research and their ability to make use of it. Thus in an instructive manner this reflects the differences in industrial structure between the two countries as well as the difficulties confronting the Social Democrats in implementing radical plans for modernizing the industrial structure.

SUCCESSFUL INDUSTRIAL POLICY?

Melander had been forced to pull back with burned fingers—it was not possible for private actors to play Wallenberg in Norway. Hence the precarious question: could it be possible for the public sector to master the role that the Wallenbergs played in Sweden—as strategists for the middle level of the economy? The efforts of the research engineers and Jens Christian Hauge to play Wallenberg and to build up a knowledge industry were not successful. The public sector's broad engagement in energy-demanding export industries, first and foremost in the building up of the primary aluminum works, was considerably more successful. As far as this goes, we can say that if there was anyone able to play Wallenberg, it would be the representatives of the public sector, Trygve Lie and Jens Bache-Wiig—within one field and one period of time. But, apart from this, the strategic empty space at the meso level remained.

The Swedish economy became "one of the most dependent on large-scale corporations in the whole industrial world," while in Norway the reverse was the case.[55] The great worry, therefore, was failure to develop anything that resembled Sweden. Nevertheless, the Norwegian form of mixed economy must be viewed as reasonably successful. Despite the fact that Norway did not

55 Jonung 2002, 11.

manage to develop a knowledge industry of any effectiveness, it did manage through public initiatives to make use of the comparative advantage that hydropower (and, later, petroleum) represented.

THE SOCIAL DEMOCRATIC URBAN LANDSCAPE

After World War II Europe was confronted with the task not only of rebuilding cities that had been destroyed during the war but also of building new dwellings for an expanding population in general, and an enormous growth of city dwellers in particular. These challenges were met with impressive building activity all over Europe. This activity was in many cases combined with a wish to break with the past and develop cities for the new society. Truly, the physical appearance of many of the European cities changed during this period; whether it was for the better can be debated.[56] The Scandinavian countries were certainly no exception in this process—on the contrary.

The 1930 Stockholm Exposition had represented "the birth of the Swedish project of the future," if we are to believe Gunnar Myrdal. This applied particularly to the design of our physical environment. For example, what should a modernist city look like? How should social functions be taken care of and organized through physical planning? Urban and regional planning were by no means new, but they took a new direction in the 1930s through functionalism. Comprehensive plans were put into effect in the years that followed 1945. Functionalism was marked by reason and plan, and especially by a functionalist aesthetic—pure forms.

If functionalism represented the new direction, then Social Democracy represented the new initiative. The Social Democrats made this new direction an integral part of their profile. It also fit into their general idea that a new society was to be developed, one that looked different, where the aesthetic was woven into practical functions. Society had to prepare for "a comprehensive and rational urban building," according to Erik Rolfsen, who led the planning of Norwegian cities and towns that were destroyed during the war and who later became urban planning chief of Oslo. He had an "exclusive position in the regulation of the Social Democratic social landscape." For Rolfsen the old cities were an old civilization in decline. He ascertained that the only people who had "occasion to rationalize their central areas in a completely thoroughgoing way" were those whose cities or towns had been "stricken from the map" during World War II; that is to say, above all, the Germans.

---

[56] Judt 2007, 385f. He emphasizes "the distinctive ugliness of urban architecture in Western Europe in these years."

Thus there was a regrettable inertia in revitalization efforts since communities could not be substantially changed unless a catastrophe were to occur. But, as Rolfsen resignedly maintained, "one does not stage one's own catastrophes."[57]

In Sweden no cities were destroyed through acts of war. Nevertheless we see that after the war Sweden staged its own "catastrophe" by undertaking a rather comprehensive leveling of both "rural towns" and the larger cities. An extensive renewal of the city center was undertaken in Stockholm, for instance. In 1965 Oslo's Social Democratic mayor, Brynjulf Bull, remarked with poorly disguised envy on "how clever the Swedes have been at solving the problem [of urban renewal], knocking down heavy buildings, building underground transportation, and raising modern business centers on top."[58] At that point, by way of following the Swedish example, Oslo faced an extensive razing of the old city quarter of Vaterland, near the Central Railway Station.

"Functional segregation" was a dominant principle in this period. Different social functions were to be carried out in different places. Work was to take place in the cities, while sleeping should occur in the suburbs. The suburban concept was characteristic of the period. It reflects the view (held by Rolfsen, for example) that the old cities represented a civilization in decline. It was best to live outside the city in rural surroundings. To a large extent the upper middle class had already moved out of the city and established itself in neighborhoods composed of villas. Now everyone was to be out in the light and the air. In the suburban towns it was possible to build freestanding apartment blocks that were clearly distinguished from the old attached row-house apartments built in quarters, with fronts facing the street and backyards hidden behind. According to the modernist urban concept, the core of an up-to-date capital city was to be reserved for businesses and large companies. There was to be a strongly concentrated central business district (CBD).

The precondition for functional segregation was to develop modern means of convenient transportation capable of carrying people between the various function-specific areas. The subway system was clearly the most important collective means of transportation when it came to linking the city together, and the city with its suburbs and satellites. In 1941 in Stockholm the decision was taken in principle to develop an underground rail network. A coherent network, the "T-bane," came into being in 1957. Oslo had its more modest T-bane network assembled by 1987.

---

[57] Slagstad 1998, 300–301.

[58] City Council Proceedings, 23 September 1965. For detailed references to the expansion of Vaterland, see Sejersted 2002a, chap. 13.

THE SUBURBAN TOWNS

The satellite towns were typical of the Social Democratic era. To secure good family dwellings for the working class was a high priority of the Social Democrats. This was carried through in both Sweden and Norway, and it explains the rapid growth in residential construction. Stockholm was in the forefront of building satellite towns or "T-bane suburbs." One of the first was Björkhagen, which was built in 1948. It was planned not to be an "independent entity" but rather a complement to the "inner city"—in keeping with the principle of functional segregation. Other T-bane suburbs followed in rapid succession. Oslo got its first satellite town, Lambertseter, in 1951.

Criticism of functional segregation began early on, with satellite towns being characterized as dormitories without life or social interaction. Against the argument that in these suburbs one could combine the advantages of the city's density and the countryside's openness, it was maintained that, to the contrary, in the suburbs one was deprived of both aspects.

The response to this criticism was to place more functions in the suburbs. The most spectacular and the best known nationally and internationally was the "ABC" town, Vällingby, west of Stockholm's inner city. ABC stands for Arbeta-Bo-Centrum (A: work, B: reside, C: center). The aim was to re-create the living city by replacing functional segregation with a new functional integration. Residences, retail stores, work, and culture should once again be combined into one entity, creating a new town for 20,000 to 25,000 inhabitants from the ground up. An effort was thus made to solve the problem of the old city—the decay of civilization—by moving the city out of the city. It was a symbolic action when Erlander's secretary, Olof Palme, the aristocrat who had grown up in Stockholm's most fashionable area and would follow Erlander as Social Democratic prime minister, moved with his family to Vällingby in 1959. Even though Vällingby was reasonably successful in many respects, when "it came to the attempt to create a 'living town,' in which Vällingby inhabitants should also to a great degree have their workplace . . . the project was less successful."[59]

The great expansion reached a climax around 1970, at the same time the Social Democratic order began to develop cracks.[60] In the middle of the 1970s many apartments in the satellite towns stood empty, particularly around Stockholm. The reasons for this were many: The shortage of housing had been overcome. The trend toward the two-income family, and a further trend toward smaller households (even solitary dwellers), had changed living

---

[59] Ingemar Johansson 1991, 549.
[60] I. Johansson 1991, 611.

Figure 11. The Social Democratic landscape. This photo shows one of the latest and largest satellite cities—Rinkeby—on the northwest outskirts of Stockholm. Today relatively many immigrants live in Rinkeby. (Photo: All Over Press.)

patterns. Furthermore, the character of satellite towns changed during the 1960s. More and more residences were squeezed into ever-larger apartment blocks. This led to a reaction against the "intensity, concentration, and regimentation of the city of stone."[61] The ideal of the "little red cottage" seems to have been completely forgotten by the planners but not by most of the population, which had negative impressions of the satellite towns. The later satellite towns stood like "a forest of buildings that give a claustrophobic at-

---

[61] I. Johansson 1991, 594.

mosphere. Compared to the charming suburbs of the 1960s they have become a frightening caricature of society."[62]

The further building of residences in the suburbs took a marked turn in the direction of row houses and small bungalows. Thus one turned back to the ideal of the old bourgeois community of villas, but "under completely different economic, organizational, and production-technical conditions, with industrial mass production and, in time, a densely populated course of development that leaves its distinctive mark."[63] We could speak of a bourgeoisification of the Social Democratic family dwelling, or should we perhaps call it a Social Democratization of the bourgeois villa?

WHO CAN SAVE THE CITY?

What should actually be done with the old city core? Indeed, it did represent decay and decline.[64] As we have seen, the background for renewal lay partly in the necessity of combating an alleged decline of the old city and partly in the new society's need for a functional capital city. Extensive plans were laid down in Stockholm in 1945 for the renewal of the city core, the Norrmalm quarter. The principle was that the municipality would own the land and rent it out on long-term leases to the private sector.

Inspired by Stockholm, Oslo revealed analogous but less extensive plans for Vaterland in 1961. Here the whole region was leased to Melander's Den norske Creditbank. Melander took up the role of national strategist—and the grand renewal plan—with enthusiasm. There was full understanding between him and the city's Social Democratic mayor, Brynjulf Bull, who remarked, "Who else should one lease it to?" That it was functional to have a CBD was in keeping with functional segregation and with a general concept that was never critically evaluated in the central planning phase.[65] No "thinking person" gave a thought to any alternative development. According to Mayor Bull, everyone agreed that it had to be developed as a commercial center.

In the 1960s the great unity of thinking came to an end. Plans were put aside in the face of thoroughgoing criticism, both in Stockholm and Oslo. The plans were criticized as being too extensive and too radical. On both economic and aesthetic grounds more attention ought to have been paid to

[62] Goldfield 1979, 150, 151.

[63] I. Johansson 1991, 607.

[64] Sejersted 2002a, 374.

[65] Thomas Hall 1979, 189. The description of the renewal of Norrmalm is largely built on T. Hall 1979.

the existing size and building density regulations, and also to the value of the urban landscape that had been created by earlier generations.[66] Doubt was also sown about the assumptions behind the CBD principle, which had been fundamental to the whole project. One of the central planners in Stockholm has since commented with a deep sigh, "Why were things so different at the beginning of the Norrmalm renewal?" At that time the first and foremost concern had to do with being "sufficiently radical."[67]

The reversal can be viewed as an early expression of "the green wave" and as part of the reaction to the plan-based management so typical of Social Democracy. The Stockholm criticism also charged that, by means of the CBD principle, the Social Democrats had cast themselves in the role of errand boys to the business world. The renewal had not been marked by democratic procedures.[68] And in Oslo Melander lost the support of the Social Democrats: a large bank was neither the right institution for solving social problems nor, it became evident, did Melander have the necessary legitimacy in this connection to perform as a national strategist, or to "play Wallenberg." For the young rebels of the 1970s, the Vaterland renewal also became a symbol of precisely what "that rotten Social Democracy" could come up with.

In Stockholm as in Oslo the plans were changed to accommodate the criticism, yet there was a great difference between them. In Stockholm planners had begun early and come further, meaning that the plan was realized, if only in a reduced and revised form. Among other things, more functions were integrated into the new city. Conversely, Oslo's previous experience with atomic energy was repeated. Because the Norwegians were late in starting, it had not been possible to implement the plans before they were capsized and stunned by the criticism. This was perhaps not so bad. The planners had already managed to carry out "the catastrophe," however. Vaterland was torn down, and it lay vacant for a generation.

One can like or dislike the form of grand functionalism and the uniform or regimented appearance that the renewal of Stockholm represents, but there is no doubt that it stands as a gigantic monument to an era that possessed a vision of a rational, planned, uniform, modern city. This was a man-made world through and through, created in order to meet the needs of the modern human being as they were generally being articulated around the middle of the twentieth century. Unlike Stockholm, Oslo did not get a comparably unique monument to the vision of the Social Democratic period in the form of a modernist functional city center.[69] It might seem that Norway lacked the

---

[66] T. Hall 1979, 196; Sidenbladh 1985, 71.
[67] Sidenbladh 1985, 65.
[68] T. Hall 1979, 220.
[69] See Sidenbladh 1985, 215.

organizational ability to carry through such grand plans. Or did they happen in any case?

History tends to have a final act that can be viewed as a form of ironic commentary. The period we are looking at—the 1950s, 1960s, and 1970s—was marked by an underlying conception that the cities were in decline and had to be saved. But then a striking change came about in the 1980s in the form of a new ideology of urbanization linked to some spectacular urban renewal projects (Fisherman's Wharf in San Francisco might stand as the ideal type). There is no doubt at all that both Stockholm and Oslo have enjoyed a new life since the 1980s. The principle of functional segregation has been replaced by the principle of integration. And urban development has been marked more by organic growth than by the type of superordinate planning that was typical of the previous decades.

But what about Vaterland? The irony is that in the 1980s Vaterland was built up at a rapid tempo and roughly in the manner laid down by the original plans. The flagship of this project was a gigantic hotel, for quite a while Scandinavia's highest building. Otherwise the area is distinguished by climate-controlled artificial shopping galleries, malls, and precincts. And the culture has also had its way, such that Oslo too got its eventual monument to the great period of Social Democratic urban planning—only it did so ten or twenty years after the period had ended.

The Social Democratic landscape was distinguished by suburban satellite towns and extensive urban renewal initiatives. Here two motives blended together. One was the great social need for new dwellings and the need to struggle against urban blight in the large cities, and the second was a planning ideology marked by functionalism—the desire to build a new society more or less from the ground up. It was a matter of being "sufficiently radical." As in so many other areas, the residential and urban renewal projects provoked a reaction. The lofty ambitions—the great visions of the society of the future—had to be adjusted, expert leadership modified, and the politics reintroduced.

THE TRIUMPH OF REASON

The period from 1945 to approximately 1970 was a time of unusually strong and consistent economic growth. It was during this era that our two societies, Sweden and Norway, took the step out of poverty and into the consumer society. It was also the period of stable Social Democratic hegemony. In this connection it is important to stress that the contradictions and conflicts had been moderated. Steen was on the right track when he maintained that this was the period of reconciliation. The whole society stood together regarding extensive projects of modernization. This applied first of all to technological and economic projects, and then to popular projects that material prosperity made realizable and that we shall return to, such as the refinement of the population through the expanded unitary school system and especially the welfare system.

It is important to capture the dominant mentality of the era. Once people had put the war behind them, optimism predominated, based on the perceived possibility of following policies that were based on objectivity and reason. The role of policy making was to administer progress and make sure that developments followed an appropriate course. The most dynamic and, at the same time, liberating force in the development of society was science and technology. The politicians relied heavily on the experts. The experts were those who could interpret the imperatives of technology and transform scientific points of view into the advancement of society. Or, if we cite again the dream of Rickard Sandler in relation to the huge atomic energy project: with the help of reason, "the demon of annihilation that lives in the nucleus of the atom" could be transformed into "a powerful, obedient servant of mankind." The most striking outcome of this mentality was the comprehensive technical modernization or industrialization that both countries underwent, each in its own way based on its own conditions.

In order to realize this policy one had to break with the past, something that implied being sufficiently radical. This never found clearer expression than it did in the great urban renewal projects where the Social Democratic landscape came into being. Here in its purest form we also meet the idea that the well-planned, man-made world is best. This lay within the extension of the view of science and technology as comprising the most dynamic force in societal development. In hindsight we are struck by the touch of hubris that informed the very core of this idea.

CHAPTER 8

The Crowning Glory

Technocracy and the Welfare State • Children and the Family • The Radicalism of the
Myrdals • The Era of the Nuclear Family • The Housewife Contract under Pressure • The
Struggle over the Compulsory General Supplementary Pension (ATP) • Agreement on
Social Security • Why Standard Security? • The "Evangian" Health Policy • Swedish Health
Policy • Good Family Housing • Social Democracy's Happy Moment

TECHNOCRACY AND THE WELFARE STATE

The concept of the welfare state in its narrower sense refers to a system "of
state or juridical plans that guarantee the individual member of society security of life, health, and well-being."[1] Building welfare states was on the political agenda all over Europe after World War II. The inspiration came especially
from Great Britain, where a bold and simple plan for the whole social security
system, the Beveridge Plan, was published in 1942. The road taken by the
different European countries varied, however.

Forms of welfare *regimes* are found in all societies. But if we confine ourselves to twentieth-century modernity we can, as a starting point, use Gøsta
Esping-Andersen's division into three types: the "liberal" of the Anglo-Saxon
countries, the "conservative" of the Continent, and the "Social Democratic"
of Scandinavia. In the liberal regimes, relatively great emphasis is placed on
the market to create security or deal with social risk; in the conservative regimes, emphasis is placed on the family. The Scandinavian Social Democratic welfare states have been regarded as particularly well-developed welfare
states insofar as the guarantee of security or managing risk is to a high degree
handed over to the state.[2]

Compared to many other welfare regimes the Scandinavian welfare states
are generous, with a high degree of tax-based financing and universality and
with comprehensive socialization of risk management. In a central area such

[1] Slagstad 1981.

[2] Esping-Andersen 1990 and Esping-Andersen 1999, 34, regarding the concept "welfare state" and
"welfare regime." For a recent, critical examination of the different types of welfare regimes, see Åmark
2005, 217f.

as family policy the Scandinavian welfare states also distinguish themselves from other welfare regimes, particularly from the familialism of conservative regimes. They do so by taking over much of the burden of elder care (and, to a lesser extent, child care) from families. In addition, these states are characterized by the fact that it is the wage earners who generally have the most comprehensive rights to social benefits. "Standard security" is an important principle. This means that social benefits to alleviate loss of income vary according to the income one has lost. This applies equally to short-term loss of income (due to factors such as illness) and long-term loss (due to, for instance, old age). Systematic standard security benefits have been realized only in Sweden, Norway, and Finland.

As we have seen, the Myrdals' 1934 book, *The Population Crisis*, provided an answer to the general crisis of reproduction in society. The drastic drop in rates of childbirth in the 1930s indicated that the family was not functioning as expected. The family was the fundamental social collective. It was the hearth of reproduction, the venue in which society reproduced itself. As such, crisis in the family was a crisis of the society at large. The Myrdals' book covers more than is suggested by its title. It represents a well-articulated vision of a Social Democratic society and an almost boundless desire for reform. The book is also characteristic of Social Democracy in that the rhetoric is that of the social engineer. Among other things, the Myrdals, without regard for the need for autonomy, recommend intervention of the public sector into the privacy of the family sphere.

Gustav Möller is considered to be the father of the Swedish welfare state. He was from a working-class background and, out of all the Social Democratic Party's leading men, has been regarded as the person most intimately in touch with the party's grass roots. As a reformer he was radical; he would not be diverted from the idea of a Socialist society, but his approach was gradual.[3] Möller became general secretary of the Social Democratic Party in 1916, a position he held until 1940. He was minister of social services between 1924 and 1926 and from 1932 to 1951 (with a short interruption during the latter period).

Bo Rothstein has stressed that Möller's view of the relationship between the state and its citizens differed from that of the Myrdals.[4] Unlike the Myrdals, he was not a technocrat. The greatest distinction between their social policy orientations was Möller's great sensitivity toward the possibility of social stigmatization. To a great extent, the reforms he fought for had to do with "children and mothers, and they were all of a type that would strengthen their

---

[3] Zander 2001, 411.
[4] Rothstein 2002, 209.

autonomy as citizens."[5] His was one of the strongest voices in support of social security benefits as a right rather than a charity, and in developing the system on that basis: the state should provide basic security to all. This meant that he adamantly adhered to the principle of universality, financing through taxation, and a unified support system. Support should be independent of the size of one's income lost; on the other hand, it should depend on the number of dependents one has. Further means testing (with the attendant social stigmatization), along with bureaucratization and centralization of the system, should be avoided. The administration of the social security system should be established through local planning efforts, allowing utilization of the institutions of civil society. As with the AMS system, the functionaries were not to be recruited through the usual career route but rather from the ranks of "street bureaucrats" from the civil institutions.[6]

It is difficult to envision a large, ambitious social construction project without an element of technocracy. A certain objectification of the clients, with a corresponding tendency toward violation of their autonomy, is perhaps unavoidable. Yvonne Hirdman, who has criticized this aspect of the Myrdals' book and has been criticized in turn for her position, has also replied that she "completely identifies with the volition and the pathos that are the consequences of social engineering." She would have preferred to "understand this modernist reason, discuss it, and above all, save it."[7] The relationship between the Myrdals and Möller and the discussion about the justification of social engineering demonstrates the dilemmas involved in bringing to fruition this great welfare project. But it also shows us the strength of the visions.

CHILDREN AND THE FAMILY

In social policy the child comes first. The obligatory comprehensive type of school that developed during the nineteenth century was the first and strongest expression of social responsibility for children. In the great nation-building project the child could not be left to the family alone. From the school system children were to acquire the necessary moral grounding as well as the knowledge that would mold them into adequate citizens. Laws were gradually developed concerning child welfare as well. From an early stage, policy relating to children was an important part of this great social integration project.

[5] Rothstein 2002, 215.
[6] Östberg 1996, 151–152.
[7] Hirdman 2000, foreword.

Social responsibility for children was expanded at the beginning of the twentieth century. The social crisis was one thing that stimulated this; it especially affected the great demographic upsurge in children and the many "illegitimate" children. In Norway the Castbergian child laws of 1915 stood as a milestone. These laws gave children born out of wedlock the right to inherit property and the family name, and allowed public help to those mothers who did not receive child support from the father. The laws were adopted after a huge fight. Here was the idea of integration, of taking care of the weakest, combined with a nationalism that demanded a healthy stock. We notice an increasing interest in the quality of the population. At the same time, as with so many other reforms, "good intentions and poor instruments" became the reality.[8] But in the later Social Democratic phase the instruments would be addressed.

The problem behind the "child laws" had been taking care of the many "extra" children. As we have seen, in the 1930s the problem was the opposite: it had to do with stimulating people to have children. This meant strengthening interest in the reproductive sphere as well as increasing the attention paid to families, particularly the mothers. This does not mean that there had not been a family policy. In Norway health insurance had been extended (in 1909 and 1915) from a principle of family insurance by giving the mothers birth assistance. This care for the nuclear family became a particular feature of Norwegian social policy and was linked to a persistent functional division between the sexes. In Sweden a similar plan for mothers' assistance was not instituted until 1931, but this did not mean that attention to the family was any weaker there.

One of the reasons that mothers' assistance took so long in Sweden was concern that direct support to mothers would make them independent, thereby undermining the responsibility of fathers as providers for their families. In other words, the result might be a weakening of the nuclear family as a functional entity. Ironically, modern women's rights activists later would also directly oppose support for the mothers because of an opposite effect: "That they receive rights by virtue of motherhood serves to retain the existing division between man and woman, and thereby raises the risk that society's gender relations are set in concrete."[9] The skepticism with regard to direct mothers' support demonstrates how closely the emancipation of women and family policy are interwoven, and the dilemmas that cropped up here were to color social development throughout the century. Should the nuclear family

---

[8] Anne-Lise Seip 1984, 190, 194.
[9] Peter Johansson 2002, 47.

be protected, and what about the emancipation of women? Where did Social Democracy stand on this question?

THE RADICALISM OF THE MYRDALS

The Myrdals argued in favor of making the private sphere public or, in other words, for public-sector intervention into everyday family life:

> The future is not going to be marked by an indifference toward what one does with one's money: which standard of living one has, what kind of food and clothing one buys, and above all, to what degree the child's consumption needs are satisfied. In any case, the tendency is toward organization and management through social policy, not only with regard to the division of incomes in society but also with regard to consumption decisions within the family.[10]

In addition to inserting the state into the family, the Myrdals also favored removing children from the family to a greater degree. In their view, the main responsibility for child rearing was to be given to society, not only guaranteeing a good upbringing for children, but also implying a freeing of the family from responsibility since "the home has ceased to be an appropriate environment for raising children":

> The child-rearing situation in the small modern family is almost . . . pathological. . . . [T]oday's child [risks] being overraised and in various ways the situation is personally unbearable: a few individuals living in narrow constricting circumstances continually wear each other out. This will put one on edge and take the joy out of living.[11]

Indeed, the Myrdals are extreme in their view of society's responsibility for the upbringing of children. Such points of view were articulated in Norway as well. The Communist Trond Hegna, who later was a Social Democratic parliamentarian for many years, wrote an article on the family.[12] Here he refers to "the abolition of the family!" as found in *The Communist Manifesto* and Engels's portrayal of the socialistic society in which "the caring for and upbringing of children will be a matter for society." But the characteristic difference was that while Hegna used a revolutionary rhetoric and thereby moved outside the general social discourse, Alva Myrdal, despite her radicalism, was part of this discourse. While Hegna spoke about a completely dif-

---

[10] Alva and Gunnar Myrdal 1934, 203.
[11] A. and G. Myrdal 1934, 303.
[12] "The Family" in *Arbeidernes leksikon* (The Workers' Encyclopedia) 1933.

ferent society, the Myrdals' attack on the family was an attack based on the principles of the existing society and was therefore potentially more effective. Alva Myrdal followed the attack by launching a model of "the great nursery" in 1935. This model might be considered an early expression of what would come to be the welfare state's "home for children" or "preliminary school," as it would later be called.

The most specifically technocratic and paternalistic—or maternalistic— view was expressed, among other places, in the Myrdals' "natural line," which argued that support for families with children should take the form of sharing goods. The mothers, on the basis of means testing, should have apportioned to them clothing, shoes, vitamins, and nutritional goods at stipulated places in the municipality.[13] By contrast, Möller uses the stigmatization argument against the natural line; that is, what the family with children needed was cash support for the household budget. There was great debate within Social Democracy on these two perspectives, with Möller's view emerging victorious.

The Myrdals felt that the nuclear family was dysfunctional. Thus their solution was to reform it through integration into a more extensive social community. They began their family policy, or rather their "antifamily policy," by maintaining that it had to do "merely with restoring to a renewed spirit of community what had become the isolated family of the transition period." This "restoring" sounded conservative, and it was. Alva Myrdal said as much herself: "Conservatism has become individualistic, while it is the radicals who are social."[14] It was the social sense of community that existed in preindustrial society, or in forms of private association, that should be reestablished. Independent of whether the foundation was liberal individualism or radical Socialism, and independent of whether the Myrdals were only cultural radicals rather than genuine Socialists, citizens could unite around the task of breaking up the isolated family by having society take over most of the caregiving. For the cultural radical this meant liberating women from the male-dominated family collective, and for the Socialist it had to do with building a sense of fellowship greater than the family or, in other words, with building another home—"the people's home," an expression characteristically borrowed from the conservatives.

Alva Myrdal eventually came to develop and modify her family policy by bringing out an extensive family program based on middle-size families. This should be achieved through public education and free access to the means of birth control as well as various public support schemes—all stemming from

---

[13] Rothstein 2002, 213.
[14] A. and G. Myrdal 1934, 320–321.

the values of social solidarity represented by the family. And not the least of these values was equality between the sexes. Alva Myrdal's family policy was too radical for Social Democracy, however.

THE ERA OF THE NUCLEAR FAMILY

"The housewife contract" dominated in both Sweden and Norway from about 1920 until around 1960. This reflects, first, not only that the nuclear family was held up as a predominant ideal, but also that it was defended and protected as a fundamental collective of society throughout the hegemonic period of Social Democracy; and, second, that the functional gender division of labor was retained. This was a feature of the Scandinavian welfare states just as it was of the other welfare regimes. Rejecting the functional division between the sexes and making room for women alongside men in working life and in the public sector was simply not one of the tasks of Social Democracy. "The 1950s stood out as the decade of the nuclear family," writes Klas Åmark. "The family still holds together, those who want to can build their own household. ... [C]hildren continue to live with their biological parents."[15] Statistics from both countries confirm this assertion.

The population crisis was overcome. During the hegemonic phase of Social Democracy, from approximately 1940 to 1970, marriage rates reached record highs. The birthrate was higher than during the 1930s, while at the same time the number of children born out of wedlock was extremely low.[16]

These developments can be regarded as vindication for those who maintained that the "individualization of the family," by way of direct support given to mothers and children, strengthened the nuclear family. Of course the most important reason for overcoming the reproductive crisis and achieving a favorable balance was not the social policy initiatives but rather the economically good times. Notwithstanding, we see a striking demonstration that the bourgeois family ideal also predominated under Social Democracy. The radical attack on the nuclear family that resulted from the population crisis of the 1930s had been effectively beaten back. As two of the leading Norwegian feminists maintain in *The Family in Class Society*, a book published in 1975, Social Democratic policy took "little account of the principal points of view that emerged from Social Democracy's own left wing and completely supported the traditional conception of the family as

---

[15] Åmark 2002, 263.
[16] For statistics, see Åmark 2002 for Sweden; for Norway, St. forh. (Parl. Proceedings) 1973–1974, St. Meld 51.

an institution that ought to be preserved. ... And in this they were in tune with general popular opinion in Norway."[17]

THE HOUSEWIFE CONTRACT UNDER PRESSURE

Even if the 1950s was the decade of the nuclear family, Åmark finds it necessary to counter the idea that this period, "above all others, was the time of the housewife."[18] A critical examination of statistics shows that women's work outside the home has been underrecorded. The domination of the "housewife contract" until sometime in the 1960s does not mean that they stayed home; they worked to an increasing degree outside the home, often in part-time jobs.[19] In 1957 Alva Myrdal, together with Victoria Klein, published the book *Women's Two Roles: Home and Work*. In this book Myrdal revises her family program, distancing herself from "the most fanatical of fighters for women's issues" and arguing that these two roles have to be played out at different phases of a woman's life.[20] As Yvonne Hirdman writes, "the sharp tensions in gender conflicts between integration and segregation" were played out most clearly in the 1950s precisely through this double role. The housewife was "half human" and "half woman."[21]

It was not a great remove from this double role to demand a reformulation of the "housewife contract" or its replacement with a "gender-equality contract" based on equal rights and responsibilities for men and women in the labor market and in the home. The 1962 Swedish-Norwegian research report *Women's Lives and Work* played a major role in getting this debate on the agenda. A brochure, *Women's Equality*, was produced in 1964 by a Social Democratic committee headed by Sweden's prime minister Erlander. Here one finds a mixture of the liberal ideas of equality and the older housewife emancipatory ideas, such as the proposal to institute a cash-support plan and another that would award pension points to women for caring for their husbands and children. The demand for equality arose within Social Democracy for the first time in 1970,[22] around the same time the nuclear family began to show cracks as society entered a new "reproduction crisis." We will later consider what this implies about family policy.

---

[17] Holter et al. 1975, 17.

[18] Åmark 2002, 264.

[19] St. forh. (Parl. Proceedings) 1973–1974, St. Meld. 51:30. We see here that what Åmark found for Sweden is also the case in Norway, that the statistics do not include married women's part-time work.

[20] Hinnfors 1992, 108.

[21] Hirdman 1998, 132.

[22] Hirdman 1998, 133–134.

This sketchy development is particularly applicable to Sweden. In Norway we find the same tendencies but in a more moderate form. Sweden had a stronger and more coordinated women's movement than did Norway. Among other things, Sweden managed to prevent the work prohibition for married women during the crisis of the 1930s. Furthermore, the war enabled mobilization of women's labor power. On the whole, the women seem to have been considered at least a usable reserve workforce. In Norway, conversely, a work prohibition for married women was implemented during the 1930s. During the war years the mobilization of women's labor power was not under consideration, and after the war, when the demand for labor was great, there was no mention of the women. Nor does it seem that the need for two incomes was great among Norwegian families.[23]

Compared to Sweden, Norway was slower to embrace the concept of the two-income family. The bourgeois nuclear family and the housewife contract were more deeply rooted there than in Sweden. It is also striking that the number of children born outside marriage was lower in Norway.[24] Sweden was quicker to assume public responsibility for child care and protection through a much more extensive day-care system.[25] On the whole, Norway consistently followed a general European trend when it came to family and gender-equality policy, while Sweden followed a more radical course. Sweden represented the avant-garde also in this field, but in a more liberal than Socialist direction.

THE STRUGGLE OVER THE COMPULSORY GENERAL SUPPLEMENTARY PENSION (ATP)

The core element in the social security system is payment for loss of income. The system has primarily been organized to provide security to those who had income-generating work at the outset. Public-sector care for those who have been unable to look after themselves—such as the mentally handicapped—is more poorly developed and has never been completely collectivized or taken over by the state, even though Scandinavian countries are rated among the foremost in this field. The system is such that many rights are only accessible through wage-paying or salaried work. This is integral to the idea of the family that remained prominent far into the postwar period: above all, security should be given to the family provider, and the family should be protected

---

[23] Arnlaug Leira 1998, 190–191.
[24] St. forh. (Parl. Proceedings) 1973–1974, St. Meld. 51:22.
[25] A. Leira 1998, 196f. Hagemann and Åmark 1999, 192.

through the provision of support for the provider. This "work approach," through which wage-paying or salaried work generates rights that others do not have, has come to characterize social policy right up to the present day. One has full social citizenship under Social Democracy only by being a wage earner.

A central question concerning these payments for loss of income is whether they should be the same for everyone (the principle of equality) or whether they should vary according to the level of the income one has lost (standard insurance). This would come to be highly disputed, especially in Sweden. The dispute began when Gustav Möller, as minister of social services, proposed a system of health insurance with equal compensation for all. Möller was successful in getting both the Social Democratic Party and Parliament behind his proposal. His victory did not last, however, since the party leadership, with Erlander and Wigforss at the head, got Parliament to postpone the reform because of the great costs involved.[26]

The dispute is highly instructive in terms of the various principles involved in social security. In the eyes of many, the fact that people had different levels of income was a consequence of market influence on working income. A system based on standard security would imply that the state contributed to maintaining and reproducing the income differences created by the market, and this ought not to be the task of the state. Intuitively, from the point of view of justice, the most obvious solution would be equal payments. Möller's arguments were reasonable enough, at least to Social Democratic ears. But the result would be the reverse.

The actual argument against Möller's proposal was that equality of payment meant the system would be too costly for the state. The issue of health insurance was not dispatched until Gunnar Sträng had taken over as minister of social services after Möller in 1951. He immediately set up commissions to investigate the questions of health, occupational injury, and unemployment insurance. Möller's position was abandoned, and the new health insurance, implemented in 1955, was based on standard insurance. This also applied to the two other security plans. Economic arguments counted for much. With an income-related system, the contributions too could be income related; at the same time, contributions from employers could be instituted, covering a significant portion of the costs. The end result for the health insurance plan was that the state would be liable for only 30 percent of the costs, as opposed to 70 percent in Möller's system. The total costs were double those envisioned in Möller's system, however, since the new system involved so much more money. As Klas Åmark writes, "Income security therefore satisfied not only

---

[26] Åmark 1999, 22.

the movement for private health insurance, but also the LO, the prime minister, and the minister of finance."[27]

The big social policy issue was the national pension plan. Sweden had established a modest state pension as early as 1913. Perhaps the most prominent task of the "harvest period" was to develop this further, creating a coordinated security system—a general system of social insurance covering all kinds of income loss. The actual result of this effort was that in addition to an expanded state pension there was an obligatory General Supplementary Pension (ATP), which was essentially intended to ensure the security of income. The ATP decision was made in 1959 after a rather intense political struggle that dominated the political arena in Sweden during the latter half of the 1950s.

The dispute was over the same question that had arisen with the health insurance plan—the choice between the principle of equality or standard insurance. In the main, the Social Democrats stood on one side and the bourgeois parties on the other. The principal issue was the role of the state in the new welfare society.[28] The leading bourgeois party between 1949 and 1958 was the Liberal Party (Folkpartiet), and the person leading the polemic against the Social Democrats was the party leader Bertil Ohlin. It is high time, he said, that "Sweden begins a new chapter since what was intended by the social insurance plan is now in its concluding phase." And this new chapter should find people less reliant on the state. When incomes are rising, and "society creates a minimum level of security, then one makes up the difference oneself; through various measures—insurance, savings and so on—one takes responsibility for one's security in whatever form one finds suitable."[29] Thus, when it came to the national pension, the state should take no responsibility for supplementary benefits.

The Social Democrats and Erlander hit back by maintaining that, to the contrary, the state's obligations had to increase with the increase in societal well being, among other reasons because the situation led to increased demand for collective goods.[30] When it came to the national pension plan, the Social Democrats maintained that the state should guarantee standard insurance, with obligatory supplementary pensions determined by income level before the loss of income.

The issue came to a dramatic finale. A constitutional proposal was put forward in 1954 from the bourgeois side concerning the rights of minorities to demand referendums. With this in the background, they now demanded

[27] Åmark 1999, 31.

[28] This political dispute is analyzed by Leif Lewin 1992, 272–311. The following account is based on Lewin.

[29] Cited by Lewin 1992, 275.

[30] Lewin 1992, 283.

a referendum on the pension question. Erlander tried to avoid this, but in the end he had to give in; yet he did so in a way such that the government and the parliamentary majority managed to formulate the alternatives. Three alternatives were put forward but none of them received a clear majority, and the situation became chaotic. The sitting coalition government of Social Democrats and the Farmers' Party resigned. An effort was made to form a bourgeois coalition government, but this was unsuccessful. The result was that Erlander formed a purely Social Democratic minority government, after which he called for a proroguing of the Second Chamber and a new election. With this election in 1958 the Liberal Party experienced a setback while the Social Democrats moved forward somewhat, but not enough to secure victory for their proposition. Thus the situation in Parliament seemed to point in the direction of victory for the non-Socialist proposal. The obligatory supplementary pension was, however, passed by one vote, with one Liberal Party member siding with the Social Democrats. The leader of the Conservative Party (Högerpartiet) immediately declared that his party would work to "demolish the ATP decision."[31] Nothing came of this, one reason being that the trade union of the functionaries (TCO) gave its approval to the decision. As soon as the decision was made, the dispute died away surprisingly quickly. The following regular election in 1961 was also a victory for the Social Democrats.

AGREEMENT ON SOCIAL SECURITY

Because of economic factors, the social policy reforms had to wait when it came to Norway. But this did not mean that Norway's gaze had shifted away from the future. In 1948 the Social Democratic government put forward a white paper on a "national insurance plan." Klas Åmark, who has carried out a thoroughgoing comparative analysis of the development of the social security systems of Sweden and Norway, characterizes this report as "an important, principled, thoroughgoing and remarkable document on modern social policy."[32] The report took as its point of departure the joint postwar general program of the parties, while it developed the principles for "an integrated social security that covers the whole population, and with common organs and simple principles of financing." At the same time, it was ascertained that the realization of such social security had to happen on the basis of future economic growth.

---

[31] Classon 1986, 163.
[32] Åmark 1999, 27.

It is noteworthy that the report distinguished in a principled way between "income security," which was to cover short-term losses of income because of illness and unemployment, and "pension security," which had to do with long-term support for the aged or infirm. The first was to be graded by income; that is, the standard insurance procedures should apply. Conversely, the second should be based on equal payments, or a minimum standard. In comparison to Sweden's approach, dividing it up in this manner seemed to be a clever solution that looked obvious after the fact, like the fabled egg of Columbus. Sweden's view seems to have been that the chosen principles had to be applicable across the entire social security system. Incidentally, that was what happened in the end.

In Norway reforms were also enacted in the 1940s. Child welfare was introduced in 1946. Health insurance was extended in 1946, and in 1949 the unemployment insurance plan was overhauled. In 1952 the national insurance issue was taken up again. This led to a united Parliament rescinding the means test for old-age security in 1957, which meant a decisive breakthrough for the principle of universality. While the struggle raged in Sweden, there was great agreement in Norway. But, naturally enough, alternative voices were also raised. One prominent member of the Conservative Party argued that in a rich society with a relatively level income differential one could do away with publicly financed social assistance. He seems to have been inspired by the arguments put forward by Ohlin in Sweden. These rather right-wing radical ideas were immediately rejected by the Norwegian Conservative Party (Høyre), however.[33] Nonetheless, there was a certain amount of conflict over standard insurance and supplementary pensions in the final phase of the development of the national insurance plan.

Above all, following the developments in Sweden it became clear to all the parties that they had to have a national insurance program by the election of 1961. Ironically it was the Swedish Liberal Party's Norwegian counterpart, the Norwegian Liberal Party (Venstre), that introduced the standard insurance plan to Norway—a plan that the Swedish Liberal Party had opposed so vehemently. Conversely, the conservative party Høyre in Norway rejected the idea of starting with a compulsory supplementary pension. Along with the Communists, the Conservatives preferred a plan with equal payments that consisted of "60 percent of normal wage income in society."[34] The Labor Party vacillated. As pointed out by Åmark, conditions were suitable for a corporative solution to the supplementary pension problem since the LO and the employers' association had progressed toward agreement on a supplement

---

[33] Sejersted 2003b, 335–337.
[34] Sejersted 2003b, 339. St. forh. (Parl. Proceedings 1960–196, S. Tid, 3596.

to the basic security model. Although such an agreement was a seemingly natural solution, the organizations put forth little effort in the end: "The civil society in Norway was thus too weak and uninterested to carry off a system based on specific agreements for different vocational groups."[35]

In the course of the Norwegian election cycle of 1961–1964 the larger parties had each ended up with the Swedish plan. The election led to a center-right unity coalition positioned to take over the government. In 1966 this government put forward a proposition that in all essentials built on the proposition from the previous Social Democratic government. National insurance—based on standard security, which had split the Swedish Parliament—was thus adopted almost unanimously by the Norwegian Parliament. In this way the two countries ended up with similar plans—arrangements that were unique to these two countries.

When it came to the financing, however, the two countries' plans differed. To a much higher degree than in Norway, Sweden based its financing on setting up reserve funds. This created conflict between the Social Democrats and the non-Socialist parties. These funds would soon reach a magnitude that gave them influence on the structure of the economy. Who should manage this significant amount of capital? In the end, a public fund (known as the AP Funds) became "the cornerstone for the control of saving and investing."[36] In Norway the social security costs would be to a much higher degree covered from the current state budget.[37] In this way Norway was much behind in terms of the "savings revolution". It was not until the petroleum income began to flow in during the 1990s that a public "oil fund" was set up and earmarked for a future fund-based form of financing for the national insurance plan. But that is another story.

WHY STANDARD SECURITY?

Why was standard security such a prominent feature of the Social Democratic order? The radicals, from Gustav Möller and the Communists on one side and the Liberals and Conservatives on the other, had all established equal payments as the basic principle. Consequently the final solution cannot be regarded as a compromise between the Socialists and the bourgeoisie. The ultimate solution was something beyond compromise—a Nordic Social Democratic system in its own right.[38]

[35] Åmark 1999, 37.
[36] Schön 2000, 412.
[37] NOU 1998:10, p. 17. In Norway there was no funding for the supplementary pensions, while Sweden had built up relatively large buffer funds.
[38] For the most part the following discussion is based on Åmark 1999.

We have seen that there were some practical and economic reasons for choosing standard security, since the disbursements could be shared in a way that was less costly for the state. Another, more important, motive was the need to capture the support of the functionaries. We have also seen that the functionaries' trade union approved the system. Pension reform was fundamentally a working-class issue since a majority of the middle class had pensions funded by their employers. It was therefore a question of justice to establish a similar plan for the workers, and this meant a system of standard security. Nevertheless, the orientation toward the functionaries' system strengthens the conclusion of those researchers who stressed the "bourgeois" or the "liberal" nature of the reform—standard security reinforces the class society. It has been called a welfare state for the middle class. That the reform implies a solution based on bourgeois premises is lent support by the fact that the real radicals, and Gustav Möller with them, opposed the system and wanted a model based on the principle of equality.

When those on the political right in Sweden supported the model based on the principle of equality and the transfer of the supplementary pensions to voluntary private plans (which also was the course taken by the conservatives in Norway at the outset), they did so because they wanted to reduce public plans. This standpoint, most clearly enunciated by Ohlin, stood in opposition to what Lewin has called "the powerful society," which implies that the welfare society required an expansive state power—that collective solutions normally implied state solutions.[39] The opposition from both the left and right factions justifies Åmark's conclusion: "Class interest was not so obviously expressed that it unambiguously points the way to a solution."[40] Thus there were also some practical-economic as well as tactical reasons for adopting the standard insurance principle.

There is a feature of standard security solutions that has played a role throughout the history of social security, namely that voluntary plans do not cover those who have the greatest need for them. There is a paternalistic element here that is in line with a general feature of Social Democracy: the state must step in and lead the wage earners through obligatory plans because the individual workers are inclined to make the wrong choices if the decisions are left to them.

Åmark, however, finds the main reason elsewhere. His starting point is that the trade unions were the driving force for carrying through the standard insurance plan, and the explanation lies in the social norms around status differences within the working class. With his principle of equality, Möller came into conflict not only with economic considerations but also with "social

---

[39] Lewin 1992, 287.
[40] Åmark 1999, 40.

ideas about equalities and inequalities among workers, and how these should be indicated and upheld."

Equality is a problematic concept. There was in the Social Democratic society a tension between the concept of equality of result and the concept of equality of opportunity. Welfare capitalism often represents a synthesis of liberal and Social Democratic thinking on equality, something that is reflected in many fields.[41] The labor movement supported variation in wages in accordance with contribution. There was nevertheless a certain degree of hesitation when it came to institutionalizing existing hierarchies by adopting standard insurance. But as Åmark so significantly notes, these doubts were overcome when cabinetmaker Axel Strand took over from sawmill worker August Lindberg as chairman of the (Swedish) LO in 1947.

The ATP in Sweden and the national insurance plan in Norway have since been considered the crowning glories in the development of the welfare state in these two countries. The conflict that raged over the Swedish plan seems to have been put to rest surprisingly quickly. It is not surprising, then, that Norway obtained its national insurance system following the pattern of the Swedish without conflict. Before the war each of the countries had developed different social security systems. After the war, however, it became almost a norm that Norway would follow the lead of Sweden.

In general there developed a close cooperation between the two countries at both the civil service and the political levels after the war. This closeness is demonstrated by the policy in each country of extending the rights enjoyed by its citizens to the citizens of the other Nordic countries as well. The breakthrough for this principle came in 1949 with an agreement about mutual old-age pension payments. In 1955, when the ATP was on the agenda, this reciprocity system was generalized with the Nordic Welfare Convention. For all practical purposes, with this convention Nordic citizens all had the same right to social disbursements as they had in their own countries.[42] This plan, although not directly having to do with the development of similar systems, had indirectly come to imprint a trend toward convergence on the process.

The critics who said that the system adopted by the Social Democrats contributed to maintaining the social order were right. In a sense, that was the point of it. But then it ought to be added that this order deviated considerably from the social order that had prevailed half a century earlier. The new social order was an order with a much higher degree of equality and well-being, with a solidarity-based wage policy. This wage policy served as a force

---

[41] Esping-Andersen 1999, 8.
[42] Wendt 1979, 145–146.

for leveling between firms and branches of the economy. This leveling did not stand in contradiction to the "differential principle" of standard security but served rather as a precondition for the implementation of standard insurance. The system of standard welfare benefits was a Social Democratic plan in its own right. It went beyond the old class contradictions, and it was closely linked to the Social Democratic notion of "the powerful society."

The fact that the Liberal Party (Venstre) introduced the system to Norway does not mean that the system did not fit into the Social Democratic order, rather on the contrary. The Social Democratic order that made its appearance in the 1950s and 1960s had historical roots that extended back beyond the Social Democratic movement. Most of the plans we consider peculiar to Social Democracy were introduced to Norway by the Liberal Party (see chapter 3), only later to be implemented, further developed, and administered by the Social Democratic hegemons. This reminds us that though the corresponding plans in Sweden were largely initiated by the Social Democrats, we cannot therefore conclude that they would not have been carried out if the Social Democrats had not taken the initiative. Whether or not the ATP system represents a welfare state for the middle class is an open question. What is certain is that the Swedish Social Democrats gained strength by this reform. Whether it was intentional or not, the reform was instrumental in capturing a substantial part of the functionaries' votes. The ATP system turned out to be the foremost symbol of the Social Democratic order.

THE "EVANGIAN" HEALTH POLICY

"In many ways it is health policy that has given Social Democracy its central ideas about the good society, once the class struggle had been taken out of the program." Trond Berg Eriksen writes this in a recently published *Norwegian History of Ideas* volume.[43] This scarcely applies to the Swedish Social Democrats. The major reason that health policy became particularly important in the Norwegian connection was due to Doctor Karl Evang, minister of health from 1938 to 1972. If Gunnar Myrdal was the prototypical social engineer of Sweden, it was Karl Evang who filled the role in Norway.

We have met Karl Evang already, as the revolutionary intellectual of the 1930s who agitated for sexual enlightenment and gave qualified support to the sterilization law. Evang was learned and energetic, possessing a sense of engagement that marked so many of the Social Democrats after 1945. They had an almost naive belief that the time had now come to bring about the

---

[43] Eriksen, Hompland, and Tjønneland 2003, 373.

good society. With great force and energy Evang approached the formulation of professional policy in his field. "With Evang, so to speak, the medical profession crept into the state apparatus; administration and policy became one."[44] He combated the traditionally powerful position of the jurists in the state administration and built a health service and hospital sector into a "medicracy" relatively isolated from the general government administration, and where the leading positions were filled by doctors. As he himself said, in general he went in for "an organic and professionally responsible construction of the state's central administration." He also rejected the "dogma" that the elective organs should have "full sovereignty over the bureaucracy." The bureaucracy ought to represent expertise, and as a body of expertise it could not be overridden by elected organs. He had an insatiable confidence in professional knowledge: "Medical science can revolutionize the world—healthy generations everywhere—if sense is allowed to prevail."[45]

Above all, Evang involved himself in preventive work, in the creation of a healthy population. This implied special care and attention to the primary health service, where the district doctor was central. This was a combined position, with responsibility for both preventive and clinical medicine. With regard to the former function, the district doctor was a public employee, and with regard to the latter, the doctor conducted a private practice (but was in practice paid from the public purse through the health insurance system). Evang never touched this system; that is, he never tried to turn clinical medicine into a purely government-run service. Even hospitals were partly organized like the medical practices of the chief physician or surgeon.

The situation in 1945 demanded new initiatives. A myth had grown up that the Norwegians had been healthier owing to the war. The opposite was the case. And it was here that Evang took charge: "The overhaul of the Norwegian people's health and labor power is a necessary condition for material and economic reconstruction. The funds expended on this field are not dead capital but are, in a very real sense, productive capital."[46] Evang spoke from within the hegemonic Social Democratic discourse and, for the most part, got what he wanted. Health policy was not something that one could postpone until better times; it was something that had to be given top priority. Money was invested over a broad spectrum—especially on prophylactic measures. By means of persuasion, upbringing, and organizing, people would be induced to get out into nature; they would take up sports, eat healthy food, and be exposed to abundant sunlight and fresh air. All this was to be initiated,

---

[44] Schiøtz 2003, 345.
[45] Cited from Slagstad 1998, 314–315.
[46] Cited from Schiøtz 2003, 309.

administered, and organized by the medical profession. The health policy of Evang can be seen as a further development of ideas from the sports movement: the body was a focal point in the Social Democratic state.

Evang took a considerable interest in the mental health of the population. People should not only be physically healthy; in addition they should be content. This too was a responsibility of the medical profession. It is symptomatic that his broad engagement in the field of mental health led to him being a witness in the celebrated case of the writer Agnar Mykle, whose novel *The Red Ruby* caused the author to be taken to court on charges of alleged "obscenity." As Berg Eriksen writes, "No one found it odd that the director of health was pulled in as a competent expert on the controversy over the value of a work of literature."[47] From the point of view of social hygiene this "obscene" book represented a positive contribution to the cultural struggle, according to Evang. For young people who were riddled with guilt complexes this was a useful book.

In addition, with his intense energy it was also natural that Evang engaged in international work for improved health. He became one of the founders of the World Health Organization, and it was he who first took responsibility for the organization's constitution, which declares: "By health it must be understood that a person is not only free of sickness and infirmity but also enjoys complete physical, mental, and social well-being."[48] Later this definition was criticized for being too extensive and leading to what has been called "medicalization"—everything in the final analysis becomes a question of health. And the doctor becomes the central professional with responsibility for bringing about the good society.

Owing to several factors, the "Evang system" came under criticism in the 1970s. The operating expenses had a tendency to grow uncontrollably. The "benefits" were a long time in coming, at least in the form of economic dividends. Dysfunctional features had developed in the system, and there was a diminishing belief that the health personnel themselves could put matters right. The high prestige of the medical profession began to weaken, and it became increasingly legitimate to question the many new demands for increased funding. "In particular, questions were raised about the medical profession's social conscience and morals, and opening forays were made into the liberal labor market of the doctors."[49]

The Evang system also became caught up in the general criticism of instrumentalism in the field of social engineering. Many thought that the reforms

---

[47] Eriksen, Hompland, and Tjønneland 2003, 112.

[48] Nordby 1989, 142–143.

[49] Schiøtz 2003, 351–352.

were based on a wrong view of human beings. People were made into clients. One of the clearest expressions of revolt against the demands of social engineering came from the Austrian-American writer Ivan Illich, who, above all, was known for his critique of schooling and health institutions in, among others, the book *Medical Nemesis: The Expropriation of Health*, which was precisely an attack on medicalization. Supposedly he held a lecture in Oslo that was attended by Evang. Evang, who viewed himself as an avant-gardist and a radical reformer in the field of health policy, had come to hear what one of the period's new critical voices might contribute to his project. When he discovered that the lecture was fundamentally an attack on his own project, he reportedly left the meeting after issuing a clearly articulated protest. He must have felt as if he had been stabbed in the back.

SWEDISH HEALTH POLICY

The development of health policy in Sweden was, in its main features and tendencies, the same as Norway's, yet without coming as close to the ideal type as the Evang system. In the Myrdals' *Population Crisis*, great attention is devoted to "physical and mental hygiene."[50] According to the Myrdals, the most important thing in the existing situation was "building the medical service into a health service." In other words, attention had to be paid to preventive work. People should be "treated" before they become sick. In their typical technocratic rhetoric the Myrdals say that "an improved health service is the most important means in the long term for raising the quality of the human material." It is characteristic that the Myrdals, like Evang, placed special emphasis on prophylactic mental health policy. This, especially, was to be carried out to prevent "criminality and general antisocial behavior, neuroses, degeneration, and deficient personal effectiveness in various respects."[51]

The year after the Myrdals published their book, the Socialist and doctor J. Axel Höjer was appointed general director of the Medical Board (Medicinalstyrelsen), a position comparable to Evang's in Norway. Sweden was an avant-garde nation when it came to a scientifically based health service organized in hospitals and related institutions.[52] During the harvest period, when Höjer was general director, this institutional system was expanded. Among

---

[50] G. and A. Myrdal 1934, 238f.

[51] G. and A. Myrdal 1934, 245, 255.

[52] Ole Berg 1980, 32, 40. Berg has made valuable suggestions regarding this section.

other things, Höjer accomplished this by establishing what were called care centers that would be owned and managed by the local county councils, and which to a large degree replaced the private-practice doctors.[53] In other words, in a manner that was more radical than that of Evang, Höjer worked to make the health and hospital systems public, or at least turn doctors into public employees to a greater degree. This implies that while Evang remained a man of his profession and shrank away from challenging it, Höjer came into sharp conflict with his own profession.

In both countries the medical profession occupied a strong position with great legitimacy. This meant that Evang and Höjer had a good starting point when it came to establishing professional administration. On the other hand, the profession was able to use its strong position to develop privileges, which it did as well, naturally enough. It was in this connection that conflicts could arise. Höjer himself tells about a conflict over expanding medical capacity by training more doctors.[54] The Swedish Medical Association (a national association of doctors) denied that there was a shortage of doctors. During a pause in a meeting a "prominent representative of the medical profession" went up to him and asked, "Are you so damned stupid that you don't understand that our opposition to you is due to concern about our undeclared incomes?"[55] Höjer's laconic commentary in his memoirs shows that of course he knew this; indeed, part of the object of the whole reform was to remove the undeclared incomes. As occurred in Norway, suspicion developed in Sweden that the medical profession's social conscience and morals were perhaps no higher than those of others, and criticism was leveled against the strong professional administration with its great ambitions. Illich's book was published in Swedish the same year that it was launched in English. But Höjer had died a year earlier, so he, at least, avoided being knifed in the back.

In both Sweden and Norway many signs of mistrust in the ability of the doctors and public health authorities to deal with people's medical and other problems gradually emerged. It was this reaction that in time would lead to such initiatives as the liquidation of the large institutions for the mentally handicapped and the mentally ill, and toward the growth of a new system of personal doctors, alternative medicine, and private hospitals. All this is in contrast to the vision forwarded by the wave of reform in which Evang and Höjer were instrumental, and which, particularly in its Evangian variant, was such a clear example of the technocratic way of thinking.

---

[53] Höjer 1975, 190.
[54] Heidenheimer 1980, 121f., discusses this conflict.
[55] Höjer 1975, 198.

GOOD FAMILY HOUSING

Provision of good housing to the working class was viewed as one of the most powerful means of struggle against the social crisis that followed the industrialization of society. Good family housing would integrate this new working class into the nation. We have followed various initiatives from around the turn of the last century, but it was not until after World War II, under the Social Democratic regime, that the issue picked up momentum, for example, in the form of the large satellite towns. In both Norway and Sweden a construction plan for extensive publicly subsidized and regulated social housing was developed, making it possible for low-income groups to obtain good housing. There was scarcely any area in which rising standards were so obvious. On the whole, housing policy was one of Social Democracy's greatest successes. But here too it would gradually be revealed that there was a downside to success.

There is a remarkable difference between Sweden and Norway in the field of housing. Sweden has a high rate of tenancy, while Norway has a higher rate of individual ownership. It has been maintained that this has a historical explanation, since the Swedish agricultural society was marked by a concentration of ownership with a large grouping of propertyless rural laborers, while the Norwegian agricultural society to a greater degree was dominated by freehold peasant-farmers.[56] This was not only an actuality that continued to make itself felt in the proprietorship structure when it came to housing, but it also left traces on the two different ideals regarding social housing. Sweden came to prioritize municipal rental units, while Norway fell into housing cooperatives. In practice the difference was not so great. In both instances this had to do with subsidized public housing construction outside the private market sector. And comprehensive regulations made the tenants and the cooperative members come out rather equally in the two countries. In addition to this social housing construction, there was also extensive private house construction in this period.

Now the lines of development in history tend to get rather gnarled and twisted. The modern housing cooperative, with its members' association and cooperative housing rights, was established by Stockholm's organized tenants in 1923. This housing cooperative gained ground, and a real national federation was formed. The initiative thus arose from the civil society but found support from the municipalities. In the 1920s Sweden also established a state-housing loan plan that would become expanded powerfully during World War II.

---

[56] Annaniassen 2000–2001. For this section a debt is owed to Erling Annaniassen, who has allowed me to use a draft chapter of his book *Eierlandet Norge* as well as making himself available for discussion.

The Swedish housing cooperative was copied by construction workers in Oslo six years later in close collaboration with the municipality. But it was not until 1946 that Norway managed to establish the system of cooperative housing, with a national federation of local cooperatives and a state-housing loan plan with government-controlled interest through the state-managed Husbanken (Housing Bank). The principle of cooperation between public financing and the housing cooperative movement was, in its major contours, borrowed from Sweden.

In 1945, however, Sweden broke with the 1930s combination of semimunicipal and semicooperative "public utility" housing as municipal societies for *tenant housing* began receiving priority. This was something that had been tried in Norway in the interwar period to a modest extent. There, in response to calls by the state, certain municipalities had assumed direct responsibility for some degree of social housing construction—which, given the difficult economic conditions, had led to many problems and much political conflict concerning the sharing of costs and the rent levels. These experiences were not good, and they contributed to the alternative form of cooperative that made a breakthrough in Norway after the war. Sweden chose direct municipal responsibility because of unfortunate experiences with speculation in the cooperative housing market, while the country did not have the unfortunate experiences that Norway (and other countries) had with direct political responsibility.[57]

Thus before World War II Sweden had tried out a publicly supported system of housing cooperatives in the form of municipal rental housing, while Norway had tried out a system of municipal tenant housing. The ironic point is that the two countries simply exchanged models when they shouldered the great burden of construction of social housing after 1945, the reason being that both had had bad experience with their respective models during the interwar period. In both countries, however, the experiences from the period following 1945 were good. Thus we see that both models functioned badly during the difficult conditions between the two world wars, but well under the economic boom that followed World War II.

The years between 1945 and 1975 were marked by extensive housing construction in both countries. In the twenty years leading up to 1970, 650,000 new residences were built in Norway. This was not far from the total number of residences existing in Norway before the war. Moreover, the new dwellings were of a higher standard than the old ones. Nevertheless, the demand was not satisfied (due, among other things, to the migration of people into the cities), and the construction continued. There had

[57] Annaniassen 2000, 169.

been a certain amount of housing construction in Sweden during the war such that the housing situation was not as precarious as it was in Norway in 1945. But Swedish housing construction became equally intensive. One driving factor was the strong urbanization that was partly the result of the systematic labor market policy with the relocation of population that this implied. Industry pressed for housing construction that was consistent with economic restructuring. This was the background for a mobilization of extra effort in 1964. In the course of ten years the building of one million new dwellings was achieved.

During the 1970s some unfortunate features of these systems became evident. The intensive construction led to poor residential environments, especially in the latest satellite towns around Stockholm. Additionally there was a corresponding social segregation as the middle class began to flee from the municipal residences in Sweden, and as later occurred among the housing cooperatives in Norway. In some parts of Sweden residences stood empty, while in Norway this happened only to an extremely limited extent. Conversely, there was growing pressure to break from the division between the regulated and the unregulated housing market, and to open a free housing market. It also became evident that the taxation rules favored home owners over renters.

In Norway during the 1970s some housing cooperatives disbanded such that the members became direct owners and could put their housing unit out on the free market. The Labor Party reacted with a change in the laws that made the dissolution of cooperatives illegal. This change in the law broke with the strong Norwegian norms of individual ownership, and in the 1980s the non-Socialist government repealed the law and brought about a general deregulation. In Sweden the "use-value system" was instituted in 1968, leading to leveling of the rent in the public utility and the private sectors of the rental market. In formal terms, the Social Democratic system still continued in Sweden, but the pressure was strong for changing to a system of private ownership.

This pressure toward freehold apartments and the free market was strengthened by the expansion of the private housing market. It is said that this increase in individual ownership in Sweden implies the realization of the "property-owning democracy" of the conservatives. Sweden thus followed Norway when it came to the importance of the dwelling as an object of individual savings and investment.[58] Social Democracy's collective solutions were being abandoned.

[58] Ljunggren 1992, 154.

Figure 12. A Social Democratic king. In 1973 the price of oil increased by 70%, which led to strong restrictions on, among other things, automobile traffic. To get out on his habitual skiing trip, King Olav of Norway used the Metro. This photo, which shows the king paying for his ticket, has gained an almost iconographic status in Norway. (Photo: Jan Greve, VG.)

SOCIAL DEMOCRACY'S HAPPY MOMENT

Instrumentalist rhetoric has led some to maintain that economic goals were the "real" driving force behind the welfare state, and that the welfare state was part of the logic of the capitalist system.[59] One example of this is the business-world demand that housing policy should aim to serve the industrial structuring processes. It might also be maintained that there was a duality or a "tension within Social Democratic ideology" between a social policy that was part of commercial policy and a condition for economic growth, on one hand, and, on the other hand, a trade and commerce policy that was a means of economic growth and thereby a precondition for the fulfillment of the real goal—namely, creating security, well-being, and general prosperity.[60]

There is no basis for reducing the driving force behind the welfare state to either economic or social factors. The welfare state, with its income security

[59] Among others, this applies to Trond Nordby 1990. See also Skeie 2003, 274.
[60] Jenny Andersson 2003, 12.

and good family housing, was certainly able to catch the interest of the business community, but it was also the result of boom times or high economic conjunctures, the input of idealistic social engineers, and—especially—of most people wanting such a society and expressing this desire through democratic elections. The welfare state, alongside democratization, was the most powerful expression of the predominant integration project. The ambition was not only to create security but also to create equality, where equality was viewed as a cornerstone for social integration. To a remarkable degree Sweden and Norway thus became redistributive states.

The strong momentum of the welfare state was due precisely to the aim that economic growth, social security, and integration should mutually support one another in harmonious cooperation. For a long period it seemed that developments justified this idea. This was Social Democracy's happy moment. Later the different aims would come into conflict with one another.

CHAPTER 9

What Kind of People Do We Need?

Sweden and Norway, One-School Nation • A Break with the Past? • What Kind of Equality? • Integration and Normality • Several Dilemmas under the Surface • An Unsuccessful Integration Drive • Marginalized Universities • Swedish University Reform • Norwegian University Reform • The Social Democratic People's Church • Church and Morals • Which Is More Important—Health or Salvation? • What Kind of Human Being?

SWEDEN AND NORWAY, ONE SCHOOL-NATION

"If we were to place the problem of the 'goal' of schooling in the simplest and most general way we might ask, 'What kind of human being do we really need in modern society?'" Thus Alva and Gunnar Myrdal posed the question in 1934. People had to be appropriately formed for the new society, and therefore schooling occupied a central place in the great Social Democratic project they had in mind. The Myrdals answered their own question succinctly: "The type of human being that is most beneficial is one who, in a personal, harmonious manner most effective for society, is able to adapt himself to life in society." They wrote of society needing "upbringing for a new world."[1]

The nine-year integrated school was to be the foundation for the education system introduced by Social Democracy. The final decision on this was made in 1962 in Sweden: "The parallel school system that was more than a century old was thereby abolished and an integrated school for all school-age children was introduced."[2] In Norway the final decision regarding a nine-year school system was taken in 1969. The integrated school system reflected a strong belief in school attendance, knowledge, and general education as the basis for "upbringing for a new world": "Why, based on a knowledge of physics, and sitting at the dinner table in, say, a farmworker's home, should one not be able to discuss the configuration of the atom? Why, during their lunch break, should masonry apprentices not be able to discuss the social conditions for

---

[1] Alva and Gunnar Myrdal 1934, 261, 262, 264.
[2] Richardson 1999, 75.

Shakespeare's creative gestalt? There are no boundaries here."[3] This quotation is from Stellan Arvidsson, who in 1946 became the influential secretary of the Swedish School Commission, the commission that created the blueprint for the Social Democratic integrated school reform in Sweden and thereby, to a considerable degree, in Norway as well.

At least equally central to the formative power of knowledge was the idea of the school as the most important instrument of social integration. All children should go to the same school for as many years as possible. Differentiation was certainly necessary, but ought to occur as late as possible, using flexible transition arrangements.

The process toward these undertakings had begun right after 1945. In Sweden the initiator was the teacher's son Tage Erlander, the newly appointed minister of education and church affairs. A 1945 entry in his diary about his "school line" supported having "all types of schooling for those younger than fifteen in the same local unit, under the same guidance. If I could only find a man to carry out an undertaking like this!"[4] He would soon become the man he so ardently desired to implement such a program. He became chairman of the School Commission of 1946 but shortly afterward had to take over as prime minister. Alva Myrdal became a commission member—"a wellspring of ideas in the School Commission in 1946, especially through her international perspectives."[5]

This development in Sweden was closely watched from Norway, as Alfred Oftedal Telhaug describes:

> This [Swedish] reform work and the introduction of experimental activity were eagerly and enthusiastically studied in Norway. The commission findings and reports were read. Leading professional pedagogues, school inspectors, and senior and ordinary teachers swarmed across the border to the neighbor country to examine the experiment with their own eyes. State Secretary Helge Sivertsen sat in the visitors' gallery of the Swedish Parliament in 1950 when it brought out its principal resolution regarding the nine-year school, which was to find its final form through experimental activity. . . . The teachers' organizations unreservedly supported the Swedish initiative.

Telhaug asserts in closing: "As a concluding characteristic of the first postwar decades of the Social Democratic regime perhaps I can say that Sweden and Norway functioned as one school-nation."[6] The original "no!" to Sweden half a century earlier had become a clear "yes!"

[3] Richardson 1999, 90.
[4] Erlander 2001, 1 October 1945.
[5] Husén 1994, 26.
[6] Telhaug 2003, 4–5, 7.

The idea of an integrated school was not new, nor was it particularly Social Democratic or Socialist. The original no! refers to Norway saying no to the old school system, Norway having introduced an integrated school almost half a century earlier. Chapter 2 describes how the Norwegian Liberal Party state brought about the integrated seven-year school, while the dominant bourgeoisie in Sweden joined with the Social Democrats in Parliament to support continuing the parallel school system. The Social Democratic minister of education and church affairs, Arthur Engberg, was no supporter of the integrated school. He was "a luminous church minister," according to Tage Erlander, who added, "but schooling did not capture his interest."[7]

The Social Democrats in Norway had also taken a skeptical position with regard to expanding an integrated school system. In relation to the large parliamentary School Commission of the 1920s, for example, we see that the radical ideologue of the Labor Party, Professor Edvard Bull, commented on a proposal to expand the primary school by maintaining that the idea of school integration was erroneous in principle: "It must certainly be considered a social advantage that the children who are not interested in book learning should be able to slip out at some reasonable age level."[8] It was left to representatives of the new younger generation of Social Democrats, those who acquired their positions after 1945, to implement the school reforms under Social Democracy, taking up the inheritance of the Norwegian Liberal Party state. The lines of development crossed one another. Sweden, with no experience as a Liberal Party state, had fallen behind Norway; then after 1945 Sweden became the leading school-nation.

The resistance in the labor movement was soon won over. The reforms themselves were to some degree an answer to the demands of the period. The proposal put forward for parliamentary ratification in Sweden in 1950 reads, "Given the course that development is taking, we are confronted with the need to find forms of organization for a new phase in the history of our popular education."[9] The political right also supported the idea of an integrated school system but hesitated to hand it over to the Social Democrats; similarly, the political left feared a turn toward the right. But in the end they managed to reach an agreement. The epoch-making parliamentary decision of 1950 was consequently the result of a political compromise.[10]

A similar process occurred in Norway. When in 1954 the Labor Party government managed to put forward a proposal in Parliament for "a common

---

[7] Erlander 1973, 234. See Rothstein 1986, 130.
[8] Cited by Fredriksen 1979, 30.
[9] Richardson 1999, 74.
[10] Richardson 1999, 73.

youth school" with a two-year extension to the existing seven-year integrated school, the representative of the Conservative Party praised the government and gave his approval to the proposal.[11]

A BREAK WITH THE PAST?

In the eyes of the leading Social Democratic reformers, it seems to have been important to mark the reforms as signifying a break with the past. The Myrdals wrote: "It was impossible for us to abandon the important task of shaping the school, and ultimately the very life of society, and allow it to follow outdated routines, nor could we embrace the harmonious liberal confidence of the 'new school' that believes society itself will somehow arrange things."[12] The alternative to outdated routines lay in modern scientific pedagogy with its emphasis on individualization and activity.

The new pedagogy was not so very new. In Norway what counts as the breakthrough to modern progressivism is the Standard Plan of 1939. This Standard Plan has almost acquired the status of Holy Writ. In it, the old-fashioned methods of obtaining knowledge were to be replaced by a pedagogy informed by experience-based educational thinking. As in Sweden, the students were to be activated and made independent.[13] But old systems tend not to be easily turned on their heads.

In Sweden there was an old central organ used to direct both primary and gymnasium schooling, the National Agency for Education (Skolöverstyrelsen). It was a tradition in Sweden to set up such central bureaucratic organs. Norway did not have a tradition of this type but in this case, following the Swedish model, it founded the Experimental Council for Education (Forsøksrådet for Skoleverket) in 1954. In relation to the impressive bureaucracy of Skolöverstyrelsen, Forsøksrådet was diminutive. Both institutions would become important arenas when it came to reform activity, however.

Erlander's School Commission was aware that the great bureaucracy of the National Agency could become an obstacle to the work of reform. This was confirmed by a submission from the National Agency to the commission. In this document the agency turned against the excessively bleak description of the existing school system. The new idea that the members of a school class should be kept together through nine years of schooling was criticized, and

---

[11] Slagstad 1998, 322.
[12] A. and G. Myrdal 1934.
[13] Telhaug and Mediås 2003, 114. Richardson 1999, 73.

skepticism was expressed toward the progressive reform pedagogy with its individualization of teaching.

The commission had tried to avoid the attitude of the National Agency with regard to experimental activity by anchoring this feature of educational reform directly in the commission itself, thus presenting the integrated school to both the National Agency and Parliament as an accomplished fact.[14] There was no guarantee of political support. The commission strategy worked in part; the nine-year integrated school was established in principle. But in terms of its continuation, the experimental work was taken over by the National Agency. And this was not without consequences for the content of the schooling.

One of the leading pedagogues in Sweden, Torsten Husén, has written that the evaluation put into action by the National Agency was based on a faulty assumption, namely that the new integrated school was to be a knowledge school similar to the old grammar/high school. In general the whole debate about the integrated school was conducted as though it had to do with a *pedagogical* problem. In reality it was not a pedagogical reform, according to Husén, but a *social and political* reform. The integrated school system was carried out relatively quickly despite the turn that the debate took. But it never became what, in their most optimistic moments, the reformers had conceived. There was scarcely any pedagogical reform; nor, if we are to believe Husén, was there a social reform. It had been a precondition that teacher education would be overhauled, but this was never done. Husén concluded that "the parallel school system was retained in teacher education."[15]

In Norway the Experimental Council would become an instrument of reform policy based on the newer pedagogical research. Research, however, seems to have been a substitute motive. In reality, as in Sweden, Norwegian reforms did not have to do with pedagogy but with political reform. The aim of the Experimental Council was to get the reforms through in the most effective manner by lifting the issue out of the ongoing political discussion. Precisely as in Sweden, it thus had to do with presenting the reform to the politicians as a fait accompli. "We saved many years here," was the later comment of education minister Helge Sivertsen.

The reform did not go seriously into the content of schooling. The skepticism of the bourgeois critics proved to be unfounded—it was never a Socialist school system. Characteristically, the pedagogical view of the Experimental Council's first powerful leader was distinguished by "moderation, by accommodation and understanding, toward both tradition and diverging

---

[14] Rothstein 1986, 163–164.
[15] Rothstein 1986, 171f.

views." He was, in short, an implementer and a developer of the liberal tradition in Norwegian schooling.[16] Thus, in Sweden. elements of the parallel school system lived on while it was the liberal tradition that lived on in Norway. The Swedish political scientist Bo Rothstein uses this issue as an example of how difficult it can be to carry through reforms with the help of an established bureaucracy.[17]

It was unclear what the new content should be, and this of course made a radical departure more difficult. Social integration was given priority and remained the most important function of schooling; the reformers emphasized the formative powers of being together, with everyone remaining in the same school as long as possible. We saw that Husén stressed the political and social nature of the Swedish reform, and it was the same in Norway. "The whole fundamental thinking in the reform is the social," Sivertsen wrote with reference to the goal of the new nine-year integrated school.[18]

Generally speaking, the reforms were carried forward by a strikingly profound optimism. The political reformers believed that a longer period of schooling would foster versatile, knowledgeable, cultured, forward-looking, and prejudice-free human beings. Being raised for life in society was given weight over equipping the youth for working life. An upbringing for democracy was advanced beyond that found in prewar society. When it came to forming human beings by means of the school system, scientific outlook and Christian faith and morals were core elements of the ideal. The latter factor betrays the staying power of tradition. Even though the basic thought was social, the element of knowledge remained important. The idea of a common European cultural heritage capable of transmission by the school system was at the substantive core of school content. There was nothing radically new here.

WHAT KIND OF EQUALITY?

The idea of *unity* is closely linked to that of *equality*. But as we have seen, equality can mean different things. In reality the unified school became *the school of equal opportunity*. The school was to contribute to sweeping away the old class divisions, so that the gifted from the lower social orders would be given the same opportunities as those from the higher social orders. It is noteworthy, however, that even the report issued by Erlander's School Com-

---

[16] Telhaug and Mediås 2003, 153.
[17] Rothstein 1986, 209f.
[18] Telhaug and Mediås 2003, 165.

mission in 1946 displays a certain degree of skepticism toward this way of thinking about equality. The report indicated that it would be unfortunate if the working class were deprived of its gifted and potentially best leaders.[19] The equal-opportunity school was a liberal idea. Here we see that the reform was in reality a further working out of the Norwegian Liberal Party state's school system.

This argument against equal opportunities comes up in a modern variant, namely in the form of a dystopia—the meritocracy, a new society divided into classes according to intelligence and education. Husén writes about "a social paradox in the society of equality—intelligence."[20] Giving priority to the advancement of the most intelligent necessarily comes into a tense relationship with the integrated school's founding idea of unity. But these considerations were shoved aside in the development of the Social Democratic integrated school system, at least in the first round.

The positive argument used in defense of concentrating on the clever was strengthened with the weight that was placed on the motive of "human capital."[21] Developing and taking care of "the reserve of the gifted" was best for society. This instrumental motive, whereby school had to serve national economic goals, was by no means a new principle, but it gained strength because it was in accord with the thinking of the new economists.

INTEGRATION AND NORMALITY

The history of the integrated school system has usually been presented as a success story of a democratic school that has been propelled forward by progressive forces. This is not an unreasonable interpretation, but it is one-sided and tends to shove the less fortunate moments under the rug. In the 1960s a criticism appeared warning that all was not well. The many dilemmas inherent in the compromises regarding the reforms gradually came to the surface. Perhaps the most important was that the system did not succeed as well as expected with regard to its supposed central function: equality or social integration.

One characteristic of Social Democracy's integrated school system was that it separated out several categories of anomalous children. Special classes and special schools for those who could not function well in the ordinary schools were established. It happened at a great tempo in Norway during the 1950s

---

[19] Husén 1994, 22.
[20] Husén 1999, 49.
[21] Husén 1988, 198.

and the beginning of the 1960s; approximately twenty thousand children received special teaching in one or another form, in special classes or special schools. The sorting was based partly on intelligence, partly on physical handicaps, and partly on behavioral criteria. It became legitimate to sort out the slow learners.[22] As has been written: "There is a paradox that this was called a nine-year *integrated school,* when in reality more and more children were differentiated out of this school."[23]

The same thing happened in Sweden, where the School Commission of 1946 was positive toward establishing assistant classes, even though there is evidence of objections to segregating students into special classes. For example, 3 percent of the students in Gothenburg in 1955 were segregated out. Originally it was intended only to have been the "mentally retarded," but in reality, as in Norway, it had increasingly to do with "deviants in a series of varying respects, intellectual, social, and often even moral."[24]

Behind the segregation lay the therapists' conceptions of treatment based on individual orientation—the deviant children were to be helped into society by means of special treatment. Social preventative logic also lay behind this thinking. By taking care of deviant children in special institutions, one could fight prevailing social problems, such as permanent poverty, criminality among the young, and prostitution.[25] The deeper motive must have lain with the unity culture of Social Democracy and its demand for unity-creating normality. Normality was interpreted in a constrictive sense; that is, the criteria were stringent for determining the kind of human beings "we need in this modern society."

SEVERAL DILEMMAS UNDER THE SURFACE

Social Democracy's commitment to education was to be overtaken by a new trend. People did not need to be persuaded; they sought out secondary and higher education in large numbers. This had to have consequences for the old gymnasium school, which had been the school system for the chosen few. The debate about the rights of the gifted died down. As Sixten Marklund writes, "the insistent demands of students and parents for higher education was no longer a question for contemplation. One no longer ques-

---

[22] Ravneberg 1999, 340. In Norway the Special Schools Act of 1951 represents a breakthrough for the policy of segregation.

[23] Bladini 1990, 10–15.

[24] Bladini 1990, 10–15.

[25] Ravneberg 1999, 153, 156.

tioned how many could go to grammar school or the gymnasium but rather asked what these schools would look like when they were attended by all or most of the students."[26]

In this situation a different equality ideal thrust its way forward; equality of result entered the picture and modified the old ideal of equality of opportunity. Everyone had to be able to take part in the education system, including secondary education. As a consequence, knowledge requirements were lowered. There arose a tendentious opposition between the social motive and the knowledge motive. But this opposition did not come to distinguish the agenda of school policy until the development optimism of the period had waned and Arvidsson's dream of an agricultural worker family being able to discuss the configuration of the atom around the dinner table had been revealed as utopian.

Around 1970 school policy was overtaken by the youth rebellion. In one recommendation the professional ambitions for the junior high school were to be adjusted to take care of "everyone." The radical reform pedagogues wanted more, however. One of the prominent younger Norwegian pedagogues argued that the plan was still preparing students for the old knowledge aims. The fact that the plan would keep the regulatory and behavioral marking system was for him a feature of authority that represented "almost grotesque pedagogical thinking and the proposing of humiliating instruments."[27]

The same year saw a secondary school proposal in Norway in which the Social Democratic representatives on the parliamentary committee put forward a demand for an ideologically active school. The aim of the school had to "include a cultural and political ideology," as it was phrased. Allusions to which ideology this should be encouraged the school historian Telhaug to write that this was "the first serious thrust made by the labor movement in Norway to make use of the school system as a means of advancing its Socialist ideas."[28] A new era was at hand, but it would not bring about a more Socialistic school.

The most important contradiction was perhaps that between rearing fellow citizens in the societal collective and the development of the individual personality. This constituted a latent tension that from time to time burst to the surface. One of these times occurred in 1958 when the Conservatives, sensing Socialism, stirred up a dispute in the Norwegian Parliament about what was included in the concept "the good social citizen." The dispute ended with

[26] Marklund 1985, 4:63. Cited by Husén 1988, 197.
[27] Cited by Hustad 2002, 29.
[28] Telhaug 1991, 179.

a compromise that shoved the problem back under the rug.[29] In reality the conservatives had little to fear. More important was the underlying tension between the collectivistic legacy of the Social Democrats and the individualistic aspects of modern progressivism.

The integrated school system was one of Social Democracy's great projects. Characteristically, it was constructed under a climate of considerable political agreement. Even if the most optimistic expectations were not reached, it is fair to say that the system was reasonably successful both in relation to the education of the many and to social integration. Yet under the surface one finds built-in contradictions that pointed beyond the fine balance that had been reached. Toward the end of the 1960s these contradictions broke through the surface, and a big struggle loomed in both Sweden and Norway. As Gunnar Richardson writes with regard to Sweden: "This has something to do with the irony of fate, that the whole project of building up the education system, whose structure was set down under conditions of great political agreement, was beset with harsh criticism at that precise moment."[30]

AN UNSUCCESSFUL INTEGRATION DRIVE

In Norway "[t]he school became the foremost laboratory for a Pan-Norwegian language as an instrument of national integration," writes Slagstad.[31] This laboratory experiment was unsuccessful, however. The struggle over language became one of the most bitter of the entire Social Democratic period in Norway, a reminder of how important language is as a mark of identity.

During Norway's Danish period, up to 1814, the Norwegian written language became Danish, and this continued into the twentieth century. With Henrik Ibsen in the lead, most of the writers from Norway's golden age wrote in Danish. But from the mid-nineteenth century a struggle arose to create a Norwegian written language that was an alternative to Danish. This mother-tongue movement was part of the radical democratic popular movement at the end of the nineteenth century. It led to the development of two official languages in Norway, *landsmål* and *riksmål* (respectively, the language of the countryside and of the realm, later referred to as *nynorsk* [new Norwegian] and *bokmål* [book language]). In this early phase the struggle over language was about which of the two forms of language represented the nation. Indeed the actual differences were so slight that people on both

---

[29] Sejersted 2003b, 349–350.
[30] Richardson 1999, 93.
[31] Slagstad 1998, 332.

sides of the language divide could relatively easily understand one another. This offered the possibility of amalgamation into a common language—Pan-Norwegian. Following the war, the language dispute was over the legitimacy of Pan-Norwegian.

The language of the countryside had its basis in the dialects of what were called the countercultural regions on Norway's west coast, or *Vestlandet*. These were areas in which the labor movement had had difficulty obtaining a foothold. Social Democrats had not been particularly engaged in the language issue. Nevertheless, they took up a powerful initiative in favor of Pan-Norwegian. The man behind this drive was one of the foremost integration ideologues in the labor movement, history professor Halvdan Koht. Koht originally belonged to the Liberal, or Venstre, Party, but early on he joined the labor movement and was a central figure in preparing the ideological basis for the development of the Labor Party into a unifying national party that was able to build on the inheritance of the radical Venstre. A Pan-Norwegian language was for him a natural step in the direction of national integration.

Pan-Norwegian was to be founded on "the basis of the people's tongue," as was the common saying. This implied combining common forms from both of the official languages with features taken from the eastern Norwegian "folk tongue." The political aim was thus an administrated amalgamation of the two official languages. Pan-Norwegian policy began with the radical orthography reform of 1938 and was continued after 1945 through the active promotion of language norms at school.

The reaction was powerful. It found organized expression through the "Parents' Reaction against Pan-Norwegian" in 1952, organized by the users of *riksmål*, the literary, Danish-influenced language. A petition campaign was organized, and the names of 400,000 opponents of Pan-Norwegian were collected. This long and bitter struggle came to an end in 1981 with a parliamentary resolution that, in reality, was a clear retreat from the administrated regulation of language development.

The language dispute is symptomatic for Social Democracy insofar as it was a large-scale attempt at leadership through technological expertise. On the other hand, this departs from the picture of the great Social Democratic reconciliation. The reaction against the Pan-Norwegian policy paralleled the reaction against the policy of economic regulation (see chapter 10). But despite the fact that the economic regulation policies affected core values in the labor movement in a way that the language policy did not, it was the laguage policy that failed in a more fundamental way. The reason for this seems to lie with the fact that linguistic amalgamation was reduced to a practical-administrative question. According to Halvard Leira, those who carried forward the Pan-Norwegian project had developed no distinct identity. "With regard to the economy and social policy one can undertake compromises, but identity was a question of either/or."[32] In any case, aspects of the counter-culture of the western regions turned out to be more deeply rooted than the working-class culture!

The language struggle created contradictions and discord for the Social Democratic school system, as it did for the wider society. The retreat on language policy first appeared on the wings of a general liberation revolution around 1980 (see chapter 12). Here the Social Democratic integration policy came up against barriers that could not be neutralized despite heroic efforts. In linguistic terms Norway is still two nations. This has been a struggle that has had no match in Sweden, where the hegemonic written culture allied itself with the nationalist efforts. Sweden did not experience a "counterculture" of corresponding strength to that in Norway.

MARGINALIZED UNIVERSITIES

There is value in the words of one of the foremost ideologues of modern Social Democracy, Gunnar Myrdal, at the beginning of the hegemonic phase of Social Democracy:

> Research and higher education are the sources of national culture. . . . The newly awakened interest, coming from all directions, in practical science must not obscure the fact that this in itself, like the remainder of our culture, is built on our universities and colleges having the freedom of investigation in the pursuit of truth, a freedom that is not governed by immediate utilitarian interests. We have to step up the safeguarding of our basic research. We must also pay attention to the humanistic sciences. In them is found the deeper cultural world, which is the soul of the nation's breeding. For my part I hope and believe that the Socialist labor movement, which is now decisively seizing political power in society, will feel its solidarity with the ideal of humanity and will see to it that our research does not become shortsightedly limited to utility.[33]

We find here an expression of the universalism of science and of its role in the formation of humanity, but at the same time we get a hint of resignation. It is obvious that Myrdal felt he had to remind his compatriots of the existence of the humanities, which indeed, above all else, ought to represent the argument for culture and formation of the social human being. What shines through is a doubt that the Social Democrats would take the culture argument seriously. Subsequent events would show that this concern was justified.

---

[32] Halvard Leira 2003, 395.
[33] Gunnar Myrdal 1945,29f. Cited by Wittrock 1989, 281.

It was some time before the Social Democrats developed what we might call a university policy. At first the universities did not interest them. Applied research, which to a large extent took place outside the universities, was more important for the project of modernization, and the school system was more important for social integration. As Thorsten Nybom writes, Swedish Social Democracy's attitude toward research and higher education could be summed up as "a programmatic and manifest parade of kindness toward research, at best combined with an almost nonexistent interest in higher academic education, and, above all, in its link to the research system."[34] During the Social Democratic period the universities continued to be relatively marginalized, just as they had been in the interwar period.

As a consequence, the universities maintained their independence. For a very long time there was no pressure to abolish the old "contract" that had been shaped at the turn of the century. The humanistic faculties continued to educate teachers in the college and secondary grammar school system. In other words, traditional humanistic ideals continued to exert their influence over the school system. This part of the system remained at the periphery of Social Democratic state-interventionist policy.

The first indication of change was the great flood of students into the universities that began in the 1950s and continued in the 1960s. During that period the universities were transformed from elite to mass institutions. A common process occurred across the Western world. This did not happen on the basis of any planned policy; above all, it was a movement from below.

The youth sought out higher education, and the system had to adapt to this as well as it could. With time this would lead to changes in views on the function of higher education, the organization of the curricula, academic requirements, and the leadership of the institutions. Developments pointed toward a cancellation of the old "contract," but this did not happen all at once.[35]

SWEDISH UNIVERSITY REFORM

In 1967 the Swedish minister of education took the initiative to launch a Commission of Inquiry into Higher Education. The background to this initiative was a growing interest in the subject through the 1960s, together with a growing criticism of the established university system. Reform policy in the education sector had now reached the field of higher education. The universities had to accommodate the huge volume of students and at the same time

---

[34] Nybom 1997, 63.
[35] Lindensjö 1981, 25.

be reformed.[36] The findings of the main report of 1973 recommended new avenues for educational policy.

The inquiry's mandate strikingly lacked an ideological perspective on education. No vaunted theses about the social functions of education were to be found.[37] Meanwhile the student rebellion and the general criticism, which was now coming from bourgeois circles as well, thrust ideological debate to the forefront. Among other things, the Social Democratic youth association demanded that reform be directed toward making education policy an integral part of the changes necessary for building a Socialist society. But this was hardly the result.

The commission's white paper played down the importance of general education and stressed the need for education relevant to working life. The dimensions of the study programs were to be geared to the demand for labor power. All study programs, in principle, should be of limited enrollment. At the same time, higher education served the progressive development of society without clearly specifying what this implied, beyond an increasing public responsibility for the economy and social services.[38]

One central motive behind this new policy was *equality*. At the same time that the commission was searching for new ways to solve old contradictions between social formation and education, it was also seeking new ways to view the significance of education for equality. The free choice of the old policy, according to Education Minister Ingvar Carlsson, was nothing other than "an effective instrument for defending the inequalities and shortcomings."[39] The system, based on what Prime Minister Palme characterized as the "rather limp and narrow thinking" about a starting point for equal opportunity, had not functioned smoothly. The white paper had slipped into thinking about *equality of results*; that is, education should function in a socially compensatory manner.[40] As Carlsson said, "Today we select the best-fitted for education; tomorrow we will have to give the worst-fitted a chance to be selected."[41]

In the course of further developments, however, even this equality ideal was pushed aside. Neither the "best suited" nor the "worst suited" would be guaranteed higher education. Higher education would be granted on the

[36] Lindensjö 1981, 62.
[37] Lindensjö 1981, 74.
[38] Lindensjö 1981, 192–193.
[39] Lindensjö 1981, 107.
[40] Lindensjö 1981, 115.
[41] Lindensjö 1981, 108. This sentence was found in a speech given by Ingvar Carlsson at an OECD conference. See *Educational Policy for the 1970's*, Conference on Policies for Economic Growth, Paris, \3–5 June 1970. General Report, OECD, Paris, 1971, 73.

basis of a lottery, the dimensions of which were to be determined by the needs of society.[42] The discussion about the criteria of choice revealed the difficulties of formulating a policy of equality within the framework of educational policy. It is also symptomatic that the optimistic and reformist spirit that had marked so much of earlier education policy had become subdued and that simultaneously political agreement had dissolved. Criticism came from both the left and the right, and from the universities themselves. Torgny Segerstedt, the high-profile chancellor of the University of Uppsala, said that the proposal constituted "a threat to higher education."[43]

Nevertheless, proposals stemming from the white paper were by and large addressed through "the great college reform" that was finally ratified by Parliament in 1977. Now, in principle, all education became vocation-oriented, with a view to preparing workers for specific labor markets. The importance of general education was de-emphasized. Free-choice study programs were done away with in principle. The college concept was expanded to include many vocational and professional education programs. External influence on college administrations was strengthened. There were tendencies toward both decentralization and centralization, the former with the establishment of regional college leadership and the latter with the central chancellorship actually being strengthened.

Internally the old professorial power and authority was dissolved in favor of a democratic-corporative structure of leadership with representation from students and administrative employees in addition to those holding scholarly and scientific positions. Meanwhile, as in the remainder of society, this democratization was to some degree outweighed by a parallel bureaucratization.[44] All this represented a radical reform for the universities, perhaps above all in terms of the emphasis now placed on work-directed education.

In certain respects the Swedish 1977 reform was "the final expression of the extreme technocratic form of planning of the 1960s."[45] Torsten Husén has an explanation of why the reform assumed this bureaucratic character and why it was being forced on the administrators of the unwilling universities. He felt that the universities had resisted all attempts at reform in the preceding decades and that this had led to "disillusionment, if not open animosity, toward the universities from the government and the top administration." And thus the time had now come to seize "power over a sector that, despite a centralized system, still enjoyed much autonomy."[46] This confirms what we

---

[42] Lindensjö 1981, 194–195.
[43] Lindensjö 1981, 161.
[44] Lennart Svensson 1980, 51.
[45] Lindensjö 1981, 73.
[46] Lindensjö 1981, 190.

have seen—at last it was the turn of the universities and colleges; the contract was to be renegotiated.

It is noteworthy that only the Swedish universities during the rather limited period of a decade beginning in 1977 became encapsulated in the Social Democratic, technocratic, state-interventionist policy. This occurred as part of the Social Democratic radicalization of the 1970s. But as we have seen, this happened after the period of harmony and represented only a last thrust before things took a new direction.

NORWEGIAN UNIVERSITY REFORM

The Swedish white paper had its counterpart in Norway with the cross-party Ottosen Committee and its recommendations issued between 1965 and 1970, prior to Social Democratic radicalization. Characteristically, the committee had made all its recommendations unanimously, emphasizing effectiveness, improvements in study progression, and expansion of vocational studies. As in Sweden, the Norwegian committee became caught up in the student revolt, and the criticism against the committee gradually became widespread. Most of the radicals viewed their criticism as part of a general critique of capitalism, which was also about higher education "satisfying the needs of the business world." It is important, however, to take note that the "effectiveness demand" was also criticized from another direction, especially within the universities.

What was most noteworthy, however, was the committee recommendation for open courses of studies and an expansion of course offerings according to individual requests for education. This contrasted sharply with what happened in Sweden. This openness and orientation to demand was explicitly linked to education as a "social benefit":

> In the society now taking shape, education in the widest sense will be regarded as one of the individual's central welfare requirements, just as central as many of the welfare demands that the society quite naturally favors today. Through education, human horizons are further expanded, greater insights are created, as are opportunities for the individual to develop abilities and interests leading to a richer life.[47]

What remains unspoken is just as interesting as what is actually stated. In contrast to Sweden, very little is said about market-economy requirements. And very little is said about the function of higher education from a general formative perspective, beyond education as a welfare requirement. Much can

[47] Ottosen-komiteen (Ottosen Committee) 1966, Report 1, 12.

be read into the committee's reasons for not saying much about the general basic values, however: "When, for example, the laws do not go further in the direction of defining which value system they should be based upon, this can in part be connected to the fact that the academic ideals of the universities/ colleges are taken for granted, partly because the political authorities have accepted an extreme self-governance of the institutions."[48]

The Swedish report was based on the opposite position in terms of autonomy. That report expressed a concern that developments could lead to a situation where "only students and teachers at the higher educational institutions would determine the aims, and thereby the effect, that education should have on society." Here we find a lack of confidence in the universities and in the traditional autonomy, something not found in the Norwegian committee's report.[49] The difference is symptomatic of the Swedish tradition of stronger political control.

Also, as in Sweden, the Norwegian committee was concerned about adult education, flexible transitional arrangements, and especially equality. Norway also went well beyond the old liberal argument about equality of opportunity in stressing that education should be a welfare requirement. Finally, in relation to the issue of limited enrollments, the Norwegian committee discussed the Swedish principle of using a lottery system as an alternative to granting admission based on grades. On this point there were disagreements within the committee, and its recommendation reveals a distaste for the lottery system. In the end it recommended open courses of study, thereby avoiding the necessity of drawing lots.[50]

The motive of equality found different treatment in the two countries. Sweden wanted to dimension according to the various needs of society and had to resort to random selection, while Norway wanted to dimension according to the study preferences of the individual. Everyone should have a chance. Such were the principles; in reality, though, the differences were not very great.

An Ottosen Committee proposal regarding formation of district colleges was followed up by the authorities. In quick succession fifteen district colleges were established, and at the same time several forms of vocational education were upgraded to college education, in conformity to what had been done in Sweden. When it came to the universities, the recommendations of the committee were only partly fulfilled. Funding for both research and advanced studies increased powerfully in the 1970s and at the beginning of the 1980s,

---

[48] Ottosen-komiteen 1970, Report 5, 33.
[49] Lindensjö 1981, 111.
[50] Ottosen-komiteen 1970, Report 5, 20–21, 25–26.

but for the most part it bypassed the universities. At the same time, the new education programs, particularly at the district colleges, came to take a market share of the university candidates. Thus the old universities remained in a backwater with respect to both funding and function.

In Sweden the universities were included within the major college reform. Consequently, as one of its arguments for district colleges, the Ottosen Committee referred to the fact that Sweden had established several university branch campuses in the districts.[51] But in Norway the universities were not drawn in. For the Norwegian universities, the advantage of not being included in the college reform was that they retained much of their traditionally strong autonomy—one factor, among others, that served to protect the humanistic disciplines. As we can see, the new reform wave came later and was weaker in the Norwegian than in the Swedish universities.

THE SOCIAL DEMOCRATIC PEOPLE'S CHURCH

Historically, both Sweden and Norway have had national Lutheran state churches to which a great proportion of the population felt a connection. How would a popular movement like the labor movement behave toward this church? The state church had been a conservative force in the development of society. But both countries had also had strong low-church movements that had the character of popular movements and played a progressive role with regard to democratization. Nevertheless, the Marxist-inspired Social Democrats began by establishing a clear front against both Christianity and the church. Consequently the situation was not like that in Great Britain, where the labor movement was closely associated with the low-church movement.

Gradually, as the Social Democrats won public support, their relationship with the church became problematic. And when the Labor parties began to form governments, they became directly responsible for the state church. As a result, "The 'people's home' became complete in the 1930s by including the Social Democratic People's Church."[52]

Originally the Social Democrats in each country had called for the dissolution of the state church. This would be combined with a neutral position regarding religion, which was proclaimed in Sweden as early as 1890—after Branting had done an about-face from the previous year's position.[53] In Norway in 1923 Labor Party ideologue Edvard Bull, among others, also

---

[51] Ottosen-komiteen 1970, Report 5, 17.
[52] Stråth 1993, 18.
[53] Stråth 1993, 17.

maintained that religion was to be a private matter.[54] This point of view was tactically motivated and demonstrates the Social Democrats' equivocal relationship to the church and Christianity.

In the Swedish labor movement Arthur Engberg, who became church minister in 1932, set the tone in these matters during the interwar period. He had clearly been against the state church but had shifted his view in 1920, the same year the movement assumed responsibility for the church when Branting formed the first Social Democratic government. In the new point of view, the state church was regarded as the organ of the state for managing the religious life of society. The dissolution of the state church was pushed into the future, to the eventual establishment of the Socialist society. The first priority was to set limits to the autonomy of the church, which was now regarded as part of the state administration. Consequently, Engberg was opposed to the individual right to leave the church, as it "in a practical way involves a withdrawal from the community of the state." As he said in Parliament in 1930: "To start with, let us get rid of the bishops and appoint a church executive, with a general director responsible for a royal board of celestial administration."[55] There were several features here that bring to mind the old state church established after the Reformation, which he also referred to. Church reforms never went that far, however.

In 1951 Sweden passed a freedom of religion law. The Social Democrats still had it written in their program that the "state church system should be dissolved." In 1960, however, this point was dropped. A pragmatic and church-tolerant position had taken over in the party. The program now called for "[t]he relationship between state and church to be regulated in accordance with the principles of democracy and religious freedom." But the presupposition remained that the state retained control over the church, since it represented an offer regarding religious service to individuals without placing any demands of personal commitment when it came to the question of faith. In this way the state church guaranteed a greater degree of religious freedom than would have been available without a state church.[56]

The ambiguity in the relationship between church and state had in no way been abolished. This is demonstrated especially in the constant confrontations over Christian teaching in the school system. In both countries the Social Democrats had gone for a nondenominational form of Christian teaching. But it can be difficult to define and put boundaries to a nondenominational form of teaching, which the constant conflict over the question has certainly

---

[54] Midttun 1995, 17.
[55] Stråth 1993, 20, 21.
[56] SOU 1968:11, pp. 76, 78, 79.

demonstrated. Moreover, it became evident that on this point they were up against strong forces within the population. This was demonstrated in 1963 when the Swedish "Petition for Christian Content" collected 2,135,000 signatures in favor of Christian teaching. Similarly, in Norway two years later 725,000 signatures were collected with the same goal. There was an obvious need for the ideologues of Social Democracy to tread carefully.

CHURCH AND MORALS

The growth and strength of the labor movement had been nurtured by moral inspiration. This was the movement of the underprivileged that to an especial degree was thought to have morality on its side. It is thus paradoxical that Göran Bexell demonstrates a falling away from morality in politics in Sweden during the Social Democratic phase.[57] It is reasonable to draw a line of consistency from the "objectivity discourse" to the strong position that instrumental reasoning occupied during the Social Democratic period. There were not as many moral arguments in political debates as there were appropriate considerations and rational arguments on which to base validity and legitimacy. There was more talk about reason than about morals.

This phenomenon was noticed by Oslo's bishop Eivind Berggrav in 1945. In a powerful piece of polemical writing he warned against the totalitarian tendencies of the times that were manifested precisely through a constant appeal to reason—"this mystifying incarnation of the divinity of the state."[58] As another central presence within the church put it, the modernist state was more dangerous than the Nazi one because it "puts everything under itself and eats its way into the spiritual realm."[59] A powerful voice from the church blended with the jurists and the liberal conservatives to warn against the all-powerful state and demand stronger constitutional limitations to its powers. But this turned out to be a cry in the wilderness in the hegemonic period of Social Democracy.

The church was viewed as though it stood, above all, for individual bourgeois, conservative morality by virtue of the weight it gave to issues such as sexual morality, women in the clergy, remarriage, and abortion. On all these issues the Social Democrats stood for individual freedom of choice.[60] It is characteristic that such moral-political questions not only involved a distance between Social Democracy and the church but also led to deep divisions

[57] Bexell 1995, 16.
[58] Berggrav 1945b, 22.
[59] Midttun 1995, 22. This refers to Stephan Tschudi.
[60] Bexell 1995, 114–124.

within the two conservative parties—between individualistic liberals and those upholding conservative values. In Norway the conflict came to the fore over the question of whether contraceptives should be issued to the Norwegian occupation forces stationed in Germany, and later—in both countries— over the issue of freedom of choice with regard to abortion.

WHICH IS MORE IMPORTANT— HEALTH OR SALVATION?

In both Sweden and Norway during the interwar period the church was considered "a state institution that, rather like other institutions, has to be managed by the state." There was to be no "clericalism." The term belonged to Johan Castberg but, like so many of his other thoughts, it suited Social Democracy well.[61] Nevertheless, in 1951 Norway's Social Democratic government put forward a proposal concerning an increase in church self-governance. After all, during the war the church had been a focal point for the resistance, and increased self-governance had been included in the parties' joint program of 1945. The proposal was rejected by the parliamentary group of the Labor Party, however, on the basis that it was the state rather than church organs that represented the silent majority, and thereby represented democracy in church affairs.

The dispute over church autonomy continued, approaching the fundamental question of dogmas. In 1953 the predominant leader of the Norwegian low-church movement gave a sermon over the radio in which he said that those who refused conversion would end up in hell. In the extensive struggle that followed it was said that the sermon was a threat to the psychic health of the population. This dispute thus illustrates the kind of difficulties that cropped up when Christian dogma collided with Social Democratic pragmatism, or when the aim of salvation collided with the aim of health. It seems that the struggle over Hades strengthened the demand for state control over the church.[62]

The church/state relationship in Sweden was also marked by ambiguity and anxiety. Even so, it seems as though a modus vivendi was reached under the Social Democratic regime. The state church was retained, resulting in a popular church suitable to the Social Democratic "people's home"—a religious service institution that met the needs of the modern individual. Even though there were collisions over various questions, the church by and large

---

[61] Midttun 1995, 22.
[62] Midttun 1995, 24–25.

kept its distance from politics in accordance with the Lutheran doctrine of dual regimes: one had to make a distinction between the spiritual and the worldly. But this would not last.

WHAT KIND OF HUMAN BEING?

This chapter opened with a reference to Alva Myrdal's question: "What kind of human being do we really need in modern society?" The school was to be an important instrument for the reformers when it came to molding and forming people for "a new world." Under Social Democracy a new, integrated nine-year school was instituted in both countries. When it came to the content of schooling, however, it was not revolutionized in the sweeping way most zealous reformers had envisioned. We find a compromise between a knowledge school and a school based on experience-pedagogy, and a compromise between individual personal development and the formation of the democratic citizen demanded by society. The principle of equality was important, but it was the equality-of-opportunity school of the liberals, or "an elitist equality," that came to dominate, particularly in higher education. But the universities were never really captured by the regulatory zeal of Social Democracy, which means that they were able to keep their traditional autonomy during the hegemonic phase of Social Democracy. And when it came to the church, the Social Democrats abandoned their traditionally radical anticlerical points of view. Christianity was to live on, in an undogmatic and passive form, and the state church got to live its life more or less as before.

Under all this apparent agreement, however, there were compromises and unanswered questions. In the phase that followed, some of these floated to the surface, creating new and more far-reaching changes.

CHAPTER 10

Capitalism, Socialism, and Democracy

Tage Erlander and Einar Gerhardsen • The Struggle over the Planned Economy in Sweden • The Struggle over the Planned Economy in Norway • A Social Democratic Constitution • Corporatism and Economic Democracy • The New Administrative Corporatism • How Democratic? •The Double Strategy of Business and Industry • An Ideological Counterthrust • Social Democracy as a Consumer Society • Taxation Socialism • Capitalism without Capitalists? • Credit Socialism or Indicative Planning? • An Order in Its Own Right

TAGE ERLANDER AND EINAR GERHARDSEN

Part II of this volume sketches a broad modernization process carried out by the Social Democrats. The resulting technical-industrial development, urban renewal, welfare state, and school system were all developed with a high degree of popular consensus, with technocrats or social engineers playing central roles. Even though Sweden remained neutral and Norway was occupied, the war opened the way for new initiatives in both countries, giving rise to a spirit of cooperation and increased awareness that a better society was possible. On the other hand, the old ideological contradictions lived on. The strong position of the Social Democrats following the wartime election in Sweden and the 1945 election in Norway created governments with the ability to act, but it also engendered mistrust and fear on the part of the bourgeoisie concerning how this newly gained power would be used.

It is important to understand the peculiar mixture of consensus and will to cooperate, on the one hand, and of fear and ideological oppositions, on the other, that was found in both countries around 1945. There has been a tendency to overlook these contradictions, particularly in Norway. Perhaps we can say that power was readily available to whoever showed the greatest ingenuity. There was a struggle over who was to administer the programs arising from this period of general agreement and intensified sense of fellowship. In more concrete terms, there was a struggle over the system of economic leadership—planned versus market economics, economic democracy, and who should control the capital. There was not only a struggle between the Social Democrats and the non-Socialist parties but also a tug-of-war within the labor movement over appropriate strategy for this new situation.

The struggle eventually calmed in response to positive developments, especially the long period of stable economic expansion. The Social Democratic welfare state is a historic example of the possibility of bringing great ambitions into reality. And successes were largely due to the development of a political culture with a high degree of consensus regarding the goals—economic growth and welfare for all—and a willingness to bet on these goals and have faith that they could be realized. Another important factor was clever leadership that contributed to building and legitimizing common ideology, thereby keeping the conflicts under control.

Both Sweden and Norway had a leading figure who came to personify the Social Democratic regime and to have national paternal qualities—Tage Erlander in Sweden and Einar Gerhardsen in Norway. Erlander was prime minister from 1946 to 1969, Gerhardsen from 1945 to 1965 (with a break of three years between 1951 and 1955, when he handed the prime ministerial post to one of his closest colleagues, and a short break in 1963, when a non-Socialist government came into power). These leaders regarded themselves as representatives of the national fellowship, while at the same time they were each anchored deeply in Social Democratic ideals. The two men possessed many personal similarities, although they came from rather different backgrounds.

It is not easy to calculate personal influence, since leadership is always practiced within a context. The two leaders were both children of their time; yet, owing especially to their respectively long periods of activity, they each came to symbolize their period, as well. Erlander and Gerhardsen were not technocrats. They were full-blooded politicians; but, as politicians, they made a place for the technocrats, using that expertise to the fullest. Transferring responsibility as much as possible to the experts was also a way of dampening the political contradictions, and dampening the contradictions was something that concerned them both deeply.

When the old "father of the nation," Per Albin Hansson, died suddenly in 1946, it was not obvious that Sweden's minister of education and church affairs, Tage Erlander, would succeed him. Many expected that the minister of social affairs, Gustav Möller, would take over, including Möller himself. But it was to be Erlander. Erlander's own surprise is evident in his journal entry:

> A terrible night. No sleep and the whole time Gustav Möller's bitter features in the field of vision. . . . Really I had never dreamed about leadership. Not until voting on the party leadership was over did I begin to understand that here there was a serious risk. . . . Unheard of—how this will turn out I do not know. To be sure the criticism is right—I have none of the great visions; not the great man of decision. I am afraid.

And six days later: "Also, the commentators of the bourgeois press perpetually pointing out my insignificance, nervousness, and smallness have cheered and encouraged me greatly. My chance lies precisely in the fact that I continue to be systematically underrated."[1]

There are grounds for taking his commentary seriously. He had not sought power, and he was unprepared for the position of prime minister. He did have political qualifications, however: he had determination and will. And he was not completely without faith in his own abilities, which is revealed in the final two sentences just quoted.

Erlander was an intellectual, the son of a teacher, and he attended the University of Lund. There was "an air of the perpetual student about him: he gradually finished enough courses to earn his degree," as biographer Olof Ruin writes. He "liked to discuss, to twist the arguments and . . . was a diligent reader; he had a debating style that reminded one of a student politician, with its snappy rejoinders, sudden shifts between the serious and the humorous." He himself was astonished that he was actually suitable to be leader of the labor movement.[2] Yet he was a political figure, but not a revolutionary.

Einar Gerhardsen was the son of a worker who, in turn, became a worker himself—in the Highways Authority, where he quickly became involved in trade union work. He developed revolutionary points of view, but when he hung up a portrait of Lenin at home, his Social Democratic father tore it down. He was shy by nature but soon gained attention in the political context with his characteristic low-key, yet urgent, sense of engagement and his organizational abilities. Martin Tranmæl, the superstrategist of the Norwegian labor movement, quickly discovered Gerhardsen's talents and netted him for the revolution. It was also Tranmæl who, when the Labor Party had abandoned Marxism, prevented Gerhardsen from becoming a Communist and piloted him into the reformist fold. In clear contrast to Erlander and to the tradition of the Swedish labor movement, Gerhardsen was deeply skeptical toward the intellectual radicals. It was Gerhardsen who staged the exclusion of the radical "student organization" Mot Dag (Toward the Day). "Allowing himself to grovel before these young intellectuals must have appeared to Gerhardsen as a caricature of the liberation of the working class," his biographer writes.[3]

Political relations in Norway during the summer of 1940, following the German invasion and occupation, were chaotic. As a result, Gerhardsen was thrust into taking responsibility for the labor movement. He was jointly responsible for a proposal to form "a Norwegian front" by establishing an independent, vigorous Norwegian leadership that could advance the goals of

[1] Erlander 2001, 10 October 1946, 16 October 1946.
[2] Ruin 1986, 31, 50.
[3] Olstad 1999, 93.

the labor movement. This took into consideration that the parliamentary system, following the flight of the king and the Nygaardvold government, had played out its role. This initiative threw a light both on the situation and on Gerhardsen personally. Gerhardsen was a clear, unequivocal anti-Fascist, but one had to face the facts: a Germanic Europe was being established and, one way or another, one had to adapt to the situation.[4] This initiative never went further than the discussion stage. It rapidly collided with German ambitions and plans, and became simply an episode in the chaotic times.

Thereafter Gerhardsen was central to the establishment of the resistance movement until his arrest by the Gestapo in the autumn of 1941. He survived imprisonment in Germany through a combination of survival skills and luck. Toward the end of the war he was sent home to imprisonment in Norway. The circumstances around his transfer are unclear, but he was likely viewed as a man needed by the new Norway, and it seems as if some clear-sighted persons must have succeeded in persuading the Germans to send him back to Norway. By virtue of his participation in the resistance struggle he had become a legend. In 1945, with this reputation and with his background as an inmate of the German concentration camps, he held great authority. In a remarkably natural way he slid into the role of Labor Party leader and new prime minister.

Erlander and Gerhardsen became the undisputed national leaders of the great epoch of Social Democracy. Despite their differences in background and personality there were also similarities between the two men. Neither of them were confrontational politicians; they both believed in and relied upon cooperation. They realized their socialistic visions by getting as many people as possible on board, even though it would take time. The close fellowship he had experienced with people from different political streams in the resistance movement and the prison camps was obviously important to Gerhardsen's development as a collaborative politician.

Erlander and Gerhardsen had one particularly important feature in common: in 1945 when they were about to take over as prime ministers, they were both considered to be weak politicians. Erlander was characterized by many as insignificant and indecisive.[5] Gerhardsen matured more naturally into the role, but he too was considered by many to be a weak politician. Gerhardsen was indeed a sympathetic person, as one of the central Social Democrats said in 1948, adding that he was weak and that he changed his opinions according to the circumstances.[6]

---

[4] Olstad 1999, 140–143.
[5] Ruin 1986, 337.
[6] Olstad 1999, 423. This was said by Olav Oksvik.

In hindsight these "weaknesses" can be viewed as strengths. The men had power and they used it, but there is reason to take them seriously when they themselves maintained that they had never aspired to this power. Neither did they allow power to go to their heads or let themselves be corrupted by it. They represented "an innocence of power"[7] that made them no less powerful; quite the reverse, it inspired confidence and thus supported their positions. Perhaps successful political leadership can be characterized by a certain attentive indecisiveness that leads to pragmatic solutions while, on another level, representing the management of deeper currents. It is not unreasonable to say that Sweden and Norway got the leaders they needed at the time they needed them.

THE STRUGGLE OVER THE PLANNED ECONOMY IN SWEDEN

In Norway planning for the postwar period was made difficult by the war itself. Such planning had to be conducted partly in secret, in the concentration camps in Norway and Germany, but also among the refugees in Sweden and Britain.

The situation was different in Sweden. The planning for the postwar period began early. In 1943 work commenced on the Labor Movement's Postwar Program. This initiative was made by a committee of the trade union central (LO) chaired by Minister of Finance Ernst Wigforss. By this point he had been in close contact with the employers' Industrial Research Institute (IUI) in order to get a clear picture of the postwar problems. The complexity of the situation found a concrete expression: "Ernst Wigforss first gave IUI a mandate from the state to carry out plans on the basis of its investigations, but only a few weeks later he found himself as the party's representative on the above-mentioned committee, with the task of challenging the basis for industry's aspirations in this field."[8] The confusing mixture of desire to cooperate and ideological contradictions that we have referred to is demonstrated here.

In 1944 the Labor Movement's Postwar Program was put forward. The inspiration came not from Socialist theories but rather from the war economy. Wartime economic policy had shown how labor and resources could be fully utilized for the common good. This presupposed a planned economy and Keynesian macropolicies. Principles governing the just allocation of resources, a higher living standard, greater effectiveness, and more democracy

[7] Ruin 1986, 349.
[8] Ekdahl 2001,136.

followed. One of the most conspicuous concrete proposals was for a state commercial bank.

It is noteworthy that there was no demand for socialization. The state's expansive and superordinate responsibility for the society's economy did not mean "that all ownership should be considered to rest in the hands of the state and all economic activity ... be directed by an economic central administration. The state's economic activity is a means of gaining the greatest possible effectiveness and is motivated precisely to the extent that it advances this purpose." The state was thus to behave in a compensatory way; in principle, it was only to become involved wherever private interests were unsuccessful. Wigforss directly stated that private enterprise should not be attacked as long as it could carry out its tasks in a satisfactory manner. None of this sounded particularly radical, at least if one also considers that the bourgeois side was at this time captivated by Keynesian expansionism.

The Swedish Social Democrats did not believe that the private sector would be able to manage the postwar problems of economic cycles and structural needs. The general expectation was that there would be a crisis after World War II, as there had been after World War I. Along with the postwar program, Gunnar Myrdal had published his well-known text titled *A Warning against Peace Optimism*. It was consequently expected that a radical intervention by the state would be necessary, not only through an expansive policy at the macro level, but also on the question of public investment. Preparations were made for a structural rationalization of commercial life under the leadership of the state. In a word, the Social Democrats were prepared for action.

Simultaneously with the launching of this program, the "Myrdal Commission" was established. Under the leadership of Gunnar Myrdal it acted as a Social Democratic shadow cabinet, capable of taking initiatives that the coalition government could not.[9] Among other things, these initiatives made recommendations, based on investigation, regarding sector-by-sector structural rationalization. The LO was also active, warning against dissolving the wartime regulated economy and arguing for effective price controls. Inspired by the Norwegian "lex Thagaard" of 1945, a proposal was put forward that producers could be instructed to shut down or produce specific products at officially set prices.[10] Even if a thoroughgoing piece of legislation like that taken in Norway never came into being, there was enough material to provoke the business world and the interests of the bourgeoisie.

From the launch of the postwar program in 1944 until the election of 1948, the business community and the bourgeois parties mobilized an intense ideo-

[9] Lewin 1992, 235.
[10] Ekdahl 2001, 186.

logical countercampaign. An important ideological inspiration came from F. A. Hayek's book *The Road to Serfdom*, the main message being that organizing the peacetime economy in the same way as the wartime economy would necessarily lead to "serfdom": the planned economy was incompatible with parliamentary democracy. The institution Næringslivets Fond (Foundation for Trade and Commerce) gave out anti-Socialist journals, pamphlets, and books at a rate never before seen. For the business world it was a question of whether to participate in the investigations and commissions that the Social Democrats initiated. Hesitantly, it decided to participate.

As it turned out, there was no postwar crisis. There are several reasons for this: international ones, first and foremost, but it was also due in part to successful initiatives taken by industry itself. Consequently, there was no need for a publicly initiated and publicly led structural rationalization process such as the Social Democrats had prepared for. Their intended strong kickoff consisted of springing into action like a lion and falling back to earth like a fur rug. "'Productive labor' triumphed over 'bureaucracy,'" as Leif Lewin wrote. In general he characterized the Social Democrats' support for a planned economy as "a political fiasco."[11]

The confrontation over the planned economy was the central feature of the election campaign of 1948. The results led to some shift in the direction of the bourgeois parties; above all, the Liberal Party doubled its number of votes and sailed forward as the leading party in the bourgeois opposition. The Communists lost ground as a result of the coup d'état in Czechoslovakia, but the Social Democrats remained at about the same level and, with a majority in both houses, managed to hold on to governmental power. Despite holding power, they decided to retreat on the question of a planned economy. It was striking how rapidly the disagreements died away and a milder current entered the political climate. The government took several initiatives to meet with business interests and establish the confidence necessary for a good collaboration. In response, the business world dropped its aggressive propaganda against the Social Democrats.

For explanation of these moves we return to the blending of contradictions and fellowship. The confrontation had been frightening. Both sides must have felt that they had more to win through collaboration; indeed, they were in agreement about the goal—full employment and economic growth through increasing efficiency and structural adjustments. Important questions could be taken out of politics and transferred to the strong new expert profession—the economists. Most economists were now "Keynesians," no matter what else they stood for. Erlander willingly listened to them, above all

[11] Lewin 1992, 247. Lewin 1967, 331.

to Gunnar Myrdal: "Gunnar Myrdal became of great importance to the work of government. His intellectual vigor, his knowledge, his contacts with leading economists—all this brought with it a vitalization."[12]

The anti-Socialist mobilization had been directed toward not only what the Social Democrats proposed or implemented in the current situation but also what they might propose next. On both sides there were some who saw the Social Democratic initiatives as only a first step on the road toward a Socialist society—a notion that brought hope to some and fear to others. This uncertainty seems to have weakened, however, once the postwar crisis failed to materialize.

THE STRUGGLE OVER THE PLANNED ECONOMY IN NORWAY

Developments in Norway had features that strikingly paralleled those in Sweden, but the confrontations over the planned economy were harsher, the contradictions penetrated more deeply, and the struggle was longer.[13] It did not end until 1953, when the Labor Party government failed to ratify the rationalization bill that had been forwarded. A relatively peaceful period followed.

The struggle began with the issue that has been named the lex Thagaard, a provisional ordinance undertaken by the coalition government while still in exile in London. This ordinance determined that the Directorate for Price Controls could forbid reduction or stoppage of production, order the production of specific goods, decide that firms should not be set up or should be closed down, and levy tariffs in order to regulate prices. It also allowed for the confiscation of unfair earnings, independent of whether or not the earnings were lawful. Thus the directorate was given far-reaching powers, more far-reaching than had ever been instituted in Sweden. It was said that this ordinance was meant to deal with the difficult transition period and that it would be used with the greatest of caution. Nonetheless, it provoked a violent reaction, with accusations that the Labor Party now wanted to implement pure Nazi-style dictatorship over economic life. In 1947 the ordinance was replaced by a provisional law that remained in effect until 1953.

---

[12] Erlander 1973, 322.

[13] The discussion among Norwegian historians concerning the laws governing prices and economic rationalization has been very extensive. See, for example, Sejersted 2001, 310–346, "Sosialdemokratiet finner sin form." Slagstad 1998, 233–250, "Da Dagbladet seiret i Arbeiderpartiet." For an overview, see Grønlie 1993 and Grønlie 1999, 181–214.

The dispute reached its peak in 1947. On top of lex Thagaard the government had brought out its first national budget in 1947—and behind this stood the new experts: the economists. Like Erlander, Gerhardsen listened to them. Myrdal's equivalent in Norway was Erik Brofoss, who became minister of finance in 1945. He was known for his long economics speeches in Parliament. "[I]nside the government too, we had the feeling he saw that it was his task 'to bring us up to scratch,'" Gerhardsen wrote, adding, "And that he did in spades."[14] The Labor Party in Norway went further than their counterparts in Sweden when it came to the national budget. One of the young Social Democratic economists would point out that "[t]he Swedish national budget was not a program for economic policy to the same extent as the Norwegian one. The budget publications, for instance, do not discuss goals for economic policy to the same degree as in Norway."[15] In other words, the Norwegian national budget had the more distinct character of a program; there were more politics and more planned economy in it, thereby creating more controversy.

The largest confrontation came in 1952 when a proposed law regulating prices and rationalization, in general much the same as lex Thagaard, was put forward by a committee chaired by the lawyer for the LO, and on which Wilhelm Thagaard was a very active member. As in Sweden, the business community mobilized a fierce countercampaign with a stream of publications, meetings, and so forth. In the end, the Labor Party government did not put forward the proposal for a rationalization law but proposed and adopted a modified version of a law relating to prices. The situation subsequently calmed down.

The retreat of the Social Democrats in Norway and in Sweden five years earlier seem rooted in the same causes. As in the Swedish case, the confrontations in Norway caused fear, and the Swedish example acted as a modifying element. Some historians have maintained that there was no retreat: the government was merely following a pragmatic policy. When a postwar crisis failed to materialize, there was no need to make the price and rationalization laws permanent; nor were they ever fully utilized. Even in Norway there was reality in the argument that the business community had actually demonstrated its ability to master the situation. However, the economic problems were more pressing in Norway, the provisional laws more far-reaching, and the ability of the business world to seize control of the situation much weaker; and thereby the conflict was sharper.

One modifying element that entered the picture was that the economic policy came under the influence of "technical assistance" linked to aid from the Marshall Plan. This was based on different premises than those forming the

---

[14] Gerhardsen 1971, 125.
[15] Cited by Slagstad 1998, 518–519, note.

basis of the regulatory law proposal. Here there was a strong element of American management thinking, focusing more on private initiatives and competition and introducing a "productivity policy" with American assistance.[16]

This American influence represented a technocratic trend. The directors of business gained greater autonomy, since they were regarded as professionals. As one writer notes, directors discovered, to their amazement, that they had arrived in paradise.[17] They could continue to act as directors while, at the same time, the regulated economy contributed to eliminating troublesome market competition. Note that this referred not to the *capitalists* but rather to the *directors*, the chief executives of companies. Managerial capitalism, or capitalism managed by professional leaders, gained considerable acceptance in the technocratic Social Democratic camp.[18]

A SOCIAL DEMOCRATIC CONSTITUTION

The great dispute over price and rationalization regulation in Norway served to awaken constitutional misgivings. In the final phase of the dispute, with a view to radical law making, law professor Johannes Andenæs wrote: "Enabling acts can in fact be used as a means of putting the constitutional democratic system out of action. This was the case in Germany when the Reichsdag, in a law dated 24 March 1933, stipulated in general that laws, in addition to the manner in which they were laid down constitutionally, also could be determined by the government. . . . Here authorization took a form chosen to give seeming legitimacy to the transfer from democracy to dictatorship."[19]

The laws regulating pricing and rationalization were the most important in a series of laws that gave the government and the administration far-reaching powers of attorney. The extraordinary postwar situation demanded extraordinary measures, but it also challenged established constitutional forms. The difficulty for the non-Socialist or bourgeois opposition lay in the fact that the extraordinary measures were in line with the general principles of the Social Democrats regarding state control. The new, young upper echelons of the Labor Party felt they were confronting great tasks. In this situation the constitutional limitations placed by permanent rules, intricate procedures, and submission of administrative initiatives to judicial reviews all seemed to be unnecessary hindrances. On the other hand, broad powers gave opportunities and freedom of action to the most innovative.

---

[16] Yttri 1995.
[17] Jens Arup Seip 1963, 37.
[18] See Sejersted 2003a, the chapter titled "Direktørkapitalismens kranke skjebne."
[19] Andenæs 1962, 289.

Opposition arose, and the struggle over constitutional principles would become severe. We have seen that supposedly sober-minded jurists went so far as to envision parallels with the establishment of the German dictatorship. Parallels were also drawn with the Leninist one-party state.

The problem of "legal protection in relation to administrative decisions" had already been on the Nordic juridical agenda for some time when it was taken up at the meeting of Nordic jurists in Stockholm in 1951.[20] The non-Socialist Andenæs presented the issue: "In the liberal constitutional state, the question of the handling of issues by the administration is not a great problem from the point of view of legal protection." In Norway there had been legislation giving reasonably clear instructions for the decisions of the administration such that these could be reviewed by the general courts. But, Andenæs continued, "The social welfare state of our day is setting itself more ambitious goals for state administration," arguing that the welfare state was "necessarily intervening in the freedom of the citizens in a completely different manner than before. This applies in particular to the freedom of enjoyment of private ownership and to the operation of private businesses."[21] But the enabling acts of the new system did not provide clear procedural instructions. Administrative resolutions in the new state were discretionary in nature—leaving questions about legal safeguards unsolved. The conservative Swedish professor of law Nils Herlitz concluded that it was "the lifeblood of our legal control over the administration that now found itself in danger."[22] The constitutional problems were very much the same in both countries.

These problems had not played the same role in "the economic planning debate" in Sweden, however, for many reasons. When Herlitz and Andenæs discussed legal safeguard problems in 1951, the Swedish Social Democrats had long since carried out their retreat, while in Norway the question was still of the greatest currency. And, most important, Sweden and Norway had different administrative traditions.

Sweden was unique in that its ministries were small and, for the most part, public administration was organized in relatively independent entities known as "boards" (*verk*), maintaining distance from their respective ministries. This implied that the administration was more independent; that traditionally it had a greater freedom of movement; and that the civil servants had a greater (political) responsibility than was the case in Norway. There was talk of the Swedish "administrative dualism" wherein the executive authority was divided in two. There was also discussion as to whether this power

---

[20] *Förhandlingarna* ... 1952.
[21] Andenæs 1952, 7–8.
[22] Nils Herlitz in *Förhandlingarna* ... 1952, 244.

wielded by the administration was, in reality, in accordance with democratic, parliamentary principles.[23]

In comparison with Norway and the dispute over enabling acts there, it is evident that substantial authority had already been issued to the administration in Sweden. It was part of the old system; thus there was no current interest in stirring up a fight in the constitutional arena. In Norway, on the other hand, this dispute over delegation of parliamentary authority by means of enabling legislation erupted with full force in relation to the pricing and rationalization laws.

According to Andenæs there were two lines that Norway could follow to guarantee legal protection in relation to the administration. There was the old way, *control by the court system*, and there were *rules for administrative management*.[24] Andenæs argued that control by the court system was hardly applicable in a modern state; therefore the necessary control should be built into better regulations for administrative management. He characterized this type of reform by saying that compensation for the control formerly exerted by the courts could occur through the introduction of court procedures into state administration.

Sweden does not only have independent administrative boards. Like most countries in Europe—with the exception of Norway—the country has a two-court system: the general and the administrative courts. Oversight of administrative decisions is thus carried out by special courts within the state administration, with the Supreme Administrative Court as the highest level of appeal. The process is simplified in relation to processes in the general courts by, among other things, the fact that the legal system itself investigates the issue. So Sweden had already instituted court procedures into state administration, while more extensive reforms were required in Norway.

In 1967 Norway passed its Public Administration Act, complete with concrete instructions regarding decision-making procedures in the administration. This covered such things as the duty to hold hearings and to provide explicit reasons for the decisions taken. Norway has never managed to establish an administrative court system but has gradually achieved a comprehensive system of courtlike appeal boards within the administration. The most important of these is the Social Security Court. These days it is rare for the general court system to pass judgment on issues that have to do with state administrative decisions.

Another initiative for defending legal safeguards in Norway's modern state administration was the establishment of the Parliament's ombudsman for public administration in 1962. The ombudsman does not have formal

---

[23] Wockelberg 2003, 17.
[24] Andenæs 1952, 7; appendix 6, p. 7.

authority to impose sanctions but can critically evaluate administrative decisions. Informal sanctions lie within the realm of the ombudsman's legitimacy, for instance the use of the general public as a forum. Already in 1809 Sweden had established a "justitia ombudsman" to defend citizens against the authorities.

In 1970 Norway eventually passed the Freedom of Information Act, giving citizens, on request, the right of access to the case documents of the public administration. This too was an old institution in Sweden, rooted in "the freedom of the press" decree of 1766. This right of access is widely used by the press. The idea of controlling the administration through general access to the case documents of the administration is unique to Scandinavia.

The ascendancy of the Social Democrats to a hegemonic position consti-tuted a regime shift that involved several incursions into the liberal structure of norms, with resulting expansion of the role and competence of the state. The dispute over the planned economy is the most conspicuous example of how Social Democracy established itself in this new position. It took place during a struggle in which the bourgeois forces mobilized to retain the old liberal normative structure, while many Socialists might have imagined more maneuvering room for the public authorities than actually resulted. Seen from the Social Democratic point of view, the struggle could be viewed as formative, as fumbling toward the eventual result—which could be consid-ered a compromise between the more extreme standpoints and an order in its own right.

This expanded leadership competence demanded a new form of demo-cratic control. The Social Democrats now bore both a liberal and a Socialist inheritance. When the legal safeguard arguments of the jurists prevailed, it was because they appealed to attitudes that were part of the Social Demo-cratic movement. It is worth noting the degree to which Sweden possessed an existing constitutional system that suited the expanded state administra-tive competence that was part of the Social Democratic regime. Independent boards, an administrative court system, a "justitia ombudsman," and public disclosure of administrative processes already existed. By contrast, Norway had to carry out relatively extensive constitutional reforms in order to estab-lish what we might call a Social Democratic constitution.

CORPORATISM AND ECONOMIC DEMOCRACY

To a considerable degree the confrontations over the planned economy related to serving the goal of full employment and an efficient economy. One motive left lying in the shadows was that of democratization. The planned economy challenged not only legal safeguards, or the "negative" defense against state power, but also democracy itself. At its outset there was nothing particularly democratic about the planned economy; the opposite was nearer reality. The democratic motive had been part of the discussion the whole way, however, and it left its traces in the proposal regarding corporatist plans.

Corporatist plans are, in themselves, nothing new, but they made a breakthrough and gained a new significance with the growth of strong interest organizations during the heyday of the Social Democratic hegemony. It can be fruitful to make a distinction between two types of corporatization: *negotiative corporatism* and *administrative corporatism*. The first involves a systematic negotiation and collaboration between organized interests in the labor market, with or without the state as an "interest" or as mediator. The main features of this form were laid down in the Main Agreement in Norway and the Saltsjöbad Agreement in Sweden during the 1930s. The development of this negotiative corporatism was dealt with in chapters 4 and 7. The plans that were brought forward in this field continued to function relatively well up to 1970; that is, they functioned well in moderating wages and restoring peace to the workplace.[25] Hence they became a model "for state regulation rather than for a democratization of working life."[26]

The most important new formation in this period was the provision for public servants to also have their right to wage agreement negotiations with their employers. This occurred in Norway with the regulatory law of 1958 and in Sweden with the regulatory agreement that came into effect in 1965 when a Board for State Agreements was instituted. Even though there were differences at the practical level, in principle the two governments had chosen the same policy: "By accepting that the state be put side by side with the organizations as a negotiating party, the main organizations could be made jointly responsible in the wage-setting process."[27] The respective Parliaments were set aside in this process but, precisely by means of this "act of abdication," reasonable control over the wage process was achieved. Here too we see that this has had as much to do with state regulation as with democratization.

Administrative corporatism implies that organized special interests are included in the public decision-making processes through testimony at hearings or through representatives sitting on public commissions, many of which

[25] Heiret et al. 2003, 141. Heiret has a different division of the period in his description of labor relations. By treating the period 1945–1977 as one, he manages to get the great changes of the 1970s (company democracy, working environment legislation) in under "the postwar period." By contrast, we set the boundary of this period at approximately 1970, such that these changes are viewed as the beginning of something new and not the conclusion of something old. Developments in the 1970s and further on will be dealt with in chapter 12.

[26] Heiret et al. 2003, 14.

[27] Åsmund Arup Seip 1998, 301, 448.

have the authority to make decisions.[28] Initiatives opening the way to development in this field also occurred in the 1930s with the crisis settlements in both countries.

Corporatization had been a typical characteristic of Fascist regimes. When the labor movements in Sweden and Norway introduced their corporatist programs in the 1940s, they went to great lengths to emphasize that they were speaking about a *democratic* corporatism that was being instituted specifically in answer to the problem of democracy. The relatively open situation during and following the war had to be utilized to forward the process of democratization. In addition to political democracy, there would now be an *economic democracy*.

The more extensive plans for such democracy first began to take form within the trade union movement: "Within the Nordic labor movement there arose a common aspiration for a jointly established democratic organ, with representation from the relevant parties at the level of the company, branch, and society."[29] A hierarchical corporatist structure was envisioned, in the form of economic councils at three levels. In Sweden it was a "troika," composed of the LO chairman, August Lindberg, the LO leader of research, Richard Sterner, and Gunnar Myrdal, that drafted the proposal and tried to implement the system.

As early as 1943 Sterner had drafted a memorandum in which he discussed "the question of expanded public control over the development, location, rationalization ... of industry," and the question of "the workers' assistance in leading production." Sterner felt that an industrial democracy within an individual firm implied a risk of "particularism," since it could create an alliance of interests between the leadership and the employees. "However, such a tendency can be countered through a corresponding 'democratization' carried through at the higher levels in the organizations as well." If the workers' participation within the company was to have a democratizing effect, and not merely create a hostage situation, it would be necessary to link this to a greater organizational system. In this way the trade unions could cooperate in the production plans for the industries as a whole.[30]

At the outset it was thought that this could be realized by negotiations. And in 1945 the LO presented a draft *three-level strategy*. A comprehensive corporatist structure was to be established with a central production council at the national level, branch councils at the confederation (industry) level, and "company committees" at the level of the firm. The Employers Associa-

---

[28] Nordby 1994.
[29] Ekdahl 2001, 175.
[30] Ekdahl 2001, 203.

tion firmly opposed such a structure, however. They were particularly provoked by the branch council proposal since they viewed it as an invasion into
a field of responsibility that belonged to the industries themselves. Meanwhile
the Employers Association undertook to set up "company committees" as a
compromise. But these were to be solely advisory, so there was hardly any
concession here. Without a link to branch councils beyond the level of the
firm, these committees represented no threat but rather an opportunity for
an alliance of interests within the company. Opposition was also mounted
against the proposition for a central production council at the national level.
This last proposition ended with only a limited expansion of competence for
the Labor Market Council.[31] Thus very little was accomplished.

When negotiations failed to move forward, a legislative approach was attempted through collaboration between the LO's Lindberg and Myrdal, who
was minister of trade. A proposal drafted from within the LO was sent to
the government in 1947. But only a few weeks later both Myrdal and Lindberg stepped down from their posts and Karin Kock, another member of the
cabinet, took over from Myrdal. This implied that "the air to a considerable
degree went out of the political–trade union offensive aimed at broadening
the state and trade union influence over industrial affairs."[32] Thus the plan
for a democratic, hierarchical corporatist structure was set aside before the
decisive confrontation regarding the planned economy that accompanied the
election of 1948. This meant that the planned economy debate did not really
deal with economic democracy but rather with the conditions necessary for
an effective economy and, behind this, the role of the state in this rich society.

Developments in Norway were once again strikingly parallel. The main
platform for a postwar program for the labor movement was put forward
in 1942 by the Norwegian LO Secretariat in Stockholm. In its subsequent
work the LO Secretariat in London played a central role. The work concluded with a program titled Norway of the Future, which was presented
in January of 1945. In this program a three-level strategy was presented,
consisting of an economic council of cooperation at the top, councils at the
branch level, and "production committees" at the company level. The coincidence of timing and content between the Swedish and Norwegian programs
was hardly accidental.

As in Sweden, the production committees (Sweden's "company committees") were established at the company level on the basis of negotiations between the parties in working life, but these committees scarcely lived up to

[31] Ekdahl 2001, 195–197.
[32] Ekdahl 2001, 210.

expectations.[33] The branch councils were established by law in 1947, but the government was cautious about using the law, ultimately choosing "the voluntary line." Nevertheless, fourteen branch councils were gradually set up. To some extent these councils fulfilled a role during the reconstruction period, when the government was pursuing a policy of "direct means." But once direct means were abandoned in the 1950s, these councils were marginalized. A national Council of Economic Coordination (Det Økonomiske Samordningsråd) was established and functioned well for some years, insofar as Prime Minister Gerhardsen utilized it with great ingenuity as a tool of leadership—by using the pronouncements of this council to get his policies through, both in his parliamentary group and in Parliament itself.[34] The council eventually refused to allow itself to be used in this way, however, leading to its disbandment in 1954. And, as in Sweden, very little was accomplished.

Lars Ekdahl stresses that the reason for the retreat on the question of economic democracy was due, on the one hand, to the business community's absolute and almost arrogant opposition and, on the other hand, to the Social Democrats' lack of will to take up an offensive policy.[35] This occurred largely because Social Democratic motives were overshadowed by the economy, which was doing well. Industry managed to deliver on its tasks through the use of indirect support from such legislation as the official labor market policy and the solidarity wage policy. The business community argued that moving a portion of the responsibility for the companies away from the traditional company leadership and over to the branch councils would only serve to create ambiguity regarding who actually possessed competence to make decisions, which in turn could harm the company.[36] Social Democrats hesitated to take responsibility for a reform that would upset a well-functioning system.

The trade union movement had advanced the notion of establishing an economic-democratic order along with political democracy, while the Social Democratic parties of both Norway and Sweden had assumed hegemony in the political sphere. This must have inspired a new attitude toward the established political system. By virtue of seizing political power, the Social Democratic parties had new means at their disposal, and they had emerged in a stronger position in relation to the trade union movement. A regulated economy based on the new hegemonic political position could be equally as good for both the party and the movement, as might the establishment of alternative structures of power, especially since the latter might easily create ambi-

[33] Trond Bergh 1973, 3.
[34] Nordby 1994, 113–115.
[35] Ekdahl 2001, 212–218.
[36] Ekdahl 2001, 213.

guities with regard to the allocation of responsibility. There was undoubtedly a power play between the business community and the labor movement, but there was also a tug-of-war within the labor movement.

In both countries the three-level strategy for economic democracy was set aside before the decisive conflict broke out over the planned economy. In addition, when it came to the planned economy, there was a retreat in each country—in Sweden in 1948 and Norway in 1952. The Social Democratic system thus became a strongly modified version of the drive for economic democracy and a planned economy that had been launched by the labor movement in the 1940s. This did not mean that the questions about economic democracy or about who should control capital had been settled once and for all. Nor did it mean that the trade union organizations and, in general, the organized special interest groups were disconnected from the policy.

THE NEW ADMINISTRATIVE CORPORATISM

Corporatism would come to be a distinctive feature of the Social Democratic order, but it would take a form other than that of the great wartime visions of a three-level structure. A "corporative pluralism" developed wherein organized special interests were stitched into different segments of the administration without any uniform, hierarchical corporatist structure, such as proposed in the three-level strategy, to attach themselves to.[37]

Administrative corporatism had its roots in the predemocratic society. In the 1930s a principled and important step forward was taken with the crisis settlement plans ratified in relation to the agricultural sector. Around 1950 there was new impetus. Above all, administrative corporatism involves the establishment of state commissions with different functions. Trond Nordby has noted eight different types of commission: commissions for investigation and preparation of legislation; boards and councils for public enterprises such as schools, institutes, and directorates; advice-dispensing organs such as the State Nutrition Council; contact and cooperation organs such as the contact committee between immigrants and the Norwegian authorities; negotiative organs; control and supervision organs; and complaint and appellate bodies, in addition to a heterogeneous group of delegations and commissions.[38] Rothstein, in his overview of administrative corporatism in Sweden, categorizes such commissions on the basis of policy areas, finding that they

---

[37] The concept "corporative pluralism" is used in different ways in the literature. See Nordby 1994, 26–33.

[38] Nordby 1994, 77–78.

exist in all areas. Thus under Social Democracy in both countries we find the development of a very tight network linking interest organizations and the administration.

Corporatization was closely linked with reform politics, which, in turn, was closely linked with the labor movement's hegemonic phase. The politicians and the administration needed legitimacy in order to carry out reforms. This could be acquired by linking oneself to those whom the reforms were directed against. Reform policy thereby became strongly marked by the strategy of negotiation and compromise—in other words, by organized class collaboration.[39] Moreover, the administration needed the help of experts. In establishing corporatist forms of collaboration, there were constant references to the need for the professional competence of the interest organizations. Legitimacy and vocational or professional competence thus became a major explanation for active network building by the administration.

In relation to constitutional reforms that followed the retreat of the three-level strategy, there are also grounds for stressing what almost became an opposing motive for cooperation, namely the need for democratic control in the face of a constantly growing and increasingly complex administration. The interest organizations thus were intended to be both collaborative partners with and controllers of the administration. The different motives point toward the same goal—corporatization, thereby strengthening the result.

What, in fact, was the result? Was it that the interest organizations obtained power over the state, or did the state gain strength through the organizations, thus consolidating its power? Who dictated to whom, and who ought to dictate? For a long time it was usual to argue that, first of all, the organizations' power grew strong. The influential Norwegian political scientist Stein Rokkan maintained such a point of view. But more recent research seems to more closely support the second view, that it was the state that became more consolidated in its position. First and foremost, corporatization served the state's control and regulation. But what served the democratic considerations best—organizational power or state power?

HOW DEMOCRATIC?

There have been different points of view as to whether or not the corporatization that took place in the Social Democratic countries was actually democratic. "Democracy requires organizational freedom, but the strength of an organization can to some degree constitute a threat to democracy," as Bo

---

[39] Rothstein 1992, 30, 32, 38–39.

Rothstein writes, adding: "In terms of international comparisons, Sweden has been a country with unusually strong interest organizations, which can also be considered to have a strong influence over public policy."[40] The historian Edvard Bull Jr. has characterized corporatist Norway as "an elite partnership," meaning that the leaders of the large organizations conspire with the leaders of politics and business. From this point of view the system is seen as a form of undemocratic state corporatism.

At its inception, the democracy argument was linked to economic democracy. There can be no doubt that the invigorating role of the trade unions in the private business sphere served to place limits on the (undemocratic) power of the owners. We have seen that corporatism had a tendency to serve state regulatory activity. But here it can be argued that when the political democracy of the state enters the economic sphere, this also involves a limiting of private proprietary power and, accordingly, constitutes a democratizing tendency. In general we can say that there evolved in the private business sphere a balance of power among the owners, the managerial bureaucracy, the trade unions, and the state as a representative of the society at large.

But the problem concerning the democratic character of corporatism remains. The organization society favors those special interest groups that are best organized. Some individuals—those who are members of strong organizations—can have "the right to double voting," both as organization members and as ordinary citizens. The organized special interests can easily shove aside the consideration of general interest or the interests of the weak. Moreover, collaboration along corporative channels can easily acquire a closed character and lead to an elite partnership. On the whole, it is not easy to judge the democratic character of corporatism.

Peter Katzenstein speaks about the "democratic corporatism" of small countries, arguing that it is rational within small countries in a large-scale world to cooperate in the form of corporative plans. In a discussion of Katzenstein's theory, Rothstein is in agreement about the democratic character but feels that it must be explained historically in relation to the integrative and reformist behavior of the labor movement before World War II.[41]

Conspicuously, into the mid-1970s there was broad political agreement about the favorable aspects of corporatization. Among other things, this agreement depended on two motives pointing in the same direction—the labor movement's need for legitimacy and competence in reform work, on the one hand and, on the other, the need by the bourgeois side to have controls on the administration through "court procedures." Bourgeois criticism

---

[40] Rothstein 1992, 11.
[41] Rothstein 1992, 74–76. Katzenstein 1985.

directed against the planned economy and the three-level strategy in Norway was only "aimed against the Labor Party's leadership ambitions, and not against the functional representation as such."[42] It seems as though the bourgeois forces in both Norway and Sweden regarded the pluralistic form that corporatism took as a preferable alternative to what they regarded as the "state capitalism" of the Social Democrats. Using agriculture in the interwar period as its example, the Norwegian Conservative Party introduced "business's self-regulation" as one of its slogans.

It is reasonable to conclude that the pluralistic form of corporatism we find in the Social Democracies had a democratic character. Nevertheless, there would later be poignant criticism that would, above all, align itself against the tendency of special interests to set aside consideration of general interests. This was part of a general criticism of the view of politics that had dominated the Social Democratic order and which we find among both politicians and social scientists—namely, that politics was concerned only with interest struggles and compromises between special interests, and not with the formation of common goals beyond the special interests. Politics, it was said, was too important to be left to the organized special interests.

THE DOUBLE STRATEGY OF
BUSINESS AND INDUSTRY

Following a period strongly colored by confrontations, the administrative corporatist system was built up, functioning from around 1950 until well into the 1970s on the basis of broad political agreement in both countries. In addition, there were informal contacts between the Social Democrats and business and industry. The Harpsund Democracy of Sweden was typical. This referred to meetings that took place between the government and (above all) the leading men of business and industry at the official summer residence of the prime minister at Harpsund Mansion. The non-Socialist parties were, by and large, excluded.

This period was not as idyllic as it might appear, however. Collaboration predominated on the political level and in the corporatist channels, but under the surface there was ideological mobilization around the question of who should control the capital. The characteristic mix of fellowship and ideological contradictions continued after the retreats and the compromises of 1948 and 1952. In real terms the business community followed a double strategy.

[42] Nordby 1994, 58.

In *The Inner Circle*, Niklas Stenlås describes how Swedish business life formed itself into an informal network to coordinate the political initiatives of trade and commerce. The network had a close inner circle whose members, based on their positions in large firms or organizations and their individual qualities and efforts, became central in the formation of ideology and strategy. In certain situations these informal networks could condense into organizations, as was found in the interwar period.[43] In the 1940s, however, the Swedish business community began to systematically organize to advance policies and opinion-driven activities.

The impulse to organize business as a political actor came, in part, from its opponents. In 1938 Ernst Wigforss, expressing the view that it was problematic to become oriented toward a business community represented by an amorphous economic elite, challenged business to organize. Formation of the Business and Industry Council resulted from this challenge. "Those industrial leaders who internally were considered the leading force in the country, and without whose thinking the others could not bring themselves to express a view about the direction of business life, had come together to form the council."[44] Ultimately the council was insignificant. This was not the case, however, with the Trade and Industry Foundation founded in 1940 in connection with the purchase of the daily newspaper *Svenska Dagbladet*. The goal had been to secure this newspaper as an organ for an independent business life, which, indeed, it became. Contact with the Conservative Party was very close. The Trade and Industry Foundation would become "one of the tools of the inner circle in Swedish politics for the remainder of the twentieth century."[45]

The foundation, above all other organizations, came to mobilize the political right in the great 1948 debate regarding the planned economy. Organizations such as the Swedish Employers Association and the Federation of Swedish Industries were considered nonpolitical, and only with difficulty could they mobilize directly for political action. There was a great degree of overlap in the leadership of the three organizations. Gustav Söderlund was thus chairman of both the Employers Association and the Trade and Industry Foundation.[46] In 1942 the foundation was busy with the establishment of the Libertas Foundation, which would support the bourgeois press. In 1946 the Guaranty Foundation was established as a direct reaction to the "taxation process" that the Social Democratic government put forward that year.

[43] Söderpalm 1976. Stenlås 1998, 14–16.
[44] Stenlås 1998, 72.
[45] Stenlås 1998, 79.
[46] Stenlås 1998, 88–89.

As noted in the invitation to participate, "real, thoroughgoing measures are required if the increasingly obvious threat to freedom of enterprise in trade and commerce is to be fended off."[47] A considerable sum was raised for this effort from far-reaching circles within the private sector.

The bourgeois parties had been supported before this period by individual actors from the private sector. Now, however, this support was coordinated on behalf of the business community through informal and partly hidden networks. This meant, first, that greater means were marshaled and, second, that the problem of expected political services in return was accentuated. The independence of the parties was threatened. We find an unusually clear expression of this when some of the younger forces within the Conservative Party managed to achieve a breakthrough for a more active social policy in a draft program of the party for 1946. In a letter to the party leader, the above-mentioned Gustav Söderlund wrote:

> I became alarmed. Alarm over the defeatism that characterizes the program. And the politi-
> cal immaturity! This ridiculous licking up of elements that, until now, Socialists and Com-
> munists have purchased successfully with the state's wherewithal, is directly repugnant, and
> is absolutely not something that will give the Right [Conservative Party] any additional
> support. . . . If this program were to be confirmed, then calls from the new Right for eco-
> nomic assistance would fall on deaf ears in all the broader circles of business life.[48]

Despite this mobilization, these bourgeois forces were, as we know, unsuccessful in their attempt to shove aside the Social Democrats, and trade and commerce gradually came to mistrust the bourgeois parties' ability to govern. Consequently, the business community changed strategy by, on the one hand, increasingly adjusting to collaborations with the Social Democrats within the contours of Harpsund Democracy and, on the other, taking up information and communication work themselves. We are back to the double strategy.

One reason for the dispute and the election of 1948 was the founding of the Study Association for Business and Society (SNS). This had its roots in both the Industrial Research Institute (IUI) and in the Trade and Industry Foundation. As Stenlås writes, the goal was "[a] more low-key and long-term formation of opinion that only indirectly had a political purpose. One was to consider that such 'prejudices' as Socialism and a planned economy could be counteracted through economic instruction. It was not necessary to make Social Democrats into non-Socialists, it was good enough to make them less Socialistic."[49]

---

[47] Stenlås 1998, 151.
[48] Stenlås 1998, 218.
[49] Stenlås 1998, 195–200.

Thus it was that the ideological contradictions were maintained through the Social Democratic phase but, over time, in a strikingly subdued form. Perhaps we could speak of a dormant preparation under conditions of relative consensus. Institutions with sharper political profiles would pop up again in the context of new ideological confrontations in the 1970s. The Trade and Industry Foundation, which was still in existence, established the think tank Timbro in 1978, as well as the publishing house Ratio, and in 1988 its new germination, the City University.

Developments in Norway had clear parallels but occurred somewhat later. In 1947 a Norwegian Libertas was established. Discussion had been taking place for some time over how the private sector could contribute to advancing a "business-friendly politics," with particular reference to the assistance that could be rendered by a business-friendly press. The Conservative Party felt that it should administer and channel financial contributions from the business world. Trade and industry's confidence in the Conservative Party was limited, however, and Libertas became the organization of the private sector, with the aim of agitating for free trade and commerce. Formally, the organization was independent of the business organizations. It was established in secret but was unmasked by the labor newspaper *Arbeiderbladet* one year after its founding: "Millions are devoted to the struggle against the government and the Labor Party. Big merchants, shipowners, and leaders of heavy industry are starting their election battle. Newspapers that are in favor of free enterprise are helped, bourgeois members of Parliament hire consultants, a large estate is purchased on Onsøy."[50] From the Conservative Party and Libertas side it was argued that the Labor Party had its own "skeleton in the closet" since it received contributions from the LO. Gerhardsen countered this by maintaining that while the bourgeois parties shamed themselves by accepting the contributions that were named in the press, the Labor Party was "proud to be receiving contributions from a broad people's organization such as the trade union federation."[51]

There was also an "inner circle" in Norway. Its actual core consisted of a triumvirate, namely the director of the Employers Association, the director of the Shipowners Association, and, especially, the general secretary of Libertas.[52] They slipped informally into the role of ideologues for the business community and its foremost representatives in the political arena. Libertas was, above all, a channeling organization, but it gradually developed into something more, and in the great dispute over the planned economy in 1952

---

[50] *Arbeiderbladet*, 16 October 1948.

[51] Sejersted 2003b, 67, 77.

[52] These were, respectively, Christian Erlandsen, John Egeland, and Trygve de Lange.

the business community set up its own organization, the Office of Information on the Pricing and Rationalization Laws. The new office vehemently agitated against the planned economy alongside the bourgeois parties, but did so in a way that created tensions with them.

As in Sweden, the storm died away after the Social Democrats retreated on this issue. But they remained the holders of government power, and there was a constant dissatisfaction within the business world with the perplexed non-Socialist opposition. As a result, the double strategy became more pronounced in Norway than in Sweden. On the one hand, business cooperated, as in Sweden, within the extensive corporative network; on the other hand, it found space for mobilizing against Socialism. In 1959 Libertas launched its action program Will to Power. The launching referred to a trend wherein the Socialists of several European countries had had "to give up government power and power arrangements," but in Norway "these political forces had not been released." A national plan for "recruiting professional politicians for, and from, business life" was announced. Libertas also launched an alternative state budget including severely reduced disbursements, sick pay only for "the more serious and long-term cases of illness," reduced subsidies to agriculture, and the selling off of shares in state companies.[53]

This drive was remarkable in that Libertas had great support from the business community. The Conservative Party had close contacts with trade and industry. This drive was, however, a clear declaration of mistrust of the Conservative Party, an attempt to capture the party. It ended with the party, under the leadership of its old chairman C. J. Hambro, successfully repulsing "the intrigues that these financially well-to-do but intellectually and politically impoverished gentlemen have conducted," as he put it.[54] After the showdown, Libertas concentrated on informational activity. But Norway never developed anything similar to the Swedish SNS.

The conflict gradually calmed down in Norway, as it did in Sweden, with Social Democratic hegemony. In the 1960s the bourgeois parties mobilized again, but the contradictions had changed. Now the strategy was to strike back at the successful Social Democrats on their own ground. In Norway there was a scramble over an initiative that, ironically, resulted in a non-Socialist coalition government carrying out the crowning glory of the Social Democratic achievements, the establishment of the national social insurance plan. Even in this phase, however, politics was not completely denuded of ideological contradictions.

[53] Sejersted 2003b, 212f., 216.
[54] Sejersted 2003b, 209.

AN IDEOLOGICAL COUNTERTHRUST

In the 1950s the British Conservatives developed the idea of a "property-owning democracy," a notion rapidly taken up by the Conservative parties in both Sweden and Norway. This was conceived as an answer to the demand for economic democratization, a demand that had been raised by the Social Democrats and accepted by the Conservatives as well. It also served as an attempt by Conservatives to extricate themselves from the braking role and go on the offensive by formulating a positive alternative to the "state capitalism" of the Social Democrats.[55] It was an attempt to establish some basis for an ideological confrontation with the Social Democrats, right in the middle of their hegemonic period.[56]

Ownership has long been associated with democracy. In nineteenth-century Norway suffrage was inter alia based on registered ownership of land. Thus the progressive liberal could struggle for democratization through the diffusion of ownership. Economic democracy also warranted its own spot in the program of the Norwegian Conservative Party in 1945, where it was written that there was need for "steadily more members of society [to] become owners of their means of production and independent in their trade."[57] This is reminiscent of the anti-industrial traditionalism that had wintered in the Conservative Party. Society would ideally consist of small, independent entrepreneurial peasant farmers and craftsmen who owned their means of production.

The conservatives of the more industrialized Sweden were not so backward-looking but, even there, "the market liberal image with its focus on the individual and the small entrepreneur was evident."[58] But a society of small peasant farmers and small enterprises was scarcely a real alternative for a modern industrial society, which speaks to the conservatives' lack of ability to find solutions to the problems of the day. But then along came this "propri-etary democracy." Once again it became possible to take up the old strategy of democratizing through the spread of proprietorship. First and foremost, the spotlight was directed to the possibility of owning one's own home, preferably with a bit of land around it. But what was new, and would become the answer to economic democracy, was the expansion of the social scope of shareholding in large modern enterprises. Thus the way to unite "the renaissance of propri-etary rights" with "the democratization of capitalism" was by urging everyone to become a capitalist.

[55] Ljunggren 1992, 132.
[56] Ljunggren 1992, 130f; Stråth 1998, 36f.; Sejersted 2003b, 192f.
[57] Sejersted 2003b, 31, 188.
[58] Stråth 1998, 37, 39.

Bo Stråth emphasizes that this form of "social conservatism" became a serious challenge to the Social Democrats. There were now two different formulations of the "people's home." Should this be realized in the form of Social Democracy or a "proprietary democracy," and which was more democratic? Stråth points out that there was a similarity between the talk of the conservatives in the 1950s and "the Social Democratic talk of the nineties with its praise of free enterprise, small business, and the small scale." There is an affinity here. Both the conservatives and the Social Democrats "appeal to deeper emotional and identity structures around the concept of 'the people.'"[59] Along with Stig-Björn Ljunggren, we might also argue that "the central element in the proprietary democratic vision of the right to ownership of one's own home has come to fruition to a considerable degree—Sweden is a proprietary democracy."[60] When it comes to owning one's own residence, Norway too is a democracy of individual ownership—and to a greater degree than Sweden.

The discussion regarding economic democratization through the spread of stockholding calmed down in the course of the 1960s. There are several reasons why the conservatives pulled back on this point. The risk of having to hold shares was too high and the democratizing effect too low; and, furthermore, the business world was not very willing to participate in the spread of stockholding.[61] Instead, the conservative forces came to rely on personal savings through tax advantages that favored saving in banks and investing in bonds, something that achieved a certain breakthrough. These advantages also came to affect savings in shares. By the end of the century there was a great expansion of stockholding in both countries with the florescence of mutual funds. We can say that eventually individual proprietary democracy also enjoyed victory in this field, but many small shareholders experienced the results of high risk when they were left sitting with their devalued shares. Nor did any actual democratizing effect emerge from such expansion.

The problem of how to achieve economic democracy was not solved by the Social Democratic order. The Social Democratic order was marked by the fact that the class society existed as a cultural construction. Through the corporatizing process the old class struggle certainly took more peaceful forms by being converted to a regular tug-of-war within an economy of negotiations. But, above all, attention had been turned toward effective solutions and the problem of allocation. The question of democratization was less pronounced.

[59] Stråth 1998, 39.
[60] Ljunggren 1992, 154.
[61] Sejersted 2003b, 196; Ljunggren 1992, 154.

In the 1960s there was a considerable level of unrest in the workplaces,[62] culminating in the Kiruna strike of 1969 in northern Sweden. This unrest attracted new attention to the working environment and economic democracy. Industrial democracy was to be a kind of "solution" to the democracy problem in the economic sphere. It did not develop during the classic Social Democratic epoch because, among other things, it presupposed the dissolution of class-conscious loyalties and the development of new loyalties within the firm.[63] And this did not happen until the next phase of development.

SOCIAL DEMOCRACY AS A CONSUMER SOCIETY

Expansionism filled much of the ideological vacuum that had arisen when the Social Democrats distanced themselves from Marxism. Expansionism pointed the way toward the consumer society, or the affluent society—something that Gunnar Myrdal had pointed out as early as 1934. The logic was that if more was to be produced, more had to be consumed. At roughly the same time, the Norwegian "three-year plan" pronounced that "[t]he transition from the economy of scarcity to the economy of affluence signified the human leap from necessity into the realm of freedom."[64] And this was the end result, as Ambjörnsson acknowledged in his claim that it was "consumerism" that had lifted his working-class parents into a new world.

The Social Democrats' inspiration, John Kenneth Galbraith, describes the "affluent society": "The individual serves the industrial system not by supplying it with savings and the resulting capital; he serves it by consuming its products. . . . In a society that so emphasizes consumption and so needs capital, the decision to save should obviously be removed from the consumer and exercised by other authority. All industrial societies do so." From his description, this is the way things have to be. He writes not about freedom but rather about coercion—the individual has to *serve the system* by consuming and refraining from saving, adding, "On no other matter, religious, political, or moral, is he so elaborately, skillfully, and expensively instructed."[65] Most people received their instructions on how to "serve the system" through advertising.

Consumption was necessary for the efficient functioning of the system and, naturally, it had to be ideologized. To some degree the orientation toward consumption would shove aside the production orientation that had been such a strong feature of the labor movements. The consumer orienta-

[62] Stråth 2000, 101, 129, 141.
[63] Stråth 1998, 122.
[64] Colbjørnsen and Sømme 1933, 131.
[65] Galbraith 1967, 49.

tion took its inspiration from America, taking root first in Sweden, then in Norway.[66] The creation of the ideology implied that individual saving was to be viewed as suspect. As the Norwegian Social Democratic ideologue Torolf Elster said, "the moral of saving, like the delight in owning solely to have ownership, has entered the world with a life-repudiating, joyless, censorious Puritanism that is one of the ugliest of capitalism's children."[67] People in the new rich industrial society should not become *petit capitalists*; they should become happy *consumers*.

Consumption or affluence was seen early on to be a problem of social morals. Among others, the problem was taken up by the German academic Socialists who had been a source of inspiration for the Scandinavian Social Democrats. Prosperity ought not to be a goal in itself; it had to be evaluated in connection with a moral view of society. This implied "moral, spiritual, sanitary, psychic, economic, and social uplifting of the masses of the population."[68] Now, the Puritanism that Elster so despised sat deep within the soul of the Scandinavian people. To a considerable degree, this was also the legacy of the labor movement. Thus it was that the consumer society represented a problem, or became a problem, of how consumption could represent the realm of freedom rather than systemic coercion. In 1945 the new Norwegian Social Democratic government allowed a series of intellectuals to write a "culture letter." The basic tone turned out to be pessimistic. They maintained that "the overwhelming mass of consumer goods" would come to create important cultural problems. The human mind was about to be dangerously harnessed to "things."[69]

The solution lay in paternalistic initiatives. These seemed to vacillate between control of consumption and the creation of the cultivated consumer. Myrdal had seen the consumer society coming, saying that this new society required "control, not only of income distribution in society, but also of the adjustment of consumption in the family."[70] The families had to be instructed in what they should buy. A more culturally optimistic point of view lay in the description of "the cultivated person," which would become a core concept in the Norwegian Labor Party's cultural program. This "idealistic classless society would end not with the affluence of the leveled-out masses, but rather with a well-formed, restrained, and democratic welfare society in which consumption rhetoric was linked to the concept of the living standard."[71]

---

[66] Myklebust 2004.
[67] St. forh. (Parl. Proceedings) 1959–1960, S. Tid. 3177. Cited by K. Willoch in the Parliament.
[68] Citation is from the academic socialist Adolph Wagner. See Ketil Gjølme Andersen 2002, 49–53.
[69] Cited by Myrvang 2004, 291.
[70] Alva and Gunnar Myrdal 1934, 203
[71] Myrvang 2004, 293–294.

The question became one of how to foster the rational, or the culturally formed, consumer. An important actor in this process was the consumer cooperative. The Swedish cooperative movement was particularly strong, defining itself as a "formative project." It was a link in the civilizing process that was to form critical citizens into rational consumers who would not be tempted by strong commercial interests. The Cooperative Association was intended to foster "independent and upright personalities," as expressed by the association president Alex Gjöres at the Cooperative Congress in 1939.[72] Through the project called "A Richer Everyday Life," attempts were also made to strengthen the aesthetic consciousness of consumers. The project successfully "consolidated the role of cooperation as the bearer of principles in the debate about the new patterns of consumption."[73]

Norway's attempts to reproduce this project did not meet with success. Conditions were not fertile for fostering an aesthetic consciousness-raising of consumers.[74] It seems that the Norwegian consumers were more difficult to train. Nevertheless, following the war a close relationship developed between Social Democracy and the consumer cooperatives in both countries. The cooperative was an important factor in addressing the problems expressed, among other places, in the "culture letter."

Opposition to this paternalistic policy gradually developed, however. Consumers did not want to be instructed, and the cooperatives, needing to satisfy the demands of consumers, soon came to resemble other department store chains. On the other hand, the state developed an active consumer policy. As early as 1946 the Swedish Parliament produced a report on quality control and the education of consumers that resulted in the establishment of the Product Description Authority in 1951. In Norway the Consumer Council was founded on the same model in 1953. This was intended to teach people to shop properly and utilize goods economically, as it was put. A new state consumer policy initiative came out in the 1970s, part of the attempt to deal with the problems that arose with the institution of a general political revitalization in 1970. Now one was to put one's "house in order to . . . utilize one's resources in a manner that best promotes the individual's physical, psychological, and social well-being."[75] This was almost an echo from, especially, the Swedish cooperative movement of the 1930s.

In addition to training consumers through the guidance efforts of its consumer policy, the state directed consumption through rationing, taxes and fees on luxury goods, subsidization of sensible goods, and directing produc-

[72] See Myrvang 2004, 285.
[73] Even Lange 2006, 382.
[74] E. Lange 2006, 382–383.
[75] E. Lange 2006, 385.

tion through quality control and other means. There was also state effort to "socialize consumption" by developing collective or common consumption through institutions such as schools, hospitals, sports clubs, parks, and so on.

One might ask whether such a paternalistic policy actually fostered trained, rational consumerism and gave priority to collective consumption. It did to some degree, perhaps, but in the long term consumers became inundated by a flood of goods, and the traditional Scandinavian Puritanism began to fade. The many initiatives intended to train the rational consumer and give priority to public consumption were just as much a sign of how the shoe pinched as they were effective moves to control consumerism.

In his 1950s book Galbraith makes the point that the affluent society is marked by public poverty and private wealth. This was generally considered to apply also to Scandinavian societies—including Sweden, which was the most heavily taxed country in the free world. And in Galbraith's book on the new industrial state, published in the late 1960s, the tone is almost one of resignation. The consumer was instructed to serve the system, and did so with obvious joy. The Social Democratic order represented a breakthrough for the consumer society. But Social democracy had difficulty incorporating consumerism into its order. The dilemma remained: Social Democracy rejected the affluent society but contributed to its realization.

TAXATION SOCIALISM

Despite what has been said about public poverty, Social Democracy brought about a vigorous growth in public expenditure. In the 1930s public expenditure in both countries constituted between 10 and 20 percent of the gross national product; in 1975 it was around 50 percent, on a par with that of several Western European countries. A significant portion of these public expenditures—approximately half—were transfers that followed the social reforms. Social Democracy was a redistributive regime: expenditures were covered by an extensive system of taxation. Since the political parties stood together regarding the welfare state, there was no real opposition to the high level of taxation, not even from the political right.[76] There was a degree of opposition, however, partly toward the forms of taxation and partly toward the taxation level. The former had its basis in disagreement over the importance of the form of taxation for conducting an effective business life, and the latter in an ideological conflict over whether savings in society should take place in the public or the private sector. Who should control the capital? We recall

[76] Uddhammar 1993, 336–337.

Galbraith's point that in the modern industrial society "the decision to save" had to be taken away from the consumer and subjected to another authority.

During the Social Democratic period both Sweden and Norway had high public and low private savings rates. As expressed in a Norwegian white paper: "In order to have a large total amount of savings and a correspondingly high level of investment that is secured simultaneously with a leveling of income, it would be necessary for the state to take in more taxes than it needs to finance the state's consumption, investments, and transfers to the private sector."[77] Initially the planned-economy aspirations of the economists ran smoothly in tandem with Socialist ideology: taxation became the domain of technical experts.[78] And it was best that the state took care of savings. Arguably, "The high taxation policy of Social Democracy that presupposed that the state, rather than the individual citizen, should save was in itself the mechanism of long-term Socialist strategy."[79]

On the other hand, "the Socialists were never able to enact policies that even faintly resembled the radical policies suggested in their early campaign rhetoric."[80] For instance, the Norwegian Labor Party program of 1922 required "an extraordinary confiscatory tax on large fortunes and a strong progressive taxation on large incomes."[81] But burdened with the responsibility of power, the party never went that far.

In the wake of the Social Democrats' takeover of government power and the Saltsjöbad agreement in Sweden in the 1930s, Finance Minister Wigforss instituted a tax reform in 1938 that was extremely favorable to the big private corporations. As a Communist member of Parliament commented: "Now the Right can be very pleased with their triumph."[82] Toward the end of the Social Democratic era there was a tendency toward radicalization. At the Swedish Labor Party Congress in 1969 the demand was raised for a significant intensification of taxation on capital. But the party leadership, with Finance Minister Gunnar Sträng at the head, warned against such a line on the basis of pragmatic economic arguments. The Social Democrats were, as always, hesitant to undermine a system that worked well. As Sträng himself put it, the policy was based on "a most practical and simple philosophy: from a fiscal point of view one ought to be concerned about Swedish free enterprise. It is better to have good enterprises that yield profits than it is to have poor enterprises that end up with losses."[83] Throughout the hegemonic period of Social

---

[77] St. forh. (Parl. Proceedings) 1960–1961, S. Meld. 54:154.

[78] Steinmo 1993, 122.

[79] Ljunggren 1992, 132.

[80] Steinmo 1993, 83.

[81] Maurseth 1987, 258.

[82] Steinmo 1993, 89–90. The details of the reform in a note on p. 220.

[83] Elvander 1972, 304, 307.

Democracy, corporate taxes in Sweden were among the lowest in Europe. According to Finance Minister Kjell-Olof Feldt, the idea was to promote rationalization of large successful companies by holding profits inside the companies, thereby forcing them "to invest instead of distributing the money among the shareholders."[84]

While the corporate taxes were well below the European average, personal income taxes and social security taxes were well above the average. Contrary to what we would expect, however, Sweden did not have a particularly progressive tax system. As pointed out by Sven Steinmo, heavy tax burdens had to be borne by all income groups in order to get the required revenues: "The key here is that Sweden, like all Social Democratic countries, has been able to build a tax system that generates huge revenues to the state. These revenues translate into public spending on housing, education, health, and welfare, and the effects of this spending are substantially more redistributive than steeply progressive taxes."[85]

In 1947 Wigforss launched a new and radical tax strategy. Income taxes were raised, but most provocative was a substantial rise in inheritance duties. As Wigforss had previously said, the inheritance tax was a means for "reconciling Socialism with liberal economic theory," wherein capital could "be transferred into the hands of society . . . without great disturbances of everyday economic life."[86] This was written in relation to the launching of a far-reaching inheritance tax by the Social Democrats with the election of 1928. That election was a setback for the Social Democrats, and Prime Minister Hansson placed part of the blame on Wigforss's radical proposal regarding death duties. But Wigforss was to come back.

In the short period between the death of Hansson in 1946 and Wigforss's departure from the post of finance minister in 1948, Wigforss took the opportunity to introduce a new "inherited estate tax" of up to 60 percent, levied against the larger fortunes. The idea was that over the long term—a couple of generations—the formation of private fortunes could be undermined. No other tax question has engendered such strong ideological confrontations as this proposition did.[87] It must be seen as part of the general radical move toward a planned economy that followed the war, peaking in 1947. The confrontational strategy was soon abandoned, and the radical inheritance tax was repealed in 1958. Nevertheless, notwithstanding the general moderation of the reform policy, time and again we can observe instances that reveal the

---

[84] Steinmo 1993, 180.

[85] Steinmo 1993, 2.

[86] Isaksson 2000, 61.

[87] Elvander 1972, 100. Sweden was not the only country to introduce heavy inheritance taxes. Indeed, they were based on the estate tax used in Britain. Steinmo 1993, 123.

underlying Socialist goal. Wigforss's vision of "public enterprises without pro-prietors never vanished."[88]

Abolition of consumption taxation, considered to be most burdensome for the lower-income groups, had been an important issue for the Social Democrats. As part of his radical reforms in 1947 Wigforss eliminated the consumption taxes. In the 1950s and 1960s, however, taxes rose mainly by expanding consumption taxation, the Social Democrats having been con-vinced by the economic experts that consumption taxes were politically the most convenient way to generate more revenues. A political controversy arose over this issue, with the non-Socialist parties and the Communists opposing the proposition. The former feared higher taxes, and the latter feared the so-cial effects. But the Social Democrats got their way by introducing a sales tax, later converted into a substantial value-added tax (VAT).[89]

In both countries the system functioned such that the taxes, under cer-tain circumstances, could exceed 100 percent of the income. This meant that even the small private companies were hit: "From the end of the sixties, the tax system was such that, in principle, high inflation made it impossible for private persons to own or run a profitable business; the real taxes exceeded 100 percent."[90] In order to prevent an unreasonably high level of taxation, both countries eventually introduced limitation rules specifying, for example, that no one should pay more than 80 percent of their income in taxes. The limitation rules had a sort of symbolic value and were a political shuttlecock throughout the whole period.[91]

Sweden's national icon Astrid Lindgren, the writer, was one of those who had to pay more than 100 percent in taxes. This prompted her to write a book titled *Pomperipossa i Monismanien*, a satirical saga in which she made fun of the system. The book became highly popular.[92] The minister of finance, Gun-nar Sträng, criticized Lindgren for incompetent calculation: she should leave the calculations to him and continue writing sagas. Lindgren's answer was that it was rather the other way round, so it would be best if they changed positions. She could be finance minister and take care of the calculations, whereas Sträng could continue to tell fanciful sagas to which he had proved competent. People still speak of the Pomperipossa Effect.

Developments in Norway were parallel to those in Sweden in many re-spects. The otherwise more radical Norwegian Social Democrats seem to have been more cautious than Wigforss, however, at least when it came to the

---

[88] Henrekson and Jakobsson 2002, 27f.
[89] Steinmo 1993, 123–128.
[90] Henrekson 2006, 1.
[91] Mosken Bergh 1990.
[92] Lindgren 1976.

taxation system. Rising taxes followed the war, and Norway never had the very low level of corporate taxes that we find in Sweden. Norwegian corporate taxes were high, but the firms discovered loopholes that almost allowed them to decide for themselves what income would be taxed.[93] And since inheritance taxation rates remained relatively low in Norway, there was never a dispute over "the inherited property tax" analogous to that in Sweden. Sales taxes were reduced in 1947 but not eliminated, as they were in Sweden. Later Norway followed Sweden in the extensive use of consumption taxes; the VAT was introduced soon after it had been introduced in Sweden.

There were, of course, recurring disputes between the Social Democrats and the non-Socialists on taxation issues. In 1947 the Norwegian finance minister Brofoss made his famous statement that "[i]t is rather odd how well people can tolerate taxes, once they have become accustomed to them."[94] The LO chairman was able to comfort those who were, nonetheless, discontent: "We all complain about the taxes, but if we study the tax systems of other countries we find, as far as I know, no other country where the capitalist class had been bled as much through taxation legislation as in our country."[95] There are circumstances indicating he could be right. The taxes increased through the 1940s, 1950s, and 1960s.[96] In 1949, for example, the net wealth tax was increased fivefold. A representative of the opposition protested: "The tax on ownership, by its very nature, amounts to confiscation, and therefore I cannot support it."[97]

In 1965 there was a non-Socialist majority in Norway's Parliament. One of the first things that the bourgeois coalition government did was to set up a taxation commission. The old system had become extremely complicated, with many unintended repercussions. Despite the high rates of taxation in both Norway and Sweden, there had been considerable possibilities for those who were smart to wriggle through the many loopholes in the laws. There was great agreement about the need for a technical revision, but there was political discord on the technicalities.

The non-Socialist government also wanted to minimize progressive taxation and change the taxation of companies in order, as it said, to increase "Norwegian capital formation—savings by firms as well as personal saving."[98] The reaction from the spokesman for the Social Democrats is symptomatic

[93] St. forh. (Parl. Proceedings) 1990–1991, S. Tid. 95–96.

[94] Morgenbladet, 25 November 1947.

[95] T. Bergh 1987, 156.

[96] St. forh. (Parl. Proceedings) 1968–1969. Ot. Prp. 17, appendix 1, Report of the Tax Commission of 1966 (1967, 117–118).

[97] St. forh. (Parl. Proceedings) 1952, S. Tid. 2071.

[98] St. forh. (Parl. Proceedings) 1968–1969, O. Tid. 606.

of the underlying conflict: the government's plan would lead to "a shift away from saving by the public sector to private saving." Moreover, the reform would increase "the power of private credit institutions in this country." He also referred to Galbraith's thesis on public poverty and private well-being, maintaining that this tendency would gain strength.[99] The initiative of the non-Socialist government can be viewed as an introduction to the sweeping readjustment of the taxation policy that would come about in both countries at the end of the 1980s.

As we saw in Sweden, the Social Democrats did have to go back on their principles (progressive taxation and consumption, inheritance, and corporate taxes) in order to expand tax revenues, react to political opposition, and support a well-functioning economic system. Sweden became the most heavily taxed country in the world.[100] Norway did not keep pace but was clearly above the average taxation level in the member states of the Organization for Economic Cooperation and Development (OECD). It is worth noting that Social Democratic Scandinavia—particularly Norway—turned out to be among the most, if not the most, egalitarian societies in the world, at least partly owing to the redistribute effects of the taxation system.

CAPITALISM WITHOUT CAPITALISTS?

Both the Social Democrats and the bourgeois side had prepared for the political processes that, over time, would lead to a new allocation of proprietorship (the non-Socialists by means of the bourgeoisie's cherished "property-owning democracy"). But the bourgeois side opposed the more brutal forms of taxation since, in contrast to the Social Democrats, they felt that saving, in essence, should be in private hands. Their policy was to address the issue of small savers. Yet, true to Social Democracy's hegemonic nature, no one really stood up for the rich, the real capitalists. It is perhaps not surprising that the capitalists were unable to constitute a group capable of being defended on moral grounds. But the general feeling seems to have been that, even from the pragmatic point of view, there was really no need to have any actual capitalists. After all, there were the executive directors. It was not easy to be a capitalist, nor should it have been. But it was possible.

Personal taxes such as the progressive income tax, the net wealth tax, and the capital gains tax, along with the inheritance tax, were all used as a policy means aimed at combating the formation of private fortunes. But what hap-

[99] St. forh. (Parl. Proceedings) 1969–1970, S. Tid. 1173. Guttorm Hansen in the Parliament.
[100] Steinmo 1993, 131.

pened to the private fortunes? To some extent taxation socialism (to which the bourgeois parties had also conceded) worked, but only to some extent. In Sweden managerial capitalism never really made a breakthrough. The rich families retained partial control through difficult times. Above all the others, this was the case for the Wallenberg family, who "in a way that was really more clever than that of the other old estate-owning families, managed to make use of the vacuum that appeared in the ranks of proprietors with the strong institutionalization of ownership during the postwar period."[101] As we have seen, this opportunity lay in the fact that the regime had a use for them because they did a good job developing Swedish industry, and that during this period the regime was careful not to occasion "great disturbances of everyday life," as Wigforss put it.

One move by the old capitalists was to place a large portion of their stock shares in self-owned foundations over which the old owners still retained a high degree of control.[102] For example, when Marcus Wallenberg died in 1982, he was "not as wealthy as the impression given by his position and his influence." The total extent of his fortune was approximately 140 million kronor ($24 million), and in the 1960s he had had a fortune of "only" 50 million ($9 million). He did, however, have control over the large Knut and Alice Wallenberg Foundation, "the nucleus of the family's holdings," as the biographer Olsson writes, which the family did not own in the juridical sense.[103] In addition, the old capitalists and in particular the Wallenbergs could use the system with A– and B– shares and the possibilities of "boxes within boxes" of ownership, where they had control of one company that in turn had control of the next, which means that with a relatively limited amount of capital they were able to control relatively many companies.

Things were different in Norway. There too the wealthy could shield their existing fortunes to some degree by allowing them to stand as working capital in the firms, but to a lesser degree than in Sweden. Those who are said to have "played Wallenberg" (Johan Melander, Trygve Lie, and Jens Bache-Wiig, for example) definitely did not have their positions by virtue of being capitalists. Managerial capitalism thus had a bigger breakthrough in Norway. On the other hand, there was a group of rich shipping magnates. The most famous of these, Anders Jahre, placed some of his fortune into foundations. But these were small in comparison to those of Sweden, and they did not function in any strategic way as the basis for control within the business world. On the other hand, it has since come to light that Jahre hid away a large fortune

---

[101] Henrekson and Jakobsson 2002, 45.
[102] Isaksson 2000, 72.
[103] Ulf Olsson 2000, 434–436.

abroad, probably with the implicit consent of the government. Thus there were means of surviving as capitalists under Social Democracy.

Limits on the ideologically tinged struggle against private fortunes were set, above all, by a certain prudence with regard to undermining an economic system that functioned reasonably well. There was also a certain sympathy among the Social Democrats for the bourgeois opposition's defense of the rights of proprietorship. Additionally, there were the needs of the economists to use taxation policy as an instrument of macroeconomic control, either through efforts to level the economic cycles, strengthen development of trade and commerce, or prepare for capital accumulation through savings. As we have seen, macroeconomic considerations neatly paralleled the aspirations of the Social Democrats initially. But here, as in many other fields, by relying on practitioners of objective science the Socialists became caught in its net. For the macroeconomists, motives such as a just distribution played a lesser role.[104] The road that led from the principle of social justice to macroeconomic control, and on to forwarding private savings and private fortunes, was indeed a short one. The great tax readjustment will be revisited later in this volume.

CREDIT SOCIALISM OR INDICATIVE PLANNING?

In both Norway and Sweden public-sector saving was channeled into the capital market as loan capital or, to a lesser degree, as proprietary capital. It was put to use for financing investments in such a way that new share issues became less common. In this way the state retained a high degree of control even though direct socialization was abandoned. There was talk of "functional Socialism" and "credit Socialism," and not without reason. In Sweden the extensive public saving was undertaken to a considerable degree through the General Pension Funds (AP Funds). These funds acted as buyers in a bond market. With the established low-interest policy, this meant, in reality, that loans obtained in this market were subsidized. The loans were granted on the basis of politically determined quotas. This was carried out, especially, through the channeling of loan capital such that the state could become involved in the structural development of business life. The effectiveness of this program is debatable. In reality it implied a system in which large and well-established firms tended to be first in the loan queue.[105] We can see the contours of collaboration between the traditional large proprietors, such as the Wallenbergs, and the official Swedish public sector. For their (successful)

---

[104] Einar Lie 1995, 363f., 444.
[105] Henrekson and Jakobsson 2002, 39; Schön 2000, 406.

strategic grip, the politicians were dependent on the large private players who could utilize capital in an effective manner.

"Credit Socialism" also gave rise to other institutions, among them the different types of public credit institutions suitable for specific goals, such as study loans, housing construction, and similar ventures, but also for the development of trade and commerce (light industry, for example). An important initiative was taken in 1967 with the founding of the state-owned Swedish Investment Bank. This was considered necessary to strengthen the competitive power of Swedish business life and accelerate rationalization. It required expanded savings and a long-term credit system that could operate under high-risk conditions. In other words, the state had to step in. The basis for increased state savings lay with the increased sales tax that had recently been introduced. The AP Funds could not meet the above-mentioned requirements, since they had to stick to low-risk products.[106] The Investment Bank served for a period of time as an instrument for state-initiated restructuring. In 1989 it was taken over by the PK Bank (later Nordbanken) and then, in a privatized form, by the financial concern Nordea.

In Norway, too, the public sector controlled the capital channeled into the market in the form of loan capital. A state-controlled bond market was established as in Sweden, along with a comprehensive system of state credit institutions. In the 1960s the public banking community was larger than the private one. New initiatives were taken in the 1970s when funds for industry were gathered in the Industry Fund, and plans were prepared to establish a public holding company. The latter was linked to the initiative to develop a Norwegian knowledge industry. As far as it went, the idea was analogous with that behind the state-owned Investment Bank in Sweden. The holding company, however, never materialized.[107]

It was obviously difficult to implement a system of state-initiated structural rationalization in Norway. For one reason, Norway did not have a structure composed of large private firms, so the system functioned differently from that in Sweden. The public sector of proprietary capital became greater owing to direct investments in the larger state corporations, such as the iron and steel mill and the aluminum plants. In other respects, when it came to public savings capital, only a lesser proportion went to private firms. In addition to the state corporation, much went for housing construction, schools, hospitals, and infrastructure.

The system of publicly organized loan capital is not uniquely Scandinavian. It has features of what has been called "indicative planning," for which France serves as a model. In this type of planning those who are willing to

[106] Uddhammar 1993, 403f.
[107] Sogner 2001, 49f.

take a chance on areas that are given priority by the public authorities have easier access to credit. Under favorable conditions this system can work well. The policy was successful in Norway insofar as Norway had a high rate of saving. On the other hand, it did not lead to a particularly high rate of growth. Capital became more productive in Sweden, perhaps because there the public sector had access to a better-developed industrial sector; in other words, there were potentially productive enterprises to invest in. There was not as much talk about better public planning as there was about utilizing the (capitalistic) system that was already in place.

AN ORDER IN ITS OWN RIGHT

The Social Democratic phase was marked by a high degree of harmony and a spirit of cooperation. After the great confrontations that broke out in both Sweden and Norway over the planned economy, the countries entered smoother waters. Leading Social Democrats such as Tage Erlander and Einar Gerhardsen tried to avoid confrontations. There was also great agreement over the propitious aspects of both negotiated corporatism and administrative corporatism. One characteristic difference between the countries in connection with negotiated corporatism was the tripartite system in Norway versus the bipartite6 system in Sweden. The role of the state as a third party in Norway was forced into being partly because of the weaker employer organization and partly because of a less centralized trade union movement. The degree to which economic democratization was achieved, however, is debatable. Nor was the situation entirely idyllic.

Class society existed as a cultural construction. It was said that Norway had reached its zenith as a class society in the 1950s.[108] Since the same can be said of Sweden, the class society thus becomes a characteristic feature of the Social Democratic order. There were ideological contradictions under the surface, and tendencies toward dual strategies on both sides of the political spectrum. On the one hand, the business community worked rather harmoniously with the Social Democrats at Harpsund and through corporative channels. On the other hand, the world of commerce prepared for long-term ideological rearmament. From the bourgeois circles, this constituted an attempt to go on the offensive with regard to economic democratization through the introduction of property-owning democracy. This must be viewed in connection with the bourgeois belief that rights of ownership over the means of production should remain with the private sector.

---

[108]   Olstad 1991, 11.

The double strategy of the Social Democrats found expression through their strategies to transfer saving in society to the state and the collective organs. Among other measures, this was done through taxation policy. They were seemingly careful not to attack the capitalist system. The policy of the Social Democrats can, however, be interpreted as a long-term strategy that could pluck the feathers from the capitalists.

Contradictions did not come to the forefront during the Social Democratic epoch. A capitalism without capitalists was not achieved, even though some efforts were made in that direction. But the mixed economy that evolved can be regarded as an order in its own right that functioned surprisingly well. An economic foundation was laid for a powerful rise in the living standard, with a high degree of equalization and a vigorous expansion of public-sector performance, especially in fields relating to education and welfare. But in the 1960s the Social Democratic order would reveal itself to be more brittle than one could imagine, at least in the form it had assumed in that decade.

PART III

1970–2000: A Richer Reality

CHAPTER 11

A Difficult Modernity

A Decade of Conflict • The Social Democrats Reply • The Risk Society • Sweden and
Nuclear Power • Norway and Natural Gas Energy • The Nordic Energy Market •
Norway Becomes an Oil Nation • Heavy-Handed Discrimination • Sweden Loses Its
Leading Position • New Policy: A Turnabout? • Successful Policy? • A Difficult Modernity

A DECADE OF CONFLICT

Something happened around 1970 that, in hindsight, appears to be rather
fundamental. The old sense of unity shattered, and a new criticism entered
the picture. There was a shift in thinking that gradually led to a course change
in the development of society, if indeed one can even speak of *one* course or
one direction. Naturally enough, the precipitating conflicts were not synchro-
nous; new conflicts arose in some areas during the 1960s and later in other
areas. But the resulting shift became tangible around 1970. Change occurred
throughout Western Europe but was especially shattering in the Scandinavian
social democracies.

We have already recorded some aspects of this shift, and thus will present
but a brief overview at this juncture before we take a closer look at the more
important aspects. In economic terms, the trade cycle experienced a turnabout. The dollar ceased to be pegged to gold in 1971, leading to new uncertainty regarding currency rates. The period of steady growth that had marked
the golden age of Social Democracy since 1945 ended, and the economy
went into crisis. The youth rebellion revealed a new generational conflict—or
was it only a student uprising? Environmental politics was now on the agenda, and expansion of energy production came under criticism: this applied
not only to nuclear energy but also to hydroelectricity and gas power plants.
Technocracy and the authority of experts (doctors and engineers, as well as
the economists) faded away.

In Scandinavia the Social Democrats lost their hegemony. Social welfare
with its crowning glory, the national insurance plan, was criticized for not
providing what it promised; and at the same time new poverty was revealed.
The work environment came under criticism. The integrated school system,
which had just been instituted with full political agreement, was now being

exposed to tough criticism. Class as a cultural construction disintegrated. The major contradiction was no longer between capital and labor; thus the basis for the system of negotiated corporatism was undermined, and new patterns of loyalty arose. Administrative corporatism was criticized as a case of the fox guarding the henhouse. The physical landscape of Social Democracy, the satellite towns, came under criticism. The housewife contract was replaced by a gender-equality contract, and the abortion issue exploded. Newspapers cut themselves free from specific political parties, and diversity was introduced into the broadcast media. The new immigration began in earnest. In Norway there was a bitter struggle over whether to join the European Union, and the list goes on.

Many of these elements were interrelated. In general there was a reaction against central aspects of the Social Democratic society, and attention shifted to new areas. "Atop the rigid and orderly pattern of industrial society there rested an air of old men's rule and past historical experience."[1] Now people began to examine the back side of the Social Democratic medallion, with varying reactions: some felt the course of developments should be reversed, while others felt that it had not gone far enough.

THE SOCIAL DEMOCRATS REPLY

The splintering of the old consensus led to sharp new political conflicts in the 1970s, and it provided a new dynamic to developments. The basis for the conflicts lay partly in the traditional ideological contradictions inherent in questions that had to do with the relationship between the individual and society, but conflicts also broke out along new ideological dividing lines. In any case, the idyll of Social Democracy's golden era had now been violated, and Social Democrats had to adapt to a new reality. For them the 1970s became a decade of hesitation and fumbling. While the Social Democratic hegemony in politics had been broken in Norway in 1965 with the formation of a bourgeois coalition government under the Center Party (formerly the Farmers' Party) leader Per Borten, the Swedish Social Democrats continued to hold government power until 1976, when the Swedish Center Party (formerly the Farmers Association) leader Thörbjörn Fälldin formed a non-Socialist coalition government.

Norway's entry into the 1970s was marked by the struggle over membership in the European Economic Community (EEC). The Borten government broke apart over this issue and the Labor Party, which favored membership, formed a government. In the 1972 referendum a majority of the public voted

[1] Andreas Hompland in Eriksen, Hompland, and Tjønneland 2003, 25.

against membership in the EEC. The Labor Party, weakened even further by internal conflicts, managed to hold on to government power throughout the 1970s. It responded to the challenges by instituting a series of very radical reforms, including "democratization" of the private banks, increased state ownership and domination of industry, the founding of a state commercial bank, placement of public representatives on the boards of private companies, public regulation of transfers of real estate ownership, prohibition of housing cooperative dissolutions, a public housing service with the right of first refusal given to the municipalities upon the sale of private houses, elimination of grading in the school system and of the Christian objects clause in the law on kindergartens—and free abortion. Some of these reforms were carried out, although many were later reversed. The most radical reform that was actually carried out (in 1977) was the democratization of the banks, meaning that publicly appointed representatives and employee representatives constituted the majority in the decision-making bodies. This reform was reversed by the non-Socialist government in the beginning of the 1980s and has never been proposed again. The struggle over such issues set the stage for political confrontations.

In Sweden the Social Democrat Olof Palme had become prime minister in 1969 and remained in office until the formation of the non-Socialist government in 1976. Similar to the Social Democratic government in Norway, the Palme government greatly enhanced the public sector in the 1970s.[2] Even so, the Palme government did not radicalize itself the way the Norwegian Social Democrats had done. When nationalization of the banks was proposed in 1972, Palme was dismissive.[3] The Swedish banks had publicly appointed representatives in their decision-making bodies, but bank democratization, as had occurred in Norway, was out of question. Nor did Palme ever become an important environmentalist politician. And when he was confronted with growing unemployment in 1971, he chose to abstain from launching an expansive initiative to deal with the situation—something that put him on a collision course with the LO (trade union central). The truly radical proposals concerned what was called the "wage-earner funds." It was proposed by the LO, partly against Palme's wishes.

Ironically, Palme acquired the reputation of a radical. As his biographer writes, it was not "improbable that his ability to take action and his ideological grasp consequently prevented the formation of a large left Socialist party standing beside that of Social Democracy. Undoubtedly, Palme seized for himself some of the dying embers of the student movement of 1968."[4] In fact, his reputation as a radical was based on his foreign policy. The Left So-

---

[2] Östberg 2002, 156: "the strongest ever upgrading of the public sector."

[3] Elmbrant 1989, 133.

[4] Elmbrant 1989, 324.

Figure 13. Olof Palme, *left*, was prime minister in Sweden from 1969 to 1976 and 1982 to 1986, when he was shot down on a street in Stockholm. An aristocrat by birth, he had the rather thankless task of leading the Social Democrats against the headwinds of the 1970s and 1980s. In this photo Norwegian Conservative prime minister Kåre Willoch looks with skepticism at Palme's pointing finger. The picture was taken in 1984 after the "Conservative wave" had swept the bourgeois forces to power in Norway. (Photo: Arbeiderbevegelsens arkiv.)

cialist Party in Norway built itself up from opposition to NATO, but Sweden was not a member of NATO. Palme, however, was an articulate opponent of the Vietnam War, while Norway's NATO membership automatically identi-fied the Norwegian Social Democrats with the policies of the United States. Nor had Sweden sought membership in the EEC at this point in time, thus managing to avoid that dispute.

THE RISK SOCIETY[5]

The economic downturn around 1970, with its higher interest rates, fluid currency rates, and increased inflation, implied that the old stability had bro-ken down. Most significantly, however, faith in the possibility of directing the

[5] The concept "risk society" is taken from Beck (1986).

economy according to the Keynesian recipe was undermined. The economists had to begin to look into the mechanisms on the supply side, things that led to structural changes. Faith in mass production technology and the superior efficiency of large industrial corporations also began to crumble. "Flexible specialization" became a new ideal linked to the new electronic industry and the circle of small firms in Silicon Valley, California. Some experts felt they could discern the contours of a new industrial revolution.[6]

Proletarianization, the shady side of the old industrial society, had been defeated, at least in the Scandinavian countries. But new shadows took its place, threatening the obvious legitimacy of industry. This happened in part because industry no longer (to the same degree) produced goods to satisfy scarcity but, rather, produced goods that contributed to abundance in the rich countries. But above all, it became increasingly evident that science and industry also "produced" hazards and pollution and contributed to unemployment through rationalization of production. In addition, some began to doubt both the possibility and the desirability of continuous economic growth. The book *The Limits to Growth*, published in 1972, became an international hit.[7] It would later be revealed that the ideology of growth was not dead, but that is another issue.

The political agenda changed. Decisions regarding production processes, types of energy utilized, and the handling of waste, for example, had been left to the leaders of industry. These items now appeared on the political agenda. New types of conflicts had to be dealt with. At the beginning of the 1970s quite a few people believed that environmental policy ought to be the great new theme and the creator of new political constellations. To a certain extent this also occurred. Environmental policy found its place, and its institutions spread throughout Europe. In Norway a Ministry of the Environment was established in 1973, along with a state body for pollution control the following year. In 1967 Sweden had already established a state "environmental authority," and it formed a Department of the Environment and Natural Resources in 1987.

The period's new environmental anxiety focused particularly on the heart of modern industrial society—energy production. Modern society was extremely energy intensive. One of the foremost features of Scandinavian Social Democracy had been what was characterized as "power Socialism," and the critique of this society was gradually leveled against all the important energy sources: water, nuclear energy, and fossil fuels. In both Sweden and Norway

---

[6] Piore and Sabel 1984.

[7] This was a report written for what was called the Club of Rome by a group of Americans and one Norwegian, Jörgen Randers.

energy policy—which came to the fore by national consensus—became a central area of conflict from the 1970s through the end of the century, although with differing emphases. In Sweden the toughest battles were fought over nuclear energy, while in Norway they were over natural gas. In both countries, however, the opening salvo had to do with waterpower.

SWEDEN AND NUCLEAR POWER

Both Sweden and Norway had initiated extensive expansion of hydroelectric power installations after 1945. Early on, this expansion was criticized on the basis of the classic principles of nature conservation linked to aesthetic values, but in the 1960s the criticism became more forceful. It took off first in Sweden, where the scarcity of untouched waterways was a more crucial issue. An agreement, the "Peace of Sarek," was undertaken in 1961 between those with interests in the expansion, represented by the state's hydropower company, Vattenfall, and the nature conservation interests. The agreement made a distinction between the waterways where expansion was allowed to occur and those that were to be protected. Evert Vedung has called the agreement "a Saltsjöbad Agreement for the hydroelectric area, a major agreement that would provide an exemplary Swedish model for future negotiations, taking into account opposing interests on the water flow question. The attitude of the political parties was characterized by the paired concepts of nonintervention and industrial fatalism. They strove to play no role other than that of the onlooker."[8]

The Sarek model was thus the corporatist Saltsjöbad Agreement, in which conflicts would be resolved via agreements reached through compromise between the affected parties, and independent of party policy and the state. The difference, however, was that while the Saltsjöbad Agreement had formed the basis for peaceful negotiations for over thirty years, the Peace of Sarek Agreement immediately led to new confrontations that politicized the issue, split the Social Democratic Party, and stretched "the tip of its paralyzed hand into the Chancellery, creating an agony of decision making and a waste of time." The dispute concerned hydroelectric construction on the Vindel River. According to the agreement, this could legitimately be undertaken, and by 1962 plans for twelve power stations were in place. But a storm of protest then arose, marking "the starting point for the present-day Swedish environmental debate."[9]

[8] Vedung and Brandel 2001, 97.
[9] Vedung and Brandel 2001, 100.

During the spring of 1969 the Vindel River project came up in the Social Democrats' parliamentary group, where a large majority voted in favor of the construction. Olof Palme, in a newspaper debate with the writer Lars Gyllensten, gave a lukewarm defense of the construction project. It was clear, however, that he had accepted Gyllensten's argument that it was wrong to destroy nature "for a drop or two of electrical energy, just when the age of atomic energy is standing in the doorway." When Palme took over as prime minister some months later, one of his first official acts was to go against the parliamentary group and stop the construction. In reality this meant that construction on all the untouched rivers was stopped and the great epoch of hydroelectric power was over.[10]

And by 1970 another epoch awaited: further development was underway on the new "pure" and inexhaustible source of power—nuclear energy—with Palme among its foremost advocates. Sweden was well advanced in terms of the technology. The nuclear power station at Oscarhamn had been under construction since 1965, and in 1968 Vattenfall was projecting reactors for Ringhals and Barsebäck. In 1969 Vattenfall launched plans for fifty possible nuclear power stations.[11] In 1970–1971 the Swedish Parliament, in an act of great unity, decided to build eleven reactors.[12]

Around 1973 there were two occurrences of importance to the future of nuclear energy: first came the OPEC oil price shock, which made nuclear power of even greater immediate interest, and then, second, the rapidly growing critical opinion regarding nuclear power, which "inundated . . . the Swedish public like a tidal wave, its size and strength barely anticipated by anyone."[13]

Politics during the latter half of the 1970s came to be marked by the nuclear energy issue. The Center Party spearheaded an agitation against nuclear energy. In 1979 a nuclear reactor accident occurred at Three Mile Island near Harrisburg, Pennsylvania. Skepticism toward nuclear energy increased further, and Palme and the Social Democrats did an about-face. They now maintained that nuclear power had to be wound down in the long term. A plebiscite was held on the question in 1980, offering a choice between three alternatives that each implied an eventual phasing out of nuclear energy. The vote favored a strong buildup in the short term followed by a long-term phaseout.[14] The phaseout line was further strengthened with the accident at the Soviet Union's Chernobyl nuclear power station in 1986 and the 1988 parliamentary decision that the phaseout of nuclear power would begin in

---

[10] Elmbrant 1989, 189.
[11] Anshelm 2000, 95.
[12] Lewin 1992, 313.
[13] Anshelm 2000, 119.
[14] Vedung and Brandel 2001, 238f.

1995. Vedung writes, "Never has Sweden been as close to phasing out nuclear power as it was in 1988."[15] But dismantling a great technical infrastructure is not easily done. There also had to be an alternative to nuclear energy, the nature of which was as yet extremely unclear.

By 1991 the Chernobyl effect had ended, and Parliament could begin what was called "the phasing out of the phaseout."[16] The decision to begin the dismantling was rapidly reversed in 1995, and the question continued to create political conflicts. In 1997 the Social Democratic government of Göran Persson put forward a proposition for a gradual dismantling of nuclear energy in favor of a new energy system. This proposition was rewarded with a storm of protest, particularly from the business sector. On the editorial page of *Svenska Dagbladet* it was stated that the "long-term consequences of Sweden abdicating its role as a modern industrial nation" would be enormous. And Per Unckel from the Conservative Party (the Coalition of Moderates) challenged the Social Democrats to "return to the faith in reason and common sense that once guided Social Democratic energy policy."[17] As Jonas Anshelm says, it became a dispute over who represented modernity and the future. The conflict has still not been resolved.

Today it seems reasonably clear that Sweden will keep nuclear energy. Its neighbor Finland has decided to build nuclear power stations and, according to the public opinion polls, a majority of the Swedish public wants to continue with nuclear energy.[18] The self-described "independently liberal" newspaper *Dagens Nyheter* questions how billions could be invested in gas power plants as an alternative to nuclear energy when nuclear energy is having "its golden age, with construction costs paid off and extraordinarily high production security."[19]

NORWAY AND NATURAL GAS ENERGY[20]

In Norway the great debate over further expansion of hydroelectric energy gained impetus around 1970 with strong protests against the proposed construction of two hydroelectric projects on the west coast. Despite the protests, and in opposition to the outcome of the Vindel River controversy in Sweden, both construction plans were ratified by Parliament. But the struggle contin-

[15] Vedung and Brandel 2001, 376.
[16] Anshelm 2000, 425f.
[17] Anshelm 2000, 476f, 490.
[18] *Svenska Dagbladet*, 27 April 2004.
[19] *Dagens Nyheter*, 22 September 2004.
[20] What follows on Norway and oil/gas is based largely on Sejersted 2002a and on Ryggvik 2000.

ued. In 1979, amid strong protests, Parliament approved a plan for hydro-electric development on the Alta River waterway in Norway's northernmost county of Finnmark. Here the situation was further complicated by charges of violation of Sami traditional rights to their land and water. After the Alta controversy, further construction of hydroelectric projects was limited. The great epoch of hydroelectric construction in Norway was over, almost a decade following its end in Sweden.

It has been said that in the closing years of the 1960s Norway had an "atomic power structure" and the only thing it lacked was the actual plants. In 1970 the government brought out a white paper that favored nuclear energy, and in 1972 Parliament ratified an atomic energy law, with the presupposition that four nuclear energy plants would be ready before 1985.[21] One year later, however, protests against nuclear power exploded in both Norway and Sweden, although neither government was knocked off its pins by this. In 1974 the Norwegians issued another white paper advocating nuclear energy.[22] When the issue was debated in Parliament a year later, however, the Social Democratic government did not even get the support of its own parliamentary group, whereupon the issue was abandoned in a backwater. Following the Three Mile Island accident in 1979, the minister of petroleum and energy announced that nuclear power would be out of the question in Norway during the current century.[23] With this, the debate over nuclear power was definitely over.

The difference between Sweden and Norway lay in the fact that Sweden built its nuclear power stations, while Norway never got that far. Not only did Norway have more hydroelectric power than Sweden, but Norway was also able to access a new energy resource in the 1970s—oil and natural gas from the rich oil fields in the North Sea. Thus, in contrast to their Swedish neighbors, Norway's Social Democratic parliamentary group could reject nuclear power in 1975. It is easier to run away from a point of view when one has not invested in it and when one has clear alternatives.

While the premises of the nuclear energy debates in Sweden and Norway were different, Norway found itself in an intensification of discussions around the natural gas alternative in the wake of the nuclear energy debate. The great worry about natural gas, the greenhouse gas effect of CO_2 emissions, reached back to the 1960s, but it was not until the Brundtland Report, *Our Common Future*, appeared in 1987 that the concerns accelerated. This report, a climate policy manifesto, was composed by an international commission of the United

[21] St. forh. (Parl. Proceedings) 1969–1970, St. Meld. 97; St. forh. 1971–1972, O. Prp. 51. Law sanctioned in May 1972

[22] St. forh. (Parl. Proceedings) 1973–1974, St. Meld. 100.

[23] St. forh. (Parl. Proceedings) 1978–1979, S. Tid. 3096f.

Nations under the leadership of the Norwegian Social Democratic prime minister Gro Harlem Brundtland. In this connection Norway's neophyte petroleum industry rapidly became the center of attention. It would, however, soon prove difficult to be an oil nation *and* to pioneer climate policy.

Natural gas was one of the great political issues of the 1990s, and the "gas argument" would come to play a central role in the Norwegian climate debate. This argument maintained that an extensive export of Norwegian gas was a means of reducing emissions; after all, natural gas would replace the much more damaging coal-fired power stations that were the most important producers of energy on the European continent. The gas argument was the "moral" alibi for repealing the goal of stabilizing emissions that was established in 1989, an agreement that CO_2 emissions should be stabilized at the 1989 level by the year 2000. In 1996 concessions were granted for the construction of two gas power plants. The environmental movement mobilized, achieving a breakthrough insofar as the pollution inspection authorities were assigned to establish permissible emission levels for the power plants, levels that were lowered to such an extent that the resulting difficulties led to postponement of the plant construction.

In 1998 the general director of the oil firm Norsk Hydro proffered claims that his company had the necessary technology to build an emissions-free gas power plant, a move that attracted great attention. It became apparent, however, that there was no new technology. The plan was based on a previously known idea: reinjecting the CO_2 back into the gas fields under the North Sea. This was technically possible but not economically feasible, so the proposal was more political in character than it was practical. It directed attention toward possible technological solutions for building an emissions-free gas power plant, however—something that would become an important feature in the course of further debate.

Following the Norwegian election in 1997, the newly formed centrist coalition government swiftly produced an energy report based on the positions of the environmental movement: environmental goals had to determine energy production, while at the same time working to limit energy consumption. This report unleashed a great political debate, which ended with the opposition overthrowing the government in 2000. A new Social Democratic government was formed, and the strict emissions demand was reversed. Initially this paved the way for construction of plants that had previously been issued licenses, but the road proved to be twisted, for both political and economic reasons.[24] Not until 2007 was it possible to begin the construction of a gas power plant—one that, to date, is not addressing the issue of CO_2 emissions.

---

[24] *Dagens Næringsliv*, 17 February 2004. Øyvind Ihlen in *Klassekampen*, 19 July 2004. Ihlen has written a thesis on natural gas energy that was published too late to be used as a basis for this description.

THE NORDIC ENERGY MARKET

Norwegian gas has largely been conveyed by pipeline to the Continent. The question of exporting Norwegian natural gas to Sweden, primarily as an alternative to nuclear energy, has been under discussion since 1988. Different alternatives, such as a gas pipeline direct from the North Sea to the Gothenburg area, have been formulated. There has also been a proposal to run the gas across the middle of Norway to Gävle, which would be the shortest route. These negotiations shut down at the beginning of 1991 because of the "phasing out of the phaseout" of nuclear energy that year, among other reasons. The plan for a Nordic "natural gas axis" was also put forward—a gas pipeline through Østlandet in southeast Norway that would supply gas to a refinery there and then be extended to the Stockholm area for regional utilization and on under the Gulf of Bothnia to Finland. A similar plan had previously been considered for gas coming from the Soviet Union across Finland to Sweden.[25] Swedish interest has been weak since 1991, and at this point no plans have been implemented.

The decision has been made to build a gas power plant at Gothenburg; the gas is not to come from Norway, however, but rather from the Danish gas fields in the North Sea. For several years a pipeline has been in operation from the North Sea, across Denmark to Malmö in Sweden and on to the Gothenburg area. This pipeline, built in response to an initiative of the Swedish government following the planned dismantling of nuclear energy production, has delivered natural gas for industrial and household purposes and heating.[26] In Sweden, too, there has been opposition to building gas power plants with CO_2 emissions, but it seems not to have had the same force as in Norway. The irony is that in Sweden, under the cover of the intense debate about nuclear energy, it has been easier to accept natural gas, while the opposition in Norway has concentrated on gas power plants and CO_2 emissions.

Whether or not gas pipelines are built, there has in any case been a steadily increasing dense network of electric power lines. These form the technical foundation and grid for a liberalizing of the energy market. Here Norway is in the lead. In 1990, "Norway acquired Europe's most modern energy law, which opened the way to visions of leading the future Europe by means of energy exchanges in open competition with other countries. This was to create growth, efficiency, and better added value in the electrical energy branch."[27] A common Swedish-Norwegian energy market was established in 1996, usher-

---

[25] An overview of the development is found in *Dagens Næringsliv*, 6 January 1992, "Norsk gass til Sverige og Finland?" and in *Energi til Europa* 1994, especially pp. 44–45.

[26] *Energi til Europa* 1994, 73.

[27] Jacobsen 1998, 182.

ing in the removal of the old border tariffs and establishment of a Swedish-Norwegian energy exchange.[28] This was later expanded into a Nordic market with branches to the Continent. Nowadays electrical energy is bought and sold relatively freely across national boundaries, which means that when there is an undersupply of electricity in the "energy country," Norway, it can be purchased from coal-fired generating stations, power stations fueled by Norwegian natural gas on the Continent, or nuclear energy plants in Sweden. The development of a European market for electrical energy has changed the terms of the great debates (about atomic energy in Sweden and natural gas energy in Norway).

NORWAY BECOMES AN OIL NATION

In 1969 the first large oil discovery was made on the Norwegian shelf in the North Sea, beginning Norway's incredible development as an oil nation. This discovery immediately gave rise to the political problem of how to go about extracting this newly found natural resource and how to organize its use. The chosen solution was the development of an oil industrial complex involving several new elements of organization and cooperation that ran counter to established Norwegian practices and would have long-term significance for Norwegian economic institutions.

Schematically, in the beginning there were two technological systems standing face-to-face. On the one hand, there was the traditional Norwegian industry and production structure distinguished by small entities, local networks, a high degree of transparency, and strong democratic norms. On the other hand, there was the oil system "out there," whose features were large scale—technologically and organizationally opaque entities dominated by the international oil companies. In order to be able to utilize the "new" oil resources, some joining of these two systems was essential yet, at the same time, obviously problematic. One seldom encounters situations of this type, in which the existing structures offer so little guidance and the future consequences will be so great.

In order to move as quickly as possible, the Norwegian policy began by clarifying the rights of proprietorship to the North Sea shelf. The policy was based on the realization that the large oil companies had the essential technological expertise and marketing and capital networks; thus it was appropriate to utilize the interests of these firms. As a result, the large petroleum firms obtained considerable influence over setting up the framework for the whole

---

[28] Jacobsen 1998, 4.

petroleum venture, including establishment of regulations regarding the sharing of concession rights. An alliance between the Norwegian state and some of the large multinational corporations thus arose from a common interest in clearly defining proprietary rights to the shelf in order to get the extraction of the oil under way. Norwegian business interests played a more modest role in this early phase.

One consequence of the petroleum activity was that the Norwegian state, by means of alliances with private interests and the division of concession rights as well as in other ways, was forced to discriminate between different private interests. This had not been done before in Norway, although Sweden had some experience along these lines. The Wallenbergs would not have been able to position themselves so well without positive discrimination and the goodwill of the Swedish state. But in Norway, even under the Social Democratic regime, nondiscrimination was viewed as a virtue—the state was not to compete with private interests.[29] Now this abstemiousness came to an end, and the state came into closer contact with current business activity. Its role as arm's-length regulator developed into that of a more actively interventionist and discriminating implementer of business policy—in the Social Democratic spirit but, paradoxically, only at the very end of the hegemonic period of Social Democracy.

No sooner had oil been discovered on Norwegian soil than the OPEC shock occurred, sending oil prices sky high and contributing to an international crisis. Norwegian traditional industry, especially the marine shipping sector, was hit by the crisis; but, for Norway as an oil nation, the oil shock was a golden opportunity. OPEC, an organization of the oil-exporting countries, had been established to get some control over the large international oil corporations. The formation of OPEC heralded a period of cold relations between states and multinational corporations. All the oil-exporting countries (with the exception of the United States) established their own national state-owned oil companies during this period—even Great Britain, despite the fact that the British state already owned half of the oil company BP.

HEAVY-HANDED DISCRIMINATION

In accordance with this new trend, Norwegian policy changed vigorously. Now the goals were to secure the rights to ground rent and "make Norwegian" the petroleum industry. The completely state-owned Statoil was established in 1972, and in 1974 Norway confronted the large oil companies with regard to

[29] Kleppe 2003,124.

taxation. Statoil was not only to be an operating oil company but, above all, a political instrument for "Norwegianization," which was to remain its function for a long time. It has been said that with such a company "one comes close to the boundary of what a capitalist state can do and still be capitalistic."[30]

Norwegianization had as its goals the integration of the oil industry into Norwegian society, the creation of a prosperous society, and the development of a sense of activity and well-being throughout the country. Originally it was even decided that all petroleum resources should be brought ashore in Norway and uses were to be found for it there. This, of course, did not happen, but it did not mean that Norwegianization was given up. For some time we can see a powerful politically led attempt to bind together the two different business systems referred to earlier: the traditional Norwegian system and the international oil system. The efforts were, however, not very successful. Norwegianization was to be given up, and petroleum activity came more or less to assume the character of an enclave.

Statoil had its "wings clipped" in the early 1980s; that is, the company was removed (or "freed") from its political functions. It was supposed that the country gained more economically by simply harvesting the ground rent and allowing Statoil to develop the petroleum resources on its own and in competition. Thus the enclave model obviously had its advantages. The politicians had not managed to live up to the expectations created in many local and district circles in society.

Nevertheless, Norway had succeeded in the most essential feature, namely to achieve, by protection of this infant industry, a significant technological development and to create independent Norwegian participation within the international petroleum field. Thus the Norwegians were now able to hob-nob with the great and the powerful, as the Swedes had long been doing. For the Norwegians, incorporation into the modern international economic structures occurred largely through participation in the petroleum business. This would certainly have happened in any case, but perhaps not in the same manner or to the same extent. The drawback was a relatively high degree of exposure to the hazards of international economic cycles and forces that were beyond Norwegian control. The Norwegian system was no longer so very Norwegian.

The oil policy was remarkable up to this point because there was an important political desire guiding the development, and the result was positive and in accord with intentions. Certainly policy was changed at times, from the period of flirtation with multinational corporations to the Norwegianization phase with its challenge to the multinational companies. The assembled

---

[30] Olsen 1989, 104.

results were good, nonetheless. Norway managed to get the oil from beneath the sea, keep the most essential part of the ground rent in Norwegian hands, build up an oil industry complex roughly as had been desired at the outset, and, for the most part, avoid the "Dutch disease" insofar as a substantial part of the large oil income was salted away in future pension funds. This can be viewed as a triumph for a planned economic initiative bearing the stamp of Social Democracy, and it stands as a striking example of how a new industry can be built up with ingenious use of positive discrimination. A positive discrimination of this kind would have been impossible after Norway joined the European Economic Area agreement in 1994. But at that time the Norwegian oil industry was capable of competing in the international markets. The history of the oil industry stands in sharp contrast to the simultaneous unsuccessful attempt to build up a Norwegian information and knowledge industry in the electronic field. Naturally enough, the conditions were different in terms of the enormous flow of money generated by oil production.

As time goes by we can gradually see how oil policy was subjected to the coercion of the system. The oil industrial complex, created in an open situation and from political desire, quickly acquired its own needs and made its own demands that would force a reordering of priorities. In other words, there was a move away from the leading and enabling Social Democratic policy and toward a policy in which, to a great degree, the premises lay outside the political system. More business-oriented considerations came to govern even the politicians.

The trajectory of this development is exemplified by the changing function of Statoil. By means of a partial depoliticization of oil policy, Statoil was no longer needed as a governing instrument. Thus Statoil was first to have its political wings clipped and then be partly privatized—while simultaneously being developed into a multinational enterprise, well supported by political authorities at home. There is irony to this relationship insofar as Statoil was originally construed as a national political tool for confrontation with the large multinational oil companies, and now it has itself become such an enterprise. In countries such as Azerbaijan, Nigeria, and Angola the company—and thereby also the state—plays a role opposite the one played in Norway during the period of Norwegianization.

SWEDEN LOSES ITS LEADING POSITION

Sweden had been "the winning nation," standing as the prime example of the successful modern industrial nation. It showed that Social Democracy could function more in accordance with the logic of industrialism than could

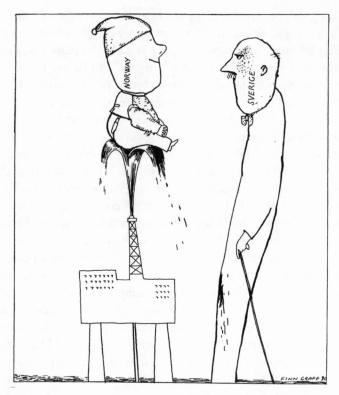

Figure 14. After Norway became an oil-producing nation and the national income per capita rose above that of Sweden, the self-image of the Norwegians seems to have been strengthened. (Drawing: Finn Graff.)

liberal capitalism. But in the 1970s things changed. The general international crisis hit the Swedish economy particularly hard, and in the course of a few years Sweden became just another European country. By the beginning of the 1980s the per capita income in Norway exceeded that of Sweden. The heavy industries, the processing industries and shipbuilding, had dominated the Swedish economy. In a little more than ten years following 1975, however, the steel plants, the mining industry, and the wood-processing industry were all reorganized and reduced to a mere fraction of what they had been; the large shipbuilding industry was as good as dead.

One of the characteristics of Swedish industrialism had been its ability to conduct restructuring and rationalization. This was clearly revealed in the 1930s when the system responded quickly and effectively to the challenges posed by the economic crisis, such that the effects of the crisis were less severe in Sweden than in other industrial countries. The Social Democrats had also been cautious about disturbing the established economic system, which continued to unfold according to its own logic. By contrast, however, in the 1970s Sweden was among the countries that managed poorly.

Lennart Schön places the blame for the 1970s result on structural relations. In the 1930s Swedish industry managed so well owing to, among other things, the continual renewal that could be undertaken within the established structure and on the basis of existing resources, competence, and institutions.[31] When we move forward to the 1970s the situation had changed. There was still a significant vitality within the enterprises but "also a constraint exerted by traditional pathways. Few new large-scale enterprises arose in Sweden after 1950. The preferred approach was to increase international specialization and to rationalize rather than to found new enterprises with new development methods."[32] Some of the abilities to innovate were lost here, in comparison with actions taken in earlier times—for example, when the Wallenbergs intervened and organized the financing of a new, extremely large, and risky project such as Norsk Hydro.

Constraints imposed by the established ways of doing things have also been blamed on weaknesses in the Swedish model. The solidarity wage policy of the Social Democrats, public saving, the management of the capital market, and (especially) the very low taxation of income that remained within the enterprise all contributed to conserving the existing structures. The option of depositing profits in foundations had the same effect of remaining tied to the established way of doing things. Furthermore, the progressive taxation system meant that returns on investment in education were low. And increased investment in human capital was precisely what the future-oriented industries required. Moreover, there were limited possibilities for defending new industries in their establishment phase through various forms of positive discrimination. (Here Norway was more ruthless when it came to favoring oil-related new industry.) But though it seems as if Swedish industry had been weighed down by its ways of doing business, this is not the whole truth.

If we return to the heavy industries—mines, steel, wood processing, and shipbuilding—we find that "at the end of the 1970s a restructuring, rationalization, and renewal process was begun that presumably had no counterpart in Swedish history. Between 1978 and 1982, huge changes in proprietary relations were carried out, as well as changes in construction size, techniques, and product selection," to cite Schön.[33] Remarkably, the most serious measures were taken in the state sector. The Swedish state essentially took over

---

[31] Schön 2000, 470–475.
[32] Schön 2000, 474.
[33] Schön 2000, 490.

and amalgamated the entire steel and shipbuilding industries within two large enterprises, Svenskt Stål AB (Swedish Steel Corporation) and Svenska Varv (Swedish Shipyards). This was done largely to provide a mechanism for closing down their operations in an orderly manner.

Initially the state had met the crisis with large sums of money to support industry, but when the nature of the crisis became clear, the state stepped in with a draft of a brutal restructuring policy. The early support given to industry has been criticized as having prolonged the crisis, but as Schön points out, if the entire process is viewed as one entity, this appraisal is "extremely doubtful."[34] Like the planned construction of the oil-related industry in Norway, these powerful structural steps in the Swedish steel and shipbuilding industries were the final (successful) examples of extensive, direct state intervention in the production sphere. We can consider this the swan song of the Social Democratic planned economy. Ironically, this intervention had to do with dismantling what had been core operations in Social Democracy's advanced industrial state.

NEW POLICY: A TURNABOUT?

The 1970s had been a decade of economic crises, unrest, and conflicting tendencies throughout Western Europe. The dominant Keynesian way of thinking was giving way to "monetarism," with its tendency to look on inflation as a greater threat to the economy than unemployment. But an established policy cannot be changed overnight, and there was a lot of fumbling in the process of deciding how the challenges should be met. We have seen how the Social Democrats in Sweden and, particularly, in Norway came up with a series of very radical proposals in the direction of more "Socialism." This proved to be a dead end. In Britain both the Conservative government up until 1974 and the subsequent Labor governments were without any real alternatives. True, in 1977 the Labor government introduced substantial cuts in public spending that resulted in a steep rise in unemployment and a wave of strikes. In the 1979 election the Conservatives were swept back into power under the leadership of an unusually strong prime minister—Margaret Thatcher. She followed up with determination what the Labor government had hesitantly tried. As Tony Judt says, she "bullied, browbeat—and seduced—the British electorate into a political revolution. . . . 'Thatcherism' stood for various things: reduced taxes, the free market, free enterprise, privatization of industries and services, 'Victorian values,' patriotism, 'the individual'"—and,

[34] Schön 2000, 493.

especially, "she destroyed forever the public influence exercised by Britain's trade unions."[35]

The year after Thatcher had taken control in Britain Ronald Reagan was elected president in the United States. Like Thatcher, he was a believer in monetarism, the free market, and reduced taxes. He also made cuts in various areas of public spending, but not enough to compensate for the rise in military spending; consequently, the federal deficit increased. But economic performance did improve—in America as in Britain. Reagan's policy was not as revolutionary in America as Thatcher's was in Britain, but it was of the same brand, and the two leaders developed a relationship of mutual respect and admiration. Together they made an imprint on policy, not only in their own countries but throughout the Western world. The 1980s and, to a certain degree, the 1990s were the decades in which "the American model" was at its height in Western Europe (also in Eastern Europe after 1989). But that does not mean that the European model or the Social Democratic model was extinct, even if it never again became exactly what it once had been.

Developments in France were also symptomatic of the changes in many European countries around 1980. The Socialist François Mitterrand was elected president in 1981. He immediately introduced what Tony Judt calls "a phantasmagoric program of 'anticapitalist' legislation," which was a bit like the policy introduced by the Social Democrats in Norway to meet the challenges of the 1970s.[36] Mitterrand's program primarily consisted of a substantial number of nationalizations that, to a certain degree, followed traditional French policy. As in Norway, this turned out to be a dead end, and by 1982 he had already done an about-face, adopting an economic strategy that, according to Judt, "would have introduced into France a dose of Thatcherism *avant l'heure*." And in 1984 he followed up by calling for "a French modernization 'à l'américaine.'"[37] Such is the European background for circumstances in Scandinavia around 1980.

The end of the 1970s marks the beginning of Swedish and Norwegian economic policy adjustment in the direction of deregulating capital and labor markets and relaxing taxation, a necessary move in order to provide relief to the world of trade and commerce. In Norway the Social Democrats held government power; in Sweden they were in the opposition. As we have seen, Sweden was worse off and was preparing to rein in public expenditure. The dispute was a struggle less among varying political groups than between the opposition and those who, for the moment, held government power.[38] Most

[35] Judt 2007, 540.
[36] Judt 2007, 552.
[37] Judt 2007, 553, 554.
[38] Urban Lundberg 2003, 79.

remarkably, the Social Democrats sacrificed some of their sacred cows, such as their regulation and interest policy. Since the 1980s the European Social Democrats have contributed to "the development of a new model of growth in which the state consequently has slowly begun to surrender responsibility for the well-being and employment of its citizens."[39] Periodically the question of employment has led to tense relations between the party and the trade union federation, particularly in Sweden.

The new policy would find its most striking expression in a report presented by the Swedish Social Democratic Party in 1981. The report was drawn up by a group under the leadership of Ingvar Carlsson. As right-hand man to Palme and his successor as prime minister, Carlsson more than anyone else came to stand for what has been called the "third way policy." This concept has been used to describe the policy of Tony Blair after the British Labor Party resumed power in 1997, but it has been used retrospectively to characterize the emerging policy of the Swedish Social Democrats in the early 1980s.[40] It was a third way policy *avant l'heure*, meaning that in Sweden—and in Norway—the Social Democrats themselves took the initiative to make the policy change. In this way they avoided the Thatcherite interlude of Britain, which was at least partly due to the fumbling of the British Labor Party.

In Sweden the third way policy meant a middle way between the traditional Swedish Social Democracy and Thatcherism,[41] representing a sort of equilibrium thinking. According to Urban Lundberg, "This had to do with finding a balance between public and private, labor and capital, international and national. The public sector was to be big, but not too big. The trade union movement ought to have power, but no more than was necessary. The taxes could be high, but not without limits. There were boundaries that could not be overstepped without reality hitting back."[42] Carlsson himself had chosen the members of the group that prepared Social Democratic Party report. Kjell-Olof Feldt, who was later finance minister, was a prominent member. "Our task was to form a new policy," as Carlsson writes, frankly and without reservation, in his memoirs. The program had necessarily to "differ from the existing program, which the labor movement had in place since the postwar period." The point was still to safeguard social welfare, but the route had to lead through a "renewed and expanded industry."[43] There were no resources

---

[39] U. Lundberg 2003, 21.

[40] The concept "third way" has been used in other connections also, for instance to characterize the reformist policy between laissez-faire liberalism and Soviet Communism between the wars. Cf. Berman 2006, 15.

[41] As pointed out by Judt (2007, 794), it was hardly a new idea in European context.

[42] U. Lundberg 2003, 113.

[43] Ingvar Carlsson 2003, 175–176.

available for new social reforms; indeed, one had to carefully control expenditure by the public sector.

Carlsson's program provoked powerful reactions within the labor movement, with accusations of weakness and undue support for the premises of capitalism and the bourgeoisie.[44] But as Carlsson writes in his memoirs: "At least to a certain degree, opinion seemed to be ready for a new message." With the following year's election, in 1982, the Social Democrats took power and set their program in motion. The conflict was increased by the dismantling of credit restrictions and the unfortunate credit expansion in 1985, and again when Carlsson became prime minister after Palme's death in 1986 and introduced a tighter economic policy. But the fiercest reaction came with the tax reforms around 1990. The harsh conflict—which has been called "the war of the roses"—was first and foremost a conflict between the Social Democratic government and the LO, which means that it affected the very basis of the Social Democratic order.

Contentions arose in Norway that the Labor Party changed course in terms of economic policy during the night of August 12, 1977. In any case, on August 13 the finance minister issued a warning that an adjustment was needed to rescue the industrial sector. The many radical proposals of the 1970s had gradually been put aside. Deregulation began, and tax policy was revised. This revised policy was continued under Kåre Willoch's non-Socialist government following the Labor Party's 1981 election loss and again under Gro Harlem Brundtland when the Labor Party returned to power in 1986.

The question of which party would be in power was obviously not the most decisive issue. The new policy of the Social Democrats was expressed in the program adopted in 1981. It is deeply symptomatic that the old formulation of the party program—"The goal of the Labor Party is a Socialist society"—was changed to "The Norwegian Labor Party builds its policy on the principles of Democratic Socialism." The man behind this new policy was Einar Førde, program committee chair, who was elected vice chair of the party in the same annual national meeting that ratified the program. "It is paradoxical that it was the former leftist oppositional Einar Førde who had to deck out Gro Harlem Brundtland's business-oriented pragmatism in ideological robes."[45] At the party's national assembly in 1987 Førde followed up with what has been called a rhetorical masterpiece of a speech: "We have to get rid of all the accusations that we are not market friendly. We are in favor of free competition where it serves the consumers and the people."[46] As a typical intellectual, Førde was a

---

[44] Jenny Andersson 2003, 109–110.
[45] Bjørgulf Braanen in *Klassekampen*, 28 September, 2004.
[46] Cited from Braanen, ibid.

strange bird inside the Norwegian Labor Party, but he played an important role in the changeover to a new policy. Perhaps it was precisely because he was a strange bird with a typically left-oriented radical background that he was able to play this role. It was difficult to fault him for having run errands for the bourgeoisie when he was advocating bourgeois policy.

As in Sweden, there was internal opposition in Norway. When the party program of 1984 was called "New Growth for Norway," it is not surprising that use of the word "growth" met with criticism. Both the leader of the La-bor Party youth organization and the Oslo branch of the party said that the idea of growth was negatively charged. The leadership got what it wanted, however. As noted in Brundtland's memoirs: "The Labor Party is the growth-oriented party. Are we to be ashamed of this?"[47] As in Sweden, there was talk of a new policy, introduced in parallel in the two countries. Carlsson's report and Førde's draft proposal for the party program were both advanced in 1981.

Both countries implemented a drastic and risky means of assisting the crisis-ridden industrial sector—namely, currency devaluation. In the autumn of 1977 the conservative government in Sweden devalued the currency by 10 percent. The following year the Social Democratic government of Norway devalued its currency by 8 percent. Following the election of 1982, the Swed-ish Social Democrats under Palme formed a new government and initiated a massive devaluation. It was intended to be 20 percent, but as a result of pressure, partly from Norway, it was "only" 16 percent.[48] The previous year Norway had acquired a non-Socialist government under Kåre Willoch, which followed a careful policy of devaluation. In 1986 Willoch had to hand the baton back to a Social Democratic government under Brundtland, which immediately set about instituting a currency devaluation of 10 percent.[49] The parallel with Sweden is striking. The devaluation policy, particularly that of Sweden, has been hotly debated. Devaluations have the character of solutions to crises when negotiation-based corporatist systems are working poorly. At the same time, they can contribute to undermining the very same systems by working in an inflationary manner.

The deregulation of the loans and credit market was equally dramatic. The "great release," as it has been called, took place in Norway on January 1, 1984, when the Willoch government lifted the loan and credit controls con-straining the banks and insurance companies. This rapidly led to a drastic, and unfortunate, expansion of credit, partly because Willoch did not manage to increase the interest rate while the Labor Party hesitated. Later, Willoch

---

[47] Brundtland 1997, 381–382.
[48] Elmbrant 1989, 261.
[49] Sejersted 2003a, 135.

Figure 15. Two of Social Democracy's leading politicians were women: Alva Myrdal, (middle, right) in Sweden and Gro Harlem Brundtland, (middle, left) in Norway. They belonged to different generations. Myrdal was an activist involved in forming the Social Democratic project during its hegemonic phase. She was an advisory cabinet minister for disarmament and member of a series of important commissions. Harlem Brundtland came to power after the hegemonic phase was over. From the late 1970s she was prime minister three times and led with a sure hand Social Democracy's adaptation to a new reality. Both occupied top international positions. The photo shows the two of them in Oslo in 1982 when Alva Myrdal won the Nobel Peace Prize. The two women are flanked by their husbands Arne Olav Brundtland (left) and Gunnar Myrdal (right). (Photo: Arbeiderbevegelsens arkiv.)

maintained that if Norges Bank (the Bank of Norway) had been in a more independent position it would have been able to increase the rate of interest and contribute to slowing down the "buying spree."[50] The Brundtland government that took over in 1986 raised interest rates and devalued the currency. The Labor Party insisted on slaughtering its own sacred cow—the low-interest policy—itself.

In Sweden the Social Democratic government of Ingvar Carlsson shortly followed Norway, dismantling credit controls via the so-called November Revolution in 1985.[51] The unfortunate outcome of the "great release" in Nor-

---

[50] Sejersted 2003a, 137, 140.
[51] Torsten Svensson 2001, 82.

way had been noted by the Swedish finance minister, Kjell-Olof Feldt, who "felt that the Bank of Sweden had learned from the Norwegian mistake."[52] But this was not the case, at least according to Carlsson. In Sweden, too, there was a regrettable expansion of credit, for which Carlsson largely blamed the Riksbanken (the Bank of Sweden, which was more independent than the Bank of Norway), feeling that it had propelled deregulation and failed to effectively control interest in the first phase.[53] The Swedish case indicates that Willoch was wrong when he said that the results would have been better if the Bank of Norway had had a tight grip on the reins in Norway. The deregulation policy was an important part of the third way policy. It indicated a drastic change from the previous hallmark of Social Democratic policy, and even though the deregulation was undertaken in a very unfortunate manner, the new policy had come to stay.

The privatization wave of the 1980s and 1990s also reached Scandinavia. The most spectacular result was the transformation of state-run monopolies within the field of public service (telecommunication, postal service, and so forth) into state-owned companies competing on the free market. Parts of these companies were subsequently sold to private interests. In 2001 the Social Democratic government in Norway also undertook a partial privatization of the big state-owned company Statoil. But after that point the privatization wave died out. It was never very substantial, since socialization had never been a preferred political strategy in the Scandinavian Social Democracies. (At present [2008] the trend is ambiguous; the non-Socialist Swedish government has taken initiatives for a further privatization, whereas the Social Democratic government in Norway is about to develop a more active ownership policy. Characteristically, the question has arisen as to whether the [partly state-owned] Norwegian telecommunication company shall buy the [partly state-owned] Swedish telecommunication company.)

Extensive taxation reforms came to both countries around 1990. These reforms have to be viewed in relation to the deregulation and internationalization of the 1980s and the global wave of tax reforms that came at the end of the 1980s, inspired by the American tax reform of 1986. The aim of these reforms had been to simplify the tax systems in order to avoid unintentional consequences and to become compatible with international developments. Taxation of capital was lowered, as were income taxes in general and marginal taxes in particular. The consequences, according to Sven Steinmo, were that "capital was given more freedom and the tax burden was redistributed downward."[54] This means that the reductions were compensated in many

[52] I. Carlsson 2003, 217.
[53] I. Carlsson 2003, 306f.
[54] Steinmo 1993, 179.

countries (particularly in countries such as Sweden and Norway) by boosting the consumption taxation. The low level of corporate taxation in Sweden was intended to lock up profits in the corporations. The system had functioned well for a long time, but during the economic downturn in the 1970s it only contributed to an unhealthy preservation of existing structures. Capital required more flexibility if Sweden was to maintain its competitiveness.

The tax reforms were in the direction of what the non-Socialists and the business community stood for, and they constituted the death of whatever "taxation Socialism" had existed. Nonetheless, to a great extent it was the Social Democrats who brought about this reorganization. In Sweden, Minister of Finance Kjell-Olof Feldt was mainly responsible for the "tax reform of the century." It is characteristic of this policy readjustment that Feldt, enthusiastic over the tactical challenges posed by the new orientation, could say, "We have expropriated the bourgeoisie's top issue—now Social Democracy has become the great reform party on the taxation front."[55] And Prime Minister Carlsson noted that "for the most part the bourgeoisie was astonished and impressed that the Social Democrats were prepared to go so far and take such a strong hold as we did."[56] As in Norway, there were apparently no scruples against stealing the opponents' policies. The marginal tax rate was reduced but, most remarkably, the Social Democrats went along with a significant reduction in the tax on capital gains.

One of the reasons that the Social Democrats took the initiative for taxation reform was that the old system was riddled with loopholes. As it was stated in the Norwegian Parliament, taxation should be according to ability to pay, not according to desire.[57] Nevertheless, it was once again possible to save, and legitimate to be a capitalist.

The new Swedish economic policy took another turn as the mild European economic setback in the early 1990s was significantly compounded in Sweden. The years from 1991 to 1993 became known as the "years of the black-of-night crisis."[58] It began with economic pressure on the Swedish krone. In an effort to support the krone, the Riksbanken undertook a dramatic increase in the interest rate, which contributed to an increase in bankruptcies and a dramatic increase in unemployment. The state intervened with extensive support for the large banks. Deficits soared in the Swedish state budget. The krone had to be allowed to float free in 1992, leading to a powerful fall in its value—in effect, a new "devaluation." The war of the roses was brought to an end, but not without leaving some scars. The general mood of crisis made it possible to intervene with political initiatives. The ambitious employment

---

[55] Uddhammar 1993, 327.
[56] I. Carlsson 2003, 272.
[57] St. forh. (Parl. Proceedings) 1990–1991, S. Tid. 95.
[58] *Svenska Dagbladet*, 14 September 2004.

policy was abandoned. as the policy had been "adapted to the European norm that developed during the 1980s, with unemployment levels of more than 10 percent."[59] Equally dramatic was the fact that in 1994 Sweden gave up much of the ATP system (the General Supplementary Pension), and it joined the European Union—both occurrences being directly related to the crisis.

SUCCESSFUL POLICY?

In the short term, the new economic policy in Sweden was hardly a success in economic terms. The question, however, is whether, in the broader perspective, it led to structural conversion that could point the way out of the crisis situation. Lars Magnusson leans in the direction that "the pressure for conversion" in the 1980s was too low.[60] On the other hand, Lennart Schön shows that during the 1980s extensive direct foreign investments were made, and export profits were high: "The usual picture of the 1980s as Sweden's decade of extravagance needs a reliable retouching."[61] In particular he points out that it was during the 1980s that a basis was laid for a decisive breakthrough for Swedish initiatives in new areas of growth—electronics and pharmaceuticals. Among others, the great industrial locomotive, the telecommunications firm L. M. Ericsson, grew with great force during the 1980s and 1990s after a restructuring crisis in the 1970s.[62]

Schön's conclusions are weakened, however, by the fact that L. M. Ericsson ran into a new deep crisis when the information technology bubble burst after the turn of the millennium, that is, right after Schön's book was published. Ericsson had to reduce its size significantly. The pharmaceutical industry also fell into difficulties. Foreign owners acquired dominant shares in the large firms of Pharmacia and Astra and moved their headquarters out of Sweden. All this occurred following the dismantling of the steel industry and shipbuilding. At this point in time the automobile industry was also under threat; in 1999 the Volvo passenger vehicle branch was sold to Ford, and the following year Saab Automobile was sold to General Motors. The crisis had reached the core of Swedish industry. All the large industrial concerns that had brought Sweden into the leading position among modern industrial nations were now profoundly affected.

Schön spoke too soon when he issued a certificate of good health to Swedish industry. Yet there were signs that today confirm his point—the crisis was

---

[59] Schön 2000, 507.
[60] Magnusson 1997, 497.
[61] Schön 2000, 501.
[62] Schön 2000, 513.

the condition for restructuring and renewed growth. In the period between 1998 and 2003, wages increased less in Sweden than in most other European countries, with the result that industrial workers' wages in Sweden came to be around the average for Europe. More important, however, the increase in Sweden's industrial productivity during this period was among the highest in Europe, which implies that productivity increased more rapidly than wages in Sweden. If Sweden has lost its leading position, the country is thus prepared for competition.

In Norway, which has been able to surf on an ocean of oil, the situation has been different. During the above-mentioned period, only Ireland has seen a greater wage increase than Norway. But Ireland began at a much lower level. Norway is ranked at the top when it comes to wage levels for industrial labor, ahead of Germany. The productivity increase in the manufacturing industries is lower than in Sweden.[63] Norway is ranked above Sweden, however, in increased productivity in the service sector.[64] The financial crisis of 2007–2008 hit Sweden hard, whereas Norway has managed surprisingly well.

A DIFFICULT MODERNITY

Environmental problems secured a place on the agenda during the 1970s. The modern industrial state came under attack from many directions, and criticism penetrated to the core of the great modernization project—energy production. Norway and Sweden met the problems in somewhat different ways, but policy was seriously affected in both countries. New divisions appeared, generating changes of government in both countries. The shift was rather dramatic as the time of optimistic and unproblematic investment in an increasingly more energy-intensive society came to an end. New worries arose about developments in general, but this did not mean that the old policy of growth and welfare was abandoned—it was pursued, but without the old optimism and joy.

On the other hand, these new worries ran together with a new (optimistic) faith that it was possible to control the development of technology. Technology was no longer seen as the "the strongest force for social development." The development of nuclear energy has been viewed as the first real example of political influence exerted over technological development.[65] Technological determinism gave way as a representative form of development; at the same

---

[63] The report *I Takt med Europa*, prepared by the trade unions within Swedish industry. Referred to in *Svenska Dagbladet*, 10 March 2004.

[64] Annual Report, Bank of International Settlements, referred to in *Dagens Næringsliv*, 29 June 2004.

[65] Sejersted 2002c, 260–261.

time, a new skepticism or distrust of experts arose. The environmental movement made use of opposing experts, and the partly scandalous ways in which the two governments had used experts were publicly exposed.[66]

In other words, we see a tendency toward (re)politicizing the development of important areas in society. In this way a dispute arose over what kind of society we ought to be turning toward—a new struggle between traditionalists and modernists, or perhaps a struggle over the content of the concept of modernity. Has the time passed for Social Democracy's "power Socialism" and the high-energy society? Does this mean we are in the process of abdicating the role of modern industrial nation, or can we talk about an "ecological modernity" based on energy conservation and uses of different sources of energy?[67] Time will tell whether the premises for this debate will change gradually as technology changes. And this applies not only to the development of alternative energy sources but also to further development of the traditional energy sources: nuclear power and natural gas energy.

The new challenges for the Social Democratic economic order did not arise solely from environmental demands but also from the general development of economic cycles and the globalization of the economy. The opportunities for dealing with these were quite different in the two countries once Norway became a petroleum nation—immediately becoming rich owing to the high oil prices that followed the oil shock. Conversely, Sweden ran into profound structural problems and lost its leading position as the rich, industrial model country. Both countries experience new limitations to the freedom of political action. In parallel with the above-mentioned repoliticization of technological development, we see an opposing tendency toward a subordination of politics to the demands of the internationally exposed economy.

As indicated earlier, the crisis of the established Social Democratic order in the 1970s and the new direction taken in the 1980s affected society more deeply than hitherto described. In the following chapters we shall look at the changes in various societal sectors. From the political perspective it was a question of how to save the core values of Social Democracy or the Scandinavian model.

---

[66] Nilsen 2001, 169, 172, 176.
[67] This expression is used by Anshelm 2000, 490.

CHAPTER 12

What Happened to Economic Democracy?

Corporatism under Pressure • Nevertheless, a Change of Model? • Industrial Democracy •
Self-determination • Wage Earner Funds—a Radical Move • Weakened Administrative
Corporatism • Labor Power for a Better Competitive Edge • Social Democracy in a
Globalized Economy • A Weak Milieu of Private Ownership • State Ownership •
An Ambiguous Development

CORPORATISM UNDER PRESSURE

Economic democracy, or the limiting of proprietary power in the economic sphere, had been a theme throughout the twentieth century. The Social Democratic order was distinguished by the fact that one had come close to a mutual understanding on where the line ought to be drawn. Gradually there was, however, a rising demand for renegotiation of this mutual understanding or "contract."

Social Democratic regimes in Sweden and Norway were noted for strong trade union organizations and far-reaching corporatist systems that had, on the whole, worked well. At the beginning of the 1970s, however, circumstances arose that would gradually lead to considerable changes regarding relations in working life. The economic downturn of the period was one important factor behind these events, but there were other factors as well. We have seen how the strong position of the LO was challenged in both countries by the organizations of salaried employees who were not under the LO umbrella. With the crumbling of the class society as a cultural construct, new bonds of loyalty arose. In addition, internationalization and globalization began to pose new challenges. We shall follow four different aspects of these developments: the state of negotiative corporatism (inherited from the Saltsjöbad Agreement and the Main Agreement); the growth of industrial democracy; the rise of participatory democracy, or self-determination in the workplace; and, finally, the weakening of administrative corporatism.

In Norway the economic downturn led to extensive demands before the wage negotiations in 1974.[1] The moderate line of the LO was challenged by the left within the labor movement, which prepared for conflict. The Social Democratic government barely managed to salvage the wage contract by way of an extremely generous package including, for example, a reduction of taxes and increased food subsidies.[2] The result was the strongest wage increase ever seen (25 percent, including local supplements). In practice, the state paid about half of the disbursements. The following year saw the move for farmers to secure incomes that were in line with those of industrial workers—an extremely costly plan. This was the period of countercyclical policy, when the government, "with the active use of the state apparatus, tried to compensate not only for weakening markets and the lack of competitive power but also for a lack of confidence between both parties: between the grass roots and the leadership in the labor movement, and especially between voters and the party."[3]

By nature such policy was situation dependent, and toward the end of the 1970s the countercyclical policy was abandoned, which, among other things, meant that the two sides in working life were increasingly left to themselves. Things were not going well, and in 1979 Parliament undertook a wage and price freeze. "This involved an ongoing suspension of the whole negotiation economy and, as far as it went, formed the prelude to the criticism that arose during the 1980s."[4] Two years later the right to negotiate was returned to the opposing parties in the workplace, but it proved difficult to get wage developments under control. In 1986 the Employers Association tried to show strength by calling a major lockout. This became a fiasco, resulting in a generous wage increase for the LO and a change in leadership for the Employers Association. The employers were too weak to play their role in the wage struggle and, without the moderating role of the state, the developments had gone out of control.[5] Thus the state had to intervene again to regulate wage developments.[6]

Around 1990 Norway was threatened with massive unemployment for the first time since World War II. The situation thrust what was called "the solidarity alternative" to the fore. First and foremost this alternative implied solidarity with the unemployed.[7] In a climate of mutual understanding, the

---

[1] Heiret et al. 2003, 165.
[2] This was the first of what were called the "Kleppe packages"; cf. Kleppe 2003, 240f.
[3] Heiret et al. 2003, 174.
[4] Nordby 1994, 70.
[5] Heiret et al. 2003, 184.
[6] Heiret et al. 2003, 191.
[7] Bjørnhaug et al. 2000, 110f.

main organizations and the government attached the solidarity concept to the policy regarding the wage agreement system. In principle, employment and internal stability were to be secured through the use of countercyclical policy tools, while inflation would be kept in check and the ability to compete would be secured through moderate wage increases. The result was a significant improvement in market competitiveness. There has been a degree of discussion about what led to the favorable economic developments of the 1990s. Was it the solidarity alternative, or was it the Brundtland government's new economic policy? In any case, the traditional Norwegian model, with the state as the third party, was now reestablished, and with good results. As has been pointed out by Jan Heiret, Norwegian Social Democracy showed itself to be robust, at least when it came to the central model for cooperation between the parties involved in working life.[8] This meant that Norway still possessed one of the most corporatist and centrally coordinated economies in the world.[9]

The 1970s were marked by sharp conflicts in Sweden as well. These were dominated by the LO's 1971 proposal regarding the wage earners' fund. This in itself affected the capitalist system and will be treated below, but it is important to keep it in mind since the proposition contributed powerfully to the warlike atmosphere during the 1970s. The OPEC shock and the subsequent depression led to an expansive economic policy that contributed "first to a profits explosion in 1973–1974 and then a wage explosion in 1975–1975—the most conspicuous failure of centralized negotiations to gear wage change to changing economic conditions."[10] The social economy had gone out of control.[11]

In 1976 the non-Socialist parties in Sweden formed a government, and in 1980 they entered a great confrontation over the wage agreement. It was obvious from the outset that a compromise settlement was needed if developments were to be brought back under control. From both sides, but particularly from the employers, a demand arose for the government to step in as a third party in the negotiations, as in Norway. But the level of mistrust was high, especially the employees' mistrust of the new bourgeois government, which had tried what Olof Palme called "a clumsy leap into the labor market."[12] This leap did not seem to cool tempers, and the employers opted for a major lockout. As a result, costs expanded exponentially. Control was not reestablished, and the outcome of the conflict was almost catastrophic for

---

[8] Heiret et al. 2003, 196f.
[9] Dølvik and Martin 2000, 280.
[10] Dølvik and Martin 2000, 300.
[11] Nycander 2002, 178.
[12] Socialdemokratiska partistyrelsens protokoll 28/3-1980. Quoted by Nycander 2002, 188.

employers. In addition, the government had been humbled. The conflict had clear ideological overtones and was reminiscent of the conflicts in the inter-war period. It was, as Nycander says, a struggle regarding "on whose premise Sweden should be run."[13]

In 1982 the Social Democrats regained control of the government, but the problems continued. "The tendencies toward disintegration in the Swedish negotiation system appeared clearly during the period 1982–1986."[14] There was also movement toward decentralizing the negotiations. This was partly due to pressure from the strong multinational corporations.[15] Kjell-Olof Feldt tried continually to draw the government in as a third party. One might say that Sweden in the 1970s and 1980s tried to institute a tripartite model that followed the pattern of Norway, Denmark, and Finland. But these attempts unleashed a wave of protest, primarily from the LO, and the government had to pull back.

Meanwhile, as economic crisis threatened in 1991, a stabilization agreement was undertaken (commonly referred to as the "Rehnberg action"). It included 111 interested parties and forbade local negotiations in 1992, among other things.[16] This agreement did not actually bring the government into negotiations as a third party, but it did indicate a breakthrough for the government insofar as government gained strong influence on decisions concerning what the economy could tolerate, along with responsibility for providing the exhaustive statistics that informed these decisions. "Both sides felt as though they had been placed under the charge of a guardian," according to Svante Nycander.[17] But control was regained. This happened about the same time as the establishment of the solidarity agreement in Norway. Under the threat of crisis, both countries managed to improve control over wage developments.

But the old questions remained in Sweden: should there be more centralization or less; should there be a dual model or a tripartite model; should settlements be based on negotiations or legislation?[18] In 1997, under a vision of the "black-of-night crisis," the stabilization agreement was followed up with the Cooperative Agreement on Industrial Development and Wage Formation. The agreement, which proved to be successful, was signed by twelve employer organizations and seven trade unions.[19] In the wake of the agreement an arbitration institute was established. With regard to wage developments,

[13] Nycander 2002, 188–190, 196.
[14] Nils Elvander. Cited from Nycander 2002, 204.
[15] Dølvik and Stokke 1998, 138.
[16] Heiret et al. 2003, 211; Nycander 2002, 208f.
[17] Nycander 2002, 211.
[18] Dølvik and Martin 2000, 309.
[19] Dølvik and Martin 2000, 310; Elvander 2002, 130.

there was a return to what had been, in its major features, the Swedish model. Sweden still has probably the strongest and most vital system for reaching agreements between labor and capital in Europe—without state intervention. And so far Swedish Social Democracy has revealed itself to be robust. After a period of restive wage developments, a well-functioning negotiative corporatism was successfully reestablished in both countries.

NEVERTHELESS, A CHANGE OF MODEL?

When it came to other features of working-life relations (for example, industrial democracy and work environment), we see a clear tendency in Sweden to get around corporatism by way of comprehensive legislation. It is a large step from the Saltsjöbad Agreement, based on free negotiations, to the legislative road of the 1970s. As the sociologist Carl von Otter writes, "Viewed from an international perspective, from being a country with unusually light regulatory intervention by law, Sweden today has ended up in the leading group."[20] And Svante Nycander treats this phenomenon under the title "When Sweden Changed Its Model of Society."

It has been generally maintained in the Swedish debate that the trade unions were the force that pushed for more legislation, "taking advantage of the Social Democrat–controlled state as an instrument."[21] But if this were so, the shift would have occurred earlier, when Social Democracy actually controlled the state. Nycander feels that the initiative did not come from the trade unions, however, but rather from the Social Democratic Party, particularly from Olof Palme himself. The offensive was political in orientation rather than trade unionist.[22] The LO was more closely tied to the old system, while the party needed issues with which to build its profile. The effect of the Kiruna strike and Palme's own engagement in issues relating to the work environment played a large role. Tampering with the old system, however, was not without cost. Nycander believes it was ill fated: "Relations in the labor market were severely damaged in the 1970s. The more the state took control of the rules of the game, the weaker the incentive became for the parties to come to an agreement. That the SAF [the employers' organization] began to consider strong employee organizations as something negative was fatal from the trade union point of view. The older LO members understood what was going on but were incapable of standing up to the pressure from the political

[20] Cited by Nycander 2002, 312.
[21] Nycander 2002, 296.
[22] Nycander 2002, 300.

side."[23] In Sweden the harmonious relationship between the different parties in working life was undermined in the 1970s, as was the relationship between these parties and the state.

INDUSTRIAL DEMOCRACY

Democratization of the economic sphere was an old demand, and it remained in evidence throughout the Social Democratic period. No resolution was found insofar as the system by and large retained its capitalistic features. One prominent proposal was to allow employee participation in the decision-making process. Such industrial democracy had long been a recurring theme, revived again in the 1960s. An ambiguous concept, it was viewed with skepticism by both employees and employers. On the one hand, it implied transferring a degree of decision-making competence to the company employees, which meant limiting the traditional decision-making authority of owners and managers. On the other hand, industrial democracy linked the employees more closely to the firm, fostering a feeling that everyone in the firm, leaders as well as workers, was "in the same boat." The employers looked on the limiting of their authority with misgivings, and on the new loyalty with sympathy, while for the trade unions it was the reverse. For them leadership participation led to double loyalties: one had to sit on both sides of the table.

The established policy, represented by the Saltsjöbad Agreement in Sweden and the Main Agreement in Norway, was a different system in principle. It was premised on a division into two parts, employees and employers, each linked to its own larger organization *beyond* the firm; loyalty was not primarily to the company but rather to class and trade union. There was also a clear boundary between the exclusive domains of the employers and the questions that could be solved through negotiated collective agreements. It was this negotiative corporatism that was adopted by Social Democracy. Nonetheless, this system was deemed unsatisfactory from a democratic perspective, and codetermination, giving the employees a voice in the decision-making process, remained a theme for discussion throughout the Social Democratic period. But it was only with the weakening of class-based loyalties around 1970 that plans for workers' participation in the decision-making process were first realized.

In 1953 the proposal concerning employee representation on company boards of directors was placed on the Norwegian Labor Party agenda. This must be viewed as an expression of a need for a radical alibi following the

[23] Nycander 2002, 314.

party retreat on the issue of price controls and the rationalization laws. The employers' reaction was not altogether negative. Following pressure from the LO, the proposal was removed from the Labor Party's 1957 program. The issue was kept warm on both sides, however. In the 1960s we can trace an international trend toward endorsement of industrial democracy. Industrial democracy reflected a common spirit of cooperation and was deemed conducive to increased productivity.

In 1968 the non-Socialist coalition government in Norway set up a broad-based committee to look into the question. A large majority supported legislation in favor of employee representation. Within the Conservative Party it became clear that property-owning democracy could not satisfy the demand for economic democracy. A committee composed of representatives from both the party and the trade unions was established within the labor movement. The committee called for an industrial democracy based on a "supervisory board" with one-third of its membership elected by the employees. The supervisory board had the authority to choose the board of directors, of which employees could make up a maximum of one-third. Following the resignation of the Conservative government in 1972, a proposal was put forward by the new Social Democratic government. Before the year was out, the law regarding employee participation in management was ratified, complete with concrete proposals from the Labor Party and LO as to the forms this representation would take.

In principle, these actions paralleled developments in Sweden. Both sides hesitated. In the Swedish situation the Liberal Party, represented particularly by Sven Wedén, was the driving force. At the outset the two sides, the LO and the SAF, wanted an agreement on the issue, but negotiations dragged on. In 1971 the SAF issued a statement that it could not decide in the matter on behalf of the companies. Marcus Wallenberg, among others, was in agreement. One of the central board members of the SAF felt that this was one of the most ill-conceived decisions the association had ever taken.[24] Despite this setback, the employees' representation was not particularly controversial at this point in time. In the end, the Social Democrats took up the initiative and, as in Norway, it was ratified into law in 1972. This action prepared the way for direct employee representation in management, with the right to have two representatives in companies with more than one hundred employees.

While in Norway the law gave employees themselves the right to direct representation, in Sweden this right was given to the trade unions.[25] Although the specific approaches of the countries and political parties differed, this

[24] Eijle Mossberg. Reported by Nycander 2002, 238.
[25] Nycander 2002, 311.

should not overshadow the fact that, in principle, there was broad political agreement on the right of employees to representation in the leading organs of management. Most remarkable is the fact that it became acceptable to sit on both sides of the table, a potentially problematic position.

SELF-DETERMINATION

There were two aspects to democracy in the workplace. One had to do with representative democracy—representation in the decision-making organs—as we have seen. The other had to do with the limit of these organs' decision-making competence in relation to individual self-determination at ground level, that is, to the individual's right to decide on appropriate actions in carrying out his/her assigned duties and maintaining personal well-being. This was a central feature of the complex of problems around work relations that had been placed on the agenda in the 1960s. Even though there had been a certain degree of dispute about self-determination for most of the twentieth century, the employer's right to direct and organize the work was an established right recognized in the old Saltsjöbad/Main Agreement complex. Attacking this point was just as radical as proposing employee representation in the decision-making organs.

Attention toward work relations became noticeably sharper during the 1960s. In Norway this gained strength in 1962 following a mining accident at King's Bay, on the Arctic island of Svalbard, in which twenty-one people were killed. The accident led to the problematization of state-owned industrial operations, a crisis of government, and the resulting rise of the first non-Socialist government since the 1930s. But it especially led to directing sharper attention to working conditions, that is, to such things as safety and security, health and well-being, and opportunities for individual development and a degree of self-determination sufficient to engender self-respect. It was thought that there had been excessive concentration on issues of production and rationalization (by the state and trade unions alike) and on the question of distribution (wages), attention that detracted from movement toward improving working conditions.

As in so many other questions, it seems that this new awareness of working conditions hit Sweden with greater force than Norway. "The great triggering factor for political engagement in working-life environmental questions" was the large LKAB strike in Kiruna, in the north of Sweden, at the end of 1969 and the beginning of 1970.[26] The Kiruna strike was not the only one of its

---

[26] Johansson and Magnusson 1998, 156.

kind, but it garnered the greatest attention. The number of wildcat strikes increased from close to 120,000 strike days in 1966–1968 to almost 400,000 days in the following three-year period. The Kiruna strike was illegal, but owing to extensive media coverage it received great sympathy; "thus a great middle-class consciousness was for the first time confronted by the working conditions of manual labor."[27] A research project on the working conditions at the Kiruna mine had actually been set in motion prior to the strike, giving the researchers a unique opportunity to follow the strike and examine its causes. The conclusion of the researchers was "not very flattering for the Saltsjöbad Agreement."[28]

The collaborative organs that were institutionalized under Social Democracy had little effect in shaping the workplace milieu. The right to direct the work at ground level had not been given a central place on trade union agendas, nor had control of the work process.[29] Not only had the uneven sharing of power between workers and employers continued to stand as it was, but in some cases the one-sided concentration on questions of productivity and rationalization had led to worsening working conditions. The criticism of working conditions also affected the principle of voluntary agreements. It became normal to maintain that improvements to working conditions should be a subject for legislation, not for employer-employee agreements. These signals were quickly intercepted. In 1970 the Swedish Parliament was engaged in a far-reaching debate that would become "the prelude to the labor market legislation that would be carried out in the 1970s, implying a move beyond the collaborative and Salsjöbad policy that dominated the labor market political scene during the three previous decades."[30]

During the 1960s the Norwegian Norsk Hydro company experimented internally with autonomous work groups in the workplace, giving workers more control over their own work process. The experiment was based on a collaboration between the company management and the LO. Moreover, it was an attempt to meet the criticism that had been raised against Taylorism and time-and-motion studies in the workplace. The Norsk Hydro project, testing "the democratic theory of organizational change," was led by Einar Thorsrud and gradually attracted international attention.[31] To a significant degree the interest in these efforts lay in the employers' camp, and early on the project was described positively in the Swedish newspaper *Arbetsgivaren*

[27] Nycander 2002, 228.
[28] Johannsson and Magnusson 1998, 156.
[29] Nycander 2002, 234.
[30] Johansson and Magnusson 1998, 159.
[31] Gustavsen 1992.

(The Employer).[32] That is to say, the aim of managerial effectiveness was given at least as much weight as the aim of democratization.

All these cooperative efforts seem to have had greater practical significance in Sweden than in Norway. As early as the end of the 1960s efforts were made in Sweden to develop "alternative forms of organizing work" at Volvo, where principles were established for a production system at the new factory in Kalmar in 1974 and in Uddevalla in 1989. The Kalmar factory was "the first of its type in the world and it showed that there were functional alternatives to the traditional rigid, steady, conveyor-belt production."[33] One could hardly speak of a general breakthrough for such self-directed groups. The system faced criticism: first, that it was inefficient and, second, that it ignored power relations and was thus not very democratic.[34]

In 1993 Volvo closed down the two plants. In this connection the newpaper *Börsveckan* (Stock Market Weekly) described the production effort as "a social experiment in the best 1970s style," one that now provided "the ultimate confirmation of the Volvo leadership's total incompetence." Christian Berggren's investigations come to the opposite conclusion, however. In his view, the Kalmar factory excelled "in terms of process development, quality, and capacity to deal with changes in models."[35] The experimental factories influenced a more gradual, step-by-step development of the production processes within the overall Volvo corporation. It can also be argued that the cooperative experiments had a positive indirect significance for the work environment legislation in both countries during the 1970s.

The many pieces of legislation on working-life conditions that came out in the latter half of the 1970s were just as important as the laws regarding employee representation. In Norway the Working Environment Act of 1977 represented a radical leap. In paragraph 12 of the law it states first that "[t]echnology, work organization, agreements on working hours, and wage systems should be worked out such that the employees are not subjected to unfortunate physical or psychic strains, nor are their opportunities for attention to issues of safety allowed to deteriorate. The conditions should be such that employees are given reasonable opportunity for professional or personal development through their work." When it came to the organizing of the actual work, the law states that account is to be "taken of the individual employee's opportunity for self-determination and professional responsibility," and that

---

[32] Nycander 2002, 225.
[33] Johansson and Magnusson 1998, 169. Citation from Parl. Proceedings.
[34] Gustavsen 1992, 110.
[35] Berggren 1993, 52.

"monotonous, repetitive work" and work that prevents the employee "him/herself from varying the tempo of work" should be avoided. Furthermore, the employee should participate in devising systems for carrying out the work, and wage incentive plans should not be used where they "can have a substantial impact on safety."

Sweden brought about the Employment Protection Act in 1974, the important Codetermination Act (Medbestämmandelagen, MBL) in 1976, and a Work Environment Act in 1978. The MBL gave employees the right of access to information about the firm and stipulated negotiations toward larger changes in the firm affecting working conditions. Beyond this, it was assumed that the codetermination process would be developed in detail through negotiations.[36] We see that legislation did not replace negotiative processes as much as it provided a framework for such processes. As was common during this period, in Sweden the rights prescribed by the laws were linked to trade union membership, while in Norway they were linked to employment.[37] In general the regulation of the work process and the working environment found a vaguer and more general expression in the Swedish laws. Its legal basis was consequently weaker. It was not until the revision of the Work Environment Act in 1991 that Sweden got provisions similar to paragraph 12 in the Norwegian Work Environment Act of 1977. From then on, the legal basis was the same in both countries.[38] And here as well we see a convergence. At the outset Norway had been a little ahead of Sweden with regard to legally binding obligations, while Sweden had been somewhat ahead when it came to worker participation. Protection against dismissal had been strongest in Norway, where a law was passed on this issue in 1936. It is symptomatic of the bipartite model of Sweden that this had not been subject to legislation but was part of the agreement system. It was not until 1974 that corresponding legislation was enacted there. Thus by following each other's example the two countries ended up with quite similar systems with regard to work relations.

We have followed the new attention paid to the work environment, or "the good job" (*det goda arbetet*, as it was described in Sweden).[39] Earlier we referred to Ingrid Millbourn's book *The Right to Ease and Comfort*. There she describes the conflict within the early labor movement between the ideal of the disciplined worker in the efficient large firm and the ideal of decentralization and self-determination as a strategy for well-being and liberation. This contradiction has always existed within the

---

[36] Johansson and Magnusson 1998, 186; Andersen and Hoff 2001, 118.

[37] Nycander 2002, 311.

[38] Gustavsen 1992, 26.

[39] Johansson and Magnusson 1998, 168.

Social Democratic movement. There has been internal opposition to the predominant technocratic way of thinking and the strong reliance on industrialization, an opposition that holds to an alternative conception of modernization.

This internal opposition was stronger in Norway and was in some circumstances linked to the name of Johan Nygaardsvold. It found its clearest expression in fishery and agricultural policy. The new attention to working conditions within industry implied an element of protest, rooted in this alternative concept of modernization. The efficient organization of work was naturally a means for creating the material basis for the good life. But the good life was not something to be achieved solely outside the workplace; it also had to be brought about through security and well-being in the work situation, or through "the good job."

WAGE EARNER FUNDS—A RADICAL MOVE

With the wage earner fund proposal, the Swedish labor movement appeared to be "on the threshold of a fundamental programmatic shift in which the organization of capitalist production would be challenged once again," wrote Gösta Esping-Andersen in 1985. The Norwegian labor movement had concentrated on industrial democracy and legislation regarding working life, but it did not have radical plans regarding economic democracy in line with those of the Swedish wage earner funds, according to Esping-Andersen.[40] Although it looked as if the time was ripe in Sweden for a large step toward some form of Socialist society, this move was unsuccessful. The reaction would be at least as spectacular as the original move: "With the threat of the fund as its great enemy, the bourgeois bloc was able to forget its petty quarrels and, led by the business community, it united as the great non-Socialist political alternative in Sweden."[41]

The proposal for the funds arose in the LO Congress of 1971. The idea, in one form or another, of collective capital accumulation in the hands of employees was not new. At the Swedish LO Congress of 1961, for example, a motion had been put forward regarding a fund for branch rationalization.[42] But the motion had floundered. The trade unions exhibited no interest in changing the role of the private owner in business life.[43] In their view, the Saltsjöbad system was functioning well enough.

[40] Esping-Andersen 1985, 291.
[41] Johansson and Magnusson 1998, 210.
[42] Johansson and Magnusson 1998, 191.
[43] Nycander 2002, 322.

By the beginning of the 1970s, however, the dysfunctional features of the old system were becoming visible. As we have seen, the restraint of the solidarity wage policy had yielded great profits to parts of the economy, the so-called "windfall profits" (*övervinsterna*). At the same time, the long period of growth and full employment had been replaced by the insecurity accompanying a new economic downturn. One could no longer have faith that the capitalists would maintain a level of investment sufficient for supporting full employment. This occurred simultaneously with the general radicalization that awakened the old desire for a socialized leadership of the economy. In contrast to earlier times, therefore, the wage earner fund propositions now resulted in a positive response within the LO. A small group was given the task of preparing a proposal, and it was the LO economist Rudolf Meidner who set the tone.

The group's proposal, published in 1975, included obligatory seizure of profits that would be converted directly into shares. These were to be assigned to employee collectives that would thereupon develop their *proprietary power*: "The wage earner funds will take over an increasingly large proportion of ownership in the individual enterprises. The speed with which the funds eat into ownership is naturally affected by how large a portion of the profit is to be placed in the fund."[44] This proposal was "almost dumbfounding in its radicalism." It was also presented in a radical rhetoric that bordered on the revolutionary: "We will dispossess the old owners of capital of their power, which they exercise through the force of their ownership." Individual obligatory saving was under discussion but was brushed aside as social romanticism and a petit bourgeois mode of thinking.[45] The goal was not primarily to access capital but to attack individual proprietary power. The proposal for such collectivization of ownership strongly affected the attitude of the Employers Association toward the LO and corporatism—as the employers little by little realized what was happening.

The Palme government had broken with the policy of negotiations on a number of legislative initiatives in areas such as the working environment and codetermination, proposing laws instead. The Social Democratic Party had thus entered the sphere of the LO. The proposal concerning wage earner funds, however, was at first a purely LO initiative—and on a question that, compared with the working environment issues, was oriented more toward politics than toward the trades or professions. The cards were shuffled, and all this came on top of the government being on a collision course with the LO on the question of employment.

[44] Cited by Johansson and Magnusson 1998, 194.
[45] Nycander 2002, 325–326.

Initially the party leadership was skeptical, but not dismissive, toward the wage earner funds, and some movement in that direction became evident in the party program, albeit vaguely worded and without obligation. But at the LO Congress of 1976 the tension was obvious. Following the congress, Palme actually distanced himself from all types of plans relating to wage earner funds that would impart a dominant economic power to the trades and professions via employee ownership.[46] The loss of the election that same year was attributed in part to unemployment problems and partly to the opposition leader Fälldin's move regarding the question of nuclear energy. The proposal regarding the wage earner funds must also take some of the blame, however. It was not supported by public opinion.[47] Palme's biographer maintains that following the election the very idea of the funds became "almost physically repugnant to Olof Palme."[48]

Yet it had become necessary to effect coordination between the party and the central trade union organization, so a joint investigative group was appointed. In 1978 the group brought out a somewhat modified version of the wage earner funds proposal, and at the party congress of that same year Palme took the issue into his own hands, charging that "a constructive solution to the question of wage earner funds is crucial to favorable economic and social development for Sweden during the 1980s and 1990s." But it had to be better defined, and a new investigative committee was appointed, this time under Kjell-Olof Feldt. The party had taken control: Feldt became the movement's external spokesman, and Meidner was excluded. The funds were now cast not primarily as a Socialist experiment in collective ownership but rather as a necessary initiative for securing the flow of capital into the economy.

In 1981 the Feldt group came out with a proposal that the Social Democrats took to the polls the following year. This was "a much watered down proposal that had nothing much in common with the radical line that had been launched in 1975–76."[49] Even so, Nycander maintains that it "aimed at a far-reaching, system-changing collectivization of proprietorship."[50] After the election Palme tried, in the old spirit of compromise, to involve the business community and the non-Socialist parties in talks. Time had run out for that type of compromise, however. Nonetheless, the proposition that was put forward in 1983 was modified yet again. There were to be five funds set up within the ATP system. They would be financed by means of taxation on

[46] Johansson and Magnusson 1998, 203.
[47] Nycander 2002, 337.
[48] Elmbrant 1989, 210.
[49] Johansson and Magnusson 1998, 209.
[50] Nycander 2002, 368.

Figure 16. Seventy-five thousand protesters demonstrated against the wage earner funds in Stockholm on October 4, 1987. It was said that this was the first time that corporate executives joined a protest march. The wage earner funds were later disbanded. The text on the poster says: "Disband the trade union's funds. Personal ownership for everybody." (Photo: Sven-Erik Sjöberg/Pressens Bild/Scanpix.)

owner profits and the wage sector. Unlike the original proposal, these funds would buy shares on the market without any means of coercion. None of the funds were to have more than 8 percent of the voting shares in any company. The proposal was "so temperate that share prices hit a record high the day after this was made public."[51]

[51] Nycander 2002, 370.

Nonetheless, the proposal led to seventy-five thousand people demonstrating against these funds in Stockholm. It was said that for the first time in history CEOs and leading capitalists took to the streets in protest. Palme considered withdrawing the proposition but came to the decision that "we will lose faith in ourselves and faith in the party as a force for reform if, after plodding along with this issue for almost ten years, we were now to drop this question."[52] The proposal was put forward and ratified without enthusiasm. Thus it was that these watered-down employee funds were established in Sweden. After the non-Socialist Bildt government took over in 1991, however, they were phased out, just as bank democratization had been phased out in Norway ten years earlier.

When the Swedish LO published its research report in 1975, the government and the party were both working on the Codetermination Act. The person responsible for this was Kjell-Olof Feldt. His reaction to the LO report reflected his commitment to codetermination: "Then I questioned this in government: we have now chosen an ideological line, that is, that *labor* has the right to have influence, it is labor that is fundamental and that is the motive and, so to say, the *moral* in this context. But now we find Rudolf [Meidner] and Anna [Hedborg] have provided a new ideology, another basis for employee influence—namely, *ownership*. There are two trains on the track now, and which one are we going to board? Indeed, we are already sitting in one of them, but are we also going to board the other one?"[53] And thus it was that the Social Democrats chose to board both, which had to be a rather difficult feat.

It is remarkable that the Norwegian trade union movement refused to follow Sweden when the wage earner funds were launched. This occurred for two reasons, the first being the economic-structural conditions. The power of private ownership was much stronger and more concentrated in Sweden, while in Norway little private ownership remained. What did exist was scattered, and the state was heavily involved. It was also referred to bank democratization as a better alternative. The second reason had to do with the different tradition followed by the Norwegian labor movement: "Among us there has always been the tradition that labor itself gives influence, but with the wage earner funds it is ownership that gives power." What was sought, then, was *labor power* rather than the power of ownership. Democratization of the system of stocks and shares was "a foreign element in the Norwegian labor movement."[54] The subtext here is the Norwegian perception that the country

[52] Ekdahl 2002, 35.

[53] Ekdahl 2002, 17. Reported by Kjell-Olof Feldt according to memory.

[54] Nyhamar 1990, 559; Langeland 1985, 123, who cites Tor Halvorsen of the LO, in *Arbeiderbladet*, 25 September 1981.

had achieved greater distance from capitalism than had Sweden. Norway had boarded the train preferred by Feldt—and Palme.

Palme's frustration with the situation found expression in 1978 when, before his major speech on the wage earner funds, he launched a proposal to radicalize the Codetermination Act of 1976 by extending the representation of employees in the decision-making bodies of the companies to 50 percent. As Meidner commented afterward, "Palme made an almost desperate attempt to sell this 50 percent representation in return for the LO giving up pursuit of the wage earner funds question."[55]

The same proposal—increased worker power by means of 50 percent representation—was recommended by a Norwegian committee under the chairmanship of Lars Skytøen of the Iron and Metal Workers Union, with Gro Harlem Brundtland as a member.[56] This was a characteristic swing in the radicalization of the Labor Party in the 1970s. In addition, Skytøen announced that the goal for the future was achievement of employee majorities in decision-making bodies. The radicalizing of industrial democracy as proposed by the Skytøen Committee was not realized, however. The crisis of the 1970s changed the atmosphere, and the committee's report was quickly sidelined by the Social Democrats themselves: building up industry's competitive edge assumed greater relevance. "The aim of further democratization was no longer to limit the employers' managerial rights, but to ensure effective leadership."[57]

Esping-Andersen has argued that there was a fundamental radicalism in the moves made by the Swedish LO in comparison to Norwegian labor movement policy. This is a dubious position, and contrary to the Norwegian labor movement's own perception. On the other hand, the violent reaction provoked by the Swedish proposals indicates that he was right. The wage earner funds (together with the nuclear energy question) came to dominate Swedish politics from the mid-1970s into the 1990s. The proposals had been presented as a radical stand against what has been the core of capitalist society—the proprietary power of the capitalists. Business life picked up the gauntlet and made the issue a symbolic question about the nature of an optimal society. Despite repeated efforts, it was impossible to agree on any compromise, the reason being that, from the very beginning, the question was of an ideologi-

---

[55] Ekdahl 2002, 32.

[56] *The Further Development of Industrial Democracy: Report from a Joint Committee of the National Trade Union Organization and the Norwegian Labor Party* (1980).

[57] Heiret et al. 2003, 187. The Skytøen Committee would be buried by the Brubakken Committee of 1985 (Engelstad et al. 2003, 284). In 1989 the Norwegian LO also took up the idea of wage earners funds. They existed at that time in Sweden in a very watered-down form. They never came into being in Norway. Cf. Nyhamar 1990, 558–559.

cal nature.[58] The Swedish and the Norwegian trade union movements each chose to climb aboard their respective trains bound toward increased workers' power. Neither reached its final destination, however.

WEAKENED ADMINISTRATIVE CORPORATISM

In the 1970s negotiative corporatism had been regulated through legislation. In addition, administrative corporatism came under criticism for not functioning adequately. The idea was that the particular partisan interests involved should take part in the relevant decision-making processes. The possibility of ignoring the general interests of society obviously existed but, remarkably enough, it had not been singled out for general criticism before this. The criticism arose first in Norway. In 1972 the first project investigating the power relations of Norwegian society had been launched. Its major perspective turned out to be that the political process did not lead to results that were any more rational than those of the unregulated market. As far as it went, this involved a criticism of the established "negotiative economy" and "mixed administration," to use terminology coined by the leader of the investigative committee, Gudmund Hernes. In the 1980s the non-Socialist government of Kåre Willoch took up the problem by strongly "reducing the boards and councils of the collegial administration," with the aim of strengthening "the interests of society as a whole."[59]

In Sweden the system had functioned more effectively, but, "From having been a largely undisputed principle, administrative corporatism became the source of both political conflicts and changes by the end of the 1980s." In 1985 a Swedish public white paper recommended, surprisingly, that the interest organizations' representatives should be removed from public boards since, in such roles, they "could be considered to represent special interests."[60] The report met with opposition, especially from the LO. By contrast, the SAF (the Employers Association) supported the conclusion, pointing out that administrative corporatism led to "double loyalties and unclear mandates." On this basis, in 1991 the SAF took the drastic step of removing itself from all state administrative bodies. As Bo Rothstein writes, thereupon "one of the cornerstones of the administrative corporatist system had fallen."[61] In 1992 the conservative prime minister Bildt followed up by excluding the other interest organization representatives from a number of public boards. (The previous

[58] Åsard 1985, 142–143.
[59] Nordby 1994, 70–71. Hernes 1978, chapter 1.
[60] Rothstein 1992, 347–348.
[61] Rothstein 1992, 349.

year the wage earner funds had been phased out, and the government initiated the stabilization alternative, giving the organizations a feeling of being taken under guardianship.) The LO's reaction was strong. According to Johansson and Magnusson, the LO now stood almost alone in support of the Swedish model, a fact that was strengthened by the unwillingness of the Social Democrats to reestablish the old order when they resumed power in 1994.[62]

In the late 1970s Norway began gradually dismantling the system. In 1991 the Employers Association considered following their Swedish colleagues, but in the end they let the system stand. The administrative corporatist system thus remains intact in Norway, although in a weakened form. In Sweden it was phased out.

The upheavals along the way were more dramatic in Sweden than in Norway. Sweden suddenly turned from a more extensive and efficient system, quickly carrying out a far-reaching demolition. In Norway the trend was the same but resulted in a careful withdrawal. It also looks as though the criticism of administrative corporatism that appeared in both countries gradually developed certain contrasting features. In Norway the main emphasis was placed on the excessive power that had been accorded the *organized special interests*, leading to irrational solutions. It seems, however, that the main argument in Sweden, at least from the SAF, was the opposite; namely, the *state* had acquired too much power, thus creating a hostage situation for the representatives from the SAF. This difference might explain why the Norwegian Employers Association did not withdraw. In any case, beginning in the 1970s there was a clear change in both negotiative and administrative corporatism, both of which had been characteristic features of the Social Democratic society.

LABOR POWER FOR A BETTER COMPETITIVE EDGE

The trade unions have not played out their role. In Sweden almost 90 percent of those employed are still members of trade unions, the highest rate in the world. In Norway the percentage is 57; this represents the highest rate internationally for countries in which unemployment insurance is not administered by the trade unions, unlike Sweden.[63] In both countries labor power, or the influence of employees and their engagement in the production process, has been increasing. But, for Sweden, critics have pointed out that this has been happening on a basis that is "liberal democratic" rather than "Social Democratic" in nature.[64]

[62] Johansson and Magnusson 1998, 328–329.
[63] Engelstad et al. 2003, 220.
[64] Dahlström 1989, 134.

We have ascertained that a shift of strategy occurred in the 1980s. "The Labor Party in Norway and the non-Socialist coalition government in Sweden were in power when the development of codetermination was subordinated to the demands of business."[65] But here the similarities end. It can be argued that the Norwegian plan involved a further working out of the Social Democratic order; that is, it built on the trusted collaboration between the different interests involved in the tripartite model. In the course of the 1970s the focus had shifted from representative democracy to participatory democracy. In the course of the 1980s there had been a further shift of emphasis from participatory democracy to better leadership. This was worked out through cooperation at the company level, in order to bring about a greater ability to adapt to changing conditions and better compete in a threatening world. In this connection there was even a tendency to believe that the formal representative plans and the traditional work of forging agreements might be a hindrance to favorable development, while participatory democracy could advance such a development.[66] The precondition was the well-developed relationship of trust in the Norwegian system.

It might sound as though Norway was idyllic. Of course it was not. In both countries the employees had great influence internally, but at the same time their opportunities to affect the external affairs of a company had decreased.[67] If we ask whether increased security and well-being were general features of working life, the answer has to be qualified. The many reforms brought about during the hegemonic phase of Social Democracy, and up to the present day, presupposed high rates of employment and stable firms. When conditions worsen, many workplaces are marked by insecurity and stress. Formal guarantees by means of such things as protection against dismissal and "the right to ease and comfort" are undermined. Such is the irony of history; the moment one is about to achieve something, the very conditions necessary for realizing those gains undergo change.

In 2000 the Norwegian LO leadership took the initiative to revise the Working Environment Act of 1977: "There are . . . reasons to ask if the law gives appropriate protection and provides answers to the challenges of today." This call to attention was relevant, but it is also symptomatic of the dilemma that was now being faced. At the LO Congress of 2001 there were many who, out of principle, warned against revising the statute—one knows what one has; one does not know what one may get. The white paper on the working environment had prepared for more flexible plans relating to working hours and temporary employment.[68] These (and other) questions were taken

[65] Tor Are Johansen 1995, 142.

[66] Heiret et al. 2003, 187.

[67] Engelstad et al. 2003, 291.

[68] NOU 1999:34. Ebba Wergeland in *Klassekampen*, 10 October 2003.

up once again by the White Paper Committee on Work Environment Law, which presented a comprehensive, but not unanimously agreed on, report in February 2004.[69]

Sweden has followed a similar process. In response to a commission from government, the Work Life Institute published its recommendations in 2003, titled *A Firm and Solid Working Life*. The same year the Committee for New Regulations Regarding Working Hours and Holidays brought out its findings. The tendency was the same in both countries—pressure in the direction of more flexibility regarding working hours and temporary employment.[70] The political conflicts over these issues have been considerable in both countries, and the final result remains unclear.[71] These processes, which were set in motion to ensure the safety and security of the workplace, really only confirm that the Social Democratic order, with its social security system, is in retreat. And indeed it was precisely this threat that pushed forward participatory democracy at the company level, in order to improve efficiency and facilitate flexible restructuring.

Even though Norway is not idyllic, it is more so than Sweden. Under the old system from the hegemonic period of Social Democracy both countries developed "something like sustained, institutionalized social pacts. During the eighties, however, Sweden broke from this tradition. At about the same time Norway seemed to be doing so too, but there was soon a return to national cooperation between employers and unions in Norway." The conclusion of Jon Erik Dølvik and Andrew Martin is that "the contrast persists between Norway, where national-level cooperation is supported by strong state intervention through mediation and occasional compulsion, and Sweden, where national-level cooperation seems to have eroded beyond repair, offset by minimal increase in state intervention through a limited expansion of the mediation function."[72] The situation in Sweden has, however, improved somewhat since Dølvik and Martin wrote their article in 2000.

SOCIAL DEMOCRACY IN A GLOBALIZED ECONOMY

The Social Democratic order had been based on the principle that successful enterprise depended not on ownership but on professional leadership and state control through political regulations. Stock markets, particularly those in Social Democratic countries, were dead institutions. As late as the 1970s one of the central Social Democratic politicians in Norway could assert that

[69] NOU 2004:5. *Arbeidslivslovutvalget.*
[70] NOU 2004:5, 45–46.
[71] *Aftenposten,* 19 July 2004.
[72] Dølvik and Martin 2000, 279, 316.

"to stimulate the stock market is like carrying oats to a dead horse." The scope of economic policy was confined to the boundaries of the nation-state, something that gave the state the opportunity to regulate the economy. Business life was a "junior partner to government," and the state could regulate and defend against, or open the way to, international competition according to need. At the same time, the firm had been a stable framework for the individual employee, and a whole series of social security plans for the welfare state were based on this stability.

From the 1970s this structure began to dissolve. A general deregulation led to the free flow of international capital. Above all this liberalization applied to capital, while other input factors, such as labor and goods, did not manage to flow as freely, despite attempts at liberalization in these areas as well. An important aspect of this development was the growth of a new international market, or what Alfred Chandler calls a "distinct business in its own right," namely, the buying and selling of companies, or parts of companies.[73] This constituted a radical break with the structure that Galbraith had described. One now had a new active proprietary capitalism, or finance capitalism. Among other things, this implied a new vigor in the stock exchanges and movement of strategic decision making out of the sphere of the firm, where the workers had their hard-won influence, and into the more internationalized sphere of finance.

We have seen how Sweden and Norway, including the Social Democrats in both countries, adapted to these developments through deregulation and freeing up the movement of capital. The reason for this policy reversal can be found in both internal and external factors. It was due not least to the fact that the crisis of the 1970s, and the more or less uncontrolled countercyclical policies undertaken to deal with the economic downturn, undermined faith in the existing system of planning and management. Successful Social Democratic capitalism had itself begun to creak at the joints. The governmental projects on power relations in both Sweden and Norway revealed that the policy of state control and regulation had not led to more rational solutions than the market had been able to achieve. The general change of mentality, the reaction to the interfering regulatory state, and a certain influence from "the American model" and Thatcher's Britain seem to have played a role as well. The change of political course implied that an array of political tools was renounced, while at the same time the new course gave rise to a whole series of new problems.

Market exposure was one facet of the new reality. Another was the growth of finance capitalism and institutional ownership. There is a growing concen-

[73] Chandler 1990, 621.

tration of ownership in the stock exchanges today among large impersonal funds such as the big private pension funds and equity funds but also public funds such as the AP Funds in Sweden, the big state pension funds in Norway, and other new huge state funds. All these funds are the result of what some have called a "savings revolution." These funds hold the money of small investors or the public. For the most part these funds want to place monies in interest-bearing paper transactions, but they have gradually become more dominant in the stock market. We can perhaps speak of a democratizing of capitalism insofar as ownership is spread out. But this does not mean that it is coordinated through a democratic decision-making process.

In most contexts it is the directors of the large funds who determine where the monies are to be placed. As one of Norway's largest private investors, Fred Olsen (who has billions at his disposal but mere peanuts compared with the current large funds) has said that in Norway there are five persons who decide what is to be invested in—namely, the directors of the five largest public and private funds.[74] Of course, unlike Fred Olsen with his small handful of billions, these five are in no way free to decide what the many billions they manage should be invested in. And this is precisely the problem. From the outset the funds are not active owners. The directors have to take into account the actual owners, who are widely dispersed, often at great distance from the business. This means that the directors have to pay inordinate attention to dividends and the stock exchange rates.

As the growth of institutional ownership gained momentum in the 1990s, the concept of "corporate governance" became widespread. It reflected a growing importance of shareholder value as opposed to the more Social Democratic idea of stakeholder value, but otherwise its meaning is unclear. An initiative has been taken within the European Union to work out "a modern EU framework for company law, which would include corporate governance."[75] In reality this initiative is a search for a formula for political control of the new internationalized finance capitalism. The main worry is not the big pension funds but rather the fast growth of private equity funds, many of which are loan based and speculative in nature. There is evidence that these funds have destroyed basically sound business enterprises.

The big, nontransparent, state-owned investment funds of China, Russia, and some of the oil-exporting countries give further cause for worry. There is a danger that funds of this kind can conceal political agendas and disrupt the general economic stability. The EU initiative has been backed by the Social Democrats in the EU Parliament. They have demanded legislation to con-

---

[74] *Aftenposten*, 21 April 2004.
[75] www.euractiv.com

trol investment funds: "We believe in the market, but we insist on creating a Socialist market economy and not a pure market economy," as they say in their report.[76] The new internationalized finance capitalism and the new institutional ownership have created large political challenges, especially for the Social Democrats.

A WEAK MILIEU OF PRIVATE OWNERSHIP

As we have seen, companies can be bought up and moved out. Even though to date there has been a reasonable balance between direct investments in and out of Sweden and Norway, there are serious concerns. Foreign owners will certainly not be governed by national considerations. The moment that the automobile industry has to be further rationalized, it could easily happen that the relatively small-scale automobile producers Volvo and Saab would disappear from Sweden. Small countries on the periphery of the large markets are vulnerable. Moreover, the national owners have themselves become internationalized. In this connection a worry has appeared that can be seen as an inheritance from Social Democracy. As Lars Jonung writes: "Had Swedish owners been richer and had the Swedish capital market been better developed, then Volvo and Saab might have managed their financing from within the country. With higher share values the Swedish auto industry could have financed its investments through the stock market. The problem of Volvo and Saab with regard to Swedish ownership was, in other words, the result of the economic policy that Sweden followed."[77]

A parallel fear was enunciated when the large Norwegian Bergesen Shipping firm was sold to a Hong Kong shipping company—that the Norwegian capital market was not large enough or strong enough to provide the proprietary capital the company required, that is, no one was rich enough to buy it. Thus the problem in both Sweden and Norway is the weakness of those circles that constitute private ownership. According to Jonung, "the mass of wealth in private ownership in Sweden amounts to very little in an international context." If this applies to Sweden, it is much more applicable to Norway. Private wealth in Sweden and Norway is relatively modest not because the countries are small. We are, after all, speaking about rich countries.

Under Social Democracy both countries followed a policy that sought to limit the power of the capitalists, although care was taken not to totally undermine this power. If a stronger environment for private ownership had been

[76] *Mandag Morgen* 14/2007.
[77] Jonung 2002, 168.

required, Sweden could have continued its positive discrimination policy from the early twentieth century. And Norway's oil industry provided a golden opportunity for building up a strong private ownership environment by allowing private national interests to retain control of at least part of the ground rent, as occurred with the much more limited petroleum enterprise in Denmark.

In the history of industrialization the ability to make use of natural resources has been a common means of building up private capitalist interests. But it was precisely such a building up that the Social Democratic countries sought to prevent. From the desire to have a just distribution in society, the wealthy were heavily taxed. Quite simply, a strong milieu of private ownership was not desired in Sweden or Norway. And the policy established to hinder such development has been partly successful, particularly in Norway. This society-leveling policy has been viewed as a particularly positive feature of the Social Democratic society. Today, however, both countries are facing a dilemma. There is now a fear that private ownership has been so weakened that it cannot meet the challenges of the globalized economy.

STATE OWNERSHIP

What role does the state play in this more globalized economic system, or what role might it play? The state is no longer the strong player it was within the Social Democratic order; the situation has changed from business being the junior partner to government to something more in the direction of government being junior partner to business. For example, how can the state guarantee the investments necessary to national business life? In various ways it could prepare the ground, tempting foreign investments to enter the country. We have seen how the nation-state has flirted with those who manage capital and technology in the global economy. Norway is well placed with regard to oil, and both countries have good infrastructure, political stability, and a highly educated labor force.

Another way of securing national interests is through direct state ownership. During the 1980s and 1990s both the Stockholm and Oslo stock exchanges enjoyed a marked upswing. The latter lagged behind, however, as the listings on the Norwegian stock exchange involved a smaller proportion of national companies than was the case in Sweden. The state is a highly involved stockholder in the Norwegian exchange, to the tune of approximately 430 billion Norwegian kroner, or about 40 percent of the total asset value on the stock exchange.[78] This is partly due to the stock market listing of such

---

[78] This is relevant to the beginning of 2005. St. forh. (Parl. Proceedings) 2006–2007, S. Meld. 13:40.

large state companies as Statoil and Telenor, where the state has retained a large proportion of the ownership. The aim was that these state portions of ownership would be gradually sold to the private sector, but the attitude toward privatizing has been changing.[79] Moreover, a sale would mean selling to foreigners since there was not a "capital base in Norway, apart from the state itself, that had the capacity to take over the state's share of ownership."[80] Both in Sweden and Norway it is nevertheless a matter of dispute between Social Democrats and non-Socialists whether privatization should be continued or reversed.

Traditional arguments for state-run operations have been advanced, such as control of national resources and national ownership as the precondition for local and national development of industry and industrial competence. When there are no private capitalists to buy up national interests, and when the state is unable to use discriminatory regulations owing to international obligations, state ownership can be the only guarantee that national interests are protected. In Sweden, too, state ownership is significant, with a collective value of stock market listings of 174 billion Swedish kronor, which makes the Swedish state the largest owner in the companies listed on the stock exchange.[81]

In addition, a new feature has entered the debate—the state has had an income problem. This is due to some degree to the fact that while taxes have been reduced to make investment attractive in the country, at the same time the welfare state constantly requires more. To address this situation, the idea has been posited that the state should secure income in the form of dividends from proprietary capital in business life. One has to take the monies wherever they are to be found![82]

It is undoubtedly ironic that socialization or state ownership and public saving have gained renewed interest in the liberalized, deregulated, and globalized economy. The reality is that in such a world it is only the power of ownership that counts. There are both political and economic reasons for taking these positions. The problem lies in how this ownership is to be exercised. How active should the state be as owner? The idea of publicly owned companies as actors in the market economy is not new. The Polish economist Oscar Lange and the Norwegian economist Leif Johansen have aired such thoughts. Indeed, this is also in accord with Ernst Wigforss's idea of a capitalism without capitalists. So was Rudolf Meidner right when, in connection

---

[79] St. forh. (Parl. Proceedings) 2001–2002, S. Meld. 44. New skepticism is found in St. forh. (Parl. Proceedings) 2001–2002, Innst. S. 264.

[80] Former general director of Norsk Hydro, Egil Myklebust, in *Aftenposten*, 7 December 2006.

[81] *Aftenposten*, 6 February 2007.

[82] *Dagens Næringsliv*, 28 May 1996 (Thorbjørn Jagland). *Svenska Dagbladet*, 16 April 2004 (Anne-Marie Lindgren). The Norwegian state took in 19 billion Norwegian kroner in share dividends in 2005.

with the wage earner funds, he said that it was only ownership that counted? Is it possible to adapt the Social Democratic order to the new, open, globalized economy after all?

AN AMBIGUOUS DEVELOPMENT

The corporatist system that had been so characteristic of Social Democracy was weakened around 1980. This applied to both negotiative and administrative corporatism. As for the former, we see that both Sweden and Norway, following a period when the old models were under pressure, returned to these models—Sweden to its dual model and Norway to its tripartite model. But something was lost along the way. The legislative drive of the Swedish government in areas formerly dominated by the LO together with the employers' organization, and the LO's provocative proposition on the wage earners funds, tended to undermine the mutual trust of the traditional system, whereas Norway has been more successful in building on the old system's existing relationship of trust.

The weakening of the corporatist system was certainly not to the advantage of economic democracy, nor was the new globalized finance capitalism with its emphasis on proprietary power, or the growth of private equity funds and state-owned investment funds in, for example, China and some of the oil-exporting countries. On the other hand, it can be argued that the increased importance of state ownership and mutual-fund capitalism in democracies such as Sweden and Norway can be viewed as pointing in the direction of democracy and political control. The same can be said about the higher degree of self-determination in the work situation. In other words, there is a certain ambiguity in the development in the two countries with regard to their democratic character and political control of the economic development.

In many ways history took a new turn around 1970 and even more markedly around 1980. It would, however, be hasty to conclude that this meant the liquidation of the Social Democratic order. The Social Democratic parties are still the biggest parties in both countries and, in spite of a certain weakening of the corporatist elements, the trade unions in general and the LOs in particular have preserved much of their strength, and large parts of the Social Democratic social contract have been retained. The reason for this is that the labor movements in Norway and Sweden have been active in adapting themselves to a new reality..

CHAPTER 13

From Equality to Freedom

The Welfare State under Pressure • The Changing Character of Social Policy • The
Hunt for the Lost Sense of Community • The Jewel Is Removed from the Crown •
Does Norway Follow Suit? • From an Emigration Society to an Immigration Society •
The Establishment of an Immigration Policy • A Political Minefield • The Policy Is
Revised • Toward the Two-Income Family • The Great Dispute over the Cash
Benefit Plan • Gender Equality Lite • A School for the Weakest • Gudmund Hernes—
a Parenthesis • Toward the Dissolution of the Comprehensive School • The Universities
and Market Logic • From Equality to Freedom

THE WELFARE STATE UNDER PRESSURE

By about 1970 the major elements of the welfare regimes in Western Europe
were in place. A particular Nordic variant can be faintly discerned among
the many different solutions chosen to meet the challenges of social and economic advance in the developed countries, a variant marked by universalism,
taxation financing, and standard social security. The difference between the
Nordic countries and the other developed nations should not, however, be exaggerated. Not unexpectedly, Sweden occupied the top position. Sweden was
among the richest countries in the world and had the most generous welfare
plans. Even during the turbulent 1970s the social expenditures continued to
mount. In 1984 Sweden used a full 33 percent of its gross national product
on social expenditures, while Norway, along with a cluster of other countries,
used 23 percent. Thereafter the Swedish growth rate tapered off, but social
expenditures relative to the gross national product remained around 33 percent up to the end of the millennium. By contrast, Norway had significant
economic growth, passing Sweden in terms of per capita gross national product. Its social expenditures have risen even more strongly, reaching 30 percent
around the turn of the millennium.[1]

[1] Hatland, Kuhnle, and Romøren 2001, 55. The 1984 figures are from an earlier edition of the book.

Undoubtedly the welfare state continues to exist, albeit in a state of crisis, according to many. Yet these feelings of crisis arise from gloomy thoughts of future insecurity rather than from an actual acute situation. One problem is that the expenditures have mounted automatically, and more forcefully than expected, giving politicians the sense of having lost control. In addition, there is worry over demographic developments. One can foresee a future with a vastly increasing number of elderly and a shrinking working-age population.

In chapter 8 we found that there was a harmonious balance between economic growth and social care during the hegemonic phase of Social Democracy. Yet this harmony broke down around 1970 with the end of the period of consistent growth. The Social Democrats, as we have seen, had difficulty maintaining the idea that the social expenditures were a productive investment, as Karl Evang had insisted. Despite these economic worries, however, the 1970s saw new initiatives in the development of social welfare plans. New demands had to be dealt with.

A new radical criticism of the welfare state, based on investigations demonstrating that the state had not satisfied expectations, had emerged at the end of the 1960s. A "residual need" continued to exist in society. The Norwegian sociologist Vilhelm Aubert had launched a program aimed at unmasking *The Hidden Society*, as his seminal book was titled. Researchers looked into areas that had remained in the shadows, such as prisons, hospitals, fishing communities in the north of Norway, and so on. There they uncovered conditions that cried out for reform. Aubert's book first appeared in English in 1965, unleashing an intense debate in Sweden in 1966.[2] It was published in Swedish in 1968 and in Norwegian in 1969.[3]

Aubert defined his program in the Norwegian edition: The reason that "the positivistic, strongly natural scientific direction" had been "more predominant in Swedish social research than in the Norwegian" was that Norwegian society was "more oppositional, relatively weakly affected by the interests of the public organs. An oppositional research has less reason to follow the methodological norms of positivism than has an applied sociology." Oppositional sociology was not as closely linked to the administration but rather addressed "another public, the educated general public, socially critical politicians, the youth."[4] There was a stronger tradition of independent and critical research in Norway, an oppositional sociology that engendered reform. There

---

[2] Johan Asplund set off the debate in Sweden on the basis of the English edition of Aubert's book from 1965; see also *Sosiologisk forskning*, 1966, nos. 2, 3 and 4.

[3] Swedish edition, *Det dolda samhället*, 1968.

[4] Aubert 1969, 192–194. See also Slagstad 1998, 386.

gradually appeared several books with characteristic titles such as *The Crippled Welfare System* and *The Myth of the Welfare State*.[5]

In addition to residual need in the hidden society, criticism also appeared regarding the development of a "new need." The modern working life did not incorporate all those who needed support. Many were left out, including those on early retirement, the homeless, the unemployed youth, single mothers, burned-out workers, immigrants and their offspring not speaking Scandinavian properly, or inhabitants of the satellite towns.[6] All these had to be included in the welfare system. The economic development that should have formed the basis for a more extensive welfare state contributed, to some degree, to creating the very problems it was intended to solve! The social welfare goals became more difficult to live up to. Nonetheless, the welfare state was maintained. As far as it goes, there was a fundamental continuity here that extended on from the hegemonic phase of Social Democracy.

Many believe there is a paradox in the welfare state model: on the one hand, the human being is viewed as a member of a collective in which the individual stands in a duty-bound relationship with others, as within a family or a "people's home." On the other hand, the ambition of the welfare state is to foster the economic and social independence of the individual from the social collectives. Consciousness of rights forcefully entered the debate around 1970. The individual and his or her specific needs were now more clearly the focus of attention—the weight was shifted "from the group to the individual."[7] We might say that there was a tendency for the welfare state to weaken the collective consciousness that had created it. These were self-destructive mechanisms.[8] This shift in mentality made people relate to the social help apparatus in a new way.

The change in mentality ran parallel to people regarding *work* in a new way. Social democracy had identified itself with the "work approach," which is deeply anchored in Scandinavian society. It is part of the puritanical outlook that we are put here on earth in order to work. The welfare state built on this outlook, linking the duty to work with the right to work. "The system could be generous since it assumed that it would not be misused," as Alf W. Johansson writes. The model "built on the inner-directed individual: scrupulous and with a well-developed sense of guilt. . . . Puritanism became a silent

[5] Inghe and Inghe 1967, and Lingås 1973.

[6] Jenny Andersson 2003, 75.

[7] Anne-Lise Seip 1994, 381.

[8] Blomqvist and Rothstein 2000, 50. They refer to this in connection with the German Ulrich Muckenberger. Cf. Lorentzen 2004, 33; Stjernø 2004, 338: "Does the welfare state undermine solidarity?"

presupposition for the social forms of life in society."[9] It was this presupposition that disintegrated in the new society.

This new mentality can also be viewed as a form of mental liberation. The new society allowed realization of an old Western dream that has stood in opposition to the puritanical legacy: the dream of freedom from the compelling character of work.[10] This liberation can be viewed as a component of mental modernization, but it led the welfare state into difficulties.

THE CHANGING CHARACTER OF SOCIAL POLICY

Gradually the Social Democrats acquired a new understanding of reality. They not only had to reject the idea that social expenditures were productive investments. As we have seen, the new criticism also held that the industrial society had contributed to the creation of social problems. Thus the radical demand was for more fundamental reorganization of the production sphere. The problematic facets of growth had to be brought under control, and the conditions for a "sustainable development" must be created. This applied equally to the social realm and the natural environment. There is no doubt that these problems occupied Social Democrats during the 1970s. Yet we must conclude that "[n]either in business policy nor in the discussion around social welfare was there anything concrete about how this restructuring of the industrial society should come about."[11] In other words, while attention was directed to the problems of the "risk society," nothing much was done to repair the shortcomings. Consequently, a new harmony between economic policy and social policy was not established.

The pressing question then became how the welfare state was to be financed. This implied that economic policy and the reconstruction of growth were being awarded top priority, meaning that there was a return to the traditional production line but, as we have seen, with one important reservation. There was "a break with the postwar Social Democratic ideological inheritance regarding productive social policy and the strong societal view of the socioeconomic effects of the public-sector production." The fact that the idea of a productive social policy had been given up became "something that slipped by without much notice."[12]

---

[9] Alf W. Johansson 2001, 11. Cf. Lindbeck 2003 as well.
[10] Sejersted 2002c, 115f.
[11] Jenny Andersson 2003, 79.
[12] Jenny Andersson 2003, 89.

The character of social policy changed. First, *effectiveness* of the public sector became central. If there was no more money for reforms, then there should be more reforms for the money. Second, we find a remarkable rebellion against the old social political ideology from the heyday of Social Democracy. This has to do with the liberation from the nanny state of the "people's home," from the "authoritarian society." As Palme said, "Now, when a powerful expansion of the public sector has occurred, another dimension of the Social Democratic idea of liberation gains great importance. Present-day efforts should be directed toward allowing the citizens to take part in the public sector's resources with a greater sense of freedom of choice."[13]

Freedom of choice was the new slogan, alongside effectiveness. It was part of a common trend within the welfare regimes. As pointed out by Rothstein, freedom of choice was taken from the world of marketing and implied a kind of quasi market.[14] The lone individual is given a greater responsibility for his or her own social situation, while at the same time an element of competition arises among those who provide the services. Consequently, such quasi markets imply not only greater freedom for the individual but also a certain control over expenditure through competition.

This was a break with the old Social Democratic ideology. It had been based on the idea of *equality*, implying that social services such as schooling, health care, and social care should be the same for all—and of high quality. One consequence of this "high-quality standard solution" had been a minimum of diversity. It had been a premise of Social Democratic paternalism that if one were given a free choice of services, this would imply inequality of results; the weakest would suffer because they would be crowded out of receiving the best services. Thus there was talk of a contradiction between freedom and equality. Or, put differently, the argument was about two different ideals of equality: the liberal ideal, which maintains that all should have the freedom to choose, and the Socialist or Social Democratic ideal, which places greater weight on equality of result—everyone should end up roughly equal. This contrast can be observed in a number of areas, especially in the debate regarding schooling but also in social policy.

THE HUNT FOR THE LOST SENSE OF COMMUNITY

In chapter 11 we saw how Ingvar Carlsson and Gro Harlem Brundtland introduced a new economic policy, referred to as the "third way," simulta-

---

[13] Jenny Andersson 2003, 114.
[14] Blomqvist and Rothstein 2000, 64.

neously in Sweden and Norway. At the same time, they also supported freedom of choice in the field of social policy, a move they both defended in their
memoirs. "I had difficulties in understanding why we citizens did not get to
choose [among an array of social services]," as Carlsson writes.[15] And Brundtland writes enthusiastically about this "new debate on freedom," how the
individual could now be placed at the center, thus creating greater freedom:
"Freedom of choice also had to be a Social Democratic affair."[16] They were
both political pragmatists, with a great sense of what motivated the times and
with great flexibility regarding tradition, even though in their rhetoric they
insisted that most of what they did as politicians was specifically Social Democratic in nature. The vice chairman of the Norwegian Labor Party, Einar
Førde, the ideologue behind the new policy, saw the possibility of a conflict
between equality and freedom but loyally followed the line of the party:

> Equality and decentralization often stand in contradiction to one another. As you know, I
> warmly support carrying forward the tradition of equality in the Norwegian labor move-
> ment. All in all, I believe it is the most valuable tradition we have. But it still does not blind
> us to the fact that in the choice between equality and decentralization, we ought more often
> to choose decentralization. . . . This might mean a little less equality, but it is a cheap price
> to pay for greater diversity and freedom.[17]

There was indeed a price to pay. And in the Swedish party's program for 1990
we discern a certain tendency toward cold feet:

> The aim of organizing welfare, the social and educational sector under public-sector aus-
> pices, and financed via taxation, is to ensure that all citizens shall share the same high-
> quality service, no matter where they live or what they earn. Therefore the labor movement
> cannot accept an increased freedom of choice if this increases segregation and injustice.[18]

The discussion about freedom of choice involved "an unmistakable sugges-
tion of the incentive discussion found in debates on system change initiated
from the right."[19] We might say that this new attention on freedom was a
concession to parts of the traditional criticism from the bourgeois side. But
it was also a concession to a new mentality of the time, a general reaction
to the increasing bureaucratization and a demand for more freedom for the
individual.

Three methods have been used to attack the problem of the automatic increases of expenditure in the social sector. The first is the method we have al-

---

[15] Ingvar Carlsson 2003, 192.
[16] Brundtland 1997, 398, 379.
[17] Cited by Sandvin 1996, 228.
[18] Blomqvist and Rothstein 2000, 72.
[19] Jenny Andersson 2003, 116.

ready examined, namely, establishing quasi markets and increasing individual responsibility for one's own welfare. The second method is to sharpen control over the use of the services; and the third is to delegate responsibility of the social services to the local and civil societies, where one might presume the existence of a greater degree of collective consciousness than in the modern society at large.

The establishment of quasi markets is a logical solution in a situation of individualization and weakened collective consciousness. This involves the use of individual forms of stimulation by, for instance, increasing the correlation between individual contribution and the services one gets in return. This can also occur directly with the imposition of user fees to cover part of the costs of providing services, or through traditional insurance plans. Such plans may be compulsory or voluntary. Thus individuals are responsible for buying their own (standard) social security. Some initiatives along these lines have been introduced.

Increased inspection and control is another way of approaching the problem. The many disbursements given through the welfare system have led almost out of necessity to a form of clientage at the level where the individual is confronted by the bureaucrats of the welfare state. Paternalism and control are intrinsic to the system. As we have seen, this is something that the fathers and mothers of the welfare state were concerned about. They saw this as a danger to be combated through universality, and later by defining benefits as individual rights. As pressure on the welfare state increased, however, it became necessary to increase the controls or sharpen the paternalistic tendencies. Among other places, we see this in the development of a rehabilitation policy.

Beginning in the 1990s in both Sweden and Norway, systematic work has been undertaken in cooperation with employers to get national insurance recipients back to work. Those who are reported to be chronically ill are to be followed up systematically. Health certificates are employed in placement services; a more comprehensive surveillance of doctors' practices has been instituted; a constriction of the grounds for disability has been carried out; there are stronger punishments for misuse of the system; employers now have the duty to give an account of how the workplace can be adjusted to the needs of the disabled, and so on.[20]

The third method is to transfer responsibility to smaller collectives. In the long-term program of the Norwegian government for the period 1900–1993 we can read the following:

---

[20] Bjørnson and Haavet 1994, 326–327. NOU 1986:22. With regard to corresponding measures taken in Sweden, see Grape 1998, 116f.

In the work of developing the welfare society it is important to improve cooperation between the public and the voluntary organizations, self-help groups, and local cooperative initiatives. In order to solve important tasks and make everyday life simpler, there are many who find their interests served by working together. Others find that life becomes more meaningful when, on a voluntary basis, they make an effort on behalf of others. This deepens and strengthens welfare; it creates solidarity, closeness, and fellowship.[21]

First we notice that the state is withdrawing. At the same time, we note what might be called a "hunt for the lost sense of community." There are many who have written about the march toward individualism in recent decades. But it is not certain that the collective consciousness is weaker, even if it is no longer linked to the national sense of community, or to the "people's home." If it is possible to find this sense of community again at a more local level or in civil society, it could be the basis for delegating greater responsibility for welfare projects to this level. And, indeed, there are clear indications of a wave of collective grassroots organizing in many European countries today, including Sweden. It seems as though there is a new awakening of the civil society. In Norway this development is not so marked, however[22]

THE JEWEL IS REMOVED FROM THE CROWN

The General Supplementary Pension (ATP) was the "jewel in the crown"[23] of the Swedish welfare state, just as the national insurance plan was in Norway. In the face of opposition, the ATP was introduced by the Social Democrats in the 1950s and came to symbolize the Social Democratic order. As Olof Palme said during the election campaign of 1982, "I am, of course, a Democratic Socialist, as was Branting when he brought in universal suffrage, as was Erlander when he built up the social security system and the ATP." And even though the non-Socialists had fought against the ATP, it had become part of established society. In both 1976 and 1979 the non-Socialist coalition government pledged to respect the ATP,[24] but in the 1990s it was transformed and phased out through a process in which the Social Democrats were the leading force.[25]

Despite the non-Socialist government's pledge to keep the ATP, it brought out a proposal as early as 1980 regarding necessary cost saving in state expen-

---

[21] St. forh. (Parl. Proceedings) 1988–1989, S. Meld. 4:45.

[22] For this information I am indebted to Håkon Lorentzen. Lorentzen indicates that the strong interests of the professionals in the social sector can be a barrier to a further development of the civil society.

[23] This phrase, and the title of this section, refers to Lundberg (2003), who used the title *Juvelen i kronan* (The Jewel in the Crown) with regard to Social Democracy's welfare schemes.

[24] Lundberg 2003, 39, 41.

[25] The following is largely based on Lundberg 2003.

ditures that affected the ATP. The economic crisis was behind this, while at the same time "the costs to the system had increased astronomically."[26] The Social Democrats' reaction to the government move in 1980 was powerful nonetheless. They proposed a no-confidence motion—which was defeated by a very close margin. The powerful reaction of the Social Democrats meant that they bound themselves to defending the pensions. It is characteristic that when Ingvar Carlsson put forward his crisis policy before the election of 1982, he did not take up the issue of the pensions. In this way the ATP obtained protected status.[27] If one were to continue to be a Social Democrat, it was still dangerous to interfere with the ATP, even in times of crisis.

After the Social Democratic victory in the election of 1982, the roles were reversed. The large monetary devaluation led to a strong increase of inflationary pressure, and the government prepared to defer pension protection, thus provoking a public outcry. Now it was the non-Socialists' turn to blame the Social Democrats for having watered down their election promises.[28] The solution, so typical of the Nordic Social Democrats' policy of compromise, was to establish a cross-party policy group to address the conflict. This large group included representation from all the parties as well as a weighty corporatist representation. Once it began its deliberations in 1984, the debate calmed down somewhat.

The group presented a thick report of its findings with an extensive body of supporting material. On the one hand, the report pointed to the decreased level of economic growth, which was unable to sustain long-term program costs. The ATP funds had increased up to 1982, but thereafter they had suffered continual losses. On the other hand, the demographic argument was stressed. Developments were necessarily leading to steadily fewer people at work; thus fewer workers had to maintain the increasing numbers of people on welfare, including the pensioners. This report prepared the way for *something* to be done but hardly gave any indication as to *what*.

The 1991 election put the issue back in the hands of the non-Socialists. The situation now invited efforts toward new approaches. The new government got the Social Democrats to go along with a rather small cross-party working group. Remarkably, this group did not include representation from interest organizations. It was now correctly assumed that the group would reach some form of collaborative solution. This achievement was possible because the crisis in Sweden had reached almost explosive levels at the begin-

[26] Lundberg 2003, 41, 44.
[27] Lundberg 2003, 120.
[28] Lundberg 2003, 129, 131, 150.

ning of the 1990s, a situation that encouraged internal unity and external legitimacy. Moreover, both sides of the political divide had been wounded by the foregoing hard struggles, in which each had, with considerable justification, been accused of watering down its election promises. They had reached a point where the desire for the fight had run itself out and the need to reach a solution had become pressing. Now the sides sought each other's support. As far as this went, we see the contours of a new and relatively autonomous political formation.[29]

Although pension systems are complicated, the changes brought by the new program can be summarized. First, it became a payment-based system, meaning that the size of the pension was not predetermined but dependent on what the economy could bear. Second, it took up the lifetime income principle. One's pension would no longer be calculated on the basis of earnings during only the highest-income years, thus lowering the cost to the state and increasing correspondence between what was paid in and what was paid out. Third, a smaller share of what was paid in would be allocated to a premium pension fund in which the pensioner would be involved in investment decisions. This feature was clearly a concession to the non-Socialists. In addition, the way was cleared for workers to earn further pension points after reaching the age of sixty-five.

The aim of these changes was to increase motivation for working and individual saving, and to raise the retirement age, thereby making the pension system more dependent on the economic development of society.[30] In short, current expenditures would be brought under control. There was a shift from a system of just results to one of just procedures.[31] This exemplifies the equality problematic that we have already outlined: everyone should have equal opportunities, but this does not necessarily yield equal results among individuals.

In June 1994 the Swedish Parliament made a decision in principle on the new pension system, based on the recommendations of the working group. With this decision the jewel fell from the crown. Once a symbol of identity for the Social Democrats, the ATP system quietly fell. The opposition leader, Social Democrat Ingvar Carlsson, did not mention this epoch-ending decision in his memoirs. He was not even present in Parliament when the vote was taken, nor was the conservative Prime Minister Carl Bildt. In a sense, the issue had been taken out of politics. Ironically enough, the politicians

[29] Lundberg 2003, 175.
[30] Lundberg 2003, 179.
[31] Lundberg 2003, 199, 293.

received praise precisely for the vote: "Wednesday's parliamentary decision is an achievement for our political system," according to the leading newspaper *Dagens Nyheter* (News Today). "The parties have surpassed expectation with regard to the heaviest part of the system of public expenditures."[32]

The pension decision attracted international attention. Many countries were facing similar problems, with social security plans that could hardly survive the future economic and demographic conditions they envisioned. Sweden became an example of a particularly well-functioning democracy that managed to reform its system in time. The irony is that the ATP system had become paradigmatic for several countries, while now it was the *phasing out* of the plan that became paradigmatic. It was carried out as smoothly and efficiently as the closing down of the shipbuilding industry had been.

The decision of 1994 did not put an end to all conflict. It seems as though the labor movement woke up only after the principal decision had been taken. "The horizontal agreement with the bourgeois parties in the working group on pensions was followed by a vertical conflict between leaders and members in the party organization."[33] Of course doing away with an identity-defining element such as the old ATP was not without controversy. The premium pension became a particular target of criticism, along with the increased degree of insecurity. There was also criticism of the principle of lifetime income, on the grounds that women would come out badly in this framework. But the race had been run. It should be added that the system had a principle of basic pension security. No one would fall *completely* out of the system. It was still mainly a public system, and still rather generous.

DOES NORWAY FOLLOW SUIT?

In 1966, eight years after Sweden had introduced the ATP system, Norway followed the Swedish model and instituted its national insurance plan. In 2004, ten years after the decision in principle to take the Swedish jewel out of the crown, came the large Norwegian Pension Commission recommendation that Norway follow Sweden away from the old plan—but not quite as far away as Sweden had gone.[34] The commission's proposal was a "half-hearted copy of the brutal [Swedish] original."[35]

The economic situations differed in Norway and Sweden, meaning that Norway did not suffer from the crisis at the beginning of the 1990s to the

---

[32] *Dagens Nyheter*, 9 June 1994. Cited by Lundberg 2003, 191.
[33] Lundberg 2003, 285.
[34] NOU 2004:1. *Modernisert Folketrygd* (Modernized National Insurance).
[35] The title of an article by Axel West Pedersen (2005).

same extent. As a result, Norway was not so ripe for radical reforms. The demographic conditions were the same, however. The birthrate was low, and a demographic bulge of elders was expected. Moreover, Norway had instituted a plan (AFP) that allowed union-organized workers to demand their pensions at the age of sixty-two rather than sixty-seven—a change that reduced the incentive to prolong one's working life. So in Norway there was also some agreement that the pension system needed revising. Some of the changes that had been undertaken since the system's inception were also motivating factors toward further change. The minimum pension had been increased several times, but the supplementary pension had been cut, and the AFP plan had been watered down.

The commission (which was not in agreement on all points) wanted to make the system partly payment based and partly income based, and it wanted to do away with the AFP system in order to stimulate people to remain in working life. Norway also followed Sweden with respect to using the worker's lifetime income as the basis for the supplementary pension. In short, "just the minimum pension" was the hallmark of the Pension Commission. The state owes workers nothing more. If they want more, they must work for it and pay for it themselves.[36] This signals a weakening of something that had been specifically Social Democratic in both the Norwegian national insurance and the Swedish ATP—the standard security of the welfare plan. A final solution has not been reached, however. The welfare reforms are still high on the political agenda.

The Social Democrats are not as fully Social Democratic as they used to be. The same thing applies to the non-Socialists; they too have become less Social Democratic. In spite of conflicts and continual attempts to maintain a show of insurmountable contradictions between the right and the left, the development of the welfare state had been a joint concern. This also applies to the modifications undertaken in its most recent phase. During some of the phases it was not of crucial significance which parties held power. What was more important to the parties was *whether* they held power.

The same problems appeared and the same solutions were launched in both countries, but the preconditions for reforming the system were different. At the beginning of the 1990s the state debt soared in Sweden, while at the same time in Norway the new oil income soared. Consequently, Sweden was forced to take more drastic measures than Norway. So far, we can say that the welfare state in the two countries developed in certain unique directions.[37]

---

[36] Ola Storeng in *Aftenposten*, 14 January 2004.
[37] Henrekson 2006, 11.

FROM AN EMIGRATION SOCIETY TO AN IMMIGRATION SOCIETY

The integration of the various population groups within national boundaries was central to the great nation-building project. Workers, farmers, women, minorities—all were to be fully valued citizens in the modern nation. They were to take part in the new rights: first, political rights with the development of democracy and, later, social rights with the development of the welfare state. On the other hand, there was a strong demand regarding adaptation to the national culture. This integration was an overarching ideology with roots far back into the 1800s, strengthened in reaction to the large-scale emigration to America. The flight from the Scandinavian countries had to be stopped. The Social Democrats inherited this overarching ideology, and their moment of success was successful not least because it took place at the high point in this national integration.

Around 1970 the two countries were drawn into the great global migration from the south to the north, movement that would contribute to the breakdown of established norms. How would the newcomers be incorporated into the nation-state? For Sweden and Norway, becoming immigration countries involved challenges to the existing social and economic integration. The old ideology of national integration was poorly suited to an immigrant society. There were signs that immigration was creating a new underclass. Equally important, attitudes toward cultural integration on a national basis were now challenged. One was forced to think afresh about integration (or adaptation or adjustment, as it was now called). Quite simply, the nation had to be defined in a new way. The question is, how far have these countries come in this process of redefinition?

Immigration was not something new. People have migrated throughout history, and our societies are formed by waves of immigration—and emigration. Migration between the neighboring countries has always been extensive. Traditionally, the greatest immigration to Norway came from Sweden, while Finnish immigration had been greatest in Sweden; and that continues to be the case at the beginning of the twenty-first century. Since 1970, however, immigration has been of a new type, partly because of increased numbers and partly because of immigration from distant regions. New minority groups have appeared in large numbers. There had always been minorities that, in terms of culture and manner of living, distinguished themselves from the greater society. But they had been few in number and thus tended to live in the shadows. And equality, or homogenization, had been an ideal, which meant there had been a rough assimilation policy directed toward the minorities. This would change with the great wave of new immigration.

There was significant labor immigration to Sweden during the long period of economic prosperity following World War II. Most workers came from the other Nordic countries, but workers for industry were actively recruited from Austria, Hungary, and Italy as early as 1947. The trade unions accepted this practice, if somewhat reluctantly.[38] Swedish immigration policy was marked by this early labor migration and the positive view of immigration acquired during those years, so Sweden became a relatively open country. It never developed a guest worker system as found, for example, in West Germany, where it was expected that labor migrants would return to the countries they had come from. In Sweden the immigrants had easy access to social security payments from the state, and many of them settled in the country. As external pressure mounted, restrictions on immigration were gradually imposed.[39] Great pressure arose from 1970 onward, with the large wave of migration from third world countries.

During the long period of postwar economic prosperity Norway was hardly touched by labor migration.[40] Thus an active immigration policy such as that of Sweden was never on its agenda. Nor, for a long time, did many refugees find their way to Norway. Norway remained a little outside the experience of neighboring countries and Europe, making it that much easier to open the borders. In 1957 the old anti-immigration law of 1927 was replaced by a new "foreign law," which in reality meant open immigration. This was confirmed in 1969 with a parliamentary white paper that was "permeated with the optimism of the prevailing condition regarding the best possible utilization of labor power, and with liberal attitudes toward international labor migration."[41]

But at the same time the worries increased. Already by 1967 there had been a program on Norwegian radio that referred to the problems Sweden was experiencing with the number of foreign workers, which had by then reached half a million. In 1968 the Swedish had to introduce stricter rules, and in 1970 a corresponding set of regulations were adopted in Norway as well.[42] The real reversal came in 1971, however. Near panic broke out that spring when six hundred Pakistanis appeared in Norway. In record time initiatives were introduced to limit immigration.

[38] Lars-Erik Hansen 2001, 15.
[39] L.-E. Hansen 2001, 108.
[40] Tjelmeland 2003, 95.
[41] Tjelmeland 2003, 79.
[42] Tjelmeland 2003, 112.

THE ESTABLISHMENT OF AN
IMMIGRATION POLICY

In the first half of the 1970s all the Western European countries replied to the wave of migration by introducing a "halt" to immigration. Sweden did so in 1972.[43] Norway followed suit in 1974 with a parliamentary white paper that, on the one hand, firmly supported the principle of minimizing hindrances to international interaction but, on the other hand, stated that Norway now required some "breathing space." In reality this meant a halt to immigration based mainly on the motive of job searching, in line with that in Western Europe. After some years the "halt" became permanent. Nonetheless, immigration continued, both in Sweden and in Norway, but on a different basis than before. Labor immigration was replaced by family immigration. In accord with human rights standards, when immigrants were allowed permanent residency they also had the right to bring in and be reunited with their families.

Toward the end of the 1970s there came the last of three migration waves, and this time with an increased number of refugees and asylum seekers. This migration came partly from far-off regions (such as Chile, Iran, and Vietnam), as a result of political conditions. The wave increased at the end of the 1980s, reaching a high point with the Bosnian refugees at the beginning of the 1990s. There were only a few migrants who qualified as political refugees, yet it had been common in both Sweden and Norway to give asylum seekers refuge on "humanitarian grounds."

There is a degree of contrast between developments in the two countries. Norway moved quickly from a condition of innocence to one of panic and immigration "stoppage." In Sweden, which had far more immigrants than Norway, we find a smoother transition, from an active policy of recruitment during the height of the economic cycle to strict regulations. Principles of immigration policy was established in Sweden by parliamentary decisions of 1975–1976. At that point there was political agreement about permanently stopping immigration. How to stop it as humanely and effectively as possible continued, however, to be a subject for discussion.

Above all, the discussion during this phase concerned integrating those who had already arrived and those who could still enter the country legally as family members or refugees. Both countries established "double policies"—strict entrance regulation was combined with equality and integration for those who managed to pass through the eye of the needle.

[43] L.-E. Hansen 2001, 108.

The ideology of the welfare state permeated immigration policy. It is important to bear this in mind in order to understand the double policy. Responsibility for maintaining the boundaries of the nation was inherited from the nation-building project. Within the borders of the nation there were to be "standard solutions of high quality." Here there would be no underclass with restricted access to universal services. This meant that immigrants obtained social rights before political ones.[44] But in the eyes of public opinion, this stance was not without problems.

Foreign policy also had significance for integration policy. What was Sweden actually doing for its own minorities? As long as official Sweden was unable to improve their conditions, it was unable to "beat its breast in terms of its international engagement." It was thus important for Sweden's foreign policy profile, and for its own self-image, that it "try to bring about a Sweden that was a leading country in the creation of constructive solutions for ethnic questions, unlike the capitalist United States with its difficult racial conflicts and great class divisions."[45]

In the beginning there was a certain breakthrough for the policy of equality. The Working Group for Equality, with Alva Myrdal at the head, pointed out that, among other things, knowledge of the Swedish language and awareness of how Swedish society functioned was necessary for the achievement of equality. The message was that immigrants had "to be adapted" to Swedish society. Any general policy of assimilation was hardly mentioned. That belonged to the past, but we could perhaps talk about a partial assimilation. Stressing equality was in the tradition of good Social Democratic thinking. Cultural differences were usually interpreted as problems of integration.

But this would soon change quite radically. The demand to adapt was considered by many in the immigrant communities as a lack of understanding of the needs of immigrants to maintain their own identity. If there was anything that the former emigration countries of Sweden and Norway ought to have understood, it was the need of the immigrants to retain their own culture. It was not at all easy to change one's identity. The immigrants thus came to maintain that cultural diversity was a positive value; they demanded the right to choose their own identity. Equality and freedom thus emerged once again as possible contradictions. We can trace the development from what we might call the traditional Social Democratic concept of equality to a new stress on positive diversity. "State-supported pluralism" was the principle on which Swedish immigration policy was to be based—and so too for Norway.

[44] Brochmann 2003, 266.
[45] L.-E. Hansen 2001, 92, 222.

The possible contradiction between the (desired) integration into Swedish society and the emphasis on cultural diversity was scarcely articulated in the early stages of transition.[46] In fact, people commonly viewed the possibility of practicing one's own culture as a condition for social integration. Teaching children in their first language became obligatory in both countries since it was felt that a good grasp of that language was the basis for developing fluency in Norwegian or Swedish. There was thus a marked shift from regarding difference as a problem of integration to regarding the cultivation of one's own distinctive character as a condition for integration. But this view was not without its problems: perceptions of integration differed across party lines.

The Social Democrats had to change their view on the equality ideal, but it is characteristic that they did not take a leading role in implementing the new policy. David Schwarz, one of the foremost advocates of ethnic diversity in Sweden, had a Social Democratic background. He came to the view, however, that the immigration policy initiatives of the bourgeois parties were more progressive than those of the Social Democrats. And this centered on the question of freedom of choice, in Sweden as in Norway.[47] As Lars-Erik Hansen comments, "Here lies an embryo of the dissolution of the equality discourse."[48] The contrast is particularly clear on the question of school policy in Sweden: the conservatives wanted to allow the immigrants to establish their own schools, while the Social Democrats did not want to give up the idea of the integrated school system. There were limits to the freedom of choice—on this issue, at least.

With the ratification of the immigration policy by the Swedish Parliament in 1975–1976, Sweden became the first country in Europe to clearly admit that its policy was influenced by a model of pluralistic state intervention. In the end, this policy was established through the cooperation of all parties. It was commonly held that in this matter Sweden was on the cutting edge. "I still believe it is correct to say that the immigration policy that Sweden is pursuing . . . is probably the most positive and most constructive pursued by any immigrant country in the world," to cite the Social Democratic chairman of the parliamentary committee studying the immigration question.[49] Norway followed in Sweden's footsteps.

[46] Borevi 2002, 97.

[47] Borevi 2002, 187. The bourgeois parties, however, wanted to use much less money in their support of ethnic diversity.

[48] L.-E. Hansen 2001, 130, 188–189.

[49] L.-E. Hansen 2001, 205. This statement was made by Yngve Möller.

A POLITICAL MINEFIELD

With the policy (or double policy) in place, one might believe that the problems were being resolved. The dilemmas have continued to ravage the field of immigration, however. Immigration did not end with the immigration halt—quite the opposite. Throughout the 1980s constant tightening of immigration requirements was required. In 1986 the Social Democrats took over the government in Norway. At this point in time a climate change was under way in the immigration debate. The Norwegian municipal elections the following year were the first in which immigration policy played a role. The right-wing Progress Party made a significant advance in this election, riding a wave of increasing dissatisfaction regarding immigration. And when the Social Democrat Brundtland took over the government, she declared, "The government is committed to restricting the liberal practices followed earlier when it comes to giving residency to asylum seekers who are not real refugees, and therefore do not fulfill the requirements for gaining asylum."[50]

In 1990 a report was published in Sweden under the title *A Comprehensive Refugee and Immigration Policy*.[51] This was followed a year later with a policy proposal that was worked out in cooperation with the UN high commissioner for refugees. This new approach aimed to strike at the roots of evil by linking immigration policy with policies on foreign aid and foreign affairs. In other words, refugee home countries or countries that had high potential for conflict would be targeted for migration prevention measures that provided assistance, negotiation and mediation, and development of human rights initiatives. Similar ideas appeared in Norway around the same time, including those of Thorvald Stoltenberg, who for a short time had been UN high commissioner before being called back to Norway in 1990 to become foreign minister in Brundtland's government. The Swedish white papers were read with scrupulous care in Norway, where in 1994 a new policy was expressed in the form of a Norwegian parliamentary white paper.[52]

By that time the stream of refugees from the former Yugoslavia was in full flood. In a very short time eighty thousand Bosnians arrived in Sweden, and in 1993 Sweden (and Denmark) instituted visa requirements that had the effect of directing the flood toward Norway. Consequently, Norway also had to institute visa requirements, the last country in Europe to do so. These requirements proved to be a very powerful tool. Moreover, the mass flight

---

[50] Brochmann 2003, 298.

[51] This report was published in English, with the above-mentioned title. Brochmann 2003, 303.

[52] St. forh. (Parl. Proceedings) 1994–1995, St. Meld. 17.

from Yugoslavia contributed to confirmation of the principle of *temporary asylum*. This was not a new principle but would now become a natural and more important part of the policy. It was assumed that the refugees would return to their home countries after a certain period of time. Temporariness created a dilemma, however, when it came to handling war refugees. Norway was the only country to choose "the two-track course"; that is, these refugees should first be integrated into Norwegian society and then later returned to their home countries. This self-contradictory policy illuminates the dilemma and, naturally enough, had to be given up after a period of time.

The increasingly restrictive asylum policy led to political confrontations. Examples of brutal rejections and expulsions of people in need gradually began to appear in the media. In Sweden an Immigration Board worker described the effects of the stricter practices. Earlier, she said, it was thought better to allow ten applicants through, although nine of the applications were perhaps based on unfounded claims, if it could save one applicant who was truly in need of protection. Now the situation was reversed; one was prepared to risk not protecting one applicant in need if that was necessary to prevent nine other people with unfounded applications from entering the country.[53] During this period there was also extensive use of church asylum—a powerful manifestation of broad engagement in the fate of individuals. When the centrist parties took over government after the 1997 election in Norway, the immigration policy was again liberalized. This attracted great attention in Europe, and it led to a great increase in immigration, which in 1999 reached a record high of twenty thousand people. It also led to a rapid pullback to a more restrictive line.

The limiting of immigration is one side of the double policy. The other is *integration*. In the 1980s adjustments were made to the integration policy. The ideal of a multicultural society began to fade, and a certain anxiety appeared "regarding the fact that the goal of freedom of choice implied that immigrants had the right to follow norms and regulations that differed from those of the rest of the population." The policy had to be based on a more limited concept of culture. The Immigrant Policy Committee established by the Swedish government in 1980 found that "[s]ociety should not aim for one long-term cultural and language assimilation," but then it continued: "nor should it, in principle, oppose the development of such."[54] Thus the possibility of tension between integration and multicultural policy began to emerge. The state ought to play a more passive role; at the same time, a lengthier assimilation seemed likely.

[53] Vestin 2002, 172.
[54] Borevi 2002, 100–102.

THE POLICY IS REVISED

During the 1990s a more thorough reevaluation of immigration policy took place. The criticism of immigration policy up to that point arose from many directions. It had "unfortunately served to divide the population into 'us' and 'them,' thus abetting the emergence of the outsider status that many immigrants and their children experience in Swedish society."[55] The integration problem ought not to be viewed as an immigrant question but, rather, as a general problem affecting the whole population. A policy that is directed only toward immigrants is always problematic from the point of view of stigmatization. *All* members of society should be integrated with one another. Under this pressure the government sought refuge in a new rhetorical strategy. "Diversity" rather than "multiculturalism" became the goal. The *Immigrant* Board was rechristened the *Integration* Board, and so on.

It had been difficult to find a language in which to discuss the problems that undoubtedly existed. The immigration debate had been marked by "the anxiety of touching."[56] Many people feared the political minefield and abstained from taking part in the debate. Even speaking about "immigrants" could be regarded as a form of stigmatization and could lead to accusations of "racism." In Norway the anxiety about touching had led to what was called by the pejorative neologism *snillisme*, which literally means "nicenessism." Quid pro quo had been a feature of the welfare state throughout its history, but now immigrants had been given access to all the support plans of the welfare state without anything being required of them in return. "Humanitarian grounds" had been given too much weight, it was held. The nicenessism debate contributed to a sudden change. "All the parties now had to 'make demands on the immigrants'—an assertion that moved from 'taboo' to cliché in a very short time." In Norway, the right-wing populist Progress Party had throughout the debate argued for a stricter immigration policy and consequently been accused of racism. Now the chairman of the party was able to say, with no little justification—you've got it at last.[57]

The integration debate continued to be a minefield. The position of women in some of the immigrant cultures is representative of a concrete problem that generated strong feelings and hot debate. Enormous attention was paid to a Swedish-Kurdish girl, Fadime, who was killed by her own father, ostensibly because she stood by her love for her boyfriend, Patrik, and her right to lead her own life. The murder was said to have been an ethnically or religiously

---

[55] Government report, cited by Borevi 2002, 126.

[56] Brochmann 2003, 337.

[57] Brochmann 2003, 338. Norway's "niceness debate" was introduced by the local government leader in Oslo, Rune Gerhardsen, a Social Democrat and son of Einar Gerhardsen.

inspired honor killing. It has since come to light that this could hardly have been the case; it was more likely merely a family dispute.[58] The attention focused on this murder nonetheless contributed to a more multifaceted discussion concerning the problem of integration. At the same time, it provided nourishment for xenophobic, partly racist positions.

In the wake of rising attention in the media to the situation of immigrant women, it was maintained that integration policy ought to engage with and be based more on a group that had largely lived a hidden life—the mothers. In general the gender-equality debate broke into the immigrant debate and gave it an extra dimension since it turned the spotlight on the rights of immigrant women as well, especially in relation to the issues of female circumcision and forced marriage.

Behind the change of policy in the 1990s we can glimpse a more flexible concept of culture. Cultures are not unambiguously determined, and they are not static; they develop through contact with one another. And what about second-generation immigrants who have one foot in each of two cultures? Perhaps we should speak about an immigrant culture in its own right, based on its own special experiences—a hybrid culture? Language is a critical part of culture and provides a case in point: we notice a tendency toward the development of a mixed language in some immigrant circles. This new diversity also raises the question of whether one can choose one's own identity. The well-known Norwegian stand-up comedian Shabana Rehman is from an immigrant background but insists that her identity is bound to being a modern Norwegian woman. But are we willing to accept and apply to ourselves a flexible concept of culture?

Integration is the policy's goal, but the meaning of the concept becomes unclear when the concept of culture becomes more flexible. It is clear, however, that the later conceptualization remains a considerable distance from the traditional integration concept that was the basis for the great national integration project with its strong demand for equality and conformity in both the economic and cultural senses. The Social Democrats have had to slaughter some holy cows. But it also lies a considerable distance from the somewhat naive, free-of-worry idea of the colorful community spoken about so frequently in the 1970s. Yet Norway and Sweden are still very cautious about imposing demands on immigrants in comparison to many other countries. In Norway Grete Brochmann considers that this restraint can, paradoxically, be a reflection of a "thick" understanding of national culture: there *is* something that is distinctively Norwegian and can be transferred to newcomers only

---

[58] Wikan 2003. For corrective interpretations see Shoaib Sultan, "Muslimhets på norsk," *Klassekampen*, 21 February 2006.

with difficulty. But when from the start one believes that it is almost impossible to become Norwegian, pressuring newcomers to become Norwegian becomes a "mission impossible."[59]

This is possibly a greater problem in Norway than in Sweden. Even though in all its major contours immigration policy has followed the same pattern in both countries, there are still some characteristic differences. First and foremost, there are relatively more people of immigrant background in Sweden than in Norway. Sweden has been one of the most liberal immigration countries in Europe, which can hardly be said of Norway. In Sweden too there is reason to believe, however, that under the liberal surface there is a generally widespread skepticism toward immigrants from other cultures, something that easily can lead to a form of everyday racism. In Sweden there are also clearer tendencies toward the formation of immigrant ghettos. In all likelihood people in both countries will have to struggle with the integration problems for a long time.

TOWARD THE TWO-INCOME FAMILY

The Social Democratic era, more than any other, was that of the nuclear family. This was the case particularly in Norway, which had not been willing to liberalize its legislation regarding marriage and divorce to the same extent that Sweden had. Norway held more firmly to the traditional (bourgeois) family.

At the end of the 1960s we find a drop in the birthrate in most European countries, but most dramatically in Scandinavia, where there was a repetition of the reproduction crisis of the 1930s. Moreover, a large, and increasing, number of children were born outside wedlock. Decreasing numbers of people spent their lives married, and there was an increasing frequency of divorce. Society's most important institution for reproduction, the nuclear family, was thus in crisis. As it had been in the 1930s, this was interpreted as a general crisis of society. But it did not necessarily mean that the nuclear family should be strengthened.

The 1970s were a period of youthful rebellion and, in general, a radical wave. Radical feminism gained momentum. The bourgeois family institutions were attacked by radical elements using the slogan "dissolve the family," referring to the family as a "community of terror," and forcefully proclaiming the wretchedness of family life.[60] This point of view was well known, having had a certain amount of diffusion during the crisis of the 1930s. We recall

[59] Brochmann 2007.
[60] Holter et al. 1975, 20–21.

attacks on the family by Trond Hegna and Alva Myrdal, and Myrdal's vision of "the maternity of society," or a greater societal collective. At the beginning of the 1970s this position produced a new and intense debate over the family and family policy—war broke out over the family.[61] A major question now, as in the 1930s, was whether the traditional family should be strengthened, or whether more of the responsibility for children should be taken over by society. Which arena of socialization was the most important? The disagreement reflects thoroughgoing differences in views about society.

The Swedish Social Democratic women gathered together with the youth association in 1966 to demand "a radical, 'liberal' contract between the sexes." The old "housewife contract" had to be replaced with a "gender-equality contract," the most revolutionary point of which was that "the care of the children should be the task of both the parents"—in short, gender equality within the family. In 1972 there came "a high point in this new articulation of gender conflict" with the Social Democratic women putting forward a program of "a Socialist family policy." This new gender-equality contract would mean equality not only within the family but also in the labor market. "Housework implies no 'freedom' for women—the woman who is homemaker is no revolutionary." Consequently, the public sector must intervene in the care and upbringing of children—"care for the up-and-coming generations is a joint responsibility for us all."[62] Day care and other types of social services had to be extended. This was an area in which Sweden had already made many advances, although Norway had not come as far. In addition to these ideological drives, it would come to light that this policy of increased social responsibility for child rearing was reinforced in both countries by practical economic considerations.

In 1972 the white paper titled *Family Support* was issued by a joint parliamentary committee in Sweden. This report established that a significant proportion of single-income families with children fell short of what was deemed an acceptable level of income. A reform was proposed to modify and expand maternal security into a more generous "parental security." As far as it went, this reform conceded that the mother was really needed at home. Nevertheless, it was clear that it would be too costly to expand support plans to single-income families sufficient to raise them to an acceptable income level—quite apart from the fact that the old single-income nuclear family was fading away as an ideal.

The conclusion was that "the strongest 'economic support' a family in this difficult situation can get is not a cash contribution. On the contrary, it is

[61] Beck and Beck-Gernsheim 2001, 85.
[62] Hirdman 1998, 134.

the opportunity the other spouse might be given to contribute to the family economy through employment outside the home."[63] By this point in time the expenditures of the public sector had become problematic. The two-income family would be the solution to an economic problem. This solution required an intensive expansion of day care and other daytime institutions for children, however. Thus the argument for getting the mothers out into the workforce was, above all, of an economic nature; but it must also have been music to the ears of the new feminists. Economic considerations supported the implementation of this new equality contract and strengthened the gender-equality policy.

In 1973 the centrist government of Norway, under a prime minister from the Christian People's Party, put forward a parliamentary white paper on the living conditions of families with children that held the same positive view of the two-income family. As in Sweden, one of the main points was that the existing support plans for families with children had not eased their economic difficulties to a sufficient degree. Thus in Norway, too, the alternative solution was to focus on the two-income family, that is, to prepare conditions that would allow mothers to join the workforce. The Social Democratic government that succeeded the center-right government would take over the recommendations of their predecessors' white paper on the family.

In light of later debate regarding cash benefits for parents who stayed at home it is remarkable that the centrist government of Norway went against expanding cash contributions and recommended the two-income family.[64] There had been some conflict within the government that ended with the prime minister (from the Christian People's Party) having to eat crow since the women's liberation point of view was victorious over the traditional family model, and the feminist position was well supported by economic arguments.[65] In this way the prime minister fell into line with the Social Democrats and their new radical model of the family, but this alliance was not to last long.

The Norwegian recommendations were met with criticism from unexpected circles. The heaviest criticism came from a research group led by one of the radical feminists of the day. Dissolving the family was out of the question: "Any policy that aims to do away with the family has the same impossible character as a political line that aims to do away with schooling on the grounds that the latter socializes children according to the ideology of the bourgeoisie. A Socialist society without one or another form of the family

[63] Hinnfors 1992, 44.

[64] St. forh. (Parl. Proceedings) 1972–1973, S. Meld. 17:63. Tove Stang Dahl 1974, 40, has wrongly maintained that the white paper (S. Meld.) prepared the way for increased cash transfers.

[65] Sæther 1985, 178.

is as inconceivable as a Socialist society without schools." (The reference to schooling is a jab at Nils Christie's book *Hvis skolen ikke fantes* [If the School Is Not to Be Found]; see below.) The main criticism focused on the report's positive proposal to "very clearly support what we . . . have called the individualization of the family situation," without discussing what is problematic about this. As these critics pointed out, it should, in any case, look into whether "the policy of the public sector ought to *strengthen* or *check* the rapid development in the direction of a family with a low level of functionality. Our point of view is that *today* we should avoid a further dissolution of the family ties."[66]

In the governmental white paper there were references to the significance of the family with regard to meeting the need for love and emotional development, and it seemed that the authors meant that these important tasks were being fulfilled so long as the individual family member was given the opportunity to realize his or her own talents and interests. The government, by overlooking the possible conflict of aims, could have its cake and eat it too. In short, the report lacked a real family policy perspective. The main message of the critics was that "one could not reduce women's oppression *and* defend the family without transferring family tasks to the husband."[67] The nuclear family should not be dissolved, but rather reformed in order to be preserved, and this ought to be achieved by means of full gender equality in both the public and private spheres.

Roughly speaking, we can say that throughout the 1970s and 1980s the Swedes relied heavily on building up the public caring professions, while the policy in Norway remained equivocal. A whole series of Norwegian initiatives pointed toward "the mother *actually* needing quite a lengthy period of time at home with the children."[68] This referred to such plans as the common widows' pension (1964) and the transitional benefits for single parents (1967 and 1974). To be sure, the further expansion of parental leave and the restructuring of maternal leave into parental leave certainly contributed to paving the way for mothers to participate in wage-paying or salaried work. But in terms of both leave and day-care coverage, Norway lagged behind Sweden to a considerable degree. And when the investment of resources in Norway's family policy really began to increase seriously in the 1980s, it was the transfer payments that increased most strongly. Nor did the Norwegian policy come to give the same priority to two-income families in the way that the Swedish policy did. Nonetheless, the participation of mothers in the labor market also

[66] The feminist was Harriet Holter. See Holter et al. 1975, 25–30.
[67] Holter et al. 1975, 30.
[68] Skrede 2004, 164–165.

increased in Norway, but it is more correct to say that this occurred in spite of family policy initiatives rather than because of them. In any case, the crisis of reproduction more or less passed. The 1980s became the decade of children in both countries. But what certainly continued was the struggle over which family model should be emphasized.

THE GREAT DISPUTE OVER THE CASH BENEFIT PLAN

Family policy is charged with ideology. This does not mean that the ties between ideological standpoints and practical plans are obvious and straightforward. No reform demonstrates this better than the question of the cash benefit plan, known in Norway as *kontantstøtte*. Cash benefits, as they were instituted in Norway in 1998 following a period of great political confrontation, applied to families with children under the age of three who were not in publicly subsidized day care. These families were eligible to receive a monthly sum per child that was equivalent to the public contribution made toward day-care placement. This involved a cash contribution of up to three thousand kroner a month (later increased) being made directly to the family—a very costly reform.

There is a prehistory to the proposal behind the cash benefit plan. We have seen that by the 1920s the conservative regime in Sweden had hesitated to introduce a form of birth support to mothers, as had already been put into place in Norway. The reasoning was that such an invasion of the private family sphere would break down the nuclear family as a social collective. This point of view was never articulated with similar clarity in Norway. During the 1930s the Norwegian Labor Party agitated for cash contributions in the form of a wage for mothers and a children's allowance plan. The major misgivings did not come from the established conservative stratum of society, however, but from the radical bourgeois women's movement, who felt that such contributions would encourage mothers to give up wage-paying work.[69] Cash contributions could thus be defended, or assaulted, from completely different ideological positions.

It is remarkable that the Swedish conservatives maintained their opposition to cash payments for such a long time. Between 1962 and 1965 the Social Democrats developed a positive attitude toward cash payments. This came to be expressed in various contexts. Among others, the chairperson of the

[69] Berven, Magnussen, and Wærness 2001, 101.

Swedish Social Democratic women's association was explicitly positive.[70] The reaction from the Conservative Party was clear. Its family program of 1963 states, "we consider it repulsive on principle that the natural function implied by parental duties should be paid for by the state."[71] And the following year the Conservative member of parliament Astrid Kristensson maintained that it was "wrong to think that because one is fortunate enough to have children, one should have a salary from the state if one chooses to stay home and take care of them."[72] Briefly, direct pay to mothers was Socialism.

Ten years later the Swedish Social Democrats and the Conservatives had switched viewpoints! The new Social Democratic point of view was formulated by cabinet minister Camilla Odhnoff in 1973. She said the party rejected "the idea of a common, watered-down cash benefit since we consider that this would check the development of child care without solving the problems faced by the many children in need of placement in day-care centers or in 'family homes.'" On the other hand, in 1975 the Conservatives, together with two centrist parties, put forward a proposal regarding cash contributions.[73] It was a non-Socialist government that came to implement the cash benefit plan in Sweden in 1994. The election that year brought the Social Democrats to power, however, and they immediately rejected the plan. So in Sweden this was only an episode. "The decision to abolish the cash benefit plan was celebrated by the parliamentary Social Democrats with a cake-and-coffee party, but certainly not celebrated by the parents of small children," the conservative Ingegerd Troedsson bitterly noted.[74]

In 1998 (the year that cash payments were instituted in Norway, in the face of Social Democratic opposition) Sweden's prime minister, Göran Persson, commented: "[T]here are day-care centers; day care is open to everyone, and it is not reasonable to subsidize those who choose a different style of life, to be home with the children."[75] The latter portion of this sentence recalls statements by the conservatives early in the 1960s, but the reason for saying so was quite the reverse. The conservatives felt they were defending the "style of life" referenced above, while Persson took a critical stand toward it—children should be in day care and mothers should be out working. This was the legacy of Alva Myrdal. Troedsson had grounds for titling her 1999 book *The Commanded Family: Thirty Years of Alva Myrdal's Family Policy.*

---

[70] Hinnfors 1992, 110.

[71] Hinnfors 1992, 99.

[72] Hinnfors 1992, 5.

[73] Hinnfors 1992, 5–6.

[74] Troedsson 1999, 79.

[75] Göran Persson in *Dagens Nyheter*, 12 September 1998. Referred to in Troedsson 1999, 190.

Ideologically different views on which family model should be advanced have been behind the many confrontations over the cash support plans. Should the nuclear family be supported by preparing the ground for mothers to stay home with their children, or should the money be used to build up the public care sector? In Sweden the Social Democrats had strongly supported public care and developed an adequate day-care system. With strong justification, the prime minister could say that "day care is open to everyone." But there was also the question of what the mothers actually wanted. Were so many engaged in wage-paying work outside the home because they wanted to be, or was it because they felt forced by economic circumstances? Would they rather be home with the children?

In both countries one found that those who were most engaged in supporting cash payments were in the centrist parties. It is worth noting that the Swedish Center Party proposed that cash support should be given only to those who in fact chose to stay home; it should be considered wages for child care and nothing more. Similar proposals also appeared in other connections. The plan, as it was proposed and undertaken in both countries, however, was as we have described in the Norwegian case. All parents of small children would have the grant, minus the public contribution for the children who went to a publicly subsidized kindergarten. Thus the parents were able to choose whether they would stay home with the children or use the contribution to pay for private care. The latter was particularly at issue in Norway where, in contrast to Sweden, publicly subsidized day care fell far short of coverage for all. The conservative parties hesitated for various reasons. One of the reasons they joined the centrist parties' stand was their regard for the non-Socialist coalition. Moreover, it was reasonably easy for them to align themselves with the principle of *freedom of choice*: the money would follow the child.

The first official move in Norway had come from the Christian People's Party in January 1992. An important argument was that, owing to the limitations of the public care system, there were many who could not participate in the public transfer funds. Free choice was a central principle, but those who presented the proposal expected that the plan would "reduce the need for increasing day-care places."[76] In Sweden it was primarily the Christian Democrats, the new counterpart of Norway's Christian People's Party, who supported the cash benefit plan. They had joined the bourgeois coalition government in 1991.

During the autumn of 1992 Sweden was hit hard by the economic crisis, which thrust forward cooperation between the government and the Social

---

[76] St. forh. (Parl. Proceedings) 1991–1992, Doc. 8:7.

Democrats regarding crisis initiatives. The cooperation almost ran aground over the cash benefit plan as the Christian Democrats held fast to their banner issue. "In my opinion it was grotesque that the promise regarding the child-care allowance would bring down the whole arrangement," writes Ingvar Carlsson of the Social Democrats.[77] In the end, the Christian Democrats had to give in, and the crisis settlement successfully weathered the storm. It was characteristic that the Christian parties strongly defended the family as the most important arena of socialization.

In Norway the cash benefit plan was one of the big issues in the election of 1997, which resulted in the formation of a minority government composed of centrist parties. With the support of the Christian People's Party, the Conservatives, and the Progress Party, the plan was introduced. The Labor Party came out against it, stating that people should not be awarded compensation for not using a social benefit that was already provided. The Labor Party and the Left Socialist Party wanted to follow the Swedish route. Their counterproposal was full day-care coverage, "day care . . . for all," by the year 2000.

Despite the rhetoric, both sides felt that the cash benefit reform would strengthen the traditional family model and the traditional gender role model. Mothers would reduce their wage-paying work outside the home. This has led some to maintain that the left was more normative than the right. The left was afraid that, given free choice, mothers would choose to stay at home.[78] This is a reflection of the old paternalism—women are inclined to return to traditional norms, and therefore they should not be given freedom of choice. As it turned out, however, this assumption proved to be wrong. The cash benefit plan has had minimal significance in the choices made by mothers regarding wage-paying work outside the home.[79] The worries of the left had been unwarranted; the mothers chose "correctly."

In contrast, however, immigrant families showed a tendency to use the cash benefits according to the intentions envisioned by the Christian People's Party. Many immigrant mothers stay home with their children, in line with their own cultural family tradition. This, however, has awakened concern in relation to the integration project—children ought to be in day care in order to meet children of another cultural background. The dispute over cash benefits is not over.

The reformers behind the cash benefit plan underestimated the parental desire for public child care. The reason that parents did not avail themselves of the option to stay home with the children is not easy to explain, since

[77] Ingvar Carlsson 2003, 496.
[78] Berven, Magnussen, and Wærness 2001, 100.
[79] Ellingsæter 2003, 5.

many families feel that they ought to have more time with their children. It points, perhaps, to the tendency to overlook the conditions of the labor market, especially the importance of the rights given to wage laborers.[80] No matter what the reason is, the consequences are that the debate has taken a new turn. There is now agreement that, in addition to the cash benefit plan, the day-care system should be built up to full coverage for all with a maximum limit on what parents are required to pay. It is possible that the preference of parents for child care will reduce the cash benefit system and that Norway will, once more, approach the Swedish conditions—in line with traditional Social Democratic policy.[81]

GENDER EQUALITY LITE

The family policy differences between Norway and Sweden are not incidental; they are anchored in traditional attitudes that ran throughout twentieth century. In the literature, too, systematic differences are commonly referred to. In an article on European social care Anttonen and Sipolä distinguish between four groups of countries on the basis of what social services they offer the elderly and children: those who commonly have generous social services, such as Sweden; those who offer such services to a very limited extent, such as Portugal; those who offer generous services to the elderly but limited services to children, such as Norway; and those who offer limited services to the elderly but are generous toward children, such as France.[82] Sweden and Norway thus fall into different categories. Both countries offer generous services to the elderly through the national pension plans. It is with regard to services offered mothers and children that they part company.

This research was undertaken before the introduction of the cash benefit plan. Since 1998 Norway has not come out so badly with regard to support for children, but there are still differences. Walter Korpi's categories differ from those of Anttonen and Sipolä.[83] He has ranked the countries into types of welfare states according to how much weight they place on direct support to families with children, versus indirect support to two-income families through public care. Sweden comes out far lower in the former ranking but is at the top in the latter. Conversely, Norway comes out relatively high in both categories. Here, as well, the two countries are in different groupings, at least insofar as Norway manages better than any other country to follow a double

---

[80] Ellingsæter 2003, 23f.
[81] Ellingsæter and Leira 2004, 21.
[82] Anttonen and Sipolä 1996.
[83] Korpi 1999, 57.

strategy. This indicates that Norway has maintained more commitment to the nuclear family than has Sweden.

Why is this so? In both countries gender equality and the need for two incomes contributed to women entering working life. But in addition to this there are two features that are unique to Sweden. First, the Marxist criticism of the bourgeois family was introduced to Swedish Social Democratic discourse by Alva Myrdal, albeit in a watered-down version. The message was that children had to get out of the family. Second, women were actively mobilized as labor power outside the home during periods when there were general shortages of labor power during World War II and through the period of economic prosperity that followed; in other words, women also had to get out of the family. None of this happened in Norway. On the contrary, warnings against moving functions away from the family came from radical circles.

Now there are tendencies toward a change in the family pattern in both countries. Nonmarital cohabitation has become common, and the number of single parents has increased. Part of the reason for these developments lies in the fact that in the Nordic countries there has been a more "defamilialized" reproduction policy than in the rest of the Western world. In other words, the policy has contributed to reducing the dependence of the individual on the family, above all by promoting women's economic independence.[84] This has been undertaken partly from the aim of advancing women's equality. Here one finds contradictions between the considerations of the traditional family and those of gender equality.

Since the radical critique of the family never managed to take root in Norway, family policy there is colored by this contradiction, or by an "internal self-contradiction."[85] On the one hand, it was said, in relation to the cash benefit plan, that priority must be given to the traditional family rather than to extensive support of gender equality. On the other hand, gender equality in the family has been advanced by, among other things, introducing certain economic incentives encouraging fathers to take a greater share of parental leave. In reality, freedom of choice rather than gender equality has received priority. As has been said, it is "all right to have gender equality as an offer—as long as parental free choice is upheld." The result is a form of "gender equality lite."[86]

On the whole, *"freedom of choice* has been the most influential metaphor for family policy."[87] Having been a community of need, where people stayed

---

[84] Ellingsæter and Leira 2004, 23–24.

[85] Skrede 2004, 172. Cf. Bergqvist (2003, 14), where she maintains that the dismissal of the cash benefit scheme in Sweden prevented a "system change" within the family sector.

[86] Skrede 2004, 172, 193.

[87] Skrede 2004, 22.

together because they needed one another, the family is now on the way to becoming a community of choice composed of independent individuals. This does not mean that the family is being dissolved but that it is acquiring a new, more fluid form.[88] This is a general tendency that extends far beyond Scandinavia, relatively independent of family policy initiatives.

A SCHOOL FOR THE WEAKEST

The nine-year integrated or unitary school of the Social Democratic epoch was implemented with a high degree of support. But criticism from both the radical left and bourgeois directions broke loose as soon as the implementation was reached at the end of the 1960s. The radical criticism found clear expression in Nils Christie's book *If the School Is Not to Be Found*, which was widely disseminated in both Norway and Sweden. Christie's main point is that the school stays outside society and real life. In opposition to this, he poses a utopia: "The dream of a school becomes the dream of a society that provides the same thing as the good school. This cannot be anything other than, precisely, the good society."

A utopia can be a useful phenomenon for revealing a way of thinking. Christie's book identifies with the progressivism found within pedagogy, and in a way is an extreme expression of it. This radical or experience-based pedagogy makes the student the subject. It is through his or her own observations and experiences that the student should learn. Experiential pedagogy arose long ago as an alternative to the old knowledge-based pedagogy that holds that the student is an object to whom knowledge should be communicated. But experiential pedagogy had never predominated. It came into the Norwegian curriculum in 1939 and gained strength with the Swedish School Commission of 1946. In practice, however, it was only a modification of the integrated school's knowledge-based pedagogy. Only around 1970 was there a real breakthrough, and that breakthrough has had consequences.

The most significant aspect was a change in the teaching role. The teacher was no longer the learned knowledge broker but, at best, an organizer. He or she was placed on the sidelines. The old school was now considered repressive, and its teacher an oppressive guardian of an undemocratic regime. The teacher had to be fought, a struggle that has very deep roots. In Norway Alexander Kielland's 1883 novel *Gift (Poison)* has become a symbolic expression of the horrors of the knowledge school. Nevertheless, it was a very long time before we could speak about a breakthrough for progressivism.

[88] Beck and Beck-Gernsheim 2001, 85–86, 98, the chapter "On the Way to a Post-Familial Family." Gullestad 1996.

In this struggle against the "repressive" school, modern pedagogy received the assistance of the new Marxist wave of the 1970s. The breakthrough for progressivism could probably not have occurred without this alliance. By the beginning of the twentieth century teachers had become the major bearers of culture and had gained great respect. Now they were in the process of being declassed. There was also a reaction against the hierarchical grading of students according to marks, the narrow concept of what constituted normality, and against the segregation that had followed the narrow concept of normality. The most spectacular uprising against this concept was the Norwegian HVPU Reform through which the institutions for the mentally handicapped were closed down. The idea was to integrate them into the normal "good" society by integrating them into the general school population. Corresponding reforms were carried out in Sweden as well. This was only the most extreme example of the new tendency toward schools serving the needs of the weakest students. In a way we can say that progressivism greatly advanced the integrated school idea about equality.

This massive criticism from the left achieved results,[89] giving weight to the integration of school and society in the 1970s through "learning from experience" and adding elements of exchange between work activity and learning.[90] In Norway we find a clear impact of this criticism on the outline plan for the primary school beginning in 1974. This represented "the first assault from the public direction on the primary school as a nation-building institution."[91]

Ironically, this pattern of development points toward a tendency to pervert the goals that lay behind it. Christie's utopian idea was based on a fusing of school and society—exactly the feature that so beautifully complemented the pedagogy of experience. Christie writes about the good society; others would have called it the Socialist society.

The old liberal, or culturally conservative, way of thinking held the opposite point of view. From this perspective, school became such an important arena of socialization and culture that the larger society was not suited to do the job. It was power and the logic of the market that held sway in society. A decent society was possible only if the youth obtained their necessary moral and democratic formation *before* they came out into "real life." School should be protected from society in order to adequately serve society. Such was the thinking.

Reaction arose spontaneously. As the Swedish school historian Bernt Gustavsson writes: "When representatives of the school authorities found teachers wandering up and down the corridors while the students themselves were

[89] In Norway the criticism found expression among other places in the journal *Praxis*; in Sweden, in *KRUT*. Richardson 1999, 104–105.

[90] Grankvist 2000, 214–215.

[91] Telhaug and Mediås 2003, 221.

able to decide the content and form of their study program it was the final straw. Initiative was taken for a countermovement labeled 'Knowledge at School' or 'the knowledge movement.'"[92] This protest movement reflected skepticism toward the devaluation of knowledge in relation to social integration, or "compulsory socialization." As in so many other fields during the 1970s, this criticism grew in strength as a reaction to the radical criticism that had appeared at the beginning of the decade and tended toward knowledge nihilism. The new criticism sought inspiration in the popular cultural-formative traditions from the beginning of the twentieth century.

This criticism of the criticism had its roots on the bourgeois side of the political spectrum. It also had its adherents among the Social Democrats, however. When Bengt Göransson was the Swedish education minister in the Social Democratic government of 1982, his task was to turn education around, away from an approach marked by knowledge decline, psychology, and therapy. The schools proposal of 1991 was given the title *Grow with Knowledge*. "There is a new belief in the importance of traditional knowledge," Gunnar Richardson writes, but goes on to add, "not primarily for training in critical thinking and the formation of public opinion but as a basis for growth and welfare."[93] Thus, with the new direction, the old aspect of forming socially competent members of society was weakened in favor of instrumental utility. Schooling was for learning useful knowledge and for individual personality development.

Developments in Norway paralleled those in Sweden. A "knowledge opposition" developed among the Social Democrats as well. When Gro Harlem Brundtland formed her second Social Democratic government in 1986, it was clear that she wanted to give priority to knowledge in relation to "the care-giving aspect." The prime minister gave a clear signal by linking with the professor of sociology Gudmund Hernes, taking him on first as adviser, then as education minister. One of the progressive pedagogues aired the frustration of the profession by stressing how the politicians, with Hernes in the lead, had "contributed to reducing pedagogy mainly to a technical question in a positivistically oriented "means-ends" model in which the ends of the macro-level economic dimension were focused on, and the social and cultural problems and challenges were underreported and subordinated to a neoclassical (instrumental) and strategic rationality."[94]

A typical expression of this new thinking about schools was *goal orientation*, instituted for the whole educational system in both countries on the basis of political agreement. This thinking was based on the notion that resources could not possibly be utilized effectively with traditional regulatory control.

[92] Gustavsson 1996, 251.
[93] Richardson 1999, 105.
[94] Hovdenak 2000, 173–174.

The principle of goal orientation was decentralization: the state would establish the goals and content of schooling. Allocations would be granted in lump sums that could be disbursed at lower levels and across sectors of the bureaucracy; by this means it should be possible to develop local variations. The results would be assessed in relation to the attainment of goals. Goal orientation swiftly came under harsh fire, however, from the teacher organizations among others, especially in relation to bureaucratization through comprehensive reporting but also on other grounds. For example, how could one measure the results of identity building, or one's disposition toward democracy? Goal orientation would surely contribute to the undermining of the school as an arena of socialization.

At the beginning of the 1990s Norway and Sweden parted ways with respect to school policy.[95] In Sweden, Minister of Education Göran Persson continued with goal orientation. Rapidly and without prior warning, he undertook a municipalization of schooling; that is, a weakening of state control. The conservative government that took over in 1991 continued the same line. Its goal was to dissolve the state monopoly and replace it with free choice for consumers. In 1997 the government subsidies granted to free schools were increased to 100 percent, such that private schools did not have to charge fees. This led to a marked increase in the number of private schools. At the national level the curriculum was confined to a description of the contents in the form of setting goals. As for the rest, the teacher was free to choose teaching material. National student evaluations would be taken at the completion of the fifth and ninth years of schooling—a far remove from the traditional Swedish centralized school. This freedom has been put to use by experimental schools that have gone a long way toward individually directed programs of study. In other words, the school community has to some degree been dissolved. Schools such as Färla School and School 2000 have done away with the ringing of bells, classrooms, and general classroom schedules. The students themselves decide how to organize their school day. Once again the teacher is sent out into the corridor. Progressivism had its way, not least in these experimental schools, in spite of the knowledge opposition.

GUDMUND HERNES—A PARENTHESIS

Norway took quite a different course. Gudmund Hernes has been the most prominent Norwegian education strategist since the days of the great comprehensive-school-system strategist Helge Sivertsen. Hernes's career as a

---

[95] The following paragraph owes much to Telhaug and Mediås 2003.

school politician began the winter he spent as a visiting professor at Harvard University. In a feature article titled "Can One Have Ambitions in Norway?" he firmly maintained that life in modern society would increasingly be based on knowledge and that Norway was poorly prepared for such a future. The article served to unleash a long newspaper debate, to which Hernes responded with an article in which he mercilessly criticized the Norwegian school system. In his view more structure, more standardization, more work discipline, and more concentration on subject matter content was needed.[96] As such, he was a supporter of the knowledge school. Hernes was also a supporter of goal orientation. His program broke away from the general trend and made Norway a different country, at least in the field of education. Unlike the Swedish politicians, the Social Democrat Persson, or the conservative Bildt, Hernes was not a *neoliberal* but a *neoconservative*.

Hernes defended the school as a cultural, nation-building, comprehensive institution, and in this way he was in opposition to the individualism of his day. He did not follow Persson's line of dismissing state control, endorsing a minimum number of free schools. He retained the state endorsement of textbooks and reduced the amount of freedom the teachers had managed to acquire in their choice of teaching material by introducing a detailed description of compulsory teaching material for every subject and every grade in the classroom system. This national general teaching material was to be clearly and concretely specified in every subject. To a certain degree he also prescribed teaching methods.

In Sweden the cultural fragmentation of the time was met with the concept of culture and competence, which would prepare students to conduct themselves well in a multicultural society. In Norway Hernes's answer to cultural fragmentation was the opposite, namely to reconstruct the common national culture.[97] He clearly broke away from the trend in the model plan of 1974. His real ambition was to amalgamate the comprehensive school with the knowledge school, something that is strongly reminiscent of school policy during the golden age of Social Democracy. He was also in line with the thinking behind the nine-year integrated school of that period by granting everybody the right to twelve years of schooling. The result was that almost everybody started high school. The problem turned out to be a high dropout rate, however.

There was much in the new policy that would find support among the teachers. At the same time, Hernes met with much criticism and opposition, perhaps because of the way he broke with what had been Social Democracy's

---

[96] Grankvist 2000, 231.
[97] Cf. Aarsæther 1997.

way of carrying out reforms, which was to make many small stepwise changes that allowed for course corrections along the way. By contrast, Hernes's reform was closer to what the philosopher Karl Popper called "utopian technique." in which the point of departure is not the existing system but rather a future utopia, and the existing pattern is ruthlessly treated. According to Popper, the utopian method butts into reality.[98] In any case, Hernes had little time, and he met with opposition; nevertheless, he managed to implement some points despite these constraints. The final curriculum of 1997 was, in reality, a compromise between his idea of a common basis of knowledge and the demands from the pedagogues and the teaching profession for a plan that would satisfy local conditions and the individual.

TOWARD THE DISSOLUTION OF THE COMPREHENSIVE SCHOOL

In 1997 a non-Socialist government assumed power in Norway. This meant that Norwegian school policy was taken in a neoliberal direction. The Hernes period had been no more than a particularly Norwegian variant—a parenthesis within the course of development. Now Norway followed Sweden on the road to neoliberalism, instituting an individualized, decentralized school system.[99] Norway exhibited greater loyalty to the classic Social Democratic tradition with its emphasis on similar opportunities and equal schooling to all, however.

It was not until Kristin Clemet, from the Conservative Party, took over as education minister that Norway once again took up its old policy of following along behind Sweden. Clemet reported:

> We have already been moving full speed away from the integrated or comprehensive school system, if by this you are thinking of a school that makes everybody clever. In fact, there are greater differences between students in Norway than there are in other European countries. We are not managing either to bring forward the weak or stimulate the strong. The comprehensive school is an old and worn concept, out of harmony with a culture that promotes diversity and individualism.[100]

Clemet dismissed the state as the school employer and municipalized the school system. In 2003 she followed the Swedish example further by opening the way for private schools and competition among schools. The fore-

---

[98] Bertil Rolf has analyzed Hernes on the basis of Popper. Cf. Rolf, Ekstedt, and Bernett 1993.
[99] Telhaug 2003.
[100] "Noise in the Classroom," *Morgenbladet*, 14–20 December 2001.

most goal, however, was to restructure the school as a knowledge school through what she called "the knowledge lift." International studies had shown that the knowledge level in Norwegian schools was low. Here Clemet was following the knowledge opposition of Gudmund Hernes and the Social Democrats. It has been maintained, however, that in reality the long-term dismantling of the knowledge school continued as Clemet turned again to the progressive pedagogues shunned by Hernes. A basic principle of this "pedocentrism" is avoidance of fixed knowledge goals to the benefit of learning competence. This means that the students themselves take responsibility for their own learning.[101]

We have noted that the knowledge opposition had support along the entire political spectrum. Thus the motive of socialization and cultural formation was dampened, but it was not eliminated. "Formation" (socialization and refinement) became a key concept in the school debate of the 1990s.[102] But it is not always clear what was being included when it came to the relationship between formation and knowledge. For example, the Swedish white paper *School for Human Formation (Skola för bildning)* of 1992 has been criticized because the "democracy" concept is not to be found. It seems to have been replaced by "science."[103]

In general it seems as though the concept of formation is being watered down "until it becomes solely an internal personal affair that has to do with the specific individual's own self-realization and freedom of growth." This is in agreement with the individualism and cultivation of individuality of Kristin Clemet and the right. It seems to have been accepted relatively free of opposition, however, by both the radicals and the progressive pedagogues. The latter have a tendency to go in the direction of psychotherapy's individually-oriented-treatment thinking. Thus they were sympathetic toward a formation process that was free of limiting factors that necessarily had to follow the more goal-oriented, collectivist formation project of the comprehensive school system and the nation-building project.[104]

The radical thinking in regard to blurring the division between schooling and society was carried further: "A fundamental ambition of the 1970s radicals was the adaptation of school and learning 'to reality' by trying to bring theory and practice closer to one another. This ambition returns during the 1990s in a completely different disguise. Now the idea is carried forward out of economic and technical motivations."[105] It was all about a general

---

[101] Lindbekk 2008.
[102] Gustavsson 1996, 253f.
[103] Gustavsson 1996, 256.
[104] Gustavsson 1996, 17–18.
[105] Gustavsson 1996, 252.

breakthrough for the instrumentalist way of thinking. The school should be based on the premises of society. As previously mentioned, the comprehensive school was grounded in the opposite idea, namely that the forms of living in society should be created through the integrated formative school system, which was regarded as an important arena of socialization. School was a central institution for society building.

Individual acquisition of knowledge and individual development of personality, rather than social integration and formation of the members of society, became the main principle of education. This is perhaps best reflected in the growth of private schools and free choice in schooling. Free choice in schooling means "free for those with the best marks, but certainly not so free for those individuals with low levels of cultural capital and poor school performance. . . . One man's freedom becomes another man's bondage."[106] Now Norway is behind Sweden when it comes to the development of private schools. In 2006 we find only 2 percent of Norwegian primary school students in private schools, compared with 7 percent in Sweden.[107]

The struggle over the school system is not over. In 2006 the Social Democratic government in Norway reversed the development toward private schools and free choice. The old comprehensive ideals have weakened, but they have not disappeared. "As for school policy, the political left, including the Labor Party, is at least as radical and mindful of the traditional Social Democratic goals as it was earlier in the postwar period."[108] Whether they will return to the ideas of Hernes remains to be seen.

The comprehensive school under Social Democracy never became a school for Socialist indoctrination, nor was it the tool of social integration that the most optimistic reformers had thought. It must nevertheless be regarded a success, representing a great forward leap in educating the population and to a certain degree also contributing to social integration. The comprehensive school had broken down the class-based pedagogy and made it possible for bright young people to undertake the class journey of upward social mobility. Many did so.

But it had originally been a school from which "problem children" were cleansed. Paradoxically, just as schools were actually becoming really comprehensive, thus suitable for the weakest students, the problem of social stratification arose once again. When the school system disappointed the bright ones, the significance of the cultural capital from the home increased.

---

[106] Løvlie 2004.
[107] *Mandag Morgen* 37, 20 November 2006.
[108] Tuastad 2006, 443.

It is important to note that the school remains a robust and conservative institution. As has been said by a well-known school historian, Egil Børre Johnsen: "the formative content and attitude has *not* changed. The learned and the administrators changed the concepts, and the curricula followed suit. But it is wrong to believe that *the school* also followed. There remains a great distance between those who make a living from thinking about schooling and those who live by working there."[109] Especially in the Norwegian school system, continuity remains up to the present day. The political confrontations are often quarrels about the inessentials.[110] The school system is better than its reputation—otherwise it would be a bad situation, indeed.

THE UNIVERSITIES AND MARKET LOGIC

The years around 1990 represent a crossroads in higher education. It was then that the Norwegian universities acquired both more resources and more functions, and consequently slipped out of the backwater in which they had languished. The man behind these reforms was Gudmund Hernes. He was, as we have seen, genuinely preoccupied with national identity and, in general, with the motive of human social formation. Nonetheless, instrumental motives arising from the weight Hernes placed on goal orientation came to dominate. As with the schools, it can also be problematic to "evaluate the quality" of the activities of the university. The predominant goal of science is to seek truth, independent of whether or not this is worth doing. But how should this truth seeking be evaluated? There is no overarching authority (a ministry of truth?) with the competence to judge whether the scientific process is "efficient," to use market rhetoric. Nor is the market able to do so.

The Swedish reforms around 1990 took the same direction as the Norwegian. But since the starting point was different, the reforms had a different significance. In Norway Hernes's reforms were experienced as a new attack on classical autonomy. Conversely, in Sweden there had not been the same degree of classical autonomy, certainly not after 1977. Therefore Richardson is able to write: "Deregulation and decentralization constitute the most characteristic features of this 'freedom revolution' that swept over the Swedish world of colleges and universities between 1988 and 1993, and which from a historical perspective is completely unique."[111] The question, however, is what this freedom consisted of.

---

[109] Johnsen 2003.

[110] Svein Ove Olsen, "Krangelen om det uvesentlig" (The Quarrel over Inessentials), *Dagbladet*, 30 November 2006.

[111] Richardson 1999, 184.

Important elements in this new policy were that the institutions acquired control over their own internal budgets and that the labor market orientation was abandoned. Student freedom of choice had now become the predominant principle in Sweden, as it had always been in Norway. The conservative education minister noted, "my principal view of universities and colleges stems from the traditional meaning of the concept *university*: an autonomous academy composed of students and teachers who freely choose one another."[112] We see the same "neoconservatism" we saw with the Social Democrat Hernes, and the same goal orientation. The institutions must ensure that "the measures they intend to undertake are conducted to secure quality." They must be designed so that progress and outcomes may be evaluated— "if undertakings are not completed, then punitive sanctions of an economic nature may be set in motion." The other element in the system of resource allocation was to be "allocation in the form of quality premiums."[113] To some degree the universities were now exposed to a quasi market. The institutional freedom eventually involved here was not the same as the classic academic freedom. Academic freedom applied to the freedom of the individual scientist or scholar, and that was something else entirely. Thus it was that *Dagens Forskning* felt it could sum up the reform under the headline "The Price of Liberation was Less Freedom."[114]

The reforms of the 1990s were hardly those of classical autonomy. The question of what this classical autonomy really consists of is in itself problematic. In principle, the reasoning is approximately the following: If the market is to function, and if democracy is to function, this presupposes a population of mature human beings. This consequently presupposes a formative process that precedes both the market and politics. And this is to be taken care of by the institutions of the civil society: the family and the educational bodies. The universities ought to be public bodies that negotiate the civil society's liberality by standing in an arm's-length relationship to both political power and the logic of the market. The universities had kept much of this function during the Social Democratic phase. The formative function was not as clear as it had been, but it had been retained, perhaps not so much on the basis of conscious political will as from negative reasons—what was one actually to do with these institutions? The irony is that the neoconservatism that we saw in the wake of the hegemonic phase of Social Democracy does not really represent these ideals since it exposed the universities to quasi markets and external controls.

[112] Riksdagsförh. (Parl. Proceedings) 1992–1993, Prp. 169:93.
[113] Riksdagsförh. (Parl. Proceedings) 1992–1993. Prp. 169:11.
[114] *Dagens Forskning*, 28–29 April 2003.

FROM EQUALITY TO FREEDOM

In the course of the 1960s it was common to argue that the goal had been reached; the welfare state had been realized in all its essentials, while the crowning glory consisted of the national pension plans that guaranteed standard security. But from the very moment the jewel was placed in the crown, criticism and difficulties having to do with the modern industrial state arose. It was said that the welfare state was a "myth," since equality had not been achieved and there were still people in need. On the other hand, the system was difficult to handle, since there were established mechanisms that led to an automatic growth of expenditures; thus the economy ran into difficulties. Unlike during periods of prosperity, it was impossible to argue that social policy was an investment in economic growth. It had become an economic burden. Discord arose, but a look at expenditures reveals that the welfare state continued to exist. The system is in a condition of relatively systematic change, however. It had to be reformed in order to be saved.

A fundamental shift in welfare thinking can be summarized as going from a principle of the greatest possible equality to a principle of the greatest possible freedom—*freedom of choice*. Of course in many fields the rhetoric of equality has been retained, but only to the extent that the equality of result of the Socialists has been exchanged for that of the liberals—equality of opportunity. Equality of opportunity or freedom of choice has to satisfy two considerations. First, it represents liberation from the "people's home" nanny state, or what Palme referred to as the "authoritarian society," where equality of result was the foremost goal. Second, freedom of choice serves as a link in the development of individual responsibility through the implementation of market mechanisms and competition. The state curtailed its responsibility toward the individual. This was a strategy for improving control over expenditures, but freedom is not always easy to bear. In many connections the price of freedom has been greater inequality and, for some, a tougher reality.

One of the most dramatic features to have occurred in Sweden and Norway since 1970 was the new immigration. This was dramatic especially insofar as it forced a revaluation of the basis for national integration—the great project inherited by the Social Democrats from the liberal modernizers. Equality or assimilation had the status of a principle. Now it was being challenged. Diversity meant freedom to pursue one's own identity within this national welfare state. This was something new. But where were the limits with regard to the minimum adaptation that was necessary? In reality, should the liberal integration policy based on diversity perhaps be viewed as a deferment of an assimilation process for the individuals?[115]

---

[115] Brochmann 2003, 209.

The two most important arenas of socialization are the family and the school. The policy in these two areas is especially important for nation building. In the Social Democratic period up to approximately 1970 there was a strikingly harmonious development in these areas. Equally striking is the discord over family and school policy that broke out around 1970. There are clear ideological conflicts here, and the struggles are still not finished. In any case, we can see here a line from the norms of equality in the comprehensive school and the close collective of the traditional family toward individualization and freedom of choice. The two arenas, family and school, have not lost their significance, but they have changed form. The building of society is undertaken today on the basis of other premises. The family and the school are confronted with demands to adapt to individualization and the new cultural diversity. With surrender of the old equality ideal in favor of the new ideal of freedom of choice, central concepts like "welfare" and "integration" have changed their content. The old Social Democratic ideals have not vanished altogether, however.

CHAPTER 14

The Return of Politics

Two Perspectives • Is Democratic Power Disintegrating? • A Weakened Party System •
New Forms of Participation • Social Democracy's Media System • The Great Release •
Threats to Independence • The Media-Biased Society • The Decay of the General Public? •
The Youth Rebellion • Feminism • Marxism-Leninism • Constitutionalism Rediscovered •
The Return of the Values Debate • Jesus—a Social Democrat? • The Common Good •
A Showdown with the Past • The Return of Politics

TWO PERSPECTIVES

It has long been common among historians, especially Scandinavian historians, to regard conflicts of interests as the driving force in the development of
politics. From such an *interest struggle perspective*, compromise is the political
ideal. Social Democracy was a historical compromise between capital and
labor, according to Walter Korpi (see the introduction). Alternatively, the political ideal can be regarded as the transcendence of political contradictions.
This transcendence is to be accomplished through open and informed discussion, which must be carried out before informed conclusions can be reached.
Such a form of politics must be analyzed from a *communication perspective*.
In many instances it should be possible to go beyond the compromises and
attain consensus on what ultimately is the best solution. From the perspective of the interest struggle, public discourse tends to be defined as noise that
veils the power struggle, but, from the communication perspective, public
discourse is the most important element in the political process.

In the 1930s the typical interest parties—the labor parties and the farmers' parties, with close connections to special interest organizations—came
into power, and we got "a glimpse of a political paradigm shift". The Social
Democratic order was subsequently institutionalized to reach compromises
between opposing special interests by way of corporatization. Ironically, this
very order became hegemonic, which means that a high degree of consensus
on the general interest was reached. The interest struggle perspective did not
capture what was actually taking place. The democratic "people's home" was

not based primarily on compromises that left the whole population only half content. Most people became a lot more than half content.

On the other hand, it is important to note that public discourse was at a low level in the heyday of Social Democracy. Consensus does not breed discussions. One of the foremost figures in Swedish public life, the writer and chief editor of *Dagens Nyheter*, Olof Lagercrantz, describes the reality experienced in the 1960s and 1970s: "In the final phase of my lessons of life it was clear to me that in our so-called democratic society there is silence where power is to be found, and noise only where power is slight or hardly visible."[1] He occupied a central position in public life in Sweden and was among those who produced the most "noise." Although he probably undervalued his own power, there were some grounds to take him seriously when he said that he felt himself to be at such a distance from power.

When criticism of the Social Democratic order was raised and interest struggle intensified again during and after the 1970s, there was a renewed liveliness in the public discourse, however. Equally interesting is the new skepticism that arose toward the institutionalization of the special interests in corporatist structures: politics should be concerned not only with compromises between special interests but also with the formation of common goals beyond the special interests. Among the political analysts there was a certain parallel shift from the interest struggle perspective toward the communication perspective.

The role of history and the social sciences in the political process is equivocal. These disciplines give us concepts with which we can describe society, but within these descriptions there is also an element of self-fulfillment. The way society is described is not without significance for actual social development. If the interest struggle perspective is dominant, politicians will have a tendency to regard themselves as representatives of special interests and behave on that basis. Conversely, if the communication perspective dominates, they can regard themselves as representing common interests. They can even see it as their duty to transcend the special interests. Politics might thus change its character.

IS DEMOCRATIC POWER DISINTEGRATING?

The major conclusion of the final white paper report of 2003 from the Norwegian governmental Power and Democracy Project is that "[d]emocratic power as a form of governance is in a state of disintegration rather than

---

[1] Boëthius 2002, 107.

conversion." One particularly important factor behind this development is the process of internationalization and Europeanization. The expanding internationalization represents a weakening of the democratic processes as it leaves our fate more dependent on distant and nontransparent powers. This development has been met with an increase in international agreements and conventions and the development of transnational institutions and judicial systems. This implies, according to the white paper, a "judicialization" of politics by making international legal authorities important points of decision making. "Democracy as a system for decision making . . . remains [however] within the nation-state."[2]

Judicializing is undertaken at the national level as well. To an increasing degree, social and cultural problems are formulated as demands for rights, which results in "judicial organs having increasing importance, at the cost of democratically elected authorities," if we are to believe the white paper findings.[3]

The mandate of the Power and Democracy Project was limited to an investigation of the formal decision-making system through majority decision and popular elective organs. If we keep to this framework, there is something in the tendencies toward democratic disintegration. We have seen how, in an internationalized world, politics becomes a junior partner to business concerns. Economic goals have shoved aside other concerns. We have also noted how the public awareness of rights has assaulted the welfare state and contributed to the weakening of political control over the direction that events have taken. In general the collective organ, the state, has been fragmented and has assumed a lesser role: "The democratically elected authorities have a shrinking playing field on which to operate."[4]

The conclusions of this committee have been criticized, largely for taking into consideration only the decision-making process. If, for example, one looks at the democratic system from the perspective of communications, one will reach other conclusions. But the criticism also extended to the interpretation of the findings.[5] Judicialization does not necessarily shove politics aside. The making of laws can be a powerful instrument in the hands of the politicians, and court procedures are part of the implementation and control of the political decisions. Moreover, it is quite possible to reverse the judicial procedures, as the Swedish Parliament did when it reformed the ATP plan in 1994. The problem concerning the relationship between the democratic organs and the court system is illustrated in Norway with the struggle over the

---

[2] NOU 2003:19. *Makt og demokrati* 2003, pp. 16 and 56. This Power and Democracy Project should not be confused with the Power Project referred to in chapter 12.

[3] NOU 2003:19, p. 30.

[4] NOU 2003:19, p. 57.

[5] Olof Petersson 2003 makes a general criticism.

enabling laws. To delegate decision making to the government administration by way of enabling laws can undermine the power of the democratic organs. The problem was at least partly solved however by implementing "court procedures within the administration.". The courts and courtlike organs can thus function as inspectors and supervisors on behalf of the democratic organs vis-à-vis executive authorities. Hence judicialization does not in itself mean that democracy is attenuated.

There is naturally a question about what kind of democratic representation is being attenuated. The Social Democratic "elite partnership" or the "one-party state," as it has been called, was perhaps not so very much more democratic than the system that developed since the 1970s. Utilizing an extended approach by attaching importance to the communications perspective, the conclusions of the white paper are turned around. It appears that popular representation as a form of governance is in a process of conversion rather than disintegration.

A WEAKENED PARTY SYSTEM

Around 1970 the Social Democratic parties lost their hegemony. Of equal importance, the old blocs or alliances of party, press, and interest organizations fell apart. The various elements went their own ways, seeking out other alliances to some degree. Through the process of corporatization the organizations had almost become part of public administration. The same could be said of the political parties.

With the exception of the conservative parties, which had their roots in the old ruling class and civil service stratum, the parties had originated from the great popular movements. The old class-based party system had been stable because so many people had voted on the basis of class allegiance without really posing any critical questions. Voting had taken on a ritual character, something that gave great power to the leadership. It is not by chance that so many researchers have come to see the Social Democratic system as having been led from the top. In Norway the expression "some people have spoken together" meant that real decisions were taken by a small, closed circle of top leaders from the hegemonic Social Democratic parties and the different interest organizations. The political parties tended to lose their character of popular movements, choosing instead a symbiotic relationship with the public administration. In this way the parties were converted "from vital parts of civil society to an outgrowth of the resource-rich public sector."[6] It is symptom-

---

[6] Amnå 2001, 216.

atic that economic responsibility for the political parties was gradually taken over by the state. This began in 1965 in Sweden and in 1970 in Norway. The number of party members declined.

The political party pattern had been created by a different reality characterized by class contradictions. In order to maintain party identity, it is still important to both the Social Democratic and the conservative parties to maintain that there is a deep abyss between them. However, changing social structures mean that the abyss is not so great any longer. This is demonstrated by the fact that a very significant number of voters are able to hop over it with ease. Another problem for the parties is that there can no longer be such a continuity of viewpoints as there was in the old class-dominated society. If a person's beliefs about a particular issue were known, conclusions could usually be drawn about party affiliation and what that person believed about other issues. This is no longer the case—the picture is more fractured.

What happens to the radical reform parties when people's subjective class consciousness is weakened and reforms have been implemented? Many believed that the goals of Social Democracy had been attained, but this did not apply to everyone. Social Democracy was split between those who felt that the goals had been reached and those who felt that they still lived within a capitalist society where radical reforms remained crucial. The situation had created uncertainty as to the very identity of the party. Which voters should they be recruiting? The danger, naturally enough, was that politics could decline into an opportunistic fishing for votes.

Nor had the old party model managed to unite differences of viewpoint regarding some of the important issues that came onto the agenda of "the new reality." This applies in part to the issue of expanding the production of energy, in which environmental protection has played a role. We have seen that the conflict over this expansion has created difficulties for all the parties, especially the Social Democrats. The big question, however, has naturally been the response toward the European Union. This is a central issue bringing to bear underlying differences in point of view about what the future society should look like, and it has led to deep divisions within the Social Democratic parties. Sweden went through an agonizing controversy that ended with EU membership. This struggle has arisen several times in Norway, and there is little to indicate that it has come to an end. The continuous dispute is particularly uncomfortable for the Labor Party of Norway. By defining the issue as something extraordinary, the party has managed to keep it out of ordinary election campaigns, thereby preventing a damaging internal dispute. But when the political parties fail to take the initiative, others step forward to do so.

NEW FORMS OF PARTICIPATION

The approach taken around the question of European Union membership is an example of what has been called "single issue participation." The European Community (later the European Union) issues were of major dimension, and the question whether to join the union or not was taken care of by ad hoc organizations, although to a certain degree in cooperation with the political parties. Such ad hoc organizations for political action have now become more common. Their members might find themselves involved in letter writing, signing petitions, demonstrations, political strikes, or similar forms of agitation. Originally these types of actions were associated with issues where the party system functioned badly or where there was a general mistrust of the political system, but this is no longer the case. Those who take part in such actions have been steadily more representative of the entire population. It is a way of acting politically that seems to suit "the postmodern human being." Such actions are not particularly demanding, especially insofar as they do not imply long-term engagement. But they usually consist of very conscious action and undoubtedly reflect political interests that extend beyond the old ritual casting of votes. This development runs simultaneously in the Scandinavian countries, yet it is the Swedish who are the most active. It seems as though the Swedes have been more interested in foreign policy and peace, while Norwegians have been most interested in environmental questions.[7]

Another difference between the two countries is that the party system is more stable in Sweden than in Norway. The Swedish Social Democrats have retained more of their position from their hegemonic phase, and new parties have difficulty in getting a foothold. We have seen how Palme prevented the formation of a strong left radical party in line with the Left Socialist Party of Norway. Nor has Sweden had a protest party with a right populist stamp comparable to the Progress Party of Norway, in spite of efforts in that direction.

The sinking membership in the parties cannot be taken as a lack of political interest, nor can the declining participation in elections (which is still not as dramatic as some would have it). More accurately, political participation is now taking new forms; people are seeking new channels for action. Research shows that there is no decrease in political interest, certainly not among the young. They often discuss politics and are positive to basic democratic values. Relying on research undertaken in Sweden, Anders Bruhn has concluded, "what is paradoxical in this context is that today the youth can generally be considered more politically competent than earlier generations, despite the fact that election participation has decreased within this group."[8]

[7] Andersen and Hoff 2001, 176.
[8] Bruhn 1999, 260. Westholm and Teorell 1999.

Still, there are certain features in these developments that give rise to concern. Contempt for politicians is often noted. A feeling of distance arises quite easily when the parties have gone from being organs of mass mobilization to being the extended arm of the administration. Here, however, Sweden and Norway differ. In Norway there is a remarkably high degree of confidence in the way the political system functions; in Sweden the mistrust is greater. In the European context, Norway is atypical.[9]

Two circumstances contribute to our understanding of Norway's continued faith in the system. Part of the explanation may lie in that the political establishment was twice defeated in EEC and EU referendums.[10] Paradoxically, faith is placed in a system in which the leaders were voted *against*. In Sweden we can say that the political establishment received a vote of confidence insofar as it received an endorsement for joining the European Union. Hence the relations between confidence and the result of the EU voting must be more complicated in Norway. It does not have to do with confidence in the establishment so much as confidence in a system where it is possible that the establishment can be defeated by means of popular voting. Indeed, the system was demonstrably capable of being led from below and, as such, was a more democratic system than that of the old Social Democracy, wherein leadership was exercised by the people at the top. It seems as though this top-down form of leadership has survived to a greater extent in Sweden.[11]

Another reason for the high degree of confidence in the Norwegian system is the existence of the relatively strong Progress Party in Norway. The Progress Party is a right-wing populist party in the sense that it has gathered support from disaffected voters who feel they are furthest from the system. This means that the Progress Party channels dissatisfaction *into* the system, something that actually has the effect of lessening dissatisfaction *with* the system. Paradoxically, the party of disaffection with the system becomes the best defender of the system.[12]

So far, it is possible to conclude that the shift of political epoch that became evident from around 1970—and has since become much clearer—has not led to a weakening of democracy. Quite the reverse: people's political interests are at least as great as previously, and the discussions in the public arena function at least as well. Central issues such as membership in the EU and environmental questions (the nuclear energy debate in Sweden and the debate over natural gas power in Norway) are being intensively discussed

[9] Andersen and Hoff 2001, 164–165.

[10] Aardal 1999, 189.

[11] When it comes to the opposition of the periphery to the European Union, there was a noticeable gap between politicians and voters in Sweden, while the Norwegian politicians more closely reflected the feelings of the voters. Communicated by Henry Valen.

[12] Aardal 1999, 178.

in the public arena, and although the different positions on these issues are not unambiguously associated with specific political parties, they have led to changes of government. The civil society is functioning, but the parties are playing a different, and less prominent, role than they did earlier. To a greater degree, the political agenda is set by others.

Bo Rothstein has pointed out that the public administration in Sweden has taken over a portion of the old party role. The state apparatus has been ideologized such that "the ideological struggle in society sometimes tends to take place between different public officials rather than between different parties or interest organizations." From being experts who could peacefully carry out reforms on the basis of their expertise and in accordance with directives issued and guidelines established by the democratic organs, the directors of public boards and other public institutions have become creators of public opinion. They have become central, publicly paid political actors who struggle to win attention for those issues slated for action. We see this most clearly with different public mandates (ombudsmen)—the Gender-Equality Commission, the Children's Commission, and others. Rothstein mentions other civil service entities as well, such as the National Institute for Public Health, the National Agency for Higher Education, the National Authority for Rural Affairs, the National Youth Administration, and others. In all likelihood this tendency of bureaucrats to play a political role in the public arena is stronger in Sweden, where there has been a tradition of relative independence among civil service authorities. The tendency is thus in the direction of a bureaucratically conducted political process: "The parliamentary-democratic chain of leadership is still spinning in Sweden, but it spins backward."[13]

In general it can scarcely be said that democracy is disintegrating. The extremist movements that found adherents through great portions of the twentieth century, creating totalitarian regimes in several European countries and leading to hot and cold wars, today do not represent any threat, at least not in the Scandinavian countries. Throughout Europe there is a strong adherence to democracy as the only acceptable form of governance.[14] Nor is a certain weakening of the party system a sign of disintegration, as long as it means *voters* have seized power. It is more a sign of a return to politics. The voters are behaving, as Erik Amnå writes, "precisely as democratic theory hopes: curious, critical and disloyal."[15] But we must then ask where these voters have gotten their views. How are attitudes generated in the new reality? We now undoubtedly have a more vital public life with many different

[13] Rothstein 2004.
[14] Dogan 2002.
[15] Amnå 2001, 215.

actors in the public arena. We must shift our attention away from the political parties and toward other elements in the dispersed blocs of parties, press, and organizations.

SOCIAL DEMOCRACY'S MEDIA SYSTEM

In the Swedish white paper on power we read that "the road to power over the thoughts of the citizens goes . . . to a substantial degree through power over the mass media."[16] The role of the media is not new, but it has been considerably strengthened: "the media have come to acquire a . . . uniquely central role in the life of society," to cite from the foreword of a book called *The Mediazation of Sweden*.[17] Written in the 1990s, the book reflects developments in the decades following the hegemonic phase of Social Democracy.

From the beginning of the twentieth century through the interwar period, the press, "as a tool of the governing parties . . . , had fused with the exercise of power by the state authorities."[18] The press was bound to the political parties, and the Social Democratic press was the most tightly bound. But the bourgeois press too was bound, or bound itself, to the parties. There were exceptions, such as *Dagens Nyheter* in Stockholm and *Dagbladet* in Oslo—liberal papers that became forums for independent intellectuals. But they were rare. This system of a party-linked press was characteristic of the Social Democratic period. It meant that politics, or the political process, was a closed and controlled shop compared with what would follow. The Norwegian professor of history Jens Arup Seip, in his 1963 lecture on the "one-party state," said that he was better informed about American politics than he was about Norwegian politics.

The broadcast media, radio and television, have their own history. Private radio broadcasts began in Scandinavia in the 1920s but were rapidly regulated by means of special legislation and agreements, and were gradually converted into a state monopoly. This strong state interest is connected to the fact that radio was looked on as potentially a promising part of a popular enlightenment project. Television was established in 1960 as a direct expansion of the state radio monopoly, the Norwegian Broadcasting Corporation (NRK). The same thing happened in Sweden when Parliament decided in 1956 that television ought to be part of the Swedish Radio Service, which simultaneously changed its name to Swedish Radio AB.

---

[16] Petersson and Carlberg 1990, 34.
[17] Björnsson and Luthersson 1997, 7.
[18] Dahl and Bastiansen 2000, 269.

While the arts and the sciences were separated into independent fields, the reverse occurred with the media. The political agenda had been established by the political parties—to an increasing degree by the Social Democratic parties. The press had no independent power in society, and the broadcast media remained monopolized under state control. Such was the media system of Social Democracy, but it would change radically.

THE GREAT RELEASE

The grounds for the media acquiring "a uniquely central role in the life of society," which we referred to in the beginning of the preceding section, lay with freeing the media from the political parties during the 1970s, following the hegemonic period of the Social Democrats. In a surprisingly short time the media became a sphere in its own right within society, which would come to have considerable consequences. The media now stepped forward as the "third estate" in Sweden, and as the "fourth estate" in Norway. (In Sweden the judicial system is not counted as a separate branch of government; it is part of the state administration.) It is symptomatic that state support for the press was instituted during this time, in 1969 in Norway and in 1971 in Sweden.[19] The collapse of newspapers had hit Sweden harder than it did Norway, and the Swedish conditions were called forward as a warning when support was ratified in Norway.[20] The press system had to be supported, and it had to be independent.

The release of the media represented a process of differentiation that was in line with general modernization processes in other spheres. Characteristic of such a development was the insistence on professionalization. The journalists wanted to win legitimacy and recognition as autonomous skilled workers. The mixture of politics and journalism had led to politics becoming very much like a closed shop. It was now a task for the journalism profession to open up this shop, and the journalists had their liberation program.[21] The public press itself led the campaign for public support, arguing that this was one of the conditions for independence. On the other hand, the political parties were happy to be freed from the responsibility of keeping up the press system. Moreover, the parties found that the press coverage they received was frequently better than before, since the remaining (larger) newspapers now functioned as arenas for public debate. But they became unfaithful servants

---

[19] Sundberg 2001, 154; Sejersted 2003b (*Opposisjon og posisjon*), 408; Hadenius 2000, 158; Engblom, Jonsson, and Gustafsson 2002, 220.

[20] Dahl and Bastiansen 2000, 275.

[21] Raaum 2001, 60, 73.

to the parties. Another factor behind this liberating process was the competition from the state-owned broadcast media, where standards were set for independence from the parties that the newspapers had to live up to.

The broadcast media were also to be set free, not from the parties, but from the state. The monopoly situation had led to a demand that coverage had to be balanced; it also led to continuous anxieties about whether broadcasts leaned too far to the right or the left. In 1971 the Swedish television system broadcast a series on the development of Social Democracy, *From Socialism to Increased Equality*, which would prove to be "the most criticized Swedish TV programming in history."[22] The criticism was that the series had a marked leftist bias, and it came most appreciably from the Social Democrats themselves. The elderly Erlander characterized the series as "a tragic mistake," claiming the viewers had been beguiled by the "independent" journalists with the intention of "combating Democratic Socialism's founding ideology."[23] This story demonstrates a dilemma, and it strengthened the demand for greater diversity of opinion over the airwaves.

There were also issues that more directly demonstrated the need for an independent and critical press, such as the conflict in Norway over membership in the EEC in 1972.[24] In Sweden the IB affair of 1973 played a similar role. In this matter, two radical journalists unmasked the existence of the secret service organization IB. These two were imprisoned, and the debate over the role of journalists gathered velocity.[25] In Norway in 1977 similar leakages occurred with regard to the secret services, and with corresponding debate about openness and the role of the press.[26] This journalistic digging was extended under the new system and was a precondition for opening the closed shop of politics. As it was put, the media had a *task of unmasking*.

As for the broadcast media, the monopoly held out a surprisingly long time. But in 1979 there was a large debate in the Norwegian Parliament in which the Conservative Party member Lars Roar Langslet argued that the monopoly was an antiquated form. The Social Democrats hesitated. Langslet's argument was based partly on the fact that it was impossible to maintain an actual monopoly, owing to technological change. It was also an ideological argument in part, from the point of view of freedom of expression. Following the Conservative election victory in 1981, Langslet became minister of

[22] The expression is from Torsten Thurén, cited by Linderborg 2001, 423.

[23] Linderborg 2001, 426.

[24] Raaum 2001, 61. For a general treatment of the death of the party press in Norway, see Dahl and Bastiansen 2000, 274.

[25] Hadenius 2000, 159.

[26] This had to do with the "Loran C Case" and the "Issue of the List"; cf. Dahl and Bastiansen 2000, 302–313.

culture. His banner issue was the dissolution of the monopoly, which occurred in 1983. Sweden followed suit in 1987 during a Social Democratic
government. Everyone was now on board. Thus, in the course of less than two
decades, the media picture had completely changed.

THREATS TO INDEPENDENCE

That the ratification of state support to the media meant liberation is a problematic position. Would we get a system with state newspapers? This threat
was revealed in Norway in 1974 when the parliamentary spokesperson responsible for the issue of press support, the Social Democrat Oddmund
Faremo, proposed setting up an organ of public control to prevent the press
from establishing itself "as an independent state power with the marketing
of its own ideas and its own leaders and central personalities."[27] Of course
this unleashed a storm of criticism from the media, but it shows that the idea
of quid pro quo from the press was in the air. The idea appeared again in
Norway and Sweden in different forms, but a control organization has never
become a reality. Quite the opposite, the press became an "independent state
power," as Faremo feared.

Criticism of the press has persisted since its inception, particularly regarding the violation of personal privacy (in Norwegian—*personvern*). The press
organizations have themselves been in favor of putting their own ethical
norms in writing and setting up their own surveillance organs. Sweden has its
Press Council, which has since been supplemented by the Press Ombudsman.
Norway has the Professional Press Committee. The fear that external control
organs would be established has driven this process forward. Thus it has the
character of "strategically induced self-administrated justice."[28] The danger of
public control has, in any case, been averted.

Liberation from the power of proprietorship or "owners' censorship" was
not eliminated with the freeing of the press from the political parties, of
course. The extensive media, which were not in need of state support, were
now possessed by capital-rich owners. There have been attempts to build defenses against the power of the owners. In Sweden editorial independence is
set down in law; in Norway it was defended by a voluntary agreement, the
declaration "Rights and Duties of the Editor," but has recently been made
law. The advertisers are another economic interest group with the ability to
threaten editorial independence. Some have maintained that "the tyranny

---

[27] Dahl and Bastiansen 2000, 278.
[28] Dahl and Bastiansen 2000, 117–118. Hadenius and Weibull 1999, 29f.

of sources" is also a great problem. In the busy everyday world, it is not unusual for the journalist to become a voluntary slave to the institutional elites.
These resource-rich sources have professionalized their information operations through the upgrading of their information workers, and in this way
have attained influence over what is published for public consumption, and
in what form.[29] In different ways, economic interests can thus threaten the
independence of the media.

The importance of the power of the owners was seen in Arne Ruth's dramatic resignation as one of the editors in chief of *Dagens Nyheter* in 1998 in
Stockholm. Ruth was one of the most prominent members of the press in
Scandinavia. The reason he gave for his departure was that the editor was
subjugated to economic demands in a way that undermined journalistic independence. This resignation was called forth by the desire of the powerful
owners of *Dagens Nyheter*, the Bonnier family and the Marieberg Group, to
take over the other large morning newspaper in Stockholm, the old, conservative *Svenska Dagbladet*. This would put the single owner in a completely
dominant position, while at the same time such a merger of two newspapers,
each with its own profile, implied that the ideals of publicizing the news
were subordinated to purely commercial concerns. Ultimately nothing came
of this plan, and the *Svenska Dagbladet* was taken over by the Norwegian
Schibsted Group. Threats against the independence of the media can be seen
as a blow against the open society, but we should turn the question around, as
well. Can the *media* constitute a threat against the open society?

THE MEDIA-BIASED SOCIETY

In 1973 the Swedish economics professor Assar Lindbeck wrote that to an
increasing degree journalists had taken over the role of the opposition and
at the same time changed it. By making the initial kickoff in particular cases
and thereby selecting which subjects to elevate as "stories," they have managed to set the political agenda. In this way the system has became a "kickoff
democracy."[30] In 1977 Gudmund Hernes in Norway followed up Lindbeck's
move when he gave his approval to the theory of kickoff democracy. At the
same time, he argued that the old debate about whether the media, particularly the broadcast monopoly, were "left-biased" or "right-biased" missed the
essential point. According to Hernes, the issue was that the media themselves
had become "media-biased."

[29] Reinton 1984; Allern 1996.
[30] Lindbeck 1974, 96f.

The selection and form of media presentation were not colored by the political points of view of the journalists but by techniques for capturing attention: that is, simplifying, polarizing, intensifying, and concretizing ideas.[31] This special form of presentation has nourished the conception of journalism as a new and special perception of society. To the extent that this form of presentation is practiced, for example, journalistic reporting can "easily become exposed to infiltration from adjoining territories, namely fiction and marketing."[32] The boundary between biased information and critical commentary, on the one hand, and entertainment, on the other, can become blurred.

That this modern form of journalism can so easily serve commercial interests is problematic. It is commonly maintained that large media concerns can be good owners since they represent professionalism and security for the journalists.[33] But the merging of interests goes beyond this. Editors and journalists, as well as owners, do well with simplification, polarization, intensification, and concretization as they collaborate on the creation of a popular and highly sellable product. Commercialization and journalism go together hand in glove. Ruth's demonstrative resignation leaves us with the impression that the match is not idyllic, however, nor perhaps *should* it be.

The new journalism has to do with form of presentation, but form and content cannot be separated. Journalism has its own way of portraying the world. It provides us with the categories that help us interpret and understand our surroundings. This process acquires its own political content, even though this was not the intention at the outset. In the Norwegian context it has been pointed out paradoxically that the media, which are populated by journalists who are hostile to the right-wing populist Progress Party, nonetheless have contributed to the party's success. Populist journalism and populist politics use the same language, a language "that most people understand without further explanation." This language avoids the more complex correlations, those that require the use of abstract categories, and instead reduces questions of society to personal questions and ad hoc problems.[34]

Thus it is not the party of protest, the Progress Party, that comes off the worst; that honor goes to the old "establishment." This new journalism has generally led to a tense relationship between the press and the politicians that bubbles to the surface from time to time. We find one example in 1998 when the state secretary, and later cabinet minister, Jan O. Karlsson exploded in the pages of *Aftonbladet*: "The Swedish journalistic corps today is one of the most

---

[31] Gudmund Hernes 1978, 188–189.
[32] Raaum 1999, 170.
[33] Eide 2000, 261.
[34] Anders Johansen 2001, 169.

repulsive packs that one can see. There one cannot help but find lying, sloppiness, laziness, alcohol, vanity, shortcuts, superficiality, and sniffing around the contours of people's genitals."[35]

The contrast between the foregoing era with its interpretations of a society based on ideologies that were linked to class, on the one hand, and the new communications perspective, on the other, is obvious. As Olof Petersson says: "Journalism has become the information society's perception of society, as opposed to the religious representations during the agrarian society and the political ideologies during industrialism."[36] Journalism has become our "knowledge regime," if we are to believe Petersson. But should we do so?

THE DECAY OF THE GENERAL PUBLIC?

The picture presented so far must be modified. The new journalism does not necessarily dominate the serious media. In addition, the journalists are not the only participants in public discussion. There are book publishers, intellectuals, writers, politicians, advertising and marketing agents, directors of public institutions, and others. Nor can one speak of only one public sphere: there are many, with their various ways of speaking about the world. And how does communication function among them? The development of the media plays a central role, but we must also broaden our perspective in order to get a view of the world within which the media exist.

In building their knowledge regime, the Social Democrats relied above all on the social sciences, which offered useful concepts for developing images of the larger world. The rhetoric of economics came to dominate political life. Maybe Olof Petersson was correct in saying that political ideologies took over as paradigms of interpretation when it came to the ways we comprehended society during the first phase of industrialization. But when we approached the second phase, when the Social Democrats had taken over the hegemonic positions and the ideologies were declared dead,[37] the social scientists, with the economists in the lead, colonized politics, and rational discourse predominated. But nothing lasts forever.

Assar Lindbeck was ahead of his time when, in 1973, he complained that the journalists had taken over the role of the opposition in political life by setting the agenda. But he was perhaps not completely conscious of the sig-

---

[35] Engblom, Jonsson, and Gustafsson 2002, 317.

[36] Cited from Eide 2001, 65.

[37] The death of ideologies was first declared by Raymond Aron in 1955. Cf. Judt 2007, 384. The idea was taken up by Daniel Bell (1960). In Scandinavia the idea was promoted by the Swedish writer Herbert Tingsten. Cf. Tingsten 1966.

nificance of his own role as leading economist when it came to laying down premises for political decision making. He was probably more powerful than any journalist, and more powerful than the editor Olof Lagercrantz, when he made his complaint about journalists. But people seldom see their own power as clearly as they see that of others.

When the political sphere opened up with the freeing of the media, the economists (and other social scientists) lost their hegemony over interpretation. This is not to say that they lost all power but that they had to share it with others, and among these the journalists. We see a revitalization of the public arena and of politics. This did not mean that, by setting the agenda, the media had taken politics out of the hands of the politicians; rather, it was taken out of the hands of the economists and the other technocrats. The communicative space was reestablished as a political arena. The economists (and others who had held a semihegemonic role) found themselves confronted with competing interpretations.

There is now a diversity and a vitality in the public arena that was absent before. Noise or continuous clamor had been obscuring power, which was precisely the reason that power could be quietly exerted. This situation had now been turned on its head. The ability to produce noise or clamor became a power resource in its own right in the new communications society. But this did not mean that all power was now in the hands of journalists. It is a great exaggeration to think that the journalistic understanding of reality now became as predominant as had the former rationality discourse. The old discourse was replaced with a new diversity.

The media must be viewed in a broader context. What is most important from a communications perspective is not what is written but how it is read or perceived. To return once more to Olof Petersson: "In the long run the journalists' dominant position is also undermined by the ongoing changes within the population. All the available research findings point out that today's citizens have become more and more knowledgeable and questioning."[38] Nor can one conclude, on the basis of interest in a medium, that people believe that medium. *Verdens Gang* (*VG*) is Norway's largest newspaper, but it receives a low score with regard to public confidence in its content. Thus there is reason to believe in the existence of a critical opinion that is not manipulated by the media. People are not so easily misled.

The threat to public discourse comes not only from above, from "authorized" interpreters such as experts or journalists, however; it can also come from below, from a growing public doubt that there can be an objective, verifiable picture of reality. Such doubt makes it difficult to develop even

---

[38] Cited from NOU 1996:12, *Medieombud*, p. 12.

minimal common understanding. We live in a fractured world where there is a tendency away from hegemonic interpretation. This tendency is strengthened by the fact that our society has become multicultural in a manner never seen before. Communication occurs within many small public spheres, but communication between these spheres is very poorly executed. Individual communication communities develop their own languages or codes. The "tribe" withdraws more and more to its own territory, whether its members be immigrants or established elites.

In addition to this splintering into many public spheres, we also see an individualistic insistence on one's own subjective feelings and interpretations. The reason that this tendency has become so clear now lies partly with the development of the media. The media orientation implies a dramatization through concentration on the individual life and the concrete episode. The large social questions that can be addressed only through the use of abstract categories are left lying in the shadows.

There is a relationship between this concentration on the individual life and the modern tendency toward wanting to live an aesthetic life. In the (post)modern society, art is perceived as creation, according to the philosopher Charles Taylor, and modern self-realization is perceived on the same terms, namely as creative art as opposed to morality. According to this view, standard morality becomes associated with stiff conventionalism. Value is what one creates for oneself, and that interpretation can give a feeling of freedom and power. Individuals step into the public sphere in order to realize themselves by becoming visible. The public arena, where previously people could debate the great social questions, increasingly becomes a stage people use to attract attention. It has become a space peopled with celebrities about whom we gradually come to know the most intimate details. Diversity can be positive, but it also has its price.

Thus it might seem that the common arena is threatened. But all this remains in the form of tendencies. As has been pointed out, there is a new vitality in public discussion. Despite the threats, the public sphere has hardly collapsed in relation to how public discussion functioned during the hegemonic phase of Social Democracy. As we have seen, with the new vitality it is rather the other way round.

THE YOUTH REBELLION

During the latter half of the 1960s and into the 1970s, in what can be called the prepolitical arena, a new diversity of movements and subcultures blossomed forth—a diversity that is difficult to summarize and that the political parties have managed to co-opt only slightly. We have looked at the envi-

ronmental movement, the immigrant cultures, and journalism—all of which
have given a certain amount of indigestion to the established political system.
But perhaps the most spectacular development around 1970 was *youth rebellion.* This was a common antiauthoritarian rebellion, a demand for freedom
from what Social Democrat Olof Palme referred to as the "authoritarian society." Ironically, this rebellion itself ended up in a totalitarian movement.
From a political perspective the rebellion was only a parenthesis, but it left
an imprint. It tugged at familiar ideas, and in countries such as Sweden and
Norway it contributed to the loosening of the Social Democratic idealized
worldview. Although the youth rebellion itself became perverted and lost is
steam, it was a particularly pronounced expression of the broad shift in mentality that came to distinguish society in the course of the turbulent 1970s.

It is not exceptional that youth rebel, and the youth rebellion around
1970 had its precursors under Social Democracy. In the Western world of
the 1950s there arose a frustrated generation of "angry young men" who had
grown up during the war and were in rebellion against the wartime generation of their parents, and against the postwar society-building initiatives with
their pressure for conformity. The rebellion was spurred by John Osborne's
play *Look Back in Anger.* It did not really take root in Scandinavia, but we
did feel the effects of some of its wave action. Thus it is that the Norwegian
writer Axel Jensen came to be characterized as one of the angry young men.
He was also known in Sweden, where he eventually lived for several years. In
his 1957 novel *Icarus,* the rebellion is aimed at the fact that "the possibilities
of development of the self are subjected to the limitations of an ever grayer
and more conformist society."[39] The book's main character describes his own
writing project as "a book that knots its fists against the welfare state. [It is
the] defiance of a generation. The falsetto shriek, and 'go to hell' daubed on
the wall in garish colors—while at the same time trying to get a toehold in a
richer reality."[40]

The rebellion of the 1970s was more comprehensive and went deeper than
that of the 1950s. No easy explanation has been given for this; it is simply
that when different lines of development cross one another, the unexpected
happens. The ground was fertilized by features that had created aversion
toward the past and a demand for liberation—the dawning environmental
movement, a new awareness of the shortcomings of the welfare state, and a
reaction against Social Democracy's ideals of unity and equality: in short, a
general dissatisfaction with the established society. The rebels were seeking "a
richer reality."

[39] Myklebust 2004.
[40] Jensen 1957, 14.

Figure 17. The 1970s were the decade of conflicts. This photo shows a demonstration of the "Red Front" on May 1, 1972, in Oslo. Norway's membership in NATO and the discussion about membership in the European Economic Community (EEC, later the European Union) gave the left opposition concrete issues to grapple with, something their compatriots in Sweden lacked. The text on the banners says: "No to the selling of Norway. Struggle against EEC." (Photo: Arbeiderbevegelsens arkiv.)

More immediately, there was a germ of anxiety about the population explosion within educational institutions. The younger generation was streaming into the academic secondary schools and the colleges and universities, which quickly became overcrowded. This forced reform proposals, around which there were many vicious disputes, to the fore. The chaotic situation at the universities contributed to the youth rebellion being, first and foremost, a student revolt. And there was the Vietnam War. We have seen how Prime Minister Palme, with his sharply articulated criticism of U.S. policy, was able to associate himself with at least parts of the rebellion. Thus there were several factors that ran together, leading toward something resembling a comprehensive uprising against the norms of the parental generation. The students were involved with "no single question, apart from dismissing the adult world in its entirety."[41]

[41] Blomqvist 1998, 12.

The student rebellion spread remarkably quickly, not only in the Western world but also on other continents. It is important to be aware of the almost global nature of the uprising. It is equally important to note the variation in its characteristics and in the concrete issues taken up by the rebellion, based on differences between countries, although the Vietnam protest certainly broke out in most places. In 1967 there were violent outbursts at the London School of Economics. In the American universities there were vast demonstrations against the Vietnam War, and in Berlin the protest developed under the charismatic leadership of Rudi Dutschke. The most dramatic protest occurred in Paris in the spring of 1968. This began with violent student demonstrations at the Sorbonne University, and the disturbances rapidly spread over the whole of Paris. There were several confrontations with the police. At one point ten million French workers protesting the French establishment joined in as well.

In Sweden the University of Lund celebrated its three hundredth anniversary under the protection of three hundred policemen, with helicopters circling over the campus. The students burned their student caps but otherwise remained peaceful.[42] At this early phase conditions in Norway were less acute than in comparable countries. Among other things, there was never talk about calling in the police.[43]

The Swedish student rebellion concentrated particularly on the criticism of imperialism, while in Norway it was at first rooted in the academic criticism of positivism. Inspired by the German philosopher Jürgen Habermas, such criticism was developed in the 1960s and directed against such fields as psychology, philosophy, and sociology, but also the Labor Party's technocratic politics. The Norwegian criticism was critical of the regime and "struck the Labor Party state precisely in its ideological center" in a different and more direct way than did the Swedish rebellion, which to some degree Palme had been able to deflect with his anti-imperialism.[44] But other forces in the youth rebellion would soon cut ahead of both Palme and the Norwegian academic critics of positivism.

FEMINISM

Out of the diversity of extraparliamentary critical movements that had sprung up in the 1960s and would leave their collective mark on so much

---

[42] Blomqvist 1998, 11.
[43] Kalleberg 1998, 52, 83, note 1.
[44] Kalleberg 1998, 65f.; Slagstad 2001, 10.

of the 1970s, the environmental movement and the women's movement had the greatest influence on politics. They also had a life that would extend beyond the decade. We have already seen how the environmental questions hit the core of the modernization project through energy policy, and we have seen how the housewife contract was replaced by the gender-equality contract, something that came to create conflict regarding the new family policy.

Around 1970 a new, more radical, and action-oriented women's movement burst into view. "If you ask me about the 1970s, that was the decade of joy, with the effervescence of marching women—the decade of sisterhood—the decade when we first spoke the word *liberation*," as one of the Norwegian activists has since put it. "Resist—Don't weep! Be joyful—Go on the offensive!" This was the headline of a leaflet handed out at a number of women's workplaces in Sweden in June 1970. It went on to say, "Do you want to work for more day care, better conditions at the workplace, free abortion? Do you want to participate in the struggle for a Socialist society? Come to Group 8's information meeting."[45]

Group 8, consisting of eight new feminists, became the focal point for an extensive new feminist mobilization around 1970. While the old women's liberation movement was liberal and worked within the political system, the new one would study the women's questions from a Marxist perspective in order to discover the reasons for the oppression of women. But it also mobilized on the basis of current issues. Free abortion and "good and free day care for all children" were central demands. Yet despite these demands, the new feminists had an unclear relationship to family policy. The difference in relation to the traditional women's movement had much to do with form and rhetoric as well as age. The new feminists were part of the youth rebellion and thereby also in rebellion against facets of the Social Democratic order.

Group 8 grew rapidly. It was antiauthoritarian and antihierarchical in structure, and based on autonomous local groups. This in itself was a protest against the hierarchical structure of male-dominated society. In their groups the women would speak about their personal experience. One of the central slogans was "The personal is political." The organization contributed powerfully to putting the liberation of women on the agenda, and concrete reforms were achieved. Yet factionalism soon broke out. Among others, Working Women was established in 1974. Marxism was set against feminism over the question of whether working-class women should be freed before reforms were sought for all women. Should it be an avant-garde or a mass

---

[45] Östberg 2002, 138. The following is based, for Sweden, on Östberg and Witt-Brattström 1975.

movement?[46] A broad spectrum of organizations, groups, and initiatives appeared. Nevertheless, we see that the tradition of public unity in support of women's rights was maintained by mobilization around concrete issues, such as day care and strong punishment for rape.[47]

Developments in Norway paralleled those in Sweden. In 1970 an organization called the New Feminists was formed. Strongly reminiscent of Group 8 with its loose nonhierarchical structure, it was able to accommodate differing ideas. "The sickness is the man, no matter which political-economic models are taken as the bases for an analysis of human existence," wrote Nina Karin Monsen in 1970.[48] This is radical enough, but it is hardly Marxism. A year later Wenche Hjellum gave a speech in which she stressed that the enemy was not men but rather "the capitalists, the owners of the means of production." This was the starting point for the formation of the Marxist-inspired Women's Front, which rapidly became the largest of the many women's organizations in Norway. The women of the Marxist-Leninist movement (see below) organized as a separate faction within the Women's Front and gained great influence. In 1975 there was a new split. As in Sweden, a broad spectrum of groups and initiatives arose. Working Women in Sweden did not in any way achieve the same dominant position in the 1970s as the Marxist Women's Front did in Norway. Later the Women's Front developed into a more isolated radical feminist movement that has remained critical of the notion of gender equality within the existing society. In Norway, too, the various women's liberation organizations tried to cooperate on the practical level, but there was no tradition of a common public arena for discussing women's issues. It is characteristic that on International Women's Day, March 8, there were for many years two processions in many Norwegian cities.[49]

The liberal-feminist movement left its mark on policy. Norway got its gender-equality law in 1978, and Sweden in 1979. Feminism had become "state feminism," a concept introduced by Helga Hernes referring to the extension of Scandinavian state functions to include incorporation of female citizens as participants in public life.[50] She identifies state feminism with Social Democracy's orientation to equality. A breakthrough came when Gro Harlem Brundtland formed her government, in which eight of the eighteen cabinet ministers were women, in 1986. This attracted attention in large parts of the Western world. Yet work still remains to be done in terms of finding gender equality in practice.

[46] Witt-Brattström 1975, 190.
[47] Östberg 2002, 143.
[48] Lønnå 1996, 235.
[49] Lønnå 1996, 238, 240–241.
[50] Helga Hernes 2004.

MARXISM-LENINISM

Generally speaking, the youth rebellion came late to Norway, but this did not mean it was any less radical there than it was in comparable countries—quite the opposite. We shall dwell on one of the rebellion's most spectacular manifestations. In 1966 Mao put the Cultural Revolution in motion in China. This was a vital impulse for the development of the Marxist-Leninist (M-L) movement in several countries, including Sweden and Norway. Under the Cultural Revolution's regime of terror, China stood as a revolutionary ideal, as did the strongly oppressive Communist regime in Albania and, in retrospect, the Stalin-era regime of the Soviet Union.

Maoism was part of the general youth rebellion. Its development would take form in different ways in Sweden and Norway, however. The Swedish M-L movement was quickly ravaged by internal factionalism. The Norwegian movement, in contrast, was unique in its unity and loyalty, and in terms of the mark it was to leave on Norwegian society in the 1970s. As Ann-Mari Skorpen says in her comparison of the movement in the two countries, the strength of the Norwegian movement was "remarkable." Compared with any other country, there were fewer sharp social divisions in Norway that seemingly would lead to the formation of a revolutionary movement.[51] The question is thus how an emphatically authoritarian movement could usurp the leadership of an antiauthoritarian rebellion in a small, peaceful, egalitarian society like that of Norway.

The Norwegian M-L movement took over the Norwegian student rebellion and dominated student politics—something that did not happen in Sweden. In 1983 the Red Election Alliance, which was the electoral organization for the M-L, among others, had thirty-four representatives on municipal councils around Norway, while in Sweden the M-L movement had a total of thirteen.[52] In contrast to the Swedish M-L movement, the Norwegians also had considerable influence in a series of "fronts" and organizations such as the "Norway Out of NATO" campaign, the Workers' Committee against the EEC and the high cost of living, and the Women's Front.[53]

There were campaigns in both countries for the movement members to proletarianize themselves. In response to party leadership directives, many of them discontinued their higher education in order to take jobs in industry, where they tried to influence the trade unions in their new workplaces. The 1970s were the decade of extensive illegal strikes in both countries. In Nor-

[51] Skorpen 1995, 5.
[52] Skorpen 1995, 39–40.
[53] Skorpen 1995, 54–55, 57.

way we can detect a certain influence from the M-L movement, but scarcely any in Sweden. In any case, in Norway the LO found it necessary to mount an action against the movement. As LO leader Tor Aspengren said, "we can no longer sit with our hands tied when individuals from extreme groups set aside all considerations, show no loyalty, and engage in methods that are completely foreign to the trade union movement." Skorpen concludes, "The conditions for growth of these ideological and structural features found in the oppositional Norwegian labor movement in the 1970s were not found in the Swedish M-L movement. The Swedish labor movement's structure formed what was almost a wall of opposition to nonloyal penetrators."[54]

There were several external factors contributing to the movement's relative strength in Norway, such as Norway's closeness to the United States through its NATO membership and the large struggle over EEC membership in 1972, where the movement was able to fish in troubled waters. As Sweden was not a member of NATO and did not seek membership in the EEC, the rebels had fewer concrete issues on which to mobilize. Skorpen seems to lay equal weight, however, on internal organization, where secrecy and what were called "cadre evaluations" played such a large role. This had to do with standardizing rituals to correct ideological missteps so that the members might be formed according to one image.[55] When some of the Swedish M-L factions tried to emulate the Norwegians on this point, their attempts led to conflict, isolation, and dissolution.[56] Perhaps they tried too late.

Was the M-L movement a political or a religious movement? Was it oriented to changing the institutions of society or changing individuals? Many of the witnesses who later came forward suggest that the Norwegian movement had particularly religious or sectlike features. Some have stressed that the movement grew from the soil of the strong, pietistically oriented countercultural movement: "In just such a way, Norwegian Maoism, from beginning to end, was grounded in a paradox. Classic Marxism was disseminated, but it was the traditional counterculture that made up the existential basis of Maoism, and it was this that lent Maoism such great support."[57] It thus had an element of the traditionalists' rebellion against modernity.

This existential longing to get away from modern society, the longing for a different, more inclusive world, is clearly expressed in one of the novels that contribute to our understanding of the character of the movement—Dag Solstad's *Arild Asnes* of 1970. In a sense, the movement came to be more conservatively retrospective than forward-looking, bringing into view an existential

---

[54] Skorpen 1995, 126, 129, 56.
[55] Skorpen 1995, 132f.
[56] Skorpen 1995, 165.
[57] Jahn Thon 2003.

emptiness and a sense of a lost past. The movement also mythologized the folk culture and itself created strong forms of cultural expression, especially in the form of lyrical ballad singing. The best-known "M-L orchestra" in Norway was called Vømmøl Spelemannslag (the Homespun Band). Corresponding Swedish ballad groups were Blå Tåget (Blue Train) and Träd, Gräs och Stenar (Tree, Grass and Stone).[58] In Norway the M-L movement was strongly represented among the young fiction writers (Dag Solstad, Edvard Hoem, Tor Obrestad, and others).

The above-mentioned features, and particularly the connection to this strong counterculture, might perhaps contribute to our understanding of the relative success of the movement in Norway. But it hardly explains the underlying paradox—namely, that an antiauthoritarian revolt could be perverted into an authoritarian movement. At the same time that the M-L movement was trying to link itself to the traditional folk culture, it became a surprisingly foreign phenomenon in the egalitarian, democratic Nordic society. But then this is not the first time in history that a revolution for liberation has been perverted in this manner.

The movement died out toward the end of the 1970s—following the death of Mao, the fall of the Gang of Four, the break between China and Albania, the end of the Vietnam War, and, gradually, the unveiling of the terror regime of Pol Pot in Cambodia. And little time passed before a series of testimonies came out from former M-L-members who, in varying degrees, distanced themselves from the movement. Geir Mork, who later would become the administrative director of the large publishing house Gyldendal Norsk Forlag, was one of those who spoke out with particular clarity: "Individually and morally, this was a period of my life that I connect with shame, and which led me into a deep crisis from which it took three or four years following 1978 to regain a form of intellectual decency. I cannot say that I have learned anything positive from those years."[59]

Maoism, with its limited membership, was a parenthesis in societal development. Yet it is worth examining the paradoxical phenomenon since, despite everything, the movement was able to win such an acceptance and to some degree left its mark on an entire decade within the deeply rooted democratic cultures of Sweden—and, especially, Norway. It looks as if the movement was symptomatic of a general dissatisfaction. Maoism can "be interpreted as part of a more common movement, a diagnostic sign of weariness and repugnance toward the values and history of Western civilization." Thus it can be interpreted as a particularly clear expression of a broad cultural-

[58] Sjølie 2002, 163.
[59] Cited by Sjølie 2002, 145.

historical process.[60] From our perspective, it is worth noting that this weariness and repugnance hit Social Democracy precisely at the moment when (many felt that) at last the Social Democratic vision had been realized.

Moreover, there are lines of development running through the rebellion and toward the social formation whose contours we see in the 1980s. Hans Petter Sjølie tentatively gives an appreciable weight to the M-L movement as a countermovement that drew "adherents who at the outset were not particularly interested in a Communistic world order. It was *hip* to join in, both as a protest and as a desire to be *where it was happening*. And the aesthetic that went along with it was political—such that politicization came to be regarded as a marker against the stifling servility of the greater society."[61] We might again refer to Charles Taylor's analysis of the modern citizen's tendency to desire the aesthetic life, that is, to emphasize self-realization in contrast to moral conventionalism. To the degree that the M-L movement involved living aesthetically, it thus points to the future and beyond , to the new freedom of self-realization that found political expression in neoliberalism. Perhaps here we glimpse the ironical dialectics of history.

CONSTITUTIONALISM REDISCOVERED

The new Marxism was a dead end. There was, however, a need among the radical left, including the Social Democrats, for an ideological renewal. We have followed how the Social Democrats, having abandoned their Marxism, got new inspiration from the expansionism of the 1930s and the industrialism of the 1960s, both ideologized by radical liberals. Confronted with the new problems of the 1970s and the new quest for freedom, with Thatcherism and the practical problems leading on to the politics of the "third way," there arose a need for new visions, a need to be on the offensive. Tony Judt talks about "the progressive Left, which was still the dominant presence in European political and cultural exchanges, being urgently in need of a different script":

> What it found, to its collective surprise, was a new political vernacular—or, rather, a very old one, freshly rediscovered. The language of rights, or liberties, was firmly inscribed in every European constitution, not least those of the Peoples' Democracies. But as a way of thinking about politics, "rights talk" had been altogether unfashionable in Europe for many years.[62]

---

[60] Tvedt 1989, 95.
[61] Sjølie 2002, 171.
[62] Judt 2007, 564.

There had been rights talk before—talk about civil rights, political rights, and social rights. We have seen how the right to social benefits invaded the thinking of the welfare state. And, in the international arena, human rights had been put on the agenda right after World War II with the UN Declaration of Human Rights in 1948. The declaration was a reaction to the human rights abuses under the regimes of Hitler and Stalin. But Judt is certainly correct that something more happened with the general legal rhetoric around the 1980s. At that time the left rediscovered the old liberal constitutionalism, which to a certain extent had wintered among lawyers and in the conservative parties.

The liberal tradition differentiates between positive and negative power, or "the power of determining action and the power of blocking action."[63] The political authorities possess positive power. In a democratic society that means the power of the majority to take action. Negative power circumscribes the positive power of the state, which means that it stands for the rights of the individual or the minority in relation to the political authorities. This negative power is linked to the liberal *constitutional state* (Rechtstaat).

For the Social Democrats (and for the legal realists), the majority in the democratic state could (in theory) make whatever decisions it wanted. For a surprisingly long time they hung on to this "decisionism," or to the old Socialist or Marxist idea that power and law were one. For them, it was a delusion or bourgeois notion to believe that rights could circumscribe the positive political power of the state, or that the law alone could protect and guarantee the rights of the individual. Only the democratic majority, or collective concern and solicitude, could do so.

Throughout most of the twentieth century political development had been characterized by a steady expansion of positive state power. Constitutional limitations were constantly under attack by the democratic movement (and even more so by the decisionism of the totalitarian regimes, of course). Social Democracy peaked this development to the extent that *state* and *society* became interchangeable concepts. We have also seen how the young, idealistic Social Democrats who took power after World War II tended to look upon constitutional limitations as unnecessary hindrances.

But this way of thinking changed dramatically in the 1980s. The problem became how to make a decent retreat from this position. The freedom revolution was a revolution of rights, a reaction to the Social Democrats' democratic decisionism (or the "brutality of the majority"). It constituted a revision of the relationship between the positive power of the Social Democrats and the negative power of the liberals, to the benefit of the latter. This revolutionary

---

[63] Buchanan and Tullock 1965, 258.

turnabout among the Social Democrats seems to have happened almost unconsciously. Suddenly they found themselves to be liberal constitutionalists.

Judt argues that what "propelled the legal rhetoric of individual rights into the realm of real politics (in the mid-1970s) was the coincident timing of the retreat of Marxism and the international Conference on Security and Cooperation in Europe, which had opened in Helsinki the same year that *Gulag Archipelago* was published in Paris."[64] In the case of Sweden and Norway we tend to lay more emphasis on internal factors. The rhetorical changes, which in time amounted to new ideological elements, began in the 1970s. They seem, however, to have been propelled by the extensive and sudden criticism of Social Democracy at that time—the failure of the strong state. This new interest in the old constitutionalism was something different from what we called "a Social Democratic constitution," which was a constitution for the strong state.

We can find a typical turnabout in Norway. In the 1970s there existed a group of radical jurists, or "critical jurisprudence," that went to extremes in relation to the dominant legal realism of the time. They held that legal arguments were only camouflaging political power. Soon afterward they found themselves using "rights talk" in opposition to the political establishment. As one jurist noted, this was, of course, a very defensive strategy. But they found that such a use of negative power worked.

More important was the systematic work on problems of constitutionalism and the development of adequate concepts that was undertaken, under the leadership of Jon Elster and Rune Slagstad, both members of the Left Socialist Party, by a group of academics of different political persuasions.[65] Their immediate influence on practical policy was minimal. On the other hand, the work of the group constituted a contribution toward changing the political rhetoric in the long run. It was all part of the general turnabout toward constitutionalism referred to by Judt.

This turnabout is connected with the turnabout in economic policy, or what was called the "third way." We saw how even the Social Democrats argued in favor of less state regulation and the use of the free market. It must not, however, be identified with Thatcherism. Liberal constitutionalism is not identical with economic liberalism. It was the former that was now adopted by the progressive left to fill an ideological vacuum. In relation to state power, economic liberalism argues for a greater role for the market,

---

[64] Judt 2007, 565. There was a parallel liberalizing or a rights revolution in the practice of the U.S. Supreme Court not least inspired by Ronald Dworkin's classic from 1977, "Taking Rights Seriously." Cf. Sandel 1996.

[65] An early contribution was Sejersted 1973. Several papers by Jon Elster finally ending up in Elster 1979; Slagstad 1978; Sejersted 2001 (first pub. 1984); Slagstad 1987. Elster and Slagstad 1988.

whereas liberal constitutionalism stands for the "rule of law" and protection and building up of civil society. While economic liberalism was more interested in limiting state power, the latter argued for binding state power and against arbitrary rule.

THE RETURN OF THE VALUES DEBATE

Social Democracy had been carried forward on wings of moral inspiration. Thus it is paradoxical that the political discourse under Social Democracy was rational rather than moralistic, but such are the quirks of history.[66] In the period after 1970, however, and running parallel with the weakening of faith in rational common sense and in technical progress, rationalist arguments were being replaced by moral arguments. Political rhetoric was changing its character. Beneath this turnover we are also able to glimpse a weakening of technological determinism and a new faith in the significance of political decisions. "The return of the debate about values" and "the return of politics" are two sides of the same coin.[67]

This remoralization found expression most noticeably through the new popular movements that by nature were more action-oriented and that came to leave their mark on public discourse. This applied to movements such as the Vietnam War protest, the Environmental movement, and the Women's movement.[68] The youth rebellion bore signs of both modernist self-realization and moralizing.

The remoralization of politics opened the way for political engagement by a radicalized church. First of all, there was a series of urgent moral-political questions facing the church, among them the issues of abortion, cohabitation, women priests, and the rights of homosexuals—traditional, individually oriented moral questions that the church had always been involved with. The restrictive position of the church in such cases had marked it as conservative and out of step with the times. These became problematic questions for the church, issues that put it on the defensive. The great debate over abortion in the 1970s is characteristic of this constellation of factors.

The abortion issue was not new, and limited access to abortion had been established in both Norway and Sweden. But the freedom revolution, par-

[66] Göran Bexell (1995) feels that the Swedish philosopher Hägerström's interpretation of ethics affected the discourse on morality under Social Democracy. In this discourse, ethics was an objective doctrine *about* morality. It was now shoved aside by the interpretation of ethics as a doctrine *of* morality.

[67] Slagstad 1998, 447, 461—where "The Return of the Debate about Values" appears as a subheading under "The Return of Politics."

[68] Bexell 1995, 125.

ticularly the women's liberation movement, made new forceful demands for elective abortion. The Social Democrats supported this, while there was strong Christian opinion against it. Part, but not all, of the politically conservative forces were also opposed. In Norway the fundamentalist circles also mobilized spectacular actions against what they called "fetus murders." In the end, laws endorsing free abortion were ratified in both countries; that is, all women who so desired could obtain an abortion. As usual, Sweden led the way, ratifying the law in 1974; Norway followed in 1975. The abortion issue clearly left its stamp on the public in the turbulent 1970s, even after the laws had been ratified.

On the other hand, a movement in the direction of radical Christian thinking and a "tolerance revolution" had its starting point in the 1960s. The church was in the process of becoming less conservative than it had been: the 1968 General Assembly of the World Council of Churches in Uppsala was important in this connection. A breakthrough had taken place there in terms of social ethics and radical Christian thinking.[69] The predominant leader of the Norwegian low-church movement, Ole Hallesby, had rejected the view that Christian morality could exist without a personal faith in Jesus Christ.[70] Now there was a more comprehensive acceptance of morality's independence from faith, opening the way for a greater degree of tolerance. The new emphasis on social ethics meant that the church could be involved when moral grounds were being reintroduced into the political arena. Luther's doctrine of two regimes had been weakened. The church was able to go on the offensive on general social questions, moving from conservatism to radicalism.

One spokesman for the new direction in Sweden was the theology professor Anders Jeffner, who believed the task of the church was "to work for the advancement of those social and international plans that promote human well-being. In a democratic country this involves a responsibility to take part in the formation of policy. . . . [A] Christian social ethic ought to propel the Christian to take on political responsibility." It was therefore natural that Archbishop Olof Sundby stood up at the annual general meeting of the corporation ASEA in 1975 to criticize the company's involvement in South Africa. "The archbishop's words were not particularly popular," writes Sören Ekström, "but, moreover, he stood ramrod straight in what was for him the somewhat unaccustomed role of expressing revolutionary inclinations! Suddenly the Swedish Church had waded into a shareholders' meeting, which until then had been foreign territory."[71]

---

[69] Bexell 1995, p. 47.
[70] Midttun 1995, 70.
[71] Ekström 2003, 194.

JESUS—A SOCIAL DEMOCRAT?

The radicalization of the church led to a change in its relationship with Social Democracy. We see this with particular clarity in Norway, where in 1973 the Labor Party appointed a commission that was to report on its relationship to Christianity. In 1975 (the same year the abortion law was passed!) this work led to Labor Party ratification of an item on its program that was favorable toward the church. The traditionally skeptical view of the party "[f]ell like an overripe fruit."[72] A trendsetting figure in this process had been the theologian Tor Aukrust, who penned large portions of the commission's report.

According to Aukrust, the church had not succeeded in providing guidance "for a new Christian lifestyle that felt adequate and binding for modern society." Aukrust's project consisted of trying to fill this ethical no-man's-land with a reinstitution of Christian social ethics.[73] The church and the Social Democrats needed one another. For the Social Democrats, the church became an ally, able to function in a regenerative manner in a difficult situation. By placing an equal sign between the Christian idea of charity and the Socialist idea of brotherhood, the Labor Party had "made Christianity part of its official ideology—that of democratic Socialism." This was not completely unproblematic, however.

First of all, it awakened negative reactions in other parts of the Norwegian political spectrum—Jesus, as it was said, had been made into a Social Democrat. Some years later the minister of church affairs, the Social Democratic Einar Førde, characterized this mixing together of Christianity and Socialism as something a bit "soppy." Later, however, another minister of church affairs for the Social Democrats, Gudmund Hernes, declared that the revised schoolteaching on Christianity was meant to turn it into an ideology of national integration for a multicultural society.[74] This is symptomatic for the role of religion at the present time. The concept of identity has taken on a new and central role.[75] In the wake of secularization Christianity (or the Christian cultural inheritance; it is not particularly easy to distinguish between them) has been making its return in an identity-formative role.

In such a Social Democratic people's church in a multicultural society, the question of faith, or confessional Christianity with its dogmatic demands, had been thrown into the shadows by issues about values and morals. This turn of events also came to affect the question of whether or not to dissolve the state church. In Sweden in 1972, under the leadership of Alva Myrdal and in line

---

[72] Midttun 1995, 120.
[73] Slagstad 1998, 401.
[74] Slagstad 1998, 404.
[75] Brekke 2002, 123.

with traditional Social Democratic attitudes, a commission had proposed the dissolution of the state church. This provoked a strong reaction. At a protest meeting in Malmö social ethicist Karl-Manfred Olsson spoke out against the commission. According to Olsson, between the "fixed, dogmatic, confessional Christians" and the "religiously uninterested nondenominational" there was a large group whose members adhered to Christian values but whose religiosity was anonymous and private. This piety could, if it were freed from dogmatic demands, carry Christian ideas and values out into social relations.[76] It is thus assumed from this perspective that there is a sort of common basic religion, a "civil religion."[77] Perhaps the church could address Christianity on this basis, as an ideology of national integration in a multicultural society, as Gudmund Hernes had thought. But this assumed an undogmatic church. Many felt that the state church model guaranteed such a church.

In 1995 the Swedish Parliament came to grips with the decision in principle that the state church should be disbanded. In Norway the discussion went on for a much longer time, ending in 2008 with something akin to a compromise. The church was given a somewhat expanded degree of self-government (most important was the right to appoint bishops, which formerly was the responsibility of the government) in return for more democratic procedures. Perhaps the difference between the two countries can be explained by the stronger High Church tradition in Sweden, in parallel with a longer and stronger free church tradition beyond the bounds of the state church.[78] In other words, the Social Democrats in Norway feel a stronger link to the established church. It has also been argued that the Christian traditions in Norway continue to feed young people with material for reflection in a way that they do not in the neighboring countries.[79] This may mean that the Norwegian state church can be used as a bearer of Christian moral values into general social relations.

THE COMMON GOOD

There are, of course, moral counterforces apart from religion. What has been called communitarianism, which found its roots in Great Britain and the United States, stands as a pronounced countercurrent. The wake of this movement has also touched the Nordic countries. The man considered to be the godfather of this movement is the philosopher Alasdair MacIntyre, with his

---

[76] Ekström 2003, 114.
[77] Brekke 2002, 110.
[78] Brekke 2002, 62–63.
[79] Pål Repstad in *Aftenposten*, 18 February 2005.

fundamental criticism of the grand liberal modernization project in its entirety, starting with the Enlightenment. The falling away of the "virtues" and the whole process of splintering and individualization that we have referred to is for him a natural consequence of this project, the result of modernity having been taken to its most extreme consequences. The core of communitarianism, or "the new moralism," is to challenge "individualist liberal opposition to the concept of a common good"—a reaction to "individualism overheated."[80] The sunshine, fresh air, and good heath that so preoccupied the Social Democrats can certainly be important, but the real aim of politics must be to go beyond the making of healthy human beings; its aim must be, as in the Athens of antiquity, to cultivate the citizens' virtue and lead the way to the "common good."

The movement, if on the whole one can call it a movement, is of course multifaceted. Not everyone rejects the legacy of the Enlightenment to the same degree as MacIntyre does. Charles Taylor, for example, has presented a fundamentally positive attitude toward modern society but believes that there are some symptoms of sickness within it—above all, an individualism that has decayed into narcissism and has given rise to a loss of meaning, and which is intimately linked to a basically instrumental attitude that exposes human beings to being treated "as raw material or instruments for our projects."[81] In contrast to MacIntyre, however, he feels that there is a common frame of reference, albeit a hidden one. What we must do is to remind one another about the original moral inspiration behind the development of our modern society, and this must be done through public discussion about morals. Taylor has been an inspiration for many Social Democrats.

The new morality has had an impact on politics. Among others, Bill Clinton and Tony Blair have both drawn inspiration from it. In Scandinavia it has had an impact on public discourse. In Norway in 1997 the non-Socialist government set up a "Commission on Values" that was intended to "contribute to a broad, value-oriented, and social-ethical mobilization to strengthen positive values of community in society." The prime minister, Kjell Magne Bondevik, from the Christian People's Party, promoted the issue.[82] Naturally enough, the commission was nondenominational but, characteristically, the initiative came from the Christian fold. In the process of establishing and carrying forward the work of the commission, the normative aspect became less conspicuous. In its first phase, emphasis was placed on laying out a description of the Norwegian values landscape and, in the following round, on ini-

---

[80] Etzioni 1997, 40–41. He is a leading communitarian.
[81] Taylor 1992, 5.
[82] Alm (1998) goes through the history of the Commission on Values.

tiating debates, thereby contributing to the development of a foundation for people's own reflections around ethical questions. "Communication with the people" was part of the strategy. The commission also prepared to challenge the institutions of power to reflect on the ethical dilemmas they encountered in their work. Among other things, the government was challenged to reflect on how it administrated the oil wealth.

The initiatives toward the people, on the one hand, and the institutions of power, on the other, were thus to be based on mapping out the landscape of values. Here the commission concentrated on making use of knowledge from the sciences, popular institutions, institutions of power, and the disputatious public sphere. By concentrating not only on one type of knowledge but also on the formation of knowledge from such different sources, the commission believed it was "in accord with something at the heart of our own times." The commission located itself explicitly in opposition to modernity thinking, which was oriented to presenting knowledge production as the systematization of only one type of knowledge.

That the normative was relegated to the background was partly due to the relatively extensive criticism that the commission itself encountered. For many, to have a publicly appointed commission for mobilizing a community of values smacked of the familiar authorized interpretations from the old closed societies. In addition, the members of the commission did not agree that there had been any attenuation of morals. A normative element was, nevertheless, part of the commission's profile.

The significance of the commission's work was rather limited. It is interesting as a phenomenon of the period, however, and its attempt to locate itself between the new morality, on the one hand, and the liberal legacy, on the other, is symptomatic of the divisive tendencies of the period. What the commission tried to establish went beyond the rationality discourse and the media-biased society. The objective was to establish diversity itself—the many types of knowledge—as a new (postmodern) knowledge regime. The question is whether, by this method, one can approach a "common good."

A SHOWDOWN WITH THE PAST

The new morality, or the return of the debate about values, has also found expression in a number of issues that represent a showdown with the past. The debate over sterilization in 1997 is a particularly good example. It was "disclosed" that Sweden, the "model state," had carried out sterilization with the view to creating a purer race (see chapter 3). Another example is the confrontation with the different attitudes during World War II. There had developed in both countries "a consensus syndrome." In Sweden it was accepted that the policy of pragmatic accommodation followed during the war was best for the nation. Conversely, in Norway a view of the fight against Nazi Germany as heroic had been cultivated. It is remarkable that both of these national self-portraits were subjected to revision in the 1980s and 1990s from a moral perspective. How heroic had one actually been in Norway, and were all the moral questions so simple when it came right down to it? And on the Swedish side, to what extent could the policy of compliance be defended morally? Should Sweden not perhaps have also participated in defeating Nazism?

In the 1980s ripples from the great German "historians' strife" reached Norway.[83] The dispute was unleashed by a new interest in the other side of World War II—that of the losers. The archives of the NS, the Norwegian Nazi-style party, were more systematically utilized by historians, and old NS members had their say in public. There was a call for a more conciliatory attitude. Many of the NS members had done nothing wrong, beyond being members of the party. They were ordinary people who, in tumultuous times, had taken the wrong step.

As early as 1945, at the beginning of the justice proceedings against the Nazis, Bishop Eivind Berggrav had warned against the segregation effect of NS membership: "We can create a pariah caste, excluding thousands, along with their children and their next of kin, thereby creating an eternal source of bitterness, a wound that might not be healed for generations . . . if good NS people cannot be won back, then we have suffered defeat."[84] Precisely what the bishop had warned about had happened after 1945.

The showdown with the past produced other provocative questions as well. Aspects of the war that had been languishing in the shadows were now brought into the light of day. What about the collaborators, all of those who had cooperated with the occupiers? What had been done to innocent victims, such as the children of the Nazis and the German occupiers? And what had the "good" Norwegians really done for the Norwegian Jews or for the Germans' prisoners of war who had been held in Norway?

This "revisionism" gave birth to a reaction, a "counterrevisionism" that left its mark on the 1990s: no matter what happened during the war, beware of going too far in the direction of relativizing. The result of this revisionist-counterrevisionist debate seems to have been that space was created for a more differentiated and nuanced presentation of the experiences of the war and the occupation. The Norwegians had not been so very morally irreproachable as they liked to think. Their self-portrait required retouching.

---

[83] Larsen 1999. In his introduction Larsen gives an overview of the debate in Norway.
[84] Berggrav 1945a.

"During the war there was a bad conscience in Sweden," writes Stig Hadenius.[85] The moral dilemma created by the policy of neutrality has been a theme taken up by many, and yet it was not until the 1990s that the relative consensus about this policy was disrupted. The public debate was sparked by a 1991 pamphlet titled *Honor and Conscience: Sweden and the Second World War*, by Maria-Pia Boëtius. First she attacked the coalition government for having followed an immoral policy, and then she attacked the historians who had failed to bring this to light. In the debate that followed, it was argued that by supplying Germany with iron ore and ball bearings, Sweden had contributed to prolonging the war, thereby making it possible for the Holocaust to extend further than it might have otherwise. In addition, Swedish banks had traded in gold that had been stolen from Jews. As in Norway, the debate swung back and forth, while at the same time, digging deeper into the sources, researchers uncovered more about the existing circumstances and the policies followed during the actual war years.

In Sweden the criticism of the conciliatory policy during the war was followed by a revelation that the country had not been as neutral during the Cold War as it had appeared: in reality it had placed itself under the NATO umbrella. Thus the authorities had been playing a double game. This was revealed along with the illegal surveillance of citizens that had taken place during the Cold War (see chapter 6). These revelations and the scandal they provoked must be viewed as an effect of the remoralizing of politics. In Sweden, too, the complacent self-portrait required retouching.

THE RETURN OF POLITICS

The beginning of a political change was in evidence around 1970. The 1970s were characterized by conflicting tendencies. Only from around 1980, however, can we discern the contours of the society-to-be. But what would these contours resemble? Owing to internationalization and other factors, room for political maneuvering had been reduced. But, on the other hand, we can observe new forms of participation and a new vitality and engagement in the public arena, in what we might call prepolitical discourse. Popular democracy had been transformed but hardly weakened.

The political parties lost their monopoly over the daily agenda and the formation of public opinion, while simultaneously there was a repoliticizing that undermined the power of experts. The formation of public opinion now took place in a more multifaceted public arena in which the media, freed

[85] Hadenius 2000, 77.

from control by political parties, played an important role. "This probably involved one of the greatest shifts of power in the twentieth century."[86] This new journalism, with its simplifying, polarizing, intensifying, and concretizing, has had an effect on the general worldview.

On the one hand, a series of new oppositional movements arose, such as the environmental movement and feminism, among others. In sum, they represented a freedom revolution that especially directed itself against the Social Democratic order with its authoritarian tendencies and emphasis on equality relative to freedom. The most manifest form of the freedom revolution was expressed by the youth rebellion. But the more lasting result of the freedom revolution is the freedom of choice (as analyzed in chapter 13), which arose from the beginning of the 1980s. Perhaps most remarkable, however, is the new interest from the political left in the old liberal constitutionalism. "Rights talk" became fashionable.

Developments leading from this freedom revolution and its fracturing of the accepted worldview can be described as following two contrary tendencies. The first is the "postmodern" tendency, the desire to live aesthetically. Here the ideals are individualization and self-realization. The second is the remoralizing of politics, the recapturing of the political arena by shoving the ideal of an objective rational discourse to one side in favor of a new insistence on the validity of moral arguments. On this basis we are also able to observe a showdown with the past. The line of development from the 1970s has thus produced rather profound changes to what we might call the prepolitical field. There are changes in institutions but, above all, changes in mentality.

---

[86] Esaiasson and Håkansson 2002, 15.

CHAPTER 15

The Last "Soviet States"?

A Large-Scale Cooperative Effort • The Volvo Agreement: Another Unsuccessful Campaign • Toward a Nordic Economic Region? • Europe • Why Did Sweden Reverse Its Policy on Europe? • The Last "Soviet States"?

A LARGE-SCALE COOPERATIVE EFFORT

On September 23, 1999, Minister of Trade Björn Rosengren was interviewed on Swedish television about the concluding negotiations on a merger between Telia and Telenor, the two large national telecommunications companies in Sweden and Norway. They had been pure state administrative companies but were now transformed into joint stock companies with significant state ownership. After the interview Rosengren, in response to the difficulties Norway had created in the negotiations by insisting on what he felt were irrelevant national political concerns, exclaimed that Norway must be "the last Soviet state." He was unaware that the television camera had not been switched off, such that his outburst received full public coverage. This of course led to much media attention. The merger issue exemplifies the relationship between the two countries, as we shall see below.[1]

When the Norwegian government had submitted to Parliament the proposal for a merger between Telia and Telenor, the primary supporting argument was that it would be "important to retain a strong, nationally anchored telecommunications company in order to secure modern and advanced telecommunications and IT services nationwide at low prices." Thus, in the eyes of Norwegians, a Swedish-dominated company with its headquarters in Stockholm would still represent a "nationally anchored" company. In the basic agreement it was, of course, established that the new company had the task of providing such a nationwide offer, as mentioned, and that initially Norway would have a "negative majority" (less than 50 percent and more than 33 percent).[2] Even so, it is unthinkable that a similar agreement could

---

[1] The Telia/Telenor merger is analyzed in Sejersted 2002b.
[2] In Sweden the basic agreement is attached to Riksdagsförh. (Parl. Proceedings) 1998–1999, R. Prp. 99, appendix 1, 23f.

have been reached with a German company, for example. This move reflects the old dream of Scandinavia as an extended home market.

There was, however, nothing about "national anchoring" in the corresponding Swedish proposition. In any case, it is worth noting that the Swedes had agreed to forming a new company that would "work to retain and develop both Telia's and Telenor's operations in their respective home markets in order to provide appropriate and effective nationwide service in these markets."[3] The political intent of the agreement goes beyond the advantage of a large home market and to a responsibility to serve this market in a certain manner.

Scandinavianism was not dead—crossing the national borders within Scandinavia was not considered to be foreign travel. And this applied especially within the field of trade and commerce. A Swedish industry analyst wrote in 1989: "The ambition of Norwegian trade and commerce was . . . increasingly to be allowed to play with its Swedish big brother" so as to facilitate "a broadening of the Norwegian industrial base, which as a *next step* could lead to needed internationalization."[4] This was exactly what the Telia-Telenor merger was leading to—playing with big brother. Note the metaphor: it is *at home* that one plays with big brother. To go to Sweden was not "internationalization."

This idea of an extended home market emerges from a strong feeling of proximity and mutual trust. This has to some degree been investigated through a Swedish study regarding the "psychic distance" of Swedish company leaders from markets in other countries. The study reveals a striking degree of proximity between Sweden and Norway in particular.[5] There also exists an EU study on confidence showing that the Swedes have the greatest confidence in the Norwegians—greater than in their own countrymen, who place second![6] Thus it should be no surprise that the Norwegian government, apparently without reflection or in any case without comment, was able to maintain that a Swedish-dominated corporation with its head offices in Stockholm, and registered as a Swedish firm that would be taxed within Sweden, could guarantee that it would become nationally anchored in Norway.

The merged corporation should not only provide advanced services to the two countries. It should also become internationalized so as to become "one of Europe's leading telecommunications operators," as was stated in the agreement.[7] Sweden has a tradition in this field that is quite different from that of Norway. Sweden was industrialized earlier and to a greater extent than Nor-

---

[3] First page in the agreement (see ibid.).
[4] Jan-Evert Nilsson 1989, 48. Italics have been added.
[5] Nordström 1991.
[6] Cited by Storvik 2000.
[7] St. forh. (Parl. Proceedings) 1998–1999, S. Prp. 58, appendix 1, 37.

way was.[8] In contrast to Norway, where light industry predominates, Swedish industry is dominated by large industrial concerns that have long operated successfully in the international arena. Moreover, it is typical of Swedish industrial development that the boundary between the private and the public is unclear. The Swedish corporate world thus has traditions as to how such issues should be handled politically. For that matter, Rosengren's description "Soviet state" fits Sweden better than Norway. In practice, the Norwegian Social Democratic state was surprisingly liberal in the sense that it did not discriminate between private interests, at least until the discovery of petroleum. And because they had a strong home base, the Swedes did not feel the same need as the Norwegians for an extended "home market." There is a question of whether some of the preconditions for the breakdown of this agreement lie here—for it would end in a breakdown. There was no merger.

THE VOLVO AGREEMENT: ANOTHER UNSUCCESSFUL CAMPAIGN

Was there something about the agreement that was predictive of the breakdown? In other words, should the collapse have been expected? There are parallels between the attempted Telia-Telenor merger and another large collaborative project that had gone on the rocks. On this occasion as well, the collaborative initiative was taken by a Swedish leader of the corporate world, Per Gyllenhammar, the head of Volvo. In January 1978 he broached with Norway's Social Democratic prime minister, Odvar Nordli, the idea of undertaking an industrial cooperation. Nordli seized on the idea and exerted much of his influence in securing its realization. In its main features the draft agreement was for Volvo to become a joint Swedish-Norwegian concern. Following the SAS model, a holding company would be established in each country. These companies would jointly own the Volvo concern, with Norway holding 40 percent and Sweden holding 60 percent of the share capital. The new concern would be required to invest between 500 million and 700 million Norwegian kroner in Norway, creating three thousand to five thousand new jobs. In return, the Swedish holding company would obtain oil production rights on the Norwegian North Sea shelf, and Norway would have a long-term duty to supply oil to Sweden.[9] The Norwegian policy was of the traditional type: namely, in exchange for providing access to its national resources, Norway

---

[8] Thus we find in 1985 that Sweden had 768,000 industrial employees as compared to 311,000 in Norway.

[9] St. forh. (Parl. Proceedings) 1978–1979, S. Prp. 69.

would receive capital and technology. In other words, Norwegians would get the help of the Swedes in the planned industrialization of Norway.

Negotiators on both sides had exhibited great enthusiasm and determination in their efforts to achieve this end. There was no lack of vision with regard to the outcome of this cooperation. In both Sweden and Norway, however, there was considerable skepticism about the grounds on which the proposal rested. The agreement was stopped by the Swedish shareholders, among them the Swedish small-scale investors who were organized into the Shareholders' Association. The main reason for the Swedish opposition to the proposed agreement, however, was doubt as to the value of the Norwegian quid pro quo. Disappointment was great among the project enthusiasts on both sides. The Norwegian chief negotiator has since summed up the reasons for failure: "Narrow-minded, short-sighted considerations, semicompetence and dilettantism, blind nationalism [on the Swedish side] and old-fashioned animosity toward Sweden [on the Norwegian side] were, in sum, strong enough to block a really vast project with long-term perspectives. This was a tragedy."[10]

In contrast to the Telia-Telenor issue, the Swedes rather than the Norwegians could be accused of "undue" nationalism in the Volvo case. In addition, the Volvo agreement was seen in light of the Nordic cooperation agreement of 1962 (the Helsinki Agreement).[11] It was meant to achieve the vision of close Nordic economic cooperation that had been expressed many times but was largely unfulfilled. There existed a disparity between the fundamental intentions and the ability to realize them.

The proposal provided for a civil law agreement between the Norwegian state, on the one hand, and a private Swedish company, on the other. In principle this implied the entrance of the public sector into the sphere of the private. We have seen that this type of discriminatory intervention was not uncommon in Sweden. It was more unusual in Norway, but it appears as though the general oil policy represents a break with earlier practice and a return to a sort of public-privilege policy in connection with the allocation of drilling rights. The Volvo draft agreement reflects this new policy of discrimination between private interests.[12]

When comparing the collapse of the Volvo agreement and the Telia-Telenor agreement, there is a notable difference. The Volvo agreement revealed Norway's respect for Swedish industry. It was an agreement in which Norwegian

---

[10] Hauge 1989, 295.

[11] This agreement sprang out of worries about Nordic cooperation that appeared when Denmark and Norway followed Great Britain and sought membership in the EEC in 1961, while Sweden, Finland, and Iceland did not. Cf. Svein Olav Hansen 1994, 155f.

[12] In the modern, globalized economy it has gradually become common to see this type of discriminatory agreement between states and large corporations. So far the Volvo agreement has been "future-oriented."

resources would be exchanged for Swedish competence and capital. This was not the case with the Telia-Telenor merger. It is indeed possible that the latter collapse stemmed from disagreement over where the greatest competence was to be found. There was no sense of lesser competence on the Norwegian side, as there had been in the Volvo negotiations. The Norwegians now believed that they had positive contributions to make with regard to organization and technology. Could it be that the Swedes had been clinging to the old idea of superior Swedish technology?

Both the Volvo agreement and the Telia-Telenor merger were initiated with great enthusiasm from both sides, but both ended in fiasco, much like the many attempts to establish a Nordic customs union. Prime Minister Odvar Nordli's bitter comment after the Volvo failure was seemingly correct: "As time goes on, a particular feature of Nordic cooperation has developed. Every attempt at large steps forward has met with failure."[13] But what about the smaller steps, and the sum of those efforts?

TOWARD A NORDIC ECONOMIC REGION?[14]

What Nordli called "failed attempts to move forward" were not totally un-successful inasmuch as they became catalysts for compensatory projects. We can see this mechanism at work in relation to the Volvo agreement. Along with the Volvo agreement, a general agreement between the Swedish and Norwegian governments on the principles for cooperation on energy and industrial policy was set out.[15] Thus the Volvo agreement was part of a more general policy, and the collapse of the Volvo agreement provided stimulus toward rescuing something from this general agreement. In concrete terms, the Swedish-Norwegian Industry Fund was established on the ruins of the Volvo agreement.

The fund was regarded as a Social Democratic creation and was conse-quently greeted with skepticism by industry. The fund did not become exactly as expected by the politicians who took the initiative. Nevertheless, during the 1980s the fund provided 336 million Swedish kronor toward financing seventy-four projects in which a total of 116 companies were involved.[16] Perhaps more important, it gradually became an experienced and valuable adviser for the many firms that desired to work together across the Swedish-Norwegian border. But the lack of symmetry between the levels of industry in

[13] Nordli 1985, 138.

[14] "Scandinavia" usually refers to Denmark, Sweden, and Norway, whereas "Norden" or the "Nordic countries" also include Finland and Iceland. Today, however, this distinction has been blurred.

[15] St. forh. (Parl. Proceedings) 1978–1979, S. Prp. 69, pkt. 2.2, 9.

[16] Storvik 2000.

the two countries was clearly revealed by the fact that in 1990 there were 800 Swedish subsidiaries in Norway, as opposed to 150 Norwegian subsidiaries in Sweden.[17] So there were grounds for worry about Swedish competition. This picture changed, however. In 2002 a Norwegian newspaper reported that Norwegians had invested five billion kroner in Sweden that year, while the Swedes had invested only two billion in Norway.[18] This was after Norway had become an oil nation and an exporter of capital.

The Nordic collaboration in banking is interesting in principle. Private banks have to some extent the character of an infrastructural system. And the scope of an infrastructural system best illustrates the idea of a "home market." As early as 1912 a collaborative effort had been made to establish a Scandinavian bank in London. During the 1960s and into the 1970s some of the largest banks of Sweden, Finland, Denmark, and Norway collaborated in establishing Nordic banks in the large international financial centers: Zurich, London, and New York.[19] The point of these banks was, above all else, to be in a position to follow their Nordic clients into the world market. Svenska Handelsbanken (the Commercial Bank of Sweden) took the initiative. It had the greatest financial muscle and had originally planned to establish its own fully owned subsidiaries abroad. In the end it preferred, however, to have a more solid basis and went for a Nordic consortium in which private banks from all four countries participated on an equal footing. This banking collaboration developed completely independent of the unsuccessful negotiations over Nordic economic cooperation at the political level.

The proposal for a *public* Nordic investment bank had been part of the many Nordic economic cooperation negotiations since 1957.[20] Norwegian Social Democrats viewed the proposal positively, expecting that such a bank would be able to bring more capital into the country. Despite the proposal arising repeatedly, like Nordic economic cooperation in general, it was shoved aside when European solutions came to be of interest. Still it is interesting that the proposal would appear again, this time as a reaction to this same European cooperation, or as a means of organizing within a broader context. It was forwarded primarily by Iceland and Finland, who were in need of imported capital. In the other Nordic countries there was considerable skepticism, as the private banking system hesitated to welcome a public competitor.

As usual, the Norwegian right opposed the initiative. The proposal, naturally enough, carried with it an aura of Social Democracy and the planned economy. Nevertheless, the bank was founded in 1976 as a publicly owned regional, multilateral financial institution following the model of the Euro-

---

[17] Lindboe 1990, 173, 175.
[18] *Aftenposten*, 16 September 2002.
[19] Sejersted 1982, 198ff.; Knutsen, Lange, and Norvik 1998.
[20] Wiklund 2000b; interview with Jannik Lindbæk; St. forh. (Parl. Proceedings) 1975–1976, S. Prp. 84.

pean Investment Bank—or, for that matter, the World Bank. The aim was to strengthen the Nordic countries as an economic unit or, as one of the Norwegian Social Democratic leaders put it, "[The bank] should strengthen common feelings through common activity in the work of linking the Nordic peoples together."[21] Norway was no longer in need of capital, but the Nordic idea was still alive.

The bank would contribute to financing projects that were "in the Nordic countries' interest." What this would mean was the subject of extensive discussions. At least it was clear that inter-Nordic projects were of interest to at least two of the five nations. But what about Nordic investments outside the Nordic countries? It is worth remarking that the bank had been criticized from a radical position. The argument was that there was no need to channel more capital into the Nordic region. The problem was more one of managing to get capital into the developing countries. To the degree that the bank has engaged itself outside the Nordic countries, it has also been involved in environmental projects in developing countries.

While the Nordic Investment Bank was one spin-off from the Nordic negotiations, there was another project that, perhaps more than any others, demonstrated the tendency toward consolidating the Nordic home market. This was the establishment of the inter-Nordic bank NORDEA between the years 1999 and 2001.[22] Today NORDEA is the largest financial concern in the Nordic countries, with the Swedish state as the biggest owner. It was created by the merger of the Swedish Nord Bank, the Finnish MERITA, the Danish Uni-Bank, and the Norwegian Christiania Bank og Kreditkasse. The idea is no longer to follow the Nordic clients out into the world but to compete with the large international banks for the Nordic market. NORDEA is only one (particularly good) example of how the Nordic solution is materializing within this new international context. Another example is the merging of what were originally national retail cooperative operations into one entity called COOP Norden.

This Nordic concept came out clearly in a report prepared in accordance with an initiative by the Nordic Industry Fund and the Nordic Council of Ministers in 2002. The conclusion was: "Mergers, takeovers, and joint ventures between enterprises in the Nordic countries are occurring frequently and are in the process of defining the Nordic countries as one coherent region of Europe. This is a result of attempts by the enterprises to obtain a strong position in a situation of increasingly sharper international competition. To an ever-increasing degree, the enterprises regard the Nordic countries as their

---

[21] St. forh. (Parl. Proceedings) 1975–1976, S Tid. 2451.

[22] www.nordea.com/eng/group/history.asp.

home bases: the Nordic countries are in the process of developing themselves into a more coherent region of trade and industry."[23]

These Nordic mergers have to take place formally through the acquisition of shares.[24] Between 1997 and 2002 the report registered four thousand acquisitions within the Nordic countries. Sweden accounts for 42 percent of these, with acquisitions in Finland being the largest portion. Norway accounts for 17 percent, of which the largest portion is acquisitions in Sweden. The general growth of direct foreign investment is thus increasingly within the Nordic countries. One concrete example is the Norwegian media concern Schibsted, which has made acquisitions in Sweden and owns the large Stockholm newspapers *Aftonbladet* and *Svenska Dagbladet*, while the large Swedish publisher Bonnier has purchased the major Norwegian publisher Cappelen. It is characteristic that when it is a question of acquiring enterprises, Sweden is the most important trading partner for Norway, while Finland is the most important for Sweden. To date there is no symmetry to the relationship between Sweden and Norway.

In spite of the "union complex" (dating back to Norway breaking out of the union with Sweden in 1905), mutual distrust, different geopolitical orientations, lack of symmetry, and spectacular setbacks for the most audacious cooperative projects, there has been an *insistence* on Swedish-Norwegian, Scandinavian, or Nordic cooperation through the whole period of modern history. The countries are always willing to try again. Naturally enough, the underlying force is a common Scandinavian identity. There is a fellowship in terms of history, culture, and language that naturalizes the idea of a Nordic entity. This also finds powerful expression in the Social Democratic Scandinavian model. Nonetheless, this common identity has to compete with strong national identities. It might seem that the idea of a Nordic community remains in an unsettled state relative to the national identities. This explains the restless cycles of movement between the Scandinavian (or Nordic) and the national in terms of self-identity. It is easy to see how cooperation can suffer in such a situation. Scandinavianism blossomed during the Swedish-Norwegian union in the nineteenth century, but nationalism led to the splitting of the union. This greatest example of a bold attempt to enforce unity ultimately created division. After the final consolidation of the nation-states in 1905 (later in Finland), we can, however, speak of a slow development of closer cooperation in several areas.

---

[23] *Over grænsen efter koncurrenceevne* (Border Crossing to Build Competitive Ability) 2002. Cited from the introductory summary.

[24] In legal terms a firm cannot be registered as "Scandinavian"; it has to be registered in one of the old nations.

EUROPE

The development of the Nordic countries as a single economic region implies a closer contact between Sweden and Norway. On the one hand, it is striking that with regard to two of the most important international organizations in this part of the world, NATO and the EU, Sweden and Norway have each gone their own way. Norway is a member of NATO but not of the European Union, while for Sweden it is the reverse. Under the influence of the Cold War, the choices regarding security policy that the two countries had to make were complicated, but the result was perhaps unsurprising given their geopolitics and wartime experiences—Sweden retained its neutrality, while Norway found its place under the North Atlantic security umbrella. When it came to the differing choices the countries made in relation to European integration, the result is perhaps more of a paradox, at least for Sweden.

We have followed the negotiations regarding European economic cooperation from the beginning of the 1970s above. Norway applied for membership in the European Economic Community (EEC) in 1972 but ultimately was rejected by a plebiscite. Sweden did not apply. It was not without hesitation that the Norwegian Social Democrats had sought membership for their country. The hesitation stemmed from the political overtones and principles found in the Treaty of Rome, the EEC's founding document, concerning the free movement of capital and the mutual right of free establishment of business enterprises among members. In the end, they opted for membership for economic reasons. The six EEC member countries had experienced a higher rate of economic growth than the seven EFTA countries (Sweden and Norway were EFTA members).

The Social Democrats' most important argument for EEC membership, however, was the potential that membership offered for political control of the economy. As the Norwegian foreign minister said, one central point was the possibility "for control in a situation where we are more and more economically dependent on other countries."[25] The Social Democrats felt that they could meet the mutual right of establishment of enterprises and the free flow of capital by means of "greater state-ownership interests." The LO stressed the possibility of exerting increased control over multinational corporations, while at the same time launching a proposal to nationalize the forests in order to meet the threat that the principle of free establishment might lead to foreigners within the EEC purchasing Norwegian natural resources.[26] Again we see how socialization became a response to the threats of a liberalized international economy.

[25] St. forh. (Parl. Proceedings) 1971–1972. S. Tid. 3178.
[26] Aardal 1979, 192, 74.

The countermeasures that the Social Democrats proposed demonstrate that the pro-membership line was not unproblematic. The issue was leading to a deep division in the party. It was somewhat less problematic for the Conservative Party, which was able to appear relatively united in its support for EEC membership. What was generally characteristic here, however, was the inability of the parties to represent the opposing interests, such that the struggle came to be organized through extraparliamentary organizations. The opposition distinguished itself, in particular, through the People's Movement against Norwegian Membership in the EEC, which was founded in 1970. This struggle was to provide a breakthrough for action democracy (see chapter 14).

Differences in the clash over EEC membership in the period leading up to the plebiscite in 1972 were extremely sharp. In opposition to the supporters' argument that membership was necessary for economic control, their opponents maintained that membership involved signing away sovereignty—the selling out of Norway. Massive opposition came from farmers and fishermen and their organizations, who believed that their position would be threatened by membership. Rational economic arguments, however, had a tendency to be overshadowed by political arguments with strong emotional appeals to the desire for national independence. The union complex (see above) was conjured up anew by the opponents.

Yet what gave depth and breadth to the EEC opposition was that it captured and made concrete the general rebellion against the modern industrial society and the authoritarian features of the regime of the Social Democrats. It was a rebellion from below against the established societal institutions. The rebellion was able to seek sustenance in the strong countercultural circles, and it was able to provide the youth rebellion with concrete tasks to fulfill. This struggle came in the middle of the general shift of mentality that occurred starting around 1970. The opposition to the EEC and the general shift in mentality served to mutually reinforce one another. The result, then, was that the vast majority of established politicians were voted down by the plebiscite—53.5 percent voted no, and Norway had to stand on the sidelines and watch as Denmark and Great Britain were admitted to the EEC.

The Norwegians like to cultivate the notion of Norway as a different kind of country, one that did not want to join with Europe when it had the chance. But this is a myth. Sweden was traditionally "the outside country." Sweden insisted on its independence whether this had to do with NATO or the EEC/EU. In contrast to Norway (and Denmark), Sweden did not knock on the door to Europe in 1967 or in 1970. As Olof Palme said in 1971 while the struggle over membership was raging in Norway: "We are not prepared to tamper with neutrality, and we are not prepared to follow a policy that would put this in doubt. We are not prepared to go into a political collaboration that stands in contradiction with this policy of neutrality. Therefore we reject membership in the EEC."[27] To stand outside was thus official policy, and there was no doubt that this policy had great support among the people. Sweden—not Norway—was "the outside country." Had there been a plebiscite in Sweden in 1972, the numbers against membership would have been considerably more decisive than they were in Norway.

The fundamental principle for Swedish foreign policy was formulated as "freedom from alliance in peacetime, with the aim of neutrality in war." Sweden would go along with EFTA in 1960, but the country could not stretch any further. The following year Sweden declared: "The government has . . . concluded that membership in the six-state market in accord with the Treaty of Rome such as it is today is not compatible with the Swedish policy of neutrality."[28] The leader of the Conservative Party (the Coalition of Moderates) conducted his election campaign according to the slogan "Yes to Europe." But as Leif Lewin comments, "Erlander and his successor, Palme, needed only to whisper about the Swedish policy of neutrality for the question to fall away again."[29]

Palme had not been completely opposed to the possibility of membership, but the developments in Norway alarmed him: "There, from the outset, a divided and weakened Labor Party clearly resembles one of the Greek tragedies of fate."[30] Most important, however, was that the EEC Council of Ministers had given its approval to a plan that assumed a common economic policy within the EEC. This was impossible to swallow for the Swedes.

Sweden avoided the agonizing conflict that had broken out in Norway. This—together with its distance from the United States since Sweden remained outside NATO, and the fact that Palme, with his ringing criticism of the Vietnam War, "took over part of the waning embers of the student movement"—meant that the shift in mentality, or the rebellion around 1970, lacked one dimension in comparison with Norway. The established outlook was challenged; there was new feminism, Marxism-Leninism, opposition to nuclear power, and much more; but still Sweden lacked the force and the energy that was so evident in Norway. Establishment Sweden occupied a stronger position. This would be revealed again when the question of endorsing the European Union (the former EEC) came up at the beginning of the 1990s. While Norway was applying for its third time, Sweden applied for its first. There were plebiscites held in both countries in 1994. Sweden became a member, while in Norway those opposing membership celebrated victory once more.

[27] Riksdagens protokoll (Parl. Proceedings), 3 November 1970, 70. Cited from Lewin 2002, 392.
[28] Lewin 2002, 391.
[29] Lewin 2002, 391–392.
[30] Elmbrant 1989, 103.

WHY DID SWEDEN REVERSE ITS POLICY ON EUROPE?

What made Sweden turn on its heel and enter the European Union in 1994? Moreover, does this throw any light on the question of why Norway remained outside? The populations in both countries were evenly divided on the matter of joining. The constellations of parties involved were also the same for the most part. The Social Democrats in both countries were deeply split over the question. It was therefore the marginal voters who proved decisive. So far, there is some basis for saying that chance circumstances led the two countries to choose different roads. If we go a little deeper into the comparison we find, however, that the result was perhaps not completely random.

We saw that Sweden's opposition to membership was linked to the policy of neutrality. The fall of the Berlin Wall in 1989 had led to the initial re-valuation of this policy, which had been linked to the desire to stay outside the formation of blocs during the Cold War and thereby remain beyond in-volvement in a major war. According to Prime Minister Ingvar Carlsson, in a Europe "where the boundaries between the blocs disappeared," the situation ought to be reevaluated and the neutrality policy adjusted in order to be open for a pan-European peace arrangement.[31] But this was in no way the main reason for the turnabout. That lay in another quarter.

The years 1991–1993 comprised a "black-of-night crisis" in Sweden, when interest rates and unemployment soared to unbelievable heights. This was Sweden's second Poltava (the Ukrainian town in which King Karl XII was defeated by Peter the Great in 1709, resulting in Sweden's loss of position as a European great power), since the country now lost its status as an industrial great power. There had been difficulties from 1970 through the 1980s (in the 1980s Norway had passed Sweden in terms of per capita income), but the real havoc came at the beginning of the 1990s when Sweden became an ordinary small state in Europe, and an atmosphere of crisis spread throughout the country. Most people felt as though they were poised at the edge of an abyss. The crisis was countered by two dramatic moves: drastically reducing the national pension plan and attaching the traditionally "outsider" country to the EU. Within the EU economic conditions had fared much better, and EU membership was considered an emergency life raft.

It is not easy to change policy, even with the pressure of external circum-stances; and credibility can easily be lost by doing so. The move has generated extensive discussion, both at the time and since. Leif Lewin has analyzed the strategy followed by Social Democratic prime minister Ingvar Carlsson,

---

[31] Lewin 2002, 398.

who began claiming that rejecting membership was never meant to apply for all eternity. More important, he employed "a well-known political strategy, namely that of *reinterpreting* the EU question. Carlsson tried to put the question in a new context, one that justified taking a new position on the basis of changing conditions, and placed the change of course in a new light."[32] And this reinterpretation consisted of turning what had been a political question into an economic one. In this manner he disconnected the question of membership from the policy of neutrality, while at the same time sidelining the membership-critical foreign minister. The question of European Union membership became an issue for the finance minister. What the issue was really about was saving the Swedish welfare state. "A political impossibility had been reinterpreted as an economic necessity." On this basis, in 1991 an overwhelming majority of the Swedish Parliament voted to seek membership. Yet during the plebiscite of 1994 a bare majority of 52.3 percent voted for admission to the EU. Nor did Carlsson get his own party on board. It was split precisely, as was the population.[33] As in Norway, the EU issue had thus led the Swedish Social Democratic Party into "a Greek tragedy of fate."

In Norway there was no crisis—not of a comparable type in any case. The oil income had begun to flow. There were many arguments for going into the European Union, but Norway needed no life raft. Thus Sweden and Norway not only exchanged positions as the rich country of Europe, but as a consequence they also exchanged policies. Norway took over Sweden's role as the rich country that had the wherewithal to remain outside.

Norway was exceptional in terms of the divisions between the politicians and the population. There the leaders had been voted down. Such a division was not found in Sweden, where the people and their politicians had stood together with regard to remaining outside, just as they stood together with regard to membership in the face of necessity. The Swedish people followed their leaders. This was the case at the macro level, but at the micro level things were more complicated. For instance, it came to light that the opposition at the periphery was better reflected through the politicians from the periphery in Norway than in Sweden.

In many ways the EU struggle in Norway in 1994 was a repetition of the old campaign twenty-two years earlier. The foremost argument from the opposition on both occasions—and apparently carried out with the same percussive force—was the issue of national sovereignty. This was the case in spite of the many external conditions that had changed over the course of twenty-two years. Internationalization had gained momentum but, most im-

[32] Lewin 2002, 399. This section is based on the analysis in Lewin 2002, 398–403.
[33] Lewin 2002, 403.

Figure 18. Prime Minister Ingvar Carlsson led Sweden to the policy of the "third way," thereby accommodating the Social Democrats to a new reality. Among other things, he maneuvered Sweden into the European Union in 1994 by making a "political impossibility" into an "economic necessity." ("Ja!" means Yes!) (Photo: Fredrik Persson/EPA/Scanpix.)

portant, the EU now consisted of twelve countries rather than six as in 1972. Right before the national plebiscite it became clear that Finland and Sweden wanted membership, and a number of formerly Communist countries had signaled that they wanted to be members as well. One difference from 1972 was that the rebellious atmosphere was not in evidence, which meant that the internal political contradictions in Norway were less sharp. Moreover, Norway had just become a member of the European Economic Area (EEA), which for many practical purposes made the country a member of the EU's internal market. But despite these changing conditions, the voting result was still approximately the same as on the previous occasion—52.2 percent were against membership. In Norway there was no basis for reinterpreting a political impossibility into an economic necessity.

Despite the different routes the two countries chose in relation to the EU question, there are grounds to stress the convergence between them in relation to the outside world. The tendency toward Nordic regionalization has brought them more closely together. Both countries are also integrated into the EEA, although in different ways. Through its membership in the EEA Norway has followed through on 1,486 of the 1,494 EU directives, which is more than Sweden, an EU member, has managed. Norway is the cleverest one in the class without even being a member.[34]

The security policies of the two countries are identical, but in a completely different way than in the past. Of course Sweden still remains outside NATO, but the fall of the Berlin Wall had led to a cautious relaxation of the neutrality policy (see above). And after the terrorist attacks on the United States on September 11, 2001, Prime Minister Göran Persson came out swiftly in support of the United States and its right to defend itself. As Professor Olof Ruin commented, "Sweden had taken its natural place in the system of common values along with other countries; one no longer heard even a mumble about neutrality. A new generation had taken over leadership in a partially new world."[35]

There is also a convergence between Sweden and Norway when it comes to humanitarian foreign policy, especially with regard to international engagement in solving conflicts within the UN system, where both countries have been deeply engaged. They are small countries on the worldwide scale, but they are important, and not only in their own eyes. They have functioned as good examples of modern democracies, and they have a tradition of using their small size to their advantage precisely in this peace-making work. No one can suspect small countries of having imperialistic aspirations. They have both been willing to make use of this position. Sometimes it even seems as though there is a certain degree of competition between them.

THE LAST "SOVIET STATES"?

When Minister of Trade Björn Rosengren came out with his deep sigh over Norway as the last Soviet state, he was obviously thinking that the Norwegians—in that special merger—were bringing in considerations that were not related to business. This sigh is symptomatic of the way things have developed. Of course neither Sweden nor Norway has ever been a Soviet state. They are, indeed, among the most stable democracies in the world. These So-

---

[34] *Dagens Næringsliv*, 20 July 2004.
[35] Ruin 2002, 164.

cial Democratic regimes have, however, been characterized as subordinating trade and commerce to national policy, particularly in the Norwegian case. The point is that they have both been *Social Democratic* states.

This identity has now faded somewhat, but it has far from disappeared. The welfare state continues to exist, and a considerable amount of state ownership remains in the business sector, for example. There are also signs that there is a growing consciousness of the positive aspects of the Social Democratic legacy.

Despite the fact that Nordic countries have made different choices when it comes to their connections with central international organizations such as NATO and the EU, the convergence of interests seems to be greater than ever before. There is a certain tendency toward consolidation of the Nordic countries as their own region in the newly internationalized world. In this consolidation we discern an ambition to preserve political control of economic development, so characteristic of Social Democracy.

After Social Democracy: Toward New Social Structures?

A Success—but Not Exclusively So • Social Democracy's Liberal Inheritance •
The Institutional Structures under Pressure • The Freedom and Rights Revolution •
What Kind of Freedom? • High Score • Toward New Structures? • Politics Matter

A SUCCESS—BUT NOT EXCLUSIVELY SO

We have seen how Socialism could be incorporated into Scandinavian society in a peaceful manner and achieve a hegemonic position through its assumption of a Social Democratic form. The Social Democratic parties achieved this position by building an alliance between the traditional farming population and the new industrial working class. After 1945 they also managed to capture a large part of the votes of the fast-growing class of salaried employees.

The Social Democrats managed to take the nation-building project out of the hands of the non-Socialist parties by indicating a way out of the social and economic crisis of the 1930s and articulating a vision of a future society that most people could subscribe to. They also managed to develop political means through which they succeeded in realizing large parts of this vision. Social Democracy in Scandinavia must be regarded a success, an almost unique historical example of how to generate and realize ideals of a good society. It should be added, however, that the hegemonic position implies that they have to share the prize for their successes with other forces for good.

The happy moment of Social Democracy in Scandinavia was marked by the rise of the working classes from poverty to affluence; a substantial increase in material well-being for almost everyone; a very high degree of equality; social security; good housing; and access to education and the best medical treatment for all. These successes were achieved in a political order characterized by a strong state, strong trade unions, a surprisingly efficient mixed economy, and—despite all talk about the "one-party state" or the "authoritarian society"—a well-established and well-functioning democratic political order. It is not by accident that the Scandinavian Social Democratic welfare states became the model society for Europe, and that "the rise of the welfare state had diffused the old political animosities" so that ideologies could be declared dead.[1] But history rolls on.

The Social Democratic parties in Norway and Sweden started out at the turn of the century as revolutionary Marxist parties and ended up in the 1930s as comprehensive, democratic "people's parties." In 1945 they gained absolute parliamentary majorities in both countries—a position they managed to hold on to for a long period. Central questions arise: How did they make use of this unique position? What became of their Socialist inheritance? We have followed how the Social Democrats developed and modified their ideas when confronted with practical political problems, how the Social Democratic order developed into an order in its own right (see introduction), and how this led up to their happy moment in the 1960s. In the 1970s, however, precisely at the order's full execution, some aspects of the reverse side of the coin became visible. Thereupon, the relative harmony cracked, and Social Democracy came in for stiff criticism.

The response of the Social Democrats to the criticism was, first of all, to try to expedite movement toward a more Socialistic society (for example, instituting the wage earner funds). This involved new attacks on the structure of liberal norms, or more paternalism, which proved to be a dead end. By the beginning of the 1980s the Social Democrats had lost their hegemonic position, and developments took a new direction. Remarkably, not only were the Social Democrats on board with the change, but they initiated much of the new political direction, referred to as "the freedom and rights revolution" or "the politics of the third way."

SOCIAL DEMOCRACY'S LIBERAL INHERITANCE

The new turn in politics in the 1980s occurred alongside extensive changes in external structural relations. But, before considering this, we should remember the important institutions on which the Social Democratic order was built. In its heyday during the 1950s and 1960s Social Democracy represented, first of all, the height of the great, long-standing, liberal nation-building project. The *nation* was the entity within which the society of the future was to be realized. The political system of control was created for this national political arena, and it was within these boundaries that political as well as economic democracy should be developed.

[1] Cf. note 37, chapter 14.

According to the regulations of the Social Democratic regime, it was within the national boundaries that the business community had to arrange its affairs. "The very nature of economics is rooted in nationalism," as the radical British economist Joan Robinson has written.[2] We might say that the business community was subordinated to politics. At the time, there existed a feeling of full political control over economic development. It was also part of Social Democratic policy to retain control by means of a certain degree of protection from internationalization and an excessively open economy.

In addition to this strong state, strong trade unions were another characteristic feature of Social Democracy. In other words, capitalistic proprietary power was balanced by two other "stakeholder" interests—the greater society, through the state, and the employees, through the trade unions. Thus within the realm of business there existed three opposing institutionalized spheres of power: the power of ownership, the power of society, and the power of labor. These powers played against one another in the national arena but also, and especially, at the middle level—within the *company*. And with positive results for both the economy and economic democracy.

From the interwar period until the 1970s the idea existed that the companies—specifically, the great industrial corporations—would gradually take over as the most important institutions of society. This was where the future lay. Joseph Schumpeter described the tendency in the 1940s: "The perfectly bureaucratized giant industrial unit not only ousts the small or medium-sized firm and 'expropriates' its owners, but in the end it also ousts the entrepreneur and expropriates the bourgeoisie as a class that, in the process, stands to lose not only its income but, of infinitely more importance, its function. The true drivers of socialism were not the intellectuals or agitators who preached it, but the Vanderbilts, Carnegies, and Rockefellers."[3]

This description of the future society, in various versions, held a dominant position right up to the 1970s. Among others, John Kenneth Galbraith had the same view of the developmental structure of the economy. It was the vision of such a social structure—the new industrial state without an economic bourgeoisie and with its large and perfectly bureaucratized units—that the Social Democrats had based their work on, and they were not alone. These ideas were generally widespread. The large corporations were considered stable institutions, and from the outset the development of the welfare state's social security system state was based on the existence of stable and preferably large-scale companies. Sweden, as one of the countries most dependent on large-scale corporations in the whole industrial world, was far advanced in

[2] Robinson 1962, 117.
[3] Schumpeter 1970, 134.

this development. In Norway, with its many small firms, there were worries that the country was lagging behind in terms of this future vision.

With the hegemonic Social Democratic parties as the "natural" governing parties, the political system in Sweden and Norway remained stable. On the other hand, it is important to note that the negotiative corporatism of the Saltsjöbad Agreement in Sweden and the Main Agreement in Norway was based on the old notion of a contradiction between capital and labor, which continued throughout the hegemonic period. The class society remained.

Furthermore, the print media were bound to the parties, and the broadcast media were controlled by the state—a legacy of the bourgeois society. The state church was also part of that legacy. Generally, large parts of the existing institutional system remained. It should be added however that precisely this institutional setup made it possible to strengthen the political control of the public sector.

The most important arenas for social integration within the nation were the *school* and the *family*. School policy and family policy were therefore important political arenas for the Social Democrats. Under Social Democracy the unitary integrated school system would be of service to social integration. Like so much else, the idea of the standardized school was a legacy of the radical liberals. In their more radical phase, before they came to power, the Social Democrats had looked with skepticism on the idea that children of the working class should be forced into long years of schooling, but nothing was heard of this after 1945. Knowledge and social integration were two sides of the same coin within the ideal of the standardized school. Yet several mechanisms of segregation had to be instituted before the standardized school could function as a knowledge school. Problem students had to be separated out.

At the basic level of society we find the family. Originally the Social Democrats had attacked the bourgeois family. The upbringing of children for the new society was too important a task to be left to the parents. The construction of day-care centers (particularly in Sweden) and reliance on the school system reflected this view. All the same, in the heyday of Social Democracy after 1945 the ideal of the bourgeois family with its housewife contract still dominated public consciousness. The small nuclear family remained the basic collective of Social Democratic society, both as an ideal and in reality.

Such was the institutional basis of the Social Democratic order—the nation, the company, class consciousness, the media system, the state church, standard schools, and the family—these central institutions were a legacy or a further refinement of the institutions of the liberal society. This institutional continuity through the heyday of Social Democracy is striking. But it was to comprise only one moment in modern history. In the 1970s the

Social Democratic parties lost their hegemonic power, and all these institutions—the whole of Social Democracy's structural framework—came under considerable pressure.

THE INSTITUTIONAL
STRUCTURES UNDER PRESSURE

It is striking how, beginning in the 1970s, class consciousness almost vanishes in Scandinavia.[4] Class consciousness, or the working class as a cultural construction, had been the basis for the development of the labor movement as a united and politically powerful movement. And even though the Social Democratic parties moved from class-based parties to broad people's parties, much of their strength during their hegemonic period lay in the fact that they remained the obvious choice of the working class. This successful policy for equalizing conditions, however, tended to undermine the subjective class consciousness of the new generations and weaken the Social Democratic order. As so often happens in history, the effect destroyed the cause. This weakening of class consciousness was followed by what seems like a paradox: when class as a cultural construction weakened, the differences again rose.

As internal societal development moved beyond the Social Democratic order as it had been realized in the hegemonic period, so did international development. Increasingly, extensive international cooperation changed the conditions regarding regulation policy, reducing the room for political maneuvering. It is difficult to imagine, though, that the (relatively) traditional demarcation of the nation-state could have been maintained. Modern technology also pushed in the direction of internationalization. On the other hand, there was clearly a choice about how far to go with it. Opposition arose, and Norway continued to remain outside the European Union.

Internationalization and deregulation move together very closely—the state pulls back, relinquishing more of the business arena to the market. Business is no longer subordinate to politics in the way it was under Social Democracy: the situation is more nearly the opposite—the government becomes junior partner to business. Government must give assistance so that business can flourish in the face of international competition and so that there is a high enough level of investment in the country to maintain employment. Up to now this has not been a problem, but it has furthered policy built on the premises of the business community.[5] It has become more difficult to conduct

[4] Valen 1981, 133f.; Bjørklund 2008; Olof Petersson 1982. According to Petersson, 77 percent said they had a class affiliation in 1968, but only 48 percent in 1976.
[5] This applies above all to policy regarding oil. See Kristoffersen 2007.

national economic policy in the way it had been done earlier. On the other hand, the expansion of transnational institutions, first and foremost the EU, represents attempts to gain political control over the internationalized business community.

The new—freely chosen or unavoidable—international competition is closely linked to changes at the institutional middle level. The company is no longer the large, stable, perfectly bureaucratized, central societal institution that had been envisaged. Among other things, the low points of the economic cycle unmasked the lack of adaptability of these big firms. This lack of adaptability had made the whole economic system rather rigid. On the other hand, the new information technology provided the basis for a wave of new, modern, progressive small firms (those of Silicon Valley, among others) that became the new symbol of the modern industrial society—small, efficient companies located in parklike surroundings.

The concept of the "industrial society" from the heyday of Social Democracy was no longer spoken of, while the concepts of the "service society," "knowledge society," and "information society" rapidly came into circulation. These societies required institutional forms different from those of the industrial society. Thus fundamental changes were occurring in the real world, but even more so in people's *ideas* about reality or, more specifically, about what society would be in the future.

The new technological conditions melded with the international revitalization of the financial sphere and the stock market. A new international market was created for buying and selling companies or parts of companies. The Social Democratic image of a world dominated by stable, bureaucratized, large corporations dissolved into thin air. Strategic-political decision making had to some extent shifted out of the spheres of the public and private bureaucracies and into the volatile internationalized financial sphere where the new capitalists operated. Proprietary power expanded at the cost of public power and labor power. The world became more fluid.

As a consequence of these changes, the stable boundaries to employees' lives weakened. And since many of the benefits of the welfare system were linked to employment, this also created insecurity—greater freedom, perhaps, but also greater insecurity. In both countries there is now a characteristic struggle over the revision of the laws governing relations at the workplace. In a new world there is a drive to defend the security previously established in the welfare society.

One of the most revolutionary developments in the wake of the Social Democratic order was the freeing of the media during the 1970s and 1980s. This had to do with giving up the state monopoly over the broadcast media and freeing the print media from their ties to the political parties. The public sphere changed character, and the political parties lost much of their function in setting the daily agenda. The freeing of the media can be viewed as a continuation of the differentiation processes of modernity—a radicalized modernity.

When we move to the central arenas of social integration, the school and the family, we find similar basic institutional changes. The standard integrated school came under sharp criticism, and the response to this criticism was to take the idea of the standard school to extremes. The mechanisms of segregation were removed. School was now really to be for everybody, including the problem students; the standard school should become a school for the weakest, it was said. At the same time, the way was opened for private schools. Ironically, this turned out to be of no benefit to either the weakest or the brightest. If there were winners, they were the students who came from resource-rich homes.

There was at the same time a war raging over the family. Childbirth rates had fallen, and the incidence of divorce had increased. Radical feminism from around 1970 onward demanded that the housewife contract be replaced with a gender-equality contract. Two-income families became both a necessity and an ideal. The old nuclear family was shaken to its foundations. Above all, war raged around the question of whether to strengthen the family or transfer more responsibility for children to society by expanding day-care facilities.

The tendency toward the dissolution of the nuclear family was an illustration of the principles of modernity driven to their most extreme consequences. As Ulrich Beck has pointed out, the autonomy of the individual is a basic principle of European modernity. In what he calls "the second modernity" this autonomy has been extended and radicalized, leading to "the institutions of the first modernity breaking down ... the structure of the normal family."[6]

Generally speaking, when the institutional structures of the first modernity were put under pressure, it was a reaction to the further development or radicalization of liberal modernity's principles under Social Democracy. The large corporations, growing inflexible and unwieldy, lost their ability to compete; the media became differentiated, and the parties lost strength; the last phase of achieving individual freedom threatens the structure of the family; and the standard school developed into a school for the weak at the same time as the educational system was opened up for private schools. Social Democracy had cultivated almost to the extreme the unity and equality that had also been central to the liberal nation-building project. The pressure on the institutional structures of Social Democracy from the 1970s and onward was not least a reaction to this cultivation of unity and equality.

---

[6] Ulrich Beck in an interview with *Klassekampen*, 14 May 2005.

THE FREEDOM AND RIGHTS REVOLUTION

The pressure on the Social Democratic institutions was manifest in the 1970s, but it is only in the 1980s that development seems to have taken a new direction. The strong state of Social Democracy had been based on a trust in the state as an incorruptible caretaker of everybody's interests right up to the point where "state" and "society" became interchangeable concepts. A growing skepticism of this almighty state led to a careful withdrawal, leaving more room for the market and the civil society.

Many felt that the ideals of unity and equality led to an unpleasant conformity and standardization. The new catchphrase was "freedom of choice." The "nanny state" of the Social Democrats had held the ideal of universal and equal publicly defined benefits that, in principle, would represent "high-quality standard solutions." But now there were to be no standard solutions. People should be able to choose for themselves between an array of offers, whether this had to do with the welfare state's social output, schooling, domestic accommodation, TV channels, or other goods and services. The new freedom was to be realized through the use of the market or quasi markets.

The protest against the welfare state in its final form was not simply to oppose standardized solutions; demands also arose for ever more extensive services. It is said that in his last days Einar Gerhardsen posed the question in a rather disillusioned way: "What has gone wrong?" The thought had been that society would be increasingly satisfied as the contributions of the welfare state gradually came into effect, but this did not happen. In Sweden Tage Erlander conceptualized these developments as "the dissatisfaction of increasing expectations." The happy expectation of at some point being able to reach the goals had gotten lost along the way. So when the goal was reached, the future was lost.[7]

The labor movement had arisen as a popular movement based on collective solidarity. But when they assumed power in society and took over the nation-building project, the Social Democrats became less rooted in the popular movement and developed into social engineers. The new freedom was not only a protest against paternalism; it went further than that as it turned against the solidarity it was grounded in. This freedom seemed to carry along with it a certain individuation, a freedom from the collective.

The freedom revolution is intimately connected with the rights revolution and rediscovery of the old constitutional way of thinking. There is a general tendency today toward continuous expansion of individual rights. All of that which is defined as a right in the constitution or in ordinary laws gives the

---

[7] Koselleck 2000; "lost future" is an attempt to translate Koselleck's concept *vergangene zukunft*.

Figure 19. The evening sun shines on Social Democracy: Einar Gerhardsen, *left*, visits Tage Erlander on August 20, 1984, during their elder days. Gerhardsen had been prime minister during most of the hegemonic phase of Social Democracy in Norway. Erlander had held a similar position in Sweden. (Photo: Per Svensson/Scanpix.)

individual extra protection from interference by political power and, consequently, greater freedom.

With its demand for greater freedom, the new mentality turns not only against the tyranny of intimacy and the old ideal of equality; it also turns against the old standardized culture by demanding greater diversity. We remember how the main character in Axel Jensen's novel *Icarus* "knots [his] fists against the welfare state. The defiance of a generation. The falsetto shriek, and 'go to hell' daubed on the wall in garish colors—while at the same time trying to get a toehold in a richer reality."

External conditions would later add fuel to the fire, initially in the form of the new long-distance immigration that was seriously under way by the 1970s. A stream of people from other cultures arrived in Scandinavia, contributing to the downfall of the old standardized culture and leading, some say, to "a richer reality." The internal protest against what many considered to be a gray and boring society thereupon found itself mixed with external influences. If "uniformity" and "standardization" had been privileged words before, the new privileged word was "diversity." The move from *equality* and *unity* to *freedom* and *diversity* implies a dramatic change of mentality, and it broke with the traditional Social Democratic mode of thinking.

Our presentation of the twentieth century has been divided into three phases, with the hegemonic phase of Social Democracy in the middle. Thus we have described two breaks in the line of development: when the Social Democrats took power in the mid-1930s, and when they lost their hegemony in the 1970s. What we see now is that the most revolutionary changes occurred not when they assumed power but when they lost their hegemonic position. It was then that the course of history changed direction.

WHAT KIND OF FREEDOM?

Today there is a tendency to debate the concept of freedom. There is a demand from the left that the term "freedom" be recaptured from the liberals, while simultaneously arguing that the freedom revolution involves many positive elements from a Socialist perspective as well.[8] When the ideological struggle blows up again (and it is in the process of doing so), there will probably be a struggle to define the concept of freedom, for it can mean so very many things.

The Social Democratic order with its welfare state was built on solidarity thinking, but its realization, paradoxically, undermined solidarity. The actual welfare state lost its quality of representing the collective interest and came to represent individual rights instead. It seems as though something got lost along the way. To cite Zygmunt Bauman: "The splendors of freedom are at their brightest when freedom is sacrificed at the altar of security."[9] The secure people's home of the welfare state fed the dream of another freedom—a richer reality beyond the welfare state.

The great successes of the Social Democratic regimes—in short, the whole welfare state—are indeed a precondition for the great liberating project of late modernity, insofar as they provided the material basis for individual freedom, that is, freedom from need. Despite the problems of the many growing demands, and despite the adjustments that were made along the way out of necessity, nobody wants to dismantle the welfare state.

We have indicated that some security has to be sacrificed for the new freedom. But it is perhaps just as difficult to reconcile freedom with equality. Freedom has been a central concept among both liberals and Socialists. When

---

[8] Marsdal and Wold 2004. This book has found inspiration from Beck and Beck-Gernsheim 2001.
[9] Bauman 1997, 3.

the Social Democratic leaders Carlsson and Brundtland launched the freedom revolution at the beginning of the 1980s, they believed it was in full accordance with Socialist or Social Democratic thinking. The strong emphasis on equality had led in the direction of a nanny state. Now equality had to be combined with freedom. Socialism is predicated on the belief that this is possible, but what kind of freedom is it? The concept of freedom had been captured by the liberal forces in society and had come to represent individual choice and the free market. But, to cite Bauman again: "What the liberal vision of the universal and equally awarded right to choose failed to take into account is that 'adding freedom of action to the fundamental inequality of social conditions will result in inequality even deeper than before.'"[10]

The many discussions about freedom will most often take Isaiah Berlin's seminal essay "Two Concepts of Liberty" as a starting point. The two concepts are "positive" and "negative" freedom. There is a tendency among liberals to define freedom exclusively as negative freedom, or independence of the individual from interference, particularly by political powers. Positive freedom, on the other hand, is most important for Socialists and Social Democrats (and conservatives). It identifies freedom with collective self-government, or some sort of democracy. It is important to develop a sense of community as a basis for democracy. This explains the weight Social Democrats placed on the school as a socializing arena. Positive freedom presupposes that the individual is part of a moral order.

The liberal attack on the concept of positive freedom is directed toward the collective aspect. According to this critique, positive freedom means that people are "forced to be free," which implies a totalitarian tendency. Reasonable adherents of the two opposing views will of course make concessions. Negative freedom is also important to Social Democrats, while liberals, although preoccupied with limiting the positive power of the state, will admit that state power and a certain unity are required as a basis for a well-functioning democracy. Nevertheless, there are some deeper differences between the two "freedoms"—the positive and the negative.[11]

There is also a third concept that some call "republican freedom."[12] It differs from negative freedom in that the point is not a limited state but a state bound to established rules. Binding of power can be compatible with an extensive state. People are free when living in a free society, which is a society freed from arbitrary or discretionary powers. There should be "the rule of law and not the rule of men," as the saying goes. The freedom and rights revolu-

---

[10] Bauman 1997, 196. Bauman is here citing Jerzy Jedlicki.
[11] Taylor 1979, 177.
[12] Pettit 1997. Labord and Maynor 2008.

tion was a reaction against the comprehensive power of the Social Democratic state *and* its tendencies toward arbitrary rule.

There is no reason to throw overboard any of the three concepts of liberty. Perhaps we can expand on what Isaiah Berlin had to say about his two concepts: These are "two [three] profoundly divergent and irreconcilable attitudes ... in practice it is often necessary to strike a compromise between them. ... But it shows a profound lack of social and moral understanding not to recognize that the satisfaction each of them seeks is an ultimate value which, both historically and morally, has an equal right to be classed among the deepest interests of mankind."[13] The paternalistic tendencies of the Social Democrats and the weight they had placed on equality and unity meant too little attention was paid to the negative and republican freedoms, consequently inviting the liberal criticism that they "forced" people to be free."[14] The freedom and rights revolution (in which the Social Democrats themselves indeed took part) led to a better balance between the different liberties, and to a better and more open society.

What complicates the picture is internationalization, which leaves our fate more dependent on distant and nontransparent powers than before. This development has been met with, as we have seen, an increase in international agreements and conventions and the development of transnational institutions and judicial systems. So far this must be regarded as a positive development bringing at least some order to the international arena. The building up of the European Union can be seen as a special case.

The rights revolution was not least a European phenomenon. The circumscription of the decision-making power of the democratically elected institutions following the rights revolution can be observed on the national level, where it represented an improvement of the democratic system. This expanded role of the courts of law is, however, more pronounced on the European level. It has considerably strengthened and expanded the scope of the European Human Rights Court, which has proved to be an undisputable success. In principle all individual Europeans can take their cases to the European court. The problem now is that the court is overloaded, the victim of its own success. This process of judicializing is even more pronounced in connection with the EU Court of Justice. The problem here is the ambiguity and lack of clarity in the many different rules on which the court is expected to base its decisions. The courts must rely on a "dynamic method of interpretation,"

[13] Berlin 1969, 166.

[14] There has been an extensive debate over this issue in connection with communitarianism. The communitarians consider the idea of democracy from Athens to Rousseau as an ideal. It stands for a common concept of "good." For liberals pluralism is good. And Robert Dahl reminds us that the "monistic ideal" of the communitarians can be found in modern times only in totalitarian regimes (Dahl 1986, 242).

which in reality means making decisions that, in principle, should have been made by political institutions. Even more problematic is the character of the transnational European political institutions. In connection with the ratification of the Lisbon agreement, the German constitutional court made a decision that *The Economist* aptly summarizes: "In effect, the [German] court said that the EU is not democratic enough to support more integration and told Germany, the largest EU member, to hit the pause button. ... The EU is not a democratic state and the European Parliament is not a proper legislature, it said."[15] It is remarkable how a national constitutional court, whose main task it is to protect the negative freedom of the individual against positive state power, takes upon itself the protection of the collective self-government, or the positive democratic power.

So this is the situation regarding the struggle over the concept of freedom. There seems to be a possibility for the pendulum to swing in the opposite direction of its position in the heyday of Social Democracy's strong state. Then there was an imbalance in favor of the positive freedom of collective self-government, with too little regard for the negative and republican freedoms. The freedom and rights revolution remedied these problems. Seen from a European perspective there is, however, a tendency for the opposite problems to arise, which reminds us that it is imperative to retain *some* of the virtues of Social Democracy in order to strike the right balance between the three freedoms. To cite Bauman again: "Community without [negative or republican] freedom is a project as horrifying as freedom without community. For better or worse, steering clear of both is all the chance of meaningful and dignified life that human individuals may reasonably hope for, however much is done by philosophers to bar them from facing the truth."[16]

HIGH SCORE

There is every reason to stress that much of what we understand as the Social Democratic order still remains, and much policy today is directed toward defending earlier achievements. So far, policy in many areas is more retrospective than future-oriented. Wage differences are still small in both Norway and Sweden, taxes are high, the public sector is large, the welfare state retains its main features, trade unions are still strong, and negotiative corporatism in working life continues to function almost as previously. Economically, things are going reasonably well—which is in conflict with economic orthodoxy maintaining that the above-mentioned features are unfortunate for the economy.[17]

[15] "Constitutional Concerns," *The Economist*, 23 July 2009.
[16] Bauman 1996, 89.
[17] See Kalle Moene in *Aftenposten*, 24 December 2006.

If we take a quick look at the many indexes comparing the performance of nations in various aspects, a positive overall picture of the Scandinavian countries is indeed substantiated. The most widely used indicator of living standards is per capita GDP. In 1975 Sweden was ranked sixth among Organization for Economic Cooperation and Development (OECD) countries (behind Switzerland, Luxembourg, the United States, the Netherlands, and Denmark), and Norway ranked ninth. In 2006 Norway had climbed to third (behind Luxembourg and the United States), thanks to oil revenues from the North Sea, whereas Sweden was ninth. These figures should, however, be compared with the level of public social spending per capita, on which Denmark, Sweden, and Norway have very high scores compared, for instance, with the low score of the United States. They should also be compared with income inequality indicators, on which Denmark and Sweden have the lowest score and Finland and Norway score somewhat higher but still well below the OECD average. The United States is well above the average.

Part of the reason industry and trade fare so well in the Nordic countries is perhaps to be found in competitiveness and governance indicators. In the Global Competitiveness Report of the World Economic Forum (rating 131 countries) the United States tops the ranking, with Switzerland second, followed by Denmark and Sweden. Norway is ranked sixteenth.[18] In the Corruption Perceptions Index of Transparency International (rating 180 countries) Denmark tops the ranking, along with Finland and New Zealand. Sweden is ranked fourth, along with Singapore, and Norway is ninth, along with Canada.[19] In the Worldwide Governance Indicators of the World Bank (rating 212 countries) the Scandinavian countries earn close to perfect scores. Here Sweden is a little ahead of Norway in Regulatory Quality and Political Stability, whereas Norway is a little ahead of Sweden in Rule of Law and Voice and Accountability. In Government Effectiveness they are on a par.[20]

The OECD publishes a wide range of social indicators for as many of its thirty member states as possible. The idea is to go beyond the economic indicators to measure development in a wider sense and "assess the progress that various countries have made in delivering improvements in the quality of life."[21] As we would expect, the Scandinavian countries have a relatively high score in almost all of these thirty-four indicators.

Most interesting perhaps are indicators concerning social cohesion. The Netherlands, Iceland, Ireland, Denmark, and Switzerland have the highest life satisfaction rates and also some of the highest happiness rates. Norway

---

[18] http://www.weforum.org.
[19] http://www.transparency.org.
[20] http://www.worldbank.org. It is doubtful whether these small differences are significant.
[21] *Society at a Glance: OECD Social Indicators 2005.* Citation from the executive summary, p. 8. All the indicators referred to are from this publication.

and Sweden are a little below these countries in life satisfaction rates but clearly above the OECD average, and Norway and Sweden's happiness rates are among the highest, along with those of the five previously mentioned countries. On life satisfaction and happiness rates, Norway received a somewhat higher score than Sweden did during the 1990s. The Nordic countries also have high scores on the extent of participation in various group activities within civil society.

We have referred to the disappointment of Erlander and Gerhardsen when confronted with the "dissatisfaction of increasing expectations." There is, furthermore, a general sense of a darker side to the Scandinavian society. In the words of Tony Judt, "Anyone familiar with Nordic culture, from Ibsen and Munch through Ingmar Bergman, will recognize another side of Scandinavian life: its self-questioning, incipiently melancholic quality—popularly understood in these years [the heyday of Social Democracy] as a propensity toward depression, alcoholism, and high suicide rates." He places some of the blame on "the all-embracing state" and the "temptation to tinker with individuals themselves."[22] (Which obviously means to interfere with individual citizens.) There is a certain parallel to our description of the Social Democratic order, and to the freedom revolution as a reaction to the "all-embracing state." But what has been achieved by today's richer reality?

As for suicide rates, both Sweden and Norway are presently below the OECD average, but not by far. In 1980 Sweden, however, had a suicide rate that was clearly higher than the OECD average. Finland and Iceland still have high rates, and Denmark is just above the OECD average. Norway has never had a very high suicide rate (despite both Ibsen and Munch being Norwegian). We should perhaps be a little cautious about placing too much emphasis on the tendency to gloomy introspection: at least Norway and Sweden fare quite well on the suicide indicators. Besides, there is every reason to place more emphasis on such measures as the happiness indicator, which, as we saw, is high for the Nordic countries. The stress factor appears comparatively low, suggesting that the trade unions must have succeeded in realizing part of what Ingrid Millbourn called "the right to ease and comfort."

It is notoriously difficult to interpret statistical findings of the sort we have presented. As the Nordic countries have a relatively high score on (almost) all the indicators, however, the general conclusion may well be that people in the Nordic countries are happier with their overall situation than people in most other countries. So even if Sweden and Norway did not turn out to be the Social Democratic paradises envisaged by Erlander and Gerhardsen,

---

[22] Judt 2007, 367–368. See also Sennett 2006, 17, where he talks about "the Nordic tendency to gloomy introspection."

the leaders would have had every reason to be content. The Scandinavian countries have succeeded in combining a strong economic performance with a low stress factor, an equitable economic distribution, social security, and a generally high quality of life, much of which is intact. And these are the reasons that the Nordic countries seem to have regained much of their status as model countries for the future.[23]

TOWARD NEW STRUCTURES?

In the wake of the partial breakdown of old institutions and the high scores on the happiness scale, the question is whether we can see anything more than simply tendencies toward the dissolution of old structures. Do we see attempts toward the formation of new institutional developments and new mentalities that will make it possible to rescue the existing resources for use in a new world? How do the old institutions fare, and can we see incipient formation of societal elements that can replace the old institutions and shore up the foundations of happiness?

The nation-state has been weakened but, despite internationalization, it still provides the most important framework for politics—and will certainly continue to do so in the foreseeable future. European cooperation has been interpreted as a strategy for capturing and defending the national basis for political control under the new conditions created by international capitalism. This cooperation, as it is put, is a strategy to save the nation-state. So far, this is an example of how new structures can replace the old and create new external conditions for economic control.[24]

In the economic structures of the new capitalism we also see features of development that point toward something other than a mere weakening of political and democratic control. We saw how governments, under the new finance capitalism, became junior partners to the business community. Power lies with the owners of capital, roughly as it did in the old pre–Social Democratic form of capitalism. But who are these owners?

On Oslo's stock exchange the Norwegian state holds almost 40 percent of the owner capital (see chapter 12). In Sweden too the state is heavily involved. It is ironic indeed that, under the new international finance capitalism, state capitalism is growing again. The state is involved partly through direct ownership and partly through large public pension funds. State capitalism is thus

[23] Sachs 2008, 15–16. See the citation from Sachs 2008 in the introduction, note 21. See also Berman 2006, 17–18: "a proper understanding of social democracy's history can offer a guide for tackling contemporary political challenges."

[24] Johan P. Olsen 2007, 31–32.

woven into the new institutional capitalism. The largest capitalists in the market today are institutional investors, the large private and public funds.

Many of the largest of these funds represent many, many small investors. At present they certainly do not point toward a more democratic capitalism, but they do perhaps represent a possibility for political control. Funds are also of many types. Within the European Union there is anxiety both that some of the private equity funds can pose a threat to economic stability in their push to earn quick money, and that the new large state investment funds, such as those of China and Russia, can have hidden political agendas. Here are new structural features that a new policy must consider.

When we drop down to the middle level, we can see that Schumpeter's and Galbraith's large, stable, perfectly bureaucratized companies definitely belong to the past. This has tended to undermine the welfare state's security system. Perhaps it is time to loosen the tight connection between work, income, and welfare benefits that is so typical of the Scandinavian "work approach."[25] This is a cultural problem just as much as it is an economic one. Change will require setting aside the strong work ethic of Protestantism and creating space to realize the old dream from antiquity: getting rid of the imperative character of work. In our rich societies, cannot freedom of choice also include an opportunity for the individual to choose to stand outside organized wage-paying work? The established-by-law right to wage-paying work might perhaps be exchanged for the right to income. Of course, cultural restraints on the strong work ethics have already been loosened somewhat. The very many—even of working age—who today live on the social security system should perhaps be regarded as a new structural feature of our society, a feature that has come to stay and which should not be regarded exclusively as something negative. A more active civil society, a stronger sense of citizenship, is required in order to include those without wage-paying work as fully valued citizens.[26]

The newly freed media system has undoubtedly meant that the public sector has become more transparent, that information flows more freely. The revolutionary development of the Internet, however, is more equivocal. Here the future is open-ended. The situation today, with bloggers and a flow of information in which it can become difficult to find trustworthy sources, brings to mind the Wild West conditions after freedom of printing was instituted in Denmark and Norway during the 1770s. But indeed, in that instance, order was gradually established. To create a serviceable institutional framework for the use of the Internet is one of the more urgent political tasks.

---

[25] The "work approach" has played an important role in Sweden and Norway. Cf. Kautto et al. 1999, 135–136.

[26] Cf. Sejersted 1997 ("Technology and Unemployment").

With regard to schooling, there is agreement around reconstructing the knowledge school framework. At the same time, the current "Red-Green" government in Norway has instituted limits to the establishment of private schools. In other words, a step backward is being taken toward a comprehensive school system, as found in a period of great unity during the heyday of Social Democracy—back when one could dream of workers and their families discussing the constellation of the atom around their dinner tables. The talk here is about reestablishing something that was lost in subsequent struggles.

Most important, however, is the development of small collectives in daily community life. Is it true that the value of community is weakening? We live in a "highly moral world, despite what the cultural pessimists try to tell us," if we are to believe Beck.[27] The requirements for living together are, however, no longer established by either tradition or traditional institutions but must be renegotiated in response to specific cases. It is not certain whether we are experiencing a deterioration of binding fellowship in our lives. The culture of freedom, as far as we can see its contours, decreases the likelihood that people find themselves in communities thrust on them by fate. They are more apt to enter fellowships that they themselves have chosen. Here perhaps we find the most important "freedom of choice" in late modern society.

Since they are fluid in form, these communities are institutionalized differently than were the old communities. This applies especially to the "post-familial family." We are just as dependent on family fellowship as before, but it no longer has the old nuclear family's strict, closed form. Our society is thus characterized not only by new institutions but also by a new type of institution in which community can be developed in a freer form. This is the new structure of freedom as seen by the great optimists. But will it take care of everyone, or will this too be a free choice that leads to deeper inequalities?

POLITICS MATTER

The story we have told is by and large a success story. We have tried to show how this success came about by following in some detail the development of Social Democracy in the two countries through approximately one hundred years. But we have also hinted that there were some preconditions further back in the history of Norway and Sweden. The Polish professor Nina Witoszek, who now lives in Norway, has perceived what she calls "an arena for reconciliation" in these societies.[28] This is substantiated by our story. There were class

---

[27] Beck and Beck-Gernsheim 2001, 212.
[28] Witoszek 1998, 65.

conflicts, but there were also an equitable distribution of wealth and a strong feeling of fellowship, which made it relatively easy to reach solutions to social problems that everybody could accept. This points to a notable characteristic to our presentation: the history of Social Democracy is the history of how politics matter. It provides an example of how, under happy circumstances, societies can be the master of history.

Social Democracy did not represent the end of the story, however. History rolls on, and Social Democracy, like all other forms of society, was overtaken by historical developments. Social Democracy had furthered the liberating project of modernity by taking over the legacy of the liberal society and further developing its institutions. Through one of the ironies of history, however, substantial changes occurred precisely as the Social Democratic order was accomplished: some of the liberal institutions that had their origins in the first phase of modernity, and had constituted the basis of Social Democracy, broke down.

The reasons for this breakdown lie to some degree in Social Democracy's perversion of liberal freedom in the direction of paternalism and (partly in reaction to this) in the parallel freedom revolution. Whether or not the freedom revolution will follow this same path, gradually losing political control of society, will be determined by the degree of success with which the new institutional reality is taken on and begins to form the basis of subsequent policy. We should learn through Per Albin Hansson how "to seize Time by her flowing locks and lead her down the right path." Then perhaps we can once more enjoy the realization that politics matter. We conclude our story by paraphrasing Urban Lundberg's comment on the changes in the welfare state—by changing the institutions, Social Democracy changed itself. Yet every shift of identity implies a form of rebirth.[29] It is a question of recapturing the future.

---

[29] Urban Lundberg 2003, 299.

BIBLIOGRAPHY

Aagedahl, Olaf. 2003. *Nasjonal symbolmakt*. Oslo: Makt- og demokratiutredningen. Rapport 55.

Aardal, Bernt. 1979. *EF-debatten i Danmark og Norge*. Oslo: Magisteravh. i statsvitenskap.

Aardal, Bernt. 1999. *Velgere i 90-årene*. Oslo: NKS forlaget.

Aardal, Bernt. 2002. "Demokrati og valgdeltakelse—en innføring og en oversikt." See Aardal, ed., 2002.

Aardal, Bernt, ed. 2002. *Valgdeltakelse og lokaldemokrati*. Oslo: Kommuneforlaget.

Aarsæther, Finn. 1997. "1990-åras danskfag, norskfag og svenskfag. Tre nordiske læreplaner." *Nordisk Pedagogikk*, vol. 17, 1/1997.

Aasland, Tertit. 1961. *Fra arbeiderorganisasjon til mellomparti*. Oslo: Universitetsforlaget.

Aasland, Tertit. 1974. *Fra landmandsorganisasjon til bondeparti*. Oslo: Universitetsforlaget.

Agrell, Wilhelm. 2000. *Fred och fruktan. Sveriges säkerhetspolitiska historia 1918–2000*. Lund: Historiska Media.

Ahonen, Sirkka, and Jukka Rantala, eds. 2001. *Nordic Lights: Education for Nation and Civic Society in the Nordic Countries, 1850–2000*. Helsinki: Finnish Literary Society.

Aléx, Peder. 1994. *Den rationella konsumenten: KF som folkuppfostrare 1899–1939*. Stehag: Brutus Östling Bokförlag Symposion.

Allern, Sigurd. 1996. *Kildens makt. Ytringsfrihetens politiske økonomi*. Oslo: Pax.

Alm, Kristian. 1998. "Verdikommisjonen." *Nytt Norsk Tidsskrift* 4/1998.

Åmark, Klas. 1998. *Solidariteten gränser. LO och industriförbundsfrågan 1900–1990*. Stockholm: Atlas.

Åmark, Klas. 1999. "Inkomsttrygghet i Norge och Sverige. Klass, arbetarrörelse och välfärdspolitik 1930–1970." *Arkiv* nr 77–78. Lund.

Åmark, Klas. 2002. "Familj, försörjing och livslopp under 1900-talet." See Bergman and Johansson 2002.

Åmark, Klas. 2003a. "Kommissionen räknade fel–200 000 var registrerade." *Dagen Forskning*, 3–4 February 2003.

Åmark, Klas. 2003b. "Universalism med undantag. Svensk socialförsäkringspolitik 1935–1960." See *Den mangfoldige velferden* 2003.

Åmark, Klas. 2005. *Hundra år av välfärdspolitik. Väfärdsstatens framväxt i Norge och Sverige*. Umeå: Boréa.

Ambjörnsson, Ronny. 1988. *Den skötsamme arbetaren*. Stockholm: Carlssons. English edition 1991, *The Honest and Diligent Worker*. Stockholm: HLS.

Ambjörnsson, Ronny. 1996. *Mitt förnamn är Ronny*. Stockholm: Bonniers Förlag.

Amnå, Erik. 2001. "Medborgarskapets dynamik: Reflektioner kring 2006 års förstegångsväljare." *Rösträtten 80 år*. Stockholm: Justitiedepartementet.

Andenæs, Johs. 1952. "Garantier for rettssikkerheten ved administrative avgjørelser." See *Förhandlingarna . . .* 1952: bilag 6.

Andenæs, Johs. 1962. "Domstolenes stilling til Stortingets delegasjon av myndighet" (lecture 7.8.1953). In Johs Andenæs, *Avhandlinger og foredrag*. Oslo: Universitetsforlaget.

Andersen, Bjørn. 2003. *Institusjonelle investorer. Makt og avmakt i aksjemarkedet*. Oslo: Makt- og demokratiutredningen. Rapportserie nr 75.

Andersen, Jørgen Goul, and Jens Hoff. 2001. *Democracy and Citizenship in Scandinavia*. Palgrave.

Andersen, Ketil Gjølme. 2002. *Den teknologiske og den økonomiske fornuften. Tysk nasjonaløkonomi mellom Bildung og rasjonalisering 1909–1939*. Oslo: Acta Humaniora, Universitetet i Oslo.

Andersen, Ketil Gjølme. 2003. "En norsk 3-årsplan. Ole Colbjørnsen, Arbeiderpartiets økonomiske politikk og den tyske krisedebatten 1932–35." Oslo: *Historisk Tidsskrift* 2/2003, pp. 113–140.

Anderson, Ivar. 1956. *Arvid Lindman och hans tid*. Stockholm: P.A. Norstedts & Söner.

Andersson, Jan A. 2000. "1950-talet. Tid att så—tid att skörda." See Sundelius and Wiklund 2000.

Andersson, Jenny. 2003. *Mellan tillväxt och trygghet. Ideer om produktiv socialpolitik i socialdemokratisk socialpolitisk ideologi under efterkrigstiden*. Uppsala: Uppsala Studies in Economic History 67. Uppsala universitet.

Andræ, Carl Göran. 1998. *Revolt eller reform. Sverige inför revolutionerna i Europa 1917–1918*. Stockholm: Carlssons.

Angell, Svein Ivar. 2002. *Den svenske modellen og det norske systemet. Tilhøvet mellom modernisering og identitetsdanning i Sverige og Noreg ved overgangen til det 20. hundreåret*. Oslo: Det Norske Samlaget.

Annaniassen, Erling. 1983. *Rettsgrunnlag og konsesjonspraksis*. Oslo: Hovedoppgave i historie.

Annaniassen, Erling. 2000 and 2001. "Realitet eller myte?" "Den nordiske boligmodellen," I–VI. *BO* 4–6/2000 and 1–3/2001. Oslo.

Anshelm, Jonas. 2000. *Mellan frälsning och domedag. Om kärnkraftens politiska idéhistoria i Sverige 1945–1999*. Stockholm/Stehag: Brutus Östlings bokförlag Symposion.

Anttonen, Anneli, and Jorma Sipolä. 1996. "European Social Care Services: Is It Possible to Identify Models?" *Journal of European Social Policy* 6/1996, pp. 87–100.

Arendt, Hannah. 1961. "What Is Authority?" In Hannah Arendt, *Between Past and Future*. London: Penguin.

Åsard, Erik. 1985. *Kampen om löntagarfonderna. Fondutredningen från samtal till sammanbrott*. Stockholm: Norstedts.

Åselius, Gunnar. 2001. "Sverige och Nazityskland." See *Om Sveriges förhållande . . .* 2001.

Ask, Alf Ole. 2004. *Hvem skal eie Norge?* Oslo: Wigestrand forlag.

Aubert, Vilhelm. 1969. *Det skjulte samfunn*. Oslo: Pax. (Thoroughly revised version of Vilhelm Aubert 1965, *The Hidden Society*, Bedminster Press).

Baklien, Bergljot, Anne Lise Ellingsæter, and Lars Guldbrandsen. 2001. *Evaluering av kontantstøtteordningen*. Oslo: Norges Forskningsråd.

Bauman, Zygmunt. 1996. "On Communitarians and Human Freedom; or, How to Square the Circle." *Theory, Culture and Society*, vol. 13, no. 2. SAGE Publications.

Bauman, Zygmunt. 1997. *Postmodernity and Its Discontents*. Oxford: Polity Press.

Beck, Ulrich. 1986. *Risikogesellschaft. Auf dem Weg eine andere Moderne*. Frankfurt a.M.: Suhrkamp.

Beck, Ulrich, and Elisabeth Beck-Gernsheim. 2001. *Individualization*. London: SAGE.

Beckman, Svante, et al. 1974. "Ekonomisk politik och teori i Norden under mellankrigstiden." In *Kriser och krispolitik i Norden under mellankrigstiden*. Uppsala: Nordiska historikermötet i Uppsala 1974. Møtesrapport.

Bell, Daniel. 1960. *The End of Ideology: On the Exhaustion of Political Ideas in the Fifties*. Glencoe: Free Press

Bengtsson, Bo, ed. 2006. *Varför så olika? Nordisk bostadspolitik i jämförande historiskt ljus*. Malmö: Égalité.

Benum, Edgeir. 1994. *Byråkratienes by. Fra 1948 til våre dager*. Vol. 5 in *Oslo bys historie*. Cappelen.

Benum, Edgeir. 1998. *Overflod og fremtidsfrykt 1970–*. Vol. 12 in *Aschehougs norgeshistorie*. Oslo: Aschehoug 1998.

Berg, Ole. 1980. "The Modernisation of Medical Care in Sweden and Norway." See Heidenheimer and Elvander 1980.

Berg, Roald. 1993. "Spitsbergen-saken 1905–1925." *Historisk Tidsskrift* 4/1993.

Berg, Roald. 1995. *Norge på egenhånd. 1905–1920*. Vol. 2 in *Norsk utenrikspolitikks historie*. Oslo: Universitetsforlaget.

Berge, Anders. 1995. *Medborgarrätt och egenansvar. De sociala försäkringarna i Sverige 1901–1935*. Lund Studies in Social Welfare X. Lund: Arkiv förlag.

Berge, Anders. 1998. "Pensions-separatismen: frågan om den svenska folkpensionens karaktär 1913–1935." *Arkiv för studier i arbetarrörelsens historia*. Lund: Arkiv förlag.

Berge, Anders, Walter Korpi, Joakim Palme, Sten-Åke Stenberg, and Klas Åmark, eds. 1999. *Välfärdsstat i brytningstid: Historisk-samhällsvetenskapliga studier om genus och klass, ojämlikhet och fattigdom*. Stockholm: *Sociologisk Forskning*, supplement.

Berggrav, Eivind. 1945a. "Folkedommen over NS menneskelig og moralsk: Hva vil være rett av oss?" Oslo: *Kirke og Kultur* 1/1945.

Berggrav, Eivind. 1945b. *Staten og mennesket*. Oslo: Land og kirke.

Berggren, Christian. 1993. *Mästarpresentationer eller mardrömsfabriker?* Stockholm: Institutionen för Arbetsvetenskap.

Bergh, Mosken. 1990. "80%-regelen—en politisk kasteball." *Tidsskrift for skatterett*. Oslo.

Bergh, Trond. 1973. *Opprettelsen og utviklingen av bransjerådene*. Oslo: Hovedoppg. historie.

Bergh, Trond. 1987. *Storhetstid (1945–1965)*. Vol. 5 in *Arbeiderbevegelsens historie i Norge*. Oslo: Tiden.

Bergh, Trond. 2009. *Kollektiv fornuft*. Vol. 3 in *LOs historie*. Oslo: Pax.

Bergh, Trond, and Knut Einar Eriksen. 1998. *Den hemmelige krigen. Overvåkning i Norge 1914–1997*. 2 vols. Oslo: Cappelen Akademisk Forlag.

Bergman, Helena, and Peter Johansson, eds. 2002. *Familjeangelägenheter*. Stockholm/Stehag: Brutus Östlings Bokförlag Symposion.

Bergqvist, Christina. 2003. "Family Policy and Welfare State Reconfiguration in Sweden." Uppsala: Paper presented at the panel Restructuring the State, Second ECPR Conference, Marburg, Germany, 18–21 September 2003.

Bergström, Villy. 1989. "Program och ekonomisk politik 1920–1988. SAP i regeringsställning." English version: "Party Program and Economic Policy: The Social Democrats in Government." See Misgeld, Molin, and Åmark 1989.

Berlin, Isaiah. 1969. "Two Concepts of Liberty." In Isaiah Berlin, *Four Essays on Liberty*. Oxford: Oxford University Press. (The essay was originally published as a booklet in 1958.)

Berman, Sheri. 1998. *The Social Democratic Moment: Ideas and Politics in the Making of Interwar Europe*. Cambridge, Mass.: Harvard University Press.

Berman, Sheri. 2006. *The Primacy of Politics: Social Democracy and the Making of Europe's Twentieth Century*. New York: Cambridge University Press.

Bernal, John D. 1969. The *Social Function of Science*. London: Penguin.

Berntsen, Harald. 1991. *I malstrømmen. Johan Nygaardsvold 1879–1952*. Oslo: Aschehoug.

Berven, Nina, May-Linda Magnussen, and Kari Wærness. 2001. "Kontantstøttereformen; en ideologisk vending i familiepolitikken?" *Tidsskrift for velferdsforskning*, vol. 4, 2/2001, pp. 91–105.

Bexell, Göran. 1995. *Svensk moralpolitik*. Lund: Lund University Press.

Bjørgum, Jorunn. 1970. *Venstre og kriseforliket*. Oslo: Universitetsforlaget.

Bjørgum, Jorunn. 1985. "Det nasjonale spørsmål i norsk arbeiderbevegelse." *Tidsskrift for Arbeiderbevegelsens Historie* 1/1985.

Bjørgum, Jorunn. 1993. "Den revolusjonære Martin Tranmæl—et barn av sin tid." In *Portretter fra norsk historie*. Oslo: Universitetsforlaget.

Bjørgum, Jorunn. 1998. *Martin Tranmæl og radikaliseringen av norsk arbeiderbevegelse 1906–1918*. Oslo: Universitetsforlaget, Acta Humaniora.

Bjørklund, Tor. 2008. "Arbeiderklassetilhørighet i Norge fra 1965 til 2001." Oslo: *Sosiologisk Tidsskrift*, vol. 16, 4/2008.

Björlin, Lars. 1974. "Jordfrågan i svensk arbetarrörelse 1890–1920." *Arbetarrörelsens årsbok*. Stockholm: Prisma.

Bjørnhaug, Inger, Øyvind Bjørnson, Terje Halvorsen, and Hans-Jakob Ågotnes, eds. 2000. *I rettferdighetens navn. LO 100 år historisk blikk på fagbevegelsens meningsbrytninger og veivalg*. Oslo: Akribe forlag.

Bjørnhaug, Inger, and Terje Halvorsen. 2009. *Medlemsmakt og samfunnsansvar*. Vol. 2 in *LOs historie*. Oslo: Pax.

Bjørnson, Øyvind. 1990. *På klassekampens grunn (1900–1920)*. Vol. 3 in *Arbeiderbevegelsens historie*. Oslo: Tiden.

Bjørnson, Øyvind, and Inger Elisabeth Haavet. 1994. *Langsomt ble landet et velferdssamfunn; trygdens historie 1894–1994*. Oslo: Ad Notam Gyldendal.

Björnsson, Anders, and Peter Lutherson, eds. 1997. *Medialiseringen av Sverige*. Stockholm: Carlssons.

Blandini, Ulla-Brit. 1990. *Från hjälpskolelärare till förändringsagent*. Göteborg: Acta Universitatis Gotheburgensis.

Blidberg, Kersti. 1984. *Splittrad gemenskap. Kontakter och samarbete inom nordisk socialdemokratisk arbetarrörelse 1931–1935*. Acta Universitatis Stockholmiensis 32. Almqvist & Wiksell.

Blom, Ida. 1980. *Barnebegrensning—synd eller sunn fornuft*. Bergen: Universitetsforlaget.

Blomqvist, Göran. 1998. "Universitetet som oroscentrum." See Hjeltnes 1998.

Blomqvist, Paula, and Bo Rothstein. 2000. *Välfärdsstatens nya ansikte. Demokrati och markanadsreformer inom den offentliga sektorn*. Stockholm: Agora.

Boëthius, Maria-Pia. 2002. *Mediernas svarta bok*. Stockholm: Ordfront.

Borevi, Karin. 2002. *Välfärdsstaten i det mångkulturella samhället*. Uppsala: Acta Universitatis Upsaliensis. Skrifter utgivna av Statvetenskapliga föreningen i Uppsala, 151.

Brekke, Torkel. 2002. *Gud i norsk politikk*. Oslo: Pax.

Brochmann, Grete. 2003. *I globaliseringens tid 1940–2000*. See Knut Kjeldstadli 2003.

Brochmann, Grete. 2007. "Til Dovre faller. Å bli norsk—å være norsk—troskapsløfte og statsborgerskap i den foranderlige nasjonen." In Gunnar Alsmark, Tina Kallehave, and Bolette Moldenhawer, eds., *Migration och tilhörighet: inklutions- och exclutionsprocesser i Skandinavien*, Centrum för Danmarksstudier, vol. 15. Göteborg.

Bruhn, Anders. 1999. "Ungdomerna, politiken och valet." See *Valdeltagande i förändring* 1999.

Brundtland, Gro Harlem. 1997. *Mitt liv*. Oslo: Gyldendal.

Buchanan, James, and Gordon Tullock. 1965. *The Calculus of Consent: Logical Foundations of Constitutional Democracy*. Ann Arbor: University of Michigan Press.

Bull, Edvard, Jr. 1985. *Arbeiderklassen blir til (1850–1900)*. Oslo: Tiden. Vol. 1 in *Arbeidebevegelsens historie i Norge*.

Bull, Edvard, Sr. 1922. *Arbeiderbevægelsens stilling i de tre nordiske land 1914–1920*. Kristiania. (Reprinted in *Tidsskrift for arbeiderbevegelsens historie* 1/1976.)

Buraas, Anders. 1972. *Fly over fly: historien om SAS*. Oslo: Gyldendal.

Byrkjeflot, Haldor, Sissel Myklebust, Christine Myrvang, and Francis Sejersted, eds. 2001. *The Democratic Challenge to Capitalism: Management and Democracy in the Nordic Countries*. Bergen: Fagbokforlaget.

Carlgren, Wilhelm M. 1973. *Svensk utrikespolitik 1939–1945*. Stockholm: Norstedts.

Carlgren, Wilhelm M. 1990. "En kommentar om Per Albin Hansson." See Huldt and Misgeld 1990.

Carlgren, Wilhelm M. 1991. "Svensk-norska regeringsrelationer under anda värdskriget." See Ekman and Grimnes 1991.

Carlsson, Ingvar. 2003. *Så tänkte jag. Politik och dramatik*. Stockholm: Hjalmarson och Högberg.

Carlsson, Sten. 1956. *Bonden i svensk historia*. Vol. 3 in E. Ingers, ed., *Bonden i svensk historia*, 3 vols. Stockholm: Lantbruksförbundets Tidskrifts Aktiebolag 1948–1956.

Carlsson, Sten. 1980. *Svensk historia*. Vol. 2, *Tiden efter 1718*. Lund: Esselte studium 1980.

Chandler, Alfred D., Jr. 1990. *Scale and Scope*. Cambridge, Mass., and London: Harvard University Press.

Childs, Marquis W. 1936. *Sweden: The Middle Way*. New Haven: Yale University Press.

Christie, Nils. 1971. *Hvis skolen ikke fantes*. Oslo: Universitetsforlaget.

Christoffersen, Svein Åge, ed. 1999. *Moralsk og moderne? Trekk av den kristne moraltradisjon i Norge fra 1814 til i dag*. Oslo: Ad Notam Gyldendal.

Classon, Sigvard. 1986. *Vägen till ATP*. Stockholm: Försikringsförbundets förlag.

Clement, Wallace, and Rianne Mahon, eds. 1994. *Swedish Social Democracy: A Model in Transition*. Toronto: Canadian Scholars' Press.

Colbjørnsen, Ole, and Axel Sømme. 1933. *En norsk 3-års plan*. Oslo: Norske arbeiderpartis forlag.

Dahl, Hans Fredrik. 1969. *Fra klassekamp til nasjonal samling. Det norske Arbeiderparti og fedrelandet i 1930-årene*. Oslo: Pax.

Dahl, Hans Fredrik, and Henrik G. Bastiansen. 2000. *Hvor fritt et land?* Oslo: Cappelen.

Dahl, Robert. 1986. *Democracy, Liberty and Equality*. Oslo: Norwegian University Press.

Dahl, Tove Stang. 1974. "Familien og regjeringen." *Kontrast 47*, 5/1974.

Dahl, Tove Stang. 1992. *Barnevern og samfunnsvern*. Oslo, Pax.

Dahlström, Edmund. 1989. *Arbetets maktföhållanden*. Stockholm: Maktutredningen.

Dahmén, Erik. 1950. *Svensk industriell företagarverksamhet*, vol. 1. Stockholm: Industriens utredningsinstitut.

Dale, Erling Lars. 2003. "Dannelsesprogram og enhetsskole." See Slagstad, Korsgaard, and Løvlie 2003.

Danielsen, Rolf. 1964. *Det norske Storting gjennom 150 år*, vol. 2. Oslo: Gyldendal.

Danielsen, Rolf. 1966. "Arvid Lindman og Hammarskjölds regjeringsdannelse 1914." *Minervas Kvartalsskrift*.

Danielsen, Rolf. 1984. *Borgerlig oppdemmingspolitikk*. Vol. 2, *Høyres historie*. Oslo: Cappelen.

Danielsen, Svend, and Peter Lødrup. 1988. "Det nordiske samarbeidet på familierettens område." Oslo: *Tidsskrift for Rettsvitenskap* 4/1988, pp. 565–585.

De nordiske land i verdensøkonomien. 1938. Oslo: Grundt Tanum.

Den mangfoldige velferden. Festskrift til Anne-Lise Seip. 2003. Oslo: Gyldendal.

Dogan, Mattei. 2002. "Dissatisfaction and Mistrust in West European Democracies." *European Review*, vol. 10, no. 1.

Dokument nr. 15. 1995–1996. "Rapport til Stortinget fra kommisjonen som ble nedsatt av Stortinget for å granske påstander om ulovlig overvåking av norske borgere (Lund-rapporten) Stortingsforhandlinger (1995–96)." Submitted 28 March 1996.

Dølvik, Jon Erik, Tone Fløtten, Gudmund Hernes, and Jon M. Hippe, eds. 2007. *Hamskifte. Den norske modellen i endring*. Oslo: Gyldendal Norsk Forlag.

Dølvik, Jon Erik, and Andrew Martin. 2000. "A Spanner in the Works and Oil on Troubled Waters: The Divergent Facts of Social Pacts in Sweden and Norway." In Guiseppe Fajertag and Philippe Pocket, *Social Pacts in Europe—New Dynamics*, pp. 279–391. Brussels: European Trade Union Institute.

Dølvik, Jon Erik, and Torgeir Aarvaag Stokke. 1998. "Norway: The Revival of Centralized Concertation." See Ferner and Hyman 1998.

Drachmann, Povl. 1931. "Om nordisk økonomisk samarbejde—og nogle fremtidsperspektiver." *Nordisk tidskrift för vetenskap, konst och industri*.

Dunning, John. 1992. *Multinational Enterprises and the Global Economy*. Wokingham: Addison-Wesley.

Dworkin, Ronald. 1977. *Taking Rights Seriously*. London: Duckworth.

Edebalk, Per Gunnar. 1996. *Välfärdsstaten träder fram. Svensk socialförsäkring 1884–1955*. Lund Studies in Social Welfare XII. Lund: Arkiv förlag.

Edling, Nils. 1994. "Staten, Norrlandsfrågan och den organiserade kapitalismen.' Stockholm: *Historisk tidskrift*, vol. 114, 2/1994, pp. 267–295.

Edling, Nils. 1996. *Det fosterländska hemmet. Eganhemspolitik, småbruk och hemideologi kring sekelskiftet 1900*. Stockholm: Carlssons.

Egge, Åsmund. 2003. "Hvorfor ble Arbeiderpartiet splittet i 1923?" Oslo: *Historisk Tidsskrift* 3/2003.

Ehn, Billy, Jonas Frykman, and Orvar Löfgren. 1993. *Försvenskningen av Sverige*. Stockholm: Natur och Kultur.

Eide, Martin. 1998. "Det journalistiske mistaket." *Sociologisk Forskning* 3–4/1998.

Eide, Martin. 2000. *Den redigerende makt.* Oslo: Norsk Redaktørforening.

Eide, Martin, ed. 2001. *Til dagsorden!* Oslo: Gyldendal.

Ekdahl, Lars. 2001. *Tysk flyktning och svensk modell.* Vol. 1 in *Mot en tredje väg. En biografi över Rudolf Meidner.* Lund: Arkiv förlag.

Ekdahl, Lars, ed. 2002. *Löntagarfonderna—en missad möjlighet?* Stockholm: Samtidshistoriska institutet, Södertörns högskola.

Ekdahl, Lars-Olof, and Hans-Erik Hjelm. 1981. "Reformismens framväxt inom svensk arbetarrörelse." In Klas Åmark, ed., *Teori och metodproblem i modern svensk historieforskning.* Stockholm: Liber förlag.

Ekman, Stig. 2001. "Inledning." See *Om Sveriges föhållande . . .* 2001.

Ekman, Stig, and Ole Kristian Grimnes, eds. 1991. *Broderfolk i ufredstid. Norsk-svenske forbindelser under annen verdenskrig.* Oslo: Universitetsforlaget.

Ekström, Sören. 2003. *Makten över kyrkan. Om Svenska kyrkan, folket och staten.* Stockholm: Verbum förlag.

Eliæson, Sven, and Ragnar Björk, eds. 2000. *Union & Secession. Perspektiv på statsbildningsprocesser och riksupplösningar.* Stockholm: Carlssons Bokförlag.

Ellingsæter, Anne Lise. 2003. "The Complexity of Family Policy Reform: The Case of Norway." Oslo, manuscript.

Ellingsæter, Anne Lise, and Arnlaug Leira, eds. 2004. *Velferdsstaten og familien. Utfordringer og dilemmaer.* Oslo: Gyldendal akademisk.

Elmbrant, Björn. 1989. *Palme.* Stockholm: T. Fisher & Co.

Elster, Jon. 1979. *Ulysses and the Sirens.* Cambridge: Cambridge University Press.

Elster, Jon, and Rune Slagstad, eds. 1988. *Constitutionalism and Democracy.* Cambridge: Cambridge University Press.

Elvander, Nils. 1961. *Harald Hjärne och konservatismen. Konservativ idédebatt i Sverige 1865–1922.* Stockholm: Almqvist & Wiksell.

Elvander, Nils. 1972. *Svensk skattepolitik 1945–1970.* Stockholm: Rabén & Sjögren.

Elvander, Nils. 1980. *Skandinavisk arbetarrörelse.* Stockholm: Liber förlag.

Elvander, Nils. 2002. "The Labour Market Regimes in the Nordic Countries: A Comparative Analysis." *Scandinavian Political Studies* 2/2002.

Elzinga, Aant. 1985. "Research, Bureaucracy and the Drift of Epistemic Criteria." In Aant Elzinga and Björn Wittrock, eds., *The University Research System: The Public Policies of the Home of Scientists.* Stockholm: Almqvist & Wiksell International.

Elzinga, Aant, Andrew Jamison, and Conny Mithander. 1998. "Swedish Grandeur: Contending Reformulations of the Great-Power Project." In Michael Hård and Andrew Jamison, eds., *The Intellectual Appropriation of Technology: Discourses on Modernity 1900–1939,* pp. 129–161. Cambridge, Mass., and London: MIT Press.

Emil, Oskar. 1911. "Sociale horisonter." In *Samtiden,* pp. 350–360. Oslo: Aschehoug.

Energi til Europa. Norsk gass til Sverige og Finland. 1994. Rapport fra konferanse 20–21 October 1994. Oslo: Voksenåsen.

Engblom, Lars-Åke, Sverker Jonsson, and Karl Erik Gustafsson. 2002. *Bland andra massmedier.* Vol. 4 in Karl Erik Gustafsson and Per Rydén, eds., *Den svenska pressens historia.* Stockholm: Ekerlids förlag.

Engelstad, Fredrik, ed. 1999. *Om makt. Teori og kritikk*. Oslo: ad Notam Gyldendal.

Engelstad, Fredrik, Espen Ekberg, Trygve Gulbrandsen, and Jon Vatnaland. 2003. *Næringslivet mellom marked og politikk*. Oslo: Makt og demokratiutredningen. Gyldendal.

Engelstad, Fredrik, Jørgen Svalund, Inger Marie Hagen, and Aagoth Elise Storvik. 2003. *Makt og demokrati i arbeidslivet*. Oslo: Makt- og demokratiutredningen. Gyldendal.

Ericson, Magnus. 2000. *A Realist Stable Peace: Power, Threat, and the Development of a Shared Norwegian-Swedish Democratic Security Identity 1905–1940*. Lund: Department of Political Science.

Eriksen, Knut Einar. 1972. *DNA og NATO*. Oslo: Gyldendal.

Eriksen, Knut Einar, and Einar Niemi. 1981. *Den finske fare*. Oslo: Universitetsforlaget.

Eriksen, Knut Einar, and Helge Pharo. 1997. *Kald krig og internasjonalisering 1945–1965*. Vol. 5 in *Norsk utenrikspolitikkes historie*. Oslo: Universitetsforlaget.

Eriksen, Trond Berg, Andreas Hompland, and Eivind Tjønneland. 2003. *Et lite land i verden 1950–2000*. Vol. 6 in *Norsk idéhistorie*. Oslo: Aschehoug.

Erikson, Robert, and John H. Goldthorpe. 1992. *The Constant Flux: A Study of Class Mobility in Industrial Societies*. Oxford: Clarendon Press.

Eriksson, Gunnar. 1978. *Kartläggarna. Naturvetenskapens tillväxt och tillempningar i det industriella genombrottets Sverige 1870–1914*. Umeå: Acta Universitatis Umensis.

Eriksson, Lena. 2002. "Att försörja en försörjare. Statliga insatser vid arbetslöshet under 1920-talet." See Bergman and Johansson 2002.

Eriksson, Nils. 1991. "I andans kraft, på sannings stråt. . . ." In *De skandinaviska naturforskarmøterna 1839–1936*. Göteborg: Acta universitatis gothoburgensis.

Erlander, Tage. 1972–1976. Memoirs in 4 volumes: *1901–1939* (1972), *1940–1949* (1973), *1949–1954* (1974), *1955–1960* (1976). Stockholm: Tiden.

Erlander, Tage. 2001–2003. *Dagböcker 1945–1949 och 1950–1951* (2001), *Dagböcker 1952* (2002), *Dagböcker 1953* (2003). Published by Sven Erlander. Hedemora: Gidlunds förlag.

Esaiasson, Peter, and Nicklas Håkansson. 2002. *Besked ikväll!* Stiftelsen etermedierna i Sverige, Skrift nr 19.

Esping-Andersen, Gösta. 1985. *Politics against Markets: The Social Democratic Road to Power*. Princeton: Princeton University Press.

Esping-Andersen, Gösta. 1990. *The Three Worlds of Welfare Capitalism*. Cambridge: Polity Press.

Esping-Andersen, Gösta. 1999. *Social Foundations of Postindustrial Economics*. Oxford: Oxford University Press.

Etzioni, Amitai. 1997. *The New Golden Rule: Community and Morality in a Democratic Society*. London: Profile.

Evang, Karl. 1934. *Rasepolitikk og reaksjon*. Oslo: Fram Forlag.

Fahlbeck, Pontus. 1917. "Ekonomisk samanslutning i Norden." *Statsvetenskaplig tidskrift för politik, statistik, ekonomi*, vol. 20, pp. 319–327. Lund.

Feldt, Kjell-Olof. 1991. *Alla dessa dagar—: i regeringen 1982–1990*. Stockholm: Norstedts.

Ferner, Anthony, and Richard Hyman, eds. 1998. *Changing Industrial Relations in Europe*. Oxford: Blackwell.

The Fertility Decline in the Nordic Countries. 1978. Scandinavian Fertility Studies 4. København: The Scandinavian Demographic Society.

Förhandlingarna å det nittonde nordiska juristmøtet i Stockholm den 23–25 augusti 1951. 1952. Stockholm.

Førland, Tor Egil. 1997. "Ungdomsopprøret: dongeri eller *Wertewandel?*" *Nytt Norsk Tidsskrift* 1/1997.

Forser, Tomas. 1993. "Oavhängiga kulturradikaler och reformradikala socialdemokrater. Utopi och besinning i folkhemmet." See Nolin 1993.

Fostervoll, Kaare. 1935. *Arbeidarskandinavismen i grunnleggingstida*. Oslo: Det norske arbeiderpartis forlag.

Frangeur, Renée. 1995. "Utanför systemet? Om genussystemteorins förklaringsvärde för (stats) feminismen på 1930-talet." Stockholm: *Historisk Tidskrift* 2/1995.

Frangeur, Renée. 1998. *Yrkeskvinna eller makens tjänerinna? Striden om yrkesrätten för gifta kvinnor i mellankrigstidens Sverige*. Lund: Arkiv.

Frängsmyr, Tore. 2000. *Svensk idéhistoria: bildning och vetenskap under tusen år*. Vol. 2, *1809–2000*. Stockholm: Natur och Kultur.

Franzén, Nils-Olof. 1985. *Hjalmar Branting och hans tid*. Stockholm: Bonniers.

Fredriksen, Peter. 1979. "Arbeiderbevegelsen, Høyre og akademikerstanden—i striden om en sosial skolepolitikk 1889–1940." Oslo: *Praxis* 39, nr 2–3.

Fridlund, Mats. 1999. *Den gemensamma utvecklingen. Staten, storföretaget och samarbetet kring den svenska elkrafttekniken*. Stockholm: Symposion.

Friedman, Robert Marc. 1989. *Appropriating the Weather: Vilhelm Bjerknes and the Construction of Modern Meteorology*. Ithaca: Cornell University Press.

Froestad, Jan. 1998. "Staten, pedagogikken og enhetsskoleprosjektet. Handikaposorg og norsk modernisering på 1800-tallet." In Rune Sakslind, ed., *Danning og yrkesutdanning. Utdanning og nasjonale moderniseringsprosjekter*. Oslo: Norges Forskningsråd, KULT skriftserie nr 103.

Frøland, Hans Otto. 1992. *Korporativt kompromiss gjennom korporativ konsert: Tariff- og inntektspolitikk i LO—NAF området 1950–1965*. Trondheim: Historisk Institutt, Universitetet i Trondheim.

Fuglum, Per. 1989. *Én skute—én skipper. Gunnar Knudsen som statsminister*. Trondheim: Tapir.

Fure, Odd-Bjørn. 1976. "Synspunkter og historieteoretiske tendenser i forskningen om den norske arbeiderklasse og -bevegelse i den radikale fase 1918–1933." *Tidsskrift for arbeiderbevegelsens historie* 1/1976.

Fure, Odd-Bjørn. 1983. *Mellom reformisme og bolsjevisme. Norsk arbeiderbevegelse 1918–1920. Teori, praksis*. Bergen: Stensil.

Fure, Odd-Bjørn. 1996. *Mellomkrigstid 1920–1940*. Vol. 3 in *Norsk utenrikspolitikks historie*. Oslo: Universitetsforlaget.

Fure, Odd-Bjørn, 1997. *Kampen mot glemslen*. Oslo: Universitetsforlaget.

Fure, Odd-Bjørn. 1999. "Norsk okkupasjonshistorie. Konsensus, berøringsangst og tabuisering," See Stein Ugelvik Larsen 1999.

Furre, Berge. 1968. *Mjølk, bønder og tingmenn. Studiar i organisasjon og politikk kring omsetningen av visse landbruksvarer 1929–1930*. Oslo: Hovedoppgave, historie.

Furre, Berge. 1992. *Norsk historie 1905–1990*. Oslo: Det Norske Samlaget.

Furuland, Lars, and Johan Svedjedal. 2007. *Svensk arbetarlitteratur*. Stockholm: Atlas.

Galbraith, John K. 1960. *The Affluent Society*. London: Hamish Hamilton. (First edition 1958.) Swedish edition 1959, *Överflödets samhälle* (Stockholm: Tiden). Norwegian edition 1970, *Overflodssamfunnet* (Oslo: Gyldendal).

Galbraith, John K. 1967. *The New Industrial State*. New York: The New American Library. Swedish edition 1969, *Den nya industristaten* (Stockholm: Wahlström & Widstrand). Norwegian edition 1968, *Det nye industrisamfunnet* (Oslo: Tiden).

Galbraith, John K. 1980. *Annals of an Abiding Liberal*. London: Andre Deutsch.

Galbraith, John K. 1996. *Min ekonomiska historia*. Stockholm: Ordfront.

Gasslander, Olle. 1956–1959. *Bank och industriellt genombrott. Stockholms Enskilda Bank kring sekelskiftet 1900*. 2 vols. Stockholm.

Geer, Hans de. 1978. *Rationaliseringsrörelsen i Sverige*. Stockholm: Studieförbundet Näringsliv och Samhälle.

Gerhardsen, Einar. 1970. *Fellesskap i krig og fred: erindringer 1940–45*. Oslo: Tiden.

Gerhardsen, Einar. 1971. *Samarbeid og strid: erindringer 1945–55*. Oslo: Tiden.

Gerhardsen, Einar. 1972. *I medgang og motgang: erindringer 1955–65*. Oslo: Tiden.

Gerhardsen, Einar. 1974. *Unge år: erindringer fra århundreskiftet fram til 1940*. Oslo: Tiden.

Gerhardsen, Einar. 1978. *Mennesker og politikk: erindringer 1965–78*. Oslo: Tiden.

Gihl, Torsten. 1951. *Den svenska utrikespolitikens historia IV, 1914–1919*. Stockholm: Norstedts.

Glete, Jan. 1991. "Ägarekonsentrationen och den politiska demokratin." In Rolf Eidem and Rolf Skog, eds., *Makten över företagen*. Stockholm: Carlssons.

Glete, Jan. 1994. *Nätverk i näringslivet. Ägande och industriell omvandling i det mogna industrisamhället 1920–1990*. Stockholm: SNS Förlag.

Goldfield, David R. 1979. "Suburban Development in Stockholm and the United States: A Comparison of Form and Function." In Hammarström and Hall 1979: 139–156.

Götz, Norbert. 2001. *Ungleiche Geschwister. Die Konstruktion von nationalsozialistischer Volksgemeinschaft und schwedischem Volksheim*. Baden-Baden: Nomos Verlagsgesellschaft.

Götz, Nobert. 2002. "Att lägga historien till rätta. Forsöket att göra folkhemmet folkhemskt." *Tvärsnitt* 1/2002.

Grankvist, Rolf. 2000. *Utsyn over norsk skole gjennom 1000 år*. Trondheim: Tapir.

Grape, Owe. 1998. "Bistånd och tvång i den svenska arbetslinjen" See Lindqvist 1998.

Grass, Martin. 1987. "Arbetarskandinavism 1912–1920: Kommittén för skandinaviska arbetarrörelsens samarbete. Några aspekter." *Årbog for arbejderbevægelsens historie*, nr 4, pp. 55–88.

Grass, Martin. 1988. ". . . den starkaste brygga mellan nordens folk för fredligt arbete. . . ." *Arbeiderhistorie 1988*. Årbok for Arbeiderbevegelsens Arkiv og Bibliotek, pp. 76–105.

Greve, Tim. 1964. *Det Norske Storting gjennom 150 år*, vol. 3. Oslo: Gyldendal.

Grøndahl, Øyvind Nordbrønd, and Tore Grønlie, eds. 1995. *Fristillingens Grenser*. Bergen: Fagbokforlaget.

Grønlie, Tore. 1991. "Velferdskommunen." See Nagel 1991.

Grønlie, Tore. 1993. *Forvaltning og fullmaktslovgivning som etterkrigshistorisk forskningsfelt*. Bergen: LOS-senter, notat 9308.

Grønlie, Tore, ed. 1999. *Forvaltning for politikk. Norsk forvaltningspolitikk etter 1945*. Bergen: Fagbokforlaget.

Gullestad, Marianne. 1996. "Verdiendringer i Norge." *Nytt Norsk Tidsskrift* 3–4/1996.

Gustavsen, Bjørn. 1992. *Dialogue and Development: Theory of Communication, Action Research and the Restructuring of Working Life*. Stockholm: Arbetslivscentrum.

Gustavsson, Bernt. 1991. *Bildningens väg. Tre bildningsideal i svensk arbetarrörelse 1880–1930*. Stockholm: Wahlström och Widstrand.

Gustavsson, Bernt. 1996. *Bildning i vår tid: om bildningens möjligheter och villkor i det moderna samhället*. Stockholm: Wahlström & Widstrand.

Haave, Per. 2000. *Sterilisering av tatere 1934–1977. En historisk undersøkelse av lov og praksis*. Oslo: Norges Forskningsråd.

Haave, Per, and Øyvind Giæver. 2000. *Sterilisering på medisinsk grunnlag og sammenhengen mellom eugenikk og humangenetikk*. Oslo: Norges Forskningsråd.

Habermas, Jürgen. 1992. "Further Reflections on the Public Sphere." In Craig Calhoun, ed., *Habermas and the Public Sphere*. Cambridge, Mass.: MIT Press.

Hadenius, Stig. 2000. *Svensk politik under 1900-talet*. Stockholm: Hjalmarson & Högberg.

Hadenius, Stig, and Lennart Weibull. 1999. *Massmedier*. Stockholm: Bonniers.

Hagemann, Gro. 2002. "Housewife or Citizen? The Dilemma of Twentieth-Century Gender Politics." In Hilde Sandvik, Kari Telste, and Gunnar Thorvaldsen, eds., *Pathways to the Past*, pp. 152–161. Oslo: Novus.

Hagemann, Gro, and Klas Åmark. 1999. "Fra 'husmorkontrakt' til 'likestillingskontrakt.'" See Engelstad 1999.

Hagtvet, Bernt. 1970. "Eliteintegrasjon. Kulturell stil og venstrefløystyrke." Manuscript.

Hagtvet, Bernt. 1973. "Intellectuals, Party Structure and Factional Power: The Norwegian and Swedish Labour-Party Elites in Comparative Perspective." Manuscript.

Hagtvet, Bernt. 1980. "On the Fringe: Swedish Fascism 1920–45." See Larsen, Hagtvet, and Myklebust 1980.

Hall, Patrik. 2000. *Den svenskaste historien. Nationalism i Sverige under sex sekler*. Stockholm: Carlssons.

Hall, Thomas. 1979. "The Central Business District: Planning in Stockholm, 1928–1978." See Hammarström and Hall 1979: 181–232.

Hallenstvedt, Abraham. 1974. "Noen refleksjoner om komitesystemets konsekvenser for vårt politiske liv." In Jorolf Moren, ed., *Den kollegiale forvaltning*. Oslo: Universitetsforlaget.

Halvorsen, Tor. 1982. *Profesjonalisering—Taylorisering. Ingeniørar mellom leiing og arbeidar-motstand*. Bergen: Hovedoppgave i offentlig administrasjon og organisasjonskunnskap.

Hambro, Carl Joachim. 1937. *Moderne mentalitet*. Oslo: Gyldendal.

Hamilton, Hugo. 1955. *Dagböcker 1911–1916*, vol. 1. Stockholm: Norstedts.

Hammarström, Ingrid, and Thomas Hall, eds. 1979. *Growth and Transformation of the Modern City*. The Stockholm Conference, September 1978. Stockholm: Byggforskningsrådet.

Hanisch, Tore Jørgen, and Even Lange. 1985. *Vitenskap for industrien. NTH—En høyskole i utvikling gjennom 75 år*. Oslo: Universitetsforlaget.

Hansen, Lars-Erik. 2001. *Jämlikhet och valfrihet. En studie av den svenska invandrarpolitikens framväxt*. Stockholm: Almqvist & Wiksell.

Hansen, Svein Olav. 1994. *Drømmen om Norden. Den norske Foreningen Norden og det nordiske samarbeidet 1919–1994*. Oslo: Ad Notam Gyldendal.

Hansson, Jonas. 2001. "Sverige och nazismen." See *Om Sveriges förhållande* . . . 2001.

Hatland, Aksel, Stein Kuhnle, and Tor Inge Romøren, eds. 2001. *Den norske velferdsstaten.* Oslo: Gyldendal Akademisk.

Hauge, Jens Chr. 1989. *Mennesker.* Oslo: Tiden.

Hayek, Friedrich A. von. 1944. *The Road to Serfdom.* London: Routledge & Kegan Paul. Swedish edition 1944, *Vägen till träldom* (Stockholm: P.A. Norstedt & Söner). Norwegian edition 1949, *Veien til trelldom* (Oslo: Dreyer).

Hayek, Friedrich A. von. 1964. *The Counter-revolution of Science—Studies in the Abuse of Reason.* London: The Free Press.

Hederberg, Hans. 2003. "Studien av inrikesspionaget ett gedigent offentliggörande." Stockholm: *Dagens Forskning* 20–21/1/2003.

Hegna, Trond. 1932–1936. "Familie." In *Arbeidernes Leksikon.* Oslo: Arbeidermagasinets forlag.

Heidenheimer, Arnold J. 1980. "Conflict and Compromises between Professional and Bureaucratic Health Interests 1947–72." See Heidenheimer and Elvander 1980.

Heidenheimer, Arnold J., and Nils Elvander, eds. 1980. *The Shaping of Swedish Health System.* London: Croom Helm.

Heiret, Jan, Olav Korsnes, Knut Venneslan, and Øyvind Bjørnson. 2003. *Arbeidsliv, Historie, Samfunn. Norske arbeidslivsrelasjoner i historisk, sosiologisk og arbeidsrettslig perspektiv.* Bergen: Fagbokforlaget.

Helgesen, Marit. 1977. *Attføring—en tjeneste i velferdsstaten, En komparativ undersøkelse av attføring i Norge og Sverige.* Bergen: Institutt for administrasjon og organisasjonsvitenskap, Rapport nr 56.

Hellevik, Tale. 2007. "Foreldres etableringsstøtte: Fra plikt til frivillighet." *Tidsskrift for samfunnsforskning* 1/2007, pp. 33–61.

Helsvig, Kim. 2005. *Pedagogikkens grenser: Kampen om norsk pedagogikk ved Pedagogisk forskningsinstitutt 1938–1980.* Oslo: Abstrakt.

Hemstad, Ruth. 2005. "Fra 'Indian Summer' til 'nordisk vinter'—nordisk samarbeid og 1905." In Øystein Sørensen and Torbjörn Nilsson, eds., *Goda grannar eller morska motståndare? Sverige och Norge från 1814 till idag.* Stockholm and Oslo.

Henrekson, Magnus. 2006. "Folkhem i brytningstid." Manuscript.

Henrekson, Magnus, and Ulf Jakobsson. 2002. "Ägarpolitik och ägarestruktur i efterkrigstidens Sverige." See Jonung 2002.

Hentilä, Seppo. 1979. *Den svenska arbetarklassen och reformismens genombrott inom SAP före 1914.* Helsingfors: Historiallisia Tutkimuskia 111.

Hermansson, C. H. 1965. *Monopol och storfinans—de 15 familjerna.* Stockholm: Raben och Sjögren.

Hernes, Gudmund. 1978. *Forhandlingsøkonomi og blandingsadministrasjon.* Oslo: Universitetsforlaget.

Hernes, Gudmund. 1991. "The Dilemmas of Social Democracies: The Case of Norway and Sweden." *Acta Sociologica*, vol. 34, no. 4. Oslo.

Hernes, Helga. 2004. "Statsfeminisme—et personlig tilbakeblikk." *Nytt Norsk Tidsskrift* 3–4/2004.

Hestmark, Geir. 1999. *Vitenskap og nasjon. Waldemar Christopher Brøgger 1851–1905.* Oslo: Aschehoug.

Hiilamo, Heikki. 2002. *The Rise and Fall of Nordic Family Policy: Historical Development and Changes during the 1990s in Sweden and Finland.* Turku: STAKES. Research Report 125.

Hinnfors, Jonas. 1992. *Familjepolitik. Samhällsförändringar och partistrategier 1960–1990.* Göteborg studies in politics no. 26.

Hirdman, Yvonne 1998. "Kvinnor—från möjlighet till problem? Genuskonflikten i välfärdsstaten—den svenska modellen." See Nagel 1998.

Hirdman, Yvonne. 2000. *Att lägga livet til rätta.* Stockholm: Carlssons. (First edition 1989.)

Hjeltnes, Guri, ed. 1998. *Universitetet og studentene. Opprør og identitet.* Universitetet i Oslo, Forum for universitetshistorie. Skriftserie 4/1998.

Hobsbawm, Eric J. 1990. *Nations and Nationalism since 1780.* Cambridge: Cambridge University Press.

Hobsbawm, Eric J. 1995. *Age of Extremes: The Short Twentieth Century 1914–1991.* London: Abacus.

Hobson, Rolf, and Tom Kristiansen. 2001. *Total krig, nøytralitet og politisk splittelse.* Vol. 3, *Norsk Forsvarshistorie.* Bergen: Eide forlag.

Höglund, Zeth. 1928–1929. *Hjalmar Branting och hans livsgärning.* 2 vols. Stockholm: Tiden.

Högnäs, Sten. 2001. "The concept of *Bildung* and the Education of the Citizen: Traits and Development in the Nordic Countries 1870–2000." In Ahonen and Rantala 2001.

Høidal, Reidun. 2003. "Folkedanning? Landsgymnaset som mothegemonisk danningsprosjekt." *Nytt Norsk Tidsskrift* 4/2003.

Höjer, J. Axel. 1975. *En läkeres väg: från Visby till Vietnam.* Stockholm: Bonnier.

Holter, Harriet, Hildur Ve Henriksen, Arild Gjertsen, and Haldis Hjort. 1975. *Familien i klassesamfunnet.* Oslo: Pax.

Holtsmark, Sven G., and Tom Kristiansen. 1991. *En nordisk illusjon? Norge og militært samarbeid i ord, 1918–1940.* Oslo: Institutt for forsvarsstudier, Forsvarsstudier 6/1991.

Holtsmark, Sven G., Helge Ø. Pharo, and Rolf Tamnes, eds. 2003. *Motstrøms. Olav Riste og norsk internasjonal historiskrivning.* Oslo: Cappelen Akademisk forlag.

Hovdenak, Sylvi Stenersen. 2000. *90-tallsreformene—et instrumentalistisk mistak?* Oslo: Gyldendal akademisk.

Høyer, Svennik. 1995. *Pressen mellom teknologi og samfunn.* Oslo: Universitetsforlaget.

Huldt, Bo, and Klaus Misgeld, eds. 1990. *Socialdemokratin och svensk utrikespolitik.* Stockholm: Utrikespolitiska institutet.

Hult, Jan, Svante Lindqvist, Wilhelm Odelberg, and Sven Rydberg. 1989. *Svensk teknikhistoria.* Hedemora: Gidlunds bokförlag.

Hundra år av medling i Sverige. 2006. Stockholm: Medlingsinstitutet.

Husén, Torsten. 1988. *Skolreformerna och forskningen.* Stockholm: Verbum Gothia.

Husén, Torsten. 1994. *Skola och universitet inför 2000-talet.* Stockholm: Atlantis.

Husén, Torsten. 1999. *Insikter och åsikter om utbildningssamhället.* Stockholm: Gothia.

Hustad, Jon. 2002. *Skolen som forsvann.* Oslo: Det Norske Samlaget.

Ihlen, Øyvind. 2004. *Rhetoric and Resources in Public Relations Strategies: A Rhetorical and Sociological Analysis of the Conflicts over Energy and the Environment.* Oslo: University of Oslo Unipub.

Illich, Ivan. 1975. *Medical Nemesis: The Expropriation of Health.* London: Calder & Boyars.

Inghe, Gunnar, and Maj-Britt Inghe. 1967. *Den ofärdiga välfärden.* Stockholm: Tiden/ Folksam.

Isaksson, Anders. 1985–2000. *Per Albin I* (1985), *Per Albin II* (1990), *Per Albin III* (1996), *Per Albin IV* (2000). Stockholm: Wahlström & Widstrand.

Isaksson, Anders. 2001. "Per Albin Hansson—Fosterlandet, Folkhemmet, Svenskmannagärningen." In Alf W. Johansson, *Vad är Sverige? Röster om svensk nationell identitet.* Stockholm: Prisma.

Jacobs, Jane. 1961. *The Death and Life of Great American Cities.* New York: Random House.

Jacobsen, Bjørn Barth. 1998. *Kampen om nasjonal og overnasjonal energikontroll.* Bodø: Interaction.

Jakobsen, Kjetil. 1994. *"Efter oss kommer overfloden." Teknokratisk moderniseringsideologi i norsk politikk og samfunnsvitenskap 1917–1953.* Hovedoppgave, historie, Universitetet i Oslo.

Jakobsen, Kjetil. 1995. "Politikkens vekslende veiveisere." *Apollon.* Tidsskrift fra Universitetet i Oslo nr 2/1995.

Jakobsen, Kjetil. 2004. *Kritikk av den reine autonomi.* Oslo: Acta humaniora, Universitetet i Oslo.

Jakobsson, Eva. 1992. "Norsk och svensk vattenkraftutbyggnad. En komparativ studie." *Polhem* 10/1992, pp. 226–264.

Jakobsson, Eva. 1996. *Industrialisering av Älvar. Studier kring svensk vattenkraftutbyggnad 1900–1918.* Göteborg: Historiska institutionen.

Jensen, Axel. 1957. *Ikaros.* Oslo: Cappelen.

Johansen, Anders. 2001. "Enkeltpersoner og kollektivpersoner." See Eide 2001.

Johansen, Tor Are. 1995. *Bedriftsdemokratisk utvikling i en økonomisk krisetid. LO, DNA og bedriftsdemokratiet 1973–1985.* Bergen: Gruppe for flerfaglig arbeidslivsforskning. Universitetet i Bergen.

Johansson, Alf O. 2000. "Solidaritet på markedets betingelser. Fremveksten av en solidarisk lønnspolitikk i Norge." See Bjørnhaug et al. 2000.

Johansson, Alf W. 1984. *Per Albin och kriget.* Stockholm: Tiden.

Johansson, Alf W. 2000. *Den nazistiska utmaningen. Aspekter på andra värdskriget.* Stockholm: Prisma, femte utvigdade upplagan.

Johansson, Alf W., ed. 2001. *Vad er Sverige?* Stockholm: Prisma.

Johansson, Anders L. 1989. *Tillväxt och klass-samarbete. En studie av den svenska modellens uppkomst.* Stockholm: Tiden.

Johansson, Anders L., and Lars Magnusson. 1998. *LO andra hakvseklet. Fackföreningsrörelsen och samhället.* Stockholm: Atlas.

Johansson, Ingemar. 1991. *StorStockholms bebyggelseshistoria.* Hedemora: Gidlunds.

Johansson, Peter. 1999. "Sjukforsäkring bortom sjukkasserörelsen? Sjukförsäkringens institutionella gränser i frågan om frivillig eller obligatorisk sjukförsäkring 1891–1931." Stockholm: *Arkiv* nr 77–78.

Johansson, Peter. 2002. "Moderskapspolitiken och den manlige familjeforsörjaren." See Bergman and Johansson 2002.

Johansson, Peter. 2003. *Fast i det förflutna. Institutioner och intressen i svensk sjukförsäkringspolitik 1891–1931.* Lund: Arkiv.

Johansson, Roger. 2001. *Kampen om historien. Ådalen 1931. Sociala konflikter, historiemedvetande och historiebruk 1931–2000.* Stockholm: Hjalmarson & Högberg.

Johnsen, Egil Børre. 1997. *Oppgavetekst og dannelse: artiumsstilens emner, formuleringer og forvaltning 1880–1991.* Oslo: Acta humaniora, Universitetsforlaget.

Johnsen, Egil Børre. 2003. "Dannelse på dagsorden." *Morgenbladet* 18–24/7/2003.

Jonung, Lars, ed. 2002. *Vem skall äga Sverige?* Stockholm: SNS Förlag.

Jörberg, Lennart. 1973. "The Industrial Revolution in the Nordic Countries." In Carlo M. Cipolla, ed., 1973. *The Fontana Economic History of Europe*, vol. 4 (2). London: Fontana.

Judt, Tony. 2007. *Postwar: A History of Europe since 1945.* London: Pimlico.

Kaartvedt, Alf. 1984. *Drømmen om borgerlig samling.* Vol. 1 in *Høyres historie.* Oslo: Cappelen.

Kaelble, Hartmut. 1999. *Der historische Vergleich.* Frankfurt: Campus.

Kaijser, Arne, and Marika Hedin, eds. 1995. *Nordic Energy Systems: Historical Perspectives and Current Issues.* Canton, Mass.: Science History Publications.

Kalleberg, Ragnvald. 1998. "Studenter i det sivile samfunn: et perspektiv på norske "studentopprørere." See Hjeltnes 1998.

Kälvemark, Ann-Sophie. 1980. *More Children of Better Quality?* Stockholm: Almqvist & Wiksell.

Karleby, Nils. 1926. *Socialismen inför verkligheten: Studier över socialdemoratisk åskådning och nutidspolitik.* Stockholm: Tiden.

Karlsson, Sten O. 2001. *Det intelligenta samhället. En omtolkning av socialdemokratins idéhistoria.* Stockholm: Carlssons.

Katzenstein, Peter, 1985. *Small States in World Markets.* Ithaca: Cornell University Press.

Kautto, Mikko, Matti Heikkilä, Bjørn Hvinden, Staffan Marklund, and Niels Ploug, eds. 1999. *Nordic Social Policy: Changing Welfare States.* London and New York: Routledge.

Kellberg, Love. 1990. "Spetsbergstraktaten blir till." See Værnø 1990.

Kilander, Svenbjörn. 1989. "Staten byter ansikte. Statsuppfattning och samhällssyn 1860–1910." In Thorsten Nybom and Rolf Torstendahl, eds., *Byråkratisering och maktfördelning.* Lund: Stundentlitteratur.

Kilander, Svenbjörn. 1991. *Den nya staten och den gamla: En studie i ideologisk förändring.* Stockholm: Almqvist & Wiksell.

Kili, Terje. 1996. *Aksjemarkedet i Norge 1880–1990.* Det nye Pengesamfunn, Rapport nr. 88. Oslo: Norges Forskningsråd.

Kinck, Hans E. 1916. "Den indre styrke. En liden opbyggelse om samhørighed i Norden." *Tilskueren*, pp. 18–39. København: Philipsen.

Kjeldstadli, Knut. 1980. "Tranmælisme. Svar til Inger Bjørnhaug, Eirik Fiva & Nils Henrik Fuglestad." *Tidsskrift for arbeiderbevegelsens historie* 2/1980.

Kjeldstadli, Knut. 1994. *Et splittet samfunn 1905–1935.* Vol. 10 in *Aschehougs norgeshistorie.* Oslo: Aschehoug.

Kjeldstadli, Knut, ed. 2003. *I globaliseringens tid 1940–2000.* Vol. 3 in *Norsk innvandringshistorie.* Oslo: Pax.

Kjeldstadli, Ole Peder. 1973. *Opprettelsen av Den Norske Arbeiderbruk og Boligbank.* Bergen: Hovedoppgave i historie.

Kjellberg, Anders. 1998. "Sweden: Restoring the Model?" See Ferner and Hyman 1998.

Kleppe, Per. 2003. *Kleppepakke. Meninger og minner fra et politisk liv.* Oslo: Aschehoug.

Knudsen, Tim. 2000. "Tilblivelsen af den universalistiske velfærdsstat." In Tim Knudsen, ed., *Den nordiske protestantisme og velfærden.* Aarhus: Aarhus Universitetsforlag.

Knutsen, Paul. 1994. *Korporatisme og klassekamp.* Oslo: Acta Humaniora. Det historisk-filosofiske fakultet, Universitetet i Oslo.

Knutsen, Sverre. 1990. *Bank, samfunn og økonomisk vekst.* Oslo: Hovedoppg. historie.

Knutsen, Sverre. 2007. *Staten og kapitalen i det 20. århundre.* Oslo: Det humanistiske fakultet, Universitetet i Oslo.

Knutsen, Sverre, Even Lange, and Helge W. Norvik. 1998. *Mellom næringsliv og politikk: Kreditkassen i vekst og kriser 1918–1998.* Oslo: Universitetsforlaget.

Knutsen, Torbjørn L. 2001. "Twentieth-Century Stories." *Journal for Peace Research.* Oslo.

Kogan, Maurice, Marianne Bauer, Ivar Bleiklie, and Mary Henkel. 2000. *Transforming Higher Education: A Comparative Study.* London and Philadelphia: Jessica Kingley Publishers. Higher education policy series 57.

Koht, Halvdan. 1937–1940. "Eit historisk syn på den norsk-svenske unionen." *Historisk Tidsskrift,* Bd 31.

Kokkvoll, Arne. 1981. *Av og for det arbeidende folk.* Oslo: Tiden.

Korpi, Walter. 1978. *Arbetarklassen i välfärdskapitalismen.* Stockholm: Prisma. Institutet för social forskning.

Korpi, Walter. 1981. *Den demokratiska klasskampen.* Stockholm: Tiden.

Korpi, Walter. 1999. "Ojämlikhetens ansikten: Genus, klass och ojämlikhet i olika typer av välfärdsstater." See Berge et al. 1999.

Koselleck, Reinhart. 2000 (1989). *Vergangene Zukunft. Zur Semantik geschichlicher Zeiten.* Frankfurt a.M.

Kristofferesen, Berit. 2007. *Spaces of Competitive Power.* Oslo: Masteroppgave i samfunnsgeografi.

Kroon, Åsa. 2003. "Den medialiserade mediekritiken: En kritisk diskussion av publikens mediekompetens och mediernas självkritik." In Martin Kylhammar and Jean-Francois Battail, eds., *Kommunikation, kunskap, makt.* Stockholm: Carlssons.

Kvisli, Kåre. 1962. *Innføring i skatteretten.* Oslo: Brødrene Tengs boktrykkeri.

Labord, Cecile, and John Maynor, eds. 2008. *Republicanism and Political Theory.* Oxford: Blackwell.

Landes, David S. 1998. *The Wealth and Poverty of Nations: Why Some Are So Rich and Some So Poor.* New York, London: W. W. Norton & Company.

Lange, Even. 1998. *Samling om felles mål 1935–70.* Vol. 11 in *Aschehougs norgeshistorie.* Oslo: Aschehoug.

Lange, Even, ed. 2006. *Organisert kjøpekraft. Forbrukersamvirkets historie i Norge.* Oslo: Pax.

Lange, Halvard M. 1937. *Arbeiderpartiets historie 1887–1905* and *Arbeiderpartiets historie 1905–1914.* In Halvdan Koht, ed., *Det norske arbeiderpartis historie 1887–1937,* 2 vols. Oslo: Det norske arbeiderpartis forlag.

Langeland, Ove. 1985. *Økonomisk demokrati og politisk økonomi. En sammenlignende analyse av arbeiderbevegelse og økonomisk demokrati i Norge og Sverige.* Hovedoppg. statsvitenskap. Universitetet i Oslo.

Larsen, Petter, and Kjell Sandvik, ed. 1980. *Arbeideren og diktningen.* Oslo: Tiden.

Larsen, Stein Ugelvik, ed. 1999. *I krigens Kjølvann.* Oslo: Universitetsforlaget.

Larsen, Stein Ugelvik, Bernt Hagtvet, and Jan Petter Myklebust, eds. 1980. *Who Were the Fascists: Social Roots of European Fascism.* Bergen: Universitetsforlaget.

Lehmkuhl, Joakim. 1920. *Rationel arbeidsledelse—en oversigt.* Bergen: Grieg.

Lehmkuhl, Joakim. 1933. *Norges vei—Et angrep på norsk borgerlig politikk—og et forslag til nasjonal arbeidsplan.* Oslo: Fedrelandslagets forlag.

Leira, Arnlaug. 1998. "En 'kvinnevennlig' velferdsstat?" See Nagel 1998: 180–204.

Leira, Halvard. 2003. "Samnorsk som identitetspolitisk prosjekt." *Nytt Nortsk Tidsskrift* 4/2003, pp. 379–400.

Lewin, Leif. 1967. *Planhushållningsdebatten*. Stockholm: Almqvist och Wiksell.

Lewin, Leif. 1992. *Ideologi och strategi. Svensk politik under 100 år*. Stockholm: Norstedts Juridik AB.

Lewin, Leif. 2002. *Ideologi och strategi. Svensk politik under 130 år*. Stockholm: Norstedts Juridik AB.

Lie, Einar. 1995. *Ambisjon og tradisjon. Finansdepartementet 1945–1965*. Oslo: Universitetsforlaget.

Lie, Haakon. 1988. *Martin Tranmæl. Et bål av vilje*. Oslo: Tiden.

Lie, Haakon. 1991. *Martin Tranmæl. Veiviseren*. Oslo: Tiden.

Liedman, Sven-Erik. 2003. "De intellektuella i Sverige och Frankrike." In Martin Kylhammar and Jean-Francois Battail, eds., *Kommunikation, kunskap, makt*. Stockholm: Carlssons.

Lindbeck, Assar. 1974. "Internationella ekonomiska konflikter i en expanderande värdsekonomi." *Ekonomisk Debatt* 7/1974, pp. 383–394.

Lindbeck, Assar. 2003. "Välfärdsstat och sosiala normer." In Birgitta Swedenborg, ed., *Varför är svenskarna så sjuka?* Stockholm: SNS Förlag.

Lindbekk, Tore. 2008. "Pisa-skolen viser politikkens maktesløshet." *Nytt Norsk Tidsskrift*.

Lindboe, Rudolf. 1990. "Økonomisk integrasjon på den Skandinaviske halvøy. Sverige og Norge—to ulike land." See Værnø 1990.

Lindensjö, Bo. 1981. *Högskolereformen. En studie i offentlig reformstrategi*. Stockholm: Stockholms Universitet, Stockholm Studies in Politics 20.

Lindensjö, Bo, and Ulf P. Lundgren. 2002. *Utbildningsreformer och politisk styrning*. Stockholm: HLS förlag.

Linder, Jan. 1997. *Andra värdskriget och Sverige*. Stockholm: Svenskt militärhistoriskt bibliotek.

Linderborg, Åsa. 2001. *Socialdemokraterna skriver historia. Historieskrivning som ideologisk maktresurs 1892–2000*. Stockholm: Atlas.

Lindgren, Astrid. 1976. *Pomperipossa i Monismanien: en saga*. Stockholm.

Lindqvist, Rafael. 1990. *Från folkrörelse till välfärdsbyråkrati. Det svenska sjukförsäkringssystemets utveckling 1900–1990*. Lund: Arkiv avhandlingsserie 33.

Lindqvist, Rafael, ed. 1998. *Organisation och välfärdsstat*. Lund: Studentlitteratur.

Lindroth, Jan, and Johan R. Norberg, eds. 2002. *Ett idrottssekel, Riksidrottsförbundet 1903–2003*. Stockholm: Informationsförlaget.

Lindström, Stefan. 1991. *Hela nationens tacksamhet. Svensk forskningspolitik på atomenergiområdet 1945–1956*. Stockholm: Statsvetenskapliga institutionen SU.

Lindström, Ulf. 1983. *Fascism in Scandinavia 1920–40*. Umeå: Umeå University, Dept. of Political Science.

Lingås, Lars Gunnar, ed. 1973. *Myten om velferdsstaten: Søkelys på norsk sosialpolitikk*. Oslo: Pax.

Ljunggren, Stig-Björn. 1992. *Folkhemskapitalismen. Högerns programutveckling under efterkrigstiden*. Stockholm: Tiden.

Lønnå, Elisabeth. 1996. *Stolthet og kvinnekamp. Norsk Kvinnesaksforenings historie fra 1913*. Oslo: Gyldendal.

Løvlie, Lars. 2004. "Et ideologisk hamskifte." Oslo: *Le Monde diplomatique* 5/2004.

Lorentzen, Håkon. 2004. *Fellesskapets fundament*. Oslo: Pax.

Lorenz, Einhart. 1991. *Samefolket i historien*. Oslo: Pax.

Lundberg, Harald. 1988. *Broderskapsrörelsen(s) i svensk politik*. Sveriges Kristna Socialdemokraters Förbund.

Lundberg, Urban. 2003. *Juvelen i kronan. Socialdemokraterna och den allmänna pensionen.* Stockholm: Hjalmarson och Högberg.

Lundh, Christer. 1987. *Den svenska debatten om industriell demokrati 1919–1924.* I. Debatten i Sverige. Skrifter utgivna av Ekonomisk-historiska föreningen, vol. 49. Lund.

Lundkvist, Sven. 1977. *Folkrörelserna i det svenska samhället 1850–1920.* Uppsala: Studia Historica Upsaliensia 85.

Lundmark, Lennart. 2002. *"Lappen är ombytlig, ostadig och obekväm."* Umeå: Norrlands Universitetsförlag.

Lundström, Gunilla, Per Rydén, and Elisabeth Sandlund. 2001. *Det moderna Sveriges spegel* (1897–1945). Vol. 3 in Karl Erik Gustafsson and Per Rydén, eds., *Den svenska pressens historia.* Stockholm: Ekerlids förlag.

Magnusson, Lars. 1997. *Sveriges Ekonomiska Historia.* Stockholm: Prisma.

Mannsåker, Lars, and Lars Sigurd Østberg. 1990. "Plaza Story." *St. Hallvard* 1/1990.

Marklund, Sixten. 1980–1990. *Skolsverige 1950–1975.* 6 vols. Stockholm: Liber/Utbildningsförlag.

Marsdal, Magnus E., and Bendik Wold. 2004. *Tredje Venstre. For en radikal individualisme.* Oslo: Oktober.

Marton, Susan Gerard. 2000. *The Mind of the State: The Politics of University Autonomy in Sweden, 1968–1998.* Göteborg: Göteborg Studies in Politics 67.

Mattson, Ingvar, and Olof Petersson, eds. 2003. *Svensk författningspolitik.* Stockholm: SNS förlag.

Maurseth, Per. 1987. *Gjennom kriser til makt (1920–1935).* Vol. 3 in *Arbeiderbevegelsens historie i Norge.* Oslo: Tiden.

Mediås, Odd Asbjørn, and Alfred Oftedal Telhaug. 2000. *Fra sentral til desentralisert styring.* Rapport 2, Utdanning som nasjonsbygging. Steinkjer-Trondheim.

Melby, Kari. 2001. "Kvinner som politiske aktører før og etter stemmeretten." In Nina Berven and Per Selle, eds., *Svekket kvinnemakt? De frivillige organisasjonene og velferdsstaten.* Oslo: Gyldendal.

Messel, Jan. 2000. "'Vi er alle lønnsmottagere.' LO og funksjonærene 1945–1965." See Bjørnhaug et al. 2000.

Meyer, Frank. 2001. *"Dansken, svensken og nordmannen. . . ."* Oslo: Unipub forlag.

Meyer, Johan Kr. 1989. "NATOs kritikere. Den sikkerhetspolitiske opposisjon 1949–1961." *Forsvarsstudier* 3/1989. Oslo: Institutt for Forsvarsstudier.

Meyer, Siri, and Thorvald Sirnes, eds. 1999. *Normalitet og identitetsmakt i Norge.* Oslo: Makt- og demokratiutredningen. Ad Notam Gyldendal.

Midttun, Jørund. 1995. *Sosialdemokrati og folkekirke. Det norske Arbeiderpartis forhold til kirke og religion.* Oslo: Norges Forskningsråd. KULTs skriftserie nr 41.

Millbourn, Ingrid. 1990. *"Rätt till maklighet." Om den svenska socialdemokratins lärprocess 1885–1902.* Stockholm/Stehag: Symposion Bokförlag.

Miller, David, ed. 1991. *Liberty.* Oxford: Oxford University Press.

Misgeld, Klaus. 1976. *Die "Internationale Gruppe demokratischer Sozialisten" in Stockholm 1942–1945.* Uppsala: Studia Historica Upsaliensia 79.

Misgeld, Klaus, Karl Molin, and Klas Åmark, eds. 1989. *Socialdemokratins samhälle. SAP och Sverige under 100 år.* Stockholm: Tiden. (A somewhat revised version with reorganized chapters was published in English in 1992: *Creating Social Democracy. A Century of the Social Democratic Labor Party in Sweden.* University Park: Pennsylvania State University Press.)

Mithander, Conny. 2000. "1905—genombrottet för en ny konservativ nationalism." See Eliæson and Björck 2000: 205–215.

Molin, Karl. 1989. "Partistrid och partiansvar. En studie i socialdemokratisk försvarsdebatt." English version: "Party Disputes and Party Responsibility: A Study of the Social Democratic Defence Debate." See Misgeld, Molin, and Åmark 1989.

Morell, Mats. 2001. *Jordbruket i industrisamhället 1870–1945.* Stockholm: Natur och Kultur/ LTs förlag.

Myklebust, Sissel. 2004. "Flukt og motstand." See Myrvang, Myklebust, and Brenna 2004.

Myrdal, Alva and Gunnar. 1934. *Kris i befolkningsfrågan.* Stockholm: Bonniers. (Much of what is discussed in this important book is presented in English in Alva Myrdal, 1941, *Nation and Family: The Swedish Experiment in Democratic Family and Population Policy,* New York: Harper.)

Myrdal, Gunnar. 1932. "Socialpolitikens dilemma." Stockholm: *Spektrum.*

Myrdal, Gunnar. 1944. *Varning för fredsoptimism.* Stockholm: Bonniers.

Myrdal, Gunnar. 1945. *Universitetsreform.* Stockholm: Tiden.

Myrvang, Christine. 1996. *Sosialistiske produksjonsidealer—"dagen derpaa." Storskala og teknokrati i norsk sosialiseringsdebatt og -teori 1917–1924.* Oslo: TMV Skriftserie nr 18.

Myrvang, Christine. 2004. "Fra knapphet til overflod. Jakten på det rasjonelle massekonsumet." See Myrvang, Myklebust, and Brenna 2004.

Myrvang, Christine, Sissel Myklebust, and Brita Brenna. 2004. *Temmet eller uhemmet. Historiske perspektiver på konsum, kultur og dannelse.* Oslo: Pax.

Nagel, Anne-Hilde, ed. 1991. *Velferdskommunen. Kommunenes rolle i utviklingen av velferdsstaten.* Bergen: Alma Mater forlag.

Nagel, Anne-Hilde, ed. 1998. *Kjønn og velferdsstat.* Bergen: Alma Mater forlag.

Nerbøvik, Jostein. 1991. *Bønder i kamp: Bygdefolkets krisehjelp 1925–35.* Oslo: Samlaget.

Nerheim, Gunnar. 1980. "Fra teknologiforskningens barndom i Norge, oppfinnelsen og utnyttelsen av Söderberg-elektroden." See Roll-Hansen, ed., 1980.

Nielsen, Henning. 1938. *Nordens enhed gennem tiderne.* 3 vols. København: Nyt Nordisk Forlag–Arnold Busck.

Nielsen, May-Brith Ohman. 2001. *Senterpartiets historie 1920–2000.* 2 vols. Oslo: Samlaget.

Nielsen, Torben Hviid, Arve Monsen, and Tore Tennøe. 2000. *Livets tre og kodenes kode. Fra genetikk til bioteknologi. Norge 1900–2000.* Oslo: Gyldendal akademisk.

Nilsen, Yngve. 2001. *En felles plattform? Norsk oljeindustri og klimadebatten i Norge fram til 1998.* Dr.art.avhandling. TIK-senteret, Universitetet i Oslo.

Nilsson, Göran B. 1990. "Den sociala ingenjörkonstens problematik. En orättfärdig dissektion av den unge Gunnar Myrdal." *Nytt Norsk Tidsskrift.*

Nilsson, Göran B. 2003. "The Harmony Liberal Era 1845–1880: The Case of Norway and Sweden." See Teichova and Matis 2003.

Nilsson, Jan-Evert. 1989. "Svenskt näringsliv—norskt näringslivs duktiga storebror." *Bergen Bank Kvartalskrift* 1/1989.

Nilsson, Torbjörn. 1994. *Elitens Svängrum.* Stockholm: Acta Universitatis Stockholmiensis. Stockholm Studies in History nr 50. Amqvist & Wicksell International, pp. 77–107.

Nilsson, Torbjörn. 2002. "Med historien som ledstjärna—Högern och demokratin 1904–1940." *Scandia* 1/2002.

Nissen, Bernt A. 1957. *Gunnar Knudsen.* Oslo: Aschehoug.

Njølstad, Olav. 1999. *Strålende forskning. Institutt for energiteknikk 1948–98.* Oslo: Tano Aschehoug.

Nolin, Bertil, ed. 1993. *Kulturradikalismen. Det moderna genombrottets andra fas.* Stockholm/ Stehag: Brutus Östlings bokförlag Symposion.

Nordby, Trond. 1983. *Venstre og samlingspolitikken 1906–1908. En studie i partioppløsning og gjenreisning.* Oslo: Novus forlag.

Nordby, Trond. 1989. *Karl Evang, En biografi.* Oslo: Aschehoug.

Nordby, Trond. 1990. "'Velferdsstaten' og 'den sosialdemokratiske stat'—norske myter i historisk lys." *Sosiologi i dag* 4/1990.

Nordby, Trond. 1994. *Korporatisme på norsk 1920–1990.* Oslo: Universitetsforlaget.

Nordli, Odvar. 1985. *Min vei.* Oslo: Tiden.

Nordlund, Sven. 1989. *Upptäckten av Sverige. Utländska direktinvesteringar i Sverige 1895–1945.* Umeå: Umeå University Studies in Economic History 12.

Nordström, Kjell A. 1991. *The Internationalization Process of the Firm—Searching for New Patterns and Explanations.* Stockholm: Institute of International Business, Stockholm School of Economics.

Noreen, Erik. 1994. *Brobygge eller blockbildning. De norska och svenska utrikesledningernas säkerhetspolitiska föreställningar 1945–1948.* Stockholm: Carlssons.

Norman, Torbjörn. 2001. "Ludvig Nordström och den svenska historiens nu." See Alf W. Johansson 2001.

NOU (Norwegian Official Report) 1986:22. *Oppfølging av langtidssykemeldte.*

NOU 1999:27. *"Ytringsfrihed bør finde Sted."*

NOU 1999:34. *Nytt millenium—nytt arbeidsliv.*

NOU 2003:19. *Makt og demokrati. Sluttrapport fra Makt- og Demokratiutredningen.*

NOU 2004:1. *Modernisert Folketrygd.*

NOU 2004:5. *Arbeidslivslovutvalget.*

Nybom, Thorsten. 1993. "The Swedish Social Democratic State in a Tradition of Peaceful Revolution." In Carsten Due-Nielsen et al., eds., *Konflikt og samarbejde.* København: Museum Tusculanum Forlag.

Nybom, Thorsten. 1997. *Kunskap, politik, samhälle. Essäer om kunskapssyn, universitet och forskningspolitik 1900–2000.* Hargshamn: Arete.

Nycander, Svante. 2002. *Makten över arbetsmarknaden. Ett perspektiv på Sveriges 1900-tal.* Stockholm: SNS Förlag.

Nyhamar, Jostein. 1990. *Nye utfordringer (1965–1990).* Vol. 6 in *Arbeiderbevegelsens historie i Norge.* Oslo: Tiden

Nylander, Gert. 1998. "Carl Goerdelers fredsstrevare via brödrerna Wallenberg." Lund: *Scandia*, vol. 64, 2/1998, pp. 245–277.

Öberg, Nils. 1994. *Gränslös rättvisa eller rättvisa inom gränser.* Uppsala: Acta Universitatis Upsaliensis. Statsvetenskapliga föreningen i Uppsala 118.

Odhner, Clas-Erik. 1989. "Arbetare och bönder formar den svenska modellen. Socialdemokratin och jordbrukspolitiken." English verion: "Workers and Farmers shape the Swedish Model: Social Democracy and Agricultural Policy." See Misgeld, Molin, and Åmark 1989.

Offe, Claus. 2006. "Social Protection in a Supranational Context: European Integration and the Fates of the 'European Social Model.'" In Pranab Bardhan, Samuel Bowles, and Michael Wallerstein, eds., *Globalization and Egalitarian Redistribution*. Princeton: Princeton University Press.

Olsen, Johan P. 1989. *Petroleum og politikk*. Oslo: Tano.

Olsen, Johan P. 2007. *Europe in Search of Political Order*. Oxford: Oxford University Press.

Olsen, Johan P., and Bjørn Otto Sverdrup, eds. 1998. *Europa i Norden. Europeisering av nordisk samarbeid*. Oslo: Tano Aschehoug.

Olsson, Oscar. 1949–1951. *Hans Larsson I–II*. Stockholm: Oskar Eklunds Bokförlag.

Olsson, Stefan. 2000. *Den svenska högerns anpassning till demokratin*. Uppsala: Acta Universitatis Upsaliensis.

Olsson, Ulf. 1986. *Bank, familj och företagande. Stockholms Enskilda Bank 1946–1971*. Stockholm.

Olsson, Ulf. 1994. "Planning in the Swedish Welfare State." See Clement and Mahon 1994.

Olsson, Ulf. 2000. *Att förvalta sitt pund. Marcus Wallenberg 1899–1982*. Stockholm: Ekerlids.

Olstad, Finn. 1987. *Forsvar, sport, klassekamp 1861–1939*. Vol. 1 in Finn Olstad and Stein Tønnesson, *Norsk Idretts Historie*. Oslo: Aschehoug.

Olstad, Finn. 1991. *Arbeiderklassens vekst og fall. Hovedlinjer i 100 års norsk historie*. Oslo: Universitetsforlaget.

Olstad, Finn. 1998. "Martin Tranmæl og radikaliseringen av norsk arbeidervbevegelse 1906–1918." *Historisk Tidsskrift* 1/1998, pp. 73–89.

Olstad, Finn. 1999. *Einar Gerhardsen—en politisk biografi*. Oslo: Universitetsforlaget.

Olstad, Finn. 2009. *Med knyttet neve. LOs historie 1899–1935*. Vol. 1 in *LOs historie*. Oslo: Pax.

Om Sveriges föhållande till nazismen, Nazityskland och förintelsen—en forskningsöversikt. 2001. Stockholm: Vetenskapsrådet.

Östberg, Kjell. 1990. *Byråkrati och reformism. En studie av svensk socialdemokratis politiska och sociala integrering fram till första värdskriget*. Lund: Studentlitteratur.

Östberg, Kjell. 1996. *Kommunerna och den svenska modellen*. Stockholm/Stehag: Brutus Östlings Bokförlag Symposion.

Östberg, Kjell. 1997. *Efter rösträtten. Kvinnors utrymme efter det demokratiska genombrottet*. Stockholm/Stehag: Brutus Östlings Bokförlag Symposion.

Östberg, Kjell. 2002. *1968 när allting var i rörelse*. Stockholm: Prisma.

Østergård, Uffe. 1997. "The Geopolitics of Nordic Identity—from Composite States to Nation States." See Sørensen and Stråth 1997: 25–71.

Østerud, Øyvind, Fredrik Engelstad, and Per Selle. 2003. *Makten og demokratiet. En sluttbok fra Makt- og demokratiutredningen*. Oslo: Gyldendal Akademisk.

Otnes, Per. 1970. *Den samiske nasjon*. Oslo: Pax.

Ottosen-komiteen. 1966–1970. *Komiteeen til å utrede spørsmål om videreutdanning for artianere og andre med tilsvarende grunnutdanning*. Innst. 1–5. Trykt som vedlegg til St.meld. nr 66 (1972–73) *Om den videre utbygging og organisering av høgre utdanning*.

Over grænsen efter konkurrenceevne. 2002. København: Oxford Research.

Palme, Sven Ulric. 1964. *På Karl Staffs tid*. Stockholm: Bokförlaget Aldus/Bonniers.

Pedersen, Axel West. 2005. "Halvhjertet kopi av brutal original." Oslo: *Tidsskrift for velferdsforskning*, vol. 7 (2).

Pedersen, Helge. 2003 "Gud har skapat svarta och vita människor, djäfulen derimot halfne-geren." *En komparativ analyse av Jon Alfred Mjøen og Herman Lundborgs rasehygeniske ideer i Norge og Sverige ca. 1900–1935.* Oslo: Hovedoppgave i historie.

Persson, Roger. 1991. "Svensk nationalrapport." *Progressivitet och proportinalitet i skattesyste-met.* Uppsala: Nordiska skattevetenskapliga forskningsrådets skriftserie.

Petersen, Klaus, and Klas Åmark. 2002. "Old Age and Supplementary Pensions in the Nordic Countries 1880–2000." Manuscript.

Petersson, Magnus, ed. 1999. *1948–49–Nordiska ödesår?* Stockholm: Försvarshögskolans Acta B11.

Petersson, Magnus. 2000. *Vapenbröder. Svensk-norska säkerhetspolitiska relationer under kalla kriget.* Oslo: Institutt for forsvarsstudier, Info 5/2000.

Petersson, Magnus. 2003a. *"Brødrafolkens väl." Svensk-norska säkerhetspolitiska relationer 1949–1969.* Stockholm: Santérus Förlag.

Petersson, Magnus. 2003b. "Man lär sig . . . 'vem man kan hålla i hand när leken blir alvar.' Svensk militär underrättelsestjänst och Norge under första delen av det kalla kriget." See Holtsmark, Pharo, and Tamnes 2003.

Petersson, Olof. 1982. "Klassidentifikation." In Kant Asp, Stig Hadenius, Sören Holmberg, Rutger Lindahl, Björn Molin, Olof Petersson, and Lennart Weibull, *Väljare Partier Mass-media. Empiriska studier i Svensk demokrati.* Stockholm: Liber Förlag.

Petersson, Olof. 2003. "Den sista maktutredningen?" *Nytt Norsk Tidsskrift* 4/2003.

Petersson, Olof, and Ingrid Carlberg. 1990. *Makten över tanken.* Stockholm: Carlssons.

Pettit, Philip. 1997. *Republicanism.* Oxford: Oxford University Press.

Pharo, Helge Ø., and Anders Jølstad. 1998. "Mellom nasjonalstaten og Vest-Europa. Norges Norden-politikk 1945–1972." See Olsen and Sverdrup 1998.

Piore, Michael J., and Charles F. Sabel. 1984. *The Second Industrial Divide: Possibilities for Prosperity.* New York: Basic Books.

Polanyi, Karl. 1944. *The Great Transformation.* New York: Ferret & Rinehart.

Raaum, Odd. 1999. *Pressen er løs.* Oslo: Pax.

Raaum, Odd. 2001. "Se opp for etterligninger." See Eide 2001.

Randen, Olav. 2002. *Brøyte seg rydning. Bureisingstid og bureisarliv.* Ål: Boksmia.

Ravneberg, Bodil. 1999. *Normalitetsdiskurser og profesjonaliseringsprosesser.* Bergen: Institutt for administrasjons- og organisasjonsvitenskap, Rapport nr 69.

Ravneberg, Bodil. 2001. "Normalskolen for normaleleven." *ARR, Idéhistorisk Tidsskrift,* 1–2/2001.

Reinton, Per Olav. 1984. "Kildenes tyranni." *Nytt Norsk Tidsskrift* 4/1984.

Richardson, Gunnar. 1996. *Beundran och fruktan. Sverige inför Tyskland 1940–1942.* Stock-holm: Carlssons.

Richardson, Gunnar. 1999. *Svensk utbildningshistoria.* Lund: Studentlitteratur.

Riksdagsproposition 1992/93:169. *Om högre utbildning för ökad kompetens.*

Riste, Olav. 1965. *The Neutral Ally: Norway's Relations with Belligerent Powers in the First World War.* Oslo: Universitetsforlaget.

Riste, Olav. 1990. "Forholdet mellom den norske og den svenske regjering under krigen." See Værnø 1990.

Riste, Olav, and Arnfinn Moland. 1997. *"Strengt hemmelig" Norsk etterretningsteneste 1945–1970.* Oslo: Universitetsforlaget.

Robinson, Joan. 1962. *Economic Philosophy.* London: Pelican.

Rokkan, Stein. 1970. *Citizens, Elections, Parties.* Oslo: Universitetsforlaget.

Rokkan, Stein. 1996. "Norway: Numerical Democracy and Corporate Pluralism." In Robert Dahl, ed., *Political Oppositions in Western Democracies.* New Haven: Yale University Press.

Roland, Kjell, Victor Norman, and Torger Reve, eds. 2001. *Rikdommens problem.* Oslo: Universitetsforlaget.

Rolf, Bertil, Eskil Ekstedt, and Ronald Bernett. 1993. *Kvalitet och kunskapsprocess i högre utbildning.* Falun.

Roll-Hansen, Nils. 1980. "Johan Hjort og motstanden mot de praktisk-vitenskapelige fiskeriundersøkelser." See Roll-Hansen, ed., 1980.

Roll-Hansen, Nils, ed. 1980. *Skandinavisk naturvitenskap og teknologi omkring år 1900.* Oslo: NAVFs Utredningsinstitutt. Seminarrrapport 1980:4.

Rönnbäck, Josefin. 2002. "Den fängslade modern. Om samhällsmoderlighet som ideologi, taktik och praktik i kampen för kvinnors rösträtt." See Bergman and Johansson 2002.

Rösträtten 80 år–Forskarantologi. 2001. Stockholm: Justitiedepartementet.

Rothstein, Bo. 1986. *Den socialdemokratiska staten. Reformer och förvaltning inom svensk arbetsmarknads- och skolpolitik.* Lund: Arkiv Avhandlingsserie 21.

Rothstein, Bo. 1992. *Den korporativa staten.* Stockholm: Norstedts.

Rothstein, Bo. 2002. *Vad bör staten göra? Om välferdsstatens moraliska och politiska logik.* Stockholm: SNS Förlag.

Rothstein, Bo. 2004. "Från reformbyråkratier till ideologiska statsapparater." *Nytt Norsk Tidsskrift* 3–4/2004.

Rovde, Olav. 2000. "Bonde-, småbrukar- og arbeidarrørsla—i konflikt og samarbeid." *Arbeiderhistorie 2000.* Oslo: Årbok for Arbeiderbevegelsens Arkiv og Bibliotek.

Rowe, Lars. 2002. *"Nyttige idioter"? Fredsfronten i Norge 1949–1956.* Oslo: Institutt for forsvarsstudier.

Rudeng, Erik. 1989. *Sjokoladekongen.* Oslo: Universitetsforlaget.

Ruin, Olof. 1986. *I välfärdsstatens tjänst. Tage Erlander 1946–1969.* Stockholm: Tiden förlag.

Ruin, Olof. 2002. *Sveriges statsminister och EU.* Stockholm: Hjalmarson & Högberg.

Runcis, Maija. 1998. *Steriliseringar i folkhemmet.* Stockholm: Ordfront.

Runeby, Nils. 1995. *Dygd och vetande. Ur de bildades historia.* Stockholm: Atlantis.

Ryggvik, Helge. 2000. *Norsk oljevirksomhet mellom det nasjonale og det internasjonale. En studie av selskapsstruktur og internasjonalisering.* Oslo: Acta humaniora, Unipub forlag.

Sachs, Jeffrey D. 2008. *Common Wealth: Economics for a Crowded Planet.* London: Alan Lane.

Sæther, Odd Jostein, ed. 1985. *Kristelig folkepartis historie 1933–1983: Samling om verdier.* Oslo: Valo.

Sainsbury, Diane. 2001. "Gender and the Making of Welfare States: Norway and Sweden." Oxford: *Social Politics,* Spring 2001.

Salmon, Patrick. 1997. *Scandinavia and the Great Powers 1890–1940.* Cambridge: Cambridge University Press.

Sandel, Michael J. 1996. *Democracy's Discontent: America in Search of a Public Philosophy.* Cambridge, Mass., and London: The Belknap Press of Harvard University Press.

Sandström, Ulf. 1989. *Arkitektur och social ingenjörskonst.* Linköping: Linköping Studies in Arts and Science.

Sandvin, Johans T. 1996. *Velferdsstatens vendepunkt.* Bodø: Nordlandsforskning.

Scheflo, Inge. 1964. "Det norske Arbeiderpartis stortingsgruppe." In *Det Norske Stortings historie,* vol. 4, pp. 250–274. Oslo: Gyldendal.

Schiller, Bernt. 1967. *Storstrejken 1909. Förhistoria och orsaker.* Göteborg: Akakdemiförlaget.

Schiller, Bernt. 1984. "At Gun Point: A Critical Perspective on the Attempts of the Nordic Governments to Achieve Unity after the Second World War." *Scandinavian Journal of History* 3/1984.

Schiøtz, Aina. 2003. *Folkets helse–landets styrke. 1850–2003.* Oslo: Universitetsforlaget.

Schön, Lennart. 2000. *En modern svensk ekonomisk historia. Tillväxt och omvandling under två sekel.* Stockholm: SNS Förlag.

Schumpeter, Joseph A. 1970. *Capitalism, Socialism and Democracy.* London: Unwin. (First edition 1943.)

Seim, Jardar. 1972. *Hvordan hovedavtalen av 1935 ble til.* Oslo: Tiden.

Seip, Anne-Lise. 1984. *Sosialhjelpstaten blir til. Norsk sosialpolitikk 1740–1920.* Oslo: Gyldendal.

Seip, Anne-Lise. 1989. "Politikkens vitenskapliggjøring." *Nytt Norsk Tidsskrift.*

Seip, Anne-Lise. 1991. "Velferdskommunen og velferdstrekanten–et tilbakeblikk." See Nagel 1991.

Seip, Anne-Lise. 1994. *Veiene til velferdsstaten. Norsk sosialpolitikk 1920–1975.* Oslo: Gyldendal.

Seip, Åsmund Arup. 1998. *Rett til å forhandle. En studie i statstjenestemennenes forhandlingsrett i Norge og Sverige 1910–1965.* Oslo: Fafo-rapport 243.

Seip, Jens Arup. 1963. *Fra embedsmannssat til ettpartistat og andre essays.* Oslo: Universitetsforlaget.

Seip, Jens Arup. 1971. *Ole Jacob Broch og hans samtid.* Oslo: Gyldendal.

Seip, Jens Arup. 1994. "Flerpartistaten i perspektiv." *Nytt Norsk Tidsskrift* 3–4/1994.

Sejersted, Francis. 1973. *Ideal, teori og virkelighet.* Oslo: Cappelen. (Included in Sejersted 2001.)

Sejersted, Francis, ed. 1982. *En storbank i blandingsøkonomien. Den norske Creditbank 1957–1982.* Oslo: Gyldendal.

Sejersted, Francis. 1997. "Technology and Unemployment." In *Creativity, Innovation and Job Creation.* OECD Proceedings

Sejersted, Francis. 2001. *Demokrati og rettsstat.* Oslo: Pax. (First edition 1984.)

Sejersted, Francis. 2002a. *Demokratisk kapitalisme.* Oslo: Pax. (First edition 1993.)

Sejersted, Francis. 2002b. "En skjult agenda? Två nordiska Sovjetstater? Telia/Telenor-saken i historisk perspektiv." In *Till en konstnärssjäl. En vänbok till Stig Ramel.* Stockholm: Atlantis.

Sejersted, Francis. 2002c. *Er det mulig å styre utviklingen?* Oslo: Pax.

Sejersted, Francis. 2003a. *Norsk idyll?* Oslo: Pax. (First edition 2000.)

Sejersted, Francis. 2003b. *Opposisjon og posisjon.* Vol. 3 in *Høyres historie.* Oslo: Pax. (First edition 1984.)

Sejersted, Francis. 2003c. *Sannhet med modifikasjoner.* Oslo: Pax.

Sejersted, Fredrik. 1998. "Nordisk rettssamarbeid og europeisk integrasjon." See Olsen and Sverdrup 1998.

Sennett, Richard. 1998. *The Corrosion of Character: The Personal Consequences of Work in the New Capitalism.* New York and London: W. W. Norton & Co.

Sennett, Richard. 2006. *The Culture of the New Capitalism*. New Haven and London: Yale University Press.

Sevje, Svein. 1977. *En uheldig hund i keglespill. Studieselskapet for norsk industri*. Oslo: Hovedoppgave, Historisk Institutt.

Shonfield, Andrew. 1969. *Modern Capitalism*. London.

Sidenbladh, Göran. 1985. *Norrmalm förnyat 1951–1981*. Stockholm: Arkitektur Förlag AB/ Liber.

Simonsen, Eva. 2001. "'Konfermert og sterelisert' Hygiene og sosial ingeniørkunst i norsk skole." *ARR, Idéhistorisk Tidsskrift*, 1–2/2001.

Simonson, Birger. 1985. *Socialdemokratin och maktövertagandet. SAP:s politiska strategi 1889– 1911*. Göteborg: Meddelanden från Historiska institutionen i Göteborg, nr 28.

Sirnes, Thorvald. 1999. "Alt som er fast, fordamper?" See Meyer and Sirnes 1999.

Sjølie, Hans Petter. 2002. *Fra raddis til kader. Kineseri i tidens ånd*. Oslo: Hovedoppg. i historie.

Sjöstedt, Charlotta. 1999. *I skuggan av ett hjälteland. Svenska frivilliga för det ockuperade Norge*. Stockholm: Hjalmarson & Högberg.

Skarpnes, Ove. 2005. "Pedosentrismens framvekst." Oslo: *Nytt Norsk Tidsskrift* 4/2005.

Skeie, Jon. 2003. "Velferdsstaten og flukten fra markedet. Gjensyn med et seiglivet paradoks." See *Den mangfoldige velferden* 2003.

Skjervheim, Hans. 1985. "Den nye mediaideologien." *Nytt Norsk Tidsskrift* 1/1985.

Skoglund, Christer. 1993. "Kulturradikalismen—arvet och förnyelsen." See Nolin 1993.

Skoie, Hans. 1985. *Norsk forskningsorganisasjon i etterkrigstiden*. Oslo: NAVFs utredningsinstitutt, Melding 1984:8.

Skorpen, Ann-Mari. 1995. *Maoisme på norsk og svensk*. Bergen: Hovedoppgave i sammenlignende politikk.

Skrede, Kari. 2004. "Familiepolitikkens grense—ved 'likestilling light'?" See Ellingsæter and Leira 2004.

Slagstad, Rune, ed. 1978. *Om staten*. Oslo: Pax.

Slagstad, Rune. 1981. "Velferdsstaten." In *Pax Leksikon*. Oslo: Pax.

Slagstad, Rune. 1987. *Rett og politikk. Et liberalt tema med variasjoner*. Oslo: Universitetsforlaget.

Slagstad, Rune. 1989. "Prøvingsretten i det norske system." *Nytt Norsk Tidsskrift* 4/1989.

Slagstad, Rune. 1998. *De nasjonale strateger*. Oslo: Pax.

Slagstad, Rune. 2000. *Kunnskapens hus*. Oslo: Pax.

Slagstad, Rune. 2001. *Rettens ironi*. Oslo: Pax .

Slagstad, Rune, Ove Korsgaard, and Lars Løvlie, eds. 2003. *Dannelsens forvandlinger*. Oslo: Pax.

Smeby, Jens-Christian, and Ellen Brandt. 1999. *Yrkesretting av høyere utdanning? En studie av offentlig politikk fra Ottosen-komiteen til i dag*. Oslo: NIFU. Rapport 6/1999.

Söderpalm, Sven Anders. 1976. *Direktörsklubben: Storindustrin i Svensk Politik under 1930- och 40-talet*. Lund: Zenith.

Sogner, Knut. 2001. *Plankeadel. Kiær- og Solbergfamilien under den 2. industrielle revolusjon*. Oslo: Andresen og Butenschøn.

Sogner, Knut. 2002. *En liten brikke i et stort spill. Den norske IT-industrien fra krise til vekst 1975–2000*. Bergen: Fagbokforlaget.

Sogner, Knut. 2003. *Skaperkraft. Elkem gjennom 100 år.* Oslo: Messel.

Solstad, Dag. 1971. *Arild Asnes, 1970: roman.* Oslo: Aschehoug.

Solstad, Dag. 1974. *25. septemberplassen: roman.* Oslo Aschehoug.

Solstad, Dag. 1990. *Medaljens forside.* Oslo: Cappelen.

Soltvedt, Kjartan. 2000. *Dør vi ut? Befolkningsspørsmålet i norsk politisk og intellektuell debatt 1900–1940.* Oslo: Oslo: Hovedoppgave i historie.

Sørensen, Øystein, and Bo Stråth, eds. 1997. *The Cultural Construction of Norden.* Oslo: Scandinavian University Press.

Sørhaug, Tian. 2004. *Managementalitet og autoritetens forvandling.* Oslo: Fagbokforlaget.

Sörlin, Sverker. 1988. *Framtidslandet: Debatten om Norrland och naturresurserna under det industrielle genombrottet.* Kungl. Skytteanska samfundets handlingar 33. Stockholm: Carlsson.

SOU 1940:35. *Organiserad Samverken inom Näringslivet* (Organized Cooperation in Business Life).

SOU 1968:11. *Svenska kyrkan och staten.*

SOU 1999:132. *Valgdeltagande i förändring.*

SOU 2002:87. *Rikets säkerhet och den personliga integriteten. De svenska säkerhetstjenesternas författningsskuddande verksamhet sedan år 1945.*

Starheimsæter, Hermann. 2003. *Nordvegen.* Oslo: Aschehoug.

Steen, Sverre. 1958. "De frivillige sammenslutninger og det norske demokrati." In Sverre Steen, *Tusen års norsk historie,* pp. 182–196. Oslo: Cappelen.

Steen, Sverre. 1977. *Frihet og liv er ett.* Oslo: Cappelen.

Steinmo, Sven. 1993. *Taxation and Democracy: Swedish, British and American Approaches to Financing the Modern State.* New Haven and London: Yale University Press.

Stenlås, Niklas. 1998. *Den inre kretsen.* Lund: Arkiv förlag.

Stephens, J. D. 1979. *The Transition from Capitalism to Socialism.* London: Macmillan.

Stjernø, Steinar. 2004. *Solidarity in Europe: The History of an Idea.* Cambridge: Cambridge University Press.

Stjernquist, Nils. 1996. *Tvåkammartiden. Sveriges riksdag 1867–1970.* Stockholm: Sverige Riksdag.

Stonehill, Arthur. 1965. *Foreign Ownership in Norwegian Enterprises.* Oslo: Statistisk Sentralbyrå. Samfunnsøkonomiske studier nr 14.

Storvik, Kjetil. 2000. "Svensk-Norsk elendighet?" *Praktisk økonomi og finans* 1/2000. Oslo: Cappelen Akademisk forlag.

Stråth, Bo. 1978. *Nordic Industry and Nordic Economic Cooperation.* Stockholm: Almqvist & Wiksell.

Stråth, Bo. 1992. *Folkhemmet mot Europa. Ett historiskt perspektiv på 90-talet.* Stockholm: Tiden.

Stråth, Bo. 1993. "Kungliga salighetsverket? Socialdemokratisk kyrkopolitik i Sverige före 1940." *Arbetarhistoria* 2–3/1993.

Stråth, Bo. 1998. *Mellan två fonder. LO och den svenska modellen.* Stockholm: Atlas.

Stråth, Bo. 2000. *Mellan medbestemmande och medarbetare.* Stockholm: Metall.

Strömberg, Thord. 1989. "Historien om bostadsmarknadens politisering. Socialdemokraterna och bostadsfrågan." English version: "The Politiciization of the Housing Market: The Social

Democrats and the Housing Question." See Misgeld, Molin, and Åmark 1989.

Sundbärg, Gustav. 1911. *Det svenska folklynnet.* Bilaga 16 til *Emigationsutredningen.* Stockholm: Norstedt.

Sundbärg, Gustav. 1913. *Betänkande i utvandringsfrågan och därmed samanhängande spørsmål.* Stockholm.

Sundberg, Jan. 2001. *Partier och intresseorganisationer i Norden.* Nord 2001:8. København: Nordisk Ministerråd.

Sundelius, Bengt, and Claes Wiklund, eds. 2000. *Norden i sicksack. Tre spårbyten inom nordiskt samarbete.* Stockholm: Santérus.

Sundin, Bo. 1981. *Ingenjörvetenskapens tidevarv.* Umeå og Stockholm: Acta universitas umensis, Almqvist & Wiksell.

Svensson, Lennart. 1980. *Universitetens omvandling från 1870talet till 1970talet.* Del 3 av *Från bildning till utbildning.* Göteborg: Sociologiska Institutionen, Göteborgs Universitet.

Svensson, Torsten. 1994, *Socialdemokratins dominans. En studie av den svenska socialdemokratins partistrategi.* Uppsala: Skrifter utgivna av Statsvetenskapliga föreningen i Uppsala.

Svensson, Torsten. 2001. *Marknadsanpassingens politik. Den svenska modellens förändring 1980–2000.* Uppsala: Srifter utgiva av Statsvetenskaplige föreningen i Uppsala.

Sverdrup, Jakob. 1996. *Inn i storpolitikken 1940–1949.* Vol. 4 in *Norsk Utenrikspolitikks historie.* Oslo: Universitetsforlaget.

Sydow, Björn von. 1997. *Parlamentarismen i Sverige. Utveckling och utformning till 1945.* Hedemora: Gidlunds förlag.

Tamnes, Rolf. 1991. "Svalbard og stormaktene. Fra ingenmannsland til kald krig, 1870–1958." *Forsvarsstudier* 7/1991. Oslo: Institutt for forsvarsstudier.

Tamnes, Rolf. 1997. *Oljealder 1965–1995.* Vol. 6 in *Norsk utenrikspolitisk historie.* Oslo: Aschehoug.

Taylor, Charles. 1979. "What's Wrong with Negative Liberty." In Alan Ryan, ed., *The Idea of Freedom: Essays in Honour of Isaiah Berlin,* pp. 175–193. Oxford: Oxford University Press.

Taylor, Charles. 1992. *The Ethics of Authenticity.* Cambridge, Mass.: Harvard University Press.

Teichova, Alice, and Herbert Matis, eds. 2003. *Nation, State, and the Economy in History.* Cambridge: Cambridge University Press.

Telhaug, Alfred Oftedal. 1991. *Norsk skoleutvikling etter 1945.* Oslo: Didakta.

Telhaug, Alfred Oftedal. 2003. "Svensk-norsk enhetsskole." Lecture, manuscript.

Telhaug, Alfred Oftedal. 2008. "Gjensyn med Nils Christies skolevisjoner. Nils Christie—uten styrthjelm og knebeskyttere." *Nytt Norsk Tidsskrift.*

Telhaug, Alfred Oftedal, and Odd Asbjørn Mediås. 2003. *Grunnskolen som nasjonsbygger.* Oslo: Abstrakt forlag.

Terjesen, Einar A. 1991. "Arbeiderbevegelse og politikk i 1890-årene." Oslo: *Arbeiderhistorie 91.*

Thon, Jahn. 2003. "Mao som litterær motkultur." *Klassekampen* 21/2/2003.

Thon, Sverre. 1961. *Skatter, velstand og konkurranseevne.* Oslo: Opplysningsinstituttet for fritt næringsliv.

Thon, Sverre. 1968. *Økonomisk politikk i Norge 1945–1965.* Oslo: Elingaard forlag.

Thue, Lars. 1994. *Statens Kraft 1890–1947. Kraftutbygging og samfunnsutvikling.* Oslo: Cappelen.

Thue, Lars. 1996. *Strøm og styring. Norsk kraftliberalisme i historisk perspektiv.* Oslo: ad Notam Gyldendal.

Thullberg, Per. 1977. *Bönder går samman. En studie i Riksförbundet Landsbygdens Folk under världskrisen 1929–1933.* Stockholm: LTs förlag.

Thullberg, Per, and Kjell Östberg, eds. 1984. *Den svenska modellen.* Lund: Studentlitteratur.

Tilton, Tim. 1990. *The Political Theory of Swedish Social Democracy: Through the Welfare State to Socialism.* Oxford: Clarendon Press.

Tingsten, Herbert. 1966. *Strid kring idyllen.* Stockholm: Norstedts.

Tingsten, Herbert. 1967. *Den svenska socialdemokratins idéutveckling I–II.* Stockholm: Bokförlaget Aldus/Bonniers. (Første utgave 1941, Stockholm: Tiden.)

Tjelmeland, Hallvard. 2003. *I globaliseringens tid.* See Knut Kjeldstadli 2003.

Torstendahl, Rolf. 1969. *Mellan nykonservatism och liberalism.* Uppsala: Svenska Bokfölaget.

Torstendahl, Rolf. 1975. *Dispersion of Engineers.* Uppsala: Almqvist & Wiksell.

Troedsson, Ingegerd. 1999. *Den kommenderade familjen. 30 år med Alva Myrdals familjepolitik.* Stockholm: Timbro.

Tuastad, Svein. 2006. *Skulen og statsmaktsspørsmålet. Stortingsdebattar 1945–2005 om religion i skulen og om private skular i lys av normativ teori.* Bergen: Universitetet i Bergen.

Tvedt, Terje, ed. 1989. *(ml). En bok om maoismen i Norge.* Oslo: ad Notam forlag.

Tveite, Tonje. 1995. "Forvaltningsselskap for statsindustri?" See Grøndahl and Grønlie 1995.

Tydén, Mattias. 2002. *Från politik till praktik. De svenske steriliseringslagerna 1935–1975.* Stockholm: Acta Universitatis Stockholmiensis. Stockholm Studies in History 63, Almqvist & Wiksell.

Uddhammar, Emil. 1993. *Partierna och den stora staten. En analys av statsteorier och svensk politik under 1900-talet.* Stockholm: City University Press.

Værnø, Grethe, ed. 1990. *Fra arvefiende til samboer. Dialog Norge-Sverige.* Stockholm/Oslo: Atlantis/Wennergren Cappelen.

Valen, Henry. 1981. *Valg og politikk—et samfunn i endring.* Oslo: NKS-forlaget.

Vallinder, Torbjörn. 1984. "Folkpartiets ideologiska och organisatoriska bakgrund 1866–1934." In *Liberal ideologi och politik 1934–1984.* Stockholm: AB Folk och Samhälle, pp. 12–79.

Vedung, Evert, and Magnus Brandel. 2001. *Vattenkraften, staten och de politiska parierna.* Nora: Bokförlaget Nya Doxa.

Vestin, Sanna. 2002. *Flyktingboken. Från Duvemåla till Fort Europa.* Stockholm: Ordfront.

Videreutvikling av bedriftsdemokrati. 1980. Innstilling fra en felleskomite mellom Landsorganisasjonen i Norge og Det Norske Arbeiderparti ("Skytøen-komiteen"). Oslo.

Vogt, Johan. 1933. *Den nye tekniske revolusjon og dens samfunnsmessige følger.* Oslo: Fram forlag.

Vogt, Johan. 1937. *Dogmenes sammenbrudd innenfor den sosialøkonomiske vitenskap.* Oslo: Aschehoug.

Wahlbäck, Krister. 1990. "Richard Sandlers nordiska politik." See Huldt and Misgeld 1990.

Waltzer, Michael. 1983. *Spheres of Justice.* London: Basic Books.

Wehler, Hans-Ulrich. 1974. "Der Aufstieg des Organisierten Kapitalismus und Interventionsstaates in Deutschland." In Heinrich August Winkler (Hg.), *Organisierter Kapitalismus—Voraufsetzungen und Anfänge,* pp. 36–57. Göttingen: Vandenhoeck & Ruprecht.

Wendt, Frantz. 1979. *Nordisk Råd 1952–1978.* Stockholm: Nordiska Rådet.

Westerståhl, Jörgen. 1945. *Svensk fackföreningsrörelse.* Stockholm: Tiden.

Westholm, Anders, and Jan Teorell. 1999. "Att bestämma sig för att vara med och bestämma. Om varför vi röstar–allt mindre." See SOU 1999:132.

Wieslander, Bengt. 1994. *The Parliamentary Ombudsman in Sweden*. Stockholm: The Bank of Sweden Tercentenary Foundation & Gidlunds Bokförlag.

Wigforss, Ernst. 1950–1954. *Minnen*. 3 vols. Stockholm: Tiden.

Wikan, Unni. 1995. *Mot en ny norsk underklasse. Innvandrere, kultur og integrasjon*. Oslo: Gyldendal.

Wikan, Unni. 2003. *For ærens skyld. Fadime til ettertanke*. Oslo: Universitetsforlaget.

Wiklund, Claes. 2000a. "1962 års Helsingforsavtal." See Sundelius and Wiklund 2000.

Wiklund, Claes. 2000b. "Femte gången gillt—Nordiska investeringsbankens tillkomst." See Sundelius and Wiklund 2000.

Wiklund, Claes. 2000c. "Nordek–planen och dess föregångare." See Sundelius and Wiklund 2000.

Witoszek, Nina. 1998. *Norske naturmytologier. Fra Edda til økosofi*. Oslo: Pax.

Witt-Brattström, Ebba. 1975. "Sverige." Under chapter titled "Kvinnebevegelsen i andre land" in *Kvinnens årbok 1976*. Oslo: Pax.

Witt-Brattström, Ebba. 1988. *Moa Martinson–Skrift och drift i trettiotalet*. Stockholm: Bokförlaget Pan, Norstedts.

Wittrock, Björn. 1989. "Universitetets idé i den sena nationalstaten." In Thorsten Nybom, ed., *Universitet och samhälle*. Stockholm: Tidens.

Wockelberg, Helena. 2003. *Den svenska förvaltningsmodellen. Parlamantarisk debatt om förvaltningens roll i styrelseskicket*. Uppsala: Skrifter utgivna av Statsvetenskapliga Föreningen i Uppsala 155.

Yttri, Gunnar. 1995. "From a Norwegian Rationalization Law to an American Productivity Institute." *Scandinavian Journal of History* 2/1995.

Zander, Ulf. 2001. *Fornstora dagar, moderna tider. Bruk av och debatter om svensk historia från sekelskifte til sekelskifte*. Lund: Nordic Academic Press.

Zaremba, Maciej. 1999. *De rena och de andra*. Stockholm: Bokförlaget DN.

INDEX

ABC towns, 235
abortion, abortion law, 286–287, 334, 335, 451, 459, 460, 461
absolute monarchy, 10, 50
action ideologues, 119, 150, 167
Ådalen, the shots in, 156-157
administrative courts, 300
administrative dualism, 299–300
AKP (m-l). *See* Marxist-Leninist (ML) movement
Albania, 453, 455
Allmänna Valmansförbundet. *See* Conservative Party
Åmark Klas, 40, 195, 196, 210, 247, 248, 250, 252, 253, 255, 256
Ambjörnsson, Ronny, 206, 207, 316
American model, 351, 382
Amnå, Erik, 438
AMS (Arbetsmarknadsstyrelsen), 221–223, 243
Amundsen, Roald, 17, 18
Andenæs, Johannes, 298, 299, 300
angry young men, 448
Anshelm, Jonas, 216, 340
antimilitarism, 194, 203, 210
antiparliamentarianism, 73–78, 123, 144, 163
Anttonen, Anneli, 417
AP Funds (Allmänna Pensionsfonderna), 254, 326, 374, 383
applied research, 279
arrogance of power, 198, 204
Arvidsson, Stellan, 268, 275
ASEA (Allmänna Svenska Elektriska Aktiebolaget), 20, 214, 215, 218, 219, 460
Aspengren, Tor, 454
ATP (Allmänna Tjenstepensionen) (general supplementary pension), 208, 251, 252, 256, 257, 358, 374, 395–398, 399, 433
Aubert, Wilhelm, 389
Aukrust, Tor, 461
Austria, 4, 126, 401
authoritarian society, authoritarian movement, authoritarian tendencies, 162, 392, 429, 448, 453, 455, 467, 477, 484
authority of experts, 333

Bache-Wiig, Jens, 230, 232, 325
bank democratization, 335, 376

Bauman, Zygmunt, 493, 494, 496
Beck, Ulrich, 490, 501
Berg, Fridtjuv, 59
Berg, Paal, 153
Berggrav, Eivind, 286, 465
Berggren, Christian, 370
Bergman, Ingmar, 498
Berlin, Isaiah, 494, 495
Berman, Sheri, 3, 4, 5, 128, 171
Bernal, John D., 211
Bernstein, Eduard, 127, 167
Beveridge plan, 242
Beveridge, William, 223
Bexell, Göran, 286
Bildt, Carl, 376, 378, 397, 423
Birkeland, Kristian, 15, 19
Bismarck, Otto von, 101
Bjørnson, Øyvind, 124
black-of-night crisis, 357, 364, 479
Blair, Tony, 352, 463
Boëtius, Maria-Pia, 466
Bondevik, Kjell Magne, 463
Borten, Per, 334
branch councils, 303–305
Branting, Hjalmar, 26, 32, 62, 66, 67, 73, 108, 110, 129, 130, 131, 132, 133, 135, 136–138, 139, 140, 141, 142, 143, 145, 148, 150, 160, 165, 172, 180, 209, 284, 285, 395
Braut, Daniel, 56, 206, 207
Bretton Woods Agreement, 198
bridge-building, 189, 198
Brochmann, Grete, 408
Brofoss, Erik, 230, 297, 323
Brøgger, Waldemar Christofer, 17
Bruhn, Anders, 436
Brundtland, Gro Harlem, 342, 353, 354, 355, 363, 377, 392, 393, 405, 421, 452, 494
Brundtland Report, 341
Brunnsvik College, 55
brutality of the majority, 457
Bucharin, Nicholai, 145
Bull, Brynjulf, 230, 234, 237
Bull, Edvard, Jr., 7, 308
Bull, Edvard, Sr., 144, 150, 269, 284
bureaucracy, bureaucratization, 217, 281, 393, 422, 486, 500

Carlsson, Ingvar, 280, 352, 353, 354, 355, 356, 357, 392, 393, 396, 397, 479, 480, 481, 494
Carlsund, Otto, 47
cash benefit plan (kontantstøtte), 411, 413–417
Castberg, Johan, 29, 55, 69, 70, 71, 103, 111, 178, 287
Castbergian child laws, 244
Center Party, Farmers Party (Bondepartiet in Norway and Bondeförbundet in Sweden; later changed to Senterpartiet, Centerpartiet), 80, 82, 84, 86, 164, 172, 208, 252, 334, 339, 415, 431
central business district (CBD), 234, 237, 238
Chandler, Alfred D., Jr., 382
Chernobyl, 339, 340
China, 453 , 455, 500
Christian Democrats, 415, 416
Christian People's Party, 411, 415, 416, 463
Christie, Nils, 412, 419, 420
church asylum, 406
church, church policy, 7, 53, 60, 268, 269, 284–288, 290, 406, 459–462, 487
cities for a new society, 233–239
civil religion, 462
civil society, 9, 90, 111, 114, 153, 175, 176, 243, 254, 262, 394, 395, 428, 434, 438, 459, 491, 498, 500
class consciousness, 206, 369, 435, 487, 488
class cooperation, class collaboration, 49, 154, 307
Clemet, Kristin, 424, 425
Clinton, Bill, 463
Codetermination, 366, 373, 376, 380; Codetermination Act, 371, 376, 377
Colbjørnsen, Ole, 169
collectivization, 134. See also ownership: collective
collective party membership, 132, 374
Comintern, 141, 145
Commission on Values, 463–464
communication perspective, 431, 432, 445, 446
Communist Party (Communists), 157, 189, 195, 209, 295, 322
communitarianism, 102, 138, 462, 463
compulsory arbitration, 72, 140, 153-154, 155, 156, 209, 226
compulsory mediation, 154. See also mediation
concession laws, 25, 27–30, 33, 34, 70–73, 131, 135
conscientious worker, 101, 102
Conservative Party, Conservatives (Allmänna Valmansförbundet, Högerpartiet and Moderata Samlingspartiet in Sweden, Høyre in Norway) 63n41; in Norway, 28, 38, 65, 69, 74, 75, 76, 77, 81, 87, 101, 111, 131, 155, 201, 253,

255, 270, 275, 309, 312, 313, 314, 315, 367, 414, 416, 434, 435, 441, 457, 477; in Sweden, 38, 63, 64, 65, 66, 67, 68, 74, 76, 77, 83, 87, 101, 108, 135, 140, 162, 208, 252, 264, 310, 311, 314, 315, 340, 354, 413, 414, 415, 422, 434, 435, 457, 478
constitutionalism, 456–460; aristocratic, 10
consumer cooperatives, 318
consumer durables: production of, 218
consumer society, consumerism, 171, 206, 316–319
consumption: new patterns of, 43
cooperative: housing, 262, 263; initiatives, 395; producer's, 81, 135
corporate governance, 383
corporatism, corporatization, 24, 81, 83, 87, 98, 114, 151, 153, 224, 302–305, 431; administrative, 302, 328, 334, 361, 378–379, 387; democratic, 305; negotiative (negotiated), 302, 328, 334, 361, 366, 378, 379, 387, 487, 496
corporative pluralism, 87, 306–309
countercyclical policy, 362, 382
cow-trade, 84-86
credit expansion, 354, 356
credit socialism, 326–328
crisis settlement, 83, 84–87, 149, 158, 303
cultivated consumer, 317, 318
cultural diversity, 403, 404, 430, 492
cultural radicalism, cultural radicals, 7, 54, 60, 246
Cultural Revolution, 453
Czechoslovakia, 189, 194, 295

Dahmén, Erik, 45
Darwinism: social, 16, 92, 93, 94, 95
death of ideologies, 445, 445n37
December Compromise, 152, 154, 158
decisionism, 457
democratic capitalism, 21, 382, 500
Denmark, 22, 89, 96, 97, 107, 134, 142, 150, 152, 173, 174, 175, 178, 179, 180, 181, 190, 192, 193, 197, 199, 200, 201, 343, 364, 385, 405, 473, 477, 497, 498, 500
devaluation, 167, 168, 354, 357, 396
differentiation, 2, 440, 490
discourse on capitalism, 49, 213; Marxian, 40
discourse on industrialism, 40, 49, 213
Dølvik, Jon Erik, 381
dual industrial structure (Norway), 228
Dutschke, Rudi, 450

economic democracy, 51, 289, 290, 301–306, 308, 314, 315, 316, 361, 367, 372, 387, 485, 486

economic liberalism. *See* liberalism
economic planning, planned economy, 38, 45, 47,
    199, 200, 221, 224, 228, 290, 293–298, 301,
    306, 311, 313, 347, 350, 473
Edén, Nils, 67, 73, 130
Edling, Nils, 104
Ekdahl, Lars, 305
Ekman, Carl G., 154
Ekström, Sören, 460
electrification, 30–35, 48
Elektrokemisk AS, 42
elite partnership, partnership of top people, 158,
    308, 434
Elster, Jon, 458
Elster, Torolf, 317
Elvander, Nils, 140, 156
emigration, 23–25, 27, 95, 105, 108
enabling acts, 72, 298, 299, 300, 434
energy socialism (power socialism), 228,
    337, 360
Engberg, Arthur, 59, 160, 285
Engels, Friedrich, 245
engineering ideology, 47, 49
England, 19, 69, 145, 176. *See also* Great Britain
Enlightenment, 2, 57, 463
environmental policy, environmental questions,
    environmental movement, 216, 333, 335,
    337, 338, 342, 359, 360, 435, 436, 437,
    447–448, 451, 459, 467, 474
equality, 6, 7, 12, 57, 59, 65, 99, 100, 207, 208,
    250, 251, 255, 256, 266, 272–273, 275, 280,
    281, 283, 288, 329, 392, 393, 397, 400, 402,
    403, 404, 408, 418, 420, 429, 430, 441, 448,
    452, 467, 484, 490, 491, 492, 493, 494, 495.
    See also gender equality
Erfurt Program, 127
Eriksen, Alfred, 131
Eriksen, Trond Berg, 257, 259
Erlander, Tage, 55, 189, 191, 193, 194, 195, 201,
    202, 208, 209, 219, 220, 235, 248, 250, 251,
    252, 268, 269, 270, 272, 290-293, 295, 297,
    328, 395, 441, 478, 491, 492, 498
Esping-Andersen, Gösta, 241, 372, 377
eugenics, 117-119
European Economic Agreement (EEA), 347,
    481, 482
European Economic Community (EEC) (later
    European Union), 5, 199, 206, 334, 335, 336,
    436, 437, 441, 454, 476, 477, 478
European Free Trade Agreement (EFTA), 199,
    200, 476, 478
European Human Rights Court, 495
europeanization, 433

European Union (EU), 199, 334, 358, 383, 435,
    436, 437, 469, 476–483, 488, 489, 496, 500;
    Court of Justice, 495
Evang, Karl, 114, 115, 118, 119, 170, 257–260,
    261
evolutionism, 138
expansionism, 46, 166–171, 294, 316, 456. *See
    also* keynesianism
Experimental Council for Education (Norway),
    270

Fabians, 4n7, 167, 168
Fälldin, Thorbjörn, 334, 374
family insurance principle, 106, 244
Faremo, Oddmund, 442
farmers' march of 1914, 66, 79
Farmers' Party. *See* Center Party
Fascism, 4, 74, 76, 77, 78, 166, 303
Fatherland Association (Fedrelandslaget), 46, 75
Fathers of Eidsvoll, 164, 166
Faxén, K. O., 222, 223
Feldt, Kjell-Olof, 321, 352, 356, 357, 364, 374,
    376, 377
feminism, feminist, 247, 409, 411, 450-452, 467,
    478, 490
finance capitalism, financial sphere, 382, 383,
    384, 387, 489, 499
Finland, 22, 95, 150, 177, 179, 180, 186,
    189, 242, 340, 343, 364, 473, 475, 481,
    497, 498
Finnish Civil War, 143
flexible specialization, 43, 337
folk college, 54–55, 60, 124, 125
folk culture, 455
folk parliament, 61
Folkpartiet. *See* Liberal Party
Førde, Einar, 353, 354, 461
France, 4, 115, 123, 351, 417
freedom: negative, 494: positive, 494; republican,
    494
freedom of choice, 286, 287, 392, 393, 404, 406,
    415, 416, 418, 428, 429, 430, 467, 491, 500,
    501
freedom of expression, 441
freedom revolution, freedom and rights revolu-
    tion, 12, 427, 457, 459, 467, 485, 491, 493,
    495, 496, 498, 502
Frisch, Ragnar, 169
Fröding, Gustav, 137
front professions model, 226–227
FSO (the central organization of salaried
    employees in Norway), 209
functional integration, 235

functionalism, 47-48, 233, 238
functional segregation, 234, 235, 237, 239
Furugård, Birger, 76

Galbraith, John Kenneth, 212–213, 220, 316,
    319, 320, 324, 382, 486, 500
Gang of Four, 455
Garborg, Arne, 55
Gaulle, Charles de, 199, 200
Gävle speech, 138
gender equality, 90, 247, 249, 408, 412, 418,
    438, 452; contract, 89, 248, 334, 410, 411,
    451, 490
general experts, 211
general supplementary pension. See ATP
Gent system, 112, 113
George, Henry, 104, 133
Gerhardsen, Einar, 35, 146, 163, 164, 193, 194,
    290–293, 297, 305, 312, 328, 491, 492, 498
German Academic Socialism (Kathedersozialis-
    mus), 138, 317
German Social Democratic Party (SPD), 127
Germany, 2, 4, 19, 21, 36, 39, 52, 95, 96, 97,
    118, 123, 126, 130, 135, 143, 167, 171, 172,
    175, 177, 180, 181, 185–188, 199, 287, 292,
    293, 298, 359, 401, 465, 466, 496
Gjöres, Alex, 318
globalization. See internationalization
goal orientation, 423
Göransson, Bengt, 421
Great Britain, 36, 62, 167, 179, 192, 199, 200,
    212, 219, 223, 241, 284, 345, 351, 382,
    462, 477
green wave, 238
Group 8, 451, 452
Grudtvig, Nikolai Fredrik Severin, 54
Gustavsson, Bernt, 420
Gustav II Adolf, 47
Gustav Wasa, 47
Gyllenhammar, Per, 201, 470
Gyllensten, Lars, 339

Haakon VII, 163, 185
Habermas, Jürgen, 450
Hadenius, Stig, 466
Hagtvet, Bernt, 76
Hallesby, Ole, 460
Hambro, Carl Joachim, 77, 313
Hamilton, Hugo, 64
Hammarskjöld, Hjalmar, 66
Hansen, Lars-Erik, 404
Hansson, Per Albin, 73, 84, 85, 119, 121, 129,
    157, 159–162, 163, 164, 165, 179, 181, 185,
    208, 290, 321, 502

happiness indicator, 498
Harpsund Democracy, 309, 311, 328
Hauge, Jens Christian, 215, 231, 232
Hayek, Friedrick A. von, 295
health policy, 257–261
Hedborg, Anna, 376
Hedin, Sven, 17
Hegna, Trond, 245, 410
Heiret, Jan, 363
Hernes, Gudmund, 378, 421, 422–424, 425,
    426, 427, 428, 443, 461, 462
Hernes, Helga, 452
hierarchical corporatist structure, 303–305
high-quality standard solutions, 392, 403, 491
Hirdman, Yvonne, 90, 243, 248
historians' strife, 465
Hitler, Adolf, 2, 130, 457
Hjellum, Wenche, 452
Hobsbawm, Eric, 4, 145
Hoel, Sigurd, 197
Högerpartiet. See Conservative Party
Höglund, Zeta, 138, 141, 147, 160
Höjer, J. Axel, 260–261
Holocaust, 466
honor killing, 408
Hornsrud, Christopher, 133-134, 143, 163
Houm, Edvard, 455
housewife contract, 89, 92, 247, 248, 249, 334,
    410, 451, 487, 490
housing cooperatives, 262, 263, 335
Høyre. See Conservative Party
human capital, 273, 349
humanistic ideals, 278, 279
Husén, Torsten, 271, 272, 273, 281
HVPU reform, 420
hydroelectric power, 15, 16, 20, 30–35, 42, 49,
    217–218, 227–228, 338–339, 341

IB affair, 441
Ibsen, Henrik, 498
Iceland, 473, 498
Illich, Ivan, 260, 261
immigration, 25, 95-96, 334, 400–409, 429,
    492; family, 402; ghettos, 409; labor, 401,
    402; of refugees and asylum seekers, 95–97,
    402, 405
imperialism, 450
indicative planning, 326, 327
individualism, 9, 88, 92, 246, 395, 423, 424,
    425, 463
individualization, 247, 270, 271, 394, 412, 430,
    463, 467
industrial democracy, 41, 303, 316, 361,
    365–367, 372, 377

industrialization, 1, 3, 11, 12, 15, 19–25, 28, 29, 30, 37, 48–49, 51, 56, 66, 70, 71, 72, 101, 104, 122, 130, 150, 199, 204, 212, 218, 221, 227, 230, 240, 262, 372, 385, 445, 471; scepticism toward, 28
Industry Foundation, Industry Fund, 231, 327
information technology, 489
innocence of power, 293
institutional ownership, institutional capitalism, 383-384, 500
instrumentalism, 2, 44, 46, 47, 48, 49, 53, 60, 155, 259, 265, 273, 286, 421, 426, 427, 463
integrated school, unitary school, comprehensive school, 56-60, 240, 267–276, 333, 404, 419, 420, 422–427, 430, 487, 490, 501
interest struggle perspective, 431, 432
internationalization, globalization, 3, 356, 360, 361, 433, 466, 469, 480, 486, 488, 495, 499
Ireland, 359
Iron Agreement (Verkstedsoverenskomsten), 152, 158
Isaksson, Anders, 138, 159, 160, 161, 162, 164, 165
Italy, 4
itinerants, 117

Jahre, Anders, 325
Jakobsson, Eva, 33
Jeffner, Anders, 460
Jensen, Axel, 448, 492
Jeppesen, Carl, 133
Johansen, Leif, 386
Johansson, Alf W., 390
Johansson, Anders L., 379
Johnsen, Egil Børre, 427
Jonung, Lars, 384
judicialization, judicializing, 433, 495
Judt, Tony, 5, 6, 9, 350, 351, 456, 458, 498

Karleby, Nils, 160, 167
Karlsson, Jan O., 444
Karlsson, Sten O., 138
Katzenstein, Peter, 308
Kautsky, Karl, 39, 127, 134, 147
Keynes, John Maynard, keynesianism, 167, 168, 169, 170, 212, 293, 294, 295, 337, 350. See also expansionism
kickoff democracy, 443
Kielland, Alexander, 419
Kierulf, Carl, 22
Kiruna Strike, 316, 365, 368–369
Kjellén, Rudolf, 25, 161
Klein, Victoria, 248

Klingenberg, Odd, 110, 111
knowledge movement, 421; opposition, 421, 422, 425
knowledge school, 57, 58, 271, 288, 419, 423, 425, 487, 501
Knudsen, Gunnar, 28, 29, 33, 68–73, 80, 153, 154
Kock, Karin, 304
Koht, Halvdan, 277
Kokkvold, Arne, 125
Korean War, 197
Korpi, Walter, 8, 417, 431
Kreuger, Ivar, 41, 42n79
Kristensson, Astrid, 414

Labor Democrats, 69, 103
Lagerkrantz, Olof, 432, 446
Lange, Halvard, 131, 189, 191, 193
Lange, Oscar, 386
Langslet, Lars Roar, 441
language movement, 52, 276–278
Larsson, Hans, 54, 55
Lassalle, Ferdinand, 138
leadership: professionalization of, 45
legal realism, 458
Lehmkuhl, Joakim, 43, 45, 46, 75
Leira, Halvard, 277
Lenin, Vladimir Ilyich, 141, 291
Leninism, 6. See also Marxist-Leninist (ML) movement
Lewin, Leif, 212, 217, 255, 295, 478, 479
lex Thagaard, 294, 296, 297
Lian, Ole Olsen, 148
liberalism, 5, 40, 63n40, 86, 160, 165, 212, 424, 456, 458, 459
Liberal Party, Liberals (Folkpartiet in Sweden, Venstre in Norway): in Norway, 27, 28, 29, 38, 52, 58, 60, 62, 67, 68, 69, 70, 73, 77, 78, 80, 81, 86, 87, 103, 104, 111, 113, 131, 132, 153, 253, 254, 257, 269, 273, 277; in Sweden, 26, 38, 61, 62, 77, 78, 87, 103, 108, 137, 140, 153, 175, 177, 208, 209, 251, 252, 254, 295, 367
Libertas, 310, 312, 313
Lie, Trygve, 165, 228, 229, 232, 325
limited liability, 11, 23
Lindahl, Erik, 167
Lindbeck, Assar, 443, 445
Lindberg, August, 256, 303, 304
Lindgren, Astrid, 322
Lindholm, Sven Olof, 76
Lindman, Arvid, 26, 32, 63–65, 66, 67, 68, 71, 75, 77, 83, 108, 140, 162, 168
Lindquist, Herman, 140
Lindström, Stefan, 215

Lindström, Ulf, 76
Lisbon agreement, 496
little red cottage, 48, 105, 236
Ljunggren, Stig-Björn, 315
LKAB (Luossavaara-Kiirunavaara AB), 26,
    30, 368
L. M. Ericsson, 20, 42, 218, 219, 358
LO (the trade union central in both Norway and
    Sweden): in Norway, 123, 148, 152, 155, 156,
    207, 209, 253, 297, 304, 312, 323, 361, 362,
    367, 369, 380, 387, 454, 476; in Sweden, 40,
    113, 123, 139, 140, 154, 187, 207, 208, 209,
    221, 223, 224, 251, 256, 293, 294, 303, 304,
    335, 353, 361, 363, 364, 365, 367, 372–377,
    378, 379, 387
Løfsnes, Knut, 196
Lo-Johansson, Ivar, 124
London School of Economics, 450
Lundberg, Erik, 213
Lundberg, Urban, 352, 502
Lundmark, Lennart, 93
Lutheran doctrine of dual regimes, 288, 460
Lutheranism, 7, 284

MacIntyre, Alasdair, 462
Magnusson, Lars, 358, 379
Main Agreement (Hovedavtalen), 87, 149, 153,
    158–159, 302, 361, 366, 368, 487
majority election, 62–63, 69
majority system, 130
managerial capitalism, 47, 298, 325
Maoism, Mao, 453, 454, 455
Marklund, Sixten, 274
Marshall, George, 198
Marshall Plan, 189, 198, 199, 297
Martin, Andrew, 381
Martinsson, Moa, 124
Marx, Karl, 133, 138
Marxism, 1, 4, 5, 121, 129, 132, 134, 149, 150,
    166, 170, 212, 291, 316, 420, 451, 452, 454,
    456, 458; categories, 132; dogmas, 132; ideas,
    457; ideology, 129; and Marxist interlude,
    135; and politital parties, 6, 129; perspectives
    of, 451; rethoric of, 138, 161; roots of, 7
Marxist-Leninist (ML) movement, 452, 453–456,
    478
materialism: historical, 128
mediation, 154, 221, 222, 223, 226, 364,
    381, 405
medicalization, 259, 260
medicracy, 258
Meidner, Rudolf, 221, 223, 373, 374, 376,
    377, 386

Melander, Johan, 229–230, 232, 237, 325
Melby, Kari, 88
Mellbye, Johan Egeberg, 80, 81, 82
Menstad confrontation, 156-157
meritocracy, 273
Meyer, Frank, 96, 97
Michelsen, Christian, 28, 68, 69, 70, 71, 72, 111
Middle Ages, 10
Millbourn, Ingrid, 128, 135, 136, 371, 498
Mitterand, François, 351
mixed economy, 232, 329, 484
Moberg, Wilhelm, 124
Moderata Samlingspartiet. *See* Conservative Party
modernity, 4, 7, 9, 30, 130, 159, 241, 340, 360,
    454, 463, 464, 490, 493, 502; ecological, 360;
    second, 9, 490
modernization, 1–4, 9, 10, 11, 12, 18, 21, 22, 23,
    25, 27, 28, 40, 45, 46, 48, 49, 56, 71, 78, 79,
    80, 88, 104, 110, 114, 115, 120, 122, 135,
    157, 173, 175, 221, 279, 289, 351, 359, 372,
    391, 440, 451, 463; democratic, political,
    11–12, 21, 61, 66, 72, 79; discourse on, 22;
    industrial, economic and technical, 11, 12,
    21, 22, 27, 30, 34, 42, 49, 60, 68, 72, 73, 78,
    120, 230, 240; less distinct concept of, 27, 49
Molin, Karl, 194
Möller, Gustav, 113, 114, 168, 242, 243, 246,
    250, 254, 255, 290
monetarism, 350, 351
Monsen, Nina Karin, 452
moral sciences, 60
Mork, Geir, 455
Moscow, 141, 147
Moscow theses, 145
Mot Dag (Toward the Day), 170, 291
Mowinckel, Johan Ludvig, 77
multiculturalism, cultural diversity, multicultural
    society, 403, 404, 406, 407, 423, 429, 430,
    447, 461, 462, 492
Munch, Edvard, 498
municipal socialism, 112
mutual funds: the florescence of, 315, 387
Mykle, Agnar, 259
Myrdal, Alva, 12, 91, 92, 102, 115, 118, 119,
    245, 246, 247, 248, 260, 267, 268, 270, 288,
    355, 403, 410, 414, 418, 461
Myrdal, Gunnar, 47, 48, 102, 115, 118, 119, 167,
    168, 171, 213, 245, 246, 257, 260, 267, 270,
    278, 294, 296, 297, 303, 304, 316, 317

Nansen, Fridtjof, 17, 74
Napoleonic Wars, 10
National Agency for Education, 270, 271

National Board of Trade (Swedish), 20

nationalism, 1, 3, 10, 16, 20, 25, 94, 131, 244, 471, 475, 486

nationalization, 26, 38, 335, 351, 476

national pension plan (national insurance plan), 65, 106, 108-112, 251, 252-254, 256, 313, 333, 395, 398, 417, 429, 479

National Unification Party (Nasjonal Samling, NS), 75, 76, 82, 188, 455

nation building, 3, 9, 10, 17, 25, 50, 64, 82, 88, 94, 96, 98, 99, 101, 102, 161, 243, 400, 403, 420, 423, 425, 430, 484, 485, 490, 491; and NATO, 74, 189, 192–193, 195, 336, 449, 453, 454, 466, 476, 477, 478, 482, 483

natural gas energy, 338, 340–341, 360

Nazism, Nazi-style party, 74, 75, 76, 171, 286, 296, 465. *See also* National Unification Party

neo-Malthusians, 115

new journalism, 444, 445, 467

nicenessism, (snillisme), 407

Nordby, Trond, 306

NORDEA, 474

Nordenskiöld, Adolf, 17

Nordgren, Olivia, 90

Nordic collaboration in banking, 473

Nordic Council, 202

Nordic Economic Cooperation (NORDØK), 200, 202, 473

Nordic Investment Bank, 473, 474

Nordic Welfare Convention, 256

Nordli, Odvar, 470, 472

Nordström, Ludvig, 47

Norsk Hydro, 15-16, 19, 22, 28, 34, 38, 42, 156, 215–216, 228, 230, 342, 349, 369

nuclear family, 244, 246, 247, 248, 249, 409, 410, 412, 413, 415, 418, 487, 490, 501

nuclear power, nuclear energy, 214–216, 333, 337–340, 341, 343, 344, 359, 360, 374, 377, 437, 478

nuclear weapons, nuclear defense, 193, 215

Nybom, Thorsten, 279

Nycander, Svante, 154, 364, 365, 374

Nygaardsvold, Johan, 73, 162–166, 372

Nyland, Håkon, 205, 206

Nyström, Per, 138

Obrestad, Tor, 455

Odhnoff, Camilla, 414

OECD (OEEC), 198, 199, 324, 497–498

Ohlin, Bertil, 167, 251, 253, 255

Olsen, Fred, the elder, 158

Olsen, Fred, the younger, 383

Olsson, Bertil, 222–223

Olsson, Karl-Manfred, 462

Olsson, Ulf, 219, 325

Olstad, Finn, 126

ombudsman, 300, 301, 438

OPEC (Organization of Petroleum Exporting Countries), 339, 345, 363

oppositional sociology, 389

organized capitalism, 19, 21, 22, 23, 37, 49, 73

Osborne, John, 448

Östberg, Kjell, 53, 90

Otter, Carl von, 365

ownership: collective, 132, 374; individual, 134, 262, 264, 315; institutional, 382, 383, 384; modern 30, 135; private, 26, 30, 104, 133, 264, 299, 376, 384, 385; state, 335, 385–387, 468, 476, 483. *See also* rights

own home (egnahemmet) movement, 24, 26, 103–105, 132, 133, 136

Palme, Olof, 235, 280, 335, 336, 339, 354, 363, 365, 373, 374, 376, 377, 329, 394, 429, 436, 448, 449, 500, 477, 478

panic laws, 28

parallel school system, 58, 59, 267, 269, 271, 272

parity policy, back-to-par policy, 36–37, 81, 167, 168

parliamentarianism, 11n 23, 51, 52, 66–67, 74, 77, 78

parliamentary democracy, 129

parliamentary form of governance, 11

parliamentary system, 50, 51, 73, 75, 76, 78, 292

participatory democracy, self-determination, self-governing groups, 136, 361, 368–372, 380, 381, 387

paternalism, 7, 12, 59, 101, 107, 108, 109, 110, 162, 212, 255, 392, 394, 416, 485, 491, 495, 502

patriarchy, 89, 90, 91

peace congress, 177

Peace of Sarek, 338

pedagogy: class based, 53, 57, 58, 59, 60, 98, 426; knowledge-based, 419; modern scientific, reform, progressive, 57, 270, 271, 275, 288, 419, 420, 425

Pehrsson, Axel (of Bramstorp), 84-86

People's Home (Folkhemmet), 6, 26, 103, 132, 136, 159, 161, 165, 246, 284, 287, 315, 390, 392, 395, 429, 431, 493

Persson, Göran, 340, 414, 422, 423, 482

Petersson, Magnus, 192

Petersson, Olof, 445

pietism, revival movement, 52–53, 54, 60, 454

planned economy. *See* economic planning

Poltava, 479
Pomperipossa Effect, 322
Popper, Karl, 424
popular movement, 50, 52, 53, 61, 98, 111,
    121, 122, 124, 125, 126, 171, 276, 284,
    434, 459, 491
popular refinement, popular education, 53–54,
    57, 59, 60, 98
positive discrimination, 20, 345, 347, 349, 385
positivism, 389, 450
post-familial family, 501
postmodernism, postmodern society, postmodern
    tendency, 3, 9, 436, 447, 464, 467
Pot, Pol, 455
pragmatism, 167, 191, 287, 353
private equity funds, 383, 387, 500
private schools, 58, 59, 422, 424, 426, 490, 501
privatization (privatizing), 327, 347, 350, 356, 386
producer cooperation, 134, 135
Progress Party (Fremskrittspartiet), 405, 407, 416,
    436, 437, 444
proletarianizing, 453
proletarian literature, 124
property-owning democracy, proprietary democ-
    racy, 264, 314, 315, 324, 328, 367
property rights. See rights
proportional election, 62–63, 67
proportional representation, 63, 67, 130
proprietary power, 308, 361, 373, 377, 387,
    486, 489
protectionism, 20
public education, 56-60, 124, 246
puritanism, 317, 319, 390, 391

quasi market, 392, 394, 428, 491
Quisling, Vidkun, 75, 76, 82, 187

race, racism, 11, 25, 116, 117, 118, 407, 408,
    409, 464
racial hygiene, 117, 118
Randen, Olav, 105, 135
Rathenau, Walter, 39
rationalization, 37, 39, 42, 44–46, 294, 295, 296,
    297, 298, 300, 303, 313, 321, 327, 337, 348,
    349, 367, 368, 369, 372
Reagan, Ronald, 351
redistribution, 45, 72
Reformation, 7, 10, 69, 285
reformism, 6, 76, 119, 121, 122, 127, 128, 129,
    132, 134, 135, 136, 137, 138, 145, 146,
    147, 148, 150, 157, 170, 171, 172, 212, 281,
    291, 308

regional policy, 223, 226
Rehman, Shabana, 408
Rehn, Gösta, 221
Rehn-Meidner Model, 221–223
Rehnberg action, 364
religious freedom, 285
reproduction crisis, population crisis, 102,
    114–116, 242, 247, 248, 260, 409, 413, 418;
    and policy, 418
research councils, 214
revisionism, 5, 128, 141, 172
revival movements. See pietism
Richardsson, Gunnar, 186, 276, 427
richer reality, 448, 492, 498
right of reversion, 29
rights, 100, 120, 139, 249, 433, 456, 458; of
    citizens, 3, 195; civil, 89, 198, 457; of homo-
    sexuals, 459; human, 2, 402, 405, 457, 495;
    individual, 77, 88, 120, 196, 390, 394, 457,
    458, 491, 493; minority, 65, 67, 251, 457; of
    ownership, 18, 29, 30, 65, 103, 133, 328;
    political, 88, 89, 400, 403, 457; property,
    71, 80, 135; proprietary, 104, 314, 344, 345;
    social, 6, 243, 400, 403, 457; women's, 88.
    See also freedom revolution
Riste, Olav, 191
Robinson, Joan, 486
Rokkan, Stein, 50, 307
Rolfsen, Erik, 233, 234
Rosengren, Björn, 468, 482
Rothstein, Bo, 83, 84. 100n2, 222, 242, 272,
    306, 307, 308, 378, 392, 438
Royal Hydro Power Authority (Sweden), 32, 34
Royal Technical College (Sweden), 17
Ruin, Olof, 291, 482
rule of law, 459, 494, 497
rural gymnasia, 56
Rusck, Åke, 216
Russia, 95, 177, 501
Russian revolution, 73, 141, 143, 145, 177
Ruth, Arne, 443, 444

SAAB, 218, 358, 384
Saba, Isak, 95
Sachs, Jeffrey, 9
Saltsjöbad Agreement, 87, 149, 153, 157, 158,
    302, 320, 338, 361, 365, 366, 368, 369,
    372, 487
Sandler, Richard, 40, 55, 98, 160, 167, 179, 180,
    181, 186, 214, 240
satellite towns, 235, 236, 239, 262, 264, 334, 390
savings revolution, 254, 383

Scandinavian Airlines System (SAS), 200-202, 470
Scandinavianism, Scandinavian identity, 147, 149, 174, 180, 201, 469, 475
Scandinavian model, 1, 4, 6, 8, 9, 360, 475
Schjelderup, Gunnar, 225, 229, 230
Schön, Lennart, 42, 349, 350, 358
Schumpeter, Joseph A., 486, 500
Schwarz, David, 404
Scientific mangement, 43–45
Second Industrial Revolution, 19
secularization, 461
Segerstedt, Torgny, Jr., 281
Segerstedt, Torgny, Sr., 187
Seip, Jens Arup, 6, 8, 439
self-determination (self-governing groups). *See* participatory democracy
September Compromise, 152
shareholder value, 383
Sipolä, Jorma, 417
Sivertsen, Helge, 268, 271, 272, 422
Sjølie, Hans Petter, 456
Skorpen, Ann-Mari, 453, 454
Skytøen, Lars, 377
Slagstad, Rune, 30, 71, 127, 150, 276, 458
snilleindustri ("enterprise of genius"), 42
SNS (Study Association for Business and Society), 311, 313
social citizenship, 99
social democratic constitution, 298–301, 458. *See also* constitutionalism
social democratic landscape, 236, 240
Social Democratic parties, origins of, 123
social engineering, 47, 48, 49, 119, 120, 243, 259, 260
social ethics, 460, 461
social housing, 262–264
social pacification, 101
Socialist People's Party, SF, 193, 195, 196, 197
socialization: of children in school and family, 410, 416, 420, 421, 422, 425, 426, 430 ; in industry and trade, 38–41, 56, 78, 143, 230, 294, 326, 356, 386, 476
Söderlund, Gustav, 310, 311
solidarity alternative (solidarity agreement), 362, 363, 364
solidarity game, 158
solidarity wage policy, 221, 223, 226, 256, 305, 349, 373
Solstad, Dag, 158, 205, 206, 454, 455
Sorbonne University, 450
South Pole, 17

Soviet Union (Soviet), 2, 44, 95, 142, 145, 151, 179, 180, 186, 189, 190, 191, 192, 193, 194, 197, 213, 339, 343, 453
sports movement, 125–127, 259
Staaff, Karl, 61, 62, 63, 64, 65, 66, 130, 137, 140, 153, 154
Staaff Laws, 61
stakeholder value, stakeholder interest, 383, 486
Stalin, Josef, 2, 457
standard security, standard insurance, 208, 242, 250, 251, 253, 254–257, 388, 399, 429
state capitalism, 72, 309, 314, 499
state church. *See* church
state commercial bank, 294, 327, 335
state socialism, 71, 72, 73
state-supported pluralism, 403-404
Statoil, 345-347, 356, 386
Steen, Sverre, 6, 8, 164
Steinmo, Sven, 321, 356
Stenlås, Niklas, 74, 310, 311
sterilization, 116–120, 257, 464
Sterner, Richard, 303
Stjernquist, Nils, 67
Stockholm Exposition, 47, 233
Stoltenberg, Thorvald, 405
Sträng, Gunnar, 221, 250, 320, 322
Strasser, Gregor, 169
Stråth, Bo, 315
street bureaucrats, 222, 243
strike, 80, 139, 145, 152, 153-157, 350, 436, 453, 369; the big strike of 1909, 62, 139–141. *See also* Kiruna Strike
Strindberg, August, 136
student rebellion, 280, 282. *See also* youth rebellion
suicide rates, 498
Sundbärg, Gustav, 24
Sundby, Olof, 460
surveillance, 194–198
sustainable development, 391. *See also* Brundtland Report
Svensson, Torsten, 208
Swedish-Norwegian Industry Fund, 472

Taylor, Charles, 447, 456, 463
Taylor, Fredrick W., 44–46
Taylorism, 43, 44–46, 75, 369
taxation socialism, 319–324
taxes, 20, 81, 101, 104, 108, 109, 110, 111, 114, 167, 223, 229, 241, 243, 264, 310, 315, 318, 319–324, 346, 350, 351, 352, 353, 375, 385, 386, 388, 393, 469, 496; capital gains, 320,

taxes (cont'd)
    324, 356, 357; consumption (sales), 322, 323,
    324, 327, 357; corporate, 320–321, 323, 324,
    349, 357; income, progressive, 320, 321, 323,
    324, 349, 356; inheritance, 321, 323, 324;
    municipal, 108, 112. See also taxation
    socialism ; tax reforms around 1990
tax reforms around 1990, 356, 357
TCO (the central organisation of salaried employ-
    ees in Sweden), 208, 252
technocracy, technocrats, technocratic policy, 39,
    46–49, 72, 119, 211, 212, 213, 214, 242,
    243, 246, 261, 281, 282, 289, 290, 298, 333,
    372, 446, 450
technological determinism, industrial fatalism,
    338, 359, 214
Telenor, 468
Telhaug, Alfred Oftedal, 58, 275
Telia, 468
temperance movements, 52, 53
Thagaard, Wilhelm, 37, 38, 297. See also lex
    Thagaard
Thatcher, Margaret, 350, 351, 382
thatcherism, 350, 351, 352, 456, 458
theory of concentration, 132, 138
theory of depletion, 132, 138
theory of purchasing power, 83, 84, 168
third way, 352, 356, 392, 456, 458, 481, 485
Thorsrud, Einar, 369
Three Mile Island, 339, 341
Thullberg, Per, 86
Tingsten, Herbert, 128, 138, 147
Torp, Oscar, 163
totalitarianism, totalitarian movement, totalitarian
    regimes, 2, 4, 6, 7, 50, 65, 74, 76, 77, 187,
    286, 438, 448, 457, 494
traditional authority, 20–21, 162
Tranmæl, Martin, 113, 143-147, 148, 150, 151,
    155, 163, 164, 291
tripartite model, 227, 328, 364, 380, 387
Troedsson, Ingegerd, 414
Trollhätte power station, 16, 31, 32
trust laws, 37–38, 39, 40
two-income family, 89, 235, 249, 411, 412,
    417, 490
Tydén, Mattias, 119
tyranny of sources, 442–443

Uddhammar, Emil, 26
Unckel, Per, 340
Undén, Östen, 189, 190, 193
unemployment, 43, 76, 83, 89, 91, 100, 105,

112–114, 166, 168, 170, 209, 212, 221,
    250, 253, 335, 337, 350, 357, 358, 362, 374,
    379, 479
union complex, union syndrome, 1905 complex,
    186, 191, 201 475, 477
Unitas, 74
United Nations (UN), 165, 228, 341–342, 405,
    457, 482
United States, America, 19, 24, 25, 36, 37, 43,
    44, 120, 144, 177, 189, 190, 192, 317, 336,
    343, 345, 351, 400, 403, 449, 454, 462, 478,
    482, 497
universality, universalism, as a priciple in social
    security systems, 6, 12, 99, 100, 101, 109,
    110, 121, 141, 243, 253, 388, 394
universal suffrage, 11, 50, 51, 52, 61-65, 66, 70,
    73, 88, 90, 108, 129, 130, 138, 139, 162, 395
university, 60–61; and policy, 278–284, 427–428
upbringing for a new world, 267
urbanization, 264; new ideology of, 239

Vattenfall (former Royal Hydropower Authority),
    32, 34, 216, 338
Vedung, Evert, 32, 338, 340
Vemork power station, 15–16, 31
Venstre. See Liberal Party
Vietnam War, Vietnam protest, 336, 449, 450,
    455, 459, 478
vocational studies, 60, 281, 282, 283
Vogt, Johan, 170–171
Volvo, 42, 201, 218, 358, 370, 384, 470, 471,
    472
Vort Land, 74, 75

wage-earner, 209; funds, 41, 335, 372–378, 379,
    387, 485
Wallenberg family, Wallenbergs, 22, 41, 325,
    345, 349
Wallenberg Foundation, 325
Wallenberg, Marcus, Jr., 201, 219, 220, 325, 367
Wallenberg, Marcus, Sr., 16
Wallenberg system, 218–221
war of the roses, 353, 357
Waterways and Electricity Authority, 34
Wedén, Sven, 367
Wehler, Hans-Ulrich, 1
welfare regimes, 241, 242, 247, 388, 392, 417
Wicksell, Knut, 133
Wigforss, Ernst, 85, 160, 166, 167, 179, 250,
    293, 294, 310, 320, 321, 322, 325, 386
Willoch, Kåre, 336, 353, 354, 356, 378
windfall profits, 373

Witoszek, Nina, 7n17, 172, 501
women's liberation, women's emancipation,
    88–92, 114, 244, 245, 411, 451, 452, 469.
    See also feminism; gender equality
work approach (Arbeidslinjen), 250, 390,
    500
work environment, 316, 333, 365, 368, 370, 371,
    373, 380, 381
work ethic, 500

worker's academies, 124
Worker's Educational Association, 125
World Health Organization, 259

Yugoslavia: former, 405, 406
youth rebellion, 205, 275, 333, 409, 447–450,
    451, 453, 459, 467, 477

Zaremba, Maciej, 120